DAVID BUSCH'S
CANON® EOS® RP

GUIDE TO DIGITAL PHOTOGRAPHY

David D. Busch

David Busch's Canon® EOS® RP
Guide to Digital Photography
David D. Busch

Project Manager: Jenny Davidson
Series Technical Editor: Michael D. Sullivan
Layout: Bill Hartman
Cover Design: Mike Tanamachi
Indexer: Valerie Haynes Perry
Proofreader: Mike Beady

ISBN: 978-1-68198-523-7
1st Edition (1st printing, September 2019)

© 2019 David D. Busch

All images © David D. Busch unless otherwise noted

Rocky Nook, Inc.
1010 B Street, Suite 350
San Rafael, CA 94901
USA
www.rockynook.com

Distributed in the UK and Europe by Publishers Group UK
Distributed in the U.S. and all other territories by Ingram Publisher Services

Library of Congress Control Number: 2019939308

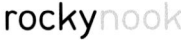

For Cathy

Acknowledgments

Thanks to everyone at Rocky Nook, including Scott Cowlin, managing director and publisher, for the freedom to let me explore the amazing capabilities of the Canon EOS RP in depth. I couldn't do it without my veteran production team, including project manager, Jenny Davidson, and series technical editor, Mike Sullivan. Also thanks to Bill Hartman, layout; Valerie Hayes Perry, indexing; Mike Beady, proofreading; Mike Tanamachi, cover design; and my agent, Carole Jelen, who has the amazing ability to keep both publishers and authors happy.

About the Author

With more than 2.5 million books in print, **David D. Busch** is the world's #1 bestselling camera guide author, and the originator of popular series like *David Busch's Compact Field Guides* and *David Busch's Quick Snap Guides*. He has written more than 100 hugely successful guidebooks for Canon and other digital camera models, including the all-time #1 bestsellers for several different cameras, as well as many popular books devoted to photography, including *Digital SLR Cameras and Photography for Dummies*. As a roving photojournalist for more than 20 years, he illustrated his books, magazine articles, and newspaper reports with award-winning images. He's operated his own commercial studio, suffocated in formal dress while shooting weddings, and shot sports for a daily newspaper and an upstate New York college. His photos and articles have appeared in *Popular Photography, Rangefinder, Professional Photographer*, and hundreds of other publications. He's also reviewed dozens of digital cameras for CNet and other CBS publications.

When About.com first named its top five books on Beginning Digital Photography, debuting at the #1 and #2 slots were Busch's *Digital Photography All-In-One Desk Reference for Dummies* and *Mastering Digital Photography*. He has had as many as 18 books listed in the Top 100 of Amazon.com's Digital Photography Bestseller list—simultaneously! Busch's 250-plus other books published since 1983 include bestsellers like *Mastering Digital SLR Photography*.

Busch is a member of the Cleveland Photographic Society (www.clevelandphoto.org), which has operated continuously since 1887. Visit his website at http://www.canonguides.com.

Contents

Chapter 2
Canon EOS RP Roadmap   **35**

Chapter 3
Recommended Settings   **53**

Chapter 4
Nailing the Right Exposure   **61**

Chapter 5
Mastering the Mysteries of Focus   111

Chapter 6
Advanced Techniques, Wi-Fi, and GPS   137

Chapter 7
Choosing Your Lens Arsenal   167

Chapter 8
Mastering Light   185

Chapter 9
Electronic Flash Basics   201

Chapter 10
Working with Wireless Flash 237

Chapter 11
Customizing with the Shooting Menu 257

Chapter 12
Customizing with the Playback Menu   319

Chapter 13
Customizing with the Set-up Menu   341

Chapter 14
The Custom Functions and My Menus   365

Chapter 15
Capturing Video   387

Chapter 16
Tips for Shooting Better Video
411

Chapter 17
Troubleshooting and Prevention
431

Index
451

Preface

At its introduction the Canon EOS RP quickly gained notice as the most compact and affordable full-frame mirrorless digital camera on the market. Veteran users of Canon digital cameras will find this new, trimmer model comfortably familiar, but also quite full of exciting enhancements made possible by its from-scratch innovative design. For newcomers to the world of Canon or the realm of mirrorless digital photography, the EOS RP can be bewildering with its sheer number of features and options. Even so, you expect more than good pictures from your sophisticated new camera: you demand *outstanding photos*. After all, the EOS RP is one of the most fully featured and versatile cameras currently in the Canon lineup. It boasts 26 megapixels of resolution, highly accurate sensor-based automatic focus, and 4K video capabilities. But your gateway to pixel proficiency is dragged down by the skimpy information offered by the minimalist manual included in the box.

You know most of what you need to know to get started is in there, somewhere, but you don't know where to start. In addition, the camera manual doesn't offer much information on photography or digital photography. Nor does it really tell you much about how mirrorless shooting might differ from the kinds of digital photography you are used to. You're probably not interested in spending hours or days studying a comprehensive book on digital photography that doesn't necessarily apply directly to the enhanced features of your EOS RP.

What you need is a guide that explains the purpose and function of the EOS RP's basic controls, lenses, and accessories from the perspective of mirrorless cameras. It should tell you how you should use them, and *why*. Ideally, there should be information about the file formats at your disposal, resolution, when to use exposure modes like Aperture- or Shutter-priority, and the use of special autofocus modes. In many cases, you'd prefer to read about those topics only after you've had the chance to go out and take a few hundred great pictures with your new camera. Why isn't there a book that summarizes the most important information in its first two or three chapters, with lots of illustrations showing what your results will look like when you use this setting or that? This is that book.

If you can't decide on what basic settings to use with your camera because you can't figure out how changing ISO or white balance or focus defaults will affect your pictures, you need this guide. I won't talk down to you, either; this book isn't padded with dozens of pages of checklists telling you how to take a travel picture, a sports photo, or how to take a snapshot of your kids in overly simplistic terms. There are no special sections devoted to "real world" recipes here. All of us do 100 percent of our shooting in the real world! So, I give you all the information you need to cook up great photos on your own!

Introduction

Despite what you might read elsewhere, the Canon EOS RP and its upscale stablemate the EOS R are not the first mirrorless interchangeable-lens cameras Canon has offered. That distinction belongs to the company's Canon EOS M product line, a series of consumer-oriented cameras which continues to be offered, but was never meant to be a tool for advanced or professional photographers. Your Canon EOS RP was carefully designed to fully meet the needs of a much different group: dedicated photo enthusiasts, semi-professionals, and professional photographers.

With the EOS RP, you're not giving up much, other than a mirror and a pentaprism/pentamirror optical viewfinder, roughly 12 ounces of weight, and quite a bit of bulk—compared to Canon full-frame dSLR models. Indeed, the EOS RP is Canon's affordable mirrorless "do-everything" camera. It has enough resolution—at 26 MP—guaranteed to please the most discerning landscape and fine-art photographers who demand amazing detail. It can capture action at up to 5 frames per second and is one of the first Canon full-frame cameras that can mount and use both EF-S and EF-mount lenses. Its 4K movie-shooting capabilities will make this camera prized by those assembling and editing serious video productions on a budget.

You may be asking yourself—*how do I use this thing?* Canon's manual, which must be downloaded in PDF form, is mind-numbingly dense, and online YouTube tutorials can't cover all these features in depth. Who wants to learn how to use a camera by sitting in front of a television or computer screen? Do you want to watch a movie or click on HTML links, or do you want to go out and take photos with your camera?

The PDF manual is thick and filled with information, but there's really very little about *why* you should use particular settings or features. Its organization makes it difficult to find what you need. Multiple cross-references send you searching back and forth between two or three sections of the book to find what you want to know. The basic manual is also hobbled by black-and-white line drawings and tiny monochrome pictures that aren't very good examples of what you can do.

I've tried to make *David Busch's Canon EOS RP Guide to Digital Photography* different from your other EOS RP learn-up options. The roadmap sections use larger, color pictures to show you where all the buttons and dials are, and the explanations of what they do are longer and more comprehensive. I've tried to avoid overly general advice, including the two-page checklists on how to take a "sports picture" or a "portrait picture" or a "travel picture." You won't find half the content of this book taken up by generic chapters that tell you how to shoot landscapes, portraits, or product photographs. Instead, you'll find tips and techniques for using all the features of your Canon EOS RP to take *any kind of picture* you want. If you want to know where you should stand to take a picture of a quarterback dropping back to unleash a pass, there are plenty of books that will tell you that. This one concentrates on teaching you how to select the best autofocus mode, shutter speed, f/stop, or flash capability to take, say, a great sports picture under any conditions.

This book is not a lame rewriting of the manual that came with the camera. Some folks spend five minutes with a book like this one, spot some information that also appears in the original manual, and decide "Rehash!" without really understanding the differences. Yes, you'll find information here that is also in the owner's manual, such as the parameters you can enter when changing your EOS RP's operation in the various menus. Basic descriptions—before I dig in and start providing in-depth tips and information—may also be vaguely similar. There are only so many ways you can say, for example, "Hold the shutter release down halfway to lock in exposure." If you need advice on *when* and *how* to use the most important functions, you'll find the information here.

David Busch's Canon EOS RP Guide to Digital Photography is aimed at both Canon and dSLR veterans as well as those who have used other mirrorless cameras and those who are total newcomers to digital or mirrorless photography. All can be overwhelmed by the options the EOS RP offers, while underwhelmed by the explanations they receive in their user's manual. The manuals are great if you already know what you don't know, and you can find an answer somewhere in a booklet arranged by menu listings and written by a camera vendor employee who last threw together instructions on how to operate a camcorder.

Family Resemblance

If you've owned previous models in the Canon digital camera line, and copies of my books for those cameras, you're bound to notice a certain family resemblance. Canon has been very crafty in introducing upgraded cameras that share the best features of the models they replace, while adding new capabilities and options. You benefit in two ways. If you used a previous Canon camera prior to switching to this latest EOS RP model, you'll find that the parts that haven't changed have a certain familiarity for you, making it easy to make the transition to the newest model. There are lots of features and menu choices of the EOS RP that are exactly the same as those in the most recent models. This family resemblance will help level the learning curve for you.

Similarly, when writing books for each new model, I try to retain the easy-to-understand explanations that worked for previous books dedicated to earlier camera models, and concentrate on expanded descriptions of things readers have told me they want to know more about, a solid helping of fresh sample photos, and lots of details about the latest and greatest new features. Rest assured, this book was written expressly for you, and tailored especially for the EOS RP.

Who Am I?

After spending many years as the world's most successful unknown author, I've become slightly less obscure in the past few years, thanks to a horde of camera guidebooks and other photographically oriented tomes. You may have seen my photography articles in the late, lamented *Popular Photography* magazine. I've also written about 2,000 articles for magazines like *Rangefinder, Professional Photographer*, and dozens of other photographic publications. But, first, and foremost, I'm a photojournalist and made my living in the field until I began devoting most of my time to writing books.

Although I love writing, I'm happiest when I'm out taking pictures, which is why I photograph two to three concerts and performances a month, and spend many days photographing landscapes, people, close-up subjects, or traveling to events, such as Native American "powwows," Civil War re-enactments, county fairs, ballet, and sporting events (baseball, basketball, football, and soccer are favorites). In recent years, I've spent a lot of time in Europe, strictly to shoot photographs of the people, landscapes, and monuments that I've grown to love. I finished this book while ensconced in my office-away-from-home in Cedar Key, Florida, to which I've fled three times to photograph the wildlife, wild natural settings, and wild people in the Sunshine State. I can offer you my personal advice on how to take photos under a variety of conditions because I've had to meet those challenges myself on an ongoing basis, using the cameras that I write about.

Like all my digital photography books, this one was written by someone with an incurable photography bug. My first Canon SLR was a Pellix back in the 1960s, and I've used a variety of newer models since then. Until the EOS RP was introduced, my favorite totable compact camera was the EOS SL2 that I still own. I've worked as a sports photographer for an Ohio newspaper and for an upstate New York college. I've operated my own commercial studio and photo lab, cranking out product shots on demand and then printing a few hundred glossy 8 × 10s on a tight deadline for a press kit. I've served as a photo-posing instructor for a modeling agency. People have actually paid me to shoot their weddings and immortalize them with portraits. I even prepared press kits and articles on photography as a PR consultant for a large Rochester, NY, company, which shall remain nameless. My trials and travails with imaging and computer technology have made their way into print in book form an alarming number of times.

Some readers who visit my blog have told me that the Canon EOS RP is such an advanced camera that few people really need the kind of basics that so many camera guides concentrate on. "Leave out all the basic photography information!" On the other hand, I've had many pleas from those who are trying to master digital photography as they learn to use their EOS RP, and they've asked me to help them climb the steep learning curve. Rather than write a book for just one of those two audiences, I've tried to meet the needs of both. You veterans will find plenty of information on getting the most from the EOS RP's features, and may even learn something from an old hand's photo secrets. I'll bet there was a time when you needed a helping hand with some confusing photographic topic.

In closing, I'd like to ask a special favor: let me know what you think of this book. If you have any recommendations about how I can make it better, visit my website at www.canonguides.com, click on the E-Mail Me tab, and send your comments, suggestions on topics that should be explained in more detail, or, especially, any typos. (The latter will be compiled on the Errata page you'll also find on my website.) I really value your ideas, and appreciate it when you take the time to tell me what you think! Some of the content of the book you hold in your hands came from suggestions I received from readers like yourself. If you found this book especially useful, tell others about it. Visit https://www.amazon.com/dp/1681985233/ and leave a positive review. Your feedback is what spurs me to make each one of these books better than the last. Thanks!

1

Thinking Outside the Box

For a photo enthusiast, nothing is quite as exciting as unboxing a new camera—particularly one as innovative as your new Canon EOS RP. That's why YouTube and Canon-oriented forums are inundated with "unboxing" videos as soon as a highly anticipated camera starts shipping. After waiting a very long time for Canon's answers to the booming trend toward compact, fully featured full-frame mirrorless cameras, many of us have been eager to see what's in the box, see what kind of accessories we have to enhance our shooting, and—finally—to start taking pictures.

If you're like me, the first thing you probably did when you first extracted your EOS RP from the box, was attach one of the available RF-mount lenses, power the beast up, and begin taking photos through a tentative trial-and-error process. Who has time to even scan a manual when you're holding some of the most exciting technology Canon has ever offered in your hands? If you're a veteran Canon shooter, you probably found many of the controls and menus very similar to what you're used to, even though the camera itself is much more compact and lighter in weight than your previous Canon and uses lenses in an entirely new lens mount.

But now that you've taken a few hundred (or thousand) photos with your new Canon EOS RP, you're ready to learn more. You've noted some intriguing features and adjustments that you need to master. Of course, on the other hand, you may be *new* to the Canon world, or the EOS RP may be your first advanced digital camera, and you need some guidance in learning to use all the creative options this camera has to offer. In either case, despite your surging creative juices, I recommend a more considered approach to learning how to operate the EOS RP. This chapter and the next are designed to get your camera fired up and ready for shooting as quickly as possible. And while it boasts both Auto and sophisticated Programmed Auto modes, the EOS RP is not a point-and-shoot model; to get the most out of your camera, you'll want to explore its capabilities fully.

So, to help you begin shooting as quickly as possible, I'm going to first provide a basic pre-flight checklist that you need to complete before you really spread your wings and take off. You won't find a lot of detail in these initial two chapters. Indeed, I'm going to tell you just what you absolutely *must* understand, accompanied by some interesting tidbits that will help you become acclimated to your EOS RP. I'll go into more depth and even repeat a little of what I explain here in the chapters that follow, so you don't have to memorize everything you see. Just relax, follow a few easy steps, and then go out and begin taking your best shots—ever.

I hope that even long-time Canon owners won't be tempted to skip this chapter or the next one. No matter how extensive your experience level is with dSLRs, your new mirrorless camera has a lot of differences from what you may be used to. Yet, I realize you don't want to wade through a manual to find out what you must know to take those first few tentative snaps. I'm going to help you hit the ground running with this chapter, which will help you set up your camera and begin shooting in minutes. Because some of you may already have experience with previous Canon cameras, each of the major sections in this chapter will begin with a brief description of what is covered in that section, so you can easily jump ahead to the next if you are in a hurry to get started.

Note

In this book you'll find short tips labeled **My Recommendation** or **My Preference,** each intended to help you sort through the available options for a feature, control, or menu entry. I'll provide my preference, suitable for most people in most situations. I don't provide these recommendations for every single feature, and you should consider your own needs before adopting any of them.

First Things First

This section helps get you oriented with all the things that come in the box with your Canon EOS RP, including what they do. I'll also describe some optional equipment you might want to have. If you want to get started immediately, skim through this section and jump ahead to "Initial Setup" later in this chapter.

The Canon EOS RP comes in an impressive box filled with stuff. The first thing to do is carefully unpack the camera and double-check the contents with the checklist on one end of the box. It's better to know *now* that something is missing so you can seek redress immediately, rather than discover two months from now that the component you didn't need right away (but now *must* have) was never in the box.

At a minimum, the box should have the following:

- **Canon EOS RP digital camera.** It almost goes without saying that you should check out the camera immediately, making sure the color LCD screen on the back isn't scratched or cracked, the memory card/battery door opens properly, and, when a charged battery is inserted and lens mounted, the camera powers up and reports for duty. Out-of-the-box defects like these are rare, but they can happen. It's probably more common that your dealer played with the camera or, perhaps, it was a customer return. That's why it's best to buy your EOS RP from a retailer you trust to supply a factory-fresh camera.

- **Lens (optional).** At its introduction the EOS RP was available as a "body only" (for about $1,299), but actually shipped with a free Canon Mount Adapter EF-EOS R and Canon EG-E1 Extension grip. It has also been offered in a variety of kit configurations, such as body plus 24-105mm f/4L lens ($2,200). Dealers were also willing to package the camera with one of the other three lenses available at introduction: the RF 35mm f/1.8 IS Macro STM ($500), RF 28-70mm f/2L USM ($3,000), and RF 50mm f/1.2L USM ($2,300). However, unless you were willing to pay out big bucks or wanted to go all in with Canon's new mirrorless system, you probably opted for the all-purpose 24-105mm optic. Some photographers with a heavy investment in Canon dSLR gear might have eschewed any RF-mount option and got one of the three available mount adapters to use with their existing lenses.

  My recommendation: You can't go wrong with the superb 24-105mm lens, which compares favorably with its Canon EF-mount 24-105mm counterpart. I'll explain your lens options in more detail in Chapter 7.

- **Battery Pack LP-E17.** You'll need to charge this 7.2V, 1040mAh (milliampere hour) battery before using it. I'll offer instructions later in this section. It should be furnished with a protective cover, which should always be mounted on the battery when it is not inside the camera, to avoid shorting out the contacts.

- **Battery Charger LC-E17/LC-E17E.** One of these chargers, described in the "Initial Setup" section that follows this one, is required to vitalize the LP-E17 battery.

- **Wide Strap.** Canon provides you with a "steal me" neck strap emblazoned with your camera model. It's not very adjustable, and, while useful for showing off to your friends exactly which nifty new camera you bought, it's probably not your best option, and also can serve to alert observant unsavory types that you're sporting a higher-end model that's worthy of their attention.

  My recommendation: I never attach the Canon strap to my cameras. I use the UPstrap shown in Figure 1.1, with a patented non-slip pad that keeps your EOS RP on your shoulder, and not crashing to the ground. I strongly prefer the UPstrap over holsters, slings, chest straps, or any support that dangles my camera upside down from the tripod socket and allows it to swing around too freely when I'm on the run. Give me a strap I can hang over either shoulder, or sling around my neck, and I am happy. Inventor-photographer Al Stegmeyer (www.upstrap-pro.com) can help you choose the right strap for you.

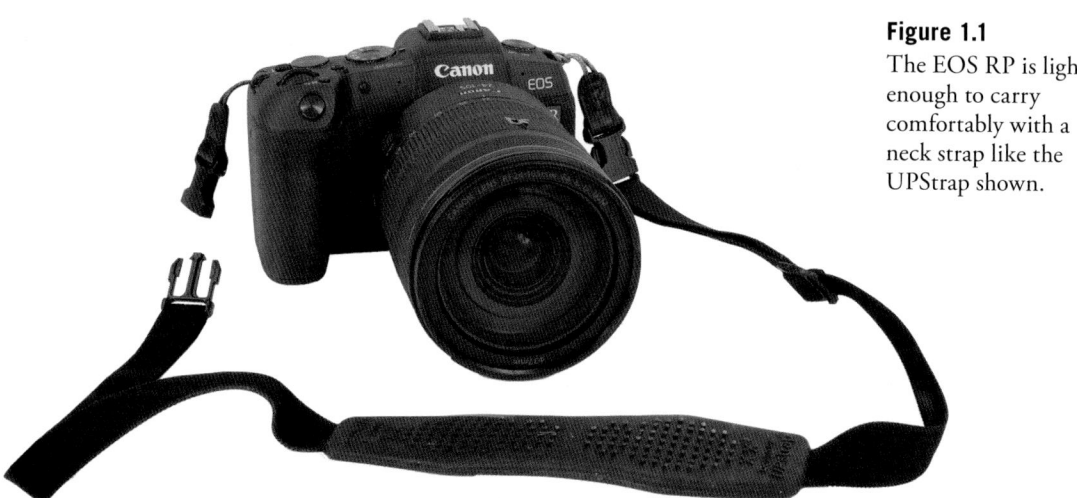

Figure 1.1
The EOS RP is light enough to carry comfortably with a neck strap like the UPStrap shown.

- **Lens accessories (if you purchased a kit).** If you purchased the EOS RP with a lens, you'll also receive accessories, including the LF-N1 rear lens cap. The lens will also be furnished with a front lens cap of appropriate diameter and may include a case. The Canon RF 24-105 f/4 L IS USM kit lens comes with a Canon E-77 II and LP1319 lens case, for example.

- **PC-GF30 body cap.** The body cap keeps dust from infiltrating your camera when a lens is not mounted. Always carry a body cap (and rear lens cap). When not in use, the body cap and rear lens cap nest together for compact storage.

- **User's manuals.** Canon still provides a basic printed manual with the EOS RP. It's small, but deceptively thick, as only one-third of it is in English, with the rest of the content repeating the same information in Spanish and French. If you need a more comprehensive manual to supplement this book, you'll have to download a PDF version, available from your country's Canon website.

- **Warranty and registration card.** Don't lose these! You can register your Canon EOS RP by mail, although you don't really need to in order to keep your warranty in force, but you may need the information in this paperwork (plus the purchase receipt/invoice from your retailer) should you require Canon service support.

There are a few things Canon classifies as optional accessories, even though you (and I) might consider some of them essential. Here's a list of what you *don't* get in the box, but might want to think about as an impending purchase. I'll list them roughly in the order of importance:

- **Memory card.** You'll need at least one memory card, as one is not furnished with the camera.

  My recommendation: For a 26-megapixel camera, you really need an SD memory card that's a *minimum* of 16GB in size, and a 32GB, 64GB, or larger card would be much better.

■ **Extra LP-E17 battery.** Your camera's sensor and either electronic viewfinder or rear panel LCD screen are active for long periods of time as you use your EOS RP, so battery life may be less than what you're used to. Canon estimates you should get approximately 250 shots from a single battery. Batteries can unexpectedly fail, too, or simply lose their charge from sitting around unused for a week or two.

My recommendation: It's easy to exceed 250 shots in a surprisingly brief period of time when shooting sports at 5 fps, when bracketing, and when taking photos at an event where a lot is going on (weddings, graduations, or amusement parks). Buy an extra (I own four, in total), keep it charged, and free your mind from worry. Canon's website says that the EOS RP's battery can also be charged inside the camera with the expensive USB Power Adapter PD-E1 (about $200 and described in the next section) connected to the camera's Type-C USB terminal, but I have not tried it.

■ **Add-on Speedlite.** Like many advanced enthusiast cameras, the Canon EOS RP does not include a built-in electronic flash. Most of the time, that's a good thing, because an internal flash is just extra weight when you're not using it. But if you use fill flash outdoors frequently, or take pictures indoors, you'll need an external Speedlite. The current top-of-the-line and most powerful Canon external flash is the Canon 600EX II-RT, the most powerful Canon external flash. If you're looking to cut down on the weight you carry around, the Canon Speedlite EL-100 is a compact unit which has more modest (but still useful) output.

My recommendation: Your add-on flash can function as the main illumination for your photo, or it can be softened and used to fill in shadows. If you do flash photography at all, consider a Speedlite as an important accessory. For the most flexibility when lighting your subject, you'll need *two* flash units: one on the camera to be used as a master, and one off-camera flash triggered wirelessly as a slave. (The two flash units mentioned above can function in either role. Canon also offers the ST-E2 and ST-E3-RT transmitter/triggers which can mount on the EOS RP's accessory shoe and serve as masters.)

■ **Interface Cable IFC-100U.** You can use this 1 meter/3.2-foot USB 3.0 Type C cable to transfer photos from the camera to your computer (not recommended), to upload and download settings between the camera and your computer (highly recommended), and to operate your camera remotely using the EOS Utility software you can download from the Support page of your country's Canon website.

My recommendation: I don't recommend using the cable to transfer images. Direct transfer uses a lot of battery power and is potentially slower. This cable has Type C connectors at either end—which means you'll need a Type C–to–Type A adapter to link to a non–Type C computer or other device. Some generic Type C–to–Type A cables I've tried do not work properly, particularly with the EOS Utility (an application that allows your computer to communicate with the camera for downloading and displaying images, remote shooting, and control of camera settings). You'll need to test yours if you're trying to save a few dollars.

■ **Mount adapters.** If you already own a collection of Canon EF and EF-S lenses, Canon offers three adapters that will let you use those lenses on your EOS RP. One is a mount adapter only, and, as I write this, is currently being bundled with the EOS RP for free. A second adds a customizable control ring to your EF/EF-S lenses like those found on the RF optics themselves, while a third includes a drop-in filter carrier that lets you use a single-size filter *behind* the rear element of the EF/EF-S lens. That includes polarizers and variable neutral-density filters, and the capability works with lenses that ordinarily can't use screw-in filters at all, such as the Canon EF 11-24mm f/4L USM or Canon Tilt/Shift TS-E 17mm f/4L lenses. I'll describe the three mount adapters in more detail in Chapter 7, which deals with your full range of lens options for the EOS RP.

■ **AC Adapter Kit ACK-E6N.** This device is used with a *DC coupler*, the DR-E18, that replaces the LP-E17 battery and powers the Canon EOS RP from AC current. Note that the ACK-E6N adapter can be used with other Canon EOS models with an appropriate coupler; the EOS R, for example, requires the DR-E6 unit.

My recommendation: There are several typical situations where this capability can come in handy: when you're cleaning the sensor manually and want to totally eliminate the possibility that a lack of juice will cause the fragile shutter to spring to life during the process; when indoors shooting tabletop photos, portraits, class pictures, and so forth for hours on end; when using your EOS RP for remote shooting as well as time-lapse photography; for extensive review of images on your television; or for file transfer to your computer. These all use prodigious amounts of power, which can be provided by this AC adapter.

■ **Remote controls.** Although the EOS RP's self-timer can be used to trigger your tripod-mounted camera without any vibration, it's more convenient to use a wired or wireless remote control to trip the shutter.

My recommendation: The EOS RP works well with the Canon BR-E1 wireless remote control, which operates using the camera's Bluetooth capability, or wired remote switch RS-60E3. For more sophisticated sequences, the TC-80N3/RA-E3 remote controller/adapter combination also functions as an interval timer. Note that previous Canon remotes that use infrared signals will not work with this camera.

■ **HDMI cable HTC-100.** You'll need this optional cable if you want to connect your camera directly to an HDTV for viewing your images.

My recommendation: I use standard HDMI mini (*not* micro) cables in 6-, 9-, and 12-foot lengths. They work fine, and I can buy several for the price of one 9.5-foot Canon-branded cable.

Initial Setup

Many EOS RP owners can skip this section, which describes basic setup steps. I'm including it at the request of ambitious photo buffs who have upgraded to this mirrorless camera after switching from a Canon dSLR, another camera brand, or an entry-level model from any manufacturer.

The initial setup of your Canon EOS RP is fast and easy. Basically, you just need to charge the battery, attach a lens, insert a memory card, and make a few settings.

Power Options

Your Canon EOS RP is a sophisticated hunk of machinery and electronics, but it needs a charged battery to function, so rejuvenating the LP-E17 lithium-ion battery pack furnished with the camera should be your first step. A fully charged power source should be good for approximately 250 shots, based on standard tests defined by the Camera & Imaging Products Association (CIPA) document DC-002.

All rechargeable batteries undergo some degree of self-discharge just sitting idle in the camera or in the original packaging. Lithium-ion power packs of this type typically lose a small amount of their charge every day, even when the camera isn't turned on. Li-ion cells lose their power through a chemical reaction that continues when the camera is switched off. So, it's very likely that the battery purchased with your camera is at least partially pooped out, so you'll want to revive it before going out for some serious shooting.

Several battery chargers are available for the Canon EOS RP. The compact LC-E17 is the charger that most EOS RP owners end up using. I like to have an extra charger in case my original charger breaks, or when I want to charge more than one battery at a time. Here's a list of your power options:

- **LC-E17.** The standard charger for the EOS RP (and also compatible with earlier cameras that use the LC-E17 batteries), this one is the most convenient, because of its compact size and built-in wall plug prongs that connect directly into your power strip or wall socket and require no cord. (See Figure 1.2, left.)
- **LC-E17E.** This is similar to the LC-E17, and also charges a single battery, but it requires a cord. That can be advantageous in certain situations. For example, if your power outlet is behind a desk or in some other semi-inaccessible location, the cord can be plugged in and routed so the charger itself sits on your desk or another more convenient spot. The cord is standard and works

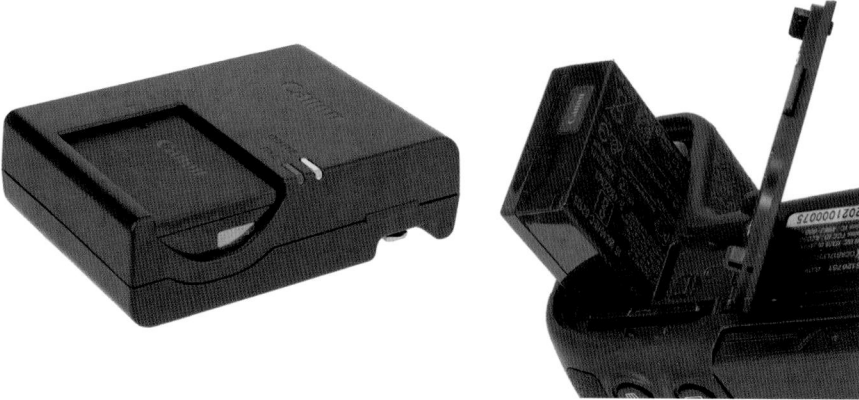

Figure 1.2
A flashing status light indicates that the battery is being charged (left). Insert the battery in the camera; it only fits one way (right).

with many different chargers and devices (including the power supply for my laptop), so I purchased several of them and leave them plugged into the wall in various locations. I can connect my EOS RP's charger, my laptop computer's charger, and several other electronic components to one of these cords without needing to crawl around behind the furniture. The cord draws no power when it's *not plugged into a charger*. Unhook the charger from the cord when you're not actively rejuvenating your batteries.

- **USB Power Adapter PD-E1.** Available separately for about $200, this adapter allows charging LP-E17 batteries without removing them from the camera over a USB Type C connection. Theoretically, you might be able to charge the batteries from a less expensive adapter or power brick if it is capable of providing higher than 5V and has USB-C output. (USB-C uses a Power Delivery specification that initially provides a "profile" that delivers 5V at 2A, but can "negotiate" with a device to provide up to 20V at 5A.) Ordinary USB chargers I've tried do not work.

    The access lamp in the lower-right corner of the camera's back panel will glow green during charging. (This is the same LED that flashes red when the EOS RP is writing to the memory card.) When charging is finished, the lamp turns off.

- **AC Adapter Kit ACK-E6/DR-E18 Coupler.** As I mentioned earlier, this device allows you to operate your EOS RP directly from AC power, with no battery required. Studio photographers need this capability because they often snap off hundreds of pictures for hours on end and want constant, reliable power. The camera is probably plugged into a flash sync cord (or radio device), and the studio flash are plugged into power packs or AC power, so the extra tether to this adapter is no big deal in that environment. You also might want to use the AC adapter when viewing images on a TV connected to your EOS RP, shooting video, or when shooting remote or time-lapse photos.

Charging the Battery

When the battery is inserted into the LC-E17 charger properly (it's impossible to insert it incorrectly), a Charge light begins flashing. It flashes on and off until the battery reaches a 50 percent charge, then blinks in two-flash cycles between 50 and 75 percent charged, and in a three-flash sequence until the battery is 90 percent charged, usually within about 90 minutes. In my experience, to be safe you should allow the charger to continue for about 60 minutes more, until the status lamp glows green steadily, to ensure a full charge. When the battery is charged, flip the lever on the bottom of the camera and slide in the battery (see Figure 1.2, right). To remove the battery from the camera, press the white retaining button.

Final Steps

Your Canon EOS RP is almost ready to fire up and shoot. You'll need to select and mount a lens, adjust the viewfinder for your vision, and insert memory card(s). Each of these steps is easy, and if you've used a previous EOS model, you already know exactly what to do. I'm going to provide a little extra detail for those of you who are new to the Canon or digital SLR worlds.

Mounting the Lens

As you'll see, my recommended lens mounting procedure emphasizes protecting your equipment from accidental damage, and minimizing the intrusion of dust. If your EOS RP has no lens attached, select the lens you want to use and loosen (but do not remove) the rear lens cap. I generally place the lens I am planning to mount vertically in a slot in my camera bag, where it's protected from mishaps, but ready to pick up quickly. By loosening the rear lens cap, you'll be able to lift it off the back of the lens at the last instant, so the rear element of the lens is covered until then.

After that, remove the body cap by rotating the cap toward the shutter release button. You should always mount the body cap when there is no lens on the camera, because it helps keep dust out of the interior of the camera, where it can settle in the interior and potentially find its way onto the sensor. (While the EOS RP's sensor cleaning mechanism works fine, the less dust it has to contend with, the better.) The body cap also protects the vulnerable sensor from damage caused by intruding objects (including your fingers, if you're not cautious).

Once the body cap has been removed, remove the rear lens cap from the lens, set it aside, and then mount the lens on the camera by matching the raised red alignment indicator on the lens barrel with the red line on the camera's lens mount. Rotate the lens away from the shutter release until it seats securely. Set the focus mode switch on the lens to AF (autofocus) and the stabilizer switch to On. If the lens hood is bayoneted on the lens in the reversed position (which makes the lens/hood combination more compact for transport), twist it off and remount so it is facing outward. A lens hood protects the front of the lens from accidental bumps, stray fingerprints, and reduces flare caused by extraneous light arriving at the front element of the lens from outside the picture area.

Adjusting Diopter Correction

Those of us with less than perfect eyesight can often benefit from a little optical correction in the viewfinder. Your contact lenses or glasses may provide all the correction you need, but if you are a glasses wearer and want to use the EOS RP without your glasses, you can take advantage of the camera's built-in diopter adjustment, which can be varied from −4 to +1 correction. With the camera powered up, rotate the diopter adjustment control located to the immediate left of the viewfinder (see Figure 1.3) while looking through the viewfinder until the indicators appear sharp.

Inserting a Memory Card

You can't take photos without a memory card inserted in your EOS RP, so your final step will be to insert a memory card. Open the battery compartment door to access the card slot. (You should only remove the memory card when the camera is switched off, but the EOS RP will remind you if the door is opened while the camera is still writing photos to the memory card.)

Insert the memory card into the slot with the label facing the back of the camera, as shown in Figure 1.4, oriented so the edge with the gold contacts go into the slot first. Close the door, and your preflight checklist is done! (I'm going to assume you remember to remove the lens cap when you're ready to take a picture!) When you want to remove the memory card later, press down on the card to make the memory card pop out.

Diopter adjustment control

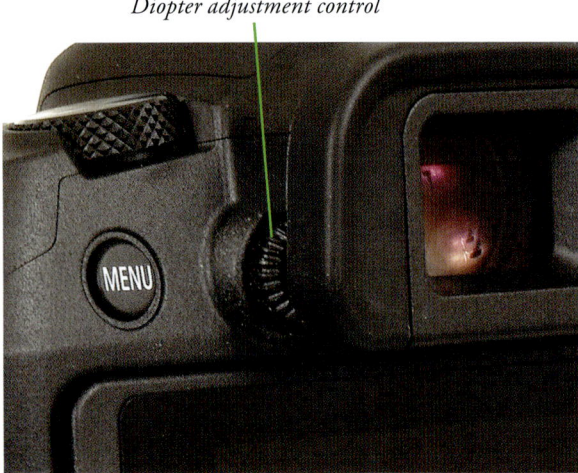

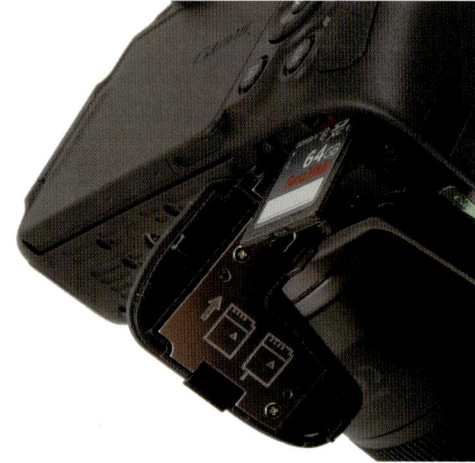

Figure 1.3 Viewfinder diopter correction from −4 to +1 can be dialed in.

Figure 1.4 Insert the memory card in the slot with the label facing the back of the camera.

Formatting a Memory Card

There are three ways to create a blank memory card for your EOS RP, and two of them are at least partially wrong. Here are your options, both correct and incorrect:

- **Transfer (move) files to your computer.** When you transfer (rather than copy) all the image files to your computer from the memory card (either using a direct cable transfer or with a card reader, as described later in this chapter), the old image files are erased from the card, leaving the card blank. Theoretically. This method does *not* remove files that you've labeled as Protected (choosing the Protect images function in the Playback menu) nor does it identify and lock out parts of your memory card that have become corrupted or unusable since the last time you formatted the card. Therefore, I recommend always formatting the card, rather than simply moving the image files, each time you want to make a blank card. The only exception is when you *want* to leave the protected/unerased images on the card for a while longer, say, to share with friends, family, and colleagues.

- **(Don't) Format in your computer.** With the memory card inserted in a card reader or card slot in your computer, you can use Windows or Mac OS to reformat the memory card. Don't! The operating system won't necessarily arrange the structure of the card the way the EOS RP likes to see it (in computer terms, an incorrect *file system* may be installed). The only way to ensure that the card has been properly formatted for your camera is to perform the format in the camera itself. The only exception to this rule is when you have a seriously corrupted memory card that your camera refuses to format. Sometimes it is possible to revive such a corrupted card by allowing the operating system to reformat it first, then trying again in the camera.

- **Setup menu format.** To use the recommended method to format a memory card, just follow these steps, shown in Figure 1.5:

  1. Press the MENU button.
  2. Rotate the Main Dial (located on top of the camera as shown) to select the Set-up 1 menu, represented by a wrench icon.
  3. Spin the Quick Control Dial (at the rear-top edge to move the highlighting down within the Set-up 1 menu.
  4. Select Format Card.
  5. Press the SET button (with the Q/SET label) on the back of the camera.
  6. Use the left/right buttons (located on either side of the SET button) to highlight OK, and press SET again to start the format. You can optionally press the Trash button first to perform an extra-thorough low-level "clean-up" format, which is a good idea if the card has been used many times.

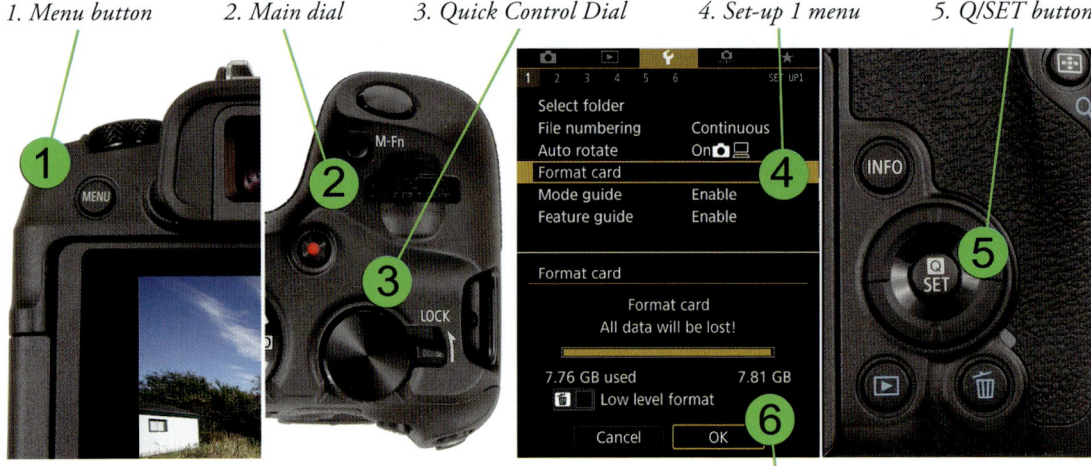

Figure 1.5 Formatting a memory card.   *6. Format screen*

Using the Physical Controls

Now that you've used the menus to format a memory card, it's a good time to introduce some of the other main controls. I will explain how to use the touch screen on the back of the camera in Chapter 2, rather than in this "quick start" chapter. First, you should become familiar with the most important of the major physical controls:

- **MENU button.** You can produce the EOS RP's main menus by pressing the MENU button, located at the far-left corner of the back of the camera (and shown at left in Figure 1.5).

- **Main Dial and Quick Control Dial.** These dials (shown at center left in Figure 1.5) move highlighting among options, say, to move left and right among the main menu heading tabs, like those seen at center right in Figure 1.5 (using the Main Dial) or to scroll down to individual entries (Quick Control Dial).

- **Quick Control/SET button.** The Quick Control/SET button (or Q/SET button) is shown at far right in Figure 1.5. When you're shooting photos, it produces a Quick Control menu screen (described later), which offers fast access to many adjustments. When you are navigating menus, it functions as a SET button (similar to a Return or Enter button on a computer) to access a sub-menu or confirm your selection.

- **Directional buttons.** The directional buttons are located on the ridged pad surrounding the Q/SET button. They are used to move things around the frame (such as autofocus points or a zoomed view of the frame) and for menu navigation. (Left/right to move between main menu tabs, and up/down to scroll among individual entries.) The official name for those four ridges on the pad surrounding the Q/SET button is "cross keys," but they are commonly simply called "directional buttons." From time to time I will also refer to them as left/right or up/down buttons.

REACH OUT AND TOUCH SOMETHING

As I noted, your Canon EOS RP has a touch-sensitive screen that is useful for navigating menus, selecting focus points, and other functions. In many cases, you can use the buttons and dials and the touch screen almost interchangeably, but for this introductory chapter I'm going to stick to using the physical controls instead of the touch controls. There are two reasons for that. First, it's important you become comfortable using the buttons and dials, because for many functions they are faster, sometimes easier, and work reliably even when your fingers are "encumbered" (say, while you're wearing gloves). In addition, this chapter is intended primarily for those new to the Canon mirrorless world. I'll explain how to use the touch screen in Chapter 2.

Setting the Time and Date

The first time you use the Canon EOS RP, it may ask you to enter the time and date. (This information may have been set by someone checking out your camera on your behalf prior to sale.) Just follow these steps:

1. Press the MENU button, located in the upper-left corner of the back of the EOS RP.

2. Rotate the Main Dial (near the shutter release button on top of the camera) until the Set-up 2 menu is highlighted. It's marked by a wrench and the message SET UP2, as shown at left in Figure 1.6.

3. Rotate the Quick Control Dial (QCD) to move the highlighting down to the Date/Time/Zone entry.

4. Press the SET button to access the Date/Time/Zone setting screen, shown at right in Figure 1.6.

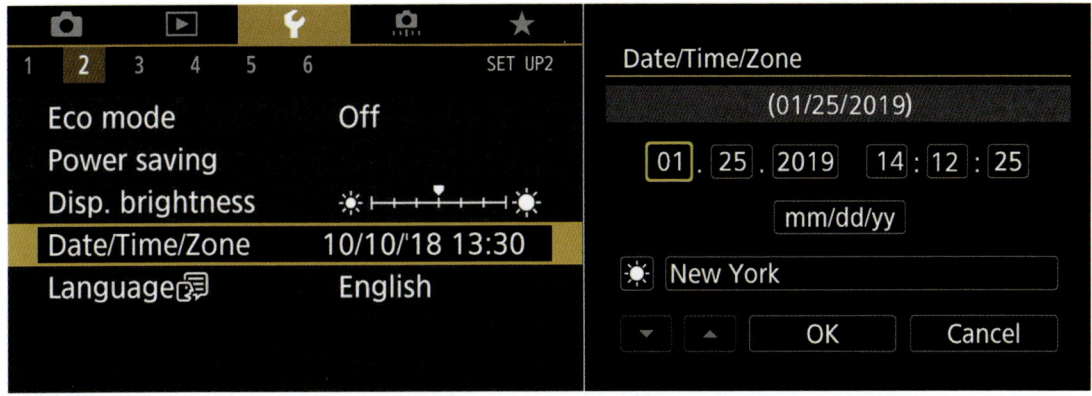

Figure 1.6 Choose the Date/Time/Zone entry from the Set-up 2 menu and set the parameters.

5. Rotate the QCD to select the value you want to change. When the gold box highlights the month, day, year, hour, minute, or second format you want to adjust, press the SET button to activate that value. A pair of up-/down-pointing triangles appears above the value.

6. Rotate the Quick Control Dial to adjust the value up or down. Press the SET button to confirm the value you've entered.

7. Repeat steps 5 and 6 for each of the other values you want to change. The date format can be switched from the default mm/dd/yy to yy/mm/dd or dd/mm/yy. You can activate/deactivate Daylight Saving Time, and select a Time Zone.

8. When finished, rotate the QCD to select either OK (if you're satisfied with your changes) or Cancel (if you'd like to return to the Set-up 2 menu screen without making any changes). Press SET to confirm your choice.

9. When finished setting the date and time, press the MENU button to exit.

Selecting a Shooting Mode

The following sections show you how to choose semi-automatic, automatic shooting, or exposure modes; select a metering mode (which tells the camera what portions of the frame to evaluate for exposure); and set the basic autofocus functions. If you understand how to do these things, you can skip ahead to "Other Settings."

Now it's time to fire up your EOS RP and take some photos. The easy part is turning on the power—that ON/OFF switch on the top-left shoulder of the camera. Turn on the camera, and, if you mounted a lens and inserted a fresh battery and memory card, you're ready to begin. You'll need to select a shooting mode, metering mode, and focus mode.

You can choose a shooting method by rotating the Mode Dial (see Figure 1.7) to select a mode. The current mode is displayed in the viewfinder and color LCD screen on the back of the EOS RP.

The camera has one fully automatic mode called Scene Intelligent Auto (A+ on the display), which makes virtually all the decisions for you (except when to press the shutter). There are also 12 Special Scene modes suitable for particular types of subjects (such as landscapes, portraits, or sports). Canon labels these as Basic Zone modes.

In addition, there are six *semi-automatic/manual* modes (what Canon calls Creative Zone modes), including Flexible-priority (Fv), Program (P), Shutter-priority (Tv), Aperture-priority (Av), Manual (M), and Bulb (B). These each allow you to provide input over the exposure and settings the camera uses. The Mode Dial also includes a Movie position to switch the EOS RP into video mode, and three camera user settings (Custom shooting modes) that can be used to store specific groups of camera settings, which you can then recall quickly by choosing C1, C2, or C3 as your shooting mode. You'll find a complete description of fully automatic and semi-automatic/manual modes in Chapter 4, as well as Custom shooting modes in Chapter 14.

Figure 1.7
The Mode Dial.

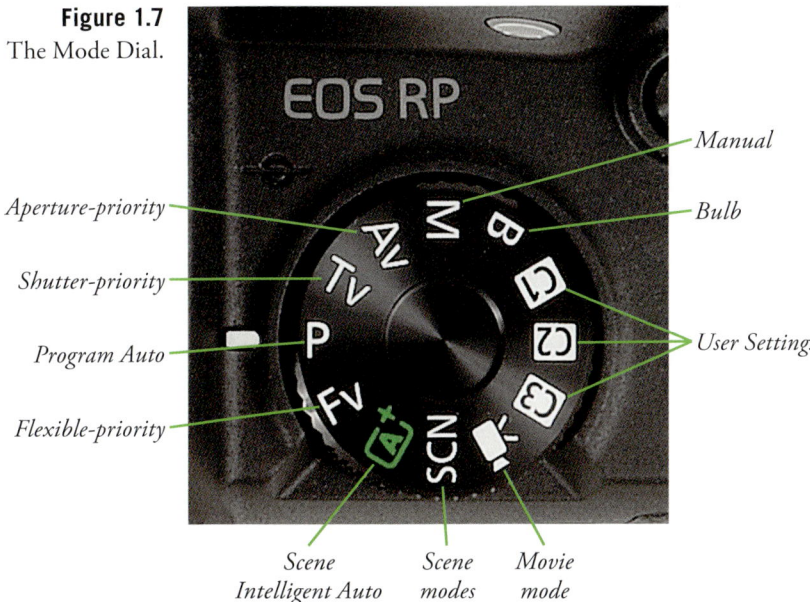

Manual

Aperture-priority

Bulb

Shutter-priority

Program Auto

User Settings

Flexible-priority

Scene Intelligent Auto

Scene modes

Movie mode

If you're very new to digital photography, you might want to set the camera to Scene Intelligent Auto (A+) or P (Program AE mode) and start snapping away. These modes will make all the appropriate settings for you for many shooting situations. Your choices follow.

Basic Zone Modes

Here is a list of the Basic Zone modes available from the Mode Dial, using the Scene Intelligent Auto and Special Scene mode positions (marked with a green A+ icon and SCN label, respectively). Unless you've disabled the default Mode Guide in the Set-up 1 menu, a screen appears explaining the functions of Scene Intelligent Auto or the Special Scene modes. (The Scene Mode guide display is shown at left in Figure 1.8.) Press the down directional button if you want more information. Press the SET button to activate Scene Intelligent Auto or proceed to scene selection, which produces a screen like the one shown at right in Figure 1.8.

■ **Scene Intelligent Auto.** In this mode, marked with a green A+ icon, the EOS RP makes all the exposure decisions for you. The camera will examine your scene and choose an appropriate mode. The type of scene chosen will be shown in the upper-left corner of the display. You can make some adjustments, such as enabling the self-timer, changing the image quality mode, and activating or deactivating Touch Shutter (which allows you to specify a focus point and take a picture by tapping an area of the touch screen).

You can also modify some of the visual features, including brightness, contrast, saturation, and color tone, using the Creative Assist Effects feature. I'll explain these options in the section following this one.

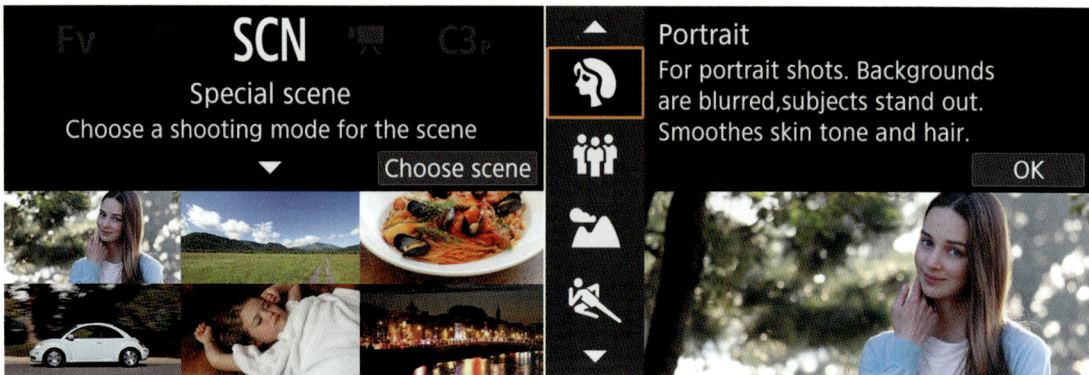

Figure 1.8 Mode Guide screens for Special Scene modes.

Note: The "scenes" chosen do not correspond exactly to the Special Scene modes described next. They take into account moving subjects, close-up, portrait subjects, backlighting (the illumination is behind the subject), and whether sky is present in the photo. The complex matrix showing the combination of 29 possible Scene Intelligent Auto icons can be found on Page 595 of your manual. I won't duplicate it here in this quick-start introduction, as I expect most of you will "graduate" from this most basic automated mode quickly as you learn to apply your own creativity to your EOS RP's settings.

■ **Portrait.** The people-friendly Portrait mode is an excellent choice when you're taking a portrait of a subject standing relatively close to the camera and want to de-emphasize the background, maximize sharpness, and produce flattering skin tones and silky-looking hair.

Note: This mode, and the 11 that follow, can be selected when the Mode Dial is set to the SCN position. Use the up/down buttons to select a mode.

■ **Group photo.** Provides settings, including a smaller f/stop, that help ensure everyone in a group shot is in acceptably sharp focus through increased depth-of-field. A wide-angle lens or zoom setting will improve your chances of deeper focus.

■ **Landscape.** Select this mode when you want extra sharpness and rich colors of distant scenes, especially in the blues and greens typical in scenic photography.

■ **Sports.** Use this mode to freeze fast-moving subjects. The EOS RP automatically looks for faces of the participants and tracks moving subjects. Multiple frames will be shot continuously as you hold down the shutter release.

■ **Kids.** Produces pleasant skin tones, with bright colors and a fast-enough shutter speed to allow sharp pictures of rampaging children. This scene mode also uses face-detection and tracking to follow fast moving children around, and captures multiple shots continuously. It's similar to Sports mode, but pays special attention to keeping skin tones warm and healthy looking.

- **Panning.** Use this mode by swiveling your camera to follow a moving subject using a panning motion. A slightly slower shutter speed will be used so that the background is blurred while the subject you are tracking is relatively sharper. Canon says it works best with lenses that support Panning mode; in plain English that simply means the lens has optical image stabilization built in that will minimize blur from up/down motion while ignoring side-to-side blur. When you select this mode, a warning message will appear on the display. Use Mode 2 if it is available on your lens.

  When Panning is active, an option will appear on the Quick Control menu screen allowing you to set the level of background motion blur from Max, to Medium, to Minimum. I'll explain the use of the Quick Control menu later in this chapter.

- **Close-up.** This mode is helpful when you are shooting close-up pictures of a subject from about one foot away or less. You'll get the best results with lenses that include macro (close-focusing) capabilities.

- **Food.** Gives you bright and vivid colors, to make your food look more appetizing than it probably was in real life. Shooting pictures of your food has become almost mandatory when dining out, thanks to Instagram. This mode, like Panning, has an Effects option in the Quick Control menu to specify a Color Tone of either Warm or Cool.

- **Night Portrait (with Tripod).** Choose this mode when you want to illuminate a subject in the foreground with an external flash mounted on the EOS RP, but still allow the background to be exposed properly by the available light. The combination avoids ending up with a totally black background. Be prepared to use a tripod or an image-stabilized (IS) lens to reduce the effects of camera shake. (You'll find more about IS and camera shake in Chapter 10.)

- **Handheld Night Scene.** If a tripod is not available to you, it's still possible to capture excellent night scenes. In this mode, the EOS RP takes four continuous shots and combines them to produce a well-exposed image with reduced camera shake. Even so, you should try to hold the camera steady. You can improve your results (especially with portraits), by using an external flash. The first image of the four captured will have supplementary illumination from the flash; the remaining three will be taken using only ambient light. Make sure your subject doesn't move between the continuously captured shots, to avoid ghost images from what is effectively a multiple exposure image. Note that in aligning the four shots, the camera will need to crop the final image slightly and a [BUSY] indicator will appear while the process is underway.

- **HDR Backlight Control.** The EOS RP takes three continuous shots at different exposures and combines them to produce a single image with improved detail in the highlights and shadows. Use this scene mode for subjects that have important detail in both the bright areas (highlights) and shadows. The [BUSY] indicator will appear for a few moments during postprocessing of your image.

■ **Silent Mode.** Your EOS RP has an electronic shutter that can capture images without the familiar ker-plunk caused by the physical mechanical shutter. You'll want to use this mode, say, to grab photos of sleeping children, or during acoustic concerts, religious ceremonies, and other "quiet zone" venues. Your main feedback that pictures are actually being taken is a white frame that is displayed briefly.

If an external flash is attached and powered up, it will not fire, and continuous shooting is not available. If you like, you can use the self-timer (explained later). The timer's normal count-down beep will be silenced, too (although the orange LED on the front of the camera will flash).

Scene Intelligent Auto Adjustments

In Scene Intelligent Auto (A+) mode, you can adjust a few of the shooting parameters, including some of the visual effects applied to your images.

■ **Shooting settings.** In A+ mode, a display similar to the one seen in Figure 1.9 appears on the LCD screen (if it does not, press the INFO button, located on the back of the camera to the right of the LCD, until it does). The icons at lower left can be tapped to change Drive mode (Single shot, plus some continuous and self-timer modes I will explain later), Image Quality, and to enable or disable the Touch Shutter feature (which allows you to specify a focus area and take a picture with a single tap). At lower right is an icon to summon the Creative Assist features, discussed next. Also shown are the Scene icons, number of possible shots remaining on your memory card, available movie shooting time, and battery status.

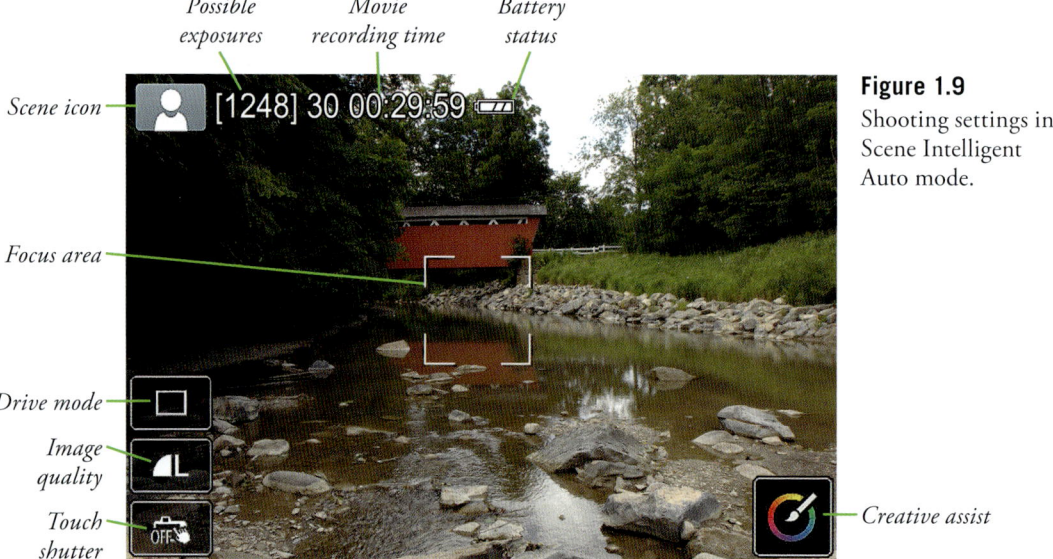

Figure 1.9
Shooting settings in Scene Intelligent Auto mode.

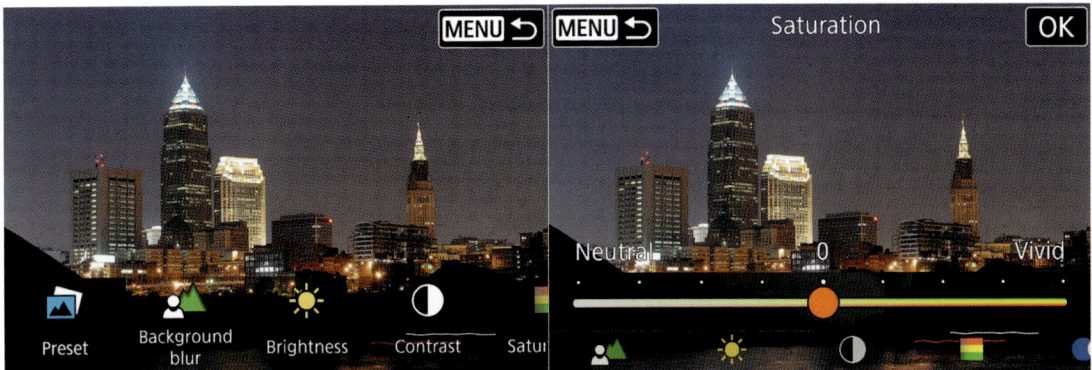

Figure 1.10 Choose a Creative Assist setting (left). Make an adjustment (right).

- **Creative Assist.** When you tap the icon at lower right, the Creative Assist screen, shown at left in Figure 1.10, appears. Along the bottom you'll find an array of creative filters you can apply to images *as you shoot*. The figure shows Preset, Background Blur, Brightness, Contrast, and Saturation. Press the left/right buttons to navigate among these and to scroll to additional choices located off-screen: Color Tone 1, Color Tone 2, and Monochrome. Press SET to adjust the application of the highlighted effect. Figure 1.10, right, shows the adjustment for the Saturation (color richness) setting, from Neutral to Vivid.

The Creative Assist effects provide adjustments similar to the EOS RP's Picture Styles, which I will detail in Chapter 11. Both change your image as you shoot, and can be redefined and saved. The current Creative Assist adjustments can be stored by pressing the INFO button and selecting OK when viewing the Creative Assist setting screen. You can also store up to three Presets as USER* settings. Once you've activated one of these effects, "* Reset" appears at lower right. Press the button marked with an asterisk (*) in the upper-right corner of the back of the camera to cancel current effects. Your choices include:

- **Preset.** Choose from 12 preset effects: None (the default, represented by an underscore character), Vivid, Soft, Warm, Cool, Green, Shine, Lime, Peach, B&W, Blue, and Purple. Each of these can be further modified using any of the effects listed next. (Saturation and Color Tone 1/2 are not available with the B&W preset.)

- **Background blur.** This setting adjusts the f/stop used, and thus its depth-of-field (the range of the image that is in focus). Choices included Blurred, Auto (which blurs the background to match the brightness of a scene), and Sharp.

- **Brightness.** Adds or subtracts exposure to brighten or darken your image.

- **Contrast.** Adjusts the contrast of the image.

- **Saturation.** Specifies the richness of the color: For example, pink is a desaturated version of a vivid red.

- **Color Tone 1.** Adjusts the bias of the color along an amber/blue axis.
- **Color Tone 2.** Adjusts color tone along a green/magenta axis.
- **Monochrome.** Captures images with a single tone: neutral Black-and white, Sepia, Blue, Purple, or Green.

CREATIVE POST-PROCESSING

The Creative Assist effects can also be applied to images you've already captured using a Playback 3 menu option or Creative Assist in the Playback version of the Quick Control menu (as described later in this chapter).

Creative Zone Modes

Your EOS RP's Creative Zone modes are the tools you can use to get, well, *creative.* These six modes give you access to the full range of your camera's shooting options. The first four listed next (Fv, P, Tv, and Av) are designed to give a great deal of versatility in specifying how the camera selects semi-automatic exposure settings. The fifth, M (Manual) makes it easy to tailor your exposure during those situations where you want to remove the camera from the exposure equation. Bulb, the final Creative Zone Mode, gives you the ability to use extra-long exposures as a special effect. **Note:** Movie mode (explained in Chapters 15 and 16), and the C1, C2, and C3 user settings (described in Chapter 13) are not considered Creative Zone modes, even though they share space on the Mode Dial.

- **Fv (Flexible-priority).** The Fv stands for *flexible value.* This is a recently introduced exposure mode that's a combination of the four described next in this list. You can manually lock in a specific shutter speed or aperture, or ISO sensitivity setting, or any combination of the three, and the other values will be set by the EOS RP. You can also allow any or all of them to be selected automatically. You can then make your images darker or lighter using exposure compensation to override your settings.

  As its name implies, this option gives you a great deal of flexibility in choosing which settings are chosen automatically, and which are specified by you manually. I recommend that beginners not use this shooting mode until they've read my complete description of how to use it easily in Chapter 4.

- **P (Program Auto Exposure).** This semi-automatic mode, usually just referred to as P or Program mode, allows the EOS RP to select the basic exposure settings, but you can still override the camera's choices to fine-tune your image.

- **Tv (Shutter-priority).** This mode (Tv stands for *time value*) is useful when you want to use a particular shutter speed to stop action or produce creative blur effects. The EOS RP will select the appropriate f/stop for you.

- **Av (Aperture-priority).** Choose when you want to use a particular lens opening, especially to control sharpness or how much of your image is in focus. The EOS RP will select the appropriate shutter speed for you. Av stands for *aperture value.*

- **M (Manual).** Select when you want full control over the shutter speed and lens opening, either for creative effects or because you are using a studio flash or other flash unit not compatible with the EOS RP's automatic flash metering.

- **B (Bulb).** Choose this mode and the shutter will remain open as long as you hold down the release button. It is useful for making exposures of indeterminate length (say, you want to capture some fireworks, and leave the shutter open until a burst appears, then release the shutter after a few seconds when the light trails have been captured). The B setting can also be used to produce exposures longer than the 30 seconds (maximum) the EOS RP can take automatically.

Choosing a Metering Mode

Metering mode is the next setting you'll want to make. Note that for this and the settings that follow, the EOS RP must be set to one of the Creative Zone modes or Movie mode, and *not* to Scene Intelligent Auto (A+). Among the four metering modes I'll describe next, the default Evaluative metering is probably the best choice as you get to know your camera.

To change metering modes, use the EOS RP's Quick Control screen, which comes in several variations and can be accessed using one of three methods. I'll explain some other capabilities of the Quick Control screen in the section that follows this one.

Option 1: While looking through the viewfinder:

- Press the Q (combined Q/SET) button. The screen shown in Figure 1.11 appears for about six seconds, waiting for your input. This is the viewfinder version of the EOS RP's Quick Control screen.

- Use the directional buttons to navigate to the Metering Mode icon, which is the fourth from the top in the left column. Then rotate either dial to select one of the four modes described next.

- Press SET to confirm.

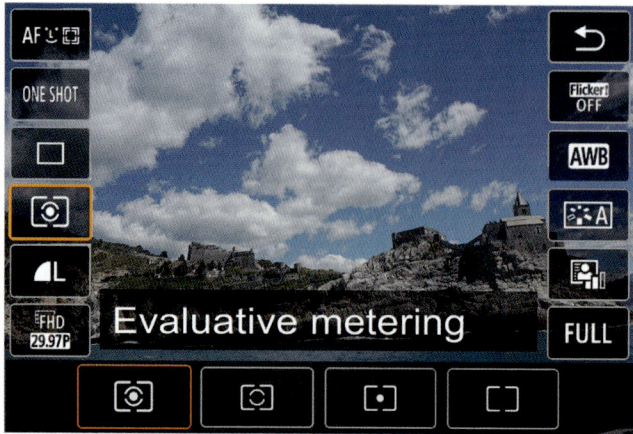

Figure 1.11
When looking through the view-finder, you can select Metering modes (left to right, bottom of the screen): Evaluative, Partial, Spot, Center-weighted.

Option 2: While looking at the LCD screen:

- The screen will display either one of several different image previews of your subject, or a graphic-based information screen. (You can cycle among these informational displays by pressing the INFO button.)

- If the graphic screen is displayed, press the Q button to see the graphic version of the Quick Control screen, shown in Figure 1.12. Navigate to the Metering Mode icon, which is in the center of the bottom row of icons. Rotate either dial to choose a mode, then press SET to confirm.

- If the image preview is displayed, press the Q button and select a metering mode from the LCD version of the Quick Control screen that appears, using the directional buttons as described above in Option 1. (See Figure 1.13.) The screen is very similar to the one shown in Figure 1.11; the chief difference is that boxes appear around the choices, which indicates you can tap them with the touch screen instead of using navigational controls, which you can use for Option 3, described below.

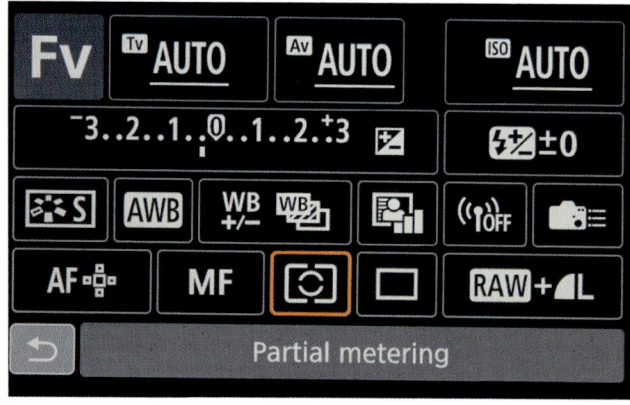

Figure 1.12
When viewing the graphic screen, Metering modes can be selected rotating either dial while the Metering Mode icon is highlighted.

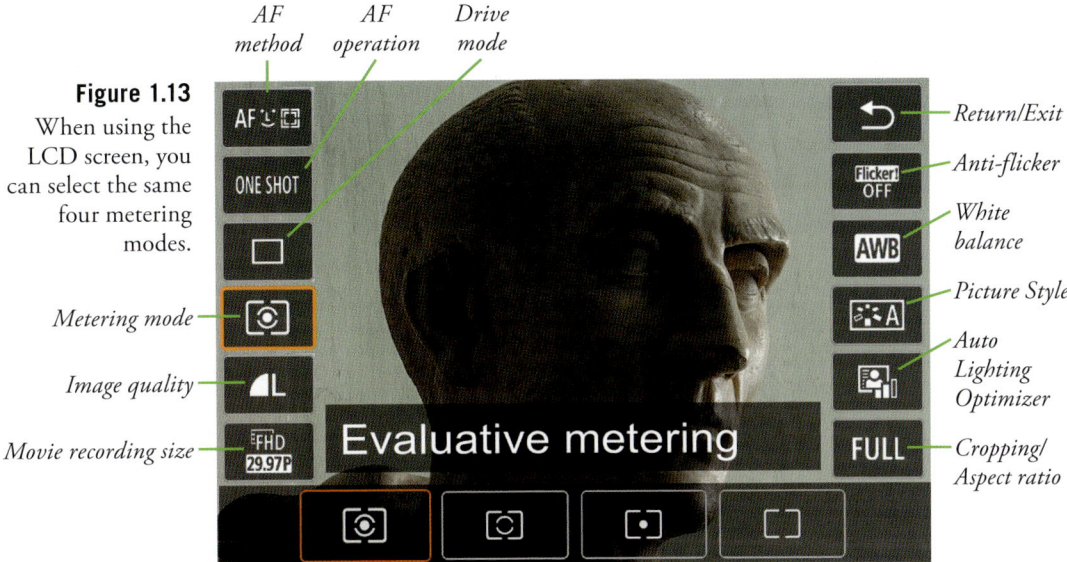

Figure 1.13
When using the LCD screen, you can select the same four metering modes.

AF method

AF operation

Drive mode

Return/Exit

Anti-flicker

White balance

Picture Style

Auto Lighting Optimizer

Metering mode

Image quality

Movie recording size

Cropping/ Aspect ratio

Evaluative metering

Option 3: When using touch controls:

- Access either the LCD or graphic versions of the Quick Control screen, as described in Option 2.
- Tap the Metering Mode icon in either screen, then tap the metering mode you want to select. Confirm and exit by tapping the "Return" arrow icon. I'll explain all your touch screen options in Chapter 2.

GETTING INFO

If at any time the expected display does not appear on the LCD screen or electronic viewfinder display in shooting or playback modes, press the INFO button several times until it is shown. One of the most frequent queries I get from new users asks why, when they follow the directions in my book, the illustrated screen isn't shown. In virtually all cases, it's because the photographer has changed the display using the INFO button on the back of the camera to the right of the viewfinder.

The four metering modes you'll be using are these:

- **Evaluative metering.** The standard metering mode; the EOS RP attempts to intelligently classify your image and choose the best exposure based on readings from a large number of zones within the image sensor.

- **Partial metering.** Exposure is based on a central spot, roughly 5.5 percent of the image area.

- **Spot metering.** Exposure is calculated from a smaller central spot, about 2.7 percent of the image area, located in the center of the frame.

- **Center-weighted averaging metering.** The EOS RP meters the entire scene, but gives the most emphasis to the central area of the frame.

You'll find a detailed description of each of these modes in Chapter 4.

Mastering the Quick Control Screen

As you've just learned, the Quick Control screen is a speedy way of making any of 11 different settings, which are called out in Figure 1.13. To access any of the adjustments, use the up/down directional buttons to move highlighting from one icon to the next one; movement will wrap around between columns. When you've highlighted the adjustment you want to make, use the left/right directional buttons or either dial to select from the options displayed at the bottom of the screen. As I noted, you can also tap their icons on the touch screen. **Note:** A second Quick Control screen is available while reviewing your images. I'll describe its options in the section on Playback later in this chapter. In shooting mode, your choices include:

- **AF method.** Choose the area of the frame which will be used to focus automatically, as described earlier in this chapter.

- **AF operation.** Choose from One-Shot or Servo modes.

- **Drive mode.** Select Single Shooting, High-Speed Continuous, Low-Speed Continuous, Self-timer: 10 sec., or Self-timer: 2 sec. You can learn more about continuous shooting in Chapter 7.

- **Metering mode.** Select the area the EOS RP uses to collect exposure information.

- **Image quality.** Choose from RAW and JPEG formats and Large, Medium, and Small resolutions.

- **Movie recording size.** Specify the resolution and frame rate of your video.

- **Anti-flicker.** Counter the flickering effects of some types of illumination, as explained in Chapter 11.

- **White balance.** Select various white balance options, such as Daylight and Incandescent.

- **Picture Style.** Apply photo-enhancing parameters to your images as you shoot, as described in Chapter 11.
- **Auto Lighting Optimizer.** Adjust shadow detail in high-contrast images.
- **Cropping/Aspect ratio.** Crop your image to 1.6X (APS-C) format; or change the proportions to 1:1, 4:3, or 16:9 aspect ratios.

Choosing a Focus Mode

You can easily switch between automatic and manual focus by moving the AF/MF switch on the lens mounted on your camera. However, if you're using a semi-automatic shooting mode, you'll still need to choose an appropriate focus mode, which tells the EOS RP *when* to focus when AF is active. (You can read more on selecting focus parameters in Chapter 5.)

To set the autofocus mode, access the viewfinder or two LCD screen versions of the Quick Control display, as described above, and navigate to the Focus Mode icon. It's located immediately to the left of the Metering Mode icon in the graphic Quick Control screen, and second from the top in the left column of the other two views. Choose one of these options, represented by the labels One-Shot or Servo.

- **One-Shot.** This mode, sometimes called *single autofocus*, locks in a focus point when the shutter button is pressed down halfway. Green boxes will appear when the image is in focus at the active focus points, or orange if the EOS RP is unable to achieve sharp focus. The focus will remain locked until you release the button or take the picture. This mode is best when your subject is relatively motionless.
- **Servo AF.** This mode, sometimes called *continuous autofocus*, sets focus when you partially depress the shutter button, but continues to monitor the frame and refocuses if the camera or subject is moved. This is a useful mode for photographing sports and moving subjects.

Selecting AF Method

The Canon EOS RP uses up to 4,779 different focus points embedded in the sensor to calculate correct focus. In Scene Intelligent Auto mode, the focus point is selected automatically by the camera, using the face detection and tracking mode I'll describe shortly. In the other semi-automatic and manual exposure modes, you can allow the camera to select the focus point automatically, or you can specify which focus point should be used.

Your camera has seven different ways of specifying which of the 4,779 focus points is selected by the camera automatically, or by the user manually. I'll describe all of them in detail in Chapters 5 and 12, and will include illustrations showing the size and coverage of each of the AF methods.

Your options are as follows:

- **Face+Tracking.** The EOS RP uses intelligent algorithms to locate human faces within the frame. The camera will then automatically focus on that face, and track it if your subject moves, refocusing as necessary. A bracketed box appears over the face to show you the active focus area. If no face is found, it will use all the focus points within the frame. As I'll explain in Chapter 5, you can select the initial position for autofocus when using Servo AF.

    I recommend Face+Tracking as your default AF focus method when starting to use your EOS RP, as it is the most versatile AF method for a wide variety of subjects. I'll provide extensive tips for choosing the other methods, and will only describe them briefly in this chapter.

- **Spot AF.** Allows you to manually select a single, reduced-size AF point.

- **1-point AF.** Allows you to manually select a single, slightly larger AF point, roughly three times the size of the Spot AF area.

- **Expand AF area.** You can manually select a single AF point, as well as the four points located above, below, and to the left/right of it.

- **Expand AF area: Around.** You can manually select a single AF point, as well as *up to* eight points surrounding it (above, below, left, right, and diagonally from the selected point).

- **Zone AF.** AF points are segregated into square-shaped zones that cover about one-sixth of the frame, and you can select which zone to use. In this Zone mode, the EOS RP will seek out faces, if present, and attempt to focus on them.

The EOS RP offers several ways of choosing the AF method. Here's a quick how-to on choosing the autofocus areas your camera will use:

1. **Press the AF point selection button.** It's located at the far right of the back of the camera. (See Figure 1.14, left.) You must press this button each time you want to change the AF area selection *mode* or when you want to select a specific AF *point* after the mode is specified.

2. **Change modes.** Within about six seconds of pressing the AF point selection button, press the M-Fn button (located on top of the camera next to the shutter release button) repeatedly to cycle among the available modes. You can *also* opt to rotate either dial or use the left/right directional buttons to cycle among the AF methods. Use whichever control is more convenient for you.

3. **Select AF area mode.** As you press the M-Fn button (or use another control) the display shown at right in Figure 1.14 appears. The highlighting will change to indicate which mode is selected. Press SET to confirm.

*AF point
selection button*

*M-Fn
button*

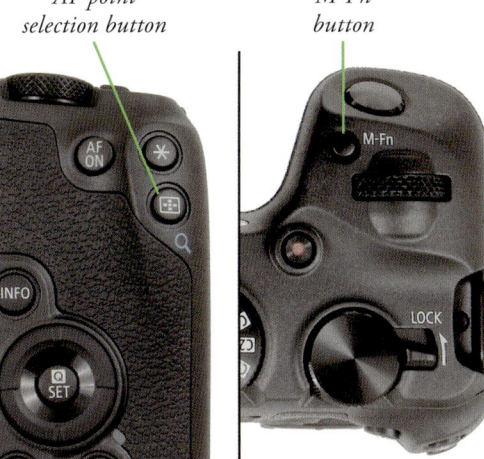

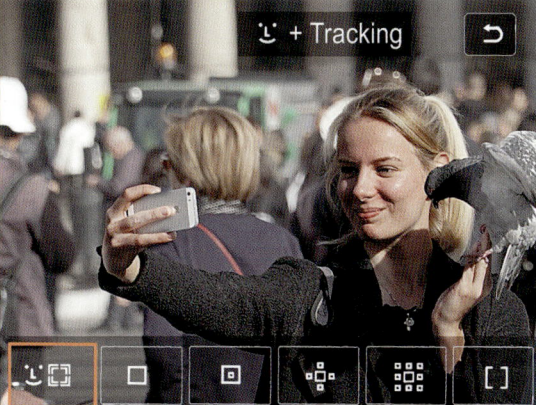

Figure 1.14 Choose AF area mode.

SIX-SECOND RULE

Many informational and settings screens will be "live" for about 6 to 14 seconds after you've pressed the relevant button. I won't repeat that information for every setting in this book; if a screen vanishes, just press the appropriate button once more.

MOVING THE AF POINT/ZONE

Once you've chosen your AF method, you can move the active focus point around the screen to a location of your choice when using any of the AF methods *except* Face+Tracking. Just press the AF point selection button, as you did before, *but do not touch the M-Fn button*. Instead, simply use the Main Dial to move the selected point, group of points, or zone left or right in the array, and the Quick Control Dial to move the point, group, or zone up or down. Or, you can use the directional buttons.

Other Settings

There are a few other options, such as white balance, using the self-timer, or working with flash. You can use these right away if you're feeling ambitious, but don't feel ashamed if you postpone using these features until you've racked up a little more experience with your EOS RP.

Adjusting White Balance and ISO

If you like, you can custom-tailor your white balance (color balance) and ISO sensitivity settings. To start out, it's best to set white balance (WB) to Auto, and ISO to ISO 100 or ISO 200 for daylight photos, and ISO 400 for pictures in dimmer light. You'll find complete recommendations for both these settings in Chapter 4.

- **ISO.** The easiest way to change ISO sensitivity is to use the M-Fn button on top of the camera. When you press it (*without first pressing the AF point selection button*), a screen appears with several functions you can adjust. Rotate the Quick Control Dial to choose which setting will be adjusted. ISO is the one located the farthest to the left. When it is highlighted, rotate the Main Dial to cycle among available ISO settings, which range from ISO Auto to ISO 100 to ISO 40000. Press SET to confirm. I'll show you how to expand those available settings from a low of ISO 50 (equivalent) to a high of ISO 102400 (equivalent) in Chapter 14.

- **White Balance.** This setting is also available from the array displayed by the M-Fn button. Rotate the Quick Control Dial until White Balance is highlighted. It's the fourth adjustment from the left. Then, rotate the Main Dial to choose a white balance setting, from among two varieties of Auto White Balance (Ambience Priority [warm] and White Priority), Daylight, Shade, Cloudy/Twilight/Sunset, Tungsten, White Fluorescent, Flash, Custom, and Color Temperature. You can also adjust white balance in the Quick Control screen, described earlier in the section on choosing a Metering Mode.

Using Drive Modes and Self-Timer/Remote

Drive modes derive their name from the days of film shooting, when physical mechanisms were used to advance the film and provide a delay before the shutter was triggered. Your EOS RP has five "drive" modes, one for taking a single shot each time the shutter is pressed, two continuous shooting modes that can capture images at up to 5.0 and 2.6 shots per second, and two self-timer/ remote modes which trip the shutter after 10 seconds or 2 seconds have elapsed.

The fastest way to choose a drive mode is with the M-Fn button, as described earlier. The Drive icon is the second from the left in the M-Fn array. Highlight it using the Quick Control Dial, and then select one of these modes using the Main Dial.

Yor options include:

- **Single shooting.** Each time you press the shutter button down all the way, the EOS RP takes one picture.
- **High-speed continuous shooting.** Hold down the shutter button to capture photos at a maximum rate of about 5 frames per second. Shooting is slower in some picture-taking modes, as I'll explain in Chapter 6.
- **Low-speed continuous shooting.** Holding down the shutter button yields shooting at up to 2.6 frames per second.
- **Self-timer: 10 sec./remote control.** The EOS RP takes a photo 10 seconds after you press the shutter release all the way, or trigger the camera using a remote control, such as the RS-60E3. You'd use this setting when you want to have enough time to get in the picture yourself.
- **Self-timer: 2 sec./remote control.** This version takes a picture after a delay of only 2 seconds. Use it when you simply want to allow the camera to stabilize after you've pressed the shutter release, minimizing camera shake (say, for long exposures).

Taking a Picture

These final sections of the chapter guide you through taking your first pictures, reviewing them on the LCD monitor, and transferring your shots to your computer.

Just press the shutter release button halfway to lock in focus at the selected autofocus point. When the shutter button is in the half-depressed position, the exposure, calculated using the shooting mode you've selected, is also locked.

Press the button the rest of the way down to take a picture. At that instant, the shutter opens, the electronic flash (if attached and enabled) fires, and your EOS RP's sensor absorbs a burst of light to capture an exposure. In fractions of a moment, the shutter closes, and the image you've taken is escorted off the CMOS sensor chip very quickly into an in-camera store of memory called a buffer, and the EOS RP is ready to take another photo. The buffer continues dumping your image onto the memory card as you keep snapping pictures without pause (at least until the buffer fills and you must wait for it to get ahead of your continuous shooting, or your memory card fills completely).

Reviewing the Images You've Taken

The Canon EOS RP has a broad range of playback and image review options. Here are the basics, as shown in Figure 1.15. I'll explain more choices, such as rotating the image on review, in Chapter 2.

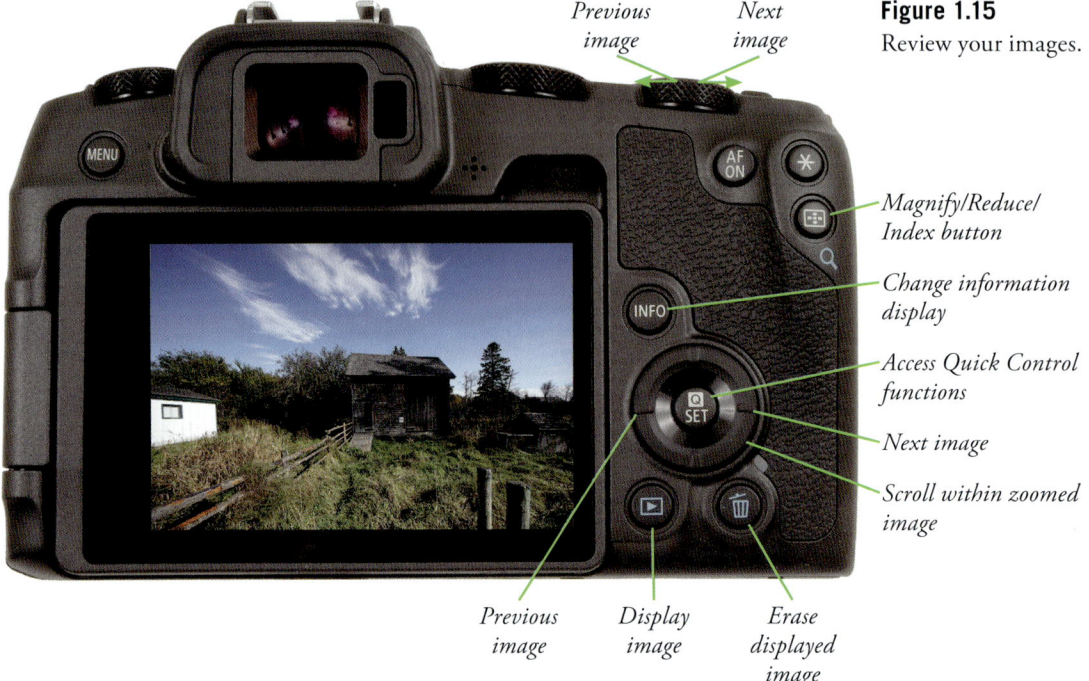

Previous image   Next image

Figure 1.15
Review your images.

Magnify/Reduce/Index button

Change information display

Access Quick Control functions

Next image

Scroll within zoomed image

Previous image   *Display image*   *Erase displayed image*

Here are the options:

- **Display image.** Press the Playback button (marked with a blue right-pointing triangle at the lower-right edge of the back of the EOS RP just to the left of the Trash button) to display the most recent image on the LCD screen in full-screen single-image mode. If you last viewed your images using the thumbnail mode (described later in this list), the Index display appears instead.

- **View previous image/next image.** Rotate the Quick Control Dial to review additional images, one at a time. Turn it to the left to review images from most recent to oldest or toward the right to start with the last image viewed and cycle forward to the newest. You can also move among images using the left/right directional buttons or the touch screen (which I'll explain in Chapter 2).

- **Jump ahead or back.** When you're using the single-image display (not zoomed or viewing reduced-size thumbnail images), you can zip through your shots more quickly to find a specific image. Just rotate the Main Dial to leap ahead or back 1, 10, or 100 images, depending on the increment you've set using the last entry in the Playback 3 menu. I find the EOS RP's use of the Main Dial is faster. You can also jump ahead by screens of images, by date, or by folder, and jump among movies, stills, and images that have been "protected" or assigned an image "rating." (You can mark favorite images to protect them from accidental erasure, or with one to four stars, as I'll explain when I show you how to select all these Playback options in Chapter 13.)

- **Change information display.** Press the INFO button repeatedly to cycle among overlays of basic image information, detailed shooting information, or no information at all.

- **Magnify/Reduce/Index button.** When an image is displayed full-screen on your LCD, press the Magnify/Reduce button. This button doubles as the AF Point Selection button, described earlier, and its Playback mode function is labeled with a blue magnifying glass icon. Rotate the Main Dial to zoom in or out. Press the Playback button to exit magnified display. I'll show you how to specify how much magnification is applied (from 2X up to 10X is available) using the Playback 4 menu, in Chapter 13. Pinching and spreading two fingers on the touch screen can also be used to zoom in and out, as described in Chapter 2.

- **View thumbnail images.** You can also rapidly move among a large number of images using the Index mode described in the section that follows this list.

- **Scroll within zoomed image.** Press the Magnify/Reduce button, then use the directional buttons to scroll around within a magnified image.

- **Access Quick Control functions.** While reviewing pictures in full-image view, you can press the Q button to produce a Quick Control screen that gives you access to many simple functions. You can protect or rate images, resize them, change the jumping method, rotate them, perform RAW image processing, enable or disable highlight alerts, search for images, and activate/deactivate AF point display. When the Quick Control screen is visible, use the directional buttons to select the function to perform. I'll explain the advantages of all these options in Chapter 3.

Cruising through Index Views

You can navigate quickly among thumbnails representing a series of images using the EOS RP's Index mode. Here are your basic options.

- **Display thumbnails.** Press the Playback button to display an image on the color LCD screen. If you last viewed your images using Index mode, an array of images appears automatically (see Figure 1.16). If an image pops up full-screen in single-image mode, press the Magnify/Reduce button once. Then, you can switch among 4, 9, 36, and 100 images, and back to single-image view by rotating the Main Dial counterclockwise. A few clicks will take you from magnified view to the four-image index view (and continuing to rotate counterclockwise will produce fewer/larger index images), whereas clockwise switches to fewer index images and back to single-image mode.

- **Navigate within a screen of index images.** In Index mode, use the QCD to move the highlight box around within the current Index display screen.

- **Check image.** When an image you want to examine more closely is highlighted, press the SET button until the single-image version appears full screen on your LCD screen.

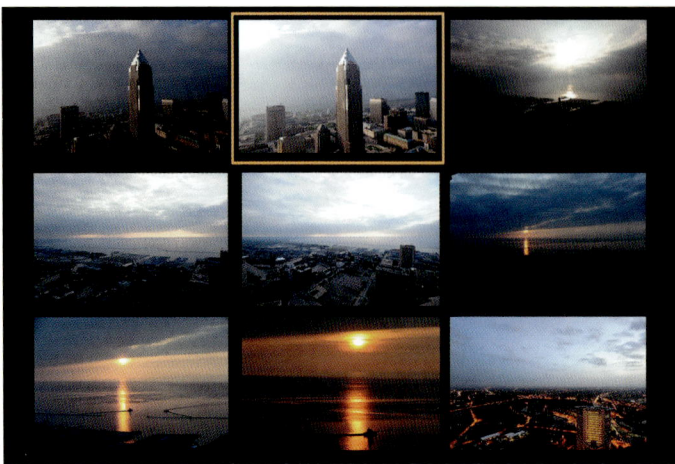

Figure 1.16
Review thumbnails of 4, 9, 36, or 100 images using Index review.

Quick Control: Playback

As I noted earlier, Playback mode also has its own Quick Control screen of functions that can be accessed quickly by pressing the Q button whenever an image you've shot is displayed. It appears in both the electronic viewfinder and on the LCD screen, and each option can be adjusted using the physical controls. Quick Control using the touch screen is, obviously, not available when viewing the Quick Control menu through the viewfinder. The options are shown in Figure 1.17. Your choices include the following, which I will explain in detail in Chapter 13:

- **Protect images.** You can protect images or groups of images from accidental erasure (but not from a card format).

- **Rotate image.** Rotate the current image on the display in 90-degree increments.

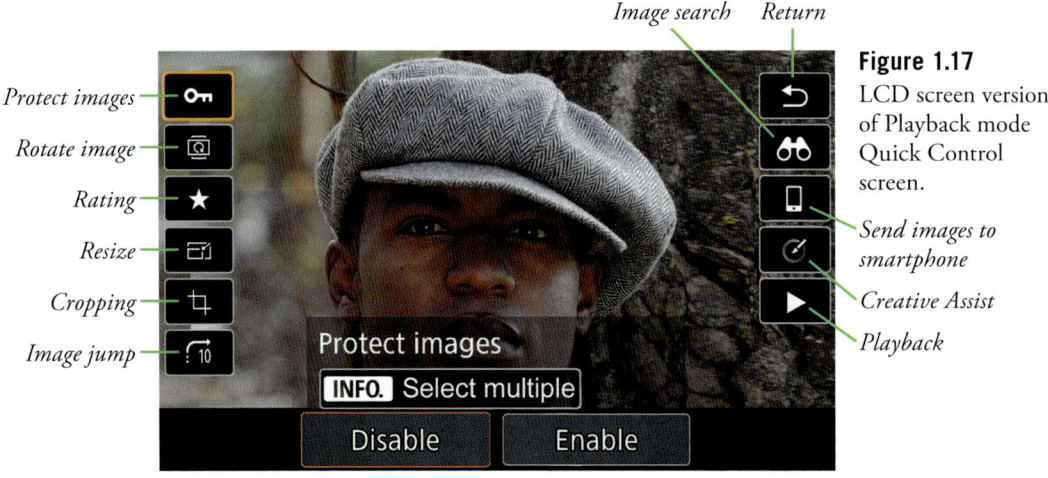

Figure 1.17
LCD screen version of Playback mode Quick Control screen.

Protect images
Rotate image
Rating
Resize
Cropping
Image jump

Image search *Return*
Send images to smartphone
Creative Assist
Playback

Protect images

INFO. Select multiple

Disable   Enable

- **Rating.** Apply one to five stars to images; these can be used to sort and search for images assigned to each rating.

- **Resize.** Convert a full-frame Large image to Medium and Small resolutions.

- **Cropping.** You can crop, straighten, or change the aspect ratio of an image, and then save a converted copy.

- **Image jump.** Jump forward or back among images during playback using leaps of 1, 10, or a specified number of images, or by date, folder name, or by movies, stills, protected, or rated image parameters.

- **Return.** Tap this icon to exit. It is available only in the LCD screen version of the Quick Control menu.

- **Image search.** You can search for images using one *or more* search parameters, including a specific rating, specified date, selected folder/protected condition, or file type.

- **Send images to smartphone.** As I'll show you in Chapter 6, you can send your shots to your smart device automatically, and select them using this option.

- **Creative Assist.** You can apply the effects discussed earlier in this chapter to your images after they have been taken.

- **Playback.** Displays most recently shot image.

Transferring Photos to Your Computer

The final step in your picture-taking session will be to transfer the photos you've taken to your computer for printing, further review, or image editing. Your EOS RP allows you to print directly to PictBridge-compatible printers and to create print orders right in the camera.

For now, you'll probably want to transfer your images either by using a cable transfer from the camera to the computer or by removing the memory card from the EOS RP and transferring the images with a card reader. The latter option is generally the best, because it's usually much faster and doesn't deplete the battery of your camera. However, you can use a cable transfer when you have the cable and a computer, but no card reader (perhaps you're using the computer of a friend or colleague, or at an Internet café).

To transfer images from the camera to a Mac or PC computer using a USB cable:

1. Turn off the camera.

2. Pry back the rubber cover that protects the EOS RP's USB terminal, and plug a USB Type C cable into the USB terminal. (See Figure 1.18.)

3. Connect the other end of the USB cable to a USB Type C terminal on your computer. (You may need to use an optional Type C–to–USB A adapter if your device lacks a USB Type C terminal.)

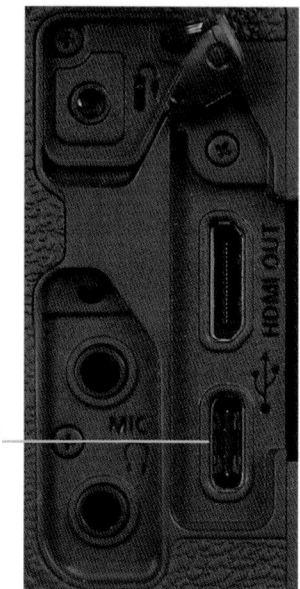

Figure 1.18
Images can be trans-
ferred to your com-
puter using a USB
cable.

USB Type C terminal

4. Turn on the camera. Your installed software usually detects the camera and offers to transfer the pictures, or the camera appears on your desktop as a mass storage device, enabling you to drag and drop the files to your computer.

To transfer images from a memory card to the computer using a card reader:

1. Turn off the camera.

2. Slide open the battery compartment door, and press down on the SD card to pop it up for removal.

3. Insert the memory card into your memory card reader. Your installed software detects the files on the card and offers to transfer them. The card can also appear as a mass storage device on your desktop, which you can open and then drag and drop the files to your computer.

2

Canon EOS RP Roadmap

Canon has simplified operation of the EOS RP by providing quick access to the most frequently adjusted commands and functions through a clever use of multi-function controls, like the Control Ring found on RF lenses and adapters, as well as the Multi-function (M-Fn) and Quick Control (Q) buttons. Canon says it's implemented this approach because the smaller size of the EOS RP doesn't lend itself to the daunting number of buttons found on traditional, large digital SLRs. Your camera has reduced the number of dedicated controls, but still minimizes the need to delve into the sometimes-confusing thicket of conventional menus.

That's a good thing. After all, while menus are easy to *learn*, because each entry describes its function in text form, their ironic disadvantage is that they are clumsy to *use*. Even though a well-designed menu system can lead you to the right commands, they require negotiating through all the various levels with multiple steps.

Your EOS RP's more limited number of controls summon concise icon-based choices you can select with the twirl of a dial and press of a button or two. Best of all, with a customizable Control Ring, M-Fn button, and Quick Control button, you can tailor the camera to work the way you want it to, rather than succumb to the manufacturer's notion of how it should work.

However, even with the EOS RP's clean, versatile design, you'll still need to learn the location, function, and application of all its parts. What you really need is a street-level roadmap that shows where everything is, and how it's used. But what Canon gives you in the comprehensive PDF user's manual is akin to a world globe with an overall view and not much information on how to use each component. Check out the Parts Names pages of the full Canon EOS RP manual (pages 31 to 38), which offer sparse black-and-white line drawings of the camera body that show front, back, two sides, and the top and bottom of the EOS RP, plus lenses, screens, and other features. There are nearly 60 callouts pointing to various buttons, dials, controls, components, and icons. If you can find the control you want in this cramped layout, you'll still need to flip back and forth among multiple pages to locate the information about them.

I originated the up-close-and-personal full-color, street-level roadmap (rather than a satellite view) that I use in this book and my previous camera guidebooks. I provide you with many different views and lots of explanation accompanying each zone of the camera, so that by the time you finish this chapter, you'll have a basic understanding of every control and what it does. I'm not going to delve into menu functions here—you'll find a discussion of your Set-up, Shooting, and Playback menu options in Chapters 11 through 14. Everything here is devoted to the button pusher and dial twirler in you.

You'll also find this "roadmap" chapter a good guide to the rest of the book, as well. I'll try to provide as much detail here about the use of the main controls as I can, but some topics (such as autofocus and exposure) are too complex to address in depth right away. So, I'll point you to the relevant chapters that discuss things like set-up options, exposure, use of electronic flash, and working with lenses with the occasional cross-reference.

NOTE

When I ask you to *press* or *tap* in this book, I mean you should press and release a button or tap the touch screen (described later). The EOS RP will then give you some time (usually about 6 seconds, depending on the function) to make an adjustment. When I am asking you to keep a button depressed while using another control, I'll say *hold*. For many functions, the camera's exposure meters must be active; just tap the shutter release button lightly to wake them up.

Front View

The front of the EOS RP is the face seen by your subjects as you snap away. For the photographer, though, the front is the surface your fingers curl around as you hold the camera, and there are really only three buttons to press, all within easy reach of the fingers of your left hand, plus the shutter button and Main Dial, which are on the top/front of the hand grip. There are additional controls on the lens itself. Figure 2.1 is a view of the front of the EOS RP with the lens detached. The other main components you need to know about are as follows:

- **Shutter release button.** Angled on top of the hand grip is the shutter release button. Press this button down halfway to lock exposure and focus (in One-Shot mode and AI Focus with non-moving subjects).

Figure 2.1

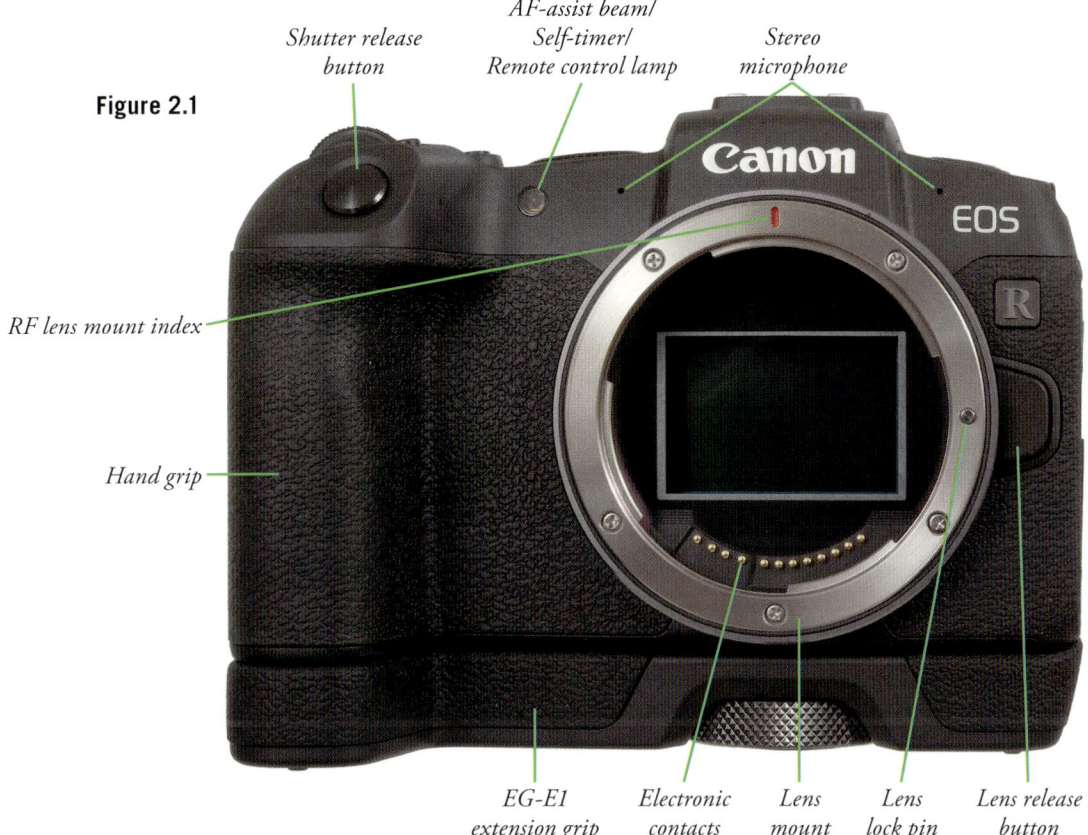

Shutter release button

AF-assist beam/ Self-timer/ Remote control lamp

Stereo microphone

RF lens mount index

Hand grip

EG-E1 extension grip

Electronic contacts

Lens mount

Lens lock pin

Lens release button

■ **AF-assist beam/Self-timer/Remote control lamp.** This LED flashes when needed to provide additional illumination to facilitate autofocus. This lamp also flashes to indicate that the remote control has connected, and when using the self-timer to mark the countdown until the photo is taken.

■ **Hand grip.** This provides a comfortable hand-hold, and also contains the EOS RP's battery and memory card.

■ **Lens mount.** This sturdy flange accepts a matching bayonet on the rear of each lens or accessory you mount on the EOS RP.

■ **Lens release button.** Press and hold this button to unlock the lens so you can rotate the lens to remove it from the camera.

■ **Lens lock pin.** This pin on the lens flange retracts when the release button is held down to unlock the lens.

- **RF lens mount index.** Line up this mark with the matching red detent on the barrel of your RF or mount adapter lens to align it as you mount it on the camera.
- **Electronic contacts.** These contacts connect to matching points on the lens to allow the camera and lens to communicate electronically.
- **Stereo microphone.** The EOS RP has a stereo microphone pair located on either side of the front of the camera slightly above the lens mount.
- **EG-E1 extension grip.** Some find that this optional extension improves the handling of the rather squat EOS RP camera. When I purchased mine, it was a free add-on: it may be an extra-cost purchase for those who buy theirs later. I'll describe this accessory in more detail later in this chapter.

You'll find more controls on the side of the EOS RP, shown in Figure 2.2. In the illustration, you can also see some of the key components of the lens that is mounted on the camera. The main elements are as follows:

- **Lens hood bayonet.** Canon offers lens hoods designed specifically for each lens; they attach to this grooved mount that rings the front of the lens, in both forward-facing and reversed positions. The hood serves to keep extraneous light, which reduces contrast and causes flare, from entering the lens. You should always use a hood when shooting, as they are your best protection from damage due to collisions and other mishaps. Filters are designed to shatter easily (that's how filter manufacturers convince you to buy more filters to "save" your lens), and are best reserved for when you want to filter something, or are working in wet or dusty environments. (Lens hoods won't disintegrate into razor sharp shards of glass, either.)

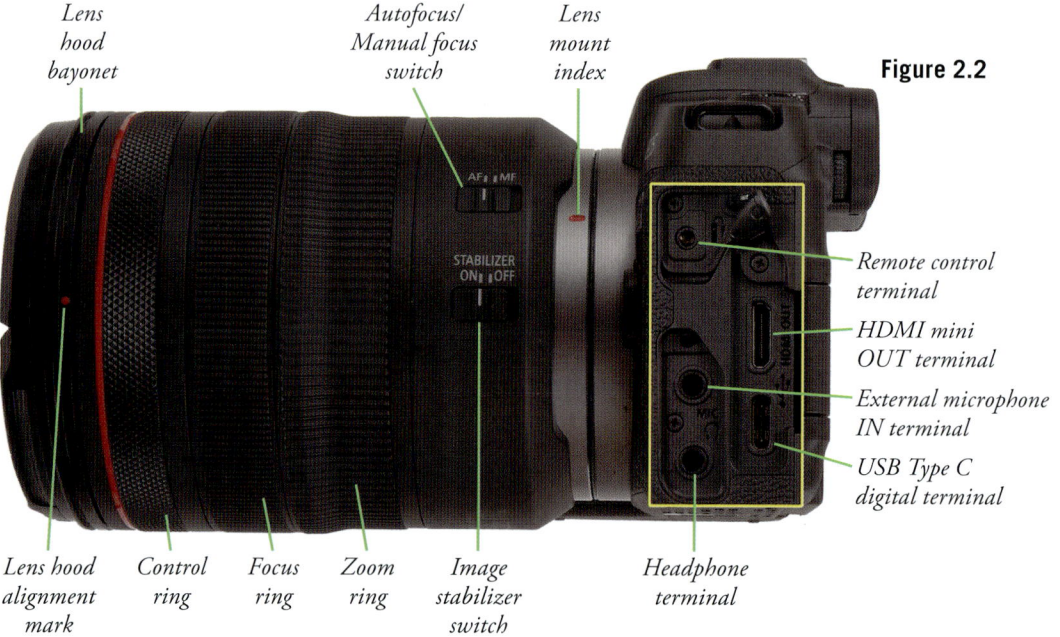

Lens hood bayonet   *Autofocus/ Manual focus switch*   *Lens mount index*   **Figure 2.2**

Remote control terminal

HDMI mini OUT terminal

External microphone IN terminal

USB Type C digital terminal

Lens hood alignment mark   *Control ring*   *Focus ring*   *Zoom ring*   *Image stabilizer switch*   *Headphone terminal*

- **Lens hood alignment mark.** Line up a matching indicator on your lens hood, and rotate the hood to fasten it securely to the front of your lens.

- **Control ring.** This brilliant new feature can be programmed to change aperture, shutter speed, ISO, and exposure compensation, as I'll explain in Chapter 14.

- **Focus ring.** Rotate this ring to focus manually or fine-tune autofocus.

- **Zoom ring.** Turn this ring to zoom in or out.

- **Image stabilizer switch.** This switch turns image stabilization on and off. You might want to disable IS when the camera is mounted on a tripod.

- **Autofocus/Manual focus switch.** Canon autofocus lenses have a switch to allow changing between automatic focus and manual focus.

- **Lens mount index.** This marking on the lens barrel is lined up with the matching mark on the lens mount.

Five terminals/ports are located under the terminal covers, as shown in the yellow box in Figure 2.2. They include:

- **Remote control terminal.** You can plug in an optional RS-60E3 wired remote switch, or TC-80N3 timer remote controller (with the required RA-E3 remote controller adapter).

- **USB Type C digital terminal.** This Type C connector accepts an optional USB cable, which you can use to transfer photos to your computer. The terminal can be used with the Wireless File Transmitter WFT-E7 II and GPS Receiver GP-E2.

- **HDMI mini OUT terminal.** You'll need to buy an accessory cable to connect your EOS RP to an HDMI-compatible television, video recorder, or other device, as one to fit this terminal is not provided with the camera. If you have a high-resolution television, it's worth the expenditure to be able to view your camera's output in all its glory. Canon's HDMI cable HTC-100, and other Type C HDMI cables are compatible.

- **Headphone terminal.** Connect headphones or other audio playback gear here. It accepts a 3.5mm stereo mini-plug.

- **External microphone IN terminal.** Connect an external stereo microphone with a 3.5mm stereo mini-plug here to bypass the internal stereo microphone pair when recording sound.

The Canon EOS RP's Business End

The back panel of the EOS RP (see Figure 2.3) bristles with more than a dozen different controls, buttons, and knobs. That might seem like a lot of components to learn, but you'll find that the camera has a reasonable number of dedicated controls that make routine adjustments more quickly than a visit to a traditional menu every time you want to change a setting.

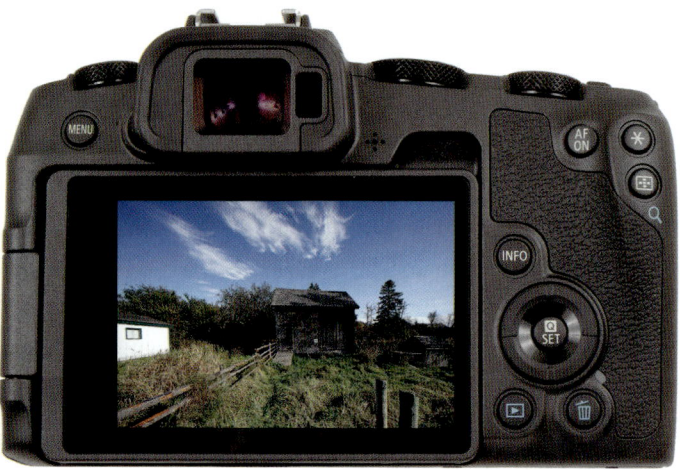

Figure 2.3

You can see the controls clustered on the upper edge of the back panel in Figure 2.4. The key buttons and components and their functions are as follows:

■ **MENU button.** Summons/exits the menu displayed on the LCD screen or electronic viewfinder of the EOS RP. When you're working with submenus, this button also serves to exit a submenu and return to the main menu.

■ **Dioptric adjustment control.** Rotate this knob while looking through the viewfinder to make adjustments for your vision, as described in Chapter 1.

■ **Viewfinder eyecup/eyepiece.** You can frame your composition by peering into the viewfinder eyepiece. It's surrounded by a soft rubber eyecup/frame that seals out extraneous light when pressing your eye tightly up to the viewfinder, and it also protects your eyeglass lenses (if worn) from scratching.

Figure 2.4

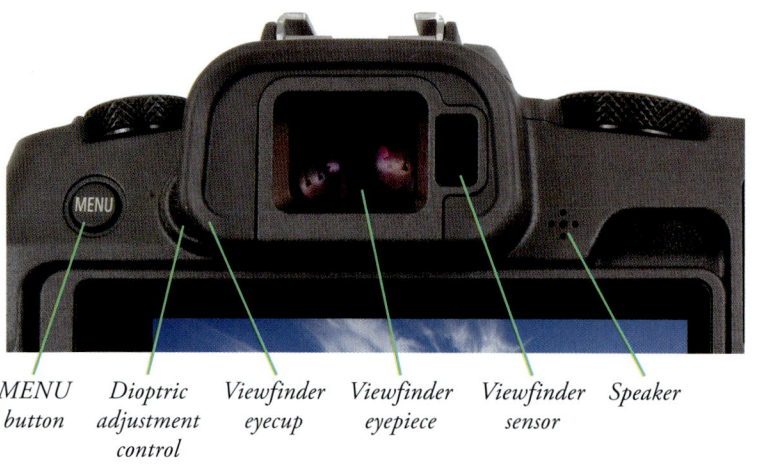

MENU   Dioptric   Viewfinder   Viewfinder   Viewfinder   Speaker
button   adjustment   eyecup   eyepiece   sensor
          control

- **Viewfinder sensor.** This sensor recognizes when your eye (or any other object) approaches the viewfinder eyepiece. By default, the EOS RP switches between the two automatically, but you can configure the camera to switch only manually, using the Display Settings entry in the Set-up 4 menu, as described in Chapter 13.

- **Speaker.** Beeps and other sounds emitted by your camera emanate from this speaker.

Right Side Controls

More buttons reside on the right side of the back panel, as shown in Figure 2.5. The key controls and their functions are as follows:

- **Quick Control Dial (QCD).** Used to select shooting options, such as f/stop or exposure compensation value, or to navigate through menus. It also serves as an alternate controller for some functions set with other controls, such as AF point selection.

- **AF-ON button.** Press this button to activate the autofocus system without needing to partially depress the shutter release. This control, used with other buttons, allows you to lock exposure and focus separately. Lock exposure by pressing the shutter release halfway, or by pressing the AE lock button; autofocus by pressing the shutter release halfway, or by pressing the AF-ON button. Functions of this button will be explained in more detail in Chapter 5.

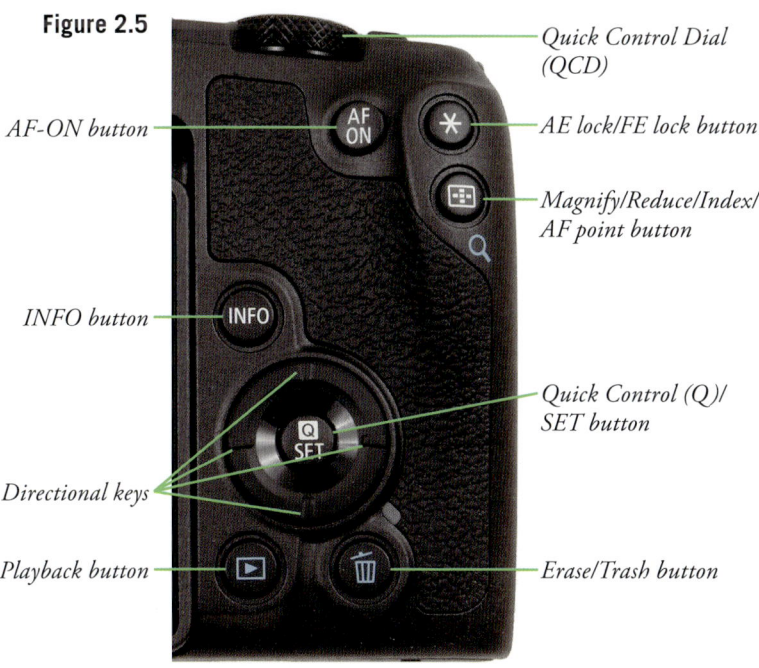

Figure 2.5

Quick Control Dial (QCD)

AF-ON button

AE lock/FE lock button

Magnify/Reduce/Index/ AF point button

INFO button

Quick Control (Q)/ SET button

Directional keys

Playback button

Erase/Trash button

- **AE/FE (autoexposure/flash exposure) lock button.** In Shooting mode, it locks the exposure or external flash exposure that the camera sets when you partially depress the shutter button. The exposure lock indication (*) appears at lower left in the display. If you want to recalculate exposure with the shutter button still partially depressed, press the * button again. The exposure will be unlocked when you release the shutter button or take the picture. To retain the exposure lock for subsequent photos, keep the * button pressed while shooting.

  When using external flash, pressing the * button fires an extra pre-flash when you partially depress the shutter button that allows the unit to calculate and lock exposure prior to taking the picture.

- **Magnify/Reduce/Index/AF point button.** This button has separate functions for Shooting and Playback modes.

  - **Shooting mode.** Press this button once, then press the M-Fn button multiple times to cycle through the available AF methods. Then, press SET to confirm your choice. (See Chapter 5 for information on setting autofocus/exposure point selection.) If you press it once *without* pressing the M-Fn button, it functions as an AF Point Selection button; you can then use the directional buttons or Quick Control and Main Dials to select the autofocus point.

  - **Playback mode.** Press this button and release it. Then rotate the Main Dial to the right to progressively zoom in on a still image. Rotate the Main Dial to the left to zoom out to full-frame mode and then to 4-, 9-, 36-, and 100-image index views. In any index or magnified view, press SET to see a full-frame view of the currently highlighted image.

- **Quick Control (Q)/SET button.** Press this button to produce the Quick Control screen, which gives you access to many features when in Shooting mode. When making choices, the button serves as a SET/Enter control to activate or confirm your selection. When you're reviewing images in Playback, a different Quick Control screen pops up that allows you to protect or rate images, change jump method, resize, crop, rotate, or perform other functions. I'll show you how to work with the two Quick Control screens later in this chapter.

- **Access lamp.** When lit or blinking, this lamp indicates that the memory card is being accessed.

- **Erase/Trash button.** In Playback mode, this button deletes the currently displayed image.

- **Playback button.** Displays the most recent image.

- **Directional keys.** Used to navigate menus and image displays and position focus point/zones.

- **INFO button.** Changes the type of information displayed in shooting and playback modes. It's also used within some menu screens to access additional information or options.

Mastering the Touch Screen

The EOS RP's versatile 3.0-inch LCD display screen is articulated so it can be positioned in multiple orientations and is also touch sensitive for rapid selection of menu and focus options. The articulation feature makes it easy to take pictures in a variety of orientations. Using the touch screen, you can perform many routine operations, including menu navigation/selection functions, by tapping the screen. This section will show you how to best make use of those features.

Flexible View

The articulated screen offers several alternative ways of previewing and reviewing your images in ways that the electronic viewfinder can't. Here are a few to consider:

- **Selfie mode.** Swing the LCD out from the body and rotate it so the screen is pointing in the same direction as the lens. Mount the EOS RP on a tripod, or any temporary resting place, then position yourself (alone or with a group) for a selfie. You can see the image the camera will capture before taking the shot with the self-timer or remote control. The camera can immediately display the photo, so you can review it and change poses before taking another shot, if you like.

- **Share the fun.** Even if you're not in the picture yourself, you can share the image you're about to take with your subject when the LCD is in the "selfie" position. (See Figure 2.6, left.) It works best if the camera is on a tripod. Your subject can evaluate the pose, adjust his or her hair, or turn to their "good" side before you shoot. When you move your eye to the viewfinder, the LCD preview will turn off, and you'll be able to see the image as you take the picture.

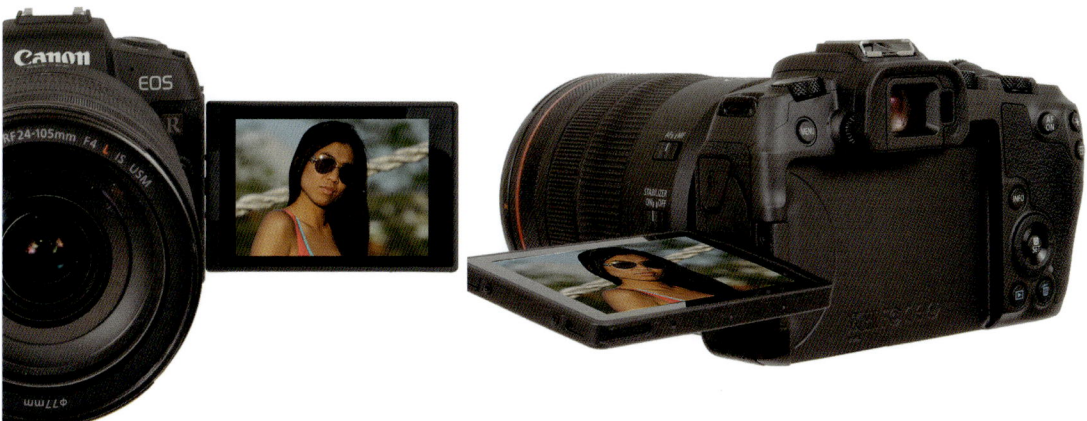

Figure 2.6 The articulated screen allows multiple views.

- **Waist-level view.** With the LCD swung out, you can tilt the screen back, giving you a waist-level preview of the picture you're about to take. That perspective can be especially useful when photographing low-lying subjects without needing to crouch or get down on your hands and knees. It's also useful for semi-stealth photography, because you don't need to bring the camera up to your eye to compose the image. (See Figure 2.6, right.)

- **Periscope view.** The screen can pivot so it is facing completely downward so you can hold the camera over your head and shoot using a periscopic perspective. Great for shooting over crowds, particularly at parades.

- **Screen protection.** Swivel the screen so the back of the LCD is facing outward, and you've got solid protection—at least from scratches and minor impacts. Even so, I'd avoid whacking the back of the camera. But it's nice to keep your screen shielded when traveling.

Touch Operation

Of course, for many veteran shooters, some touch-friendly tasks, such as navigating through menus, may be no quicker than the button/dial procedures we are used to, and can even be more awkward for those with large fingers or who need/want to wear gloves. However, there are several uses for the touch screen that border on outstanding as you become more accustomed to working with the EOS RP's screen. You can even use it while viewing through the electronic viewfinder! Here are some of the things you can do:

- **Move focus point while using the EVF.** You can touch the screen with one finger and drag to move the AF point or Zone AF frame around as you preview your image through the viewfinder. You just need to activate the Touch & Drag AF feature in the Shooting 7 menu and choose one of several alternative methods for specifying the active area of the screen and how the point or zone moves. I'll explain how to use this feature in Chapter 5.

- **Touch focus point/shutter.** While viewing the touch screen you can specify the exact focus point (or zone) you want by tapping the screen. The camera can focus at the point you just selected, or even take a picture if you've activated the Touch Shutter feature (using an icon located at lower left on the screen). If you'd prefer to drag the point around the screen to the desired location, press the point selection button, and then swipe your finger around the touch screen to move the focus point. (See Chapter 5 for more on this.)

- **Menu navigation.** You may find some menu operations are easier to complete using the touch screen, although, as I noted, many of us prefer old-school directional buttons and dials.

- **Text entry.** If you've ever had to type in copyright information, tried to rename the My Menu tab, or performed any other text-entry operation using the EOS RP's buttons and dials, you'll appreciate the ability to just tap on the virtual keyboard to input your data (See Figure 2.7.)

- **Playback.** As you'll see, you can scroll through images rapidly during review, zoom in and out, and perform other functions that are much clumsier with buttons and dials—even if you've had years of experience and are adept with the traditional methods.

Figure 2.7
The EOS RP's virtual keyboard makes text entry easy.

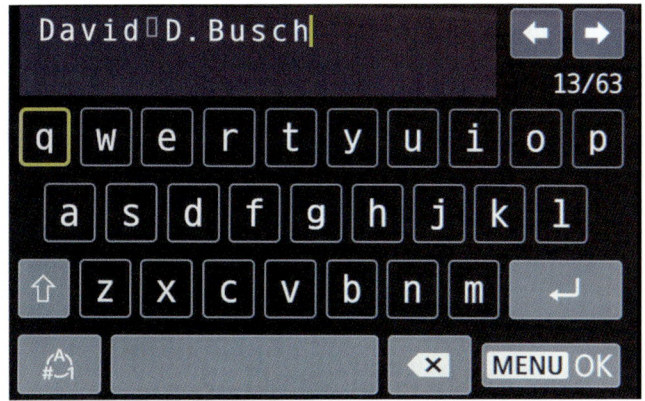

When you've activated the touch screen using the Touch Control entry in the Set-up 3 menu (as described in Chapter 13), you have a large range of capabilities available to you with a simple tap on the screen (represented by the green/red circles shown in Figure 2.8). Here's a quick overview of the options:

1. **Quick Control menu.** Tap the Q icon in the upper right of the screen and the Quick Control menu (which I first showed you in Figure 1.11 in the first chapter) pops up. You can adjust any of the options shown in the left and right columns in Figure 2.8. I'll show you more Quick Control options at the end of this chapter.

2. **Touch shutter.** Tap here to turn the touch shutter feature on or off. When active, tapping the screen tells the EOS RP to focus at the point you've specified and take a picture.

3. **Adjust shutter speed or aperture.** You can adjust any parameter with a box around it. The camera is set for Tv shooting mode (Shutter-priority), so you can tap the box displaying the current shutter speed, then rotate either dial or use the left/right directional buttons to change the shutter speed. In Av (Aperture-priority) mode, you can change the f/stop; in M (Manual) mode, both shutter speed and aperture can be adjusted.

Figure 2.8
Tap any of the boxed icons to change that function's settings.

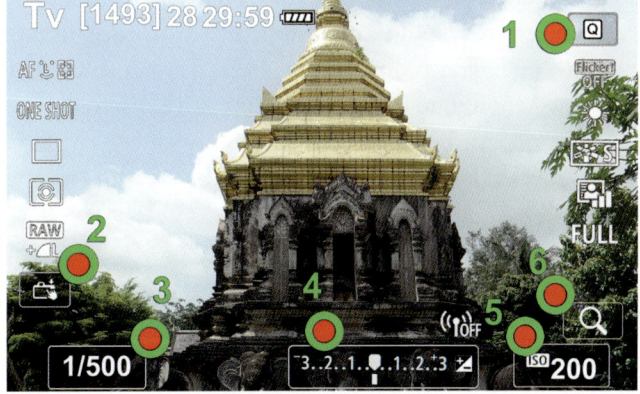

4. **Exposure compensation.** Tap this scale and use the dials/directional buttons (or tap the scale itself) to add or subtract from the metered exposure. I'll explain exposure compensation in more detail in Chapter 4.

5. **ISO sensitivity.** Tap the ISO icon to select a fixed ISO setting or ISO Auto.

6. **Zoom.** Tap the magnifying glass immediately above the ISO icon to zoom in on your image.

TIP: YOUR CHOICE

Throughout this book, I may not explicitly say "tap the screen, or use the button, or visit the menu" for every single operation. Given the large number of how-to entries in this book, that would require unnecessarily long descriptions and extra verbiage. I'm going to assume that once you master the touch screen using the information in this section, you'll make your own choice and use whichever method you prefer. I'll generally stick to using the physical controls that we're all accustomed to. But, unless I specifically say to use the touch screen or physical controls, assume I mean you can use either one.

Meaningful Gestures

When a main menu, adjustment screen, or the Quick Control menu is displayed, you will often elect to use the touch screen to make your changes. Optionally, you can resort to the physical controls that provide the equivalent functions, including the available buttons and navigational buttons. However, I think that once you become familiar with the speed with which the touch screen allows you to make these adjustments, you'll be reluctant to go back to the "old" way of doing things.

The EOS RP's touch screen is *capacitive* rather than *resistive*, making it more like the current generation of smartphones than earlier computer touch-sensitive screens. The difference is that your camera's LCD responds to the electrical changes that result from *contact* rather than the force of *pressure* on the screen itself. That means that the screen can interpret your touches and taps in more complex ways. It "knows" when you're using two fingers instead of one, and can react to multi-touch actions and gestures, such as swiping (to scroll in any direction), and pinching/spreading of fingers to zoom in and out. Since you probably have been using a smartphone for a while, these actions have become ingrained enough to be considered intuitive. Virtually every main and secondary function or menu operation can be accessed from the touch screen. However, if you want to continue using the buttons and dials, the EOS RP retains that method of operation.

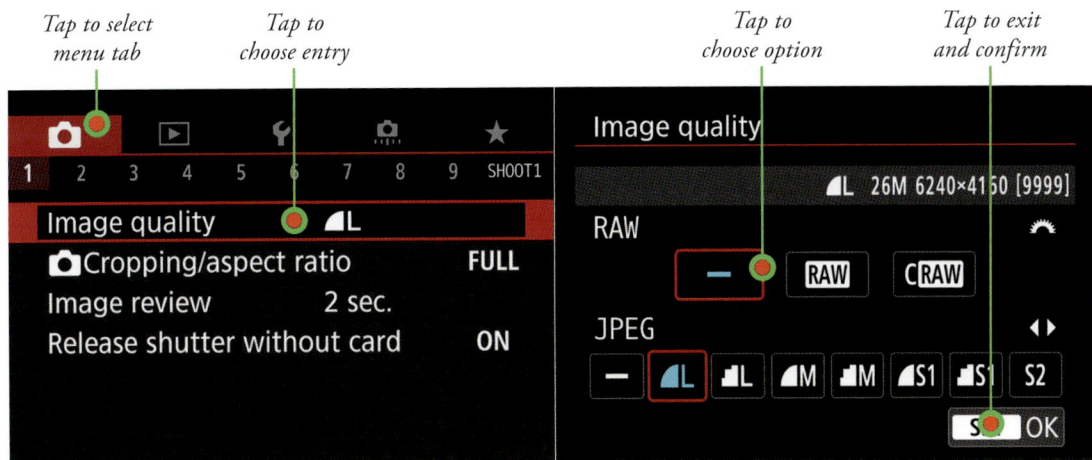

Figure 2.9 Select a menu tab and entry (left) and change settings (right).

Here's what you need to know to get started:

■ **Tap to select.** Tap (touch the LCD screen briefly) to select an item, including a menu heading or icon. Any item you can tap will have a frame or box around it. Figure 2.9 shows the taps needed to select a menu tab and specific entry within that menu and then make your adjustments on the screen that appears. On settings screens, tappable items will have a box around them.

■ **Drag/swipe to select.** Many functions can be selected by touching the screen and then sliding your finger to the right or left until the item you want is highlighted. For example, instead of tapping, you can slide horizontally along the main menu's tabs to choose any Shooting, Playback, Custom, Set-up, or My Menu tab. However, you can't slide vertically to choose an individual menu entry; tap the desired entry instead.

■ **Drag/swipe to adjust scales.** Screens that contain a sliding scale can be adjusted by dragging. In Figure 2.10, left, the arrows show how you can drag along the scale to adjust LCD screen brightness, and at right, to add/subtract exposure compensation. You can also tap the minus/plus buttons, and exit by tapping the SET/OK icon. Even when you are using the touch screen, you can still opt for the Main Dial or QCD to make your changes.

■ **Pinch/spread to reduce/enlarge.** During playback, you can use two fingers to "pinch" the screen to reduce/shrink the image, from, say, single-image to index view. Tap on a thumbnail to view it full size. Spread those two fingers apart to enlarge an image, to zoom in from, say, a 9-image index array to the 4-image display, then to single image. If you continue spreading, you can magnify the image up to about 10X. Tap the return icon to resume single-image display. (See the arrows in the top half of Figure 2.11, left.)

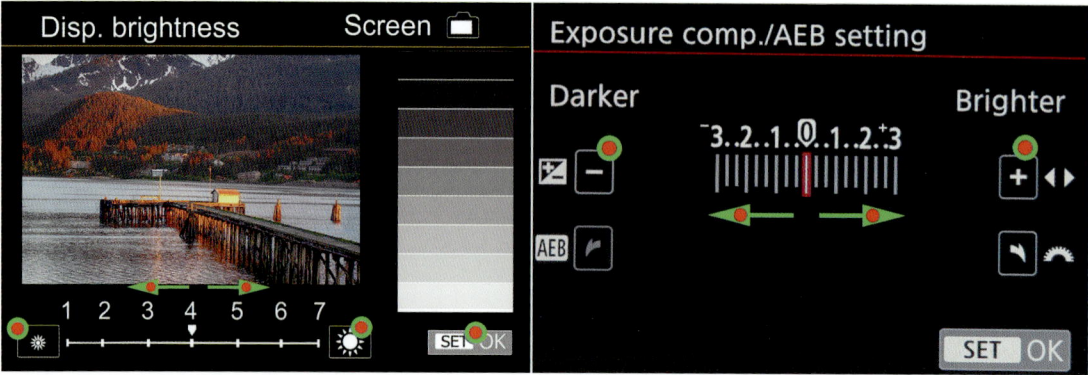

Figure 2.10 Use sliding scales or tap icons to make adjustments in screen brightness (left) and exposure compensation (right).

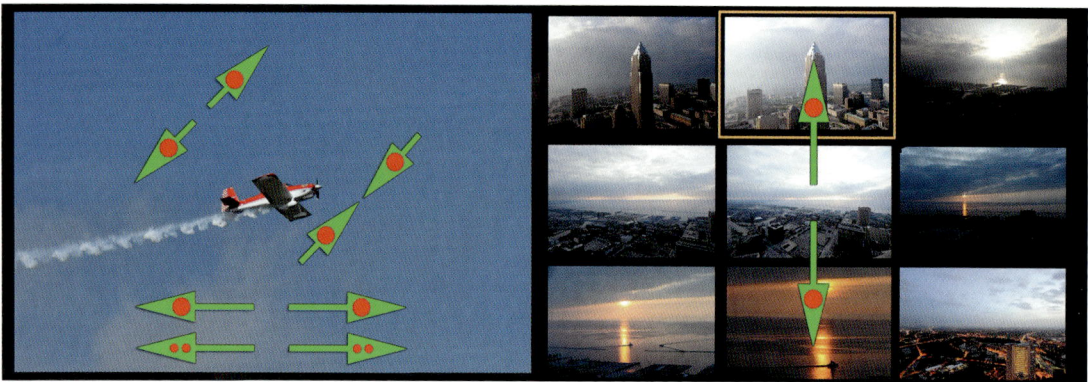

Figure 2.11 In Playback, pinch or spread fingers to magnify or reduce images (top left), and swipe/drag to move/jump among them (bottom left). You can scroll among thumbnails, too (right).

- **Drag/swipe to scroll among single images.** In Playback single-image mode, as you review your images, you can drag your finger left and right to advance from one image to another, much as you might do with a smartphone or tablet computer. Use one finger to scroll one image at a time, and two to jump using the image jump method you've chosen in the Playback 3 menu, as described in Chapter 13. The arrows at the bottom of Figure 2.11, left, represent this function.

- **Drag to scroll among thumbnails.** When viewing thumbnails, you can drag through the thumbnail screen to quickly move among sets of index images, as represented in Figure 2.11, right.

■ **Fine-tune touch features.** As I'll explain in Chapter 9, you can enable or disable touch operation and change sensitivity from Standard to Sensitive in the Set-up 3 menu under the Touch
Control entry. The click sound the touch feature makes can be turned on or off using the Beep
setting in the Set-up 3 menu.

■ **Avoid "protective" sheets, moisture, and sharp implements.** The LCD uses capacitive technology to sense your touch, rather than pressure sensitivity. LCD protectors or moisture can
interfere with the touch functions, and styluses or sharp objects (such as pens) won't produce
the desired results. I have, in fact, used "skins" and thin tempered glass shields on my EOS RP's
LCD with good results (even though the screen is quite rugged and really doesn't need protection from scratches), but there is no guarantee that all such protectors will work for you.

As I noted, the choice of whether to use the traditional buttons or touch screen is up to you. I've
found that with some screens, the controls are too close together to be easily manipulated with my
wide fingers. The touch screen can be especially dangerous when working with some functions,
such as card formatting. In displays where the icons are large and few in number, such as the screen
used to adjust LCD brightness, touch control works just fine. Easiest of all is touch operation during
Playback. It's a no-brainer to swipe your finger from side to side to scroll among images and pinch/
spread to zoom out and in.

Going Topside

The top surface of the Canon EOS RP has its own set of frequently accessed controls. The key
controls, and two additional lens control features, are shown in Figure 2.12:

■ **Zoom scale.** Shows the current zoom focal length. (Only available on zoom lenses!)

■ **Zoom lock.** When the zoom has been set to its widest position, you can flip this switch
to keep the zoom locked there. This avoids possible "zoom creep" when the lens is pointed
downward.

■ **Shutter button.** Partially depress this button to lock in exposure and focus. Press all the way
to take the picture. Tapping the shutter release when the camera has turned off the autoexposure and autofocus mechanisms reactivates both. When a review image is displayed on the
back-panel color LCD, tapping this button removes the image from the display and reactivates
the autoexposure and autofocus mechanisms.

■ **M-Fn button.** This multi-function button can be used to change the autofocus area selection
mode (as described in Chapter 5). You can assign any of 40 different functions to this control
using the Custom Controls feature, as described in Chapter 14.

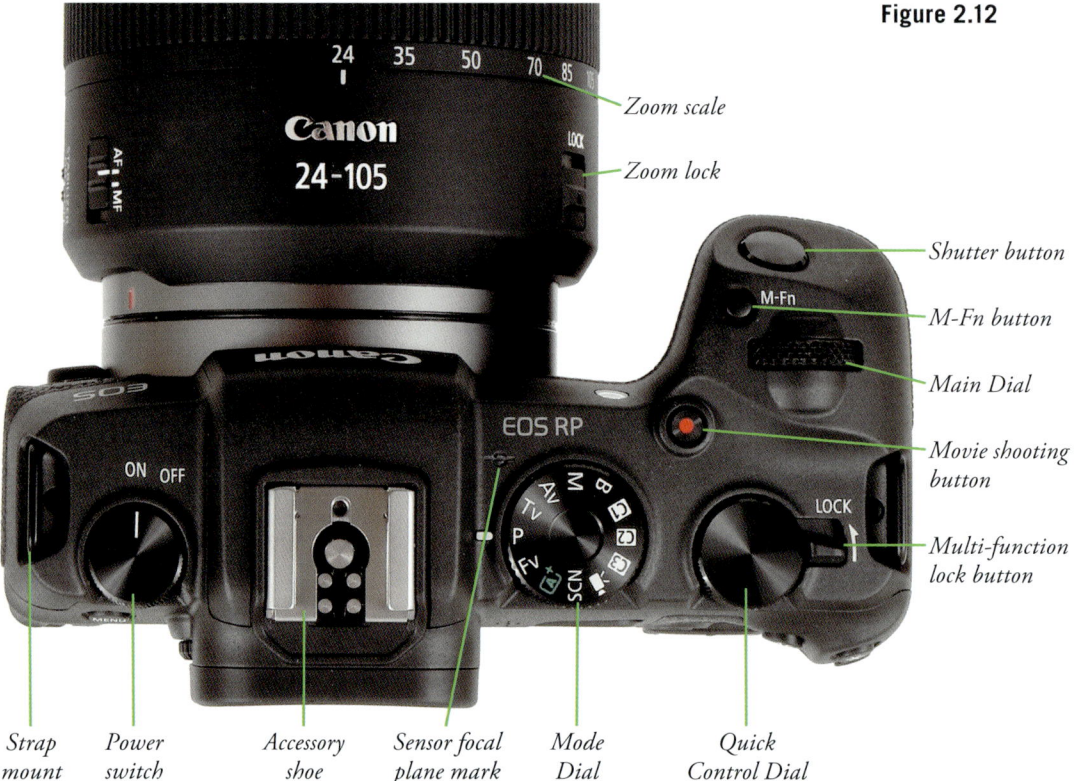

Figure 2.12

Zoom scale

Zoom lock

Shutter button

M-Fn button

Main Dial

Movie shooting button

Multi-function lock button

Strap mount

Power switch

Accessory shoe

Sensor focal plane mark

Mode Dial

Quick Control Dial

- **Main Dial.** This dial is used to make many shooting settings. When settings come in pairs (such as shutter speed/aperture in Manual shooting mode), the Main Dial is used for one (for example, shutter speed), while the Quick Control Dial is used for the other (aperture). When an image is on the screen during playback, this dial also specifies the leaps that skip a particular number of images during playback of the shots you've already taken. Jumps can be 1 image, 10 images, 100 images, jump by date, or jump by screen (that is, by screens of thumbnails when using Index mode), date, or folder. (Jump method is selected in the Playback 3 menu, as described in Chapter 13.) This dial is also used to move among tabs when the MENU button has been pressed, and is used within some menus (in conjunction with the Quick Control Dial) to change pairs of settings.

- **Movie shooting button.** Press to start capturing video; press again to stop. You can redefine this button to perform any of 40 other functions if you like.

- **Multi-function lock button.** Pressing this button can be set to lock certain controls to prevent them from being changed accidentally. Press again to unlock those controls. You can choose to lock any or all of the following: Main Dial, Quick Control Dial, M-Fn bar, control ring, or touch screen panel. Choose which of these to lock using the Multi Function Lock entry in the Set-up 6 menu.

- **Quick Control Dial.** Used to select shooting options, such as f/stop or exposure compensation value, or to navigate through menus. It also serves as an alternate controller for some functions set with other controls, such as AF point selection.

- **Mode Dial.** Rotate this dial to cycle among the available semi-automatic/manual exposure and Special Scene modes, Movie mode, and to choose one of the camera user settings (C1, C2, or C3).

- **Accessory shoe.** Slide an electronic flash into this multi-purpose accessory shoe when you need an external Speedlite. A dedicated flash unit, like those from Canon, can use the multiple contact points shown to communicate exposure, zoom setting, white balance information, and other data between the flash and the camera. There's more on using electronic flash in Chapters 9 and 10.

- **Sensor focal plane mark.** Precision macro and scientific photography sometimes requires knowing exactly where the focal plane of the sensor is. The symbol on the side of the penta-prism marks that plane.

- **Strap mount.** A neck strap fastens to this mount, with a matching mount on the other side of the camera.

- **Power switch.** Rotate to turn the EOS RP on or off.

Underneath Your EOS RP

There's not a lot going on with the bottom panel of your EOS RP. Here, you'll find, as shown in Figure 2.13:

- **Tripod socket.** Secures the camera to a tripod and is also used to lock on the optional EG-E1 Extension Grip.

- **Battery/Memory card compartment cover/cover lock.** Slide the cover lock latch toward the center of the camera to open the compartment cover and access the LP-E17 battery and memory card. (See Figure 2.13).

- **Accessory positioning holes.** Fit matching studs on the EG-E1 Extension Grip (available in black-, red-, and blue-accented models).

  To mount the grip, slide the battery cover lock to open the door, then push the black battery compartment door release lever toward the back of the camera. That will let you remove the battery door. Then attach the extension grip to the underside of the camera (see Figure 2.14, left), the two pins on the grip with the accessory positioning holes. Tighten the grip's tripod socket knob (see Figure 2.14, right) to lock the grip onto the bottom of your EOS RP.

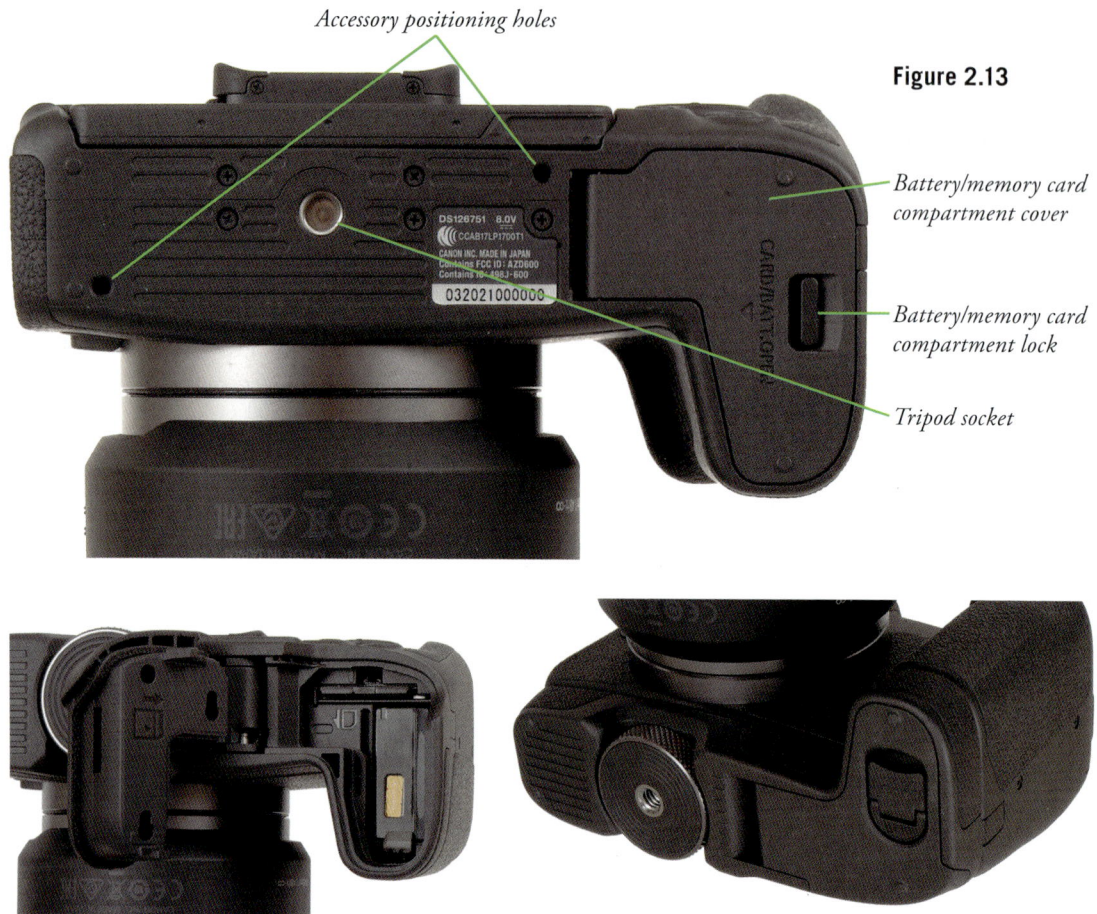

Accessory positioning holes

Figure 2.13

Battery/memory card compartment cover

Battery/memory card compartment lock

Tripod socket

Figure 2.14

Note that Canon does not currently offer a battery/vertical grip for the EOS RP (although one is available for the EOS R). The camera lacks electrical contacts on the bottom that would make a grip with a full array of vertically oriented controls available. However, the removable door and accessory mounting holes do mean that Canon could design a *battery-only* grip, if there is a significant demand for one. Third-party vendors like Meike have built such grips and included a remote control jack that plugs into the camera's own remote connector, allowing the grip to include a shutter release button. So far I haven't heard any rumors about either possibility, but additional bottom-mounted accessories are technically possible.

3

Recommended Settings

This chapter is purely optional, especially for those who are new to an advanced Canon at the EOS RP's level, who should skip it entirely for now, and return when they've gained some experience with this full-featured camera. This section is for the benefit of those who want to know *now* some of the most common changes I recommend to the default settings of your EOS RP. Canon has excellent reasons for using these settings as a default; I have better reasons for changing them.

Changing Default Settings

Even if this is your first experience with a Canon digital SLR, you can easily make a few changes to the default settings that I'm going to recommend, and then take your time learning *why* I suggest these changes when they're explained in the more detailed chapters of this book. I'm not going to provide step-by-step instructions for changing settings here; I'll give you an overview of how to make any setting adjustment, and leave you to navigate through the fairly intuitive EOS RP menu system to make the changes yourself. Or, you can jump ahead to Chapters 11 to 14 for more detailed instructions on a particular setting.

Resetting the Canon EOS RP

If you want to change from the factory default values, you might think that it would be a good idea to make sure that the Canon EOS RP is set to the factory defaults in the first place. After all, even a brand-new camera might have had its settings changed at the retailer, or during a demo. Most of the time, however, you'll prefer to use the Clear All Camera Settings option in the Set-up 6 menu, which returns most settings (other than Custom Functions) to their default values. The tables that follow show the settings defaults after using the Clear All Camera Settings menu option. Not all menu entries are shown, as some menu items are functions rather than settings. For example, in the Playback menu, non-settable entries are found in the Playback 1–3 menus. You'll find the default values and settings options for Movie Shooting in Chapter 15.

Table 3.1 Shooting Menu Defaults

Image quality	Large, Fine	WB Shift/Bracket	0,0/+−0
Cropping/Aspect ratio	Full	Color space	SRGB
Image review	2 seconds	Picture Style	Standard
Release shutter without card	On	Long Exposure Noise Reduction	Disable
Lens aberration correction		High ISO Speed Noise Reduction	Standard
Peripheral illumination correction	Enable		
Distortion correction	Disable	Dust Delete Data	Erased
Digital lens optimizer	Enable	Touch Shutter	Disable
External Speedlite control		Multiple exposure	Disable
Flash firing	Enable	HDR mode	Disable HDR
E-TTL II flash metering	Evaluative	Focus bracketing	Disable
Slow synchro	1/180th–1/60th Auto	Interval timer	Disable
Safety FE	Enable	Bulb timer	Disable
ISO speed settings		Anti-flicker shooting	Disable
ISO speed	Auto	High-speed display	Disable
Range for stills	Min: 100, Max: 40,000	AF operation	One-Shot
		AF method	1-point AF
Auto	Min: 100, Max: 12,800	Eye Detection AF	Disable
Minimum shutter speed for Auto	Auto	Continuous AF	Disable
Auto Lighting Optimizer	Standard	Touch & drag AF settings	
Disabled in M or B modes	Disabled	Touch & drag AF	Disable
		Positioning method	Relative
		Active touch area	Right
Highlight Tone Priority	Off	Lens electronic MF	Disable after One-Shot
Metering timer	8 seconds		
Exposure simulation	Enable	AF assist beam firing	Enable
White balance	AWB (Ambience-priority)	MF peaking settings	
		Peaking	Off
		Level	High
Custom white balance	Canceled	Color	Red

Table 3.2 Playback Menu Defaults

Playback information display	All enabled	Playback grid	Off
		View from last seen	Enable
Highlight alert	Disable	Magnification (approximate)	2X
AF point display	Disable		

Table 3.3 Set-up Menu Defaults

Select folder	N/A	HDMI resolution	Auto
File numbering	Continuous	HDMI HDR output	Off
File name	N/A	Shooting information display	N/A
Auto rotate	Camera+ Computer	Viewfinder performance	Smooth
Format card	N/A	Viewfinder display format	Display 1
Mode guide	Enable	Display settings	Auto
Feature guide	Enable	Shutter button func. for movies (Half-press)	Metering+ Servo AF
Eco mode	Off	Help text size	Small
Power saving		Wireless communications settings	Various
Display off	1 minute		
Auto power off	1 minute	GPS device settings	Disable
Viewfinder off	3 minutes	Multi-Function lock	Main Dial
Display brightness	0	Custom Shooting mode	(C1–C3)
Language	Varies by country	Clear All Camera Settings	N/A
Video system	NTSC or PAL	Copyright information	Erased
Touch control	Standard	Manual/Software URL	Unchanged
Beep	Enable	Certification Logo Display	Unchanged
Battery info.	N/A	Firmware	Unchanged
Sensor cleaning	N/A		

Table 3.4 Custom Functions Defaults

Exposure level increments	1/3 stop	Initial AF point set for Face+Tracking	Automatic
ISO speed setting increments	1/3 stop	Customize buttons	Unchanged
Bracketing auto cancel	Enable	Dial direction during Tv/Av	Normal
Bracketing sequence	0–+	Control ring rotation	Normal
Number of bracketed shots	3	Focus ring rotation	Normal
Safety Shift	Disable	RF lens MF focus ring sensitivity	Varies with rotation speed
AE Lock metering mode after focus	Erased	Customize dials	Unchanged
Tracking sensitivity	Balanced (0)	Release shutter without lens	Off
Accel/decel tracking	Balanced (0)	Retract lens on power off	On
AF point auto switching	Standard (0)	Audio compression	Enable
Lens drive when AF impossible	Continue focus search	Clear all Custom Functions	N/A
Limit AF methods	All enabled	Clear customized settings	N/A
Orientation linked AF point	Same for vertical/horizontal		

Recommended Default Changes

Although I won't be explaining how to use the Canon EOS RP's menu system in detail until Chapters 11 to 14, you can make some simple changes now. These general instructions will serve you to make any of the setting changes I recommend next. It's likely that experienced photographers won't need the settings tables that follow, but I'm including some basic recommendations for those who want some guidance in shooting particular types of subjects. You'll find specific types for functions like autofocus and other features later in this book.

The EOS RP divides its menu entries into "tabbed" sections—Shooting, Playback, Set-up, Custom Functions, and My Menu. All but Custom Functions and My Menu have separate pages. The available pages can vary, depending on your shooting mode, as I'll explain in Chapter 11.

To access menus, tap the MENU button. Use the Main Dial to move from menu to menu, and the Quick Control Dial to highlight a particular menu entry. Press the SET button to select a menu item. You can also navigate with the directional buttons or use the touch screen. When you've highlighted the menu item you want to work with, press the SET button to select it. The current settings for the other menu items in the list will be hidden, and a list of options for the selected menu item (or a submenu screen) will appear. Or, you may be shown a separate settings screen for that entry. Within the menu choices, you can scroll up or down with the Quick Control Dial; press SET to select the choice you've made; and press the MENU button again to exit.

Once you've made changes for a specific type of shooting, you should store each set of parameters in one of the Custom Shooting mode user slots C1, C2, or C3 in the Set-up 4 menu, as explained in Chapter 13. Here are some recommended settings to consider. Note that these tables don't correspond to entire menus; I'm listing only the settings that need attention. If a particular parameter is not listed, you can use a setting of your choice.

Table 3.5 Default, All Purpose, Sports: Outdoors, Sports: Indoors				
	Default	**All Purpose**	**Sports: Outdoors**	**Sports: Indoors**
Exposure mode	Your choice	Your choice	Tv	Tv
Autofocus mode	One-Shot	Servo AF	Servo AF	Servo AF
Drive mode	Single Shooting	Single Shooting	Continuous Shooting	Continuous Shooting
Beep	Enable	Enable	Enable	Enable
Image review	2 sec.	2 sec.	Off	Off
Metering mode	Evaluative	Evaluative	Evaluative	Evaluative
Color Space	sRGB	sRGB	sRGB	sRGB
Picture Style	Standard	Auto	Standard	Standard
ISO speed	Auto	Auto	800–3200	800–3200
ISO speed range	(Camera shows 100–40000 as default)	100–12800	200–3200	200–12800
Auto ISO range	100–12800	100–6400	200–6400	400–12800
ISO Auto minimum shutter speed	Auto	Auto	1/250	1/250
Long exposure NR	Off	Disable	Disable	Disable
High ISO speed NR	Standard	Standard	Standard	Standard
Highlight Tone Priority	Disable	Disable	Disable	Disable
AF assist beam	Enable	Enable	Disable	Disable
AF method	1-point AF	Face+Tracking	Face+Tracking	Zone AF

Table 3.6 Stage Performances, Long Exposure, HDR, Portrait

	Stage Performances	Long Exposure	HDR	Portrait
Exposure mode	Your choice	Manual/Your choice	One-Shot	One-Shot
Autofocus mode	One-Shot	One-Shot	One-Shot	Servo AF
Drive mode	Continuous Shooting	Single Shooting	Continuous Shooting	Continuous Shooting
Beep	Disable	Enable	Enable	Enable
Image review	Off	Off	Off	2 sec.
Metering mode	Spot	Center-weighted	Evaluative	Center-weighted
Color Space	Adobe RGB	Adobe RGB	Adobe RGB	Adobe RGB
Picture Style	User—Reduce contrast, add sharpening	Neutral	Standard	Portrait
ISO speed	800–3200	800–3200	Auto	Auto
ISO speed range	100–32000	100–12800	200–3200	200–1600
Auto ISO range	100–12800	100–6400	200–6400	100–3200
ISO Auto minimum shutter speed	Auto	Auto	1/250	1/250
Long exposure NR	Disable	Disable	Disable	Disable
High ISO speed NR	Standard	Standard	Standard	Standard
Highlight Tone Priority	Disable	Disable	Disable	Disable
AF assist beam	Disable	Disable	Disable	Disable
AF method	1-point AF	1-point AF	Expand AF	1-point AF

Table 3.7 Studio Flash, Landscape, Macro, Travel, E-Mail

	Studio Flash	Landscape	Macro	Travel	Email
Exposure mode	Manual	Av	Tv	Tv	Av
Autofocus mode	One-Shot	One-Shot	Manual	One-Shot	One-Shot
Drive mode	Single Shooting	Single Shooting	Single Shooting	Single Shooting	Single Shooting
Beep	Disable	Enable	Enable	Enable	Enable
Image review	2 sec.	2 sec.	2 sec.	2 sec.	2 sec.
Metering mode	Evaluative	Evaluative	Spot	Evaluative	Evaluative
Color Space	Adobe RGB	Adobe RGB	Adobe RGB	Adobe RGB	Adobe RGB
Picture Style	User— Reduce contrast, add sharpening	Landscape	Auto	Landscape	Auto
ISO speed	100–400	100–1600	100–1600	Auto	Auto
ISO speed range	100–32000	100–12800	200–3200	200–1600	100–3200
Auto ISO range	100–12800	100–6400	200–6400	100–3200	100–6400
ISO Auto minimum shutter speed	Auto	Auto	1/250	1/250	Auto
Long Exposure NR	Disable	Disable	Disable	Disable	Disable
High ISO speed NR	Standard	Standard	Standard	Standard	Standard
Highlight Tone Priority	Disable	Enable	Disable	Enable	Enable
AF assist beam	Disable	Disable	Disable	Disable	Disable
AF method	Expand AF Area	Zone AF	Manual Focus	Expand AF Area: Around	Expand AF Area

4

Nailing the Right Exposure

As you learn to use your EOS RP creatively, you're going to find that the right settings—as determined by the camera's exposure meter and intelligence—need to be *adjusted* to account for your creative decisions or to fine-tune the image for special situations.

For example, when you shoot with the main light source behind the subject, you end up with *backlighting*, which results in an overexposed background and/or an underexposed subject. The EOS RP recognizes backlit situations nicely, and can properly base exposure on the main subject, producing a decent photo. Features like Highlight Tone Priority and the Auto Lighting Optimizer can fine-tune exposure to preserve detail in the highlights and shadows.

But what if you *want* to underexpose the subject, to produce a silhouette effect? Or, perhaps, you might want to use an external electronic flash to fill in the shadows on your subject. The more you know about how to use your EOS RP, the more you'll run into situations where you want to creatively tweak the exposure to provide a different look than you'd get with a straight shot.

This chapter shows you the fundamentals of exposure, so you'll be better equipped to override the EOS RP's default settings when you want to, or need to. After all, correct exposure is one of the foundations of good photography, along with accurate focus and sharpness, appropriate color balance, freedom from unwanted noise and excessive contrast, as well as pleasing composition.

The EOS RP gives you a great deal of control over all of these, although composition is entirely up to you. You must still frame the photograph to create an interesting arrangement of subject matter, but all the other parameters are basic functions of the camera. You can let your EOS RP set them for you automatically, you can fine-tune how the camera applies its automatic settings, or you can make them yourself, manually. The amount of control you have over exposure, sensitivity (ISO settings), color balance, focus, and image parameters like sharpness and contrast make the EOS RP a versatile tool for creating images.

In the next few pages, I'm going to give you a grounding in one of those foundations, and explain the basics of exposure, either as an introduction or as a refresher course, depending on your current level of expertise. When you finish this chapter, you'll understand most of what you need to know to take well-exposed photographs creatively in a broad range of situations with the EOS RP.

Getting a Handle on Exposure

This section explains the fundamental concepts that go into creating an exposure. If you already know about the role of f/stops, shutter speeds, and sensor sensitivity in determining an exposure, you might want to skip to the next section, which explains how the EOS RP calculates exposure.

In the most basic sense, exposure is all about light. Exposure can make or break your photo. Correct exposure brings out the detail in the areas you want to picture, providing the range of tones and colors you need to create the desired image. Poor exposure can cloak important details in shadow, or wash them out in glare-filled featureless expanses of white. However, getting the perfect exposure requires some intelligence—either that built into the camera or the smarts in your head—because digital sensors can't capture all the tones we can see. If the range of tones in an image is extensive, embracing both inky black shadows and bright highlights, we often must settle for an exposure that renders most of those tones—but not all—in a way that best suits the photo we want to produce.

As the owner of an EOS RP, you're probably aware of the traditional "exposure triangle" of aperture (quantity of light and light passed by the lens), shutter speed (the amount of time the shutter is open), and the ISO sensitivity of the sensor—all working proportionately and reciprocally to produce an exposure. The trio is itself affected by the amount of illumination that is available to work with. So, if you double the amount of light, increase the aperture by one stop, make the shutter speed twice as long, or boost the ISO setting 2X, you'll get twice as much exposure. Similarly, you can increase any of these factors while decreasing one of the others by a similar amount to keep the same exposure.

Working with any of the three controls involves trade-offs. Larger f/stops provide less depth-of-field, while smaller f/stops increase depth-of-field (and potentially at the same time can *decrease* sharpness through a phenomenon called *diffraction*). Shorter shutter speeds do a better job of reducing the effects of camera/subject motion, while longer shutter speeds make that motion blur more likely. Higher ISO settings increase the amount of visual noise and artifacts in your image, while lower ISO settings reduce the effects of noise. (See Figure 4.1.)

Exposure determines the look, feel, and tone of an image, in more ways than one. Incorrect exposure can impair even the best-composed image by cloaking important tones in darkness, or by washing them out so they become featureless to the eye. On the other hand, correct exposure brings out the detail in the areas you want to picture, and provides the range of tones and colors you need to create the desired image. However, getting the perfect exposure can be tricky, because digital sensors can't capture all the tones we can see. If the range of tones in an image is extensive, embracing both inky black shadows and bright highlights, the sensor may not be able to capture them all.

Figure 4.1

The traditional exposure triangle includes aperture, shutter speed, and ISO sensitivity.

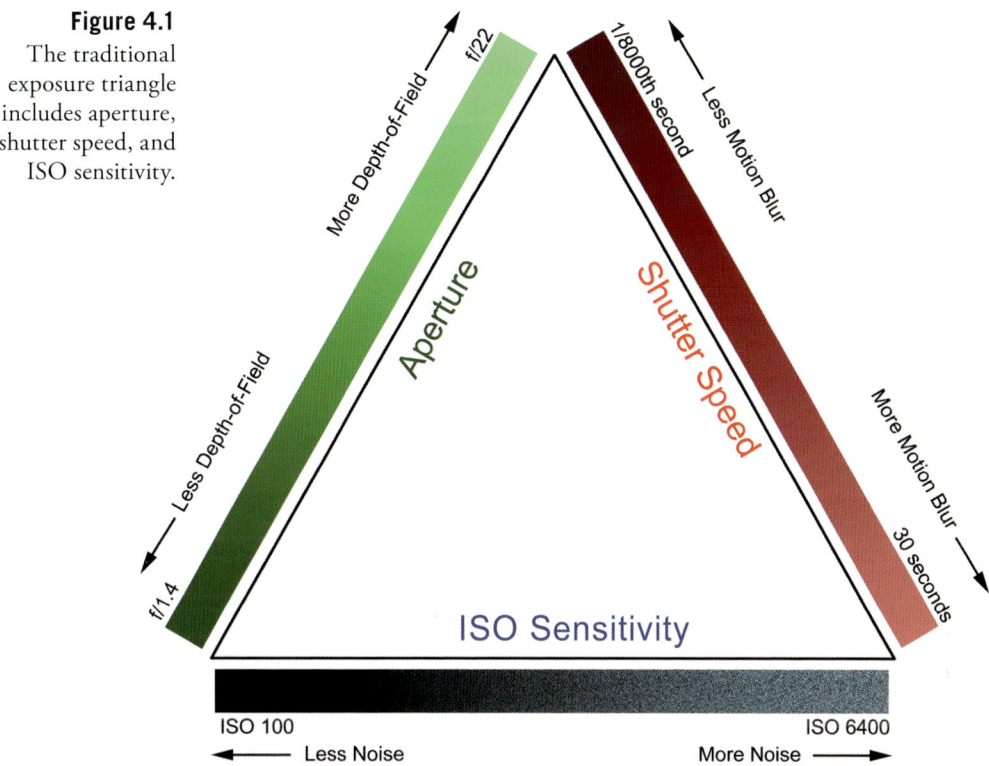

Sometimes, we must settle for an exposure that renders most of those tones—but not all—in a way that best suits the photo we want to produce. You'll often need to make choices about which details are important, and which are not, so that you can grab the tones that truly matter in your image. That's part of the creativity you bring to bear in realizing your photographic vision.

For example, look at two bracketed exposures presented at top in Figure 4.2. For the image at upper left, the highlights are well exposed, but the shadow areas are seriously underexposed. The version on the upper right, taken an instant later with the tripod-mounted camera, shows detail in the shadow areas of the structure, but the highlights are completely washed out. The camera's sensor simply can't capture detail in both dark areas and bright areas in a single shot.

With digital camera sensors, it's tricky to capture detail in both highlights and shadows in a single image, because the number of tones, the *dynamic range* of the sensor, is limited. The solution, in this case, was to resort to a technique called High Dynamic Range (HDR) photography, in which the two exposures from Figure 4.2 were combined in an image editor such as Photoshop, or a specialized HDR tool like Photomatix and Aurora HDR (both about $100 from www.hdrsoft.com and www.skylum.com, respectively). The resulting shot is shown at bottom in Figure 4.2. I'll explain more about HDR photography later in this chapter. For now, though, I'm going to concentrate on showing you how to get the best exposures possible without resorting to such tools, using only the features of your EOS RP.

To understand exposure, you need to understand the six aspects of light that combine to produce an image. Start with a light source—the sun, an interior lamp, or the glow from a campfire—and trace its path to your camera, through the lens, and finally to the sensor that captures the illumination.

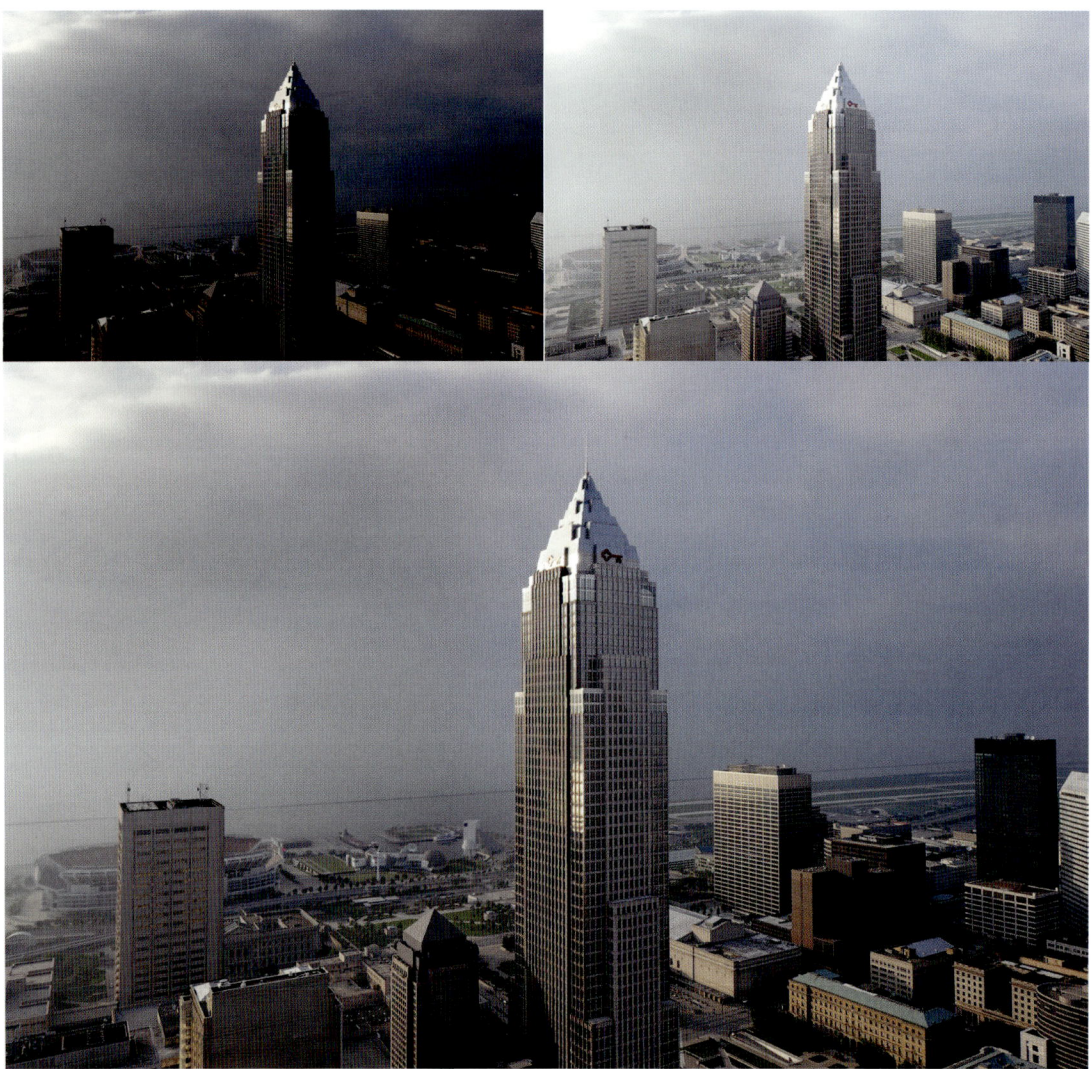

Figure 4.2 The image is exposed for the highlights, losing shadow detail (upper left). At upper right, the exposure captures detail in the shadows, but the background highlights are washed out. Combining the two exposures produces the best compromise image (bottom).

Here's a brief review of the things within our control that affect exposure.

■ **Light at its source.** Our eyes and our cameras—film or digital—are most sensitive to that portion of the electromagnetic spectrum we call *visible light.* That light has several important aspects that are relevant to photography, such as color and harshness (which is determined primarily by the apparent size of the light source as it illuminates a subject). But, in terms of exposure, the important attribute of a light source is its *intensity.* We may have direct control over intensity, which might be the case with an interior light that can be brightened or dimmed. Or, we might have only indirect control over intensity, as with sunlight, which can be made to appear dimmer by introducing translucent light-absorbing or reflective materials in its path.

■ **Light's duration.** We tend to think of most light sources as continuous. But, as you'll learn in Chapter 9, the duration of light can change quickly enough to modify the exposure, as when the main illumination in a photograph comes from an intermittent source, such as an electronic flash.

■ **Light reflected, transmitted, or emitted.** Once light is produced by its source, either continuously or in a brief burst, we can see and photograph objects by the light that is reflected from our subjects toward the camera lens; transmitted (say, from translucent objects that are lit from behind); or emitted (by a candle or television screen). When more or less light reaches the lens from the subject, we need to adjust the exposure. This part of the equation is under our control to the extent we can increase the amount of light falling on or passing through the subject (by adding extra light sources or using reflectors), or by pumping up the light that's emitted (by increasing the brightness of the glowing object).

■ **Light passed by the lens.** Not all the illumination that reaches the front of the lens makes it all the way through. Filters can remove some of the light before it enters the lens. Inside the lens barrel is a variable-sized diaphragm that dilates and contracts to vary the size of the aperture and control the amount of light that enters the lens. You, or the EOS RP's autoexposure system, can control exposure by varying the size of the aperture. The relative size of the aperture is called the *f/stop.*

■ **Light passing through the shutter.** Once light passes through the lens, the amount of time the sensor receives it is determined by the EOS RP's shutter, which can remain open for as long as 30 seconds (or even longer if you use the Bulb Timer setting in the Shooting 6 menu) or as briefly as 1/4000th second.

■ **Light captured by the sensor.** Not all the light falling onto the sensor is captured. If the number of photons reaching a particular photosite doesn't pass a set threshold, no information is recorded. Similarly, if too much light illuminates a pixel in the sensor, then the excess isn't recorded or, worse, spills over to contaminate adjacent pixels. We can modify the minimum and maximum number of pixels that contribute to image detail by adjusting the ISO setting. At higher ISOs, the incoming light is amplified to boost the effective sensitivity of the sensor.

F/STOPS AND SHUTTER SPEEDS

If you're *really* new to more advanced cameras (and I realize that many soon-to-be-ambitious photographers do purchase the EOS RP as their first digital SLR), you might need to know that the lens aperture, or f/stop, is a ratio, much like a fraction, which is why f/2 is larger than f/4, just as 1/2 is larger than 1/4. However, f/2 is actually *four times* as large as f/4. (If you remember your high school geometry, you'll know that to double the area of a circle, you multiply its diameter by the square root of two: 1.4.)

Lenses are usually marked with intermediate f/stops that represent a size that's twice as much/half as much as the previous aperture. So, a lens might be marked f/2, f/2.8, f/4, f/5.6, f/8, f/11, f/16, f/22, with each larger number representing an aperture that admits half as much light as the one before.

Shutter speeds are actual fractions (of a second), but the numerator is omitted, so that 60, 125, 250, 500, 1,000, and so forth represent 1/60th, 1/125th, 1/250th, 1/500th, and 1/1000th second. To avoid confusion, Canon uses quotation marks to signify longer exposures: 2", 2"5, 4", and so forth representing 2.0-, 2.5-, and 4.0-second exposures, respectively.

These factors—the quantity of light produced by the light source, the amount reflected or transmitted toward the camera, the light passed by the lens, the amount of time the shutter is open, and the sensitivity of the sensor—all work proportionately and reciprocally to produce an exposure. That is, if you double the amount of light that's available, increase the aperture by one stop, make the shutter speed twice as long, or boost the ISO setting 2X, you'll get twice as much exposure. Similarly, you can increase any of these factors while decreasing one of the others by a similar amount to keep the same exposure.

Most commonly, exposure settings are made using the aperture and shutter speed, followed by adjusting the ISO sensitivity if it's not possible to get the preferred exposure; that is, the one that uses the "best" f/stop or shutter speed for the depth-of-field (range of sharp focus) or action stopping we want (produced by short shutter speeds, as I'll explain later). Table 4.1 shows equivalent exposure settings using various shutter speeds and f/stops.

Table 4.1 Equivalent Exposures

Shutter Speed	f/stop	Shutter Speed	f/stop
1/30th second	f/22	1/500th second	f/5.6
1/60th second	f/16	1/1000th second	f/4
1/125th second	f/11	1/2000th second	f/2.8
1/250th second	f/8	1/4000th second	f/2

How the Camera Calculates Exposure

When the EOS RP is set for P (Program) mode, the metering system selects the correct exposure for you automatically, but you can change quickly to an equivalent exposure by locking the current exposure (hold the shutter release down halfway, or press the * button), and then spinning the Main Dial until the desired *equivalent* exposure combination is displayed. You can use this standard Program Shift feature more easily if you remember that you need to rotate the dial toward the *left* when you want to increase the amount of depth-of-field or use a slower shutter speed; rotate to the *right* when you want to reduce the depth-of-field or use a faster shutter speed. The need for more/less DOF and slower/faster shutter speed are the primary reasons you'd want to use Program Shift. I'll explain Program mode exposure shifting options in more detail later in this chapter.

In Aperture-priority (Av) and Shutter-priority (Tv) modes (or Fv mode when you opt to choose either aperture or shutter speed manually), you can change to an equivalent exposure using a different combination of shutter speed and aperture, but only by either adjusting the aperture in Aperture-priority mode (the camera then chooses the shutter speed) or shutter speed in Shutter-priority mode (the camera then selects the aperture). I'll cover all these exposure modes and their differences later in the chapter.

Correctly Exposed

The image shown in Figure 4.3, left, represents how a photograph might appear if you inserted the patches shown at bottom left into the scene, and then calculated exposure by measuring the light reflecting from the middle gray patch, which, for the sake of illustration, we'll assume reflects approximately 12 to 18 percent of the light that strikes it. The gray patch also happens to be similar in reflectance to the background behind the subject. The exposure meter in the EOS RP sees an object that it thinks is a middle gray, calculates an exposure based on that, and the patch in the center of the strip is rendered at its proper tonal value. Best of all, because the resulting exposure is correct, the black patch at left and white patch at right are rendered properly as well.

When you're shooting pictures with your EOS RP, and the meter happens to base its exposure on a subject that averages that "ideal" middle gray, you'll end up with similar (accurate) results. The camera's exposure algorithms are concocted to ensure this kind of result as often as possible, barring any unusual subjects (that is, those that are backlit, or have uneven illumination). The EOS RP has four different metering modes (described in the next section), each of which is equipped to handle certain types of unusual subjects, as I'll outline.

Overexposed

Figure 4.3, center, shows what would happen if the exposure were calculated based on metering the leftmost, black patch, which is roughly the same tonal value of the darkest areas of the subject's hair. The light meter sees less light reflecting from the black square than it would see from a gray middle-tone subject, and so figures, "Aha! I need to add exposure to brighten this subject up to a middle gray!" That lightens the "black" patch, so it now appears to be gray.

But now the patch in the middle that was *originally* middle gray is overexposed and becomes light gray. And the white square at right is now seriously overexposed and loses detail in the highlights, which have become a featureless white. Our human subject is similarly overexposed.

Underexposed

The third possibility in this simplified scenario is that the light meter might measure the illumination bouncing off the white patch, which roughly corresponds to the subject's blouse, and try to render *that* tone as a middle gray. A lot of light is reflected by the white square, so the exposure is *reduced*, bringing that patch closer to a middle-gray tone. The patches that were originally gray and black are now rendered too dark. Clearly, measuring the gray patch—or a substitute that reflects about the same amount of light, such as the standard Kodak gray card sold in many photo stores— is the only way to ensure that the exposure is precisely correct. (See Figure 4.3, right.)

As you can see, the ideal way to measure exposure is to meter from a subject that reflects 12 to 18 percent of the light that reaches it. If you want the most precise exposure calculations, the solution is to use a stand-in, such as the evenly illuminated gray card I just mentioned. But, because the standard Kodak gray card reflects 18 percent of the light that reaches it and, as I said, your camera is calibrated for a somewhat darker 12 percent tone, you would need to add about one-half stop *more* exposure than the value metered from the card.

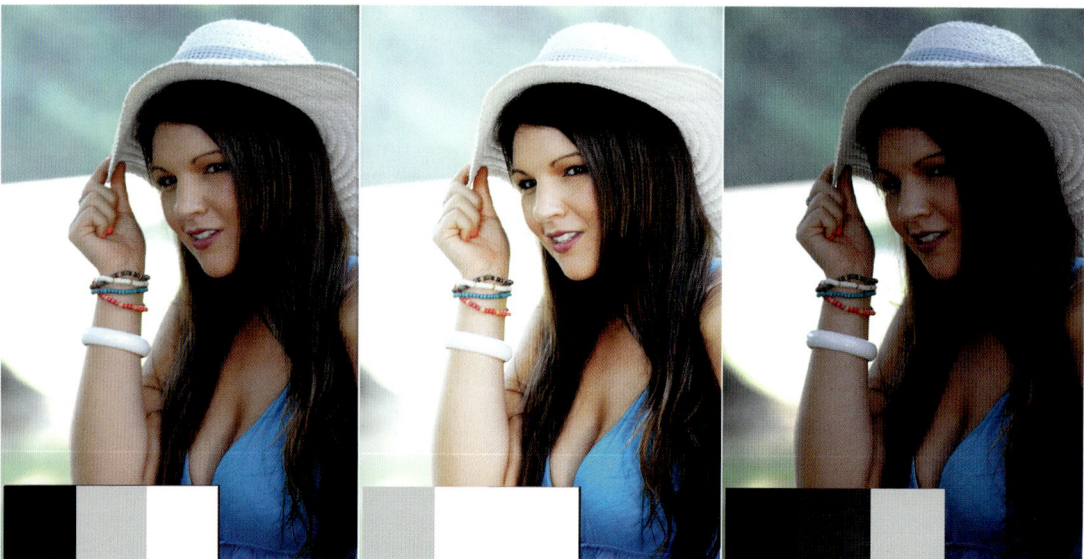

Figure 4.3 Left: When exposure is calculated based on the middle-gray tone in the center of the card, the black and white patches are rendered accurately, too. Center: When exposure is calculated based on the black square, the black patch looks gray, the gray patch appears to be a light gray, and the white square is seriously overexposed. Right: When exposure is calculated based on the white patch on the right, the photo is underexposed.

In some very bright scenes (like a snowy landscape or a lava field), you won't have a mid-tone to meter. Another substitute for a gray card is the palm of a human hand (the backside of the hand is too variable). But a human palm, regardless of ethnic group, is even brighter than a standard gray card, so instead of one-half stop more exposure, you need to add one additional stop. That is, if your meter reading is 1/500th of a second at f/11, use 1/500th second at f/8 or 1/250th second at f/11 instead. (Both exposures are equivalent.)

Or, you might want to resort to using an evenly illuminated gray card mentioned earlier. Small versions are available that can be tucked in a camera bag. Place it in your frame near your main subject, facing the camera, and with the exact same even illumination falling on it that is falling on your subject. Then, use the Spot metering function (described in the next section) to calculate exposure.

But, the standard Kodak gray card reflects 18 percent of the light while, as I noted, your camera is calibrated for a somewhat darker 12 percent tone. If you insisted on getting a perfect exposure, you would need to add about one-half stop more exposure than the value provided by taking the light meter reading from the card. Of course, in most situations, it's not necessary to do this. Your camera's light meter will do a good job of calculating the right exposure, especially if you use the exposure tips in the next section. But, I felt that explaining exactly what is going on during exposure calculation would help you understand how your EOS RP's metering system works.

ORIGIN OF THE 18 PERCENT MYTH

Why are so many photographers under the impression that camera light meters are calibrated to the 18 percent "standard," rather than the true value, which may be 12 to 14 percent, depending on the vendor? You'll find this misinformation in an alarming number of places. I've seen the 18 percent myth taught in camera classes; I've found it in books, and even been given this wrong information from the technical staff of camera vendors. (They should know better—the same vendors' engineers who design and calibrate the cameras have the right figure.)

The most common explanation is that during a revision of Kodak's instructions for its gray cards in the 1970s, the advice to open up an extra half stop was omitted, and a whole generation of shooters grew up thinking that a measurement off a gray card could be used as-is. The proviso returned to the instructions by 1987, it's said, but by then it was too late. Next to me is a (c)2006 version of the instructions for KODAK Gray Cards, Publication R-27Q (still available in authorized versions from non-Kodak sources). The current directions read (with a bit of paraphrasing from me in italics):

■ For subjects of normal reflectance increase the indicated exposure by 1/2 stop.

■ For light subjects use the indicated exposure; for very light subjects, decrease the exposure by 1/2 stop. *(That is, you're measuring a subject that's lighter than middle gray.)*

■ If the subject is dark to very dark, increase the indicated exposure by 1 to 1-1/2 stops. *(You're shooting a dark subject.)*

EXTERNAL METERS CAN BE CALIBRATED

The light meters built into your EOS RP are calibrated at the factory. But if you use a handheld incident or reflective light meter, you *can* calibrate it, using the instructions supplied with your meter. Because a handheld meter, of both the reflective and incident type, *can* be calibrated to the 18 percent gray standard (or any other value you choose), my rant about the myth of the 18 percent gray card doesn't apply.

Choosing a Metering Mode

To calculate exposure automatically, you need to tell the EOS RP *where* in the frame to measure the light (this is called the *metering mode*) and *what controls* should be used (aperture, shutter speed, or both) to set the exposure. That's called *exposure mode,* and includes Program (P), Shutter-priority (Tv), Aperture-priority (Av), Flexible-priority (Fv), or Manual (M) options, plus Scene Intelligent Auto. I'll explain all these next.

But first, I'm going to introduce you to the four metering modes. You can select any of the four if you're working with P, Tv, Av, Fv, or M exposure modes; if you're using Scene Intelligent Auto, Evaluative metering is selected automatically and cannot be changed.

Choose a metering mode by pressing the Q button and navigating to the Metering Mode icon, which is fourth from the top in the left column. (See Figure 4.4.) Then use either dial to select the mode you want and press SET to confirm.

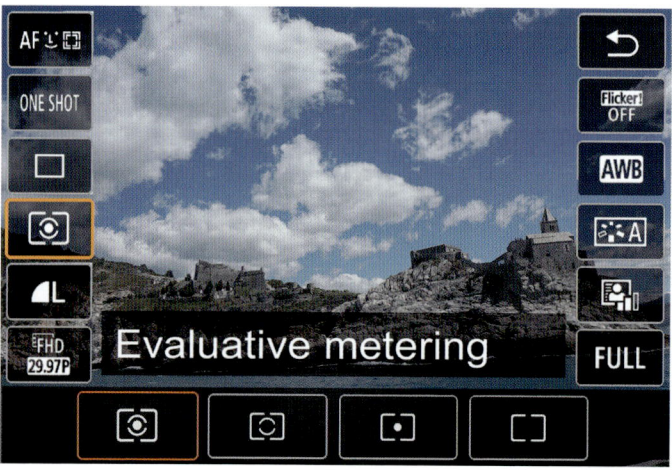

Figure 4.4
Use the Quick Control menu to choose a metering mode.

Available modes include:

- **Evaluative.** The EOS RP slices up the frame into 384 different zones (a 24 × 16 matrix), shown as yellow rectangles in Figure 4.5. (Don't confuse these zones with the 4,779 *autofocus* points or zones; they are different.)

  The exposure zones used are linked to the autofocus system such that as the camera evaluates the measurements, it gives extra emphasis to the metering zones that indicate sharp focus. From this data, it makes an educated guess about what kind of picture you're taking, based on examination of thousands of different real-world photos in the camera's database. For example, if the top sections of a picture are much lighter than the bottom portions, the algorithm can assume that the scene is a landscape photo with lots of sky. This mode is the best all-purpose metering method for most pictures. I'll explain how to choose an autofocus/exposure zone in the section on autofocus operation later in this chapter.

- **Partial.** This is a *faux* spot mode, using roughly 5.5 percent of the image area to calculate exposure, which, as you can see in Figure 4.6, is a rather large spot, represented by the larger yellow circle. Use this mode if the background is much brighter or darker than the subject, as in the figure.

- **Spot.** This mode confines the reading to a limited area in the center of the viewfinder, as shown in Figure 4.7, making up only 2.7 percent of the image. This mode is useful when you want to base exposure on a small area in the frame, such as the gray portions of the structure in the figure. If that area is in the center of the frame, so much the better. If not, you'll have to make your meter reading and then lock exposure by pressing the shutter release halfway, or by pressing the AE lock (*) button. Note that spot metering is *not* linked to the focus point.

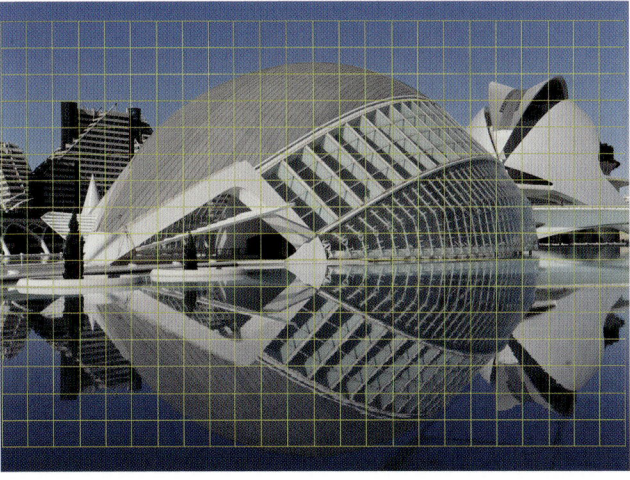

Figure 4.5
Evaluative metering uses 384 zones and is effective for interpreting evenly lit scenes.

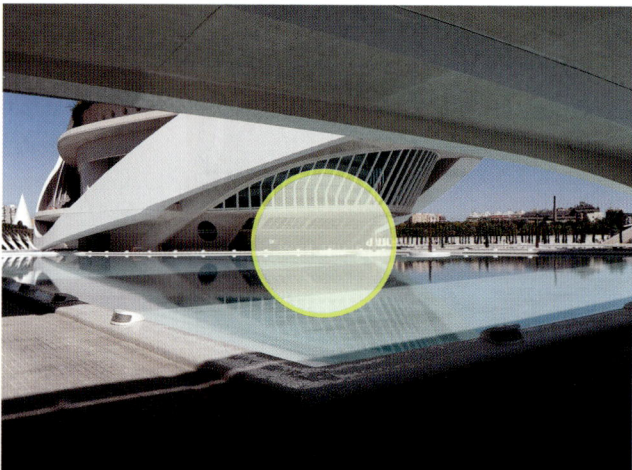

Figure 4.6
Partial metering uses a center spot that's roughly 5.5 percent of the frame area and is excellent for images with the most important areas in the center.

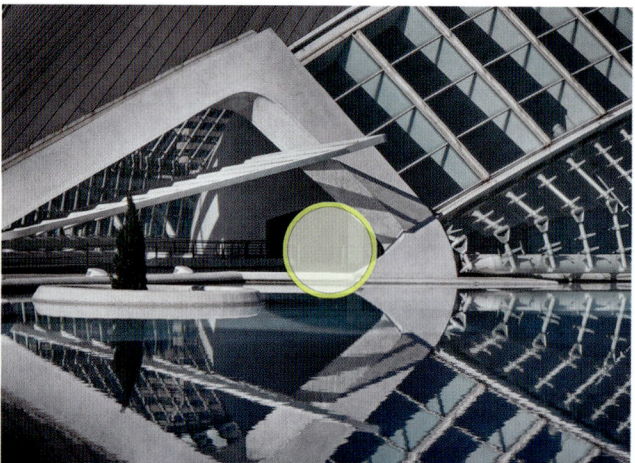

Figure 4.7
Spot metering calculates exposure based on a center spot that's only 2.7 percent of the image area and allows measuring specific areas, such as the gray portions of this structure.

- **Center-weighted averaging.** In this mode, the exposure meter emphasizes a zone in the center of the frame to calculate exposure, as shown in Figure 4.8, on the theory that, for most pictures, the main subject will be located in the center. Center-weighting works best for portraits, architectural photos, and other pictures in which the most important subject is located in the middle of the frame, as in the figure. As the name suggests, the light reading is *weighted* toward the central portion, but information is also used from the rest of the frame. If your main subject is surrounded by very bright or very dark areas, the exposure might not be exactly right. However, this scheme works well in many situations if you don't want to use one of the other modes.

Figure 4.8
Center-weighted metering calculates exposure based on the full frame, but emphasizes the center area. Exposure for the example image was calculated from the large area in the center of the frame, with less emphasis on the darker surroundings.

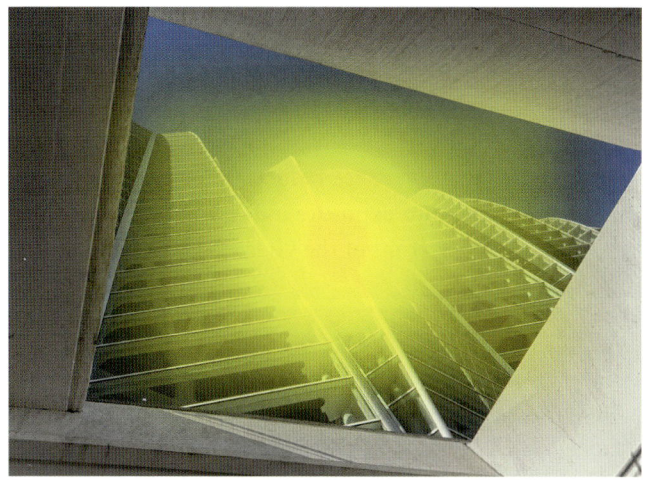

Choosing a Shooting Mode

You'll find six methods for choosing the appropriate shutter speed and aperture, including: Scene Intelligent Auto (A+), Program (P), Shutter-priority (Tv), Aperture-priority (Av), and Manual (M). The sixth, Flexible-priority (Fv) can mimic any of the previous four. To select one of these modes, just rotate the Mode Dial located at the top-right side of the camera to choose the method you want to use. (See Figure 4.9.) Your choice of which exposure/shooting mode is best for a given shooting situation will depend on things like your need for more/less depth-of-field, a desire to freeze action

Figure 4.9
Select a Shooting mode.

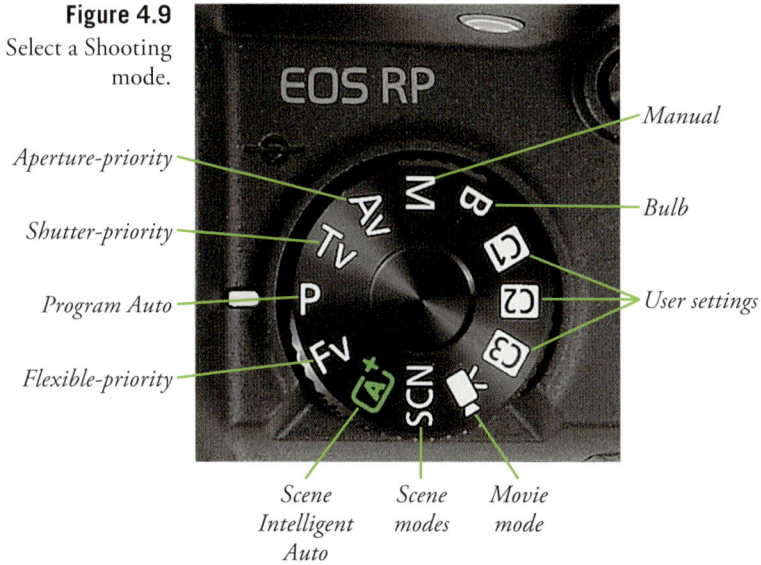

Aperture-priority

Shutter-priority

Program Auto

Flexible-priority

Manual

Bulb

User settings

Scene Intelligent Auto

Scene modes

Movie mode

or allow motion blur, or how much noise you find acceptable in an image. (Remember that exposure triangle at the beginning of the chapter.) Each of the EOS RP's exposure methods emphasizes one of those aspects of image capture or another. This section introduces you to all of them.

In Scene Intelligent Auto mode, the EOS RP selects an appropriate ISO sensitivity setting, color (white) balance, Picture Style, color space, noise reduction features, and use of the Auto Lighting Optimizer. Use the Scene Intelligent Auto exposure mode when you hand your camera to a friend to take a picture (say, of you standing in front of the Great Wall of China), and want to be sure they won't accidentally change any settings.

Scene Intelligent Auto Mode

On first consideration, including an exposure mode with few user options might seem counterintuitive on a camera as advanced as the EOS RP, because it essentially transforms a sophisticated pro/enthusiast camera into a point-and-click snapshooter. Delve deeper, and you'll discover that there is method in Canon's madness, and that Scene Intelligent Auto is a lot more than a less versatile version of Program mode. The key is the *Intelligent* part of the mode's nomenclature.

With P mode, only the shutter speed and aperture are determined by the camera. You can change the metering mode, autofocus mode, white balance, and virtually all other settings. In Scene Intelligent Auto mode, the EOS RP will analyze your scene, even to the extent of evaluating whether or not your subject is static or moving, and then intelligently choose optimum settings without any input from you. The settings the camera has to work with include:

- **ISO speed.** The camera will choose an ISO sensitivity automatically.
- **Picture Style.** The A (automatic) Picture Style is active, and the camera will choose appropriate settings. Note that if you have made changes to the Auto Picture Style (I'll show you how to do that in Chapter 11), they will be ignored in Scene Intelligent Auto.
- **White balance.** White balance is set automatically and cannot be changed.
- **Auto Lighting Optimizer.** Always active in Scene Intelligent Auto mode.
- **Color space.** Forced to sRGB.
- **Autofocus.** By default, Servo AF is always used, and AF area selection modes cannot be specified. AF point selection is always automatic, and the AF-assist beam is activated. If you prefer to use One-Shot AF, you can use the A+ Auto Servo entry in the Shooting 4 menu to disable Servo AF and force the use of One-Shot AF instead. **Note:** This version of the Shooting 4 menu appears *only* when Scene Intelligent Auto has been selected as your Shooting mode.
- **Metering mode.** Evaluative metering is always used.

Things that you *can* choose in Scene Intelligent Auto mode include:

- **Manual focus.** Manual focus can be chosen by toggling the AF/MF switch on the lens to Manual.

- **Drive mode.** You use the Quick Control screen to choose from single shooting, high-/low-speed continuous shooting, silent single shooting, silent continuous shooting, and 10 sec./2 sec. self-timer modes.

- **Image quality/size.** Press the Q button to select among your RAW, JPEG, and other image size options.

- **Touch shutter.** You can enable or disable the Touch Shutter feature, which allows you to specify a focus area and take a picture with a single tap. At lower right is an icon to summon the Creative Assist features, as explained in Chapter 1.

- **Creative Assist.** The Creative Assist options include an array of creative filters you can apply to images *as you shoot.* They include a selection of Presets, plus controls for Background Blur, Brightness, Contrast, Saturation, Color Tone 1, Color Tone 2, and Monochrome. I showed you how to apply these in Chapter 1.

- **Non-exposure Menu Items.** A selection of other shooting options, not related to determining focus, and described next.

Some shooting options are available from the truncated three-tab menu system offered in Scene Intelligent Auto mode. While some Playback and Set-up menu choices are accessible, those you most commonly might need to access while taking pictures—particularly some that apply to auto-focus settings—are those in the Scene Intelligent Auto's version of the Shooting 1–4 menus, which are described in more detail in Chapter 11 and (for the Movie options) in Chapter 15:

Shooting Menus

- Image Quality
- Image Review Duration
- Release Shutter without Card
- Retain Creative Assist Data
- Touch Shutter
- Interval Timer
- Eye Detection AF
- Continuous AF
- Touch & Drag AF Settings

- AF-assist Beam Firing
- A+ Auto Servo
- Focus Guide
- MF Peaking Settings
- Movie Recording Size
- Sound Recording
- Movie Digital IS
- Move Servo AF

Aperture-Priority Mode

In Av mode, you specify the lens opening used, and the EOS RP selects the shutter speed. Aperture-priority is especially good when you want to use a particular lens opening to achieve a desired effect. Perhaps you'd like to use the smallest f/stop possible to maximize depth-of-field in a close-up picture. Or, you might want to use a large f/stop to throw everything except your main subject out of focus, as in Figure 4.10. Maybe you'd just like to "lock in" a particular f/stop smaller than the maximum aperture because it's the sharpest available aperture with that lens. Or, you might prefer to use, say, f/2.8 on a lens with a maximum aperture of f/1.4, because you want the best compromise between speed and sharpness.

Aperture-priority can even be used to specify a *range* of shutter speeds you want to use under varying lighting conditions, which seems almost contradictory. But think about it. You're shooting a soccer game outdoors with a telephoto lens and want a relatively high shutter speed, but you don't care if the speed changes a little should the sun duck behind a cloud. Set your EOS RP to Av, and adjust the aperture until a shutter speed of, say, 1/1000th second is selected at your current ISO

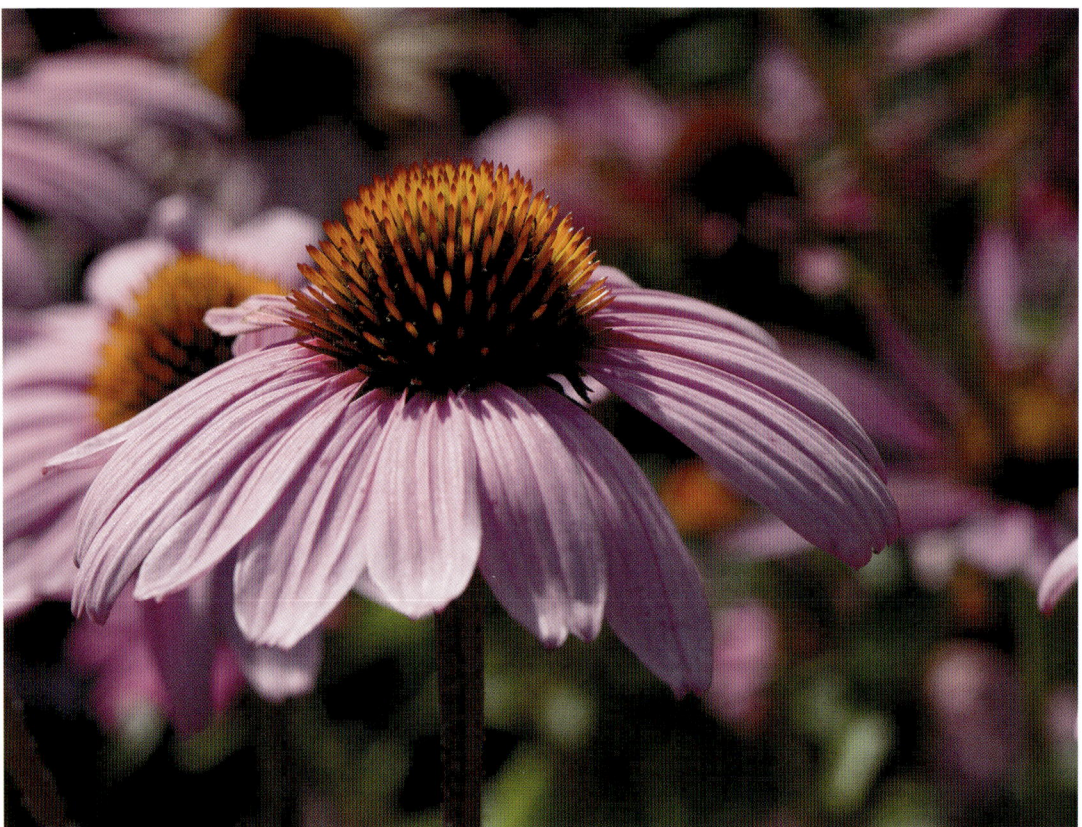

Figure 4.10 Use Aperture-priority to "lock in" a large f/stop when you want to blur the background.

setting. (In bright sunlight at ISO 400, that aperture is likely to be around f/11.) Then, go ahead and shoot, knowing that your EOS RP will maintain that f/11 aperture (for sufficient DOF as the soccer players move about the field), but will drop down to 1/750th or 1/500th second if necessary should the lighting change a little.

If the shutter speed in the viewfinder or on the Shooting Settings screen is blinking, that indicates that the EOS RP is unable to select an appropriate shutter speed at the selected aperture and that overexposure (the 4000 is blinking) or underexposure (the 30 shutter speed is blinking) will occur at the current ISO setting. To correct overexposure, select a smaller aperture (if available) or choose a lower ISO sensitivity. Fix underexposure conditions by choosing a larger aperture (if possible) or a higher ISO setting.

That's the major pitfall of using Av: you might select an f/stop that is too small or too large to allow an optimal exposure with the available shutter speeds. For example, if you choose f/2.8 as your aperture and the illumination is quite bright (say, at the beach or in snow), even your camera's fastest shutter speed might not be able to cut down the amount of light reaching the sensor to provide the right exposure. Or, if you select f/8 in a dimly lit room, you might find yourself shooting with a very slow shutter speed that can cause blurring from subject movement or camera shake. Aperture-priority is best used by those with a bit of experience in choosing settings. Many seasoned photographers leave their EOS RP set on Av all the time. The Safety Shift feature can be used to automatically override your selected aperture if the camera is unable to obtain a correct exposure. Safety Shift operates even when you're using flash. I'll show you how to configure that setting, which can also be used with P, Tv, and Fv modes, in Chapter 11.

When to use Aperture-priority:

- **General landscape photography.** The EOS RP is a great camera for landscape photography, of course, because its 26 MP of resolution allows making huge, gorgeous prints, as well as smaller prints that are filled with eye-popping detail. Aperture-priority is a good tool for ensuring that your landscape is sharp from foreground to infinity, if you select an f/stop that provides maximum depth-of-field.

  If you use Av mode and select an aperture like f/11 or f/16, it's your responsibility to make sure the shutter speed selected is fast enough to avoid losing detail to camera shake, or that the EOS RP is mounted on a tripod. One thing that new landscape photographers fail to account for is the movement of distant leaves and tree branches. When seeking the ultimate in sharpness, go ahead and use Aperture-priority, but boost ISO sensitivity a bit, if necessary, to provide a sufficiently fast shutter speed, whether shooting hand-held or with a tripod.

- **Specific landscape situations.** Aperture-priority is also useful when you have no objection to using a long shutter speed, or, particularly, *want* the EOS RP to select one. Waterfalls are a perfect example. You can use Av mode, set your camera to ISO 100, use a small f/stop, and let the camera select a longer shutter speed that will allow the water to blur as it flows. Indeed, you might need to use a neutral-density filter to get a sufficiently long shutter speed. But Aperture-priority mode is a good start.

- **Portrait photography.** Portraits are the most common applications of selective focus. A medium-large aperture (say, f/5.6 or f/8) with a longer lens/zoom setting (in the 85mm-135mm range) will allow the background behind your portrait subject to blur. A *very* large aperture (I frequently shoot wide open with my 85mm f/1.2 lens) lets you apply selective focus to your subject's *face.* With a three-quarters view of your subject, as long as their eyes are sharp, it's okay if the far ear or their hair is out of focus.

- **When you want to ensure optimal sharpness.** All lenses have an aperture or two at which they perform best, providing the level of sharpness you expect from a camera with the resolution of the EOS RP. That's usually about two stops down from wide open, and thus will vary depending on the maximum aperture of the lens. My 85mm f/1.2 is good wide open, but it's even sharper at f/2.8 or f/4; I shoot my 70-200mm f/2.8 wide open at concerts, but, if I can use f/4 instead, I'll get better results. Aperture-priority allows me to use each lens at its very best f/stop.

- **Close-up/Macro photography.** Depth-of-field is typically very shallow when shooting macro photos, and you'll want to choose your f/stop carefully. Perhaps you need the smallest aperture you can get away with to maximize DOF. Or, you might want to use a wider stop to emphasize your subject, as I did with the photo of the cone flower in Figure 4.10. Av mode comes in very useful when shooting close-up pictures. Because macro work is frequently done with the EOS RP mounted on a tripod, and your close-up subjects, if not living creatures, may not be moving much, a longer shutter speed isn't a problem. Aperture-priority (Av mode) can be your preferred choice.

Shutter-Priority Mode

Shutter-priority (Tv) is the inverse of Aperture-priority: you choose the shutter speed you'd like to use, and the camera's metering system selects the appropriate f/stop. Perhaps you're shooting action photos and you want to use the absolute fastest shutter speed available with your camera; in other cases, you might want to use a slow shutter speed to add some blur to a sports image that would be mundane if the action were completely frozen. Motor sports and track-and-field events particularly lend themselves to slower speeds, as you can see in Figure 4.11. Shutter-priority mode gives you some control over how much action-freezing capability your digital camera brings to bear in a particular situation.

You'll also encounter the same problem as with Aperture-priority when you select a shutter speed that's too long or too short for correct exposure under some conditions. I've shot outdoor soccer games on sunny Fall evenings and used Shutter-priority mode to lock in a 1/1000th second shutter speed, which triggered the blinking warning, even with the lens wide open.

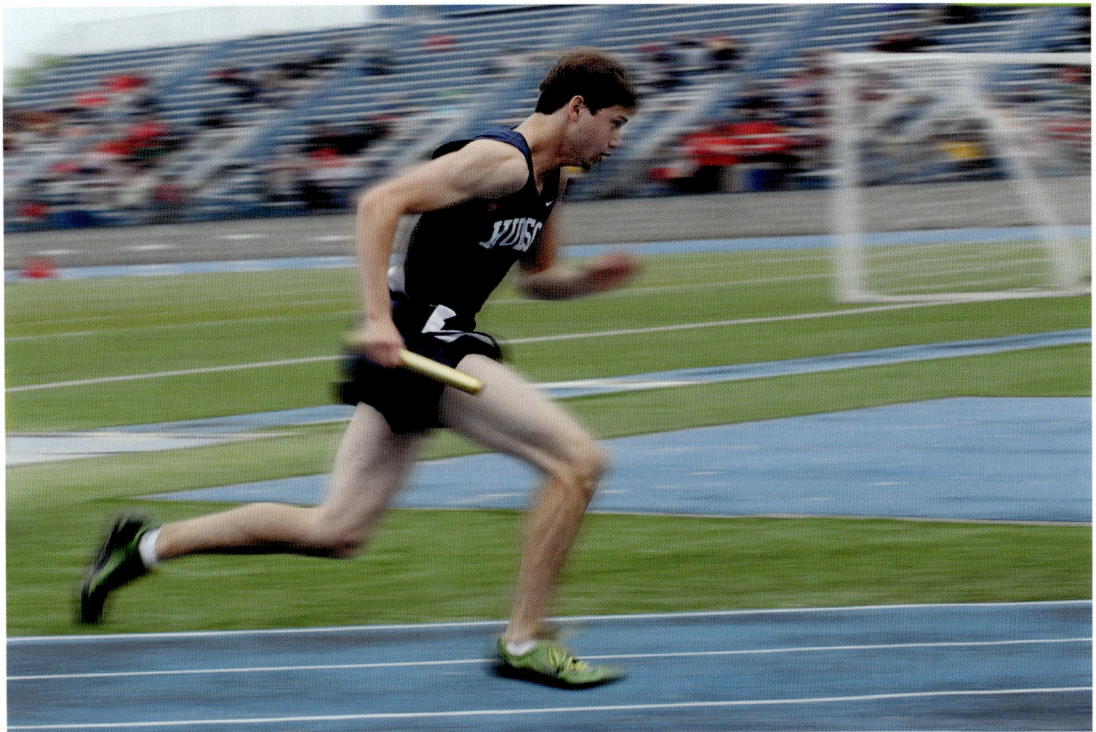

Figure 4.11 Lock the shutter at a slow speed to introduce a little blur into an action shot, seen here in this panned image of a relay runner.

Like Av mode, it's possible to choose an inappropriate shutter speed. If that's the case, the maximum aperture of your lens (to indicate underexposure) or the minimum aperture (to indicate overexposure) will blink. To fix, select a longer shutter speed or higher ISO setting (for underexposure), or a faster shutter speed/lower ISO setting (for overexposure), or use Safety Shift, mentioned previously.

When to use Shutter-priority:

- **To reduce blur from subject motion.** Set the shutter speed of the EOS RP to a higher value to reduce the amount of blur from subjects that are moving. The exact speed will vary depending on how fast your subject is moving and how much blur is acceptable. You might want to freeze a basketball player in mid-dunk with a 1/1000th second shutter speed, or use 1/250th second to allow the spinning wheels of a motocross racer to blur a tiny bit to add the feeling of motion.

- **To add blur from subject motion.** There are times when you want a subject to blur, say, when shooting waterfalls with the camera set for a one- or two-second exposure in Shutter-priority mode.

- **To add blur from camera motion when *you* are moving.** Say you're panning to follow a pair of relay runners. You might want to use Shutter-priority mode and set the EOS RP for 1/60th second, so that the background will blur as you pan with the runners. The shutter speed will be fast enough to provide a sharp image of the athletes.

- **To reduce blur from camera motion when *you* are moving.** In other situations, the camera may be in motion, say, because you're shooting from a moving train or auto, and you want to minimize the amount of blur caused by the motion of the camera. Shutter-priority is a good choice here, too.

- **Landscape photography hand-held.** If you can't use a tripod for your landscape shots, you'll still probably want the sharpest image possible. Shutter-priority can allow you to specify a shutter speed that's fast enough to reduce or eliminate the effects of camera shake. Just make sure that your ISO setting is high enough that the EOS RP will select an aperture with sufficient depth-of-field, too.

- **Concerts, stage performances.** I shoot a lot of concerts with my 70-200mm f/2.8 lens, and have discovered that, when image stabilization is taken into account, a shutter speed of 1/180th second is fast enough to eliminate blur from hand-holding the EOS RP with this lens, and also to avoid blur from the movement of all but the most energetic performers. I use Shutter-priority and set the ISO so the camera will select an aperture in the f/4-5.6 range.

Program AE Mode

Program Auto Exposure mode (usually just called *Program* or *P* mode) uses the EOS RP's built-in smarts to select the correct f/stop and shutter speed using a database of picture information that tells it which combination of shutter speed and aperture will work best for a particular photo. If the correct exposure cannot be achieved at the current ISO setting, the shutter speed or aperture indicator in the viewfinder will blink, indicating under- or overexposure. You can then boost or reduce the ISO to increase or decrease sensitivity.

The EOS RP's recommended exposure can be overridden if you want. Use the EV setting feature (described later, because it also applies to Tv and Av modes) to add or subtract exposure from the metered value. And, as I mentioned earlier in this chapter, you can change from the recommended setting to an equivalent setting (as shown in Table 4.1) that produces the same exposure, but using a different combination of f/stop and shutter speed. To accomplish this:

1. Press the shutter release halfway to lock in the current base exposure, or press the AE Lock button (*) on the back of the camera (in which case the * indicator will illuminate in the viewfinder to show that the exposure has been locked).

2. If the camera cannot select an appropriate exposure, the shutter speed and aperture display will blink:

- **Underexposure.** The 30 shutter speed indicator will flash, along with the maximum (largest) aperture of the lens. (The exact number will vary, depending on which lens you are using.) To compensate, you must either use a higher ISO setting or provide additional illumination, such as electronic flash.

- **Overexposure.** The 4000 shutter speed indicator will flash, along with the minimum (smallest available) f/stop, such as f/16, f/22, or f/32, depending on the lens you are using. You can usually compensate for this by reducing the ISO speed to a lower setting. Your scene must be *very* bright indeed to trigger overexposure at a shutter speed of 1/4000th second and the lowest L (ISO 50 equivalent) sensitivity setting. But if you're photographing, say, a blast furnace, and still have an overexposure situation, you can resort to a neutral-density filter or find some way to reduce the amount of illumination.

3. Once an exposure is set, you can spin the Main Dial to change to a different combination of settings. Rotate left to select a longer shutter speed/smaller aperture, or to the right to choose a faster shutter speed/larger aperture.

Your adjustment remains in force for a single exposure; if you want to change from the recommended settings for the next exposure, you'll need to repeat those steps.

When to use Program mode priority:

- **When you're in a hurry to get a grab shot.** The EOS RP will do a pretty good job of calculating an appropriate exposure for you, without any input from you.

- **When you hand your camera to a novice.** Set the EOS RP to P, hand the camera to your friend, relative, or trustworthy stranger you meet in front of the Eiffel Tower, point to the shutter release button and viewfinder, and say, "Look through here, and press this button."

- **When no special shutter speed or aperture settings are needed.** If your subject doesn't require special anti- or pro-blur techniques, and depth-of-field or selective focus aren't important, use P as a general-purpose setting. You can still make adjustments to increase/decrease depth-of-field or add/reduce motion blur with a minimum of fuss.

Flexible-Priority Mode

Flexible-priority (Fv) takes a little getting used to, because, at least among veteran photographers, the shooting modes P, Tv, Av, and Manual (discussed later) are ingrained in our workflow. Fv almost seems counter-intuitive until you've used it a few times and the realization comes that it is probably the most intuitive shooting mode of all. Flexible-priority gives you all four modes with full control of the three legs of the exposure triangle, all within a single setting.

In a nutshell, Fv, by default, acts like Program AE with Auto ISO activated. That is, the EOS RP selects shutter speed, aperture, and ISO setting for you automatically. But you can elect to manually specify any or all of those three, and the EOS RP's shooting mode magically transforms from P to Av, Tv, or Manual. With the mode set to Fv:

- **Tv mode.** In Fv mode, rotate the Quick Control Dial until an orange icon representing the Main Dial appears next to the shutter speed. You can then rotate the Main Dial to manually select the shutter speed, and the aperture and ISO will continue to be changed automatically. In effect, you have Tv mode with Auto ISO. (See Figure 4.12.)

- **Av mode.** In Fv mode, rotate the Quick Control Dial until an orange icon representing the Main Dial appears next to the aperture, then rotate the Main Dial to manually select the f/stop. The EOS RP behaves just like it would in Av mode with Auto ISO.

- **Manual mode.** In Fv mode, rotate the Quick Control Dial to the shutter speed and aperture icons and choose a manual setting for each. Now the EOS RP acts as if it were in Manual exposure mode with shutter speed, and the aperture and ISO will continue to be changed automatically. In effect, you have Tv mode with Auto ISO.

- **Fixed ISO.** If you want to disable Auto ISO in Fv mode, rotate the Quick Control Dial to highlight the ISO icon and select a fixed ISO value of your choice.

- **Exposure compensation.** Highlight the exposure scale at the bottom of the screen and rotate the Main Dial to add or subtract Exposure Compensation.

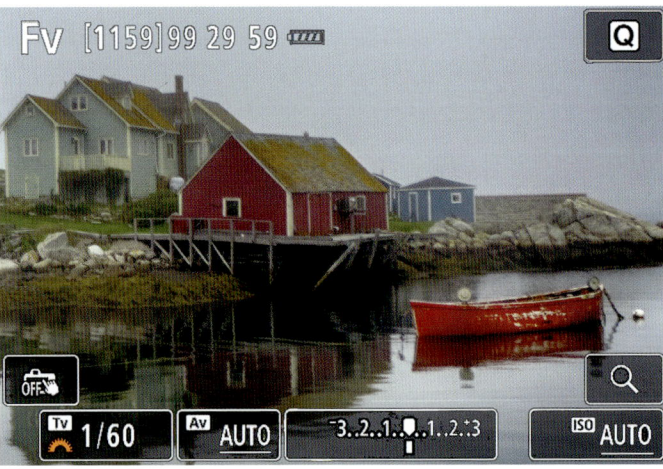

Figure 4.12
An exposure scale is shown at the bottom of the display.

Manual Exposure Mode

Part of being an experienced photographer comes from knowing when to rely on your EOS RP's automation (including Scene Intelligent Auto or P mode), when to go semi-automatic (with Tv or Av), and when to set exposure manually (using M). Some photographers actually prefer to set their exposure manually most of the time, as the EOS RP will be happy to provide an indication of when its metering system judges your settings provide the proper exposure, using the analog exposure scale at the bottom of the display (see Figure 4.12) and on the status LCD.

Manual exposure can come in handy in some situations. You might be taking a silhouette photo and find that none of the exposure modes or EV correction features give you exactly the effect you want. Or, you might be looking for a certain moody look, as I was when I was taking photos early one rainy, foggy morning that was punctuated by a motorboat gliding across the Gulf of Mexico. My camera was mounted on a tripod, and I captured the image shown in Figure 4.13. There was no way any of my EOS RP's exposure modes would be able to interpret the scene the way I wanted to shoot it, even with Spot metering. I had already taken a couple test exposures, and set the exposure manually using the exact 1/2 second shutter speed and f/22 aperture I needed.

Or, you might be working in a studio environment using multiple flash units. The additional flash are triggered by slave devices (gadgets that set off the flash when they sense the light from another flash, or, perhaps from a radio or infrared remote control). Your camera's exposure meter doesn't compensate for the extra illumination, and can't interpret the flash exposure at all, so you need to set the aperture manually.

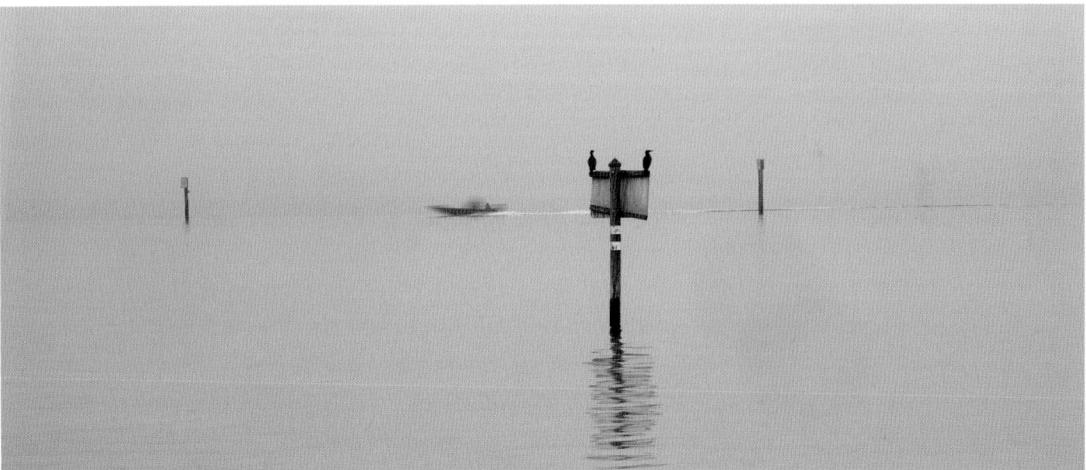

Figure 4.13 Manual exposure allows selecting both f/stop and shutter speed, especially useful when you're experimenting, as with this shot a foggy Gulf of Mexico waterfront in Keaton Beach, Florida.

Because, depending on your proclivities, you might not need to set exposure manually very often, you should still make sure you understand how it works. Fortunately, the EOS RP makes setting exposure manually very easy. Just rotate the Mode Dial to select Manual exposure, then turn the Main Dial to set the shutter speed, and the QCD to adjust the aperture. Press the shutter release halfway or press the AE Lock (*) button, and the exposure scale in the viewfinder shows you how far your chosen setting diverges from the metered exposure.

If you activate ISO Auto, you can add or subtract Exposure Compensation. Just tap the exposure scale at the bottom of the touch screen, use the Quick Control screen's Exposure Compensation function in the graphical screen, or use the Exposure Compensation/AEB entry in the Shooting 3 menu.

When to use Manual exposure:

- **When working in the studio.** If you're working in a studio environment, you generally have total control over the lighting and can set exposure exactly as you want. The last thing you need is for the EOS RP to interpret the scene and make adjustments of its own. Use M and the shutter speed, aperture, and (as long as you don't use ISO-Auto) ISO setting are totally up to you.

- **When using non-dedicated flash.** External Canon-dedicated flash units are cool, but if you're working with a non-compatible flash unit, particularly studio flash plugged into a PC/X adapter mounted on the hot shoe, the camera has no clue about the intensity of the flash, so you'll have to dial in the appropriate aperture and shutter speed manually. (And remember not to use a shutter speed that's faster than the EOS RP's maximum sync speed, as I'll explain in Chapter 9.)

- **If you're using a hand-held light meter.** The appropriate aperture, both for flash exposures and shots taken under continuous lighting, can be determined by a hand-held light meter, flash meter, or combo meter that measures both kinds of illumination. With an external meter, you can measure highlights, shadows, backgrounds, or additional subjects separately, and use Manual exposure to make your settings.

- **When you want to outsmart the metering system.** Your EOS RP's metering system is "trained" to react to unusual lighting situations, such as backlighting, extra-bright illumination, or low-key images with murky shadows. In many cases, it can counter these "problems" and produce a well-exposed image. But what if you don't *want* a well-exposed image? Manual exposure allows you to produce silhouettes in backlit situations, wash out all the middle tones to produce a luminous look, or underexpose to create a moody or ominous dark-toned photograph.

Adjusting Exposure with ISO Settings

Another way of adjusting exposures is by changing the ISO sensitivity setting. Sometimes photographers forget about this option, because the common practice is to set the ISO once for a particular shooting session (say, at ISO 100 or 200 for bright sunlight outdoors, or ISO 800 when shooting indoors) and then forget about it. ISOs higher than ISO 100 or 200 are seen as "bad" or "necessary evils." However, changing the ISO is a valid way of adjusting exposure settings, particularly with the Canon EOS RP, which produces good results at ISO settings that create grainy, unusable pictures with some other camera models.

Indeed, I find myself using ISO adjustment as a convenient alternate way of adding or subtracting EV when shooting in Manual mode, and as a quick way of choosing equivalent exposures when in Auto or semi-automatic modes. For example, I've selected a Manual exposure with both f/stop and shutter speed suitable for my image using, say, ISO 200. I can change the exposure in 1/3-stop increments by pressing the M-Fn button on top of the camera highlighting ISO with the QCD, and spinning the Main Dial one click at a time. The difference in image quality/noise at the base setting of ISO 200 is negligible if I dial in ISO 100 to reduce exposure a little, or change to ISO 400 to increase exposure. I keep my preferred f/stop and shutter speed, but still adjust the exposure.

Or, perhaps, I am using Tv mode and the metered exposure at ISO 200 is 1/500th second at f/11. If I decide on the spur of the moment I'd rather use 1/500th second at f/8, I can press the M-Fn button, select ISO with the QCD, and spin the Main Dial to switch to ISO 100. Of course, it's a good idea to monitor your ISO changes, so you don't end up at ISO 1600 accidentally. ISO settings can, of course, also be used to boost or reduce sensitivity in particular shooting situations.

When not using Scene Intelligent Auto (which sets ISO automatically), the EOS RP can set ISO speeds manually for stills. (In video mode, Auto ISO must be used in all modes except Manual exposure.) The ISO Speed Settings entry in the Shooting 3 menu allows you to specify what speeds are available and how they are used:

- **ISO Speed.** This scale allows you to choose from the enabled ISO speeds, plus Auto, using a sliding scale that can be adjusted using the QCD, directional buttons, or the touch screen. Pressing INFO when the scale is visible activates Auto.

- **Range for Stills.** You can specify the minimum and maximum ISO sensitivity available, including "expanded" settings such as Low (ISO 50 equivalent) and H1 or H2 (ISO 51200 and 102400 equivalent, respectively). I find myself using this feature frequently to keep me from accidentally switching to a setting I'd rather not use (or need to avoid). For example, at concerts I may switch from ISO 1600 to 6400 as the lighting changes, and I set those two values as my minimum or maximum. Outdoors in daylight, I might prefer to lock out ISO values lower than ISO 100 or higher than ISO 800.

Tip

The Lo, H1, and H2 settings enables *ISO expansion,* which may produce excessive noise, irregular colors, banding, and lower resolution. Use them with caution.

- **Auto Range.** This is the equivalent "safety net" for Auto ISO operation. You can set the minimum no lower than ISO 100 and the maximum to ISO 40000, and no further. Use this to apply your own "smarts" to the Auto ISO setting.
- **Minimum Shutter Speed.** You can choose whether to allow the EOS RP to select the slowest shutter speed used before Auto ISO kicks in. The idea here is that you'll probably want to boost ISO sooner if you're using a long lens with P and Av modes (in which the camera selects the shutter speed). If you specify, for example, a minimum shutter speed of 1/250th second, if P or Av mode needs a slower shutter speed for the proper exposure, it will boost ISO instead, within the range you've specified with Auto Range.

This setting has two modes. In Auto mode, the camera decides when the shutter speed is too low. You can fine-tune this by choosing Slower or Faster on the scale (–3 to +3) that appears. Or, you can manually select the "trigger" shutter speed, from 1 second to 1/4000th second.

Tip

By default, both the exposure level increments (size of shutter speed or f/stop changes) are in 1/3-stop jumps. In the Custom Functions 1 menu, you can set exposure level increments to 1/3 or 1/2 stops, and ISO changes to 1/3- or 1-stop increments. The larger 1-stop step for ISO allows rapid switching through ISO 100, 200, 400, 800, and so forth.

Find yourself locked out of ISO settings lower than 200 or higher than 40000? You've probably set Highlight Tone Priority to Enable in the Shooting 3 menu, as described in Chapter 11.

Dealing with Visual Noise

Visual image noise is that random grainy effect that some like to use as a special effect, but which, most of the time, is objectionable because it robs your image of detail even as it adds that "interesting" texture. Noise is caused by two different phenomena: high ISO settings and long exposures.

High ISO noise commonly first appears when you raise your camera's sensitivity setting above ISO 3200. With Canon cameras, which are renowned for their good ISO noise characteristics, noise is usually fairly noticeable at ISO 6400 and above. At the H1 and H2 settings (ISO 51200 and 102400 equivalents), noise is usually quite bothersome, which is why those lofty sensitivity ratings are disabled by default and must be activated with ISO expansion. This kind of noise appears as a result of the amplification needed to increase the sensitivity of the sensor. Because your sensor has twice as many green pixels as red and blue pixels, such noise is typically worse in areas that have red, blue, and magenta tones, because the green signals don't have to be amplified as much to produce detail. While higher ISOs do pull details out of dark areas, they also amplify non-signal information randomly, creating noise.

A similar noisy phenomenon occurs during long time exposures, which allow more photons to reach the sensor, increasing your ability to capture a picture under low-light conditions. However, the longer exposures also increase the likelihood that some pixels will register random phantom photons, often because the longer an imager is "hot," the warmer it gets, and that heat can be mistaken for photons. There's also a special kind of noise that CMOS sensors like the one used in the EOS RP are potentially susceptible to. With a CCD, the entire signal is conveyed off the chip and funneled through a single amplifier and analog-to-digital conversion circuit. Any noise introduced there is, at least, consistent. CMOS imagers, on the other hand, contain millions of individual amplifiers and A/D converters, all working in unison. Because all these circuits don't necessarily process in precisely the same way all the time, they can introduce something called fixed-pattern noise into the image data.

Fortunately, Canon's electronics geniuses have done an exceptional job minimizing noise from all causes in the EOS RP. Even so, you might still want to apply the optional long exposure noise reduction that can be activated in the Shooting 5 menu. This type of noise reduction involves the EOS RP taking a second, blank exposure, and comparing the random pixels in that image with the photograph you just took. Pixels that coincide in the two represent noise and can safely be suppressed. This noise reduction system, called *dark frame subtraction,* effectively doubles the amount of time required to take a picture, and is used only for exposures longer than one second. Noise reduction can reduce the amount of detail in your picture, as some image information may be removed along with the noise. So, you might want to use this feature with moderation. Some types of images don't require noise reduction, because the grainy pattern tends to blend into the overall scene.

To activate your EOS RP's long exposure noise reduction features, go to the Shooting 5 menu, as explained further in Chapter 11.

You can also apply noise reduction to a lesser extent using Photoshop or Canon Digital Photo Professional and when converting RAW files to some other format, using your favorite RAW converter, or an industrial-strength product like Noise Ninja (www.picturecode.com) to wipe out noise after you've already taken the picture.

Making EV Changes

Sometimes you'll want more or less exposure than indicated by the EOS RP's metering system. Perhaps you want to underexpose to create a silhouette effect, or overexpose to produce a high-key look. It's easy to use the EOS RP's exposure compensation system to override the exposure recommendations, available in any non-automatic mode except Manual. There are three ways to make exposure value (EV) changes with the EOS RP.

- **Display/Quick Control Dial.** When looking at the display, you can add/subtract exposure compensation +/− 3 stops by tapping the shutter release halfway (you don't have to hold it down) and then rotating the Quick Control Dial. Turn clockwise to add exposure, or counterclockwise to reduce exposure. The exposure scale at the bottom of the screen will indicate the amount of exposure compensation you've dialed in.

- **Quick Control screen.** With the shooting information screen displayed (see Figure 4.14), press the Q button and navigate to the exposure scale. Then rotate the QCD. Rotate clockwise to add exposure, or counterclockwise to reduce exposure. (As always, you can use the touch screen to access these controls.) The exposure scale on the screen will indicate the amount of exposure compensation. You can also press SET when the scale is highlighted to view the full exposure compensation/autoexposure bracketing screen, discussed next.

- **Shooting 3.** Press the MENU button and rotate the Main Dial to select the Shooting 3 menu. Then highlight the Expo. Comp/AEB entry at the top. Press SET to access the screen shown in Figure 4.15. Then rotate the QCD or slide a finger across the scale to select the amount of exposure compensation. The screen has helpful labels (Darker on the left and Brighter on the right) to make sure you're adding/subtracting when you really want to.

Note that this method has an advantage: you can specify automatic exposure bracketing from this screen just by rotating the Main Dial. I'll explain bracketing in more detail next.

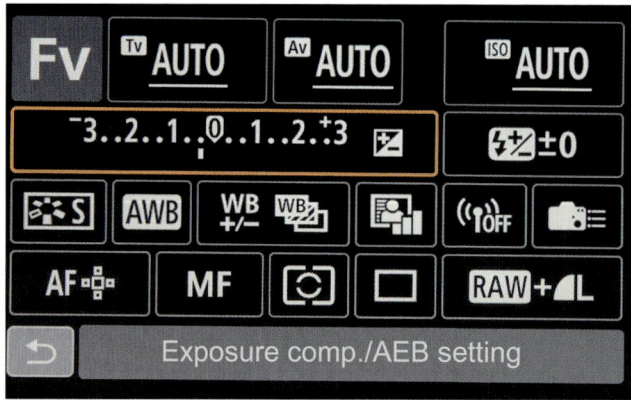

Figure 4.14

Setting exposure compensation using the Quick Control screen.

Figure 4.15
The full exposure compensation/auto exposure bracketing screen.

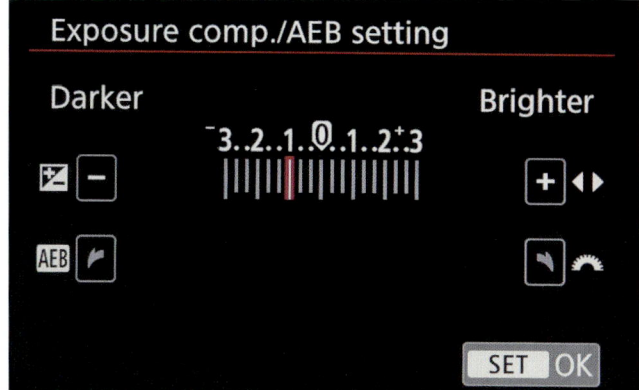

Bracketing Parameters

Bracketing is a method for shooting several consecutive exposures using different settings, as a way of improving the odds that one will be exactly right. Before digital cameras took over the universe, it was common to bracket exposures, shooting, say, a series of three photos at 1/125th second, but varying the f/stop from f/8 to f/11 to f/16. In practice, smaller than whole-stop increments were used for greater precision. Plus, it was just as common to keep the same aperture and vary the shutter speed, although in the days before electronic shutters, film cameras often had only whole-increment shutter speeds available. Figure 4.16 shows a typical bracketed series.

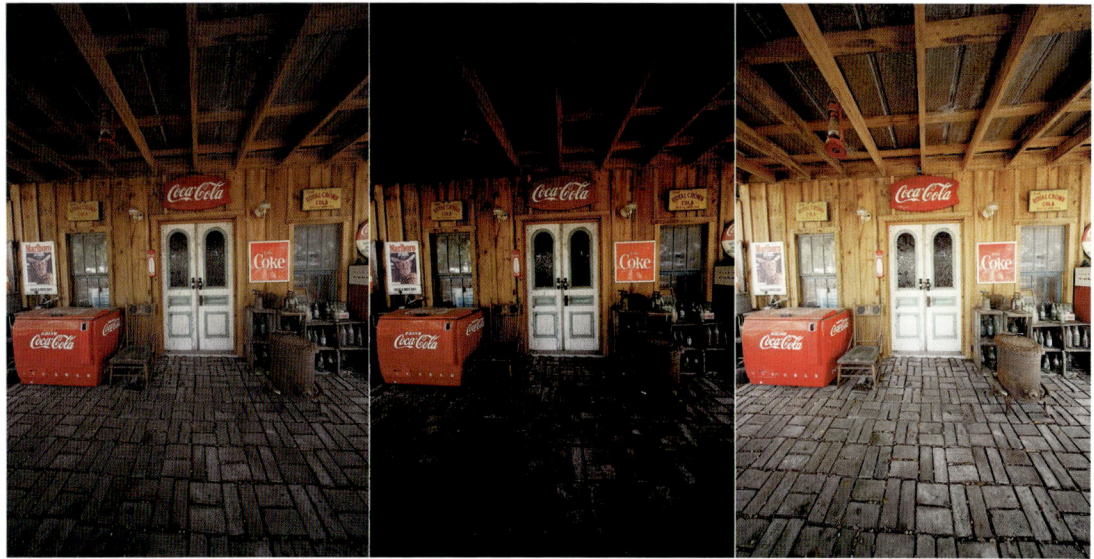

Figure 4.16 In this bracketed series, you can see metered exposure (left), underexposure (center), and overexposure (right).

Today, cameras like the EOS RP can bracket exposures much more precisely, and bracket white balance as well (using the WB Shift/Bkt entry found in the Shooting 4 menu and described in Chapter 11). While WB bracketing is sometimes used when getting color absolutely correct in the camera is important, autoexposure bracketing (AEB) is used much more often. When this feature is activated, the EOS RP takes a series of shots, all at a different exposure value—one at the standard exposure, and the others with more or less exposure. (See Figure 4.16.) In Av mode, the shutter speed will change, whereas in Tv mode, the aperture speed will change. The next sections will explain the parameters you can select.

Bracketing Auto Cancel

The C.Fn I-3 menu entry (Bracketing Auto Cancel) tells the EOS RP when to turn off an active bracketing setup. When you activate bracketing (in the Shooting 3 menu, described shortly), the EOS RP continues to shoot bracketed exposures until you manually turn the bracket feature off, assuming you have this setting disabled. That's a good thing. If you're out shooting a series of bracketed exposures (especially for HDR), it's convenient to have your bracket setting be "sticky" and still be active even if you turn your camera off. Some shooters like to bracket virtually *everything* and leave bracketing on routinely.

However, much of the time you'll want to turn bracketing off, and you may not want to visit the Shooting 3 menu to deactivate it manually. Set Bracketing Auto Cancel to Enable in the Custom Function I-3 entry, and bracketing is cancelled when you turn the EOS RP off, change lenses, use the flash, or change memory cards. When this setting is set to Disable, bracketing remains in effect until you manually turn it off *or use the flash*. The flash still cancels bracketing, but your settings are retained.

Bracketing Sequence

In the C.Fn I-4 (Bracketing Sequence) entry you can specify the order in which the autoexposure bracketing series are exposed. Your choice will depend both on personal preference and what you intend to do with the bracketed shots. The options include:

- **0 – +:** The exposure sequence is standard exposure, decreased exposure, increased exposure. With this default value, your base exposure will be captured and saved first on your memory card, followed by the progressively reduced exposure images, then the shots with increased exposure. You might prefer this order if you expect your standard exposure will be the preferred image and arranged first in the queue of each bracket set, and want the alternate exposures to follow.

- **– 0 +:** The sequence is decreased exposure, standard exposure, increased exposure. This order is the most logical to use if you're shooting with the intention to combine images using HDR (high dynamic range) techniques in your image editor or HDR utility. The final bracketed array is stored on your memory card starting with the most underexposed shot, and progressing to the best exposed, and then on to the overexposures. That makes it easy to use all of your bracketed shots in the HDR sequence, or to select only some of them to combine.

■ **+ 0 –:** This sequence is the inverse of the last one, progressing from increased exposure to standard exposure and decreased exposure. You might prefer this order if you expect to see your best exposures on the plus side of the exposure sequence, and want them to be displayed first.

Number of Exposures

In the Custom Function menu, C.Fn I-5 (Number of Bracketed Shots) entry, you can elect to bracket 2, 3, 5, or 7 shots:

■ **2 shots.** The EOS RP will capture one image at the *base* or standard exposure (which can be the metered exposure, or one that's more or less than the metered exposure, as I'll explain shortly). It then takes one additional shot that provides either *more* or *less* exposure relative to that "base" image. Rotate the QCD to the right to specify more exposure for the second shot, or to the left to specify less exposure. The *amount* of additional/less exposure is determined by the increment you select. (Read on! I'll tie all the parameters together in an upcoming section.)

■ **3, 5, 7 shots.** The camera captures one image at the base exposure, and then two, four, or six shots bracketed around that exposure, respectively. That translates to one over/one under at the 3-shot setting, two over/two under at the 5-shot setting, and three over/three under when using the 7-shot option.

Increment Between Exposures

You can choose the size of the jump between each of the bracketed exposures. To do that, you'll need to visit the Expo. Comp./AEB entry in the Shooting 3 menu. There, you can select from +/–1/3 to 3 full stops in 1/3-stop increments, by rotating the Main Dial. The next section provides instructions for producing a bracketed set.

Creating a Bracketed Set

Using autoexposure bracketing is trickier than it needs to be, but has been made more flexible than with some earlier Canon models. With the EOS RP you are not limited to only three exposures (up to seven shots can be taken), and you can choose to bracket only overexposures or underexposures—a very useful improvement! Just follow these steps:

1. **Specify number of exposures and sequence.** Choose the number of bracketed exposures you want and the sequence in which they will be shot in the C.Fn I-5 entry, as described earlier.

2. **Activate the Expo. Comp./AEB screen.** Press the MENU button and navigate to the Shooting 3 menu, where you'll find the Expo. Comp./AEB option. Press SET to select this entry.

3. **Set the bracket range/increment.** Rotate the Main Dial to spread out or contract the three bars to include the desired range and exposure increment you want to use. The wider the spread, the larger the increment and the larger the range of bracketed shots you'll end up with. The Main Dial will allow you to set the bracket range to up to three stops on either side of the standard (middle) exposure.

For example, in Figure 4.17, the left and right red highlighted bars are separated from the center bar by two marks, each representing 1/3rd stop, so the bracketing will produce one image at 2/3rds stop *less* than the zero point (the large center bar), one at the zero point, and at 1/3rd and 2/3rds stop more than that.

4. **Adjust zero point/standard exposure.** By default, the bracketing is zeroed around the center of the scale, which represents the correct exposure as metered by the EOS RP. But you might want to have your three bracketed shots *all* biased toward overexposure or underexposure. Perhaps you feel that the metered exposure will be too dark or too light, and you want the bracketed shots to lean in the other direction. Use the Quick Control Dial to move the bracket spread toward one end of the scale or the other. Figure 4.18 (top) shows the bracketing biased toward overexposure, while in 4.18 (bottom), the zero point is clustered around underexposure.

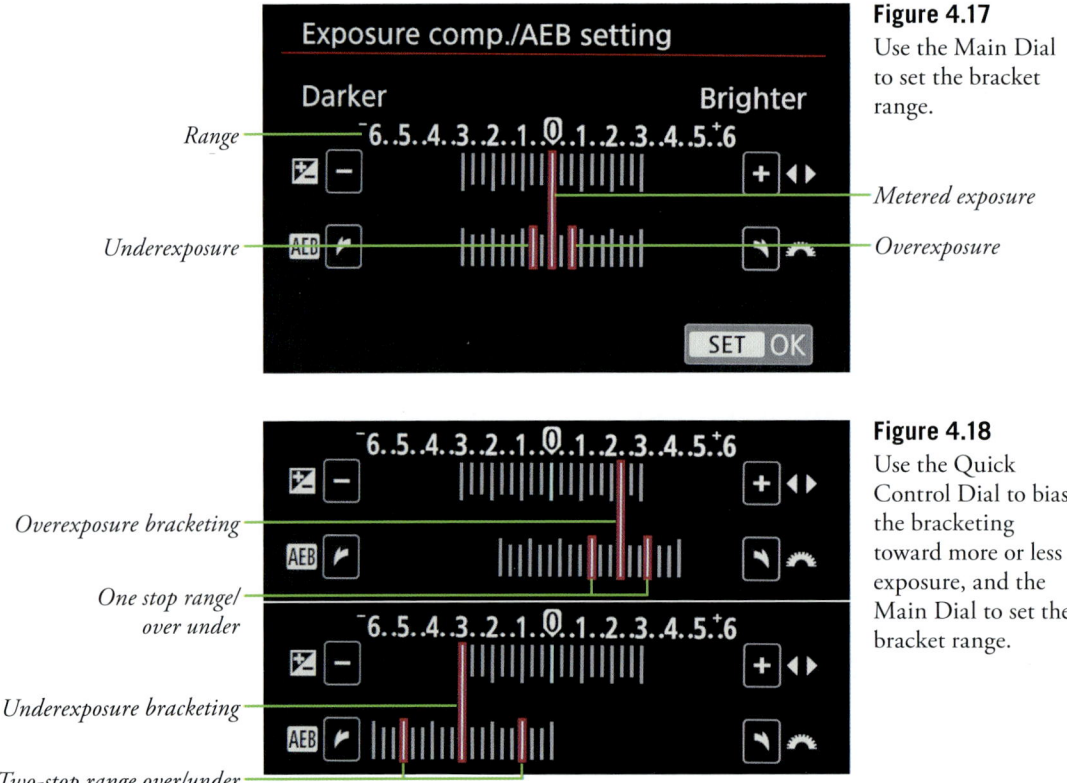

Figure 4.17
Use the Main Dial to set the bracket range.

Figure 4.18
Use the Quick Control Dial to bias the bracketing toward more or less exposure, and the Main Dial to set the bracket range.

NON-BRACKETING IS EXPOSURE COMPENSATION

When the three bracket indicators aren't separated, using the QCD, in effect, adds or subtracts exposure compensation. You'll be shooting a "bracketed" set of one picture, with the zero point placed at the portion of the scale you indicated. Until you rotate the Main Dial to separate the three bracket indicators by at least one indicator, this screen just supplies EV adjustment. Also, keep in mind that the increments shown will be either 1/3 stop or 1/2 stop, depending on how you've set Exposure Level Increments in the Custom Function 1 menu.

5. **Confirm your choice.** Press the SET button to enter the settings.

6. **Take your photo sequence.** Press the shutter release to start capturing the bracketed sequence. The drive mode you select will determine when they are taken:

   - **Single shooting/Silent single shooting.** Press the shutter release one time for each exposure in the sequence.

   - **High-speed continuous/Low-speed continuous/Silent continuous.** You can hold down the shutter release and all the shots in the sequence will be exposed. The EOS RP stops shooting when the series is complete.

   - **10 sec./2 sec. self-timer modes.** After the appropriate delay, all the shots in the sequence will be taken.

7. **Monitor your shots.** As the images are captured, three indicators will appear on the exposure scale in the viewfinder, with one of them flashing for each bracketed photo, showing when the base exposure, underexposure, and overexposure are taken.

8. **Turn bracketing off when done.** Bracketing remains in effect when the set is taken so you can continue shooting bracketed exposures until you use the electronic flash, turn off the camera, or return to the menu to cancel bracketing. That's true even if you have set Bracketing Auto Cancel to Enable in the Custom Function 1 menu. If bracketing were actually auto canceled, you'd have to respecify bracketing for each sequence you took; instead, the EOS RP remembers your bracketing settings until you cancel manually, or until you power down or begin to use electronic flash.

NOTE

AEB is disabled when you're using flash, Multi Shot Noise Reduction, taking long time exposures with the Bulb setting, or if you have enabled the Auto Lighting Optimizer in the Shooting 3 menu (in which case the optimizer will probably override and nullify bracketing).

Working with HDR

High dynamic range (HDR) photography is quite the rage these days, and entire books have been written on the subject. It's not really a new technique—film photographers have been combining multiple exposures for ages to produce a single image of, say, an interior room while maintaining detail in the scene visible through the windows.

Suppose you wanted to photograph a dimly lit room that had a bright window showing an outdoors scene. Proper exposure for the room might be on the order of 1/60th second at f/2.8 at ISO 200, while the outdoors scene probably would require f/11 at 1/400th second. That's almost a 7 EV step difference (approximately 7 f/stops) and effectively beyond the dynamic range of any digital camera, including the EOS RP.

Until camera sensors gain much higher dynamic ranges (which may not be as far into the distant future as we think), special tricks like Active D-Lighting and HDR photography will remain basic tools. With the EOS RP, you can create in-camera HDR exposures, or shoot HDR the old-fashioned way—with separate bracketed exposures that are later combined in a tool like Photomatix or Adobe's Merge to HDR Pro image-editing feature. I'm going to show you how to use both.

The EOS RP's in-camera HDR feature is simple, flexible, and surprisingly effective in creating high dynamic range images. It's also remarkably easy to use. Although it combines only three images to create a single HDR photograph, and while it's not always as good as the manual HDR method I'll describe in the section after this one, it's a *lot* faster.

Figure 4.19 shows you a typical situation in which you might want to use this setting. When the exposure is set for the interior of this covered bridge, the foliage surrounding it is overexposed

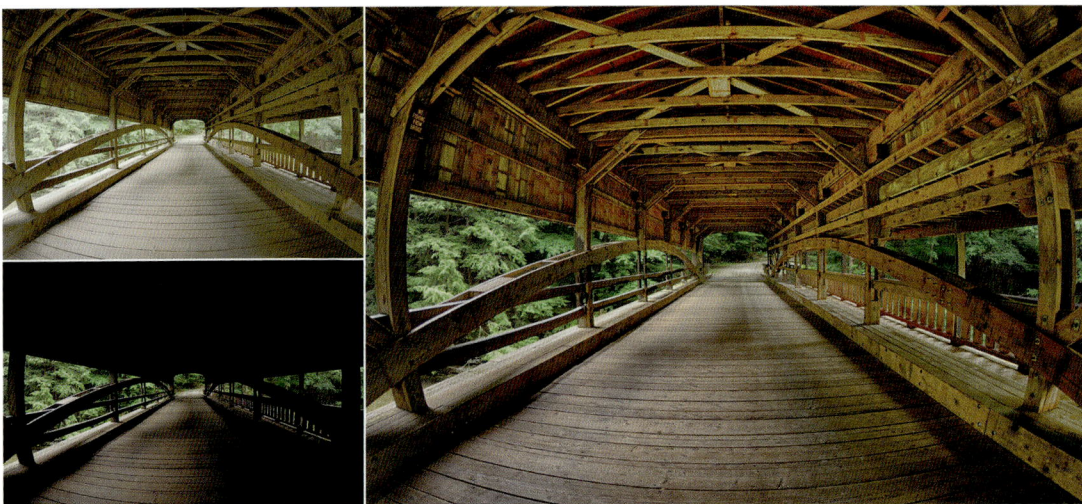

Figure 4.19 HDR combined the two images at left to produce the final version at right.

(upper left). When the exposure is adjusted to produce detail in the foliage, the interior of the bridge goes dark (lower left). HDR allows combining the detail from multiple images—not just the two shown at left, but as many as you want, if you combine them manually (as I'll show you later) to get the image shown at right.

However, a quickie solution is to use the EOS RP's HDR mode, described next. It captures three consecutive images and then merges them as a JPEG image that preserves both highlight and shadow detail.

Using HDR Mode

Here are some tips for using this feature:

- **Use a tripod if possible.** Because there may be some camera movement between the continuous shots, you'll get better results if you mount the EOS RP on a tripod.

- **Moving objects may produce ghosts.** In this case, there may be some *subject* motion between shots, producing "ghost" effects.

- **Misalignment.** If you *don't* use a tripod, when Auto Image Align is activated, this mode does a good job of realigning your multiple images when they are merged. However, it can't do a perfect job, particularly with repetitive patterns that are difficult for the camera's "brains" to sort out. Some misalignment is possible.

- **Shutter speeds vary.** The camera brackets by adjusting the shutter speed within the increment range selected, *even if you're using Tv or M modes and have specified a shutter speed.* Changing the f/stop while shooting an HDR photo alters the focus and possibly image size, and so is not compatible with HDR.

- **Unwanted cropping.** Because the processor needs to be able to shift each individual image slightly in any (or all) of four directions in Auto Align mode (described next), it needs to crop the image slightly to trim out any non-image areas that result. Your final image will be slightly smaller than one shot in other modes.

- **Weird colors.** Some types of lighting, including fluorescent and LED illumination, "cycle" many times a second, and colors can vary between shots. You may not even notice this when single shooting, but it becomes more obvious when using any continuous shooting mode, including HDR mode. The combined images may have strange color effects.

- **Can't use any RAW mode or ISOs higher than 40000.** Your image will be recorded as a Large JPEG only, and HDR is disabled when you're using ISO expansion to enable sensitivity settings higher than 32000. While you can use HDR mode if Auto Lighting Optimizer has been enabled, the camera will disable it while shooting your HDR images, then re-enable it when you turn HDR mode off.

- **The process takes time.** Forget about firing off a large number of HDR shots in a row. After the EOS RP captures its three images, it takes a few seconds to process them and save your final image. Be patient.

You can locate HDR Mode in the Shooting 5 menu. Press the SET button, and you'll be taken to the menu shown in Figure 4.20.

This menu has four separate entries:

- **Adjust Dynamic Range.** There are five choices in this entry. Select Disable HDR to turn HDR completely off. The others select the number of stops of dynamic range improvement the HDR feature will provide. Choose Auto to allow the EOS RP to examine your scene and select an appropriate EV range. As you gain experience you might want to select the range yourself, in order to achieve a particular look. You can choose +/– 1, 2, or 3 EV.

- **Effect.** If you've worked with HDR utilities (such as Photomatix) in the past, you know that various parameters can be adjusted while combining HDR images to produce various effects. These include the amount of color saturation (the "richness" of the hues); the boldness of the edge transitions between portions of the image (producing mild to distinct outlines); brightness of the resulting image; and contrast/tone. Various combinations of these settings produce what can only be called special effects. Select from what Canon terms Natural, Art Standard, Art Vivid, Art Bold, or Art Embossed. Note that these effects are *added* to the settings of any Picture Style currently in use.

- **Continuous HDR.** Choose 1 Shot Only if you plan to take just a single HDR exposure and want the feature disabled automatically thereafter, or Every Shot to continue using HDR mode for all subsequent exposures until you turn it off.

- **Auto Image Align.** HDR images are ideally produced with the camera on a tripod, in order to reduce the ghosting effects from a series of pictures that each aren't perfectly aligned with the other. You can choose Enable to have the camera attempt to align all three HDR exposures, or select Disable when using a tripod. The success of the automatic alignment will vary, depending on the shutter speed used (higher is better), and the amount of camera movement (less is better!).

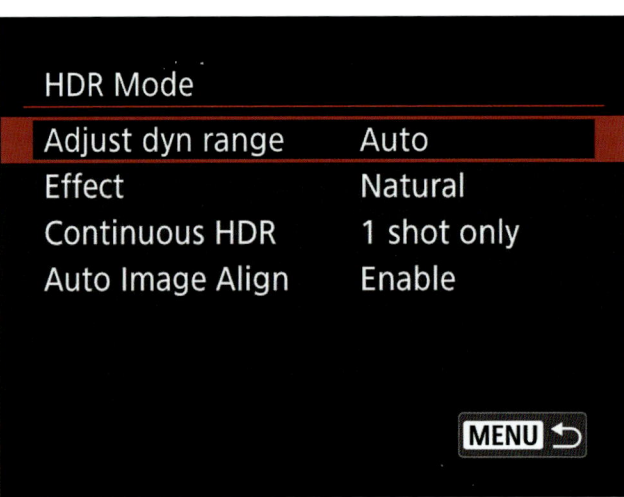

Figure 4.20
The HDR mode menu has four entries.

SPECIAL HDR EFFECTS

The Effect parameters generate five different special effects (see Figure 4.21):

- **Natural.** Provides the most useful range of highlight and shadow details.
- **Art Standard.** Offers a great deal of highlight and shadow detail, but with lower overall contrast and outlines accentuated, making the image look more like a painting. Saturation, bold outline, and brightness are adjusted to the default levels, and tonal range is lower in contrast.
- **Art Vivid.** Similar to Art Standard, but the saturation is boosted to produce richer colors, and the bold outlines are not as strong, producing a poster-like effect.
- **Art Bold.** Even higher saturation than Art Vivid, with emphasized edge transitions, producing what Canon calls an "oil painting" effect.
- **Art Embossed.** Reduces saturation, darker tones, and lower contrast, and gives the image a faded, aged look. The edge transitions are brighter or darker to emphasize them.

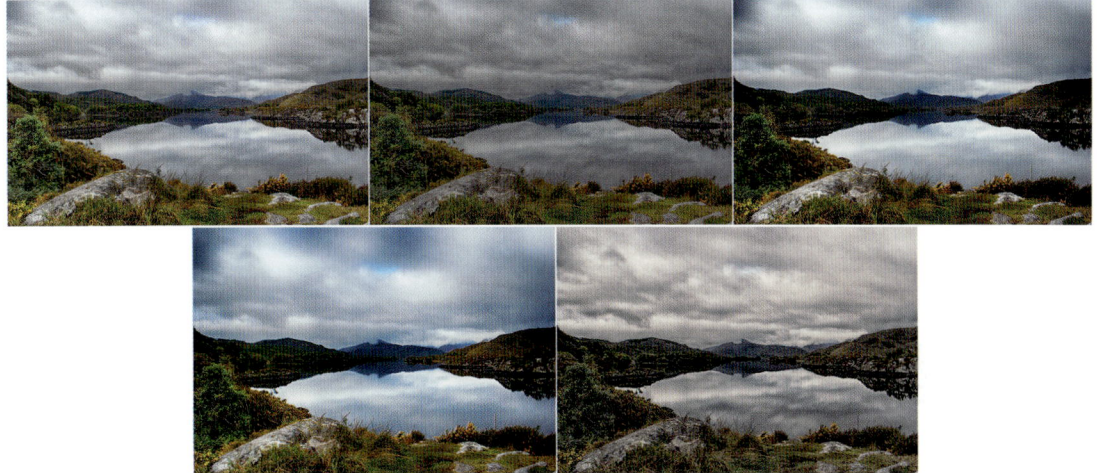

Figure 4.21 Top row (left to right): Natural, Art Standard, Art Vivid; bottom row: Art Bold, Art Embossed.

Bracketing and Merge to HDR

HDR (high dynamic range) photography was, for a while, an incredibly popular fad. There are even entire books that do nothing but tell you how to shoot HDR images. Everywhere you looked there were overprocessed, garish HDR images that had little relationship to reality. I've been able to resist the temptation to overdo my landscape and travel photography (unlike the deliberately awful example I created for Figure 4.22). The phony-looking skies, the unnatural halos that appear at the edges of some objects, and the weird textures are usually a giveaway. My rule of thumb is that, if you can tell it's HDR, it's been done wrong—unless your intent was to show off what HDR can do.

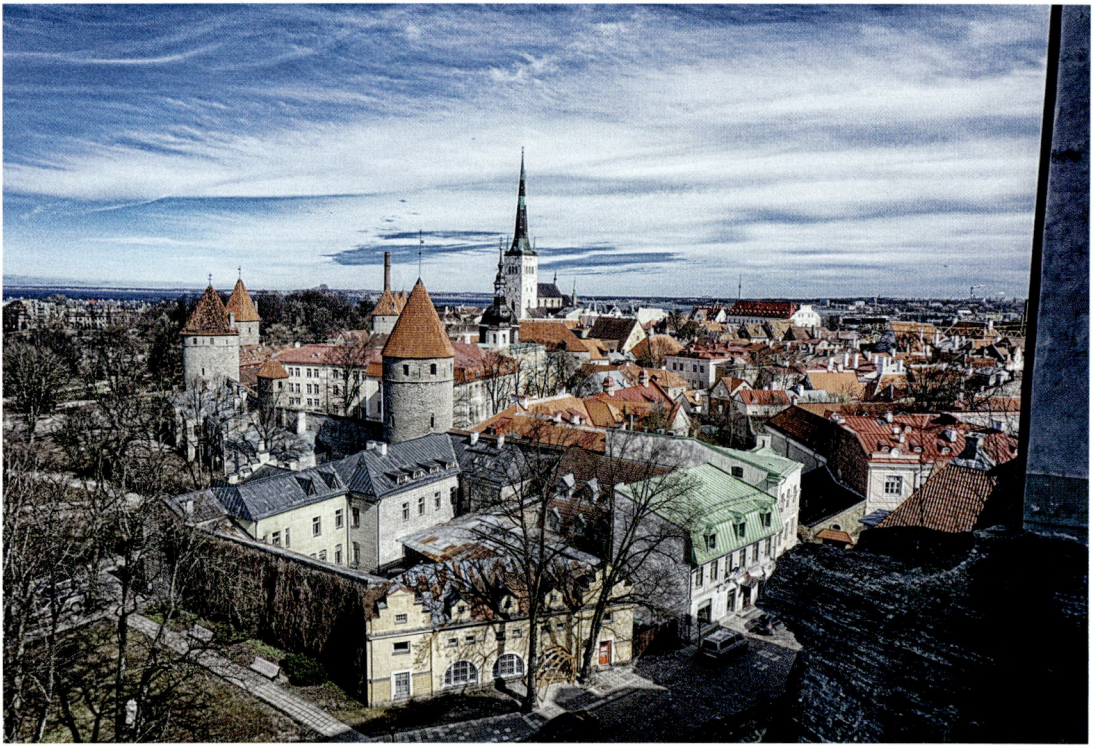

Figure 4.22 A deliberately overcooked HDR photo.

The technique does have its uses, especially if done subtly, or as a special effect. That's what I was looking for when I shot Alastair Greene, guitarist for the Alan Parsons Project for Figure 4.23. I wanted an edgy, posterlike quality, and so applied HDR liberally, but with the hope that the effect might not be evident on first glance.

Although the EOS RP does have its built-in HDR feature, you can usually get much better, more tasteful results if you create your high dynamic range images manually. You can use a tool such as Photoshop's Merge to HDR Pro feature, a stand-alone HDR utility, or a third-party Photoshop plug-in.

When you're using Merge to HDR Pro in Adobe Photoshop (similar functions are available in other programs, including the Mac/PC utility Photomatix [www.hdrsoft.com; free to try, $39 to $99 to buy, depending on the version you select]) and Aurora HDR (www.skylum.com, $99), you'd take and combine several pictures. As I mentioned earlier, one would be exposed for the shadows, one for the highlights, and perhaps one for the midtones. Then, you'd use the Merge to HDR command (or the equivalent in other software) to combine all of the images into one HDR image that integrates the well-exposed sections of each version. You can use the camera's bracketing feature to produce those images.

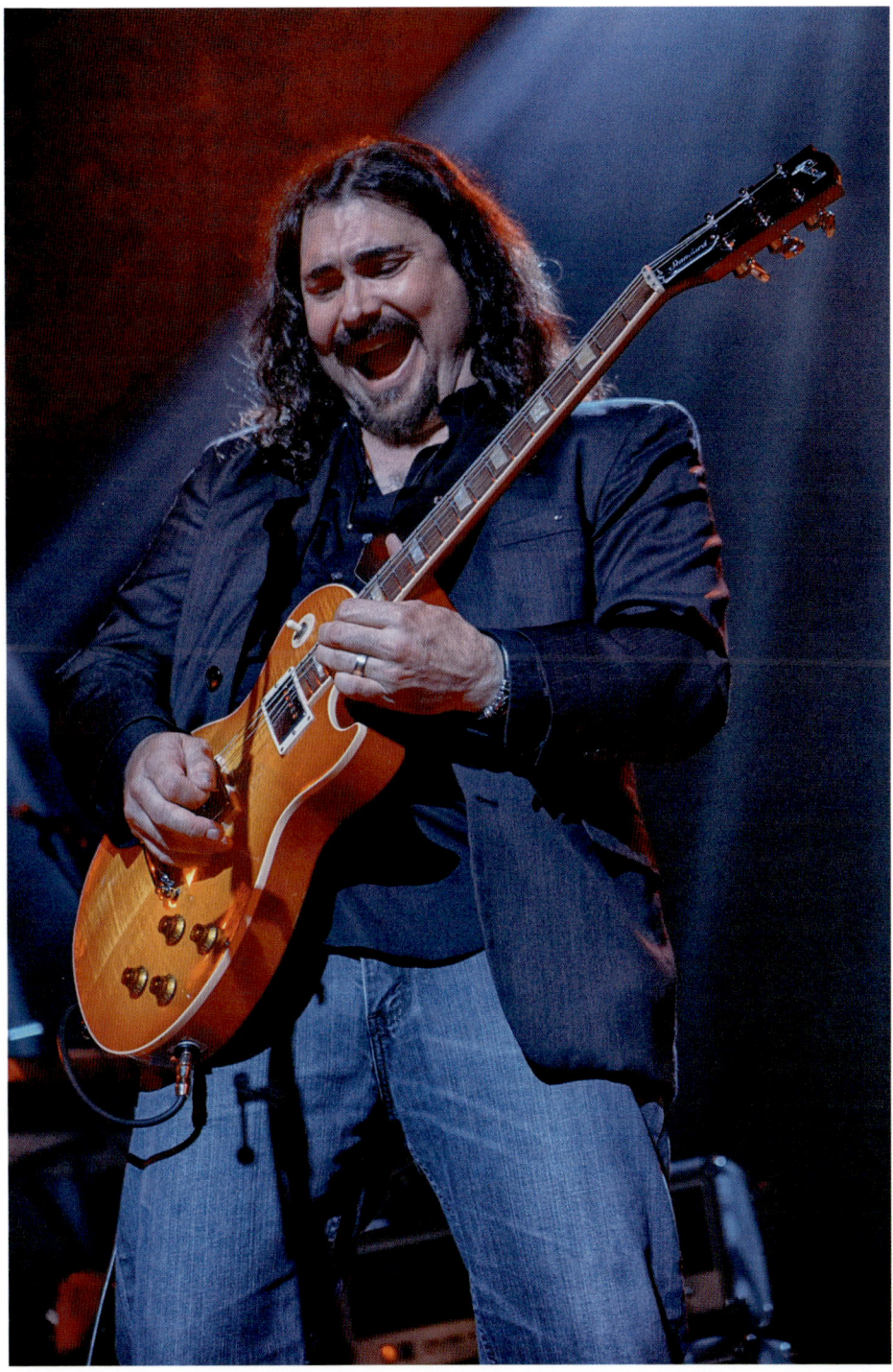

Figure 4.23 In this case, HDR added a desired poster-like effect.

The next steps show you how to combine the separate exposures into one merged high dynamic range image. The sample images in Figure 4.24 show the results you can get from a three-shot (manually) bracketed sequence. The images should be as identical as possible, except for exposure. So, as with HDR mode, it's a good idea to mount the EOS RP on a tripod, use a remote release, and take all the exposures at once. Just follow these steps:

1. **Set up the camera.** Mount the EOS RP on a tripod.

2. **Choose an f/stop and Av mode.** Select an aperture that will provide a correct exposure at your initial settings for the series of bracketed shots. *And then leave this adjustment alone!* You don't want the aperture to change for your series, as that would change the depth-of-field, and, subtly, the size of some elements of the image as they move more or less out of focus. You want the EOS RP to adjust exposure *only* using the shutter speed.

3. **Choose manual focus.** You don't want the focus to change between shots, so set the EOS RP to manual focus, and carefully focus your shot.

4. **Choose RAW exposures.** Set the camera to take RAW files, which will give you the widest range of tones in your images.

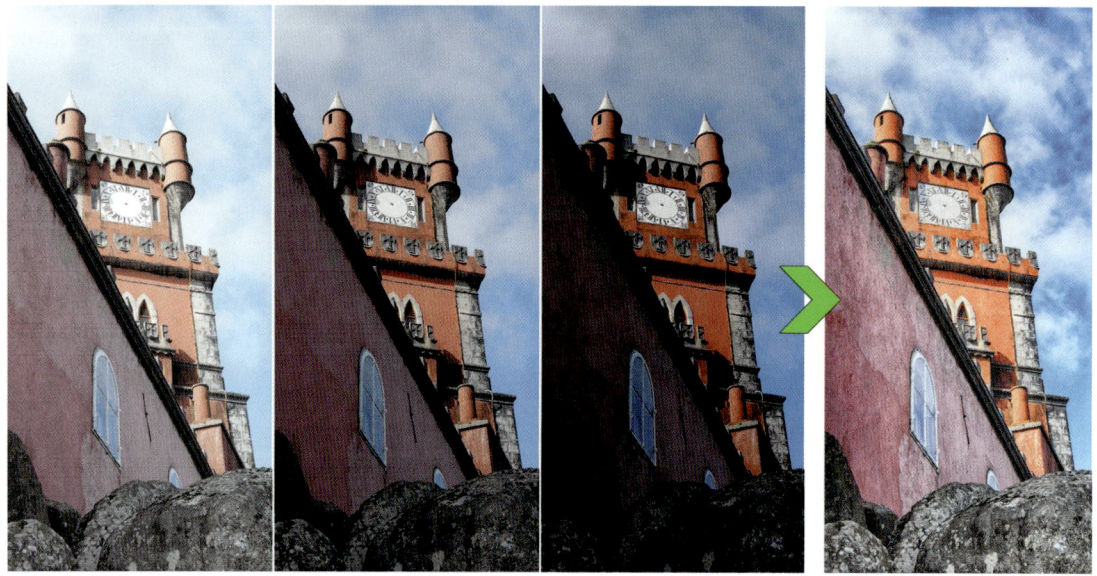

Figure 4.24 Three bracketed photos should look like this (left). The finished image is shown at right.

5. **Set up your bracketed set.** Use the instructions earlier in this chapter to set the number of bracketed images you take, and the increment between them. After you've created your first few manual HDR photos, you'll learn to judge what increment is best (larger isn't always better). However, the more shots you have to work with, the better your results can be.

6. **Take your photos.** With the camera in continuous shooting mode, press the button on the remote (or carefully press the shutter release or use the self-timer) and take the set of bracketed exposures.

7. **Continue with the Merge to HDR Pro steps listed next.** You can also use a different program, such as Photomatix, if you know how to use it.

The next steps show you how to combine the separate exposures into one merged high dynamic range image.

1. **Copy your images to your computer.** If you use an application to transfer the files to your computer, make sure it does not make any adjustments to brightness, contrast, or exposure. You want the real raw information for Merge to HDR Pro to work with.

2. **Activate Merge to HDR Pro.** Choose File > Automate > Merge to HDR Pro.

3. **Select the photos to be merged.** Use the Browse feature to locate and select your photos to be merged. You'll note a checkbox that can be used to automatically align the images if they were not taken with the camera mounted on a rock-steady support. This will adjust for any slight movement of the camera that might have occurred when you changed exposure settings.

4. **Choose parameters (optional).** The first time you use Merge to HDR Pro, you can let the program work with its default parameters. Once you've played with the feature a few times, you can read the Adobe help files and learn more about the options than I can present in this non-software-oriented camera guide.

5. **Click OK.** The merger begins.

6. **Save.** Once HDR merge has done its thing, save the file to your computer.

What if you don't have the opportunity, inclination, or skills to create several images at different exposures, as described? If you shoot in RAW format, you can still use Merge to HDR, working with a *single* original image file. What you do is import the image into Photoshop several times, using Adobe Camera Raw to create multiple copies of the file at different exposure levels.

For example, you'd create one copy that's too dark, so the shadows lose detail, but the highlights are preserved. Create another copy with the shadows intact and allow the highlights to wash out. Then, you can use Merge to HDR to combine the two and end up with a finished image that has the extended dynamic range you're looking for. (This concludes the image-editing portion of the chapter. We now return you to our alternate sponsor: photography.)

Fixing Exposures with Histograms

While you can often recover poorly exposed photos in your image editor, your best bet is to arrive at the correct exposure in the camera, minimizing the tweaks that you have to make in post-processing. However, you can't always judge exposure just by simply looking at the preview image on your EOS RP's display before the shot is made, nor the review image in Playback. Ambient light may make the monitor difficult to see, and the brightness level you've set for the monitor and viewfinder in the Set-up menu can affect the appearance of the image.

Instead, you can use a histogram, which is a chart shown on the EOS RP's display that shows the number of tones that have been captured at each brightness level. Histograms are available in real time on your display as you shoot and in the review image during playback, but they are available only when enabled. I'll show you how to enable histograms and select from among the various options available for histograms in Chapter 13. To view histograms in shooting mode or playback mode, press the INFO button until a screen with the histogram appears.

Histograms come in various flavors. Photographers are generally concerned only with two types: a brightness or *luminance* histogram, which deals only with the relative overall intensity of the tones in the image (see Figure 4.25, top), and a *color* histogram that displays the intensity of each individual color channel in a particular color space. Photographers most often work with an RGB histogram that displays values for red, green, and blue pixels in an image, but other varieties exist, such

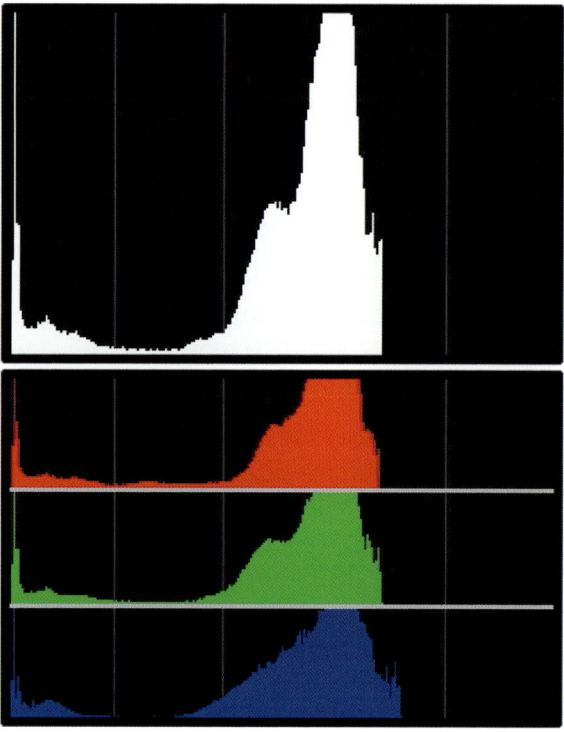

Figure 4.25
Brightness histogram (top), RGB histogram (bottom).

as CMYK (for cyan, magenta, yellow, and black hues) and HSL/HSV (hue, saturation, and lightness/value), which are alternate ways of representing the RGB color space.

To get you up to speed with histograms, the next few sections will deal only with the brightness/luminance histogram variety.

Tonal Range

Histograms help you adjust the tonal range of an image, the span of dark to light tones, from a complete absence of brightness (black) to the brightest possible tone (white), and all the middle tones in between. Because all values for tones fall into a continuous spectrum between black and white, it's easiest to think of a photo's tonality in terms of a black-and-white or grayscale image, even though you're capturing those tones in three separate color layers of red, green, and blue.

Because your images are digital, the tonal "spectrum" isn't really continuous: it's divided into discrete steps that represent the different tones that can be captured. Figure 4.26 may help you understand this concept. The gray steps shown range from 100 percent gray (black) at the left, to 0 percent gray (white) at the right, with 20 gray steps in all (plus white).

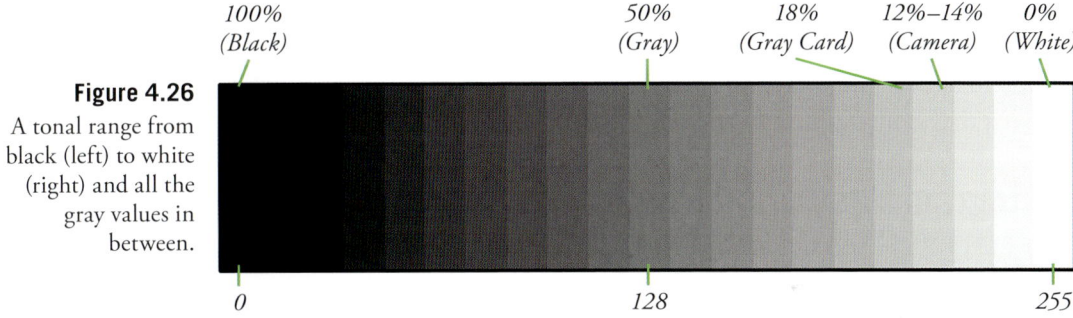

Figure 4.26

A tonal range from black (left) to white (right) and all the gray values in between.

Along the bottom of the chart are the digital values from 0 to 255 recorded by your sensor for an image with 8 bits per channel. (8 bits of red, 8 bits of green, and 8 bits of blue equal a 24-bit, full-color image.) Any black captured would be represented by a value of 0, the brightest white by 255, and the midtones would be clustered around the 128 marker. The actual information captured may be "finer" and record say, 0 to 4,094 for an image captured when the EOS RP is set to 14 bits per channel for a RAW file (see Chapter 11 for more detail on that option).

Grayscale images (which we call black-and-white photos) are easy to understand. Or, at least, that's what we think. When we look at a black-and-white image, we think we're seeing a continuous range of tones from black to white, and all the grays in between. But, that's not exactly true. The blackest black in any photo isn't a true black, because *some* light is always reflected from the surface of the print, and if viewed on a screen, the deepest black is only as dark as the least-reflective area a computer monitor can produce. The whitest white isn't a true white, either, because even the lightest areas of a print absorb some light (only a mirror reflects close to all the light that strikes it), and, when viewing on a computer monitor, the whites are limited by the brightness of the display's LCD or LED picture elements. Lacking darker blacks and brighter, whiter whites, that continuous set of tones doesn't cover the full grayscale tonal range.

The full scale of tones becomes useful when you have an image that has large expanses of shades that change gradually from one level to the next, such as areas of sky, water, or walls. Think of a picture taken of a group of campers around a campfire. Since the light from the fire is striking them directly in the face, there aren't many shadows on the campers' faces. All the tones that make up the *features* of the people around the fire are compressed into one end of the brightness spectrum—the lighter end.

Yet, there's more to this scene than faces. Behind the campers are trees, rocks, and perhaps a few animals that have emerged from the shadows to see what is going on. These are illuminated by the softer light that bounces off the surrounding surfaces. If your eyes become accustomed to the reduced illumination, you'll find that there is a wealth of detail in these shadow images.

This campfire scene would be a nightmare to reproduce faithfully under any circumstances. If you are an experienced photographer, you are probably already wincing at what is called a *high-contrast* lighting situation. Some photos may be high in contrast when there are fewer tones and they are all bunched up at limited points in the scale. In a low-contrast image, there are more tones, but they are spread out so widely that the image looks flat. Your digital camera can show you the relationship between these tones using a *histogram*.

Histogram Basics

Your EOS RP's histograms are a simplified display of the numbers of pixels at each of 256 brightness levels, producing an interesting "mountain range" shape in the graph. Although separate charts may be provided for brightness and the red, green, and blue channels, when you first start using histograms, you'll want to concentrate on the brightness histogram.

Each vertical line in the graph represents the number of pixels in the image for each brightness value, from 0 (black) on the left to 255 (white) on the right. The vertical axis measures that number of pixels at each level.

Although histograms are most often used to fine-tune exposure, you can glean other information from them, such as the relative contrast of the image. Figure 4.27, top, shows a generic histogram of an image having normal contrast. In such an image, most of the pixels are spread across the image, with a healthy distribution of tones throughout the midtone section of the graph. That large peak at the right side of the graph represents all those light tones in the sky. A normal-contrast image you shoot may have less sky area, and less of a peak at the right side, but notice that very few pixels hug the right edge of the histogram, indicating that the lightest tones are not being clipped because they are off the chart.

Figure 4.27

Top: This image has fairly normal contrast, even though there is a peak of light tones at the right side representing the sky. Center: This low-contrast image has all the tones squished into one section of the grayscale. Bottom: A high-contrast image produces a histogram in which the tones are spread out.

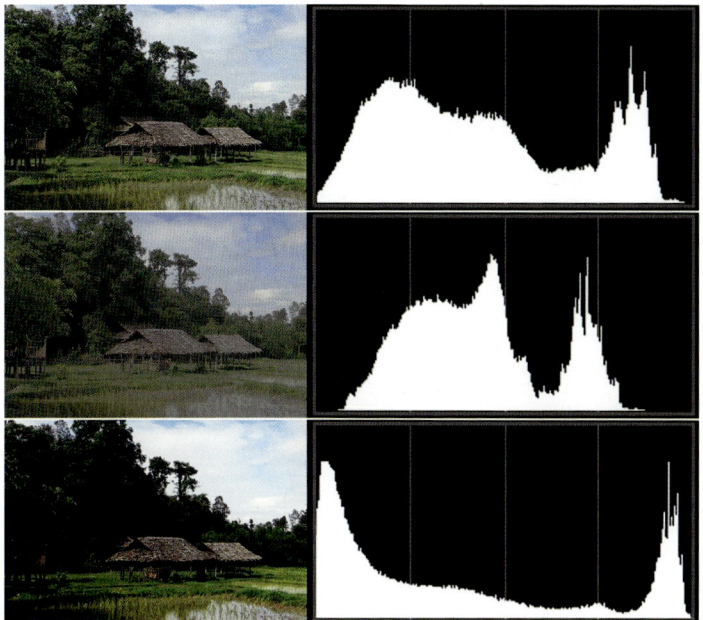

With a lower-contrast image, like the one shown in Figure 4.27, center, the basic shape of the previous histogram will remain recognizable, but gradually will be compressed together to cover a smaller area of the gray spectrum. The squished shape of the histogram is caused by all the grays in the original image being represented by a limited number of gray tones in a smaller range of the scale.

Instead of the darkest tones of the image reaching into the black end of the spectrum and the whitest tones extending to the lightest end, the blackest areas of the scene are now represented by a light gray, and the whites by a somewhat lighter gray. The overall contrast of the image is reduced. Because all the darker tones are actually a middle gray or lighter, the scene in this version of the photo appears lighter as well.

Going in the other direction, increasing the contrast of an image produces a histogram like the one shown in Figure 4.27, bottom. In this case, the tonal range is now spread over the entire width of the chart, but, except for the bright sky, there is not much variation in the middle tones; the mountain "peaks" are not very high. When you stretch the grayscale in both directions like this, the darkest tones become darker (that may not be possible) and the lightest tones become lighter (ditto). In fact, shades that might have been gray before can change to black or white as they are moved toward either end of the scale.

The effect of increasing contrast may be to move some tones off either end of the scale altogether, while spreading the remaining grays over a smaller number of locations on the spectrum. That's exactly the case in the example shown. The number of possible tones is smaller and the image appears harsher.

Understanding Histograms

The important thing to remember when working with the histogram display in your EOS RP is that changing the exposure does *not* change the contrast of an image. The curves illustrated in the previous three examples remain exactly the same shape when you increase or decrease exposure. I repeat: The proportional distribution of grays shown in the histogram doesn't change when exposure changes; it is neither stretched nor compressed. However, the tones as a whole are moved toward one end of the scale or the other, depending on whether you're increasing or decreasing exposure. You'll be able to see that in some illustrations that follow.

So, as you reduce exposure, tones gradually move to the black end (and off the scale), while the reverse is true when you increase exposure. The contrast within the image is changed only to the extent that some of the tones can no longer be represented when they are moved off the scale.

To change the *contrast* of an image, you must do one of four things:

- **Change the EOS RP's contrast setting** using the menu system. You'll find these adjustments in your camera's Picture Styles options in the Shooting 4 menu, as explained in Chapter 11.
- **Use your camera's shadow-tone and highlight "boosters."** Auto Lighting Optimizer and Highlight Tone Priority, also discussed in Chapter 11, can help you adjust contrast.
- **Alter the contrast of the scene itself,** for example, by using a fill light or reflectors to add illumination to shadows that are too dark.
- **Attempt to adjust contrast in post-processing** using your image editor or RAW file converter. You may use features such as Levels or Curves (in Photoshop, Photoshop Elements, and many other image editors) or work with HDR software to cherry-pick the best values in shadows and highlights from multiple images.

Of the four of these, the third—changing the contrast of the scene—is the most desirable, because attempting to fix contrast by fiddling with the tonal values is unlikely to be a perfect remedy. However, adding a little contrast can be successful because you can discard some tones to make the image more contrasty. Yet, the opposite is much more difficult. An overly contrasty image rarely can be fixed, because you can't add information that isn't there in the first place.

What you *can* do is adjust the exposure so that the tones *that are already present in the scene* are captured correctly. Figure 4.28, top, shows the histogram for an image that is badly underexposed. You can guess from the shape of the histogram that many of the dark tones to the left of the graph have been clipped off. There's plenty of room on the right side for additional pixels to reside without having them become overexposed. So, you can increase the exposure (either by changing the f/stop or shutter speed, or by adding an EV value) to produce the corrected histogram shown in Figure 4.28, center.

Figure 4.28
Top: A histogram of an underexposed image may look like this. Center: Adding exposure will produce a histogram like this one. Bottom: A histogram of an overexposed image will show clipping at the right side.

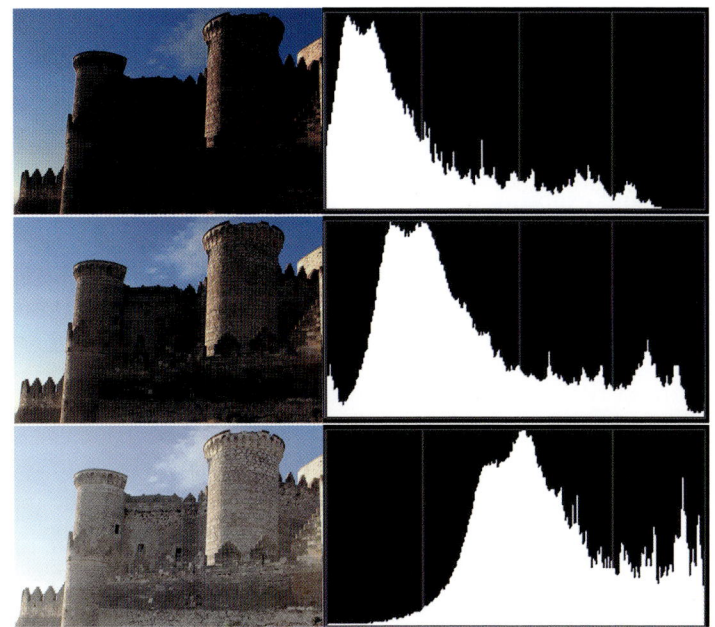

Conversely, if your histogram looks like the one shown in Figure 4.28, bottom, with bright tones pushed off the right edge of the chart, you have an overexposed image, and you can correct it by reducing exposure. In addition to the histogram, the EOS RP has its Highlights option, which, when activated, shows areas that are overexposed with flashing tones (often called "blinkies") in the review screen. Depending on the importance of this "clipped" detail, you can adjust exposure or leave it alone. For example, if all the dark-coded areas in the review are in a background that you care little about, you can forget about them and not change the exposure, but if such areas appear in facial details of your subject, you may want to make some adjustments.

In working with histograms, your goal should be to have all the tones in an image spread out between the edges, with none clipped off at the left and right sides. Underexposing (to preserve highlights) should be done only as a last resort, because retrieving the underexposed shadows in your image editor will frequently increase the noise, even if you're working with RAW files. A better course of action is to expose for the highlights, but, when the subject matter makes it practical, fill in the shadows with additional light, using reflectors, fill flash, or other techniques rather than allowing them to be seriously underexposed.

A traditional technique for optimizing exposure is called "expose to the right" (ETTR), which involves adding exposure to push the histogram's curve toward the right side *but not far enough to clip off highlights.* The rationale for this method is that extra shadow detail will be produced with a minimum increase in noise, especially in the shadow areas. It's said that half of a digital sensor's response lies in the brightest areas of an image, and so require the least amount of amplification (which is one way to increase digital noise). ETTR can work, as long as you're able to capture a satisfactory amount of information in the shadows.

Exposing to the Right

It's easier to understand exposing to the right if you mentally divide the histogram into fifths (unfortunately, the EOS RP's histogram uses quarters instead). And, for the sake of simplicity and smaller numbers, assume you're shooting in 14-bit RAW. Any 14-bit image can record a maximum of 16,383 different tones per channel. However, each fifth of the histogram does *not* encompass 3,277 tones (one-fifth of 16,383).

Instead, the right-most fifth, the highlights, shown in Figure 4.29, accounts for 8,192 different captured tones. Moving toward the left, the next fifth represents 4,096 levels, followed by 2,048 levels, 1,024 levels, and, in the left-most section where the deepest shadows reside, only 512 different tones are captured. When processing your RAW file, there are only 512 tones to recover in the shadows, which is why boosting/amplifying them increases noise. (The effect is most noticeable in the red and blue channels; your sensor's Bayer array has twice as many green-sensitive pixels as red or blue.)

Instead, you want to add exposure—as long as you don't push highlights off the right edge of the histogram—to brighten the shadows. Because there are 8,192 tones available in the highlights, even if the RAW image *looks* overexposed, it's possible to use your RAW converter's Exposure slider (such as the one found in Adobe Camera Raw) to bring back detail captured in that surplus of tones in the highlights. This procedure is the exact opposite of what was recommended for film of the transparency variety—it was fairly easy to retrieve detail from shadows by pumping more light through them when processing the image, while even small amounts of extra exposure blew out highlights. (**Note:** I've rounded the numbers a bit for simplicity.) You'll often find that the range of

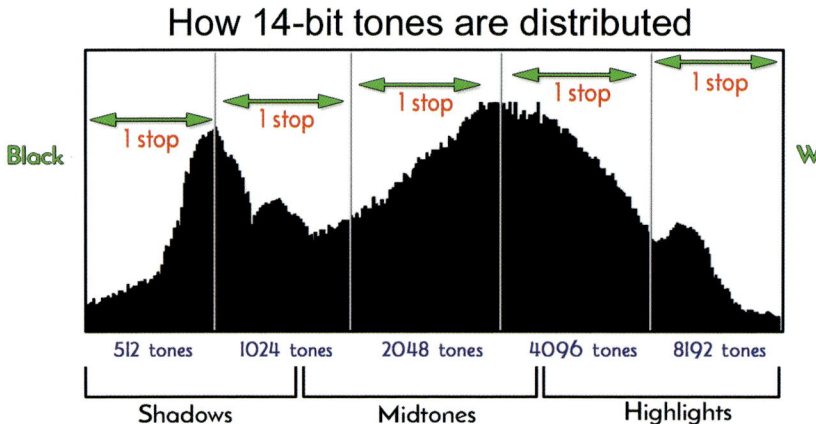

Figure 4.29
Tones are not evenly allocated throughout a histogram.

tones in your image is so great that there is no way to keep your histogram from spilling over into the left and right edges, costing you both highlight and shadow detail. Exposing to the right may not work in such situations. A second school of thought recommends *reducing* exposure to bring back the highlights, or "exposing to the left." You would then attempt to recover shadow detail in an image editor, using tools like Adobe Camera Raw's Exposure slider. But remember, above all, that this procedure will also boost noise in the shadows, and so the technique should be used with caution. In most cases, exposing to the right is your best bet.

Dealing with Channels

The more you work with histograms, the more useful they become. One of the first things that histogram veterans notice is that it's possible to overexpose one channel even if the overall exposure appears to be correct. For example, flower photographers soon discover that it's really, really difficult to get a good picture of a red rose, like the one shown at left in Figure 4.30. The exposure looks okay—but there's no detail in the rose's petals. Looking at the histogram (see Figure 4.30, right) shows why: the red channel is blown out. If you look at the red histogram, there's a peak at the right edge that indicates that highlight information has been lost. In fact, the green channel has been blown, too, and so the green parts of the flower also lack detail. Only the blue channel's histogram is entirely contained within the boundaries of the chart, and, on first glance, the white luminance histogram at top of the column of graphs seems fairly normal.

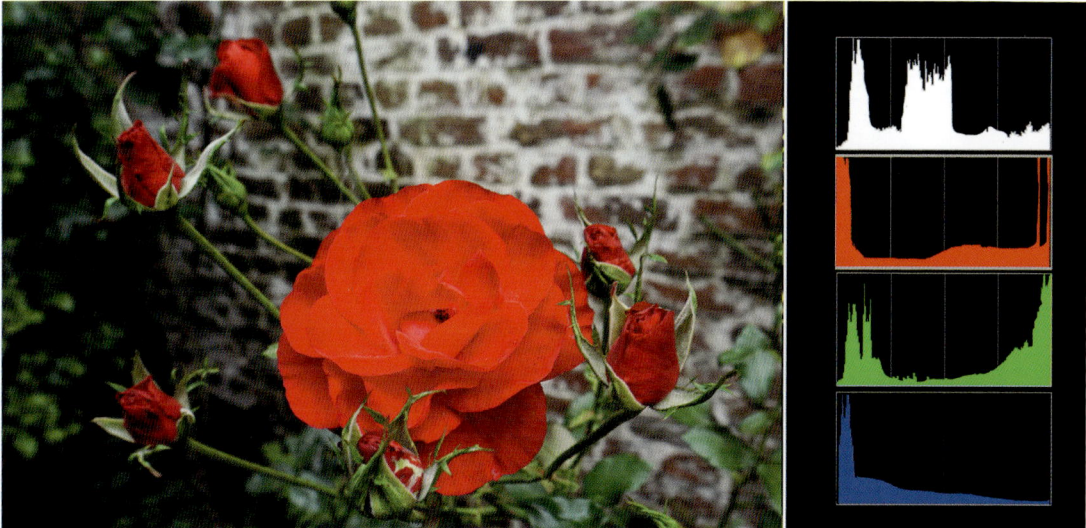

Figure 4.30 It's common to lose detail in bright red flowers because the red channel becomes overexposed even when the other channels are properly exposed (left). The RGB histograms show that both the red and green channels are overexposed, with tones extending past the right edge of the chart (right).

Any of the primary channels—red, green, or blue—can blow out all by themselves, although bright reds seem to be the most common problem area. More difficult to diagnose are overexposed tones in one of the "in-between" hues on the color wheel. Overexposed yellows (which are very common) will be shown by blowouts in *both* the red and green channels. Too-bright cyans will manifest as excessive blue and green highlights, while overexposure in the red and blue channels reduces detail in magenta colors. As you gain experience, you'll be able to see exactly how anomalies in the RGB channels translate into poor highlights and murky shadows.

The only way to correct for color channel blowouts is to reduce exposure. As I mentioned earlier, you might want to consider filling in the shadows with additional light to keep them from becoming too dark when you decrease exposure. In practice, you'll want to monitor the red channel most closely, followed by the blue channel, and slightly decrease exposure to see if that helps. Because of the way our eyes perceive color, we are more sensitive to variations in green, so green channel blowouts are less of a problem, unless your main subject is heavily colored in that hue. If you plan on photographing a frog hopping around on your front lawn, you'll want to be extra careful to preserve detail in the green channel, using bracketing or other exposure techniques outlined in this chapter.

5

Mastering the Mysteries of Focus

How far we've come! My first professional job was as a reporter/sportswriter/photographer for a daily newspaper (back when a backslash really *meant* something), and focusing to achieve a sharp image was a manual process accomplished by turning a ring or knob on the camera or lens until, in one's highly trained professional judgment, the image was satisfactorily in focus. Manual focus was particularly challenging when shooting sports.

Today, modern digital cameras like the EOS RP can identify potential subject matter, lock in on human faces, if present, and automatically focus faster than the blink of an eye. Usually. Of course, sometimes a camera's AF will zero in on the *wrong* subject, become confused by background patterns, or be totally unable to follow a fast-moving target like a bird in flight. While autofocus *has* come a long way in the last 30-plus years, it's still a work-in-progress that relies heavily on input from the photographer. Your Canon EOS RP can calculate and set focus for you quickly and with a high degree of accuracy, but you still need to make a few settings that provide guidance on three of the Ws of autofocus: *what, where,* and *when.* Your decisions in how you apply those choices supplies the fourth W: *why.* This chapter will provide you with everything you need to put all four to work.

Auto or Manual Focus?

Advances in autofocus technology have given photographers the confidence to rely on AF most of the time. For the average subject, a camera like the EOS RP will do an excellent job of evaluating your scene and quickly focusing on an appropriate subject. Interestingly enough, however, the switch to mirrorless technology has actually revived interest in old-school manual focus.

There are five reasons why manual focus is being used more by creative photographers.

- **WYSIWYG.** *What you see* (in the viewfinder or LCD monitor) *is what you get*, in terms of sharp focus. When focusing manually with the EOS RP, you're evaluating the exact same sensor image that will be captured when you press the shutter release. Traditional single-lens reflex (SLR) cameras use a mirror to direct the image to a separate focusing screen (when not in live view mode), which can be coarser, not as bright, and possibly out of alignment.

- **WYSIWYW.** Focusing manually can mean that *what you see is what you want,* that is, *you* can select the precise plane of focus you desire for, say, a macro photo or portrait, rather than settle for what the camera *thinks* you want. Your camera doesn't have any way of determining, for certain, what subject you *want* to be in sharp focus. It can't read your mind (at least, not yet). Left to its own devices, the EOS RP may select a likely object—often the one nearest the camera—and lock in focus with lightning speed, even though the subject is not the one that's the center of interest of your photograph.

- **Less confusion.** Canon has given us faster and more precise autofocus systems, with many more options, and it's common for the sheer number of these choices to confuse even the most advanced photographers. If you'd rather not wade through the AF alternatives for a given shot, switch to manual focus and shoot. You won't have to worry about whether the camera locks focus too soon, or too late.

- **Focus aids.** You can zoom in on the sensor image as you focus manually, use split-image comparison of two parts of the image simultaneously, and use a feature called *manual focus peaking,* which Canon also refers to as "outline emphasis" to accentuate in-focus areas with distinct colored outlines. The camera also has a "focus guide" that helps you judge how much out-of-focus the image is, and which direction you need to focus to achieve a sharp image. I'll explain all these options later.

- **More lenses.** All mirrorless cameras—and not just the Canon R-series—have had a limited number of lenses available when they were introduced. But fortunately, the reduced flange-to-sensor distance (which I'll explain in more detail in Chapter 7) offers plenty of room to insert an adapter that allows mounting an extensive number of existing lenses, including those from manufacturers other than Canon. Many of those third-party optics are inexpensive manual focus lenses, or lenses intended for other camera platforms which function only in manual focus on the R-series models. A whole generation of photographers who grew up using nothing but autofocus have discovered that focusing manually is a reasonable tradeoff for access to this wide range of optics.

How Focus Works

Simply put, focus is the process of adjusting the camera so that parts of our subject that we want to be sharp and clear are, in fact, sharp and clear. We can allow the camera to focus for us, automatically, or we can rotate the lens's focus ring manually to achieve the desired focus. Manual focusing is especially problematic because our eyes and brains have poor memory for correct focus. That's why your eye doctor conducting a refraction test must shift back and forth between pairs of lenses and ask, "Does that look sharper—or was it sharper before?" in determining your correct prescription. Too often, the slight differences are such that the lens pairs must be swapped multiple times.

Similarly, manual focusing involves jogging the focus ring back and forth as you go from almost in focus, to sharp focus, to almost focused again. The little clockwise and counterclockwise arcs decrease in size until you've zeroed in on the point of correct focus. What you're looking for is the image with the most contrast between the edges of elements in the image.

The Canon EOS RP's autofocus mechanism, like all such systems found in modern cameras, also evaluates these increases and decreases in sharpness, but it is able to remember the progression perfectly, so that autofocus can lock in much more quickly and, with an image that has sufficient contrast, more precisely. Unfortunately, while the camera's focus system finds it easy to measure degrees of apparent focus at each of the focus points in the viewfinder, it doesn't really know with any certainty *which object* should be in sharpest focus. Is it the closest object? The subject in the center? Something lurking *behind* the closest subject? A person standing over at the side of the picture? Using autofocus effectively involves telling the EOS RP exactly what it should be focusing on.

Learning to use the EOS RP's modern autofocus system is easy, but you do need to fully understand how the system works to get the most benefit from it. Once you're comfortable with autofocus, you'll know when it's appropriate to use the manual focus option, too.

As the camera collects focus information from the sensors, it then evaluates it to determine whether the desired sharp focus has been achieved. The calculations may include whether the subject is moving, and whether the camera needs to "predict" where the subject will be when the shutter release button is fully depressed and the picture is taken. The speed with which the camera is able to evaluate focus and then move the lens elements into the proper position to achieve the sharpest focus determines how fast the autofocus mechanism is. Although your EOS RP will almost always focus more quickly than a human eye, there are types of shooting situations where that's not fast enough. For example, if you're having problems shooting a sport with many fast-moving players because the EOS RP's autofocus system manically follows each moving subject, a better choice might be to switch Autofocus modes, or shift into Manual and prefocus on a spot where you anticipate the action will be, such as a goal line or soccer net.

Autofocus is generally achieved using two different technologies called contrast detection autofocus (CDAF) and phase detection autofocus (PDAF). I'm going to provide a quick overview of contrast detection first, and then devote much of the rest of this chapter to the complexities of the phase detection system used in the EOS RP.

Contrast Detection

This is a slower, but potentially more accurate mode, best suited for static subjects, and was originally the only kind of autofocus available for mirrorless cameras and for dSLRs when shooting in their live view and movie modes. The recent innovation of adding phase detection pixels to the sensor itself (as I'll describe shortly) converted contrast detection from a main system into a fine-tuning option for designers creating a hybrid system that used both. It's important to note that, unlike the AF systems found on some competing cameras, the EOS RP *does not* use contrast detection at all. Autofocus is achieved entirely using phase detection.

That's actually a significant achievement on the part of the Canon engineers. I'm going to give you a brief overview of how contrast detection works, which will help you appreciate the sophisticated PDAF system found in your EOS RP.

Contrast detection is very easy to understand, and is illustrated by Figure 5.1, a close-up of some weathered wood. At top in the figure, the transitions between the edges found in the image are soft and blurred because of the low contrast between them. Whether the edges are horizontal, vertical, or diagonal doesn't matter in the least; the focus system looks only for contrast between edges, and those edges can run in any direction at all.

At the bottom of Figure 5.1, the image has been brought into sharp focus, and the edges have much more contrast; the transitions are sharp and clear. Although this example is a bit exaggerated so you can see the results on the printed page, it's easy to understand that when maximum contrast in a subject is achieved, it can be deemed to be in sharp focus. Although achieving focus with contrast

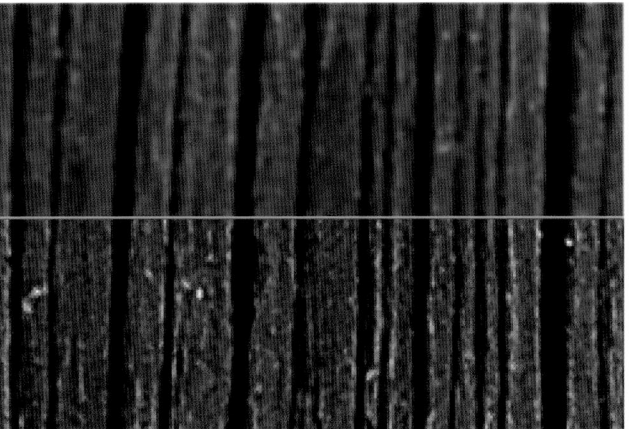

Figure 5.1

Focus in contrast detection mode evaluates the increase in contrast in the edges of subjects, starting with a blurry image (top) and producing a sharp, contrasty image (bottom).

detection is generally quite a bit slower, there are several advantages—and disadvantages—to this method:

- **Works with more image types.** Any subject that has edges will work with CDAF.

- **Focus on any point.** With contrast detection, any portion of the image can be used to focus: you don't need dedicated AF sensors. Focus is achieved with the actual sensor image, so focus point selection is simply a matter of choosing which part of the sensor image to use. It's easy to move the focus frame around to virtually any location.

- **Potentially more accurate.** Contrast detection is clear-cut. The camera can clearly see when the highest contrast has been achieved, as long as there is sufficient light to allow the camera to examine the image produced by the sensor. However, some "hunting" may be necessary. As the camera seeks the ideal plane of focus, it may overshoot and have to back up a little, then re-correct if the new focus plane is not optimal. However, once CDAF settles on the ideal focus plane, the results are generally very accurate. Contrast detection is an excellent way of fine-tuning focus that has been achieved through PDAF. However, Canon engineers say the EOS RP does not use contrast detection. I'm describing it only because many are more familiar with that type of technology, and understanding it helps you see how phase detection AF differs.

Phase Detection

The phase detection pixels in the EOS RP's sensor split incoming photons arriving from opposite sides of the lens into two parts, forming a pair of images, exactly like the rangefinders used for surveying and in rangefinder-focusing cameras like the venerable Leica M series. The dual images are separated when out of focus, and then gradually brought together to achieve sharp focus, as shown from top to bottom in Figure 5.2.

Figure 5.2
In phase detection, parts of an image are split in two and compared (top). When the image is in focus, the two halves of the image align, as with a rangefinder (bottom).

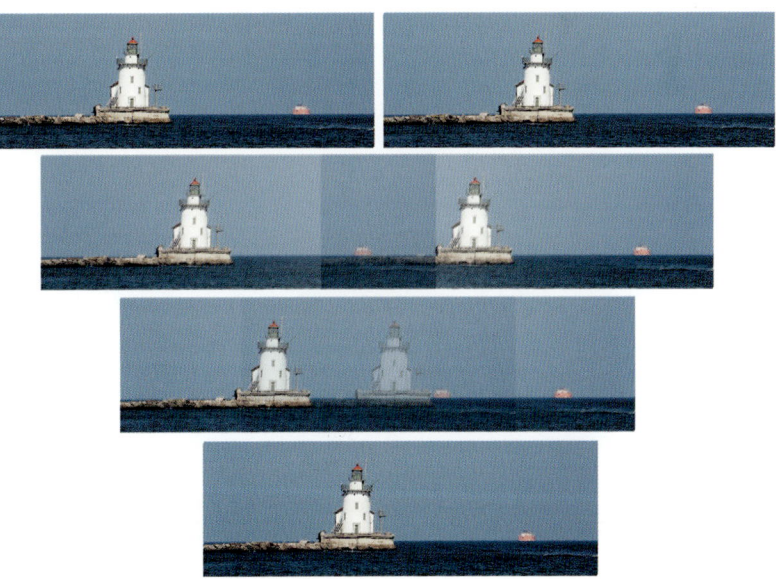

This process tells the camera when the image pair are "in phase" and aligned. The rangefinder approach of phase detection tells the EOS RP exactly how out of focus the image is, and in which direction (focus is too near, or too far) thanks to the amount and direction of the displacement of the split image. The camera can quickly and precisely snap the image into sharp focus and match the lines.

The PDAF sensors in the EOS RP are all *line sensors,* horizontally oriented, which means they work best with features that transect the sensor either perpendicularly or at an angle, as visualized in Figure 5.3, top. It's easy to detect when the two halves of the vertical lines of the weathered wood—actually a 19th century outhouse—are aligned. However, when the same sensor is asked to measure focus for, say, horizontal lines that don't split up quite so conveniently, or, in the worst case, subjects such as the sky (which may have neither vertical nor horizontal lines), focus can slow down drastically, or even become impossible. One such scenario is pictured in Figure 5.3, bottom left. A possible solution is to incorporate vertically oriented AF sensors, which can easily focus horizontal subject matter (Figure 5.3, bottom right). The line sensors arranged perpendicularly to each other are called "cross-type" sensors.

However, the EOS RP has no cross sensors, as such PDAF pixels are difficult to embed in today's image sensors. The company feels that the high density of AF positions virtually insures that the line sensors will still find enough detail crossing the sensor at an angle conducive to autofocus. In other cameras, a given sensor pixel must be either a PDAF detector or an imaging pixel—not both. But Canon's Dual Pixel technology means that any given sensor can include *both* an AF sensor and

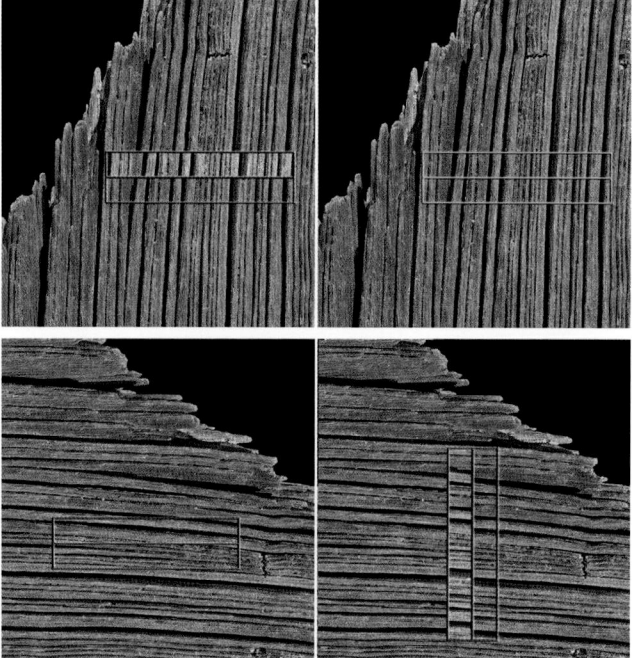

Figure 5.3
When an image is out of focus, the split lines don't align precisely (top left). Using phase detection, the EOS RP is able to align the features of the image and achieve sharp focus quickly (top right). Horizontal lines aren't ideal for horizontally oriented sensors (bottom left) and require vertically oriented AF sensors (bottom right).

an imaging photo diode and perform both tasks, so they have fewer limitations on the placement and number of PDAF detectors included in a sensor like the one found in the EOS RP. I'll tell you more about the Dual Pixel technology later in this chapter.

Of course, as with any rangefinder-like function, phase detection accuracy is better when the "base length" between the two images is larger. (Think back to your high school trigonometry; you could calculate a distance more accurately when the separation between the two points where the angles were measured was greater.) For that reason, phase detection autofocus is more accurate with larger (wider) lens openings—especially those with maximum f/stops of f/2.8 or better—than with smaller lens openings, and may not work at all when the f/stop is smaller than f/8. As I noted, the EOS RP is able to perform these comparisons very quickly.

Layout of the EOS RP'S AF System

Figure 5.4 is my rough approximation of the layout of the EOS RP's autofocus pixels, based on Canon's descriptions. Because of the flexibility of the Dual Pixel technology, Canon has been able to spread the AF area to fill nearly 100 percent of the vertical frame, and about 88 percent of the horizontal area, when working with RF (native) lenses. EF-mount lenses attached using a mount adapter may not produce that full coverage; Canon says some may provide only 80 percent horizontal coverage.

The red dots represent the manually selectable positions you can move among when you choose your own focus point, area, or zone. These positions number 4,779, to be exact, allocated in an array 87 positions horizontally and 65 positions vertically. That doesn't mean that the EOS RP's sensor has 4,779 phase detect pixels. That humongous figure enumerates just the locations you can use to specify your focus point using 1-point AF. When the camera is choosing an AF area, it

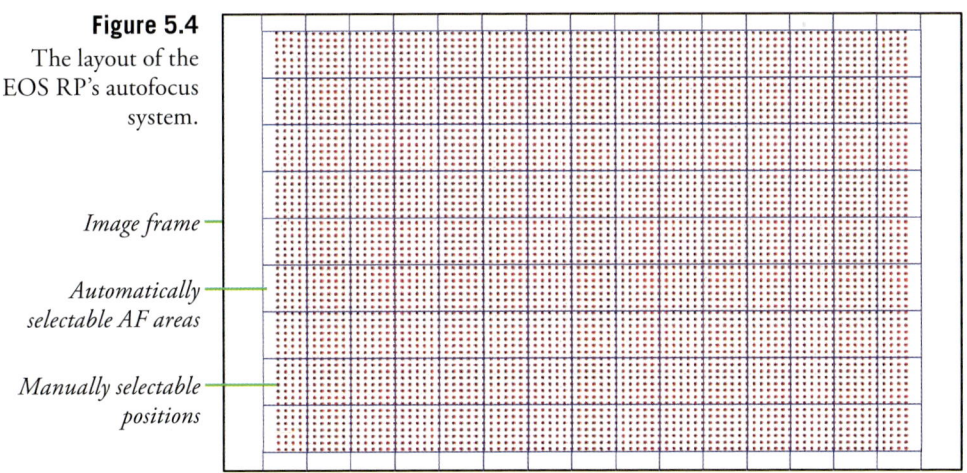

Figure 5.4
The layout of the EOS RP's autofocus system.

Image frame —

Automatically selectable AF areas —

Manually selectable positions —

will use a smaller number of sections of the sensor, roughly represented by the blue squares. Canon's PDAF system has many of the strengths formerly the province of contrast detection AF technology:

- **Works with all image types.** Because it has so many AF point positions on the sensor it's unlikely that the area being examined will lack the edges needed to achieve sharp focus.
- **Focus on any point.** While contrast detection can examine virtually any position on the sensor, the large number of AF points on the EOS RP's sensor means it, too, is capable of using almost any area of the sensor to focus, and you can, of course, move the 1-point AF point almost anywhere you please.
- **Just as accurate.** The large number of PDAF points means that it can be virtually as accurate as contrast detection, and without the hunting and slowness.

Dual Pixel CMOS AF

Understanding contrast and phase detection helps you appreciate the marvel that is Canon's Dual Pixel CMOS AF system. Used while shooting both stills and movies, as I've noted, it works much more quickly than traditional contrast detection systems.

The sensor's pixel array includes special pixels that provide the same type of split-image rangefinder phase detection AF that all PDAF modules use. The most important aspect of the system is that it doesn't rob the camera of any imaging resolution. It would have been possible to place AF sensors *between* the pixels used to capture the image, but that would leave the sensor with less area with which to capture light. Keep in mind that CMOS sensors, unlike earlier CCD sensors, have more on-board circuitry which already consumes some of the light-gathering area. Microlenses are placed above each photosensitive site to focus incoming illumination on the sensor and to correct for the oblique angles from which some photons may approach the imager. (Older lenses, designed for film, are the worst offenders in terms of emitting light at severely oblique angles; newer "digital" lenses do a better job of directing photons onto the sensor plane with a less "slanted" approach.)

With the Dual Pixel CMOS AF system, the same photosites capture both image and autofocus information. Each pixel is divided into two photodiodes, facing left and right when the camera is held in horizontal orientation (or above and below each other in vertical orientation; either works fine for autofocus purposes). Each pair functions as a separate AF sensor, allowing a special integrated circuit to process the raw autofocus information before sending it on to the EOS RP's digital image processor, which handles both AF and image capture. For the latter, the information grabbed by *both* photodiodes is combined, so that the full photosensitive area of the sensor pixel is used to capture the image.

While traditional contrast detection frequently involves frustrating "hunting" as the camera continually readjusts the focus plane trying to find the position of maximum contrast, adding Dual Pixel CMOS AF phase detection allows the EOS RP to focus smoothly, which is important for speed, and essential when shooting movies (where all that hunting is unfortunately captured for posterity). Movie autofocus tracking is improved, allowing shooting movies of subjects in motion.

Circles of Confusion and Focus

You know that increased depth-of-field brings more of your subject into focus. But more depth-of-field also makes autofocusing (or manual focusing) more difficult because the contrast is lower between objects at different distances. This is an added factor *beyond* the rangefinder aspects of lens opening size in phase detection. An image that's dimmer is more difficult to focus with any type of focus system, phase detection, contrast detection, or manual focus.

So, focus with a 200mm focal length may be easier in some respects than at a 28mm focal length (or zoom setting) because the longer lens has less apparent depth-of-field. By the same token, a lens with a maximum aperture of f/1.8 will be easier to autofocus (or manually focus) than one of the same focal length with an f/4 maximum aperture, because the f/4 lens has more depth-of-field *and* a dimmer view. That's yet another reason why lenses with a maximum aperture smaller than f/5.6 can give your EOS RP's autofocus system fits—increased depth-of-field joins forces with a dimmer image that's more difficult to focus using phase detection.

To make things even more complicated, many subjects aren't polite enough to remain still. They move around in the frame, so that even if the EOS RP is sharply focused on your main subject, it may change position and require refocusing. An intervening subject may pop into the frame and pass between you and the subject you meant to photograph. You (or the EOS RP) have to decide whether to lock focus on this new subject, or remain focused on the original subject. Finally, there are some kinds of subjects that are difficult to bring into sharp focus because they lack enough contrast to allow the EOS RP's AF system (or our eyes) to lock in. Blank walls, a clear blue sky, or other subject matter may make focusing difficult.

If you find all these focus factors confusing, you're on the right track. Focus is, in fact, measured using something called a *circle of confusion.* An ideal image consists of zillions of tiny little points, which, like all points, theoretically have no height or width. There is perfect contrast between the point and its surroundings. You can think of each point as a pinpoint of light in a darkened room. When a given point is out of focus, its edges decrease in contrast and it changes from a perfect point to a tiny disc with blurry edges (remember, blur is the lack of contrast between boundaries in an image). (See Figure 5.5.)

Figure 5.5
When a pinpoint of light (left) goes out of focus, its blurry edges form a circle of confusion (center and right).

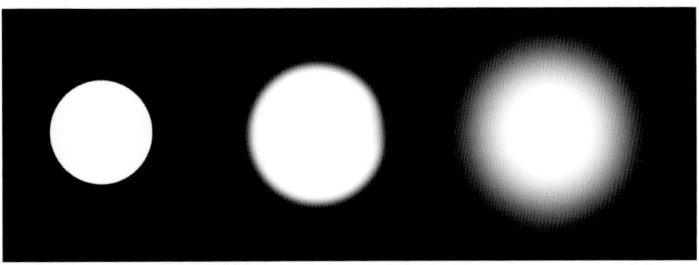

If this blurry disc—the circle of confusion—is small enough, our eye still perceives it as a point. It's only when the disc grows large enough that we can see it as a blur rather than a sharp point that a given point is viewed as out of focus. You can see, then, that enlarging an image, either by displaying it larger on your computer monitor or by making a large print, also enlarges the size of each circle of confusion. Moving closer to the image does the same thing. So, parts of an image that may look perfectly sharp in a 5 × 7–inch print viewed at arm's length, might appear blurry when blown up to 11 × 14 and examined at the same distance. Take a few steps back, however, and it may look sharp again.

To a lesser extent, the viewer also affects the apparent size of these circles of confusion. Some people see details better at a given distance and may perceive smaller circles of confusion than someone standing next to them. For the most part, however, such differences are small. Truly blurry images will look blurry to just about everyone under the same conditions.

Technically, there is just one plane within your picture area, parallel to the back of the camera (or sensor, in the case of a digital camera), that is in sharp focus. That's the plane in which the points of the image are rendered as precise points. At every other plane in front of or behind the focus plane, the points show up as discs that range from slightly blurry to extremely blurry until the out-of-focus areas become one large blur that de-emphasizes an unattractive textured white background.

In practice, the discs in many of these planes will still be so small that we see them as points, and that's where we get depth-of-field. Depth-of-field is just the range of planes that include discs that we perceive as points rather than blurred splotches. The size of this range increases as the aperture is reduced in size and is allocated roughly one-third in front of the plane of sharpest focus, and two-thirds behind it. The range of sharp focus is always greater behind your subject than in front of it.

Working with the AF System

Now that you understand the basics of how the EOS RP's autofocus system works, it's time to jump into the actual settings and options you have at your disposal. To achieve tack-sharp focus every time, you'll need to master focus modes (*when* to evaluate a scene and lock in focus) and focus area selection (you or the camera decides *what* to focus on).

AF Operation

The AF Operation focus modes tell the camera *when* to evaluate and lock in focus. They don't determine *where* focus should be checked; that's the function of other autofocus features. Focus modes tell the camera whether to lock in focus once, say, when you press the shutter release halfway (or use some other control, such as the AF-ON button), or whether, once activated, the camera should continue tracking your subject and, if it's moving, adjust focus to follow it.

The EOS RP has manual focus, plus magnified (up to 10X manual focus), and two AF modes: One-Shot AF (also known as single autofocus) and Servo AF (continuous autofocus). I'll explain all of these in more detail later in this section. Choosing the right autofocus mode and the way in which focus points are selected is your key to success. Using the wrong mode for a particular type of photography can lead to a series of pictures that are all sharply focused—on the wrong subject.

When I first started shooting sports with an autofocus SLR (back in the film camera days), I covered one game alternating between shots of base runners and outfielders with pictures of a promising young pitcher, all from a position next to the third base dugout. The base runner and outfielder photos were great, because their backgrounds didn't distract the autofocus mechanism. But all my photos of the pitcher had the focus tightly zeroed in on the fans in the stands behind him. Because I was shooting film instead of a digital camera, I didn't know about my gaffe until the film was developed. A simple change, such as locking in focus or focus zone manually, or even manually focusing, would have done the trick.

To save battery power, your EOS RP doesn't start to focus the lens until you partially depress the shutter release (unless you've activated Continuous AF in the Shooting 7 menu). But, autofocus isn't some mindless beast out there snapping your pictures in and out of focus with no feedback from you after you press that button. There are several settings you can modify that return at least a modicum of control to you. Your first decision should be whether you set the EOS RP to One-Shot or Servo. With the camera set for one of the non-auto modes, use the Q button to summon the Quick Control menu and navigate to AF Operation (second from the top in the left column). Then spin either dial to toggle between One-Shot or Servo. (The AF/M switch on the lens must be set to AF before you can change autofocus mode.)

One-Shot AF

In this mode, also called *single autofocus*, focus is set once and remains at that setting until the button is fully depressed, taking the picture, or until you release the shutter button without taking a shot. This mode is best for subjects that are not moving around a great deal. So, for non-action photography, this setting is usually your best choice, as it minimizes out-of-focus pictures (at the expense of spontaneity). The drawback here is that you might not be able to take a picture at all while the camera is seeking focus; you're locked out until the autofocus mechanism is happy with the current setting. One-Shot AF/single autofocus is sometimes referred to as *focus-priority* for that reason. Because of the small delay while the camera zeroes in on correct focus during focus-priority operation, you might experience slightly more shutter lag. This mode uses less battery power than the other autofocus modes.

When sharp focus is achieved, the selected focus point will flash green in the viewfinder and the camera will beep (unless you've disabled Beep in the Set-up 3 menu). If you're using Evaluative metering, the exposure will be locked at the same time. By keeping the shutter button depressed halfway, you'll find you can reframe the image while retaining the focus (and exposure) that's been set. You can also use the AE Lock/FE Lock button to retain the exposure calculated from the center AF point while reframing.

Servo AF

This mode, also known as *continuous autofocus,* is the mode to use for sports and other fast-moving subjects, and is often used with continuous shooting modes. Once the shutter release is partially depressed, the camera sets the focus on the point that's selected (by the camera or by you manually), but continues to monitor the subject, so that if it moves or you move, the lens will be refocused to suit. When focus is achieved, the AF point turns blue; there is no Beep signal however, as it would be intrusive if it chirped each time the EOS RP refocused. As you might expect, focus and exposure aren't really locked until you press the shutter release down all the way to take the picture. You'll find that Servo AF produces the least amount of shutter lag of any autofocus mode: press the button and the camera fires. It also uses the most battery power, because the autofocus system operates as long as the shutter release button is partially depressed.

You'll often see continuous autofocus referred to as *release-priority,* because that's the way it has been traditionally used. In that mode, if you press the shutter release down all the way while the system is refining focus, the camera will go ahead and take a picture, even if the image is slightly out of focus. Servo AF uses a technology called *predictive AF*, which allows the EOS RP to calculate the correct focus if the subject is moving toward or away from the camera at a constant rate. It uses either the automatically selected AF point or the point you select manually to set focus.

Manual Focus

Manual focus is possible if you slide the AF/MF switch on the lens to the MF position. Your EOS RP then lets you set the focus yourself. There are some advantages and disadvantages to this approach. While your batteries will last longer in manual focus mode, it will take you longer to focus the camera for each photo, a process that can be difficult. Canon does give you some help in focusing manually.

- **Focus peaking.** You can also use MF Peaking in the Shooting 8 menu to emphasize the outlines of your image with a contrasting color. In Chapter 12, I will show you how to choose a color (from red, white, or yellow) so areas that are in focus appear outlined in that hue. (See Figure 5.6.) You can also select how much peaking is used (from High, Medium, or Low) to get effects like that seen in Figure 5.7. Peaking is not shown during magnified display.

- **Magnified view.** Manual focusing is much easier if you use the magnified view (also available in autofocus modes) as described in the section that follows.

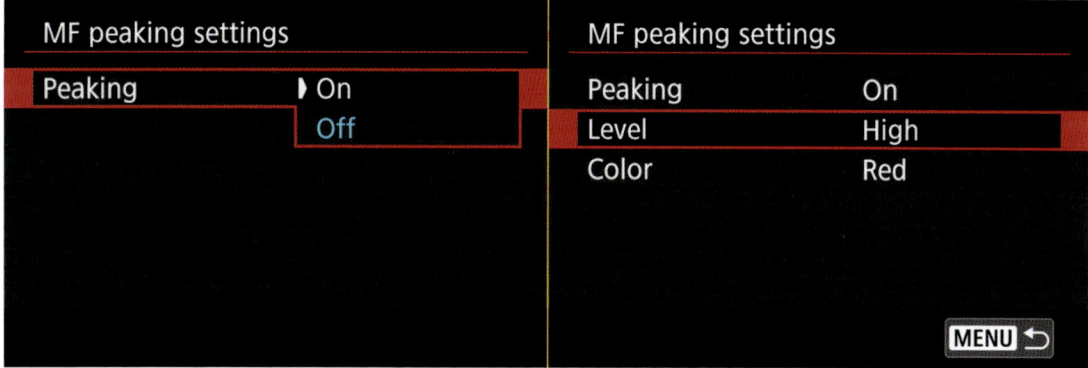

Figure 5.6 Focus peaking.

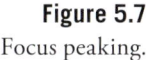
Figure 5.7
Focus peaking.

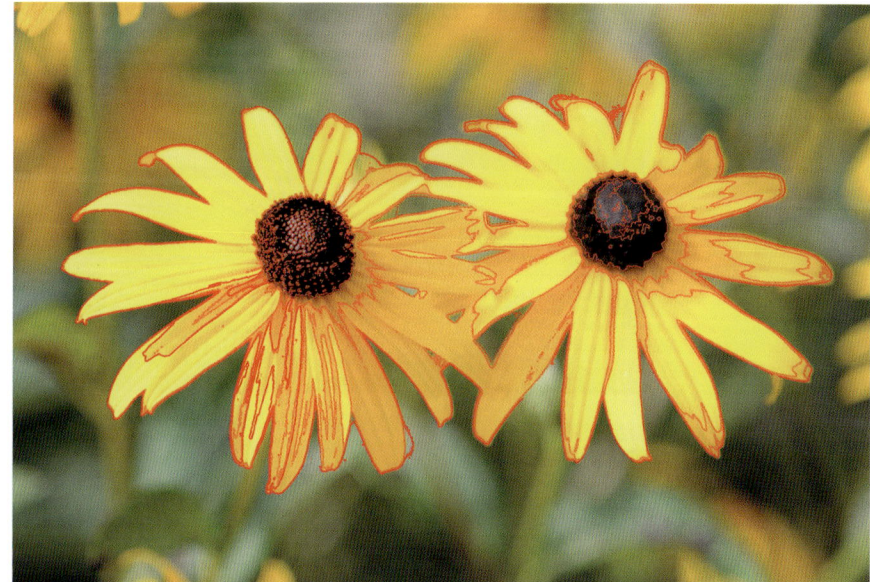

AF Method

What Canon dubs the "AF Method" is actually a feature that specifies *which areas of the frame* are used to collect autofocus information. There are five *AF area modes* you can use to select the initial point or zone of points (with variations on what additional points will also be deployed, if needed). A sixth mode allows *the camera* (not you) to select from among all the useable points (up to 4,779 total) to specify the initial focus point automatically.

You can check focus with 5X and 10X magnified views by pressing the Magnify/Reduce button in all modes (including Manual focus), except Face+Tracking. Just press the Magnify/Reduce button, followed by the INFO button once or twice to view your image magnified 5X and 10X (respectively). When zoomed in, rotate the Main Dial to move the magnified area horizontally and the vertical position using the QCD. The directional keys also can be used. Press the Trash button to center the magnified area in the middle of the frame. (See Figure 5.8.)

Switching among the six AF modes is easy: press the AF selection button on the upper-right corner of the camera's back panel (below the * button), and then press the M-Fn button repeatedly while the available modes cycle on the display similar to the one shown in Figure 5.9. If you generally use only a few of the six total modes, Canon gives you the ability to "hide" the others using the Limit AF Methods entry in the C.Fn II-5 entry, as described in Chapter 14.

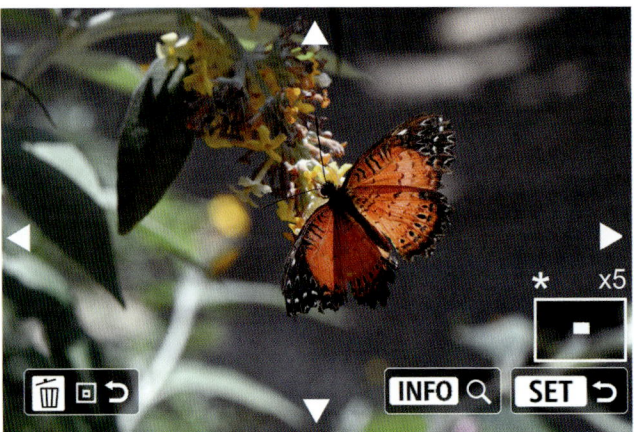

Figure 5.8
Magnified views of 5X and 10X can be used when focusing manually or in any AF mode except for Face+Tracking.

Face+Tracking AF

If you choose this mode, the camera will search for and focus on faces; if none are found, the entire autofocus area will be used. A box appears around a located face, and the EOS RP tracks it as it moves around the frame. (See Figure 5.9.) When using Servo AF mode, you can specify the initial AF point. The camera will first use the AF point you have set, and if no face is found will search elsewhere in the frame. That could be useful when shooting a series of photos when you know that your main subject will *probably* be located in a particular area of the frame, but still want the camera to refocus as the subject moves. This helps reduce AF confusion from movement elsewhere in the frame that is not your main subject.

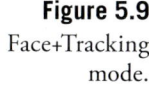

Figure 5.9
Face+Tracking
mode.

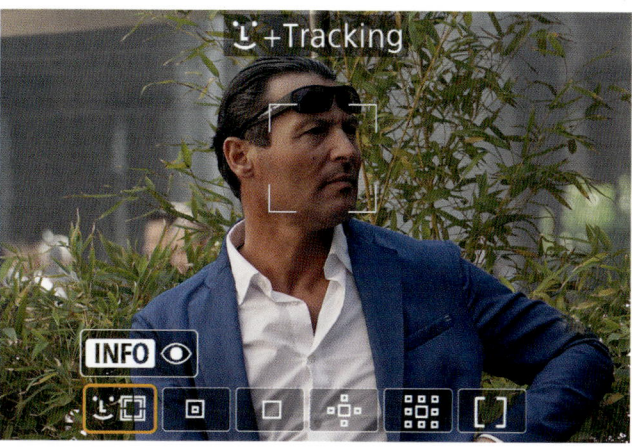

EYE DETECTION

If you've activated Eye Detection AF in the Shooting 7 menu, in One-Shot mode the camera will display an additional smaller box around an eye. You can also tap the LCD screen to select an eye. You can turn eye detection on or off when you activate Face+Tracking by pressing the INFO button to toggle between enable and disable. While using Face+Tracking, you can enable or disable eye detection on the fly by pressing the AF Point Selection button, then the M-Fn button, followed by the INFO button.

You have three choices for the initial Face+Tracking focus point, which can be specified using the C.Fn II-7 Initial Servo AF Point for Face+Tracking entry, as described in Chapter 14.

- **Auto.** The initial AF point for Servo AF when using Face+Tracking is determined by the camera. This default option is the simplest and least prone to unintended errors.

- **A point you specify.** You can choose a specific position within the frame that will always be used first when working with Face+Tracking, in Servo AF mode using the Initial AF Point for Face+Tracking entry option.

- **Retain manual point used for 1-point AF, Expand AF Area, Expand AF Area: Around.** If you are using one of these three AF methods, and *then* switch to Face+Tracking, Servo AF initially uses the AF point you specified in the previous mode.

Spot AF

In this mode, you can zero in and focus on a small box displayed on the screen (see Figure 5.10). This focus area can be moved in tiny increments to nearly any location on the screen using the directional buttons or QCD and Main Dials. (Figure 5.4 shows the selectable positions.)

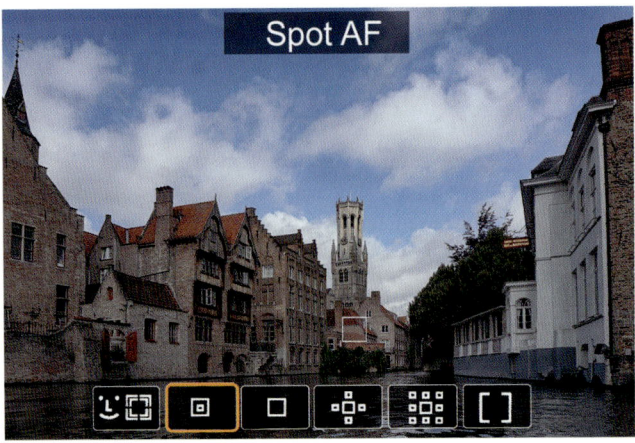

Spot AF

Figure 5.10
Focus on a single area within the frame.

This precision can be too much of a good thing, however; camera movement (as when shooting hand-held, especially with a front-heavy long lens) and subject movement can easily move the focus spot away from your primary subject. This mode may be your best choice when you want to focus precisely on a subject that is surrounded by fine detail. It is most practical for scenes where you want to focus on a certain point, but your subject may be moving slowly. Position the active focus point with the controls. You can use Spot AF for everyday shooting where precision is needed, and the subject contains sufficient detail within the area covered by the sensor. If such a small area of your subject is a bit amorphous, you'll want to use one of the selection modes described next, which allow the AF system to take into account surrounding focus points as well as the manually selected point.

1-point AF

In this mode, you can zero in and focus on a box that is roughly 3X larger displayed on the screen (see Figure 5.11). When speed is important, but you still want to specify the focus location with some degree of precision, this option is probably your best choice. I use it for sports when I want to be able to single out specific players who are not moving a great deal (say, an infielder covering third base).

Expand AF Area

In this mode, the focus point you select is used, along with the points immediately above, below, and to either side of it (until the manually selected point reaches the edge of the array and one or more of the additional points scroll off). (See Figure 5.12.) This mode is better for moving objects, because the larger effective zone makes it easier to track subjects that are moving within the frame. As the subject moves outside the area defined by the selected focus point, three to four of the surrounding focus points can pick up and track the movement. In One-Shot AF mode, the manually selected focus point and expanded point used will be displayed.

Figure 5.11
Focus on a single area within the frame.

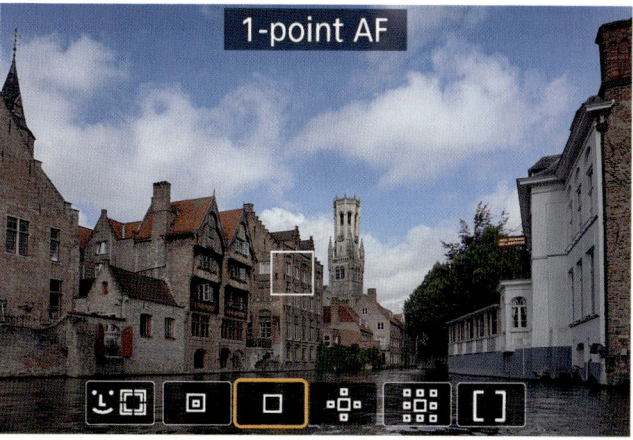

Figure 5.12
A larger AF area when using Expand AF area allows autofocus of moving subjects.

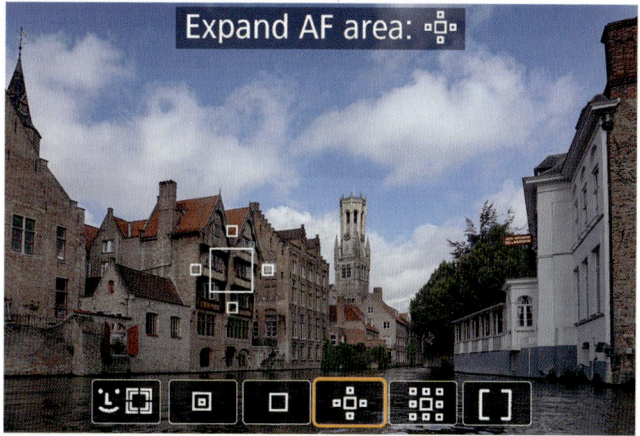

Expand AF Area: Around

This mode is similar to the one above, except that the four points located diagonally in relation to the manually selected point are included in the focusing array. It is slightly better for subjects that don't contain a lot of detail at the manually selected focus point, and the additional points surrounding the initial focus point improve your results. This mode is also better for larger moving objects, even though it offers a bit less precision. As always, while the active points are shown in the center of the frame in the figure, you can move the active area around while viewing the display. (See Figure 5.13.)

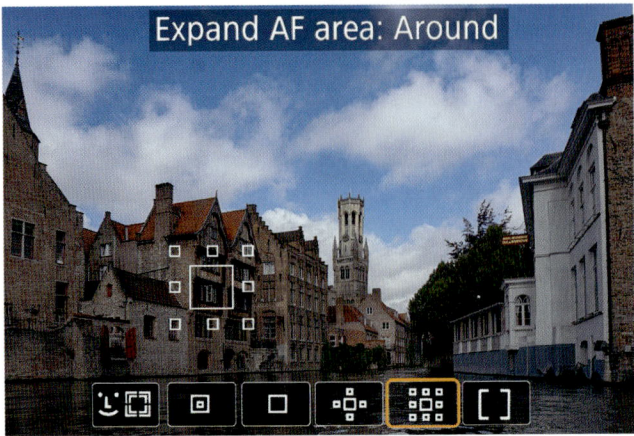

Figure 5.13
Four additional focus points are active in this mode.

Zone AF

This is a zone-oriented point selection method, in which the AF points are divided in a zone, covering roughly one-sixth of the frame. When you move the focus "point" using the controls, you are actually simply moving the zone from one position to the next within the frame. This mode works well when you know the approximate area where your subject will reside, and want to cover a particular zone. This mode usually focuses on the nearest subject, and so lacks the precision of the other AF methods described so far. However, the camera will attempt to focus on any faces detected within the AF frame. (See Figure 5.14.)

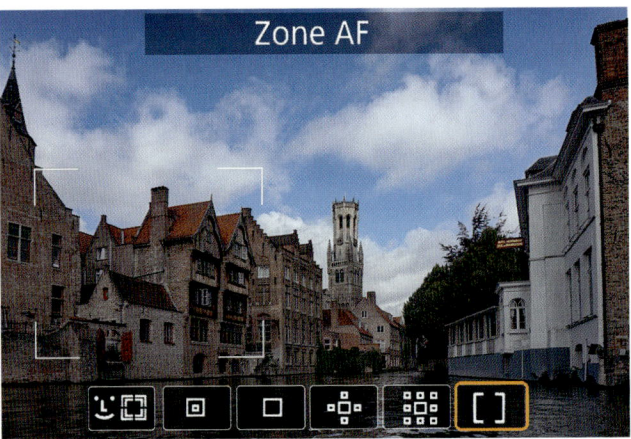

Figure 5.14
Zone AF uses a larger focus area.

Fine-Tuning Your Autofocus

The options available for the Canon EOS RP's autofocus can be overwhelming at times, which is why I'm devoting this full chapter, and portions of two others, to explaining them. I'm covering all the key concepts of autofocus in this chapter. Most of what you need to know to find and use the EOS RP's individual options is found in the bulleted list below.

If you want to know more, I provide additional detail in Chapter 11 (which deals with all the Shooting menus) and Chapter 14, which explains how to make settings in the Custom Functions menus, including the C.Fn II Autofocus entries. Your options include:

- **Continuous AF.** The EOS RP will constantly refocus, even when using One-Shot mode, until you press the shutter release halfway. Then, focus in One-Shot mode locks, and will continue refocusing in Servo AF mode, until you press the shutter release all the way to take a picture. This setting's pre-focus activity can speed up AF as you take pictures, at the expense of some battery drain. You'll find this setting in the Shooting 7 menu.

- **Touch & Drag.** You can use the touch screen to position the focus point even while composing your image in the viewfinder. In Chapter 12, I'll show you how to specify the most useful positioning method, and whether the entire LCD screen is active, or only a portion of the panel is used. This entry is also located in the Shooting 7 menu.

- **AF-assist beam firing.** This setting determines when bursts from a compatible external electronic flash or the camera's built-in LED are used to emit a pulse of light that helps provide enough contrast for the EOS RP to focus on a subject. You'll find this entry in the Shooting 8 menu.

- **Tracking sensitivity.** This determines how quickly the AF system switches to a new subject entering the focus area. Your choices are –2 (Locked On) to +2 (Responsive). Negative numbers allow you to retain focus on the original subject even if it briefly leaves the area covered by the focus points, making tracking easier. The drawback is that if the camera selects the wrong subject, there is a longer delay before the correct subject is captured. Positive numbers cause the AF system to more quickly switch to a new subject. However, such a quick response can cause the camera to focus on the wrong subject. These options are found in the C.Fn II-1 entry.

- **Acceleration/deceleration tracking.** This parameter determines how the AF system responds to sudden acceleration, deceleration, or stopping. Your choices are 0 (for subjects that move at a constant speed) to 2 (for faster reactions to subjects that suddenly change speed). Lower values can cause the camera to be "fooled" if a subject that was moving consistently suddenly stops; focus may change to the position where the subject *would* have been if it'd kept moving. A higher value may cause inconsistent focus with subjects that move at a constant speed. These options are found in the C.Fn II-2 entry.

- **AF point auto switching.** This setting determines how quickly the AF system changes from the current AF point to an adjacent one when the subject moves away from the current point, or an intervening object moves across the frame into the area interpreted by the current point. Your choices are 0 (switch more slowly so focus is stable, with slower tracking response) to 2 (switch to an adjacent point quickly). These options are found in the C.Fn II-3 entry.

- **When focus is difficult.** Low-contrast scenes and dim light levels can give the EOS RP's autofocus fits. This is often the case with long telephotos or lenses with a relatively small maximum aperture. The Lens Drive When AF Impossible setting (C.Fn II-4) can tell the EOS RP either to keep trying to focus, or to stop.

- **Limit AF methods.** If you don't use every AF method, you can make them invisible in the selection screen, so that switching among the ones you do use is faster. As described in Chapter 12, you can enable any or all methods, or have only one or two available. The 1-point AF mode cannot be disabled. These options are found in the C.Fn II-5 entry.

- **Orientation Linked AF point.** If you have a preference for a particular manually selected AF point when composing vertical or horizontal pictures, you can specify that preference using this menu entry (C.Fn II-6), by choosing Separate AF Points: Point Only. Or, you can indicate that you want to use the same mode/point in all orientations (Same for Both Vert/Horiz). (See Figure 5.15.) If you'd like to differentiate, the Separate AF Points: Point Only option gives you different orientations to account for, one horizontal and two vertical:

  - **Same for both vertical and horizontal.** The AF point or zone that you select manually is used for both vertical and horizontal images.

  - **Separate AF points: Point Only.** You can specify a different AF point in manual point selection modes for each of three orientations. The specified point will remain in force even if you switch from one manual selection mode to another. The orientations are as follows:

    - ◆ **Camera held horizontally.** This orientation assumes that the camera is positioned so the viewfinder/shutter release are on top.

    - ◆ **Camera held vertically** with the grip/shutter release above the Mode Dial.

    - ◆ **Camera held vertically** with the Mode Dial above the grip/shutter release.

- **Initial Servo AF Point for Face+Tracking.** I described this option for the Face+Tracking AF method earlier. You'll find the choices in the C.Fn II-7 entry.

FOCUS GUIDE

The guide frame can be moved by tapping the screen, pressing the AF Point button first, and then using the cross keys, or centered by pressing the Trash button. If the AF Method is Face+Tracking and Eye Detection AF has been enabled, the guide frame will appear near any eyes that are detected for the main subject.

Figure 5.15

Orientation-linked AF point: Same for vertical and horizontal (top); separate AF points for horizontal and two vertical orientations (bottom).

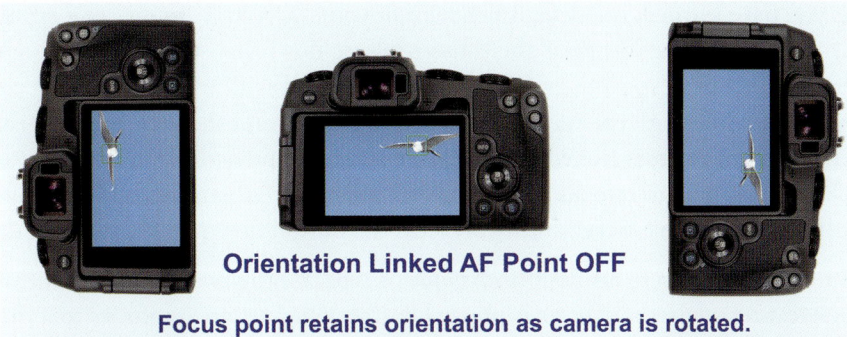

Orientation Linked AF Point OFF

Focus point retains orientation as camera is rotated.

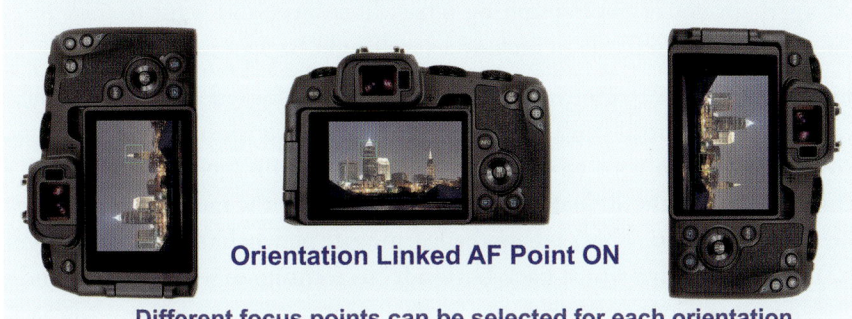

Orientation Linked AF Point ON

Different focus points can be selected for each orientation.

Back-Button Focus

Once you've been using your camera for a while, you'll invariably encounter the terms *back focus* and *back-button focus*, and wonder if they are good things or bad things. Actually, they are *two different things,* and are often confused with each other. *Back focus* is a bad thing, and occurs when a particular lens consistently autofocuses on a plane that's *behind* your desired subject. This malady may be found in some of your lenses, or all your optics may be free of the defect. The good news is that if the problem lies in a particular lens (rather than a camera misadjustment that applies to *all* your lenses), it can be fixed.

Back-button focus, on the other hand, is a tool you can use to separate two functions that are commonly locked together—exposure and autofocus—so that you can lock in exposure while allowing focus to be attained at a later point, or vice versa. It's a *good* thing, although using back-button focus effectively may require you to unlearn some habits and acquire new ways of coordinating the action of your fingers.

As you have learned, the default behavior of your EOS RP is to set both exposure and focus (when AF is active) when you press the shutter release down halfway. When using One-Shot AF mode, that's that: both exposure and focus are locked and will not change until you release the shutter button, or press it all the way down to take a picture and then release it for the next shot. In Servo AF mode, exposure is locked and focus set when you press the shutter release halfway, but the EOS RP will continue to refocus if your subject moves for as long as you hold down the shutter button halfway. Focus isn't locked until you press the button down all the way to take the picture.

What back-button focus does is *decouple* or separate the two actions. You can retain the exposure lock feature when the shutter is pressed halfway, but assign autofocus to a different button. So, in practice, you can press the shutter button halfway, locking exposure, and reframe the image if you like (perhaps you're photographing a backlit subject and want to lock in exposure on the foreground, and then reframe to include a very bright background as well).

But, in this same scenario, you *don't* want autofocus locked at the same time. Indeed, you may not want to start AF until you're good and ready, say, at a sports venue as you wait for a ballplayer to streak into view in your viewfinder. With back-button focus, you can lock exposure on the spot where you expect the athlete to be, and activate AF at the moment your subject appears by pressing the AF-ON button. That's where the learning of new habits and mind-finger coordination comes in. You need to learn which back-button focus techniques work for you, and when to use them.

Back-button focus lets you avoid the need to switch from One-Shot to Servo AF when your subject begins moving unexpectedly. You retain complete control. It's great for sports photography when you want to activate autofocus precisely based on the action in front of you. It also works for static shots. You can press and release your designated focus button, and then take a series of shots using the same focus point. Focus will not change until you once again press your defined back button. (See Figure 5.16.)

Want to reframe after focus is achieved? Use back-button focus to zero in focus on that location, then reframe. Focus will not change. Don't want to miss an important shot at a wedding on a photojournalism assignment? If you're set to *focus-priority* your camera may delay taking a picture until the focus is optimum; in *release-priority* there may still be a slight delay. With back-button focus you can focus first, and wait until the decisive moment to press the shutter release and take your picture. The EOS RP will respond immediately and not bother with focusing at all.

Here are some things to consider when using back-button focus:

- **Great for unwanted subjects in action photography.** Earlier in this chapter I talked about using the tracking sensitivity settings to minimize the camera locking onto an intervening object (in football, that might be a yard line marker, another player, or a ref) during an action shot. With back-button focus, you can not only initiate focus whenever you want, you can *pause* focus temporarily by releasing the back button and then pressing it again when the intervening subject is no longer in the frame.

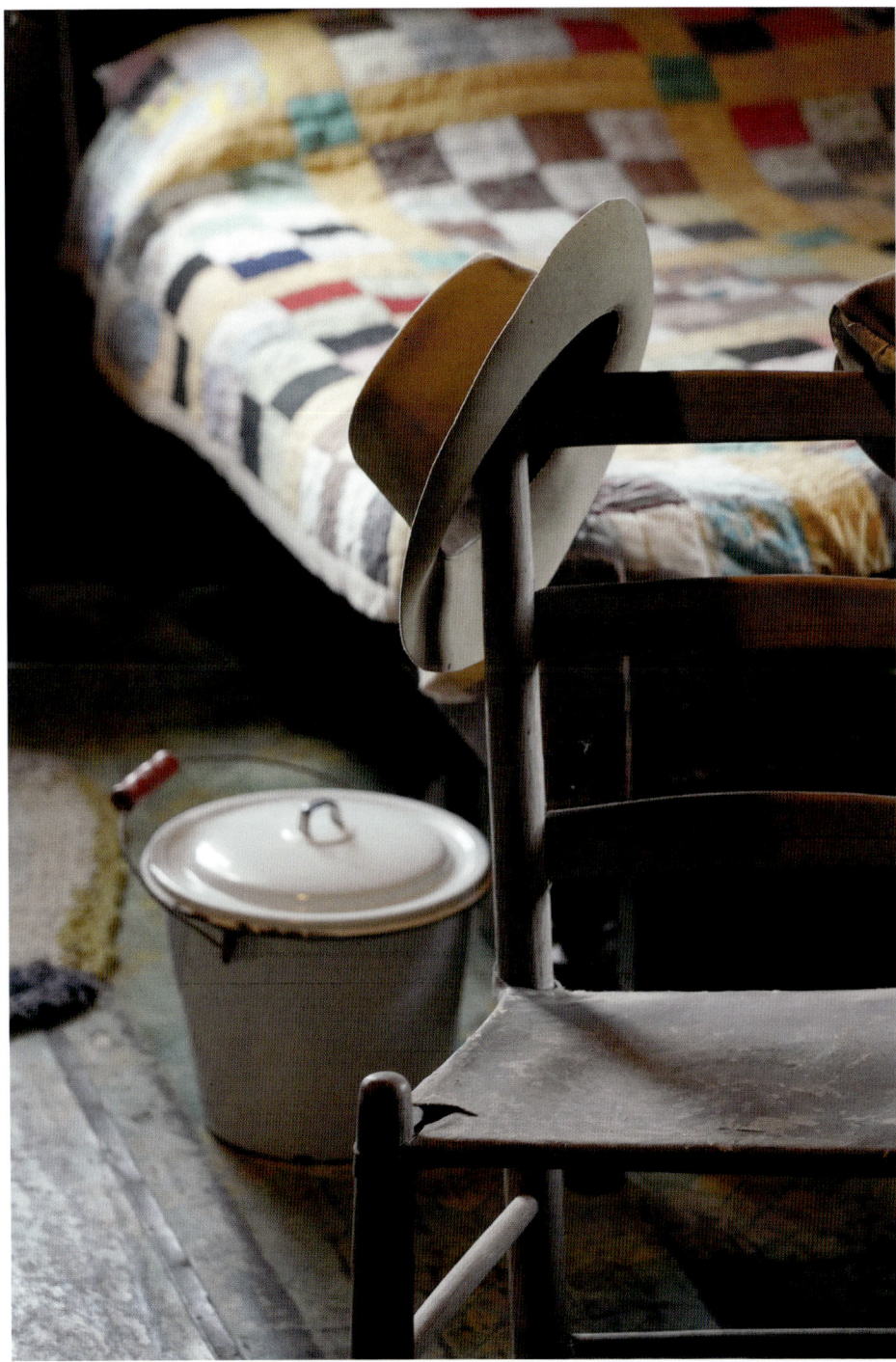

Figure 5.16 Lock your exposure for the room, but lock focus only when you've decided on your main subject.

■ **Exact timing of focus.** Sports and action photographers also like the ability of back-button focus to allow them to focus at a decisive moment. Perhaps you're shooting a scenic waterscape when a playful dolphin suddenly begins a series of leaps a few yards from you. You can lock exposure with a half-press of the shutter button, and then frame the area in which you think the dolphin may next appear. At the right moment, press the back button to focus on the creature quickly and the shutter button to take the picture. (See Figure 5.17.) Or, you may be shooting a football game and following the action through the viewfinder, seeking a subject to capture. You decide to capture an image of a wide receiver reaching out for the ball. Frame the receiver in the viewfinder and press the back button to lock in focus, and then press the shutter release all the way to actually take the picture.

■ **Reframing.** As I mentioned earlier, you can lock focus with the back button, then release the button and reframe before taking the picture with the shutter release button. The camera will not refocus when the shutter button is pressed.

■ **Fine-tuning focus.** Many Canon lenses allow you to fine-tune focus even when the lens is set for autofocus. With those lenses, you can go ahead and initiate autofocus using the back button; then, if you want to fine-tune focus manually, release the button and rotate the focusing ring. The camera will not refocus when you press the shutter release button, and you won't have to switch the lens' AF/MF switch to Manual. This technique works particularly well for macro photography, which often benefits from precise manual focusing on the exact plane that you want to be sharpest. Go ahead and pre-focus using the autofocus feature, then release the back button and manually set your focus. It's faster than focusing entirely in manual focus mode.

Activating Back-Button Focus

The EOS RP implements back-button focus slightly differently from some other cameras, because it doesn't allow you to assign AF Start (only) to a button like the AF-ON button. When you press AF-ON, the camera focuses *and* meters. But there's a way to work around that.

The easiest way to activate back-button focus is to make a quick trip to the Customize Buttons entry in the Custom Functions III-5 menu, as described in Chapter 14. Once you've activated this feature, you press the shutter release down halfway to lock exposure, and the AF-ON button when you're ready to autofocus. Here's what you need to do:

1. **Redefine the shutter release button.** In Customize Buttons, highlight the Shutter Button entry, as shown at left in Figure 5.18. Press SET.

2. **Choose Metering Start.** When selected, pressing the shutter release button down all the way meters and locks exposure, but *not* autofocus as the shutter is tripped. Press SET to confirm. (See Figure 5.18, right.)

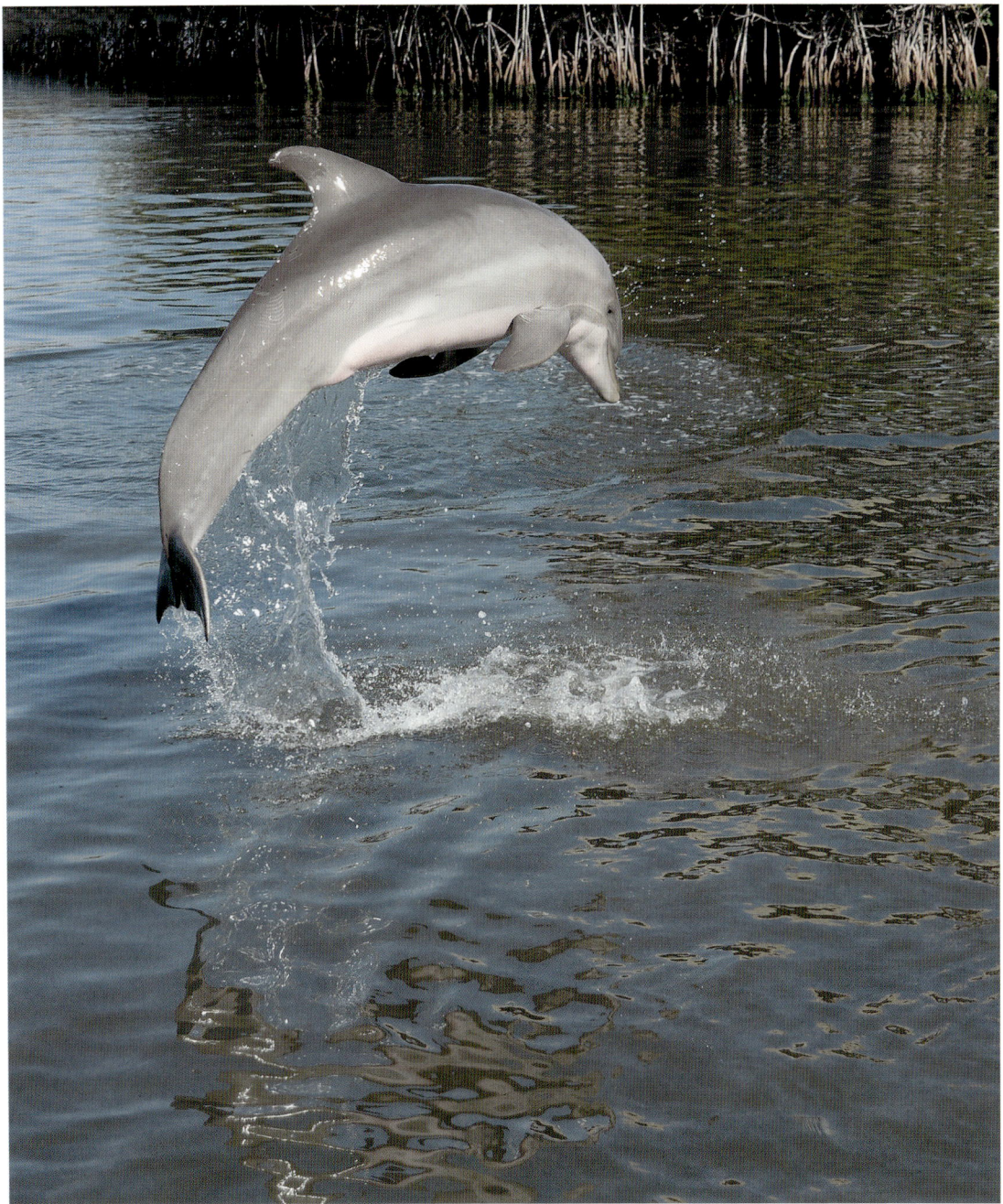

Figure 5.17 Back-button focus is great for timing the exact moment of focus.

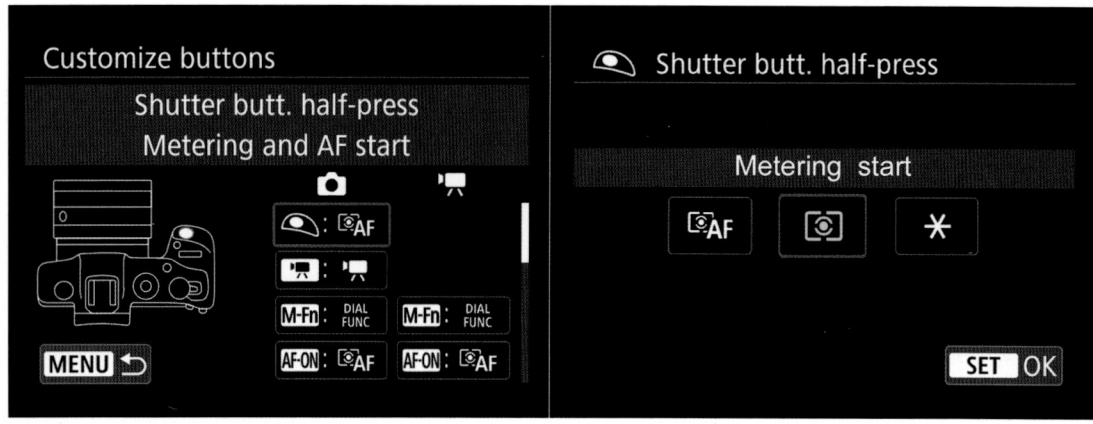

Figure 5.18   Activating back-button focus.

3. **Select Back Button.** The default value for the AF-ON button works fine. When you press the AF-ON button, autofocus will initiate *and* metering will be performed, continuously updating both until you release the button. When the shutter release button is pressed, metering will take place and the exposure will be locked. If you want to lock exposure before the picture is taken, press the AE Lock (*) button.

   Alternatively, you can define some other button with the Metering and AF Start function and use that for back-button focus instead, if you find it more comfortable to access with your thumb.

4. **Turn off continuous focus.** You'll be using One-Shot AF with back-button focus, and you'll also want to turn off Continuous AF in the AF 1 menu.

6

Advanced Techniques, Wi-Fi, and GPS

You can happily spend your entire shooting career using the techniques and features already explained in this book. Great exposures, sharp pictures, and creative compositions are all you really need to produce great shot after great shot. But, those with enough interest in getting the most out of their Canon EOS RP who buy this book probably will be interested in going beyond those basics to explore some of the more advanced techniques and capabilities of the camera. Capturing the briefest instant of time, transforming common scenes into the unusual with lengthy time exposures, and working with new tools like GPS and Wi-Fi are all tempting avenues for exploration. So, in this chapter, I'm going to offer longer discussions of some of the more advanced techniques and capabilities that I like to put to work.

Continuous Shooting

The Canon EOS RP's continuous shooting mode reminds me how far digital photography has brought us. The first accessory I purchased when I worked as a sports photographer many years ago was a motor drive for my film SLR. It enabled me to snap off a series of shots in rapid succession, which came in very handy when a fullback broke through the line and headed for the end zone. Even a seasoned action photographer can miss the decisive instant when a crucial block is made, or a baseball superstar's bat shatters and pieces of cork fly out. Continuous shooting simplifies taking a series of pictures, either to ensure that one has more or less the exact moment you want to capture or to capture a sequence that is interesting as a collection of successive images.

The EOS RP's "motor drive" capabilities are, in many ways, much superior to what you get with a film camera. For one thing, a motor-driven film camera can eat up film at an incredible pace, which is why many of them are used with cassettes that hold hundreds of feet of film stock. At three frames per second (typical of film cameras), a short burst of a few seconds can burn up as much as half of an ordinary 36-exposure roll of film. Digital cameras, in contrast, have reusable "film," so if you waste a few dozen shots on non-decisive moments, you can erase them and shoot more. Save only the best shots, like the series shown in Figure 6.1.

To use the EOS RP's continuous shooting mode, press the Q button and navigate to the Drive icon, which is the third from the top in the left column. You can also access Drive mode from the M-Fn button's Dial Functions; press the button and rotate the QCD until Drive mode is highlighted, then rotate the Main Dial to select. In both cases, you can choose High-speed continuous shooting (up to 5 frames per second) or Low-speed continuous shooting (approximately 2.6 fps).

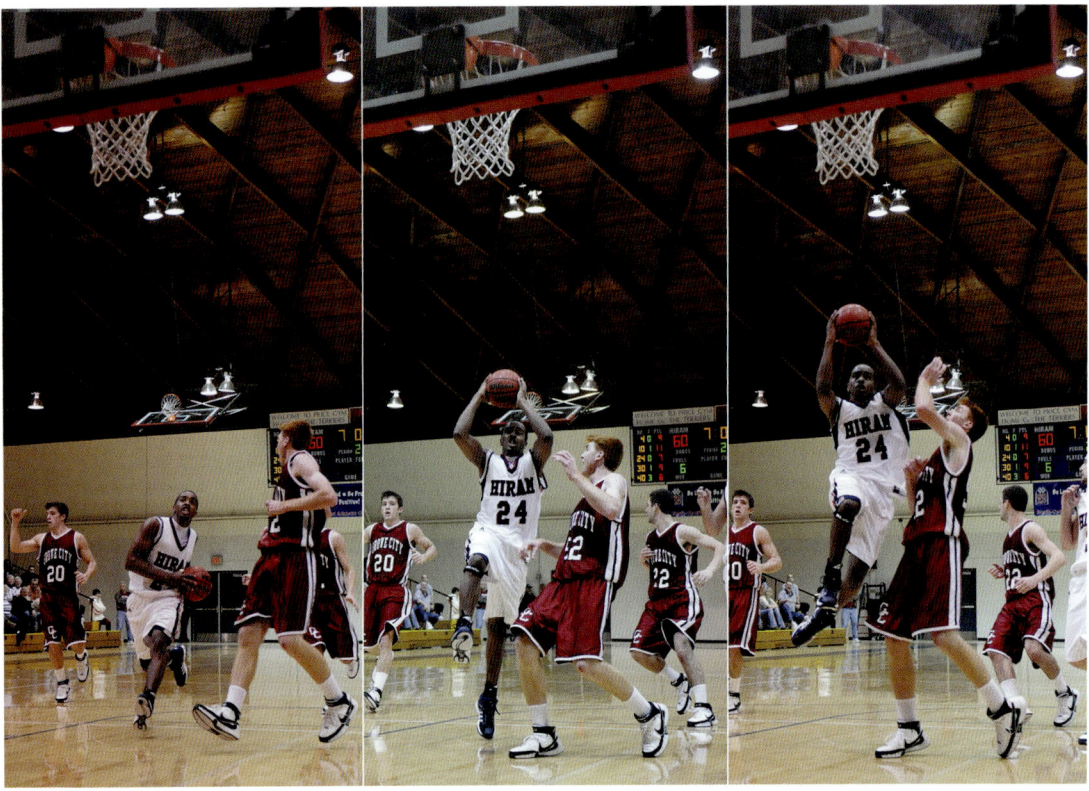

Figure 6.1 Continuous shooting allows you to capture an entire sequence of exciting moments as they unfold.

Actual frames per second in either mode may be reduced when flicker control is enabled, you've activated Servo AF, or when you're working with electronic flash. Other factors can come into play when shooting in high-speed mode, which is also affected by many shooting settings, including shutter speed, aperture, autofocus mode, silent live view shooting, or even the type of lens you are using. A cold or nearly dead battery can also reduce shooting speeds. With Servo AF, you may get only 4 fps; with flash, just 2.3 fps.

When you partially depress the shutter button, a number representing the maximum number of shots you can take at the current quality settings is displayed. In the viewfinder, that number is located to the left of the battery status indicator at lower right, immediately above the Possible Shots value. On the LCD screen, the maximum burst is located to the immediate right of the Possible Shots indicator at upper left.

The display shows a maximum of 99 shots remaining; it's possible that the camera can take more than that, so the 99 will remain lit until the actual number remaining drops below that value. When the internal buffer is full, a "BUSY" indicator will be shown. When the EOS RP's internal buffer fills, the camera will stop capturing images until enough pictures have been written to the memory card to allow shooting to resume. As you might expect, the number of continuous shots you can fire off before that happens varies with the format you choose and the write speed of your card.

The reason the size of your bursts is limited by the buffer is that continuous images are first shuttled into the EOS RP's internal memory, then doled out to the memory card as quickly as they can be written to the card. Technically, the EOS RP takes the RAW data received from the digital image processor and converts it to the output format you've selected—either JPG or CR3 (RAW), or both—and deposits it in the buffer ready to store on the card.

This internal "smart" buffer can suck up photos much more quickly than the memory card and, indeed, some memory cards are significantly faster or slower than others. You'll get the best results when using a shutter speed of 1/500th second, the widest opening of the lens, One-Shot autofocus, and when image stabilization is turned off. However, when One-Shot AF is active, the EOS RP will focus only once at the beginning of the sequence, and then use that focus setting for the rest of the shots in the burst. If your subject is moving, you can use Servo AF instead, at a slightly slower continuous frame rate.

Setting High ISO Speed Noise Reduction to High also limits the length of your continuous burst. You'll also see a decrease if lens aberration correction is active, or you have the camera set to do white balance bracketing. (In such cases, the EOS RP stores multiple copies of each image snapped, slowing down the burst rate.) Anti-flicker shooting and Dual Pixel RAW also reduce the continuous shooting speed. While you can use flash in continuous mode, the camera will wait for the flash to recycle between shots, slowing down the continuous shooting rate.

BURSTS NOT JUST FOR ACTION

I often use continuous shooting mode even when I'm not busy shooting action. As I've mentioned before, bursts make sense when you're shooting HDR or bracketing. But here's a technique you might not have thought of—continuous shooting can give you sharper images!

When I'm photographing concerts, I enjoy greater mobility by not using a monopod (and a tripod would be even more of a ball-and-chain, even if not forbidden by the venue). I'm generally shooting at around 1/180th second, which is usually fast enough to eliminate blur from the performers' motion. IS has no effect on stopping *their* movement, of course, and it does a fairly good job of eliminating camera/photographer shake. However, I invariably find that if I shoot in continuous, one of the middle frames in a sequence will be sharpest. Even the most seasoned photographer will add a little bump to the camera when they squeeze (not stab) the shutter release.

More Exposure Options

In Chapter 4, you learned techniques for getting the *right* exposure, but I haven't explained all your exposure options just yet. You'll want to know about the *kind* of exposure settings that are available to you with the Canon EOS RP. There are options that let you control when the exposure is made, or even how to make an exposure that's out of the ordinary in terms of length (time or bulb exposures). The sections that follow explain your camera's special exposure features, and even discuss a few it does not have (and why it doesn't).

A Tiny Slice of Time

Exposures that seem impossibly brief can reveal a world we didn't know existed. In the 1930s, Dr. Harold Edgerton, a professor of electrical engineering at MIT, pioneered high-speed photography using a repeating electronic flash unit he patented called the *stroboscope*. As the inventor of the electronic flash, he popularized its use to freeze objects in motion, and you've probably seen his photographs of bullets piercing balloons and drops of milk forming a coronet-shaped splash.

Electronic flash freezes action by virtue of its extremely short duration—as brief as 1/50,000th second or less. You can read more about using electronic flash to stop action in Chapter 9.

Of course, the EOS RP is fully capable of immobilizing all but the fastest movement using only its shutter speeds, which range all the way up to 1/4000th second. Indeed, you'll rarely have need for such a brief shutter speed in ordinary shooting. If you wanted to use an aperture of f/2.8 at ISO 100 outdoors in bright sunlight, for some reason, a shutter speed of 1/4000th second would more than do the job. You'd need a faster shutter speed only if you moved the ISO setting to a higher sensitivity (but why would you do that?). Under less than full sunlight, 1/4000th second is more than fast enough for any conditions you're likely to encounter.

Most sports action can be frozen at 1/2000th second or slower, and for many sports a slower shutter speed is actually preferable—for example, to allow the wheels of a racing automobile or motorcycle, or the propeller on a classic aircraft to blur realistically.

But if you want to do some exotic action-freezing photography without resorting to electronic flash, the EOS RP's top shutter speed is at your disposal. Here are some things to think about when exploring this type of high-speed photography:

- **You'll need a lot of light.** High shutter speeds cut very fine slices of time and sharply reduce the amount of illumination that reaches your sensor. To use 1/4000th second at an aperture of f/6.3, you'd need an ISO setting of 800—even in full daylight. To use an f/stop smaller than f/6.3 or an ISO setting lower than 800, you'd need *more* light than full daylight provides. (That's why electronic flash units work so well for high-speed photography when used as the sole illumination; they provide both the effect of a brief shutter speed and the high levels of illumination needed.)

- **Don't combine high shutter speeds with electronic flash.** You might be tempted to use an electronic flash with a high shutter speed. Perhaps you want to stop some action in daylight with a brief shutter speed and use electronic flash only as supplemental illumination to fill in the shadows. Unfortunately, under most conditions you can't use flash in subdued illumination with your EOS RP at any shutter speed faster than 1/180th second. That's the fastest speed at which the camera's focal plane shutter is fully open: at shorter speeds, the flash will expose only the small portion of the sensor exposed by the opening in the shutter during its duration. (Check out "Avoiding Sync Speed Problems" in Chapter 9 if you want to see how you *can* use shutter speeds shorter than 1/180th second with certain Canon Speedlites, albeit at much-reduced effective power levels.)

Working with Short Exposures

You can have a lot of fun exploring the kinds of pictures you can take using very brief exposure times, whether you decide to take advantage of the action-stopping capabilities of your external electronic flash or work with the Canon EOS RP's faster shutter speeds. Here are a few ideas to get you started:

- **Take revealing images.** Fast shutter speeds can help you reveal the real subject behind the façade, by freezing constant motion to capture an enlightening moment in time. Legendary fashion/portrait photographer Philippe Halsman used leaping photos of famous people, such as the Duke and Duchess of Windsor, Richard Nixon, and Salvador Dali to illuminate their real selves. Halsman said, "*When you ask a person to jump, his attention is mostly directed toward the act of jumping and the mask falls so that the real person appears.*" Try some high-speed portraits of people you know in motion to see how they appear when concentrating on something other than the portrait. (See Figure 6.2.)

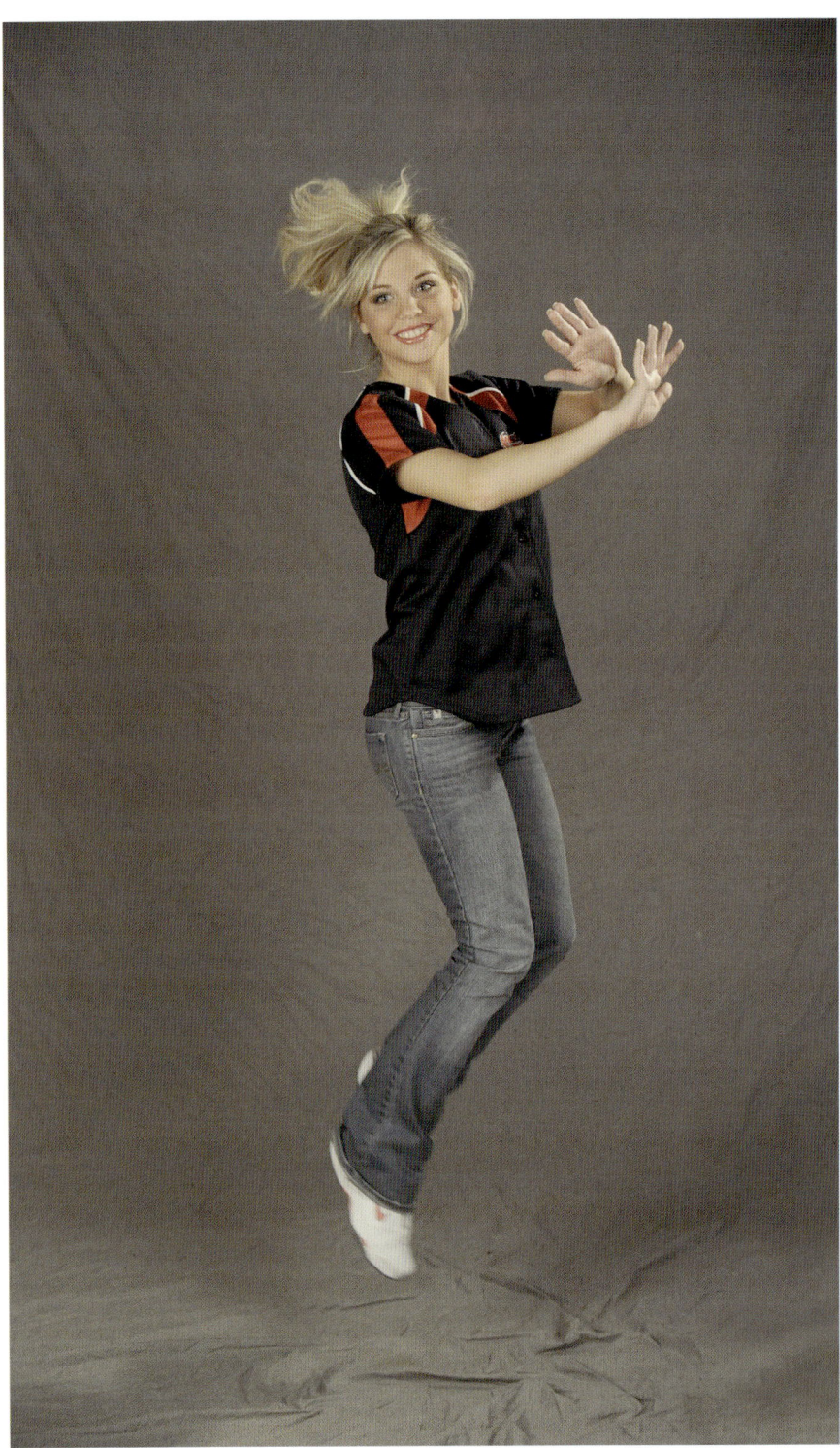

Figure 6.2
When your subjects leap, the real person inside emerges.

■ **Create unreal images.** High-speed photography can also produce photographs that show your subjects in ways that are quite unreal. A helicopter in mid-air with its rotors frozen makes for an unusual picture. Figure 6.3 shows a pair of pictures. At top, a shutter speed of 1/1000th second virtually stopped the rotation of the chopper's rotors, while the bottom image, shot at 1/200th second, provides a more realistic view of the blurry blades as they appeared to the eye.

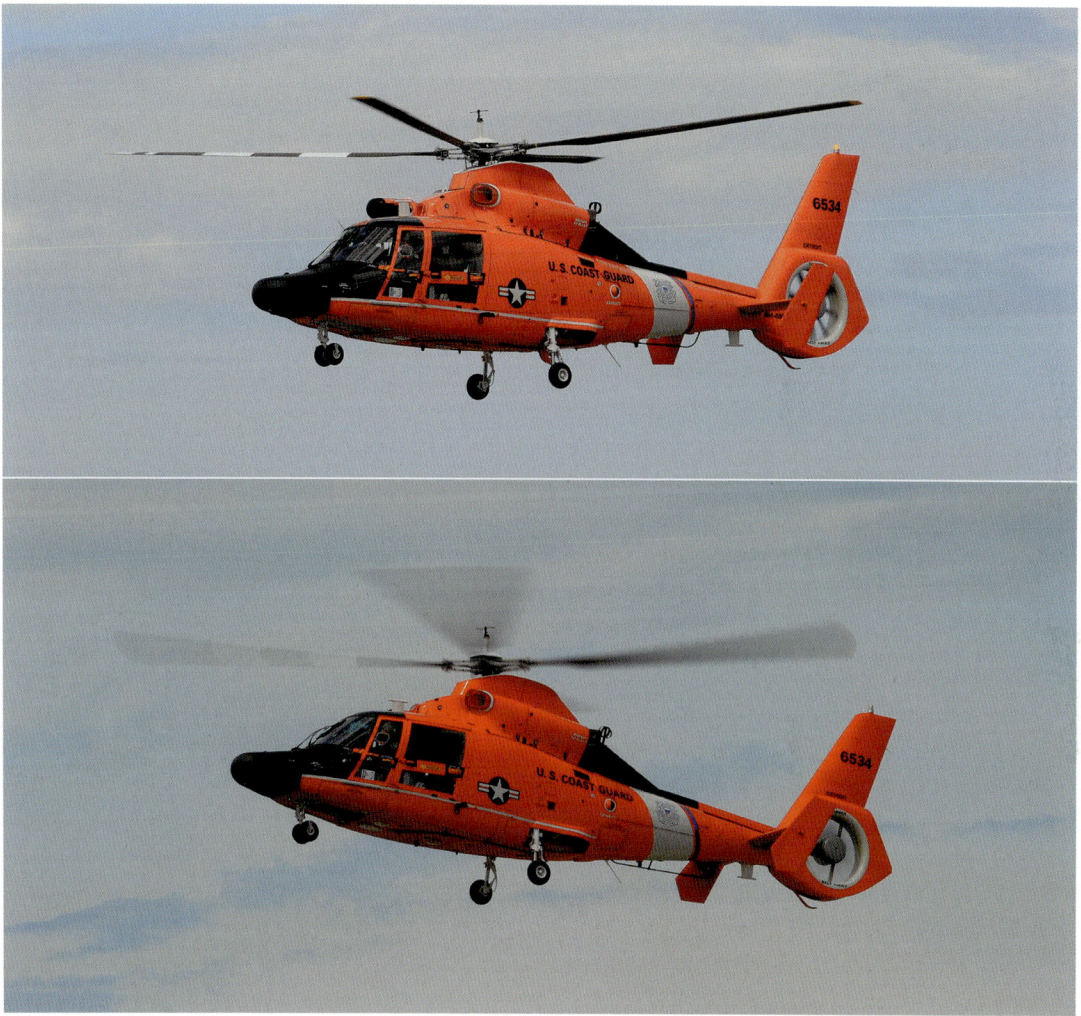

Figure 6.3 Top: the chopper's blades are frozen at 1/1000th second; bottom: a more realistic blurry rendition at 1/200th second shutter speed.

■ **Capture unseen perspectives.** Some things are *never* seen in real life, except when viewed in a stop-action photograph. Edgerton's balloon bursts were only a starting point. Freeze a hummingbird in flight for a view of wings that never seem to stop. Or, capture the splashes as liquid falls into a bowl, as shown in Figure 6.4. No electronic flash was required for this image (and wouldn't have illuminated the water in the bowl as evenly). Instead, a clutch of high-intensity lamps and an ISO setting of 1600 allowed the camera to capture this image at 1/2000th second.

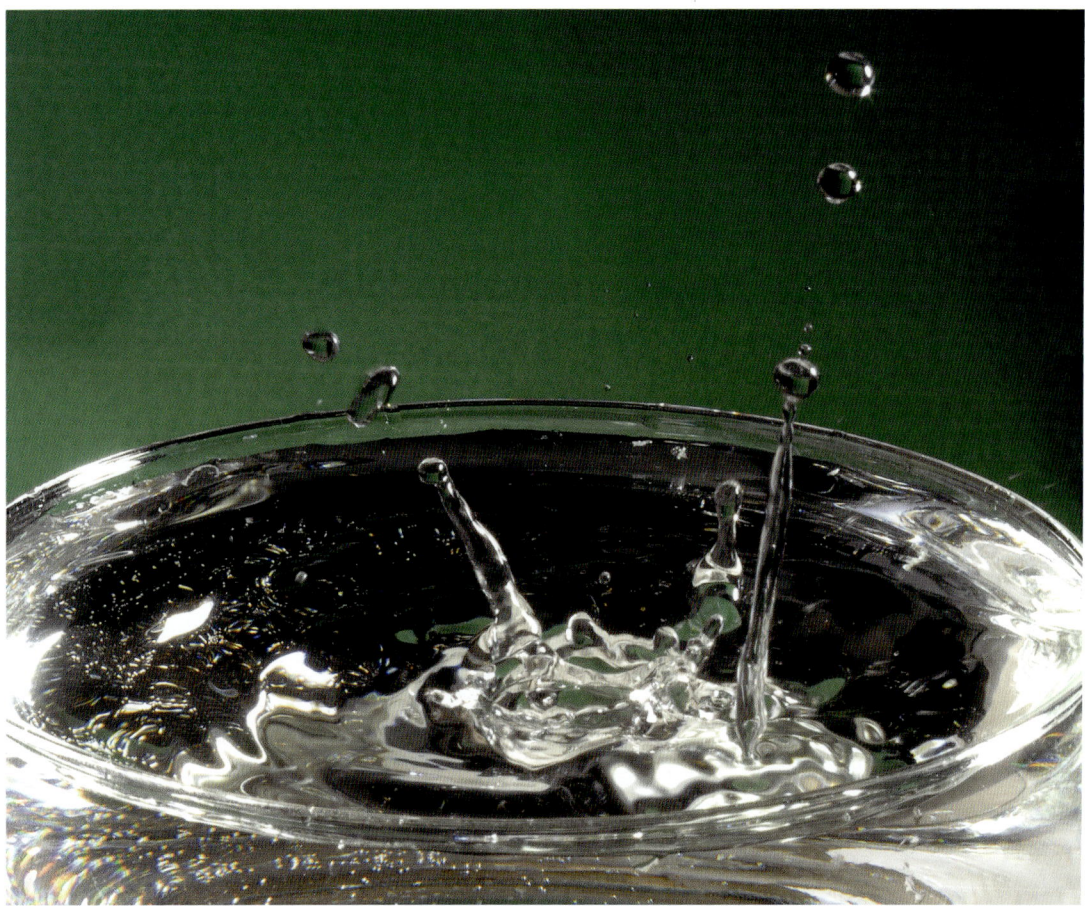

Figure 6.4 A large amount of artificial illumination and an ISO 1600 sensitivity setting allowed capturing this shot at 1/2000th second without use of an electronic flash.

■ **Vanquish camera shake and gain new angles.** Here's an idea I mentioned earlier in this chapter that's so obvious it isn't always explored to its fullest extent. A high enough shutter speed can free you from the tyranny of a tripod, making it easier to capture new angles, or to shoot quickly while moving around, especially with longer lenses. I tend to use a monopod or tripod for almost everything when I'm not using an image-stabilized lens, and I end up missing some shots because of a reluctance to adjust my camera support to get a higher, lower, or different angle. If you have enough light and can use an f/stop wide enough to permit a high shutter speed, you'll find a new freedom to choose your shots. I have a favored 500mm lens that I use for sports and wildlife photography, almost invariably with a tripod, as I don't find the "reciprocal of the focal length" rule particularly helpful in most cases. (I would *not* hand-hold this hefty lens with a 1/500th second shutter speed under most circumstances.) However, at 1/2000th second or faster, and with a sufficiently high ISO setting (I recommend ISO 800–1600) to allow such a speed, it's entirely possible for a steady hand to use this lens without a tripod or monopod's extra support, and I've found that my whole approach to shooting animals and other elusive subjects changes in high-speed mode.

Long Exposures

Longer exposures are a doorway into another world, showing us how even familiar scenes can look much different when photographed over periods measured in seconds. At night, long exposures produce streaks of light from moving, illuminated subjects like automobiles or amusement park rides. Extra-long exposures of seemingly pitch-dark subjects can reveal interesting views using light levels barely bright enough to see by. At any time of day, including daytime (in which case you'll often need the help of neutral-density filters, which reduce the amount of light passing through the lens, to make the long exposure practical), long exposures can cause moving objects to vanish entirely, because they don't remain stationary long enough to register in a photograph.

Three Ways to Take Long Exposures

There are actually three common types of lengthy exposures: *timed exposures*, *bulb exposures*, and *time exposures*. The EOS RP offers all three. Because of the length of the exposure, all of the following techniques should be used with a tripod to hold the camera steady.

■ **Timed exposures.** These are long exposures from 1 second to 30 seconds, measured by the camera itself. To take a picture in this range, simply use Manual or Tv modes and use the Main Dial to set the shutter speed to the length of time you want, choosing from preset speeds of 1.0, 1.5, 2.0, 3.0, 4.0, 6.0, 8.0, 10.0, 15.0, 20.0, or 30.0 seconds (if you've specified 1/2-stop increments for exposure adjustments), or 1.0, 1.3, 1.6, 2.0, 2.5, 3.2, 4.0, 5.0, 6.0, 8.0, 10.0, 13.0, 15.0, 20.0, 25.0, and 30.0 seconds (if you're using 1/3-stop increments). The advantage of timed exposures is that the camera does all the calculating for you. There's no need for a stopwatch. If you review your image on the LCD and decide to try again with the exposure doubled or halved, you can dial in the correct exposure with precision. The disadvantage of timed exposures is that you can't take a photo for longer than 30 seconds.

■ **Bulb exposures.** This type of exposure is so-called because in the olden days the photographer squeezed and held an air bulb attached to a tube that provided the force necessary to keep the shutter open. Traditionally, a bulb exposure is one that lasts as long as the shutter release button is pressed; when you release the button, the exposure ends. To make a bulb exposure with the EOS RP, set the camera on B using the Mode Dial. Then, press the shutter to start the exposure, and press it again to close the shutter.

■ **Time exposures.** This is a setting found on some cameras to produce longer exposures. With the EOS RP, it's actually an enhancement of the Bulb exposure feature. With the camera's mode set to Bulb, locate the Bulb Timer setting in the Shooting 6 menu. Press SET, and in the screen that pops up, highlight Enable. Press INFO, and a screen appears that will allow you to set an exposure time of up to 99 hours, 59 minutes, and 59 seconds. You'll rarely need extra-long exposures (unless you're shooting continuous star trails), but many exposures longer than 30 seconds are quite useful. For example, if many star photographers shoot multiple one-minute exposures (any longer than that, and the star pinpoints become blurs) and then merge them together to get a different kind of sky photograph.

When using this type of Bulb exposure, you can press the shutter release button, go off for a few minutes, and come back to take your next shot (assuming your camera is still there). The disadvantages of this mode are exposures must be timed manually, and with shorter exposures, it's possible for the vibration of manually opening and closing the shutter to register in the photo. For longer exposures, the period of vibration is relatively brief and not usually a problem—and there is always the release cable option to eliminate photographer-caused camera shake entirely.

Working with Long Exposures

Because the EOS RP produces such good images at longer exposures, and there are so many creative things you can do with long-exposure techniques, you'll want to do some experimenting. Get yourself a tripod or another firm support and take some test shots with long exposure noise reduction both enabled and disabled using the entry in the Shooting 5 menu, as explained in Chapter 11 (to see whether you prefer low noise or high detail), and get started. Here are some things to try:

■ **Make people invisible.** One very cool thing about long exposures is that objects that move rapidly enough won't register at all in a photograph, while the subjects that remain stationary are portrayed in the normal way. That makes it easy to produce people-free landscape photos and architectural photos at night or, even, in full daylight if you use a neutral-density filter (or two or three) to allow an exposure of at least a few seconds. At ISO 100, f/22, and a pair of 8X (three-stop) neutral-density filters, you can use exposures of nearly two seconds; overcast days and/or more neutral-density filtration would work even better if daylight people-vanishing is your goal. They'll have to be walking *very* briskly and across the field of view (rather than directly toward the camera) for this to work. At night, it's much easier to achieve this effect with the 20- to 30-second exposures that are possible, as you can see in Figure 6.5.

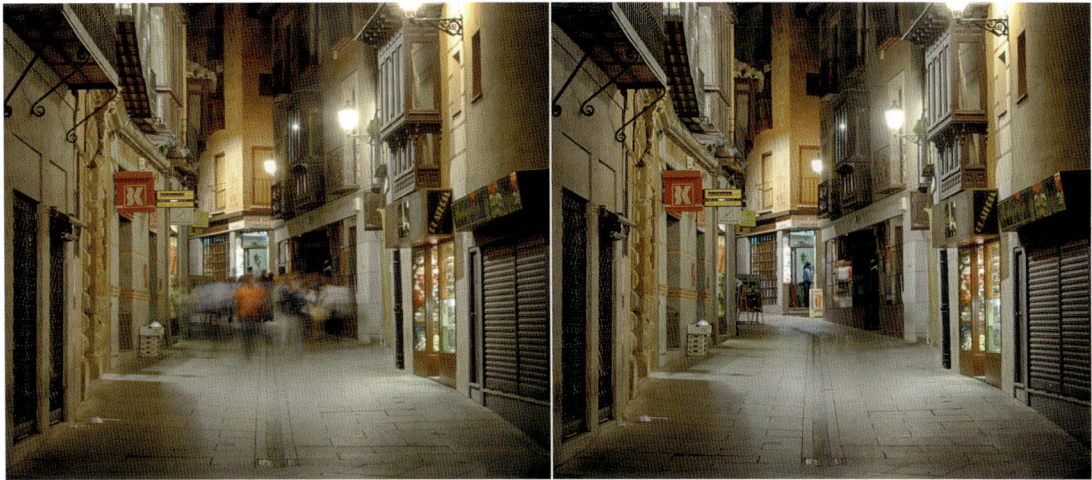

Figure 6.5 This alleyway is thronged with people, as you can see in this two-second exposure using only the available illumination (left). With the camera still on a tripod, a 30-second exposure rendered the passersby almost invisible (right).

■ **Create streaks.** If you aren't shooting for total invisibility, long exposures with the camera on a tripod or monopod can produce some interesting streaky effects, as you can see in Figure 6.6. You don't need to limit yourself to indoor photography, however. Even a single 8X ND filter will let you shoot at f/22 and 1/6th second in full daylight at ISO 100.

Figure 6.6
These dancers produced a swirl of movement during the 1/8th second exposure.

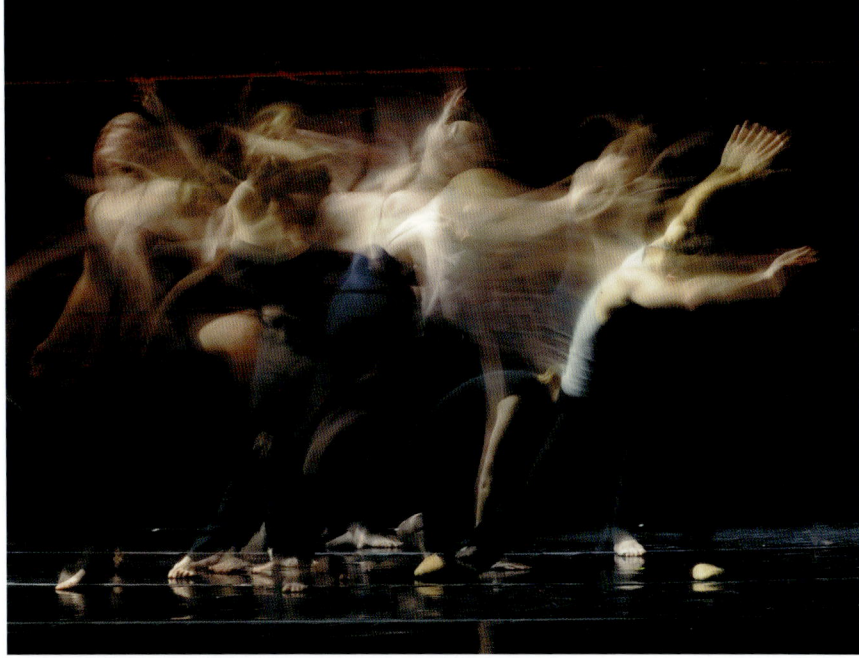

- **Produce light trails.** At night, car headlights and taillights and other moving sources of illumination can generate interesting light trails. Your camera doesn't even need to be mounted on a tripod; hand-holding the EOS RP for longer exposures adds movement and patterns to your trails. If you're shooting fireworks (preferably with a tripod), a longer exposure of several seconds may allow you to combine several bursts into one picture. Or, you can record the movement of a Ferris wheel, as shown in Figure 6.7.

- **Blur waterfalls, etc.** You'll find that waterfalls and other sources of moving liquid produce a special type of long exposure blur, because the water merges into a fantasy-like veil that looks different at different exposure times, and with different waterfalls. Cascades with turbulent flow produce a rougher look at a given longer exposure than falls that flow smoothly. Although blurred waterfalls have become almost a cliché, there are still plenty of variations for a creative photographer to explore, as you can see in Figure 6.8.

- **Show total darkness in new ways.** Even on the darkest nights, there is enough starlight or glow from distant illumination sources to see by, and, if you use a long exposure, there is enough light to take a picture, too. Figure 6.9 shows San Juan, Puerto Rico late at night.

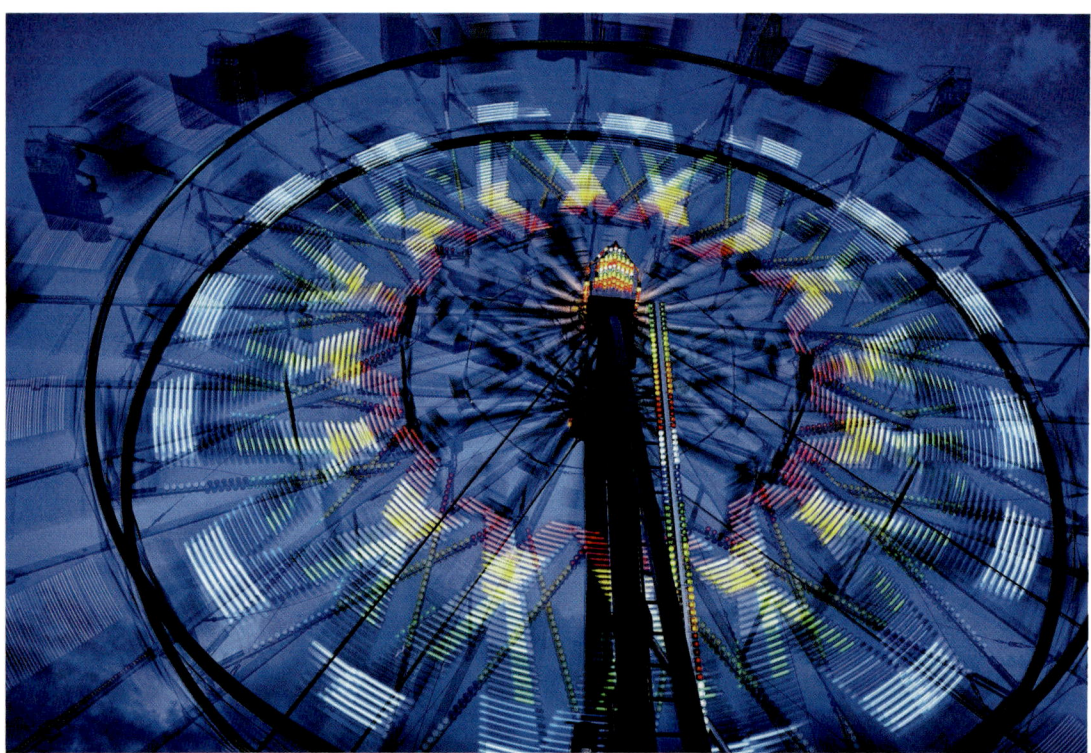

Figure 6.7 A long exposure of several seconds allows capturing the movement of this Ferris wheel.

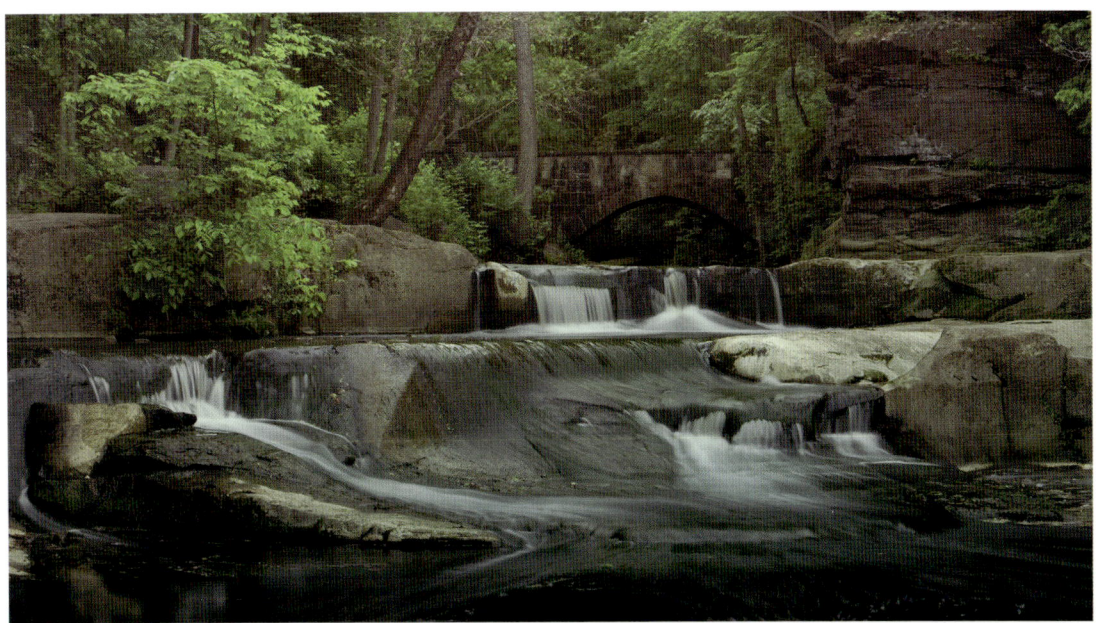

Figure 6.8 A 1/4-second exposure blurred the falling water.

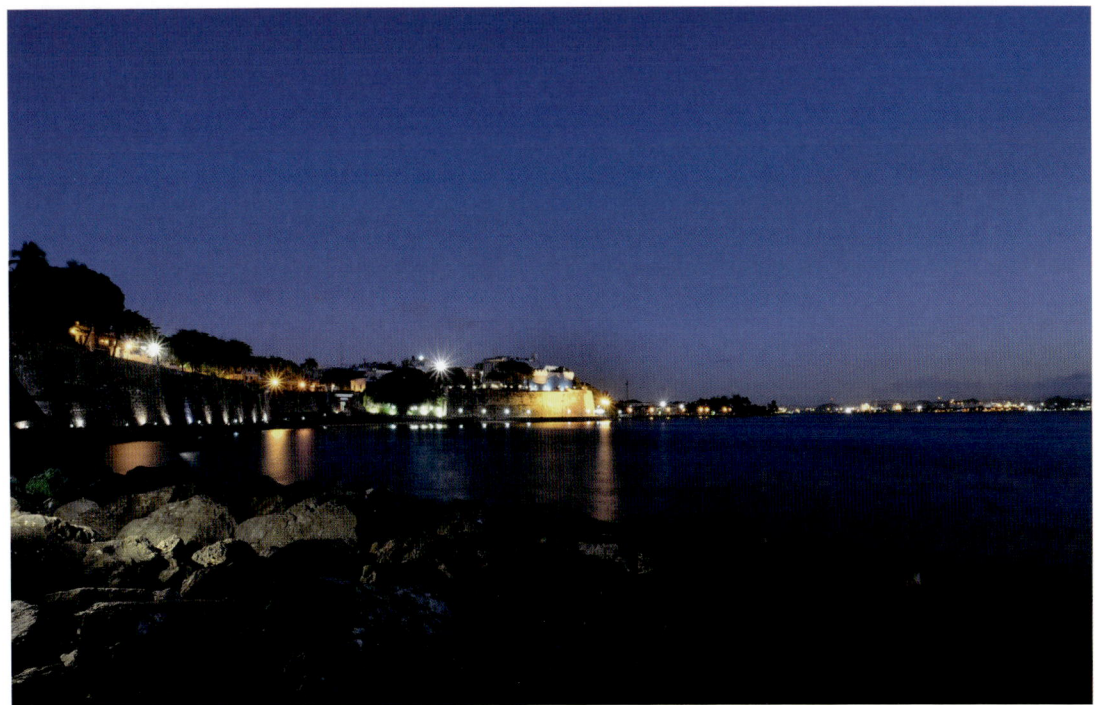

Figure 6.9 A 20-second exposure revealed this view of San Juan, Puerto Rico.

Delayed Exposures

Sometimes it's desirable to have a delay of some sort before a picture is actually taken. Perhaps you'd like to get in the picture yourself, and would appreciate it if the camera waited 10 seconds after you press the shutter release to actually take the picture. Maybe you want to give a tripod-mounted camera time to settle down and damp any residual vibration after the release is pressed to improve sharpness for an exposure with a relatively slow shutter speed. It's possible you want to explore the world of time-lapse photography. The next sections present your delayed exposure options.

Self-Timer

The EOS RP has a built-in self-timer with 10-second and 2-second delays. Activate the timer by pressing the DRIVE-AF button and rotating the QCD to select the drive modes. Press the shutter release button halfway to lock in focus on your subjects (if you're taking a self-portrait, focus on an object at a similar distance and use focus lock). When you're ready to take the photo, continue pressing the shutter release the rest of the way. The lamp on the front of the camera will blink slowly for eight seconds (when using the 10-second timer) and the beeper will chirp (if you haven't disabled it in the Shooting menu, as described in Chapter 11). During the final two seconds, the beeper sounds more rapidly and the lamp remains on until the picture is taken.

This is something you might want to do if you're shooting close-ups, landscapes, or other types of pictures using the self-timer, to trip the shutter in the most vibration-free way possible. Forget to bring along your tripod, but still want to take a close-up picture with a precise focus setting? Set your digital camera to the self-timer function, then put the camera on any reasonably steady support, such as a fence post or a rock. When you're ready to take the picture, press the shutter release. The camera might teeter back and forth for a second or two, but it will settle back to its original position before the self-timer activates the shutter. The self-timer remains active until you turn it off—even if you power down the EOS RP, so remember to turn it off when finished.

Interval/Time Lapse Photography

The EOS RP is capable of both time-lapse video (summoned from the Movie Shooting 2 menu) and interval photography (for still pictures, available from the Shooting 6 menu). Who hasn't marveled at interval stills, shot moments or minutes apart to document an event, or wasn't enrapt by a time-lapse movie of a flower opening, a series of shots of the moon marching across the sky, or one of those extreme interval or time-lapse photography productions showing something that takes a very, very long time, such as a building under construction.

You probably won't be shooting such construction shots, unless you have a spare EOS RP you don't need for a few months (or are willing to go through the rigmarole of figuring out how to set up your camera in precisely the same position using the same lens settings to shoot a series of pictures at intervals). However, other kinds of time-lapse photography are entirely within reach.

The EOS RP has built-in features that allow you to shoot time-lapse *movies* easily. You can also take stills at fixed intervals, using the Interval Timer setting. Before I explain how to use these features, here are a few things to keep in mind:

- **Use AC power.** If you're shooting a long sequence, consider connecting your camera to an AC adapter, as leaving the EOS RP on for long periods of time will rapidly deplete the battery. The optional Canon DC Coupler DR-E6 and AC Adapter AC-6N are perfect for this application. While shooting time-lapse movies, auto power off will not take place.

- **Disabled functions.** While capturing time-lapse movies, ISO must be ISO 6400 or slower; shooting and menu functions and playback are disabled, along with Movie Servo AF. You can't shoot time-lapse movies if digital zoom is enabled, and sound is not recorded.

- **Make sure you have enough storage space.** Unless your memory card has enough capacity to hold all the images you'll be taking, you might want to change to a higher compression rate or reduced resolution to maximize the image count.

- **Protect your camera.** If your camera will be set up for an extended period of time (longer than an hour or two), make sure it's protected from weather, earthquakes, animals, young children, innocent bystanders, and theft.

- **Vary intervals.** Experiment with different time intervals. You don't want to take pictures or frames too often or less often than necessary to capture the changes you hope to image in your movies or still series.

Time-lapse Movies

The EOS RP's time-lapse movie facility is actually a still photography mode that shoots images at intervals you specify, and then stitches them together automatically to create an MP4-format movie in Full HD (1920 × 1080) and 4K formats (3840 × 2160) at a playback rate of 30/25 fps (NTSC/ PAL). To create a time-lapse movie, just follow these steps:

1. **Switch to Movie mode.** Rotate the Mode Dial to the Movie position. Press SET and choose Movie Auto Exposure (you can also use Movie Manual Exposure, a mode I'll describe in Chapter 15). Even though time-lapse clips are compiled from a series of stills, you must be in Movie mode to access the feature. Even though individual images are still photographs, no stills are stored; the EOS RP converts them to a movie file even if you take only one shot in time-lapse mode.

2. **Navigate to the Shooting 2 (Movie) menu.** Select Time-Lapse Movie and press SET.

3. **Enable Time-Lapse.** Highlight Time-lapse at the top of the screen that appears (see Figure 6.10, upper left). Press SET.

4. **Choose Scene Type or Custom.** Your EOS RP can recommend an interval between shots and number of shots to take, depending on the type of scene you are capturing. Choose Scenes 1, 2, 3, or scroll down to choose Custom. (See Figure 6.10, upper right.) In all four cases, you can then specify the interval between shots and number of total shots captured, within the limitations described next. (See Figure 6.10, lower left.)

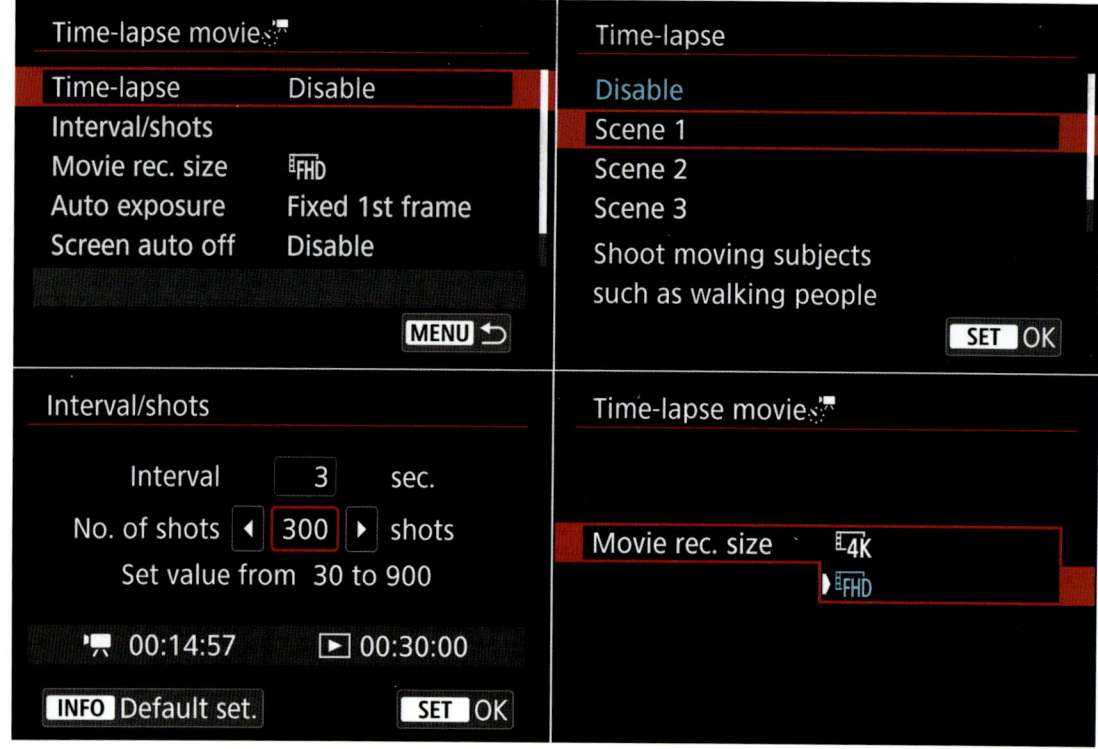

Figure 6.10 Enable/disable and check settings on these screens.

5. **Specify interval and number of shots.** The interval and shot numbers vary by type of subject selected:

   - **Scene 1.** Recommended to produce smooth sequences involving moving subjects. The default values are 3-second intervals and 300 shots (which produces a 10-second sequence that takes 14 minutes and 57 seconds to capture and is speeded up 10X from real-time during playback). However, you can select intervals from 2 to 4 seconds, and as many as 900 total shots (for a 30-second sequence). (I'm going to let you do the math henceforth.)

   - **Scene 2.** Use this to capture subjects that are moving quite slowly, such as the majestic journey of clouds across the sky. The default interval is 5 seconds for 240 shots, but you can select from 5 to 10 seconds (the latter producing more rapid apparent movement of the clouds or other subject) and from 30 to 720 individual frames.

   - **Scene 3.** This setting captures the slowest moving subjects, such as flower buds opening over a long period. The default interval is 15 seconds, and 240 total shots, but you may choose intervals from 11 to 30 seconds, and 30 to 240 shots.

   - **Custom.** Choose this for the most flexibility. You can choose intervals from 2 seconds to 60 minutes and from 2 to 3600 shots.

NOTE

You can press INFO to reset values to their defaults (for Scenes 1, 2, and 3). The total capture and playback times will be displayed at the bottom of the Time-Lapse Movie screen once you've completed your interval/shots settings.

6. **Confirm interval and number of shots.** Choose OK to confirm your choice and return to the settings screen. The total expected elapsed time will be shown. The max, available if you choose Custom and specify 60 minutes and 3600 shots, "shooting time" will be 150 days and the playback time will be an entire 2 minutes!

7. **Choose Movie Recording Size.** Highlight the entry directly under Interval/Shots and choose a Movie Recording Size, either 4K (29.97p ALL-I Ultra High Definition) or FHD (29.97p ALL-I for Full High Definition). Note that these are NTSC specifications; PAL frame rates are 25p instead, and will be specified automatically if you've selected For PAL in the Video System entry of the Set-up 3 menu.

8. **Select Exposure Setting.** Highlight Auto Exposure and press SET. You can then choose:
   - **Fixed 1st Frame.** Metering takes place and the exposure is set for the first frame, and used for all subsequent frames. You'd use this setting when you want the exposure to remain constant, even if lighting changes.
   - **Each frame.** Metering is performed for each shot in the sequence. A time-lapse movie of a city skyline from dawn to dusk will reflect the correct exposure for each stage of the day.

9. **Screen Auto Off.** Choose this setting to specify whether you want each captured image to be displayed.
   - **Disable.** The sensor image will be displayed at all times during capture, except during the moment of exposure. The screen will eventually turn off roughly 30 minutes after shooting started.
   - **Enable.** The screen turns off 10 seconds after shooting begins. This gives you a chance to monitor the first shot so you'll know the scene is framed and exposed as you intend.

10. **Specify beeper.** After setting Screen Auto Off, you can enable or disable the Beep As Image Taken feature to provide feedback that the sequence is still underway. Because the electronic shutter is used, there is no other indicator that an exposure has been made.

11. **Confirm.** When finished setting each parameter, highlight OK and press SET to confirm.

12. **Exit menu and test settings.** Press MENU to exit the menu system. A message appears on the LCD monitor advising you to make your exposure settings and press the shutter release to take a test shot. Note that you can use a full range of shutter speeds from 1/4000th to 1/30th second and if you've selected a speed slower than 1/60th second, when capture ends the camera will change to a shutter speed allowable for movie shooting.

13. **Exit setup.** When satisfied with your exposure settings, press OK to exit the set-up screen.

14. **Start time-lapse.** When ready to begin, press the Movie button to commence your time-lapse movie.

15. **Turn on screen (optional).** You can check your settings by pressing the INFO button to turn the screen on or off.

16. **Stop capture.** While the time-lapse movie is recording, you can return to the Time-lapse menu setting and switch to Disable. When time-lapse shooting ends, the settings are cleared and the EOS RP resumes normal Movie shooting mode.

Interval Timer Photography

Using the Interval Timer feature found in the Shooting 6 menu works much like time-lapse movie capture. You'll end up with a series of still photos instead of a video clip. The set-up screens for the Interval Timer are similar, but much simpler, with only two options to worry about:

- **Interval:** Choose an interval from 1 second to 99:59:59 (hours:minutes:seconds). If you're taking long exposures, the interval should be greater than the shutter speed; that is, you can't capture 30-second exposures with an interval of 20 seconds. (D'oh!) Also, be aware that the interval must be longer than the time it takes the EOS RP to save each shot to the memory card. If you're using flash, the interval should be longer than the flash recycling time.

- **Number of shots.** You can specify from 1 to 99 shots, or, if you set the number of shots to 00, the camera will continue to capture images at the set interval indefinitely until you stop the process manually.

You can combine interval timer photography with autoexposure or white balance bracketing, multiple exposures, and HDR mode if you want to enhance your still images. It's a good idea to use manual focus, because if the camera has difficulty autofocusing at any point, that shot may not be taken.

Once you've made your settings, just press the shutter release to begin capture. A TIMER indicator will blink on the display while shooting is in progress. Don't be alarmed if the EOS RP turns itself off during an interval. If Auto Power Off is enabled in the Power Saving entry of the Set-up 2 menu, the camera will go to sleep if the specified auto-power-off time has elapsed. It will turn on again about one minute before the next scheduled shot. This behavior preserves your battery power. You can disable Auto Power Off if you want to keep the camera active between shots. (You can still take photos while interval timer photography is underway and not interrupt the sequence: just press the shutter release.)

To end interval timer shooting, just turn the camera off; rotate the Mode Dial to C1, C2; or C3, or return to the menu setting and choose Disable.

Introducing Wi-Fi

Your EOS RP has built-in wireless communications capabilities that allow you to link the camera to multiple devices. The various permutations and features are complex, to the extent that Canon includes nearly 100 pages of information in the Wi-Fi manual as part of its basic EOS RP product guide. This book concentrates on still photography rather than information technology and, obviously, I can't devote 100 pages to Wi-Fi topics in this book. However, I think you'll find enough information in the following sections to get you started with the basics. You'll want to study the Canon guide for advanced networking techniques and settings.

First, here is a list of the connections you can make with the EOS RP's built-in Wi-Fi:

■ **Phones and tablets.** You can connect to a smartphone or tablet and use an app on the device to operate the camera remotely or review images on your memory card. Both Android and iOS are supported.

■ **Connect and control your camera from your computer.** The EOS Utility will allow you to connect your EOS RP to your computer over Wi-Fi and operate it remotely. The Image Transfer Utility 2 can be used to send images from the camera automatically to your computer.

■ **Print images.** If you have a PictBridge-compatible printer with wireless local area network (WLAN) features, you can print images directly from your camera.

■ **Web upload.** The free Canon iMage Gateway can be used to share your images with colleagues, family, or friends over the Internet.

I'll explain all of these in the next sections, but first you need to consider some general guidelines for the EOS RP's built-in wireless functions:

General Bluetooth/Wi-Fi Guidelines

Here are some general tips for using the EOS RP's built-in Bluetooth and Wi-Fi functions:

■ **Conserve processing power.** Wi-Fi uses some of your camera's internal CPU's processing muscle, so when the EOS RP is busy communicating with another device, give Wi-Fi top priority. Don't press the shutter release, rotate the Mode Dial, or review images with the Playback button. If you do, Wi-Fi functions may be interrupted.

■ **Some functions are disabled.** When Wi-Fi is enabled, the EOS RP cannot communicate with a computer, printer, external monitor, GPS, or other device with a direct (cable) connection, USB, or HDMI cable link. For example, if you're viewing your camera's output on a monitor using an HDMI connection, the monitor will go dark during Wi-Fi communication.

■ **No auto shutoff.** When using Wi-Fi, the camera's power-saving shutdown feature is disabled.

■ **Monitor connection status.** Wi-Fi status can be seen within the information displays on both the camera's LCD monitors. When Wi-Fi is disabled, or enabled but no connection is available, an OFF indicator is shown in both places. When a connection is available, the indicators are animated when data is being transmitted, and blink if the camera is waiting for a reconnection or there is a connection error.

Connecting to a Smartphone via Wi-Fi

When you connect your EOS RP to your smart device using Wi-Fi you can:

■ View Images on the camera on the phone, or save them to the phone.

■ Operate the camera remotely to take pictures or change camera settings using the phone.

■ Send images to the phone from the camera.

■ Establish a Wi-Fi connection through an Access point.

Connecting to a Bluetooth-compatible Smartphone

Connecting your smart device to your EOS RP is most easily done using a Bluetooth connection, which is available on virtually all smart devices introduced within the last three or four years. Make sure your phone's Bluetooth and Wi-Fi capabilities are enabled, and then just follow these steps:

1. Navigate to the Wireless Communications Settings entry at the top of the Set-up 5 menu.

2. In the Wireless Communications Settings screen that appears (see Figure 6.11, upper left), select Bluetooth Function. From the screen that appears next, select Bluetooth Function (again) and choose Smartphone from the next screen (see Figure 6.11, upper right). Press SET to confirm and MENU to exit.

3. Back at the settings screen, you can choose a new nickname or accept the default name, EOSRP. Enter using the EOS RP text-entry screen. (See Figure 6.11, lower left.) Press MENU when finished and OK to confirm.

4. Press MENU to return to the Wireless Communications Settings screen.

5. Next, choose the third entry from the top, Bluetooth Function, and select Smartphone. (See Figure 6.11, upper right.)

6. Back at the Bluetooth function screen, choose Pairing. (See Figure 6.11, lower right.)

7. At this point you can opt to install the Canon Camera Connect application, if you have not already done so. The screen shown in Figure 6.12, left appears.

   • If you have already installed Camera Connect, choose Do Not Display and proceed to the next step.

   • If you *have not* installed Camera Connect, choose either Android or iOS (depending on the operating system of your device) to display a QR code you can capture to access and install the application on your phone from the appropriate store.

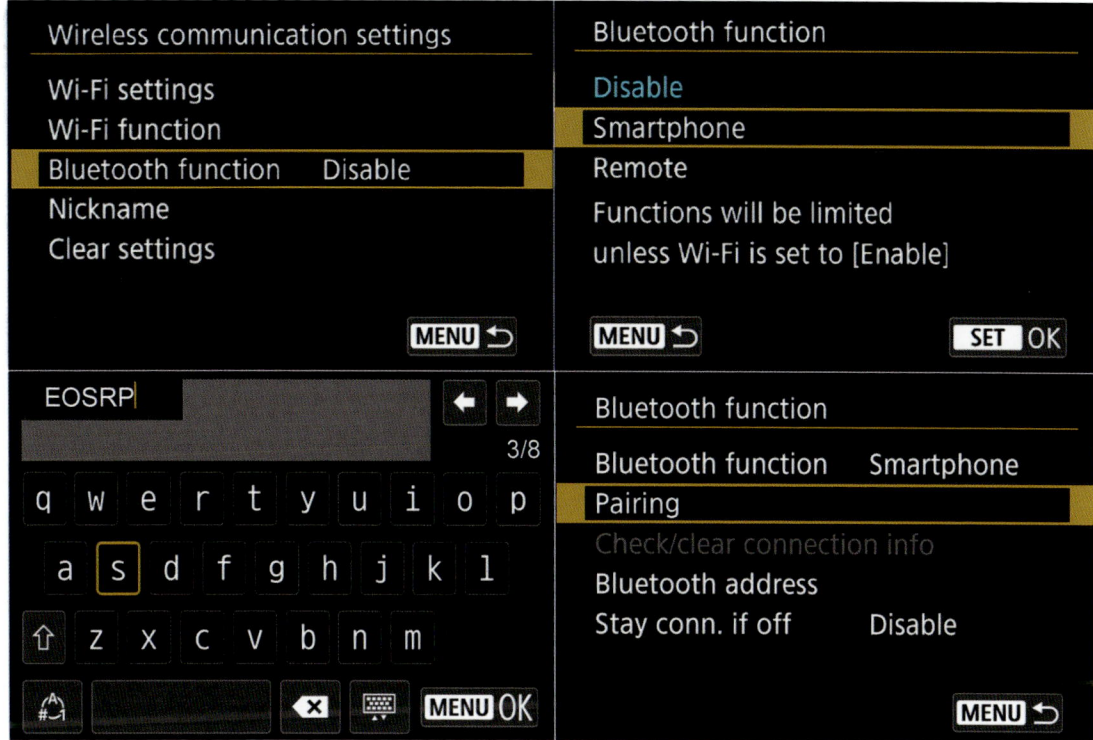

Figure 6.11 Connecting your camera and smart device using Bluetooth.

8. Pairing will now begin and you will need to carry out some subsequent steps on your smart device.

9. On your device, turn on the phone/tablet's Bluetooth feature.

10. Start the Camera Connect app on your device.

11. A message on the order of "New Bluetooth Enabled Camera Found. Choose Camera for Pairing" will appear.

12. The iOS device will next display a Bluetooth Pairing Request screen. Tap Pair. The screen shown in Figure 6.12, center, will appear.

13. Your Camera Connect will now display a screen like the one shown at right in Figure 6.12. Tap to connect to the camera and produce a confirmation screen. A message "Wi-Fi On" will be displayed on the camera along with Bluetooth and Wi-Fi icons on the Camera Connect screen.

Once you've connected using Bluetooth you can easily keep in touch. Just choose Stay Connected If Off in the Bluetooth Function menu, and the EOS RP will remain connected to your device *even if you turn the camera off.* Low-energy Bluetooth requires very little power, so you can safely enable the camera and device to remain connected when they are in range of each other. Just launch

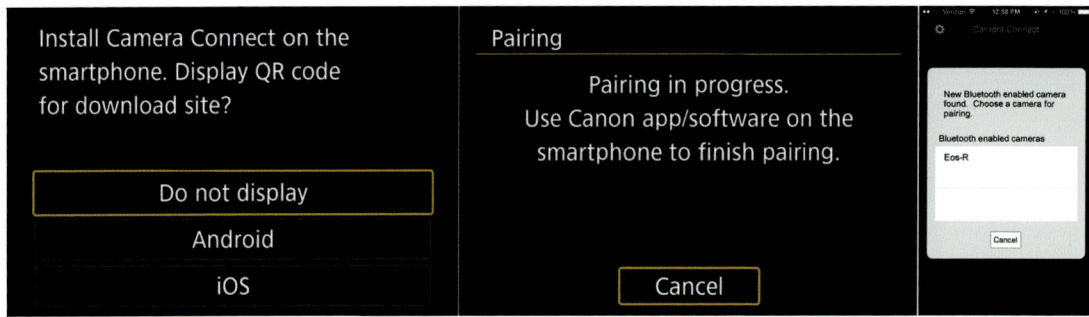

Figure 6.12 Final connection steps.

Camera Connect on your device, select Images on Camera (tap Join if using iOS), and you'll be able to view a list of images on the camera.

Camera Connect is easy to use. It has three main screens. The screen shown at left in Figure 6.13 allows you to view Images On Camera, use Remote Shooting, or adjust Camera Settings. In Images on Camera mode, you'll be shown a screen of thumbnails of pictures on the EOS RP that you can select to download to your smart device (you can also choose them on the camera and initiate transfer there). Remote Shooting allows you to make the most important camera adjustments and control your camera from the smart device. The Camera Settings screen allows you to make camera settings like date and time, and transfer them to the EOS RP.

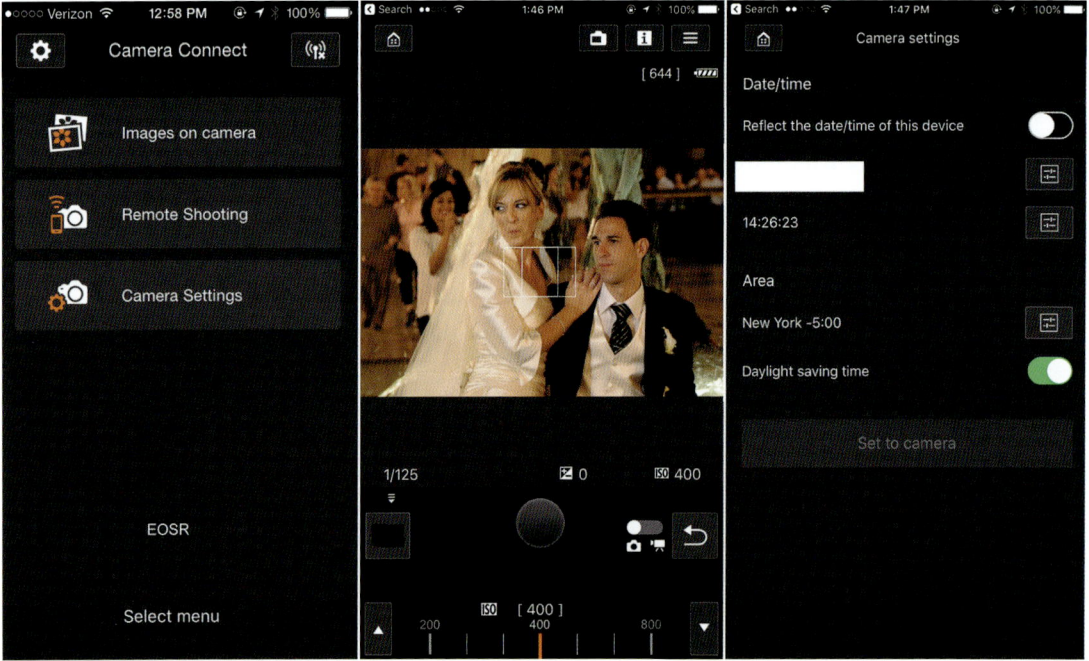

Figure 6.13 Using Camera Connect.

Remote Control with EOS Utility

While you can control your EOS RP using the Camera Connect app on your smartphone as described above, you can also use a laptop or desktop computer to wirelessly operate your camera using the free EOS Utility that can be downloaded from the Canon website.

Connection is done in a similar way:

1. Choose the Wireless Communications Settings entry in the Set-up 5 screen, and from the screen that appears (it was shown earlier at upper left in Figure 6.11), select Wi-Fi Function.

2. The Wi-Fi Function screen seen at left in Figure 6.14 will pop up. (If the history screen appears instead, press the left/right directional buttons to switch.) Choose the center icon in the top line Remote Control (EOS Utility).

3. The Select a Device For Connection screen appears next. Choose Register a Device for Connection and press SET.

4. Check the network name (SSID) of the camera and Password (which will appear only if Password is not set to None under Wi-Fit Settings (also shown at upper left in Figure 6.11).

5. Access your particular computer/operating system's wireless settings. Keep in mind that while virtually all laptops have wireless built-in, not all desktop computers do. The screen shown for my Windows 10 OS appears in Figure 6.15.

6. Select the camera's SSID from the list and enter the password/encryption/network security key (if required).

7. Start the EOS Utility 3 on your computer, and select Pairing Over Wi-Fi/LAN.

8. Choose OK when the Start Pairing Device notice shows up on the EOS RP. Then follow the prompts on the camera.

9. When pairing is accomplished, you will be able to access the camera wirelessly using the EOS Utility.

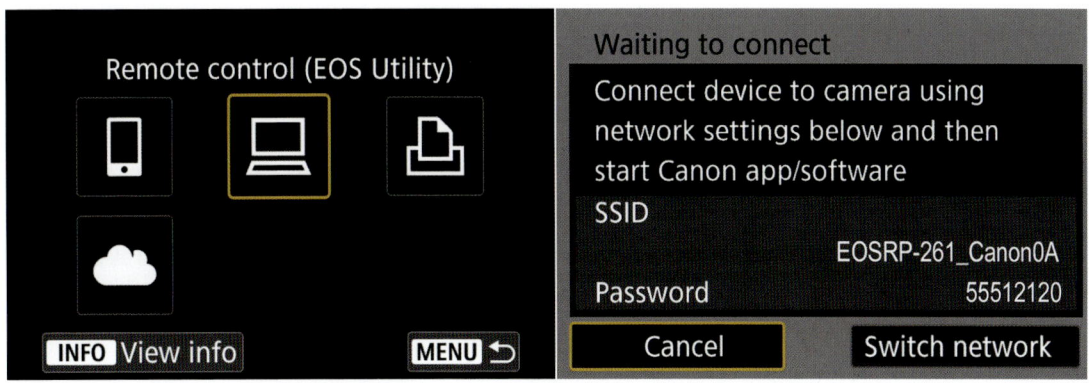

Figure 6.14 Choose the camera's SSID from your operating system's network connections screen.

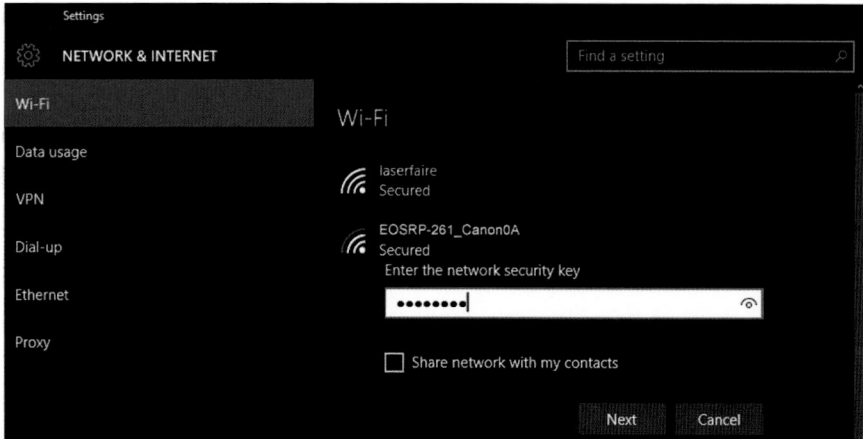

Figure 6.15
Connect wirelessly
on your computer.

Printing from Wi-Fi Printer

Many (perhaps most) printers today have built-in wireless capabilities, allowing you to print out directly from your computer without a physical link between the computer and printer. The EOS RP adds the same function to your camera/printer setup, so you can make hard copies of your images from files in your camera without the bother of transferring them to a computer first. All you need is your EOS RP and a PictBridge-compatible printer that conforms to the DPS over IP standard. (More alphabet soup: *Digital Photo Solutions* and *Internet Protocol*.) To use this feature, you must:

- **Configure your printer for wireless printing.** The instructions vary from printer to printer, so you should consult your printer manual for the procedures. Once you've done this, you'll be able to print photos from your camera, plus files from your computer and other compatible devices, such as smartphones. Wireless printing is *not* limited to camera-to-printer communications.

- **Link your camera to the printer.** The procedures are the same as those mentioned earlier. You can use your camera's connection or connect to your local area network (*infrastructure network*). A list of detected printers is displayed, and, as before, you can save the camera-printer connection to a setting for re-use later. Multiple printer connections can be registered.

  If your printer *does not* connect wirelessly, you can still connect to the camera using your LAN, as described previously.

- **Printing images.** Once linked, you can print by pressing the Playback button and scrolling to the image you want to output. Select printing parameters, number of prints, and other settings just as you would for printing over a wired connection to a PictBridge printer.

Uploading to a Web Service

This wireless option allows you to select images and upload them to the Canon iMage Gateway, which is a free-of-charge service. You can register online through your computer and through this entry. Once you've become a member, you can upload photos, create photo albums, and use other Canon Image Gateway services. The site also can interface with other web services you have an account with, including e-mail, Twitter, YouTube, and Facebook.

All you need is your EOS RP and a computer with the EOS Utility installed. Before you can interface with the Canon gateway wirelessly, you must connect your camera and computer using the conventional digital/USB connection, log onto the Gateway through the "globe" icon, and configure the camera's settings to allow access to the web services. (Remember that Wireless capabilities must be set to Disable any time you want to use a wired connection between your camera and computer.)

Then, you can remove the direct link, turn wireless features back on, and connect to your computer through the wireless access methods described earlier in this chapter. Still images can be uploaded to the Gateway, and movies to YouTube. Images can be uploaded directly to Facebook, or shared with Facebook and Twitter users by posting a link back to the Canon Image Gateway location of the files. As with the image transfer features described earlier, you can resize images before uploading, and send photos one by one or in batches.

Geotagging

Geotagging is most important as a way to associate the geographical location where the photographer was when a picture was taken, with the actual photograph itself. Geotagging can also be done by attaching geographic information to the photo after it's already been taken. This is often done with online services which allow you to associate your uploaded photographs with a map, city, street address, or postal code. When properly geotagged and uploaded to compatible sites, users can browse through your photos using a map, finding pictures you've taken in a given area, or even searching through photos taken at the same location by other users.

You EOS RP can work with the Canon GP-E2 GPS Receiver. It records locational data such as latitude, longitude, and altitude, and saves it to the EXIF metadata in your image files, where it can be retrieved by compatible software to plot to maps or insert into your uploads to Flickr or other sites. You can even track your trajectory of movement with the receiver's logging function.

If your familiarity with GPS is limited to that gadget that sits atop your dashboard, you'll be pleasantly surprised at the things that a GPS-equipped camera can do with locational information. When active, the GPS system records the latitude and longitude of each location where a picture is snapped, the elevation, Coordinated Universal Time Code (UTC), and the satellite reception status. This information is embedded in the EXIF metadata included in each photo, where it can be read and manipulated by compatible software. That includes Canon utilities, such as the Map Utility, Digital Photo Professional, and ImageBrowser EX programs; third-party image-editing software, including iPhoto for the Mac and the Map Module in Lightroom; and many photo-sharing sites that can display the location where each image was taken when you upload your pictures to an online album. Google Earth can also use your EXIF data.

You can view GPS data on the EOS RP's display as you review images. Press the INFO button until the view with a histogram appears, then scroll down using the directional buttons until you reach the screen shown at left in Figure 6.16. When the GPS is active, you can also view the information for your current location in the GPS menu, as I'll describe shortly. I often use this feature when I am traveling around and want to record a specific site that I want to return to at a later time. I can view the latitude and longitude and enter them into my portable Garmin Etrex GPS, or the GPS in my car, and then return by accessing the data I've saved. While GPS data is most often used to pinpoint the shooting location of individual images, the receiver's logging function allows you to re-create the route you took in capturing those photos, thanks to the Canon Map Utility.

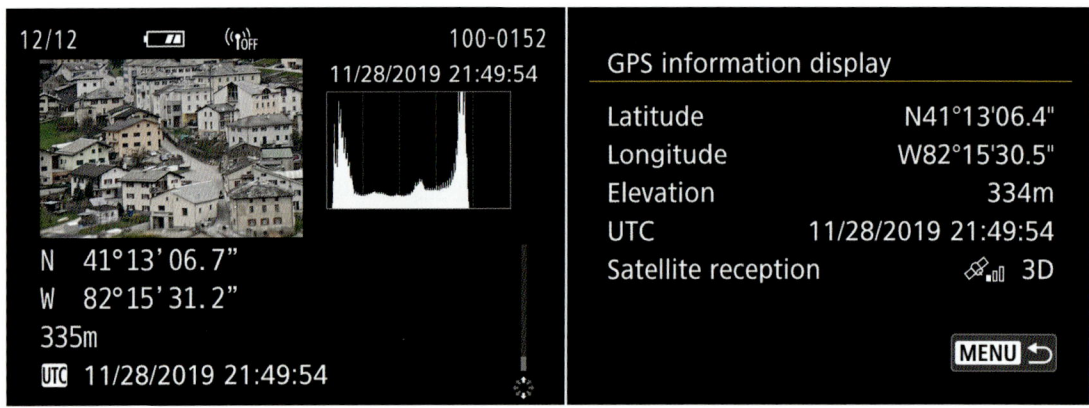

Figure 6.16 Display GPS information about an image (left) or your camera's current location (right).

Using the GP-E2 Receiver

To activate your EOS RP's external GPS receiver, just follow these steps:

1. **Navigate to the Set-up 5 menu and choose GPS Settings.** The screen shown in Figure 6.17 appears.

2. **Set GPS mode.** You can disable GPS here (to save power) or choose one of two modes:

   - **Mode 1.** When the camera is powered down, the GPS receiver still functions at intervals, keeping track of your location. That's useful if you'll be using GPS a lot during a shooting session and don't want to wait for the receiver to re-acquire GPS satellites (it can take valuable seconds or even minutes). The penalty is that the EOS RP draws power continually and your battery life is shortened. Carry plenty of extra batteries if you use this mode.

   - **Mode 2.** When you turn the camera off, GPS is turned off too and no longer drains power. However, if the camera goes to "sleep" due to your auto power off setting, the GPS will receive signals at intervals and draw some power. This mode uses less power than Mode 1, but gives you the option of shutting off the GPS when you know you won't be using it for a while, but not disabling it when your auto power off setting kicks in.

3. **Choose time update.** With the Auto time setting option, the EOS RP can use time data embedded in the GPS signal to set the camera's internal clock accurately. You can choose Auto Update to set the time automatically whenever the camera is powered up and GPS data is available; disable this function, or Set Now to update immediately. The receiver must be able to link with at least five GPS satellites for the time function to operate; when activated, the time setting in your camera will maintain +/– 1-second accuracy. (This feature is great for synchronizing several GPS-equipped cameras, especially when shooting and editing videos and still shots contemporaneously.)

Figure 6.17
GPS settings.

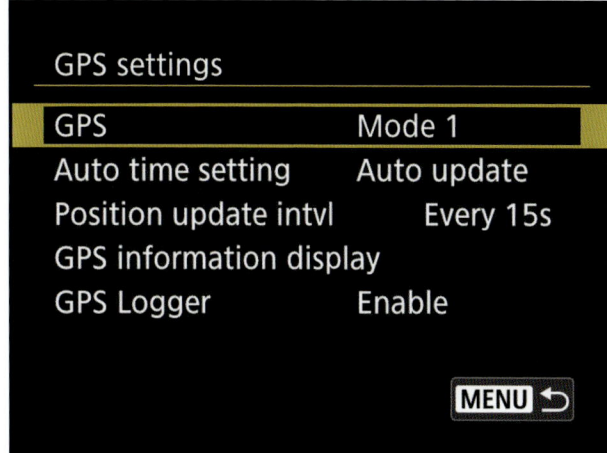

4. **Position update timing.** Use this to specify the interval the GPS device uses to update position information. Choose from every 1, 5, 10, 15, or 30 seconds, or every 1, 2, or 5 minutes. Select a shorter interval when you are moving and/or accuracy is critical, or a longer interval to save power, when GPS reception is not optimal, or you are shooting from one position for a longer period.

5. **GPS information display.** This entry simply displays a screen of current GPS information, including latitude, longitude, elevation, UTC time (essentially Greenwich Mean Time), and Satellite reception strength/status, as shown earlier in Figure 6.16, right.

6. **GPS logger.** Allows you to enable or disable tracking of GPS position data, transfer log data to your memory card for later manipulation by an appropriate software program, or to delete the camera's current GPS log. (See Figure 6.18.) Nature and wildlife photographers (now, *where* did I photograph those rare flowers?), law enforcement personnel, business users, and anyone wandering through a strange city during a vacation will love the ability to track not only individual locations but the routes taken to get from one shooting spot to another.

Your Canon Map Utility, when connected to the Internet through your computer, can easily trace a path for you on a standard road map or satellite view (see Figure 6.19). The logger's NMEA-0813 format log file, which includes all the information for a single day's shooting, can be converted by the utility to a .KMZ file and uploaded to Google Earth, where it can be shared and viewed. A new log is created each day, or each time you change time zones. Depending on how often the position update timing is recorded (from every second to every five minutes), the EOS RP can store from less than a week to as much as 100 days' worth of data. However, you'll probably use the Transfer Log Data to Card option more often than that.

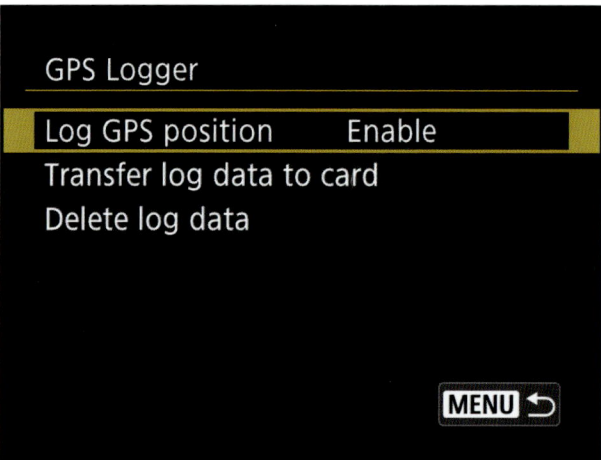

Figure 6.18
Enable, disable logger; transfer log data to a memory card; delete log data.

7. **Begin using GPS.** After a delay of about 30 to 60 seconds while the receiver connects to the optimum number of satellites, GPS functions will be activated, and remain so until you return to the menu to disable GPS features. If you turn the camera off, it will automatically re-acquire the satellites within a few seconds when it's powered up again, assuming that GPS reception is available at that location.

Figure 6.19
Canon's Map Utility can display the GPS data for an image (top), or show you the log data for a shooting session (bottom).

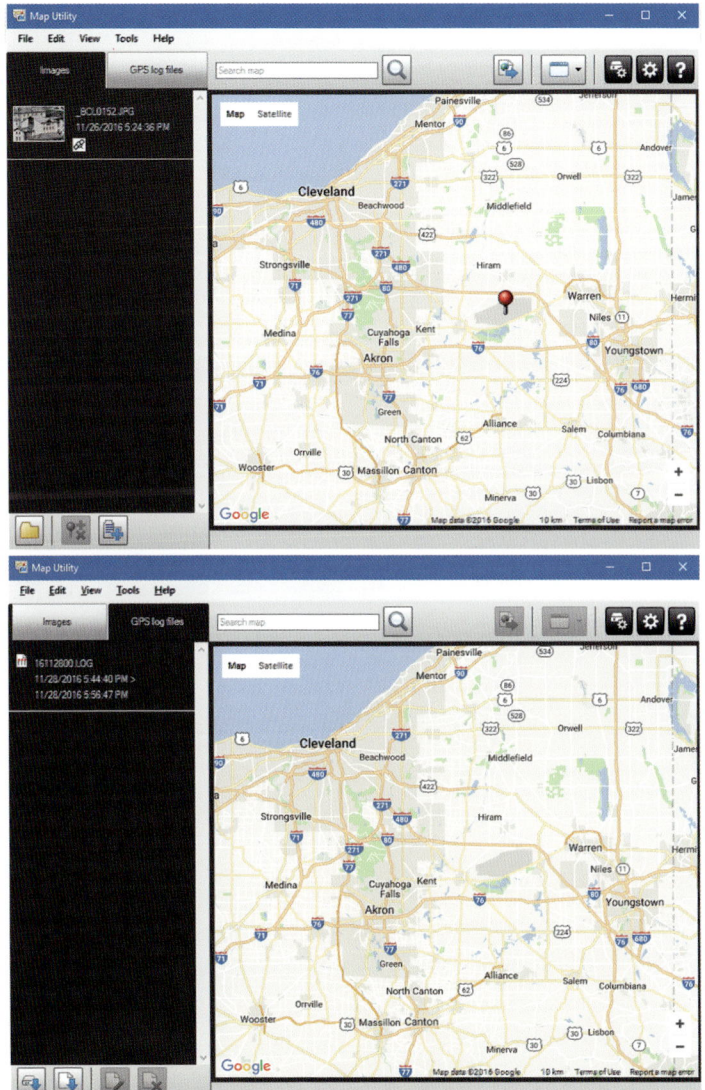

7

Choosing Your Lens Arsenal

It's not an overstatement to say that Canon has built its reputation on its expertise in lenses. Since the company began producing its own lenses for Canon cameras in mid-1947, it has pioneered many innovations, including the world's first 10X zoom lens, the first lenses to include optical image stabilization, and the first super-telephoto lens to include a built-in tele-extender.

Indeed, it's not widely known that Canon was one of the very first companies to offer autofocus lenses, even before the EOS system was introduced. The company produced a total of four AF lenses for its FD-mount cameras. Only one, the FD 35-70mm f/4 AF, worked on all Canon FD cameras; the other three (a 50mm f/1.8, a 35-70mm f/3.5-4.5, and a 75-200mm f/4.5) were compatible only with the Canon T80 camera.

Of course, in the ensuing years Canon has also developed even more advanced camera technology, too, combining its proficiency in both optical and digital arenas to produce the new EOS R and EOS RP mirrorless cameras and RF-series lenses. Because of the quality of Canon optics, photographers who started out using Canon camera bodies and lenses have tended to hang onto their lenses for many years, even as they upgraded to newer camera bodies with more features. Indeed, many of us have stuck with the Canon brand at least partially because we were able to use our existing kit of lenses with our latest and greatest camera. After all, an enthusiast's optics collection can easily have cost many times the price of the body itself.

Potential compatibility with older EF and EF-S lenses is part of what makes the EOS RP's all-new RF mount so interesting and exciting. Canon has sold more than 140 million EF lenses, and millions more are available from third parties like Tamron, Sigma, and Tokina. A large number of them are compatible with your new camera, thanks to the three mount adapters I'll be discussing later in this chapter.

So, introducing the brand-new RF-mount for Canon's first full-frame mirrorless camera could have been a risky proposition, and perhaps not worth the possibility that current Canon owners might migrate instead to a different mirrorless platform, including current industry leader Sony and full-frame rivals Nikon, Leica, Panasonic, and Sigma. Fortunately, Canon anticipated this possibility, and announced the three Canon mount adapters at the same time as the EOS RP camera. The availability of these adapters was essential to the success of the R and RP cameras for these reasons:

- **Dearth of native lenses.** The adapter compensates for the tiny number of native RF-mount lenses available for the EOS RP at introduction. Only four lenses were available, all previously introduced with the RP's upscale sibling, the EOS R: the RF 28-70mm f/2L, RF 24-105mm f/4L, RF 50mm f/1.2L, and RF 35mm f/1.8 Macro IS STM. (I'll decipher Canon's lens nomenclature later in this chapter.) In February 2019, with the unveiling of the EOS RP, six additional lenses were slated for availability by the end of the year: the RF 15-35mm f/2.8L IS USM, RF 24-240mm f/4-6.3 IS USM, RF 24-70mm f/2.8L IS USM, RF 70-200mm f/2.8L IS USM, RF 85mm f/1.2 USM DS ("defocus smoothing"), and RF 85mm f/1.2L USM. Scheduled for 2020 are an RF 24mm f/1.4L USM and RF 135mm f/1.8L.

  Note that most of the announced lenses have L (Luxe) designations, showing that Canon is serious about producing the highest-quality lenses for the new RF mount. However, even though native-mount lenses for the EOS RP are scarce, the huge number of legacy EF/EF-S-mount lenses—which many early EOS RP owners will already possess—allows Canon to introduce its additional RF-mount optics at a reasonable pace. Meanwhile, most of us are delighted we can use our favorite EF-mount lenses on the EOS RP or can purchase and use specialty lenses that may not be introduced in RF mount for some time.

- **Current owner loyalty.** Many current Canon dSLR owners have been coveting the lighter weight, compact size, and other advantages of mirrorless cameras, and while there have been some defections, a large number of us have been waiting for an alternative from Canon more suited to the enthusiast's needs than the current EOS M line. (Although the EOS M5 is one of the most popular cameras in Japan, buyers in other countries have not been so quick to buy into the M-series.) Canon expects current Canon dSLR fans to make up the bulk of purchases for the EOS R and EOS RP. The three adapter options makes the adoption of either new RF-mount camera much more seamless and less painful.

- **Technical innovations.** Canon could have, perhaps, provided the EOS R/RP cameras with a lens mount that would accept EF- or EF-S-mount lenses without an adapter. However, that would have meant larger lenses, and the submitting to the technical restrictions imposed by the 1987-era legacy lens system. The EF-mount, designed for film cameras, has a 54mm "throat" and a flange to focal plane (*registration*) distance of 44mm. These dimensions impose severe restrictions on lens design, including the maximum size of the largest aperture, and the angles at which photons can approach the sensor.

The RF-mount's diameter is also 54mm, and the flange/registration distance a mere 20mm. The reduced flange dimension means there is plenty of room between the sensor and the rear mount of many lenses designed for other camera platforms to be accommodated by additional adapters.

■ **EF-S lenses on a full-frame Canon!** Until the introduction of the original EOS R, it was impossible to use an EF-S lens (designed for the smaller APS-C format) on a full-frame Canon dSLR. Although EF-S lenses use the same lens mount, the rear elements of some lenses extend backward into the mirror box. All Canon's APS-C cameras use a "half" mirror that accommodates this, but its full-frame dSLR cameras do not.

Since the EOS R/RP *have* no mirror, all three mount adapters allow safely attaching an EF-S lens. The cameras automatically switch into 1.6X "crop" mode that captures only an APS-C-sized area of the sensor, as no EF-S lens will cover the full frame at all focal lengths. As a bonus, this automatic crop means your EF-S lens gets a 1.6X magnification boost, extending your telephoto "reach" (while reducing your wide-angle perspective, too). However, you end up with a 3888 × 2592 pixel, 10 MP image as a tradeoff. (See Figure 7.1.)

The current hybrid situation, in which there are not many RF-mount lenses for the EOS RP—but plentiful compatible lenses in the existing EF and EF-S mount lineup—means that this chapter will be a hybrid, as well. For this book, at least, I'm going to embrace both RF-mount and EF/EF-S-mount products, so that I can explain the real-world options—especially to those who may be new to the Canon world. After all, even if you did not own any Canon lenses when you purchased your EOS RP, you probably will consider both types as you expand your optical horizons, because RF mount and legacy lenses work seamlessly with your camera. A vast number of affordable pre-owned EF/EF-S-mount lenses are available from sources like www.keh.com.

Figure 7.1
The EOS RP's 1.6X crop option yields a magnification boost, but only a 10-megapixel image.

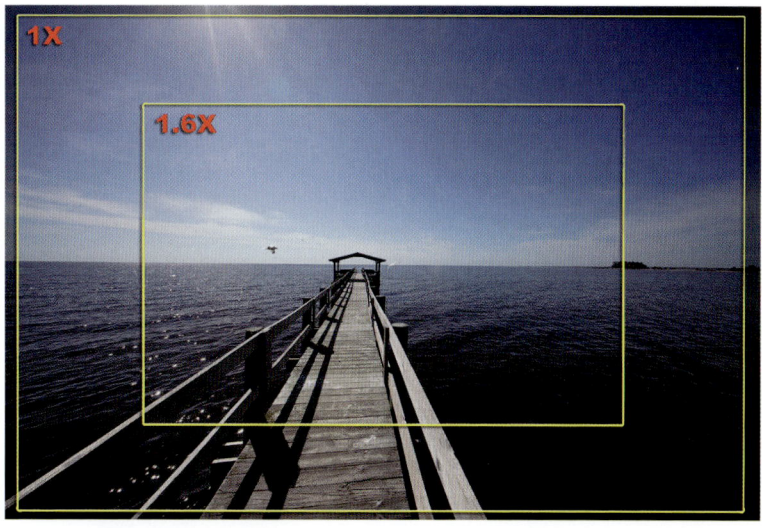

Later in this chapter, I'll have more details on how adapted lenses work with the EOS RP and the three mount adapters. It's true that there is a mind-bending assortment of high-quality lenses available to enhance the capabilities of your camera. These lenses can give you a wider view, bring distant subjects closer, let you focus closer, shoot under lower-light conditions, or provide a more detailed, sharper image for critical work. Other than the sensor itself, the lens you choose for your EOS RP is the most important component in determining image quality and perspective of your images. This chapter explains how to select the best lenses for the kinds of photography you want to do.

Your First Lenses

Back in ancient times (the pre-zoom, pre-autofocus era before the mid-1980s), choosing the first lens for your camera was a no-brainer: you had few or no options. Canon cameras (which used a different lens mount in those days) were sold with a 50mm f/1.4, a 50mm f/1.8, or, if you had deeper pockets, a super-fast 50mm f/1.2 lens. It was also possible to buy a camera as a body alone, which didn't save much money back when a film SLR like the Canon A-1 sold for $435—*with lens*. This explains why, during my photojournalist days, I owned 12 film camera bodies and eight 50mm f/1.4 lenses.

Today, your choices are more complicated, and Canon lenses, which now include zoom, autofocus, and, more often than not, built-in image stabilization (IS) features, tend to cost a lot more compared to the price of a camera. (Adjusted for inflation, that $435 A-1 costs more than $1,000 in today's dollars.)

The Canon EOS RP is frequently purchased with a lens, even now, usually the new Canon RF 24-105mm f/4L IS USM lens introduced with the camera in 2018 (see Figure 7.2). It has image stabilization, almost no vignetting in the corners, a 9-blade circular aperture with incredible bokeh (creamy background blur), and a coating that does a better job of reducing flare and ghost images.

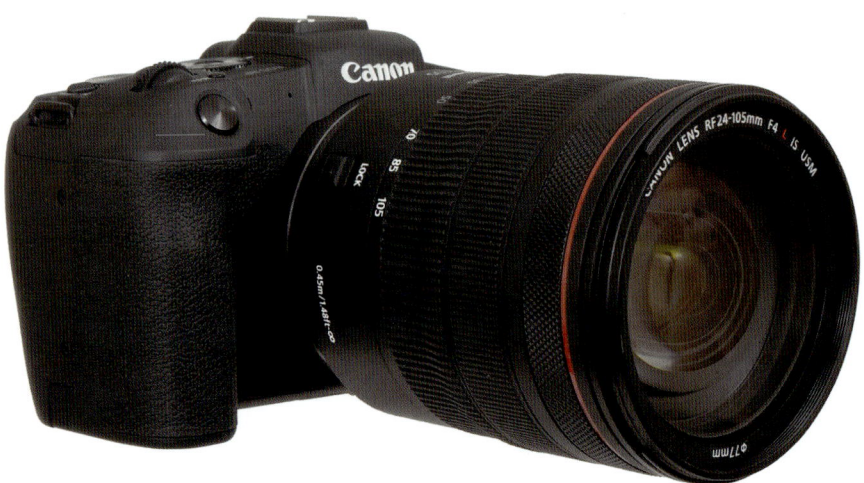

Figure 7.2
The Canon RF 24-105mm f/4L IS USM lens is often packaged with the EOS RP in a kit.

It compares favorably with Canon's EF-mount version with roughly the same optical and mechanical specifications, but it is significantly smaller and lighter.

However, the EOS RP can also be purchased with other lenses or in a body-only configuration, because advanced shooters and professionals may buy several bodies in order to have a backup, and don't need a kit lens for every body they purchase.

Note

Throughout this chapter, I'm going to use the current Canon manufacturer suggested list price (MSRP) when it's available. (I'll use the Canon store price if it's not.) You should know that many lenses are available for less at the Canon store for your country or at retailers, and that prices can (and will) change throughout the life of this book.

If you are switching platforms and don't already own a lens compatible with your EOS RP, you can't go wrong with the 24-105mm optic. Many photographers, especially old-school film shooters, prefer working with prime (fixed focal length) lenses as much as they can, and may prefer a "normal" lens, like the RF 50mm f/1.4L ($2,299 MSRP).

So, depending on which category you fall into, you'll need to make a decision about what lens to buy, or decide what other kind of lenses you need to fill out your complement of Canon optics. This section will cover "first lens" concerns, while later in the chapter we'll look at "add-on lens" considerations. When deciding on your initial lens purchases, there are several factors you'll want to consider:

■ **Cost.** You might have stretched your budget a bit to purchase your EOS RP, so you might want to keep the cost of your add-on lenses fairly low. Even if you already own many EF/EF-S optics, I don't recommend buying only a body and trying to work only with legacy lenses and a mount adapter, even though that would be the lowest-cost way of building a fledgling EOS RP system. The RF 35mm f/1.8 Macro IS STM lens will set you back only $450, and some retailers are packaging it in an EOS RP kit. But if you need multiple focal lengths and want to cut costs, the 24-105mm lens is the best way to go.

■ **Zoom range.** If you have only one lens, you'll want a fairly long zoom range to provide as much flexibility as possible. As I write this, only two RF-mount zooms are available. Again, the 24-105mm has been the best bet since the EOS RP was introduced; the awesome RF 28-70mm f/2L has a useful, but much more limited zoom range, and is saddled with a $3,000 price tag. By the time this book is published, prices for the other zooms slated for introduction may be known, but the RF 24-70mm f/2.8L IS USM and RF 15-35mm f/2.8L IS USM seem like the best bets for everyday shooting, people pictures, and some types of sports. The RF 24-240mm f/4-6.3 IS USM has the longest zoom range among announced lenses.

- **Adequate maximum aperture.** You'll want an f/stop of at least f/3.5 to f/4 in any lens you buy to allow shooting under fairly low-light conditions. The thing to watch for is the maximum aperture when the lens is zoomed to its telephoto end. You may end up with no better than an f/6.3 maximum aperture. That's indeed the case with the RF 24-240mm f/4-6.3 optic. That's not great, but you can often live with it.

- **Image quality.** Your starter lens should have good image quality, befitting a camera with 26 MP of resolution, because that's one of the primary factors that will be used to judge your photos.

- **Size matters.** A good walking-around lens is compact in size and light in weight. My favorite, the 24-105mm f/4 isn't tiny, but having it mounted on the camera most of the time isn't a burden, either. Considering its image quality and zoom range, I think it's worth every ounce.

- **Fast/close focusing.** Your first lens should have a speedy autofocus system (which is where the ultrasonic motor/USM or STM found in nearly all current moderately priced lenses is an advantage). Close focusing (to 12 inches or closer) will let you use your basic lens for some types of macro photography.

Canon RF-Mount Lenses

If you don't own many EF/EF-S lenses, or want to use RF-mount optics as much as possible, you should pay attention to Canon's RF "lens road map," which lists current and announced lenses that are available or in development (and expected for delivery between now and 2021). Here's a quick overview, based on what we know now:

- **RF 28-70mm f/2L USM.** This $3,000 lens has a useful focal length from modest wide-angle to short telephoto and a fast f/2 constant aperture, which means you can use it for everything from architecture and street photography to indoor sports and portraiture. It focuses down to about 1.28 feet and has nine rounded diaphragm blades for excellent bokeh (defocused highlights). This lens's customizable Control Ring is built-in, so you can adjust exposure settings, including shutter speed, aperture, ISO, and exposure compensation without removing your hands from the lens. It's hefty at more than three pounds, and that wide aperture calls for expensive 95mm filters. There's no image stabilization, which can be a drawback in low-light situations where you'll be using longer shutter speeds.

- **RF 24-105mm f/4L.** This all-around lens costs about $1,100 if purchased separately, and does feature five-stop image stabilization to minimize the effects of camera shake. Its hybrid autofocus system (which includes both USM and STM components; see my explanation later in this chapter) allows near-silent AF and full-time manual focus adjustments in One-Shot mode. It focuses down to roughly 18 inches for close-up work, uses "standard" 77mm filters, and has the configurable Control Ring.

■ **RF 50mm f/1.2L USM.** At $2,300, this lens is pricey for a fixed focal length ("prime") lens, but it has exquisite image quality, even wide open at f/1.2. It has the customizable control ring and weather-resistant sealing found in typical Canon L-series lenses. While this normal lens has no image stabilization, its fast f/1.2 maximum aperture allows you to use faster shutter speeds in many situations. It weighs about 2 pounds, and uses the standard 77 filter size.

■ **RF 35mm f/1.8 Macro IS STM.** This is the least expensive RF-mount lens available as this book is written, at about $500, and it's not an L lens, but it has a lot to offer, including a fast maximum aperture which, combined with five-stop image stabilization, makes it a great lens for low-light street photography. You'll find the Control Ring especially useful for changing exposure settings on-the-fly in stealth shooting situations. As a macro lens, it has close focusing down to about 6.7 inches for half life-size reproduction. The quiet STM motor is smooth and accurate, making it especially suitable for video. It's a lightweight lens, too, at about 11 ounces and measuring about 3 × 2.5 inches when mounted on the EOS RP.

■ **RF 15-35mm f/2.8L IS USM.** This lens is likely to be one of the first of the additional RF-mount optics to be introduced, probably not long after this book is published. Price and other details are unknown at this point, but its 15-35mm focal length and f/2.8 maximum aperture are likely to be perfect for landscape and architectural photography (particularly interiors). Those engaged in street photography may find it to be their ideal walk-around lens.

■ **RF 24-240mm f/4-6.3 IS USM.** I'm always wary of extreme zooms, which tend to embrace a broad range of focal lengths, while being a master of none. But given the optical design flexibility the new RF mount offers, this lens could be a winner. It's likely to be very heavy, and obviously is quite slow (f/6.3) at the 240mm zoom setting. Other vendors have positioned lenses with these specs as moderately priced walk-around optics, while some have designed them as more upscale lenses for video production. We'll see.

■ **RF 24-70mm f/2.8L IS USM.** This lens looks as if it may be a moderately priced general-purpose zoom. (I've got my fingers crossed for a price in the $1,800–$2,200 range.) However, it is an L lens and includes the image stabilization that its 28-70mm f/2 sibling lacks, and so may be more expensive than I expect. It should be smaller, though, and more suitable for everyday use with a compact camera like the EOS RP.

■ **RF 70-200mm f/2.8L IS USM.** In the Canon EF realm, there are three lenses that are considered the "holy trinity" of must-have optics. The set generally includes the EF 16-35mm f/2.8L III USM, EF 24-70mm f/2.8 II USM, and EF 70-200mm f/2.8L IS USM lenses. The more compact RF version of the 70-200mm f/2.8 lens is likely to be one of the most popular among working pros, who will use it for everything from portraits to sports. Expect it to cost from $2,200–$3,000, and be worth every penny.

- **RF 85mm f/1.2L USM.** Every Canon photographer I come in contact with who does fashion or portrait photography owns the EF-mount 85mm f/1.2 lens. This version for the EOS RP should be a virtual cream machine in terms of background bokeh, is sharp enough wide open to allow stunning selective focus effects, and focus close enough for tight face-only portraiture. I know early adopters of the EOS RP are already drooling over this one, which was introduced early in May 2019, and priced at $2,699. It's the first RF lens to feature Canon's Blue Spectrum Refractive (BR) optics, which are elements placed between concave and convex elements to eliminate longitudinal chromatic aberration (the leading cause of purple and green fringing). It also has Canon's Air Sphere Coating (ASC) to minimize flare and ghosting.

- **RF 85mm f/1.2L USM DS.** Price is likely to be no object for this upscale version, too, which is promised to include Canon's defocus smoothing technology, which will provide even better bokeh, and, possibly, the ability to adjust the effect as you shoot. Expect well-heeled portrait photographers to snap this one up as soon as it appears. Canon said in May 2019, that this lens is still under development.

Using Adapted Lenses

As I noted at the beginning of the chapter, Canon wisely elected to provide the ability to use legacy EF and EF-S lenses on the EOS RP, with full compatibility with image stabilization, autofocus, and autoexposure. The key to using your existing lenses (or new EF-mount optics you decide to purchase because no RF equivalent is available) are three mount adapters, which I'll describe shortly.

The adapters are your entry to relatively inexpensive, high-quality EF lenses, which have been in production since 1987 and are easily found in excellent condition on the used market. (I own a large number of EF lenses that I bought from keh.com in Smyrna, Georgia.) Perhaps you need a fast 50mm lens and aren't ready to pay the $2,000 tariff on the RF model. The 50mm f/1.8 II EF lens pictured in Figure 7.3 is available in Excellent-Plus condition at keh.com for $89. I purchased the 100-300mm f/5.6 Macro EF lens seen in Figure 7.4 for only a few hundred bucks. Lenses that don't date back to the EOS dark ages, like the current model 75-300mm f/4-5.6 III lens pictured (at the 75mm zoom position at left, and extended to 300mm at right) in Figure 7.5 are available brand new for less than $200. Usable lenses don't have to empty your wallet.

Even if you currently own no Canon lenses at present, you can't ignore the value of using adapted lenses. It's certain that lenses that some photographers absolutely must have will be slow in coming to the RF system, or may be prohibitively expensive. So, you may want to purchase an EF lens to get the features you need, or because the EF equivalent can be had for much, much less in the used equipment market. For example, Canon's array of perspective control (TS-E) tilt-shift lenses may be moderately easy to release in RF-mount configurations, because those lenses are manual focus and would not require re-engineering to incorporate AF features. However, demand for such specialized optics among EOS RP owners is likely to be low enough that any RF perspective control optics may be very slow in coming. While TS-E lenses are not cheap, they are available from time to time in excellent condition, used.

Figure 7.3
Canon's EF 50mm f/1.8 lens is an affordable "normal" lens.

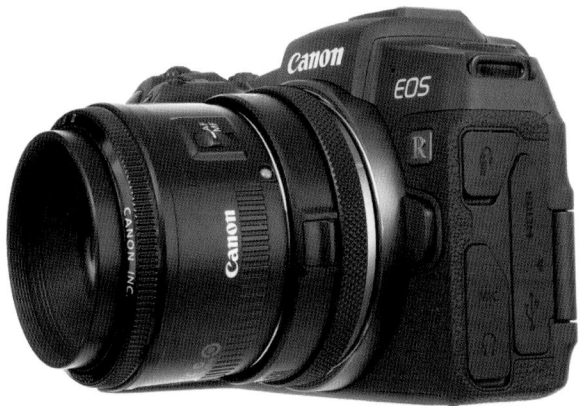

Figure 7.4
A legacy lens like this 100-300mm zoom can offer an affordable telephoto option.

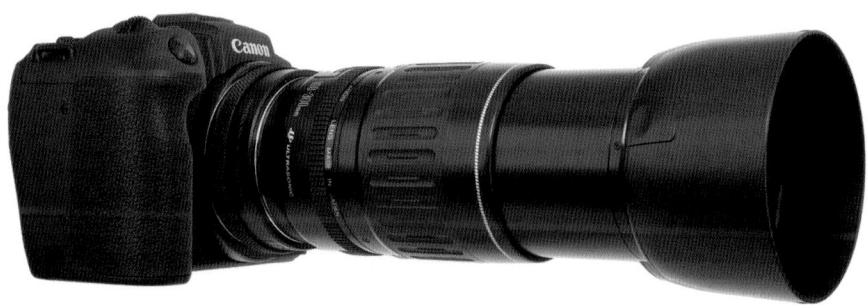

Figure 7.5
Canon offers affordable current telephoto zooms like this 75-300mm lens, shown in retracted (left) and extended (right) positions.

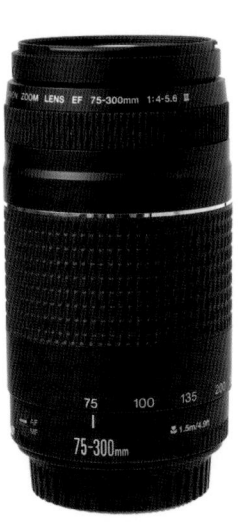
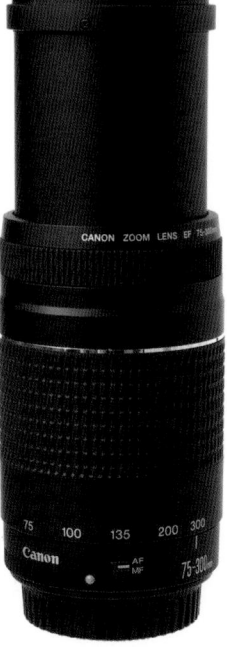

Another example might be Canon's EF 8-15mm f/4L Fisheye USM zoom lens. This autofocus lens would be more difficult to convert to RF-mount, would probably enjoy only modest popularity, and is readily available as an EF lens for $1,250 or less (used). If you need one of these, why wait for an RF version—just grab the EF fisheye zoom, mount it with an adapter, and start shooting.

As I mentioned earlier, the three mount adapters also let you, for the first time, safely attach an EF-S lens to a full-frame EOS RP model. The rationale is flawed—you end up with a low-resolution (in these days) 11.6 MP image—but if you already have a large collection of EF-S lenses, you can use them with your EOS RP for as long as you decide to keep them.

Because the EOS RP's registration distance is a scant 20mm, there is plenty of room to insert other third-party adapters aft of other vendors' zoom and prime lenses, too. You'll probably find an abundance of these by the time this book is published, allowing you to use Nikon, Sony A-mount, and even pre-EF-mount Canon lenses on your EOS RP with ease.

Canon RF-Mount Adapters

Canon announced three mount adapters at the same time as the EOS RP, each with different attributes. Your choices are as follows:

- **Mount Adapter EF-EOS R.** This bare-bones adapter costs just $99, and it has several useful characteristics. It's lightweight (four ounces), but made of metal and its exterior design matches that of EF lenses. (Third-party adapters may include plastic or poorly machined parts, and look ugly.) It's dust- and water-resistant, and like the other mount adapters, has all the electrical contacts you need for smooth operation of your EF and EF-S lenses.

- **Control Ring Mount Adapter EF-EOS R.** Priced at a modest $199, this version is the one you should definitely opt for, as it includes a Control Ring like that found on RF-mount lenses. Once you use the Control Ring, you won't want to do without it. It's only a fraction heavier than the basic adapter at 4.6 ounces.

- **Drop-in Filter Mount Adapter EF-EOS R.** You can purchase this adapter with either a circular polarizing filter ($299) or a variable neutral-density (ND) filter ($399). A thumb wheel on the filter holder allows rotating the filter to achieve the desired amount of polarization or neutral density. The ND filter can reduce light reaching the sensor by 1.5 to 9 f/stops (ND3 to ND500), although, like all the variable neutral-density filters I've used, color tinges and density irregularities can be a problem. Canon says these effects are noticeable at ND250 settings or higher. The advantage of using drop-in filters is clear (so to speak): while a large number of EF lenses take standard 77mm filters, some require 82mm or 95mm filters (or larger), or may not accept filters at all. With this adapter every legacy-mount lens you use can work with the same polarizer or ND filter.

Legacy Options

Any of the mount adapters will allow you to use the EF or EF-S lenses you already own, so you can shoot now, and expand later. Because this chapter is necessarily a hybrid—due to the current lack of RF-mount optics—I'm going to devote some space to summarizing some of your options.

One important thing to re-emphasize is that Canon has been producing EF lenses for a very long time, and some excellent lenses have been replaced with newer models, or dropped from the Canon lineup entirely. If you want to choose from the broadest variety of lenses at reduced prices, you definitely should consider buying gently used optics.

As I mentioned earlier, I highly recommend KEH Camera in Smyrna, Georgia, as a source for affordable used gear. I've purchased many lenses from their website (www.keh.com). Their prices may not be the lowest available, but you'll save significantly from the new price for the same lens, and the company is famous for exceeding their own lens grading standards: the lenses I've purchased from them listed as Excellent were difficult to tell from new, and their "Bargain" optics often show only minor wear and near-perfect glass. For each lens you're considering, you can usually select from three or more different grades, plus choose lenses with or without hoods and/or front and rear caps. Because of the ready availability of used and discontinued lenses for Canon full-frame models, I'm going to cast a broad net when making my recommendations for lenses you should consider. Canon's best-bet lenses are as follows:

■ **Canon EF 17-40mm f/4L USM lens.** Not everyone needs a wide-angle to medium telephoto lens, and this $799 optic is perfect for those who tend to see the world from a wide-angle perspective. It provides a broader 104-degree field of view than your typical walk-around lens (which usually starts at around 24mm), and zooms only to a near-normal 40mm. Its f/4 *constant maximum aperture* (it delivers f/4 at every zoom position) is large enough for much low-light shooting, particularly since it is sharp wide open. It focuses down to about 11 inches.

■ **Canon Zoom Wide-Angle-Telephoto EF 24-70mm f/2.8L II USM lens.** I couldn't leave the latest version of this premium lens out of the mix, even though it costs $1,899. As part of Canon's L-series line, it offers better sharpness over its focal range than many of the other lenses in this list. Best of all, it's fast (for a zoom), with an f/2.8 maximum aperture that *doesn't change* as you zoom out. Unlike some other lenses, which may offer only an f/5.6 maximum f/stop at their longest zoom setting, this is another constant aperture lens, which retains its maximum f/stop. The added sharpness, constant aperture, and ultra-smooth USM motor are what you're paying for with this lens.

■ **Canon EF 24-85mm f/3.5-4.5 USM Autofocus Wide-Angle Telephoto Zoom lens.** If you can get by with wide-angle to short telephoto range, this older ("classic") consumer-grade lens might suit you. It can often be found used in the $300 price range and offers a useful range of focal lengths.

■ **Canon EF 28-105mm f/3.5-4.5 II USM Autofocus Wide-Angle Telephoto Zoom lens.** Discontinued only a few years ago, this lens is a little slower than its 28-105mm L-class counterpart, but it's priced roughly in the range of the 24-85mm lens mentioned earlier and offers more reach.

■ **Canon EF 28-135mm f/3.5-5.6 IS USM Image-Stabilized Autofocus Wide-Angle Telephoto Zoom lens.** Image stabilization is especially useful at longer focal lengths, which makes this lens worth its $479 price tag. Several retailers are packing this lens with the EOS RP as a kit.

■ **Canon EF 28-200mm f/3.5-5.6 USM Autofocus Wide-Angle Telephoto Zoom lens.** If you want one affordable lens to do everything except ultra-wide-angle photography, this discontinued 7X zoom lens can be found used for around $250.

■ **Canon EF 55-200mm f/4.5-5.6 II USM Telephoto Zoom lens.** This one goes from normal to medium-long focal lengths. It features a desirable ultrasonic motor. Best of all, it's very affordable at an MSRP of $349.

■ **Canon EF 40mm f/2.8 STM lens.** This fairly fast prime lens (less than $200) has the quiet STM motor, making it perfect as a wide/normal lens for video. It's cheap enough to keep around as a "pancake" walk-around lens for street photography.

■ **Canon EF 50mm f/1.8 STM lens.** If a "normal" lens is not your cup of tea for everyday use, you can skip Canon's f/1.4 and f/1.2 options, and add this $125 lens to your kit for less than you might pay for a high-quality 77mm polarizing filter.

Ingredients of Canon's Alphanumeric Soup

The actual product names of individual Canon lenses are fairly easy to decipher; they'll include the RF, EF, or EF-S designation, the focal length or focal length range of the lens, its maximum aperture, and some other information. Additional data may be engraved or painted on the barrel or ring surrounding the front element of the lens, as shown in Figure 7.6. Here's a decoding of what the individual designations mean:

■ **EF/EF-S/RF.** RF lenses are those designed for the EOS R and RP. They cannot be mounted on any other EOS cameras, other than future mirrorless models not yet announced. If the lens is marked EF, it can safely be used on any Canon EOS camera, film or digital, but requires a mount adapter to use with the EOS R and RP. If it is an EF-S lens, it should be used only on an EF-S-compatible camera, or an EOS mirrorless model with a mount adapter. Again, if you use an EF-S lens on the EOS RP, the camera will automatically crop the image to 10 MP.

■ **Focal length.** Given in millimeters or a millimeter range, such as 60mm in the case of a popular Canon macro lens, or 24-105mm, used to describe a medium-wide to short-telephoto zoom.

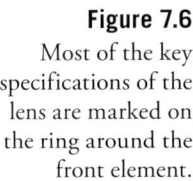

Figure 7.6
Most of the key specifications of the lens are marked on the ring around the front element.

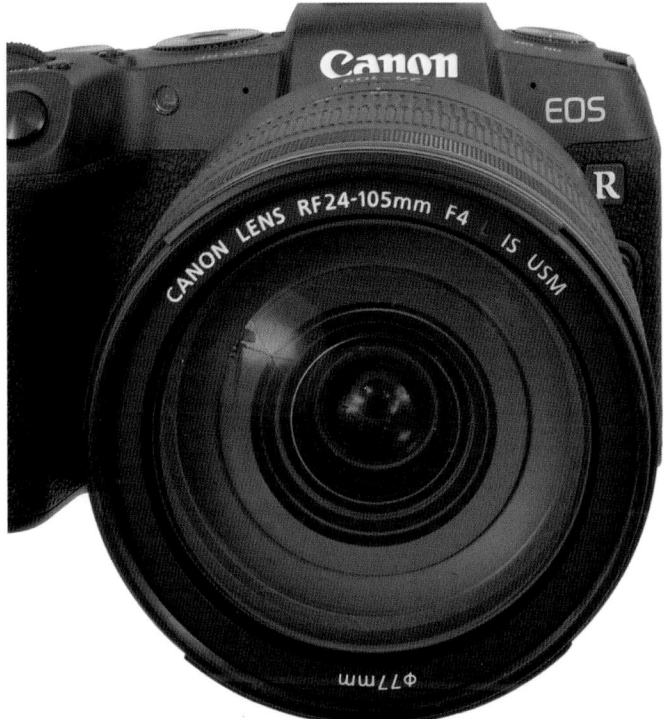

■ **Maximum aperture.** The largest f/stop available with a particular lens is given in a string of numbers that might seem confusing at first glance. For example, you might see 1:1.8 for a fixed-focal length (prime) lens, and 1:4.5-5.6 for a zoom. The initial 1: signifies that the f/stop given is actually a ratio or fraction (in regular notation, f/ replaces the 1:), which is why a 1:2 (or f/2) aperture is larger than a 1:4 (or f/4) aperture—just as 1/2 is larger than 1/4. With most zoom lenses, the maximum aperture changes as the lens is zoomed to the telephoto position, so a range is given instead: 1:4.5-5.6. (Some zooms, called constant aperture lenses, keep the same maximum aperture throughout their range.)

■ **DS (Defocus Smoothing).** This is Canon's terminology for technology that allows improved bokeh (out-of-focus highlights).

■ **Autofocus type.** Most newer Canon lenses that aren't of the bargain-basement type use Canon's *ultrasonic motor* autofocus system (more on that later) and are given the USM designation. If USM does not appear on the lens or its model name, the lens may use the less-sophisticated AFD (arc-form drive) autofocus system or the micromotor (MM) drive mechanism. The newer STM designation indicates a stepper-motor drive, which is quieter and especially useful for video.

SORTING THE MOTOR DRIVES

Incorporating the autofocus motor inside the lens was an innovative move by Canon, and this allowed the company to produce better and more sophisticated lenses as technology became available to upgrade the focusing system. As a result, you'll find four different types of motors in Canon-designed lenses, each with cost and practical considerations. Some RF lenses are hybrids, incorporating both USM and STM technology.

- **AFD (Arc-form drive)** and **Micromotor (MM)** drives are built around tiny versions of electromagnetic motors, which generally use gear trains to produce the motion needed to adjust the focus of the lens. Both are slow, noisy, and not particularly effective with larger lenses. Manual focus adjustments are possible only when the motor drive is disengaged.

- **Micromotor ultrasonic motor (USM)** drives use high-frequency vibration to produce the motion used to drive the gear train, resulting in a quieter operating system at a cost that's not much more than that of electromagnetic motor drives. With the exception of a couple lenses that have a slipping clutch mechanism, manual focus with this kind of system is possible only when the motor drive is switched off and the lens is set in Manual mode. This is the kind of USM system you'll find in lower-cost lenses.

- **Ring ultrasonic motor (USM)** drives, available in two different types (*electronic focus ring USM* and *ring USM*), also use high-frequency movement, but generate motion using a pair of vibrating metal rings to adjust focus. Both variations allow a feature called Full Time Manual (FTM) focus, which lets you make manual adjustments to the lens's focus even when the autofocus mechanism is engaged. With electronic focus ring USM, manual focus is possible only when the lens is mounted on the camera and the camera is turned on; the focus ring of lenses with ring USM can be turned at any time.

- **Stepper motor (STM) drives.** In autofocus mode, the precision motor of STM lenses, along with a new aperture mechanism, allows lenses equipped with this technology to focus quickly, accurately, silently, and with smooth continuous increments. If you think about video capture, you can see how these advantages pay off. Silent operation is a plus, especially when noise from autofocusing can easily be transferred to the camera's built-in microphones through the air or transmitted through the body itself. In addition, because autofocus is often done *during* capture, it's important that the focus increments are continuous. USM motors are not as smooth, but are better at jumping quickly to the exact focus point. You can adjust focus manually, using a focus-by-wire process. As you rotate the focus ring, that action doesn't move the lens elements; instead, your rotation of the ring sends a signal to the motor to change the focus.

- **Series.** Canon adds a Roman numeral to many of its products to represent an updated model with the same focal length or focal length range, so some lenses will have a II or III added to their name. The revamped EF 24-70mm f/2.8L II USM lens is an example of a series update.

- **Pro quality.** Canon's more expensive lenses with more rugged construction and higher optical quality, intended for professional use, include the letter L (for "luxe" or "luxury") in their product name. You can further differentiate these lenses visually by a red ring around the lens barrel and the off-white color of the metal barrel itself in virtually all telephoto L-series lenses. (Some L-series lenses have shiny or textured black plastic exterior barrels.) Internally, every L lens includes at least one lens element that is built of ultra-low dispersion glass, is constructed of expensive fluorite crystal, or uses an expensive ground (not molded) aspheric (non-spherical) lens component.

- **Filter size.** You'll find the front lens filter thread diameter in millimeters included on the lens, preceded by a Ø symbol, as in Ø67 or Ø77. One advantage of Canon's L lenses is that many of them use 77mm filters, so you don't have to purchase a new set (or step-up/step-down adapter rings) each time you buy a lens.

- **Special-purpose lenses.** Some Canon lenses are designed for specific types of work, and they include appropriate designations in their names. For example, close-focusing lenses incorporate the word *Macro* into their name. Lenses with perspective control features preface the lens name with T-S (for tilt-shift). Lenses with built-in image-stabilization features, such as the nifty EF 28-300mm f/3.5-5.6L IS USM Telephoto Zoom include *IS* in their product names.

More Interesting Optics

There are lots of interesting lenses that belong in your camera bag, and this chapter wouldn't be complete without me mentioning some of them. The next sections will give you a quick summary of some potential objects of your Lens Lust.

The Magic Three

As I mentioned earlier, if you cruise the forums, you'll find the same three lenses mentioned over and over, often referred to as "The Trinity," "The Magic Three," or some other affectionate nickname. They are the three lenses you'll find in the kit of just about every serious Canon photographer (including me). They're fast, expensive, heavier than you might expect, and provide such exquisite image quality that once you equip yourself with the Trinity, you'll never be happy with anything else.

There are actually dual versions of each focal length, and I've arbitrarily divided them into two groups, the (relatively) affordable versions, and the deluxe, top-of-the-line trio.

The Affordable Magic Three

Neither lens trio is cheap, but these three lenses carry relatively reasonable price tags for anyone with the means to spring for a camera like the EOS RP. All of them share a number of attributes. All are full-frame L-series lenses; all have f/4 maximum apertures; and they each cost up to half the price of their top-of-the-line stablemates.

- **EF 17-40mm f/4L USM lens.** This lens is often used as a "kit" lens for wide-angle shooters because of its moderate $799 price tag, but it can be an integral part of anyone's three-lens kit. When I am shooting landscapes, doing street photography, or some types of indoor sports, this lens can go on my camera and never come off.

- **EF 24-70mm f/4L IS USM lens.** The f/4 maximum aperture of this $899 lens isn't truly a handicap, because it includes image stabilization. This lens is wonderfully sharp, and well-suited for anything from sports to portraiture that falls within its focal length range. It focuses down to 1.25 feet, so you can get decent magnification by moving close to your subjects at 70mm.

- **EF 70-200mm f/4L IS USM lens.** Canon offers no fewer than *four* EF-mount 70-200mm zooms, and this $1,099 version is your best bet among the affordable alternatives. While you can also choose one of two others with an f/4 or f/2.8 maximum aperture (for $599 and $1,249, respectively), neither have image stabilization. Unless you absolutely *must* have the largest possible maximum aperture (or need to save some bucks), this one is the best overall choice. It is perfect for some indoor and many outdoor sports, on a monopod, or hand-held, and can be used for portraiture, street photography, wildlife, and even distant scenics. I use it for concerts, too, alternating between this lens and my 85mm f/1.2. It takes me in close to the performer, and can be used wide-open or at f/5.6 with good image quality. Its chief drawbacks are that it focuses only down to about 4 feet, and uses 67mm filters.

The Reigning Magic Three

It's unlikely a new EOS RP owner will have around $6,500 burning a hole in their pockets, and it makes little sense to purchase the top tier of the Canon EF line. But if you already own these primo lenses, they can work very well with the EOS RP and a mount adapter. If their 6.6-pound heft seems like a lot compared to a lightweight mirrorless camera like the EOS RP, remember that this trio of lenses embraces every focal length from 16mm to 200mm, with maximum apertures of f/2.8 over the full range. The deluxe lineup looks like this:

- **EF 16-35mm f/2.8L III USM lens.** The image quality of this $2,199 lens is incredible, with very low barrel distortion (outward bowing at the edges) and very little of the chromatic aberrations common to lenses this wide. It focuses down to about 11 inches, allowing for some interesting close-up/wide-angle effects. The downside? The outward curving front element requires the use of large, expensive, 82mm filters—of course, as the use of polarizers, in particular, would be problematic at wider focal lengths. The polarizing effect would be highly variable because of this lens's extremely wide field of view. You could always use this with the Polarizer Mount Adapter and avoid the filter expense.

■ **EF 24-70mm f/2.8 II USM lens.** This lens, at $1,899 MSRP, provides outstanding image quality thanks to its single Super UD lens element paired with two UD elements to minimize chromatic aberrations. But if you have the cash and opportunity to purchase this newer lens, you won't be making a mistake. Some were surprised when it was introduced without the IS feature, but Canon has kept the size of this useful lens down, while maintaining a reasonable price for a "pro" level lens. It's another lens that uses 82mm filters, making the Polarizer or ND Mount Adapter an attractive choice.

■ **EF 70-200mm f/2.8L IS USM lens.** This $2,100 optic is many photographers' all-time favorite Canon lens. I'm a telephoto/selective focus kind of shooter. There's an older version, also with IS, for less, and, as I mentioned earlier, an f/2.8 version with no stabilization at all. But of Canon's three 70-200mm f/2.8 lenses (which all take 77mm filters), this one is the sharpest, focuses the fastest and closest, and is more ruggedly built. You might end up making this your workhorse, as I have.

More Winners

Although all the five or six dozen readily available Canon lenses are beyond the scope of this book, the company makes a variety of other interesting lenses. Here are some of my favorites.

■ **EF 8-15mm f/4L Fisheye USM lens.** Yup, a fisheye *zoom*. For a mere $1,249 you can buy the coolest lens you'll own, and start capturing some mind-bending images, or just add some interest to a simple landscape shot, like the one in Figure 7.7.

Figure 7.7

Because lines at the center of the frame aren't bent, some fisheye shots don't look like fisheye images on first glance.

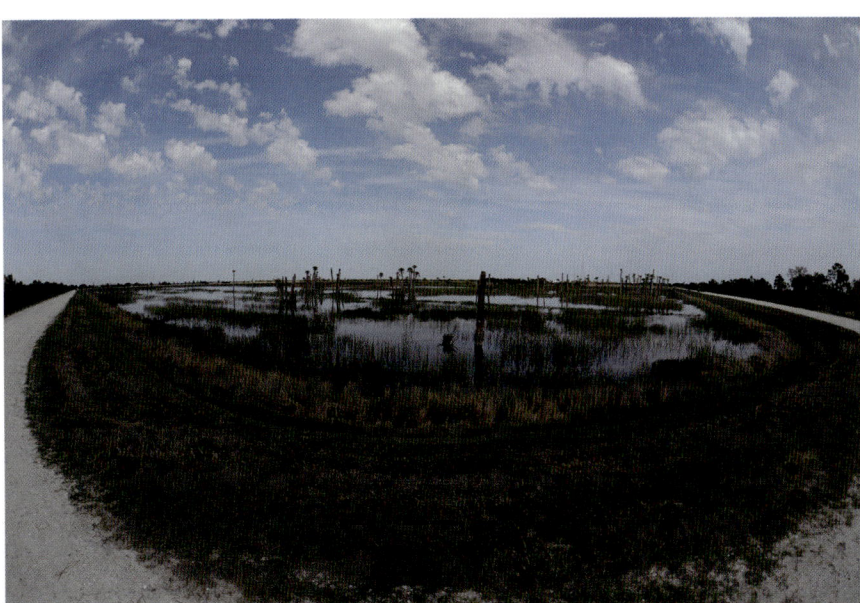

- **EF 100-400mm f/4.5-5.6L II USM lens.** A 400mm lens really comes in handy when shooting field sports, wildlife, and other distant subjects. This $2,199 lens is long enough and fast enough to prove useful in a variety of demanding situations. And, it's a lot more affordable than Canon's "exotic" lenses in this range, such as the EF 400mm f/2.8L II USM lens ($9,999). Although, at three pounds, this lens isn't really the boat anchor you might think it is; you'll want to mount it on a sturdy tripod (for wildlife) or monopod (for sports) to get the sharpest images.

- **EF 85mm f/1.2L II USM lens.** This exquisite lens is the perfect optic for head-and-shoulders portraits, with its remarkable bokeh, excellent sharpness, and shallow depth-of-field for selective focus effects. The $1,999 MSRP lens's huge maximum aperture means you can hand-hold it for sports, portraits, or other types of shooting. As I write this, there are rumors that Canon is about to introduce an updated 85mm f/1.4L lens. Price and other specs are unknown, but the new lens is sharper wide open and has comparable bokeh; many photographers will be willing to give up the f/1.2 versions slight maximum aperture advantage for an all-new design.

- **TS-E 90mm f/2.8 lens (or any other tilt-shift lens).** Manual focus won't bother you with this lens, because the most exciting capability of any tilt-shift lens is to let you manipulate the plane of focus in useful and/or interesting ways. Whether you want to correct the focal plane for architectural images, create "miniature" special effects, or produce unusual selective focus in portraits, these lenses offer interesting capabilities. The 90mm f/2.8 optic at $1,399 is relatively affordable, but Canon also offers 17mm, 24mm, and 45mm TS-E lenses for around $1,399 to $2,149.

- **A macro.** Canon offers an assortment of full-frame macro lenses, priced at less than $400 to less than $1,399, including the unique MP-E 65mm f/2.8 1-5X macro for close-up use only (it doesn't focus to infinity). All are non-zooms and they range in focal length from 50mm to 180mm, and one (the EF 100mm f/2.8L Macro IS USM) includes image stabilization for hand-held work. Choose your lens based on how close you want to work from your subject, and their closest focusing distance. Everybody needs a macro, especially for a rainy day when you want to photograph your collection of salt-shakers rather than venture out into the elements.

8

Mastering Light

The key tool we use to create and shape our images is light itself, in all its many forms and textures. Indeed, it's said that Sir John Herschel coined the term "photography" from the Greek words for "writing with light" in a paper read before the Royal Society in March 1839. Our dependence on the qualities of the light we use to produce our images is absolute. An adept photographer knows how to compensate for too much or too little illumination, how to soften harsh lighting to mask defects, or increase its contrast to evoke shape and detail. Sometimes, we must adjust our cameras for the apparent "color" of light, use a brief burst of it to freeze action, or filter it to reduce glare.

The many ways we can work with light deserve three full chapters in this book. This chapter introduces using *continuous* lighting (such as daylight, incandescent, LED, or fluorescent sources). I'll cover the brilliant snippets of light we call *electronic flash,* in Chapters 9 and 10.

Light That's Available

You'll often hear the term *available light,* meaning the ambient light at a scene, including whatever illumination is present outdoors during the day or at night, and that provided by lighting fixtures, windows, and other sources. In practice, available light includes any sort of illumination that's available, and can include supplementary lighting added by the photographer in the form of additional lamps, reflectors, or studio continuous light sources.

For our purposes, available light is exactly what you might think: uninterrupted illumination that is available all the time during a shooting session. Daylight, moonlight, and the artificial lighting encountered both indoors and outdoors count as continuous light sources (although all of them can be "interrupted" by passing clouds, solar eclipses, a blown fuse, or simply by switching a lamp off).

Indoor continuous illumination includes both the lights that are there already (such as incandescent lamps or overhead fluorescent lights indoors) and fixtures you supply yourself, including photoflood lamps or reflectors used to bounce existing light onto your subject.

Continuous lighting differs from electronic flash, which illuminates our photographs only in brief bursts. Flash, or "strobe" light is notable because it can be much more intense than continuous lighting, lasts only a moment, and can be much more portable than supplementary incandescent sources. It's a light source you can carry with you and use anywhere. There are advantages and disadvantages to each type of illumination. Here's a quick checklist of pros and cons:

- **Lighting preview—Pro: continuous lighting.** With continuous lighting, thanks to the EOS RP's real-time sensor image through the viewfinder or LCD screen, if you've opted to set Exposure Simulation to Enable in the Shooting 3 menu, you'll always know exactly what kind of lighting effect you're going to get—including color balance—and, if multiple lights are used, how they will interact with each other. If the natural light present in a scene is perfect for the image you're trying to capture, you'll know immediately (see Figure 8.1).

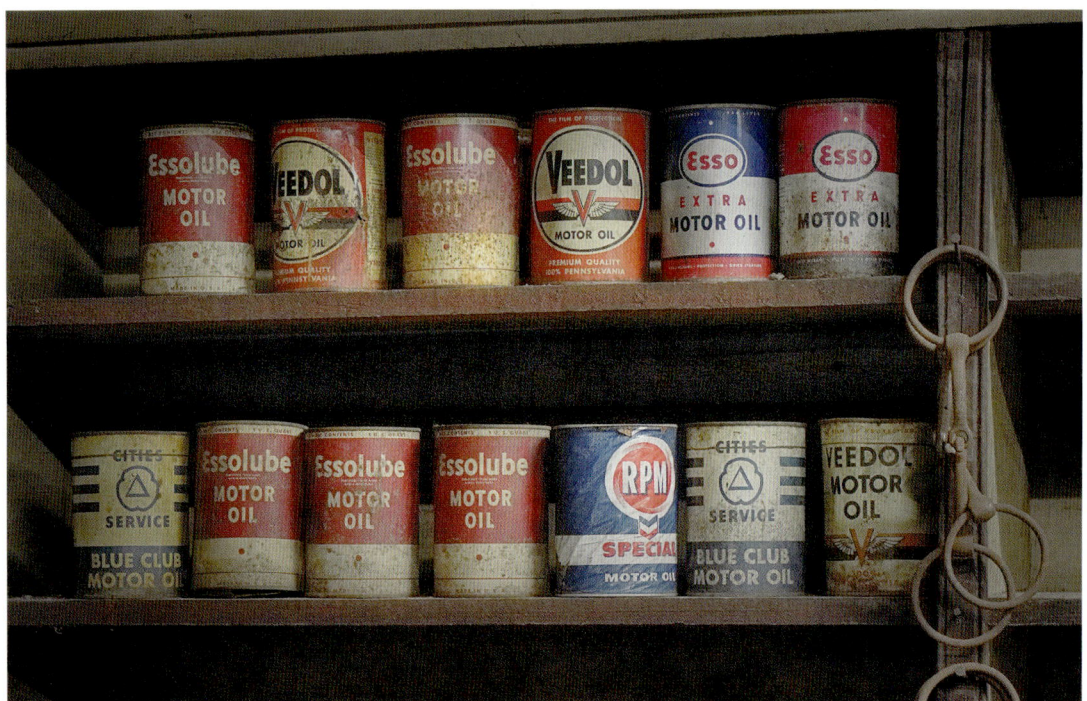

Figure 8.1 You always know how the lighting will look when using continuous illumination.

■ **Lighting preview—Con: electronic flash.** With electronic flash, unless you have a modeling light built into the flash, the general effect you're going to see may be a mystery until you've built some experience, and you may need to review a shot, make some adjustments, and then reshoot to get the look you want. (In this sense, a digital camera's review capabilities replace the Polaroid test shots pro photographers relied on in decades past.) An image like the one in Figure 8.1 would have been difficult to achieve with an off-camera battery-powered flash unit, because it would be tricky to provide the subtle illumination with the light from the flash. While the modeling light feature offered by some Canon flash units can be helpful, it's not a true continuous modeling light.

■ **Exposure calculation—Pro: continuous lighting.** Your EOS RP has no problem calculating exposure for continuous lighting, because it remains constant and can be measured directly from the light reaching the sensor. The amount of light available just before the exposure will, in almost all cases, be the same amount of light present when the shutter is released. The EOS RP's Spot metering mode can be used to measure and compare the proportions of light in the highlights and shadows, so you can make an adjustment (such as using more or less fill light) if necessary. If you want the utmost precision, you can even use a hand-held light meter to measure the light yourself, and then set the shutter speed and aperture to match in Manual exposure mode.

■ **Exposure calculation—Con: electronic flash.** Electronic flash illumination doesn't exist until the flash fires, and so can't be measured by the EOS RP's exposure sensor at the moment of exposure. Instead, the light must be measured by metering the intensity of a *pre-flash* triggered an instant *before* the main flash, as it is reflected back to the camera and through the lens. If you have a do-it-yourself bent, there are hand-held flash meters, too, including models that measure both flash and continuous light, so you need only one meter for both types of illumination.

■ **Evenness of illumination—Pro/con: continuous lighting.** Of the continuous light sources, daylight, in particular, provides illumination that tends to fill an image completely, lighting up the foreground, background, and your subject almost equally. Shadows do come into play, of course, so you might need to use reflectors or fill in additional light sources to even out the illumination further. But, barring objects that block large sections of your image from daylight, the light is spread fairly evenly. Indoors, however, continuous lighting is commonly less evenly distributed. The average living room, for example, has hot spots near the lamps and overhead lights, and dark corners located farther from those light sources. But on the plus side, you can easily *see* this uneven illumination and compensate with additional lamps.

- **Evenness of illumination—Con: electronic flash.** Electronic flash units, like continuous light sources such as lamps that don't have the advantage of being located 93 million miles from the subject, suffer from the effects of their proximity. The *inverse square law*, first applied to both gravity and light by Sir Isaac Newton, dictates that as a light source's distance increases from the subject, the amount of light reaching the subject falls off proportionately to the square of the distance. In plain English, that means that a flash or lamp that's twelve feet away from a subject provides only one-quarter as much illumination as a source that's six feet away (rather than half as much). This translates into relatively shallow "depth-of-light." I'll discuss this aspect again in Chapter 9.

- **Action stopping—Pro: electronic flash.** When it comes to the ability to freeze moving objects in their tracks, the advantage goes to electronic flash. The brief duration of electronic flash serves as a very high "shutter speed" when the flash is the main or only source of illumination for the photo. Your EOS RP's shutter speed may be set for 1/180th second during a flash exposure, but if the flash illumination predominates, the *effective* exposure time will be the 1/1000th to 1/50000th second or less duration of the flash, as you can see in Figure 8.2, because the flash unit reduces the amount of light released by cutting short the duration of the flash. The only fly in the ointment is that, if the ambient light is strong enough, it may produce a secondary, "ghost" exposure, as I'll explain in Chapter 9.

- **Action stopping—Con: continuous lighting.** Action stopping with continuous light sources is completely dependent on the shutter speed you've dialed in on the camera. And the speeds available are dependent on the amount of light available and your ISO sensitivity setting. Outdoors in daylight, there will probably be enough sunlight to let you shoot at 1/2000th second and f/6.3 with a non-grainy sensitivity setting for your EOS RP of ISO 400. That's a fairly useful combination of settings if you're not using a super-telephoto with a small maximum aperture. But inside, the reduced illumination quickly has you pushing your EOS RP to its limits. For example, if you're shooting indoor sports, there probably won't be enough available light to allow you to use a 1/2000th second shutter speed (although I routinely shoot indoor basketball with my EOS RP at ISO 1600 and 1/500th second at f/4). In many indoor sports situations, the lack of available light, and the EOS RP's increased visual noise at settings of ISO 6400 and above, you may find yourself limited to 1/500th second or slower.

- **Cost—Pro: continuous lighting.** Incandescent, fluorescent, or LED lamps are generally much less expensive than electronic flash units, which can easily cost several hundred dollars. I've used everything from desktop high-intensity lamps to reflector flood lights for continuous illumination at very little cost. There are lamps made especially for photographic purposes, too. Maintenance is economical, as well: many incandescent or fluorescents use bulbs that cost only a few dollars, and LED lamps are not only much less costly to operate, they are virtually immortal.

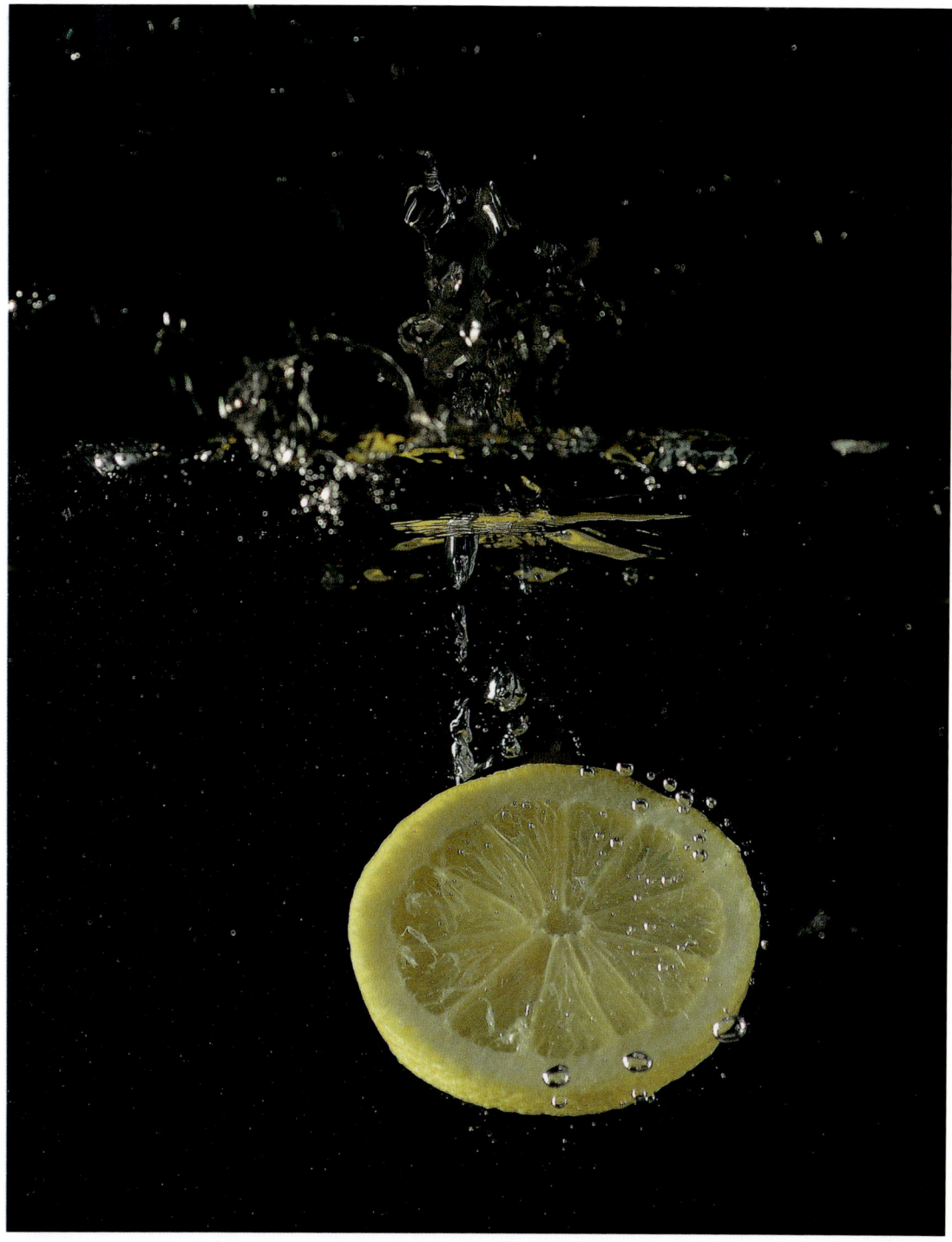

Figure 8.2 Electronic flash can freeze almost any action.

- **Cost—Con: electronic flash.** Electronic flash units aren't particularly cheap. The lowest-cost dedicated flash designed specifically for the Canon EOS cameras is about $200 (the EL-100). Such basic units are limited in features, and intended for those with entry-level cameras. Plan on spending some money to get the features that a sophisticated electronic flash offers.

- **Flexibility—Pro: electronic flash.** Electronic flash's action-freezing power allows you to work without a tripod in the studio (and elsewhere), adding flexibility and speed when choosing angles and positions. Flash units can be easily filtered, and, because the filtration is placed over the light source rather than the lens, you don't need to use high-quality filter material. For example, Roscoe or Lee lighting gels, which may be too flimsy to use in front of the lens, can be mounted or taped in front of your flash with ease.

- **Flexibility—Con: continuous lighting.** Because incandescent and fluorescent lamps are not as bright as electronic flash, the slower shutter speeds required (see "Action stopping," above) mean that you may have to use a tripod more often, especially when shooting portraits. The incandescent variety of continuous lighting gets hot, especially in the studio, and the side effects range from discomfort (for your human models) to disintegration (if you happen to be shooting perishable foods like ice cream). The heat also makes it more difficult to add filtration to incandescent sources. (It's no wonder that LED illumination is rapidly becoming the go-to continuous light source for photography.)

Continuous Lighting Basics

While continuous lighting and its effects are generally much easier to visualize and use than electronic flash, there are some factors you need to take into account, particularly the color temperature of the light, how accurately a given form of illumination reproduces colors (we've all seen the ghastly looks human faces assume under mercury-vapor lamps outdoors), and other considerations.

One important aspect is color temperature. Of course, color temperature concerns aren't exclusive to continuous light sources, but the variations tend to be more extreme and less predictable than those of electronic flash, which output relatively consistent daylight-like illumination.

Living with Color Temperature

In practical terms, color temperature is how "bluish" or how "reddish" the light appears to be to the digital camera's sensor. Indoor illumination is quite warm, comparatively, and appears reddish to the sensor. Daylight, in contrast, seems much bluer to the sensor. Our eyes (our brains, actually) are quite adaptable to these variations, so white objects don't appear to have an orange tinge when viewed indoors, nor do they seem excessively blue outdoors in full daylight. Yet, these color temperature variations are real and the sensor is not fooled. To capture the most accurate colors, we need to take the color temperature into account in setting the color balance (or *white balance*) of the EOS RP—either automatically using the camera's intelligence or manually using our own knowledge and experience.

While Canon has been valiant in its efforts to smarten up the EOS RP's ability to adjust for color balance automatically, an entire cottage industry has developed to provide us additional help, including gadgets like the ExpoDisc filter/caps (see Figure 8.3) and their ilk (www.expoimaging.com), which allow the camera's add-on external custom white balance measuring feature to evaluate the illumination that passes through the disc/cap/filter/Pringle's can lid, or whatever neutral-color substitute you employ. (A white or gray card also works.) Unfortunately, to help us tangle with the many different types of non-incandescent/non-daylight sources, Canon has provided the EOS RP with only a single White Fluorescent setting (some competing models offer more than a half-dozen different presets for fluorescents, sodium-vapor, and mercury vapor illumination). When it comes to zeroing in on the exact color temperature for a scene, your main tools will be custom white balances set using neutral targets like the ExpoDisc, and adjustment of RAW files when you import photos into your image editor.

Figure 8.3
The ExpoDisc is placed on a lens and used as a neutral subject for measuring white balance.

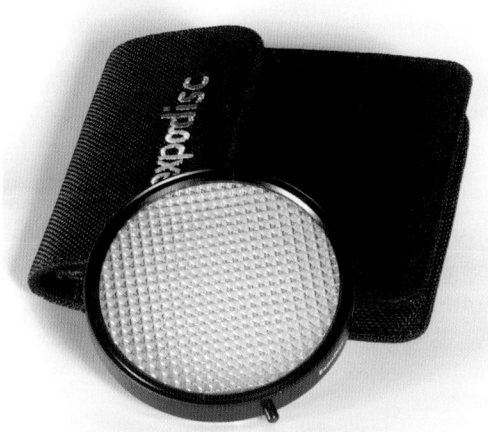

The only time you need to think in terms of actual color temperature is when you're making adjustments using the Color Temp. setting in the White Balance entry of the Shooting 4 menu, as I'll describe in Chapter 11. It allows you to dial in exact color temperatures, if known. You can also shift and bias color balance along the blue/amber and magenta/green axes, and bracket white balance.

In most cases, however, the Auto setting in the Shooting menu's White Balance entry will do a good job of calculating white balance for you. Auto can be used as your choice most of the time. Use the preset values or set a custom white balance that matches the current shooting conditions when you need to.

Remember that if you shoot RAW, you can specify the white balance of your image when you import it into Photoshop, Photoshop Elements, or another image editor using Adobe Camera Raw, or your preferred RAW converter. While color-balancing filters that fit on the front of the lens exist, they are primarily useful for film cameras, because film's color balance can't be tweaked as extensively as that of a sensor.

White Balance Bracketing

When using WB bracketing, the EOS RP takes a single shot, and then saves multiple JPEG copies, each with a different color balance. It's not necessary to capture multiple shots, as the camera uses the raw information retrieved from the sensor for the single exposure and then processes it to generate the multiple different versions. The bracketing adjustments are made only on the amber/blue axis (no bracketing in the magenta/green bias is possible), but you can select whether the bracketed shots are spread in the blue *or* amber directions (that is, each one bluer/less blue or yellower/less yellow) or balanced to provide both blue- and amber-oriented brackets. (See Figure 8.4.)

Making these adjustments are the only times you're likely to be confused by a seeming contradiction in how color temperatures are named: warmer (more reddish) color temperatures (measured in degrees Kelvin) are the *lower* numbers, while cooler (bluer) color temperatures are *higher* numbers. It might not make sense to say that 3,400K is warmer than 6,000K, but that's the way it is. If it helps, think of a glowing red ember contrasted with a white-hot welder's torch, rather than fire and ice.

The confusion comes from physics. Scientists calculate color temperature from the light emitted by a mythical object called a black body radiator, which absorbs all the radiant energy that strikes it, and reflects none at all. Such a black body not only *absorbs* light perfectly, but it *emits* it perfectly when heated (and since nothing in the universe is perfect, that makes it mythical).

At a particular physical temperature, this imaginary object always emits light of the same wavelength or color. That makes it possible to define color temperature in terms of actual temperature in degrees on the Kelvin scale that scientists use. Incandescent light, for example, typically has a color temperature of 3,200K to 3,400K. Daylight might range from 5,500K to 6,000K. Each type of illumination we use for photography has its own color temperature range—with some cautions.

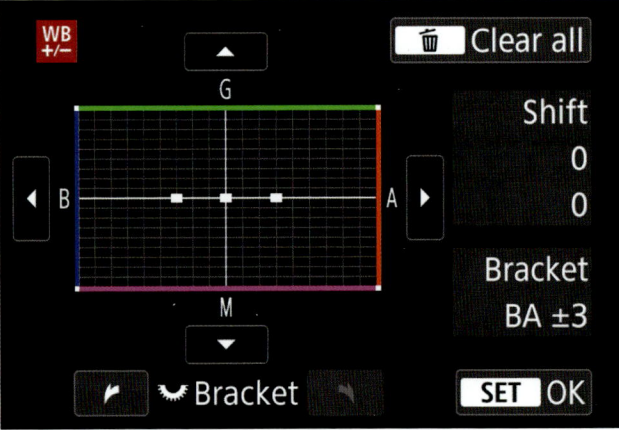

Figure 8.4
White balance bracketing can be done only along the amber/blue axis.

Daylight

Daylight is produced by the sun, and so is moonlight (which is just reflected sunlight). Daylight is present, of course, even when you can't see the sun. When sunlight is direct, it can be bright and harsh. If daylight is diffused by clouds, softened by bouncing off objects such as walls or your photo reflectors, or filtered by shade, it can be much dimmer and less contrasty.

Daylight's color temperature can vary quite widely. It is highest in temperature (most blue) at noon when the sun is directly overhead, because the light is traveling through a minimum amount of the filtering layer we call the atmosphere. The color temperature at high noon may be 6,000K. At other times of day, the sun is lower in the sky and the particles in the air provide a filtering effect that warms the illumination to about 5,500K for most of the day. Starting an hour before dusk and for an hour after sunrise, the warm appearance of the sunlight is even visible to our eyes when the color temperature may dip to 5,000K–4,500K, as shown in Figure 8.5.

Because you'll be taking so many photos in daylight, you'll want to learn how to use or compensate for the brightness and contrast of sunlight, as well as how to deal with its color temperature. I'll provide some hints later in this chapter.

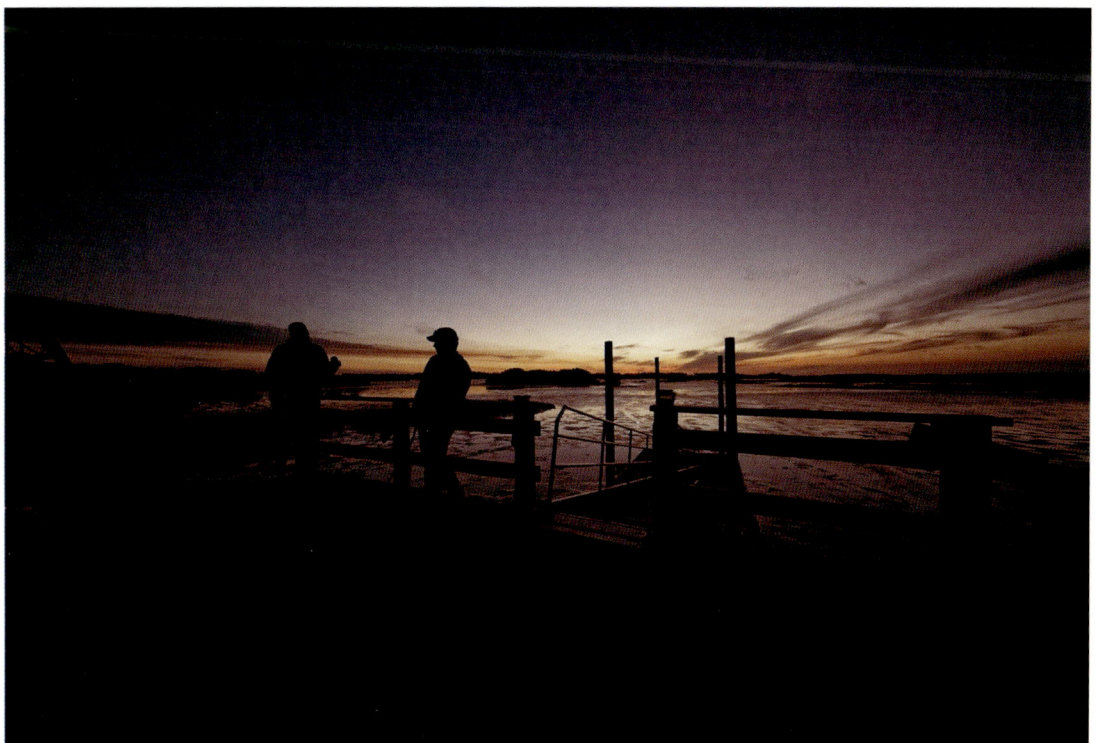

Figure 8.5 At dawn and dusk, the color temperature of daylight may dip as low as 4,500K.

Incandescent/Tungsten/Halogen Light

The term incandescent or tungsten/halogen illumination is usually applied to the direct descendents of Thomas Edison's original electric lamp. Such lights consist of a glass bulb that contains a vacuum, or is filled with a halogen gas, and contains a tungsten filament that is heated by an electrical current, producing photons and heat. Tungsten-halogen lamps are a variation on the basic light bulb, using a more rugged (and longer-lasting) filament that can be heated to a higher temperature, housed in a thicker glass or quartz envelope, and filled with iodine or bromine ("halogen") gases. The higher temperature allows tungsten-halogen (or quartz-halogen/quartz-iodine, depending on their construction) lamps to burn "hotter" and whiter. Although popular for automobile headlamps today, they've also been used for photographic illumination.

Although incandescent illumination isn't a perfect black body radiator, it's close enough that the color temperature of such lamps can be precisely calculated and used for photography without concerns about color variation (at least, until the very end of the lamp's life). As I noted earlier, the color rendering index of such lamps tends to be very high, so you need to account only for the color temperature.

Of course, old-style tungsten lamps are on the way out, at first replaced either by compact fluorescent lights (CFL) or newer, more energy-efficient (and expensive) tungsten and halogen lights, and, eventually, by LED illumination. It appears that LED illumination is on track to supplant all of these for most applications in the near future. The other qualities of this type of lighting, such as contrast, are dependent on the distance of the lamp from the subject, type of reflectors used, and other factors that I'll explain later in this chapter.

Fluorescent Light/Other Light Sources

Fluorescent light has some advantages in terms of illumination, but some disadvantages from a photographic standpoint. This type of lamp generates light through an electro-chemical reaction that emits most of its energy as visible light, rather than heat, which is why the bulbs don't get as hot. The type of light produced varies depending on the phosphor coatings and type of gas in the tube.

Color Rendering

Faithful color rendition goes beyond color temperature. So-called "white" light is produced by a spectrum of colors that, when added together, provide the neutral color needed for accuracy. Artificial light sources don't necessarily offer the same balanced spectrum found in sunlight. Some portions of the spectrum may be deficient or truncated, or include gaps with certain wavelengths missing entirely. Astronomers use their knowledge of which elements absorb which colors of light to calculate the makeup of distant stars using spectrographs. In photography, the analysis of spectra is used to calculate the color rendering index, which measures how accurately colors are presented.

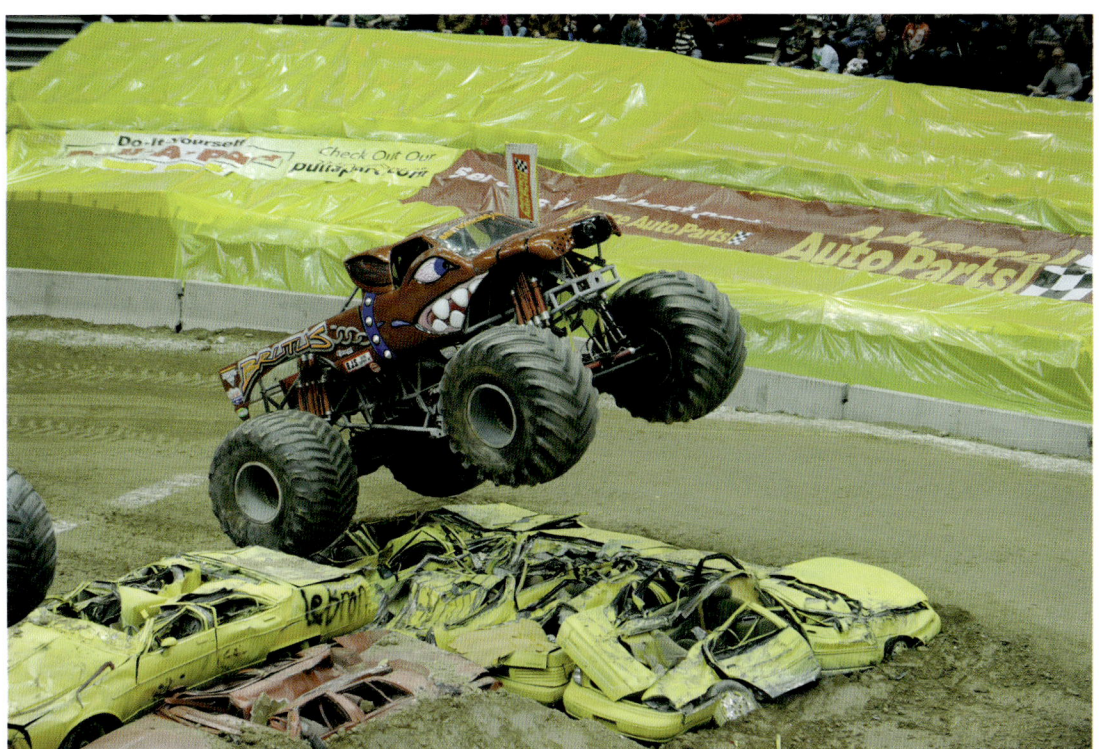

Figure 8.6 The uncorrected fluorescent lighting in the arena added a distinct greenish cast to this image when exposed with a daylight white balance setting.

All artificial light sources have a color rendering index (CRI). That figure is calculated by rating eight different colors on a scale of 0 to 100, based on how natural the color looks compared to a perfect or "reference" light source at a particular color temperature. A CRI of 80-plus is considered acceptable; for critical applications like photography, a CRI higher than 93 is best. Incandescent and halogen bulbs typically have a CRI of 100 compared to a reference light source at the same color temperature. Standard LED lamps are rated at 83, although some can have CRIs as high as 98. Many types of fluorescent lights fall into the CRI 50–75 range.

Vendors, such as GE and Sylvania, may actually provide a figure known as the color rendering index on the packaging using a scale of 0 (some sodium-vapor lamps) to 100 (daylight and most incandescent lamps). Daylight fluorescents and deluxe cool white fluorescents suitable for photography might have a CRI of about 79 to 95, which is perfectly acceptable for most photographic applications. Less desirable are warm white fluorescents, which may have a CRI of 55. White deluxe mercury-vapor lights are even less suitable with a CRI of 45, while low-pressure sodium lamps can vary from CRI 0 to 18. If you're using such a source not intended for photography, it may be worth your while to determine its color rendering index before you shoot. Fluorescent lights, discussed next, are an excellent example.

Fluorescent Light/LEDs

Fluorescent light has some advantages in terms of illumination, but some disadvantages from a photographic standpoint. This type of lamp generates light through an electro-chemical reaction that emits most of its energy as visible light, rather than heat, which is why the bulbs don't get as hot. The type of light produced varies depending on the phosphor coatings and type of gas in the tube. So, the illumination fluorescent bulbs produce can vary widely in its characteristics.

That's not great news for photographers. Different types of lamps have different "color temperatures" that can't be precisely measured in degrees Kelvin, because the light isn't produced by heating. Worse, fluorescent lamps have a discontinuous spectrum of light that can have some colors missing entirely. A particular type of light source can lack certain shades of red or other color, which is why fluorescent lamps and other alternative technologies such as sodium-vapor illumination can produce strange hues, as in the figure, and ghastly looking human skin tones. Their spectra can lack the reddish tones we associate with healthy skin and emphasize the blues and greens popular in horror movies. As I mentioned earlier, their color rendering indexes are far from ideal.

Compact fluorescent lights (CFLs) are those spiraling bulbs that became popular as old-school tungsten bulbs were phased out. However, CFLs don't work in all fixtures and for all applications, such as dimmers (even if you purchase special "dimmable" CFLs), electronic timer or "dusk-to-dawn" light controllers, some illuminated wall switches, or with motion sensors. Only certain types of CFLs (cold cathode models) operate outside in cold weather; they emit IR signals that can confuse the remote control of your TV, air conditioner, etc.

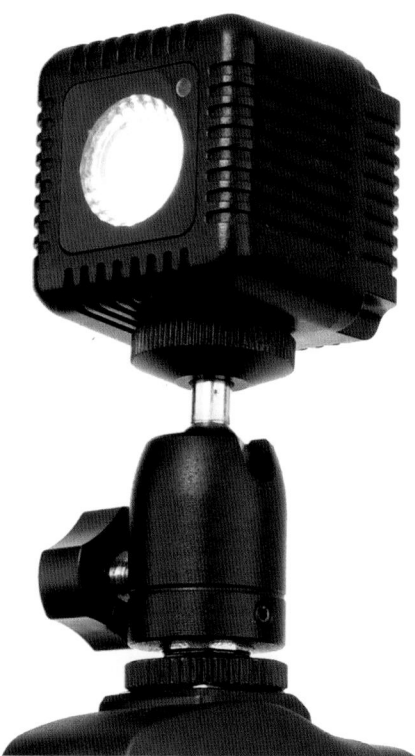

Gaining in popularity are LED light sources, particularly for movies, in the form of compact units that clip onto the camera and provide a continuous beam of light to fill in shadows indoors or out, and/or to provide the main illumination when shooting video inside. Several vendors have introduced LED studio lights that are bright enough for general-purpose shooting. It's become obvious that LED illumination will soon become the most widely used continuous light source. They've already made dramatic inroads in the automotive industry for taillights, headlights, and interior illumination. Innovations like the Lume Cube, a brilliant $80 waterproof variable-brightness LED lamp that can be triggered wirelessly, will find broader use. (See Figure 8.7.)

Figure 8.7 The Lume Cube.

Other Lighting Accessories

Once you start working with light, you'll find there are plenty of useful accessories that can help you. Here are some of the most popular that you might want to consider. These all work well with both continuous lighting, discussed in this chapter, as well as with electronic flash, which will be our focus in the chapter that follows this one.

Do-It-Yourself Lighting

The cool thing about continuous lighting is that anything that lights up can be used as a lighting tool for your EOS RP. Flashlights (for "painting with light" techniques), shop work lights, or even desktop high-intensity lamps, like the one seen in Figure 8.8, left, can be pressed into service at little or no cost (if you already happen to own something that will work). I used that desk lamp to shoot the image seen in Figure 8.8, right, simply because the lamp was bright enough to let me use a small f/stop to maximize depth-of-field, and it was really easy to see the lighting effect and move the lamp an inch or two to get different effects.

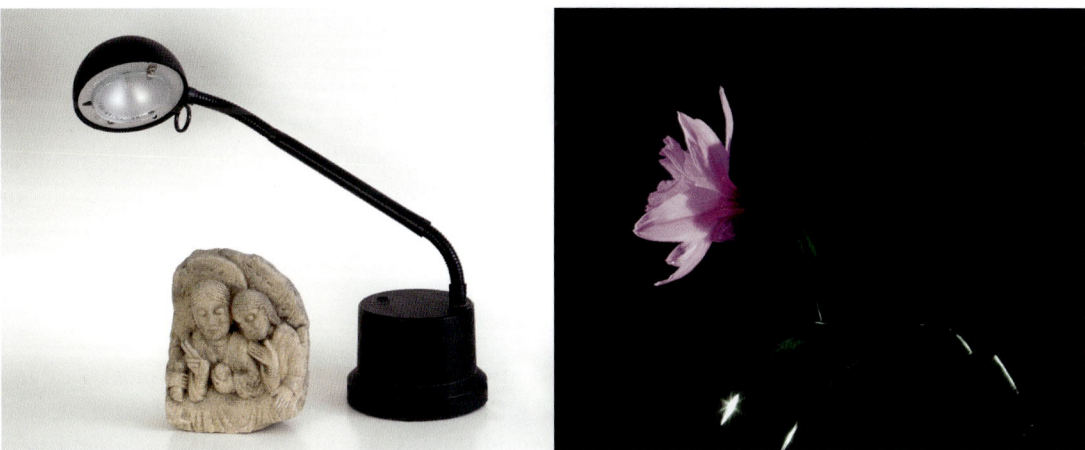

Figure 8.8 A desk lamp can be pressed into service as a light source for tabletop and macro photography.

Umbrellas

Umbrellas are just what you might think, a variation on those trusty shields-on-a-stick that protect us from the ravages of sun, rain, snow, or other elements of nature. Whether we know them as parasols (for the sun) or paraguas (for the water) on the Costa del Sol, as parapluies/ombrelles on the Riviera, or Sonnenschirme/Regenschirme (gotta love those Germans!), these inexpensive accessories are just as versatile for reflecting light as blocking it.

Indeed, you can use umbrellas in multiple roles:

- **Light reflector.** A silver umbrella can provide a softer, but not *too* soft light source, or a much softer source of illumination when a non-shiny white umbrella is used. The quality and quantity of the light that your EOS RP sees can be further adjusted simply by moving the umbrella closer to your subject (for a softer illumination) or farther away (for more contrast).

- **Light diffuser.** A white umbrella diffuses and softens light, but a translucent white umbrella (of the "shoot-through" variety) can be reversed so that the illumination passes through the fabric and becomes even more soft and diffuse.

- **Light blocker.** Some umbrellas have a white or silver interior surface, and a black cover that prevents any light from leaking through the umbrella. Those models can be used to *block* light from other sources of illumination—even outdoors in daylight—to allow you to create subtle lighting effects.

- **Light colorizer.** Umbrellas may have a shiny golden, silver, or blue interior surface (as do many flat reflectors), and so can be used to add a rich warm tone, neutral sheen, or cold bluish cast to an image or shadows. You can use umbrella "colorizing" to create an effect or balance multiple light sources.

- **Soft box in an instant.** Many umbrellas can be fitted with a cover over their front that transforms them into a soft box. This conversion is more practical for use with electronic flash (covered in the next chapter) than for some kinds of continuous lighting, because of heat build-up. "Colder" forms of continuous lighting, such as fluorescent lights designed specially for photographic applications, can be used in soft box mode, however. Figure 8.9, left, shows both an umbrella and a soft box.

Tents

Tents, like the one seen in at right Figure 8.9, are useful for photographing shiny objects or any subject where you want to reduce the shadows and reflections to a minimum. The fabric of the tent is translucent, so you place the light sources around the sides or above, and a soft glow filters through to illuminate the image. You can still maintain subtle lighting effects by choosing to light up—or not light up—individual sides of the cube.

The lens of the EOS RP protrudes through a hole or slit in the tent, so you can photograph the shiniest subject without having you or your camera show up in the final picture.

Soft Boxes

Soft boxes are also handy for photographing shiny objects. They not only provide a soft light, but if the box itself happens to reflect in the subject (say you're photographing a chromium toaster), the box will provide an interesting highlight that's indistinct and not distracting.

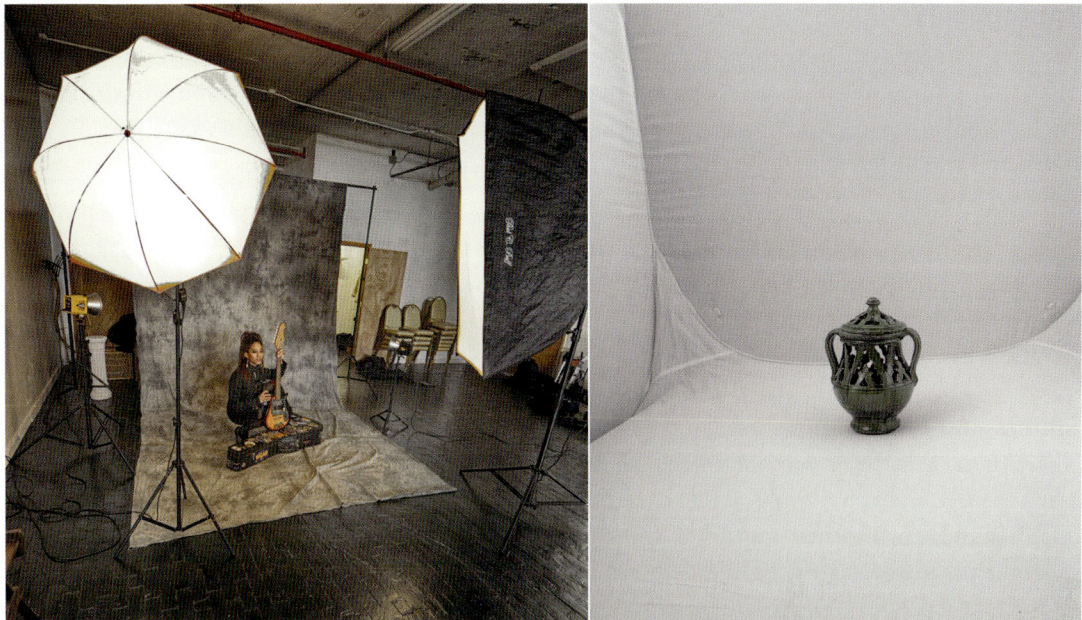

Figure 8.9 Umbrellas and soft boxes, seen at opposite sides of the frame, provide a soft, diffuse light source (left). Tents provide shadowless lighting for shiny objects (right).

You can buy soft boxes or make your own. Some lengths of friction-fit plastic pipe and a lot of muslin cut and sewed just so may be all that you need. Soft boxes are large square, rectangular, or round or octagonal devices that may resemble an umbrella with a front cover, and produce a similar lighting effect. They can extend from a few feet square to massive boxes that stand five or six feet tall—virtually a wall of light. With a light source or two inside a soft box, you have a very large, semi-directional light source that's very diffuse and very flattering for portraiture and other people photography.

Light Stands

Both electronic flash and incandescent lamps can benefit from light stands. These are lightweight, tripod-like devices (but without a swiveling or tilting head) that can be set on the floor, tabletops, or other elevated surfaces and positioned as needed. Light stands should be strong enough to support an external lighting unit, up to and including a relatively heavy flash with soft box or umbrella reflectors. You want the supports to be capable of raising the lights high enough to be effective. Look for light stands capable of extending six to seven feet high. The nine-foot units usually have larger, steadier bases, and extend high enough that you can use them as background supports. You'll be using these stands for a lifetime, so invest in good ones. I bought my light stands when I was in college, and I have been using them for decades.

Backgrounds

Backgrounds can be backdrops of cloth, sheets of muslin you've painted yourself using a sponge dipped in paint, rolls of seamless paper, or any other suitable surface your mind can dream up. Backgrounds provide a complementary and non-distracting area behind subjects (especially portraits) and can be lit separately to provide contrast and separation that outlines the subject, or which helps set a mood.

I like to use plain-colored backgrounds for portraits, and white or gray seamless paper backgrounds for product photography. You can usually construct these yourself from cheap materials and tape them up on the wall behind your subject, or mount them on a pole stretched between a pair of light stands.

Snoots and Barn Doors

These fit over the flash unit and direct the light at your subject. Snoots are excellent for converting a light source into a hair light, while barn doors give you enough control over the illumination by opening and closing their flaps that you can use another flash as a background light, with the capability of feathering the light exactly where you want it on the background.

9

Electronic Flash Basics

Until you delve into the situation deeply enough, it might appear that serious photographers have a love/hate relationship with electronic flash. You'll often hear that flash photography is less natural looking, and that the built-in flash in most cameras should never be used as the primary source of illumination because it provides a harsh, garish look. Indeed, many advanced cameras like the Canon EOS RP don't have a built-in flash at all. Available ("continuous") lighting is praised, and built-in flash photography seems to be roundly denounced.

In truth, however, the bias is against *bad* flash photography, the kind produced when you clamp a flash on top of the camera (as shown in Figure 9.1) and point it directly at your subject. In that mode, you'll often end up with well-exposed (thanks to Canon's e-TTL II metering system), but

Figure 9.1
An add-on flash is a versatile accessory.

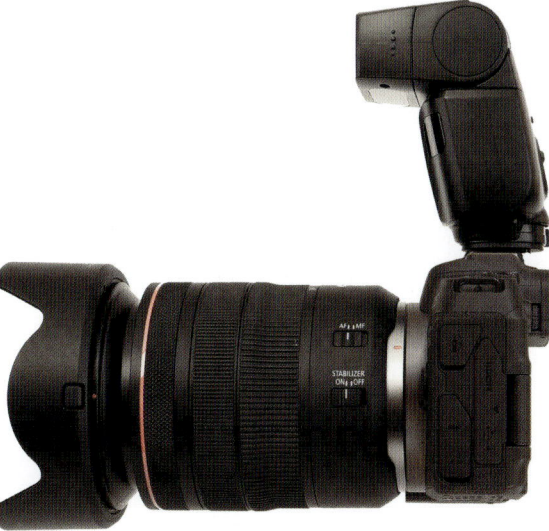

harshly lit images. Yet, in other configurations, flash has become the studio light source of choice for pro photographers, because it's more intense (and its intensity can be varied to order by the photographer), freezes action, frees you from using a tripod (unless you want to use one to lock down a composition), and has a snappy, consistent light quality that matches daylight. (While color balance changes as the flash duration shortens, some Canon flash units can communicate to the camera the exact white balance provided for that shot.) And even pros will cede that an external flash has some important uses as an adjunct to existing light, particularly to illuminate dark shadows using a technique called *fill flash*. Moreover, creative photographers can use an external Speedlite with their EOS RP in remarkably creative ways, especially in wireless and multiple flash modes (which I'll explain in Chapter 10).

But electronic flash isn't as inherently easy to use as continuous lighting. As I noted in Chapter 8, electronic flash units are more expensive, don't show you exactly what the lighting effect will be (unless you use a second, relatively continuous source called a *modeling light* for a preview), and the exposure of electronic flash units is more difficult to calculate accurately.

How Electronic Flash Works

The bursts of light we call electronic flash are produced by a flash of photons generated by an electrical charge that is accumulated in a component called a *capacitor* and then directed through a glass tube containing xenon gas, which absorbs the energy and emits the brief flash. For a typical external flash attached to the EOS RP, such as the top-of-the-line Speedlite 600EX II-RT, the full burst of light lasts about 1/1000th of a second and provides enough illumination to shoot a subject 12 feet away at f/16 using the ISO 100 setting.

Because the duration of the burst is so brief, if the external flash is the main source of illumination, the effective exposure time is short, typically 1/1000th to 1/50000th second, freezing a moving subject dramatically, as shown in Figure 9.2. These short bursts can also be repeated, producing multiple-exposure/stroboscopic effects, as described later in this chapter.

An electronic flash is triggered at the instant of exposure, during a period when the sensor is fully exposed by the shutter. The EOS RP has a vertically traveling shutter that consists of two curtains. The first curtain opens and moves to the opposite side of the frame, at which point the shutter is completely open. The flash can be triggered at this point (so-called *first-curtain sync*), making the flash exposure. Then, after a delay that can vary from 30 seconds to 1/180th second (with the EOS RP; other cameras may sync at a faster speed), a second curtain begins moving across the sensor plane, covering up the sensor again. If the flash is triggered just before the second curtain starts to close, then *second-curtain sync* is used. In both cases, though, a shutter speed of 1/180th second is the maximum that can be used to take a photo (unless you're using high-speed sync, discussed later in this chapter).

Figure 9.2
An external flash placed to the left and slightly in front of the dancer produced a brief burst that froze her en pointe.

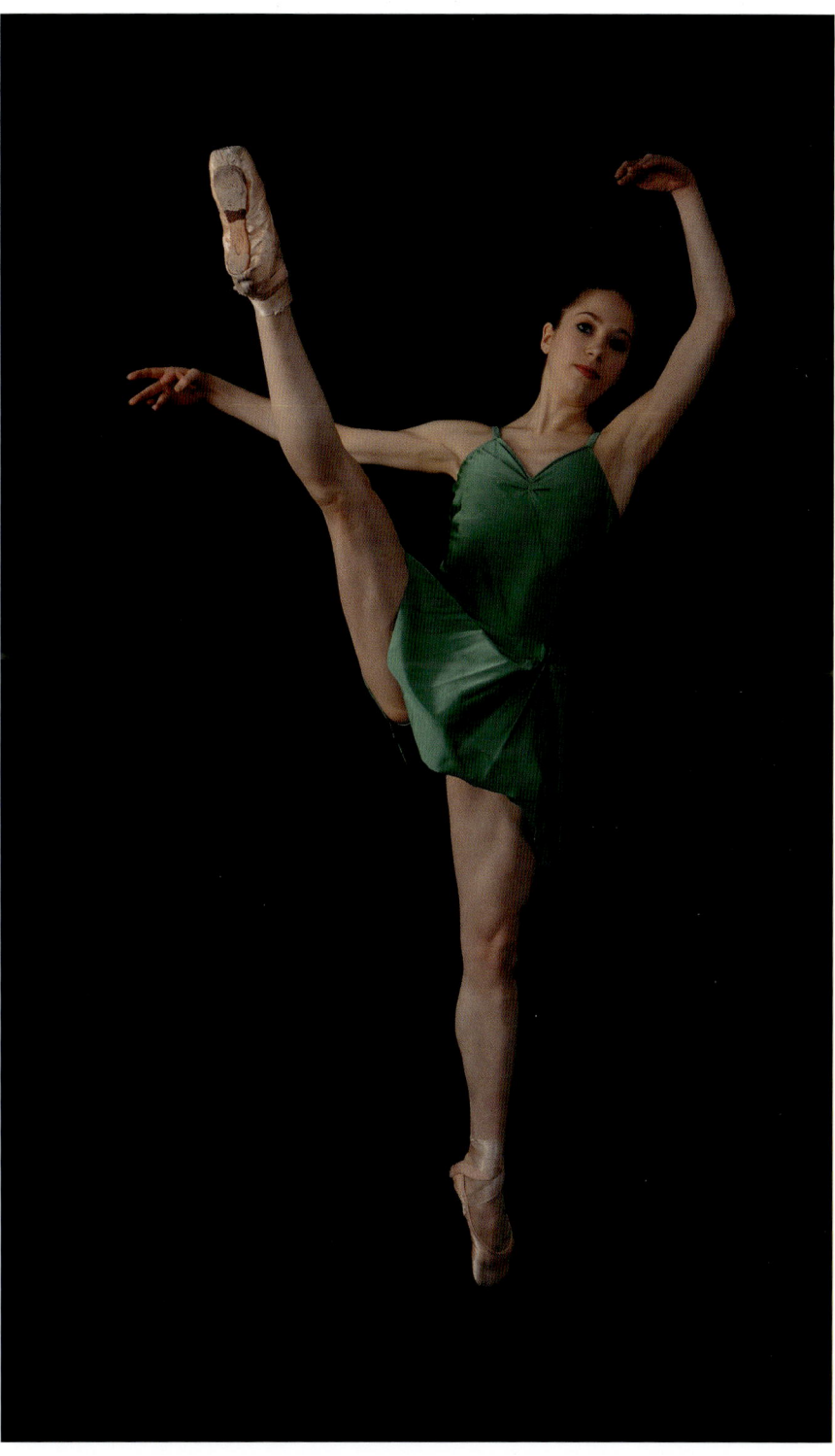

Figure 9.3 illustrates how this works. At upper left, you can see a fanciful illustration of a generic shutter with both curtains tightly closed. (Your shutter does not actually look like this.) At upper right, the first curtain begins to move downward, starting to expose a narrow slit that reveals the sensor behind the shutter. At lower left, the first curtain moves downward farther until, as you can see at lower right in the figure, the sensor is fully exposed.

When first-curtain sync is used, the flash is triggered at the instant that the sensor is completely exposed. The shutter then remains open for an additional length of time (from 30 seconds to 1/180th second), and the second curtain begins to move downward, covering the sensor once more. When second-curtain sync is activated, the flash is triggered *after* the main exposure is over, just before the second curtain begins to move downward.

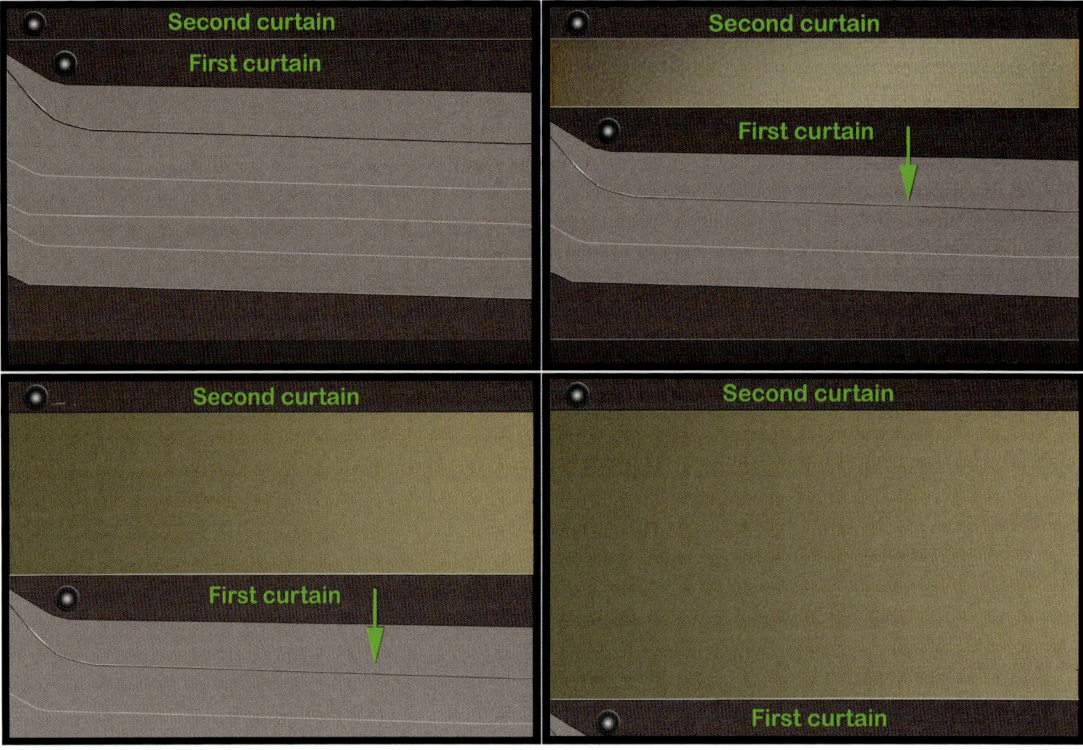

Figure 9.3 A focal plane shutter has two curtains, the upper, or front curtain, and a lower, second curtain.

Ghost Images

The difference between triggering the flash when the shutter just opens, or just when it begins to close might not seem like much. But whether you use first-curtain sync (the default setting) or second-curtain sync (an optional setting) can make a significant difference to your photograph *if the ambient light in your scene also contributes to the image.* You can set either of these sync modes in the Shooting 2 menu, under External Speedlite control, where you'll find the Flash Function setting option.

At faster shutter speeds, particularly 1/180th second, there isn't much time for the ambient light to register, unless it is very bright. It's likely that the electronic flash will provide almost all the illumination, so first-curtain sync or second-curtain sync isn't very important. However, at slower shutter speeds, or with very bright ambient light levels, there is a significant difference, particularly if your subject is moving, or the camera isn't steady.

In any of those situations, the ambient light will register as a second image accompanying the flash exposure, and if there is movement (camera or subject), that additional image will not be in the same place as the flash exposure. It will show as a ghost image and, if the movement is significant enough, as a blurred ghost image trailing in front of or behind your subject in the direction of the movement.

As I noted, when you're using first-curtain sync, the flash's main burst goes off the instant the shutter opens fully (a pre-flash used to measure exposure in auto flash modes fires *before* the shutter opens). This produces an image of the subject on the sensor. Then, the shutter remains open for an additional period (30 seconds to 1/180th second, as I said). If your subject is moving, say, toward the right side of the frame, the ghost image produced by the ambient light will produce a blur on the right side of the original subject image, making it look as if your sharp (flash-produced) image is chasing the ghost. For those of us who grew up with lightning-fast superheroes who always left a ghost trail *behind them*, that looks unnatural (see Figure 9.4).

So, Canon uses second-curtain sync to remedy the situation. In that mode, the shutter opens, as before. The shutter remains open for its designated duration, and the ghost image forms. If your subject moves from the left side of the frame to the right side, the ghost will move from left to right, too. *Then*, about 1.5 milliseconds before the second shutter curtain closes, the flash is triggered, producing a nice, sharp flash image *ahead* of the ghost image. Voilà! We have monsieur *Speed Racer* outdriving his own trailing image.

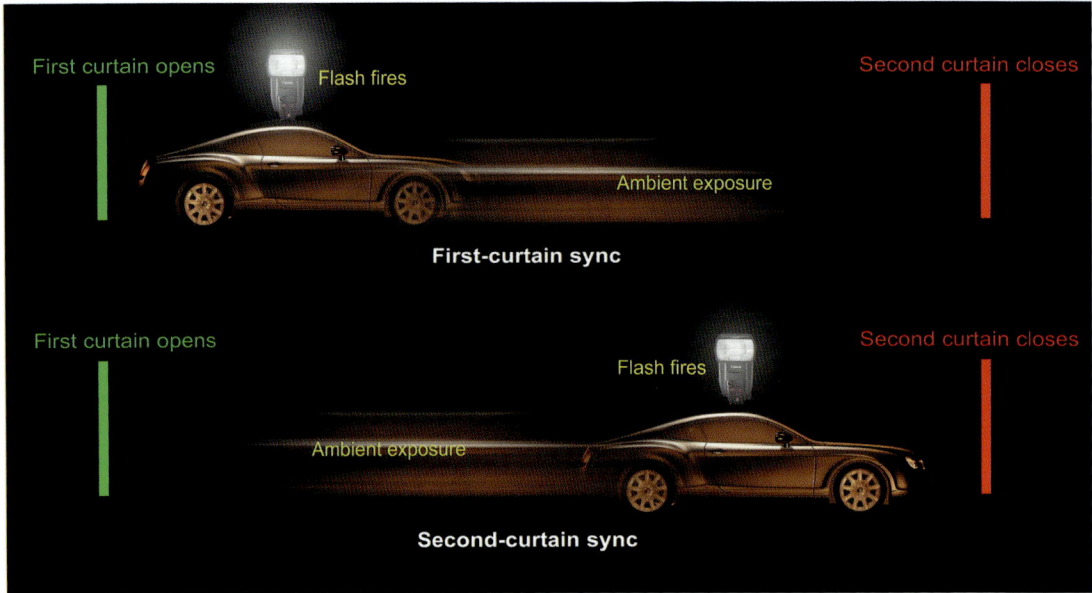

Figure 9.4 First-curtain sync produces an image that trails in front of the flash exposure (top), whereas second-curtain sync creates a more "natural-looking" trail behind the flash image.

Avoiding Sync-Speed Problems

Using a shutter speed faster than 1/180th second can cause problems. Triggering the electronic flash only when the shutter is completely open makes a lot of sense if you think about what's going on. To obtain shutter speeds faster than 1/180th second, the EOS RP exposes only part of the sensor at one time, by starting the second curtain on its journey before the first curtain has completely opened, as shown in Figure 9.5. That effectively provides a briefer exposure as a slit, narrower than the full height of the sensor, passes above its surface. If the flash were to fire during the time when the first and second curtains partially obscured the sensor, only the slit that was actually open would be exposed.

You'd end up with only a narrow band, representing the portion of the sensor that was exposed when the picture is taken. For shutter speeds *faster* than 1/180th second, the second curtain begins moving *before* the first curtain reaches the bottom of the frame. As a result, a moving slit, the distance between the first and second curtains, exposes one portion of the sensor at a time as it moves from the top to the bottom. Figure 9.5 shows three views of our typical (but imaginary) focal plane shutter. At left is pictured the closed shutter; in the middle version you can see the first curtain has moved down about 1/4 of the distance from the top; and in the right-hand version, the second curtain has started to "chase" the first curtain across the frame toward the bottom.

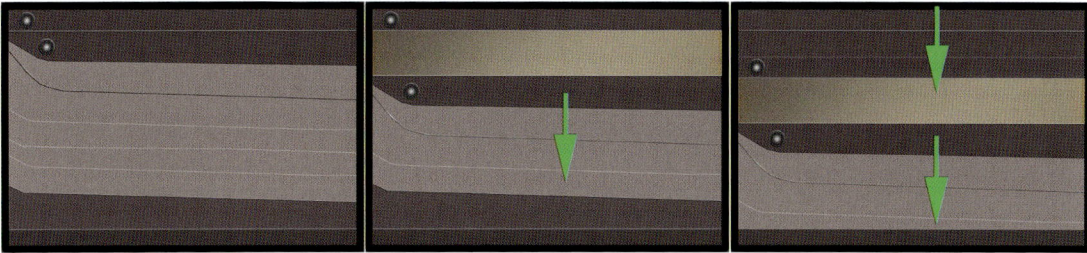

Figure 9.5 A closed shutter (left); partially open shutter as the first curtain begins to move downward (middle); only part of the sensor is exposed as the slit moves (right).

If the flash is triggered while this slit is moving, only the exposed portion of the sensor will receive any illumination. You end up with a photo like the one shown in Figure 9.6. Note that the band across the bottom of the image is black. That's a shadow of the second shutter curtain, which had started to move when the flash was triggered. Sharp-eyed readers will wonder why the black band is at the *bottom* of the frame rather than at the top, where the second curtain begins its journey. The answer is simple: your lens flips the image upside down and forms it on the sensor in a reversed position. You never notice that, because the camera is smart enough to show you the pixels that make up your photo in their proper orientation. But this image flip is why, if your sensor gets dirty and you detect a spot of dust in the upper half of a test photo, if cleaning manually, you need to look for the speck in the *bottom* half of the sensor.

Figure 9.6
If a shutter speed faster than 1/180th second is used, you can end up photographing only a portion of the image.

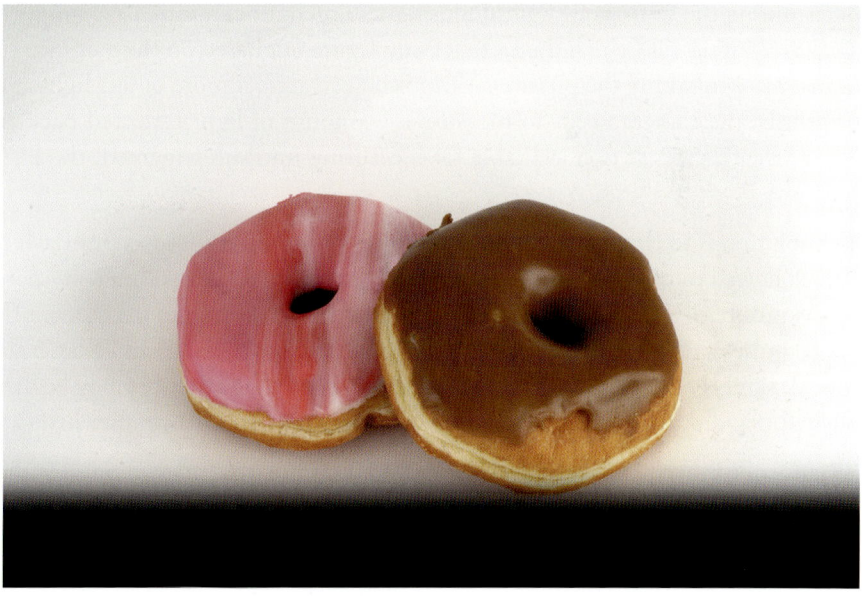

I generally end up with sync-speed problems only when shooting in the studio, using studio flash units rather than my EOS RP's Canon-dedicated Speedlite. That's because if you're using a "smart" (dedicated) flash, the camera knows that a strobe is attached, and remedies any unintentional goof in shutter speed settings. If you happen to set the EOS RP's shutter to a faster speed in Fv, Tv, or M mode, the camera will automatically adjust the shutter speed down to 1/180th second. In Av, P, or Scene Intelligent Auto modes where the EOS RP selects the shutter speed, it will never choose a shutter speed higher than 1/180th second when using flash. In P mode, shutter speed is automatically set between 1/60th and 1/180th second when using flash.

But when using a non-dedicated flash, such as a studio unit plugged into a PC/X adapter (an accessory that fits into the flash shoe and provides a "dumb" flash connector) the camera has no way of knowing that a flash is connected, so shutter speeds faster than 1/180th second can be set inadvertently. Note that the EOS RP can use a feature called *high-speed sync* that allows shutter speeds faster than 1/180th second with certain external dedicated Canon flash units. When using high-speed sync (HSS), the flash fires a continuous series of bursts at *reduced power* for the entire exposure, so that the duration of the illumination is sufficient to expose the sensor as the slit moves. High-speed sync is set using the controls on the attached and powered-up compatible external flash. I'll explain HSS later.

Determining Exposure

Calculating the proper exposure for an electronic flash photograph is a bit more complicated than determining the settings by continuous light. The right exposure isn't simply a function of how far away your subject is (which the EOS RP can figure out based on the autofocus distance that's locked in just prior to taking the picture). Various objects reflect more or less light at the same distance so, obviously, the camera needs to measure the amount of light reflected back and through the lens. Yet, as the flash itself isn't available for measuring until it's triggered, the EOS RP has nothing to measure.

The solution is to fire the flash multiple times. The initial shot is a pre-flash that can be analyzed, then followed by a main flash that's given exactly the calculated intensity needed to provide a correct exposure. If the main flash is serving as a master to trigger off-camera flash units, additional coded pulses can convey settings information to the slave flashes and trigger their firing. Of course, if *radio* signals rather than optical signals are in play, the sequences may be different. I'll cover various radio and optical wireless flash modes in Chapter 10; this chapter just explains the basics.

Because of the need to abbreviate or quench a flash burst in order to provide the optimum exposure, the primary flash may be longer for distant objects and shorter for closer subjects, depending on the required intensity. This through-the-lens evaluative flash exposure system is called E-TTL II, and it operates whenever you have attached a Canon dedicated flash unit to the EOS RP.

Guide Numbers

Guide numbers, usually abbreviated GN, are a way of specifying the power of an electronic flash in a way that can be used to determine the right f/stop to use at a particular shooting distance and ISO setting. In fact, before automatic flash units became prevalent, the GN was actually used to do just that. A GN is usually given as a pair of numbers for both feet and meters that represent the range at ISO 100. For example, consider the Canon Speedlite 270EX II, the least powerful of Canon's current external flash units (aside from the mini 90EX, primarily intended for use on Canon's non-dSLR models). The 270EX II has a GN of 89 at ISO 100. That Guide Number applies when the flash is set to the 50mm zoom setting (so that the unit's coverage is optimized to fill up the frame when using a 50mm focal length on a *full-frame* camera body like the EOS RP). (The effective Guide Number is just 72 when the flash is mounted on a "cropped" sensor camera like the EOS 7D II.) If you're using the 270EX II set to the 28mm zoom position, the light spreads out more to cover the wider area captured at that focal length, and the Guide Number of the unit drops to 79.

Of course, the question remains, what can you *do* with a Guide Number, other than to evaluate relative light output when comparing different flash units? In theory, you could use the GN to calculate the approximate exposure that would be needed to take a photo at a given distance. To calculate the right exposure at ISO 100, you'd divide the guide number by the distance to arrive at the appropriate f/stop. (Remember that the shutter speed has no bearing on the *flash* exposure; the flash burst will occur while the shutter is wide open, and will have a duration of *less* than the time the shutter is open.)

Again, using the 270EX II as an example, at ISO 100 with its GN of 89, if you wanted to shoot a subject at a distance of 11 feet, you'd use f/8 (89 divided by 11). At approximately 16 feet, an f/stop of f/5.6 would be used. Some quick mental calculations with the GN will give you any particular electronic flash's range. You can easily see that the 270EX II would begin to peter out at about 32 feet, where you'd need an aperture of roughly f/2.8 at ISO 100. Of course, in the real world you'd probably bump the sensitivity up to a setting of ISO 400 so you could use a more practical f/5.6 at that distance.

You should use Guide Numbers as an *estimate* only. Other factors can affect the relative "power" of a flash unit. For example, if you're shooting in a small room. Some light will bounce off ceilings and walls—even with the flash pointed straight ahead—and give your flash a slight boost, especially if you're not shooting extra-close to your subject. Use the same flash outdoors at night, say, on a football field, and the flash will have less relative power, because helpful reflections from surrounding objects are not likely.

So, today, guide numbers are most useful for comparing the power of various flash units. You don't need to be a math genius to see that an electronic flash with a GN of, say, 197 (like the 600EX II-RT) would be *a lot* more powerful than that of the 270EX II. You could use f/12 instead of f/5.6 at 16 feet. That's slightly more than two full f/stops' difference. As a Canon EOS RP owner, we can safely assume you'll be using one of the more powerful flash units in the Canon line (or perhaps a similar unit from a third-party vendor).

Getting Started with Electronic Flash

The Canon EOS RP's accessory flash is one of the most useful add-ons you can have. I'll include detailed explanations of your flash settings options later in the chapter. This section will get you started quickly.

When you're using Scene Intelligent Auto, P, Av, Tv, Fv, B, or Manual exposure modes, attach the flash and turn it on. The behavior of the external flash varies, depending on which exposure mode you're using:

- **Scene Intelligent Auto.** When the EOS RP is set to this mode, the flash will fire automatically, if it is attached and powered up.

- **P.** In Program mode, the EOS RP fully automates the exposure process, giving you subtle fill flash effects in daylight, and fully illuminating your subject under dimmer lighting conditions. The camera selects a shutter speed from 1/60th to 1/180th second and sets an appropriate aperture.

- **Av.** In Aperture-priority mode, you set the aperture as always, and the EOS RP chooses a shutter speed from 30 seconds to 1/180th second. Use this mode with care, because if the camera detects a dark background, it will use the flash to expose the main subject in the foreground, and then leave the shutter open long enough to allow the background to be exposed correctly, too. If you're not using an image-stabilized lens, you can end up with blurry ghost images even of non-moving subjects at exposures longer than 1/30th second, and if your camera is not mounted on a tripod, you'll see these blurs at exposures longer than about 1/8th second even if you are using IS.

  To disable use of a slow shutter speed with flash, access the Slow Synchro option in the External Speedlite Control entry in the Shooting 2 menu, and change from the default setting (Auto) to either 1/180–1/60sec. auto or 1/180sec. (fixed).

- **Tv.** When using flash in Tv mode, you set the shutter speed from 30 seconds to 1/180th second, and the EOS RP will choose the correct aperture for the correct flash exposure. If you accidentally set the shutter speed higher than 1/180th second, the camera will reduce it to 1/180th second when you're using the flash.

- **Fv.** In this mode, you can specify shutter speed, aperture, and ISO sensitivity either manually or automatically, and the EOS RP will adjust the remaining parameters. That means when using flash, the camera will behave as if it were in Program mode (if you don't choose a shutter speed or aperture manually), or Tv mode (if you select only a shutter speed), or Av mode (if you choose only the aperture), or M mode (if you select both).

■ **M/B.** In Manual or Bulb exposure modes, you select both shutter speed (30 seconds to 1/180th second) and aperture. The camera will adjust the shutter speed to 1/180th second if you try to use a faster speed with a flash. The E-TTL II system will provide the correct amount of exposure for your main subject at the aperture you've chosen (if the subject is within the flash's range, of course). In Bulb mode, the shutter will remain open for as long as the release button on top of the camera is held down, or the release of your remote control is activated. If you use the Bulb timer, you can specify long exposures.

Flash Exposure Compensation and FE Lock

If you want to lock flash exposure for a subject that is not centered in the frame, you can use the FE Lock (the * button) to lock in a specific flash exposure. Just center the viewfinder on the subject you want to correctly expose and press the * button. The pre-flash fires and calculates exposure. The EOS RP remembers the correct exposure until you take a picture, and the FEL indicator, a lightning bolt with an * next to it in the lower-left corner of the display, is your reminder. If you want to recalculate your flash exposure, just press the * button again. When you're ready to shoot, recompose your photo and press the shutter down the rest of the way to take the picture.

You can also manually add or subtract exposure to the flash exposure calculated by the EOS RP on the camera itself, without needing to touch the flash. When using any of the exposure modes *except* Scene Intelligent Auto (that is, Program AE, Aperture-priority, Shutter-priority, Flexible-priority, or Manual), you can access flash exposure compensation (FEC) in four different ways, with two of them illustrated in Figure 9.7.

■ **Set FEC on the flash.** Consult your Speedlite manual to see if you can set flash exposure compensation on the flash. See the sidebar which follows. Note that when you specify FEC on the flash, you cannot change it using the camera's controls.

■ **Use the Quick Control screen.** If you've enabled the Quick Control screen, display it by pressing the INFO button until the shooting settings screen appears. Then press Q to switch to the text/graphics version and highlight the FEC icon at the far right of the second row. Then use either dial to make the adjustment. (See Figure 9.7, top.)

■ **Press the M-Fn button.** Press the button once to pop up the functions. Rotate the Quick Control dial until the Flash Exposure Compensation item is highlighted (it's at far right), then rotate the Main Dial to set exposure compensation plus or minus three stops in one-third stop increments.

■ **Access External Speedlite Control.** Find it in the Shooting 3 menu, press SET, and, if your flash is attached and powered up, select Flash Function settings. Then navigate to the Flash Exposure Compensation icon in the second row of the screen. You might go this route if you were making multiple settings, including FEC, from that screen. See Figure 9.7, bottom.

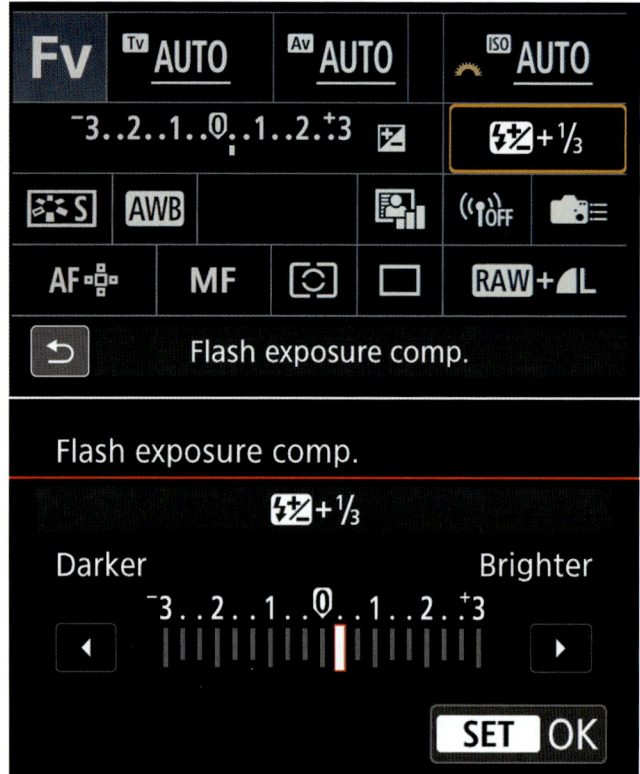

Figure 9.7
Flash exposure compensation can be set from the Shooting 2 menu's External Speedlite Control options or the Quick Control screen.

SETTING FEC ON THE FLASH

While setting flash exposure compensation within the camera is usually most convenient, with some Canon Speedlites (such as the 600EX II-RT), you can set exposure compensation on the external flash instead. With the 600EX II-RT, in ETTL, M, or MULTI modes, press the #2 button to highlight the +/– FEC indicator, then rotate the flash's Select dial to set the specific amount. Press the Select/SET button to confirm your choice.

If you want to avoid accidentally changing the FEC value on the flash, say, while making other adjustments, use either flash unit's C.Fn-13 setting (not to be confused with the EOS RP's own Custom Functions). When set to the default, 0, rotating the Select dial specifies the amount; change to 1, instead, and you must *first* press the Select/SET button before rotating the dial.

Flash exposure compensation can work in tandem with non-flash exposure compensation, so you can adjust the amount of light registered from the scene by ambient light even while you're tweaking the amount of illumination absorbed from your flash unit. As with non-flash exposure compensation, the compensation you make remains in effect for the pictures that follow, and even when you've turned the camera off, remember to cancel the flash exposure compensation adjustment by reversing the steps used to set it when you're done using it.

Tip

If you've enabled the Auto Lighting Optimizer in the Shooting 3 menu, it may cancel out any EV you've subtracted using flash exposure compensation. Disable the Auto Lighting Optimizer if you find your images are still too bright when using flash exposure compensation.

Flash Range

The illumination of the EOS RP's external flash varies with distance, focal length, and ISO sensitivity setting.

■ **Distance.** The farther away your subject is from the camera, the greater the light fall-off, thanks to the inverse square law discussed in Chapter 8. Keep in mind that a subject that's twice as far away receives only one-quarter as much light, which is two f/stops' worth. (See Figure 9.8.)

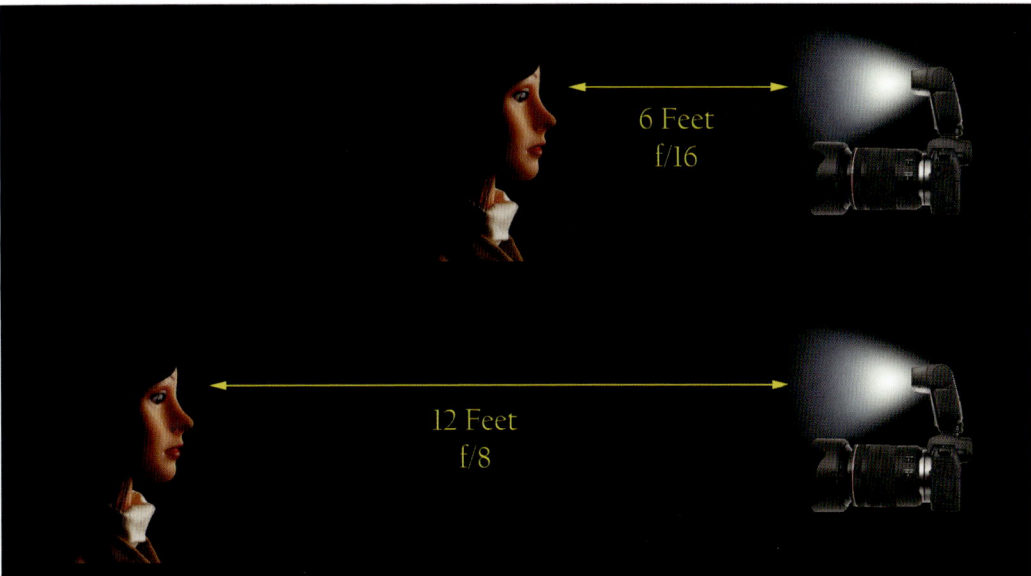

6 Feet
f/16

12 Feet
f/8

Figure 9.8 Because of the inverse square law, a subject that's twice as far away receives two stops worth less illumination.

- **Focal length.** A non-zooming flash "covers" only a limited angle of view, which doesn't change. So, when you're using a lens that is wider than the default focal length, the frame may not be covered fully, and you'll experience dark areas, especially in the corners. As you zoom in using longer focal lengths, some of the illumination is outside the area of view and is "wasted." (This phenomenon is why some external flash units, such as the 600EX II-RT or 580EX II, automatically "zoom" to match the zoom setting of your lens to concentrate the available flash burst onto the actual subject area.)

- **ISO setting.** The higher the ISO sensitivity, the more photons captured by the sensor. So, doubling the sensitivity from ISO 100 to 200 produces the same effect as, say, opening up your lens from f/8 to f/5.6.

External Speedlite Control

The Shooting 2 menu's External Speedlite control menu offers six options, plus Clear Settings (see Figure 9.9). The next sections will explain your choices.

Flash Firing

This menu entry has two options: Enable and Disable. It can be used to activate or deactivate any attached external electronic dedicated flash unit. When disabled, the flash cannot fire even if you have an accessory flash attached and turned on. However, you should keep in mind that the AF-assist beam can still be used. If you want to disable that, too, you'll need to turn it off using the AF-Assist Beam Firing entry in the Shooting 8 menu.

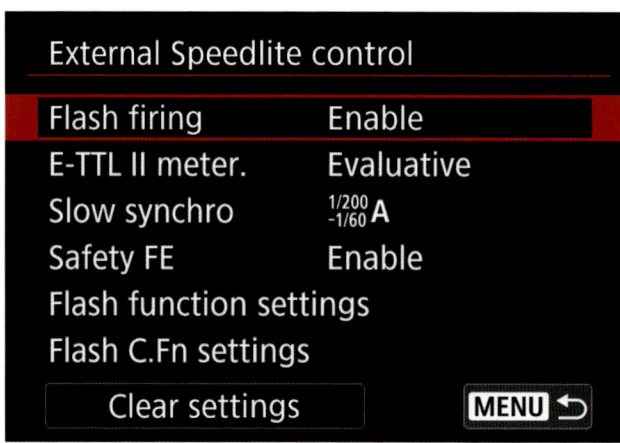

Figure 9.9

The External Speedlite control menu has six options, plus Clear Settings.

E-TTL II Meter.

When you're using E-TTL II mode, you can specify whether the EOS RP uses Evaluative (Matrix) or Average metering modes for the electronic flash exposure meter. Evaluative metering intelligently looks at selected areas in the scene and compares its measurements to a database of typical scene "layouts" to calculate exposure, while Average calculates flash exposure by reading the entire scene. Your choice becomes active when you select E-TTL II as your flash mode, using the entry listed first on this menu screen, and described in more detail in the next section.

Slow Synchro

You can select the flash synchronization speed that will be used when working in Aperture-priority mode. In Aperture-priority mode when using flash, you specify the f/stop to be locked in. The exposure is then adjusted by varying the output of the electronic flash (rather than by adjusting the shutter speed, which is the norm with non-flash images). Because the primary exposure comes from the flash, the main effect of the shutter speed selected is on the *secondary* exposure from the ambient light within the scene.

Auto is your best choice under most conditions. The EOS RP will choose a shutter speed that balances the flash exposure and available, ambient light. The 1/180th–1/60th second setting locks out slower shutter speeds, preventing blur from camera/subject movement in the secondary ("ghost") exposure. However, the background may be rendered dark, if the flash is not strong enough to illuminate it. The 1/180th second (fixed) setting further reduces the chance of getting those blurry ghosts, but there is more of a chance the background will be dark.

- **Auto.** The camera selects the shutter speed from 30 seconds to 1/180th second; however, high-speed sync (HSS) can also be activated at the flash with a compatible flash unit.

- **1/180–1/60 auto.** Only shutter speeds from 1/180th to 1/60th second will be used. This locks out shutter speeds slower than 1/60th second, and is useful when you want to avoid blur in the secondary, ambient light exposure due to subject movement and/or camera shake. The EOS RP will always expose the main subject correctly using the flash, but, as noted earlier, the unavailability of slower shutter speeds may mean that the camera is unable to balance the flash with ambient illumination, making the background too dark. HSS is not possible in Av mode with this setting.

- **1/180 sec. (fixed).** A shutter speed of 1/180th second will be used with flash at all times. Use this setting when you want to make sure that the highest flash sync speed is used, minimizing the possibility of blur in the secondary, ambient light exposure. As with the previous setting, using a fixed 1/180th second shutter speed may cause the background to appear darker because less of the ambient light can be used to balance the exposure. HSS is not possible in Av mode with this setting.

Safety FE

When you use the flash in daylight (usually to fill in shadows) or from close proximity to your subject in any environment, the flash illumination can result in overexposure. When this feature is enabled, the EOS RP can determine that overexposure is likely and automatically reduce ISO sensitivity when set to ISO Auto. This is a setting you can usually leave enabled most of the time, and disable it only if you find your images are coming out too dark when using flash.

Flash Function Settings

This entry (see Figure 9.10) provides access to functions that may differ between different flash units. Because the available features may vary, you can't access this screen unless the Speedlite you'll be using is attached and powered up; the EOS RP needs to know what flash it is working with to properly display this submenu. It has six sections that can be used to adjust flash mode, wireless functions, zoom head coverage, shutter sync, flash exposure compensation, and flash exposure bracketing.

- **Flash mode.** This entry offers several choices, depending on the modes your flash offers (check your Speedlite's manual to see the full list of specialized flash modes for your unit):
  - **E-TTL.** This E-TTL II is the standard mode for EX-series Speedlites.
  - **M.** This Manual flash can be used to set a fixed flash output, from full power (1/1) to 1/128th power.
  - **MULTI.** This MULTI flash is used to produce stroboscopic effects.
  - **CSP.** If your flash offers the continuous shooting priority mode, the flash output will be automatically decreased by one stop, ISO sensitivity is set to Auto, and Safety FE is automatically enabled. These adjustments allow you to shoot continuously if you need to, and conserve your flash's battery power in both continuous and single-shot modes. Because of the adjustments the camera makes for you in this mode, you should check your ISO and Safety FE settings after you stop using the flash, and reset them to your preferred values if necessary.

- **Wireless functions.** Functions vary, depending on the attached Speedlite. If you're not working with wireless flash, your only choice is Wireless: OFF. If you do want to use an attached flash (or a flash trigger unit) as a master flash, multiple additional options may appear, such as select Wireless: Optical Transmission; Wireless: Radio Transmission; and, with either of those two, additional functions, such as mode, channel, firing group, and other options become available. These options are explained in Chapter 10.

- **Zoom.** When using a compatible (zoomable) flash, select this entry and press the SET button. Then, you can rotate the Quick Control Dial to choose Auto (the flash zooms to the correct setting based on information about focal length supplied to the flash by the camera), or 24, 28, 35, 50, 70, 80, or 105mm (available with the older 580EX II) plus 135 and 200mm (with the 600EX II-RT).

Figure 9.10

The entries in the
Flash Function
Settings screen.

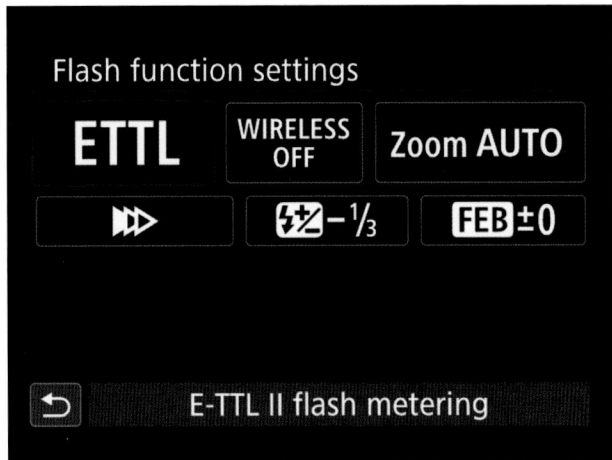

- **Shutter sync.** You can choose first-curtain sync (which fires the main flash as soon as the shutter is completely open) or second-curtain sync (which waits until just before the shutter starts to close to fire the main flash). If you have a compatible Canon Speedlite attached, you can also select high-speed sync (HSS), which allows using shutter speeds faster than 1/180th second.

- **Flash exposure compensation.** If you'd rather adjust flash exposure using a menu than with the Quick Control screen or by using the M-Fn button, you can do that here. Select this option with the SET button, then dial in the amount of flash EV compensation you want using the Quick Control Dial. The EV that was in place before you started to make your adjustment is shown as a blue indicator, so you can return to that value quickly. Press SET again to confirm your change, then press the MENU button twice to exit. Keep in mind that using this entry overrides any flash exposure compensation you might set using the ISO-Exposure compensation button on top of the camera, or with any flash function settings.

- **Flash exposure bracketing (FEB).** This option is available with flash units that support Flash Exposure Bracketing. It operates similarly to regular exposure bracketing, discussed in Chapter 4. Highlight this entry, press SET, and you can rotate the Quick Control Dial to specify up to three stops of compensation over/under the metered exposure for a set of three flash pictures.

If you enable wireless flash, additional options appear in this menu. I'll cover these in more detail in Chapter 10:

- **Channel.** All flashes used wirelessly can communicate on one of four channels. This setting allows you to choose which channel is used. Channels are especially helpful when you're working around other Canon photographers; each can select a different channel so one photographer's flash units don't trigger those of another photographer.

- **Sender flash firing.** You can enable or disable use of the external flash as the master controller for the other wireless flashes. When set to enable, the attached external flash is used as the master.

- **Flash Firing Group.** Multiple flash units can be assigned to a group. This choice allows specifying which groups are triggered, A/B, A/B plus C, or All. The 600EX-RT/600EX II-RT offer additional groups when using radio control mode, Groups D and E.
- **A:B fire ratio.** If you select A/B or A/B plus C, this option appears, and allows you to set the proportionate outputs of Groups A and B, in ratios from 8:1 to 1:8, as explained in Chapter 12.
- **Group C exposure compensation.** If you select A/B plus C, this option appears, too, to the right of the Fire Ratio icon, allowing you to set flash exposure compensation separately for Group C flashes.

Flash C.Fn Settings

This menu entry produces a screen that allows you to set any available Custom Functions in your flash, *from the camera.* The functions available will depend on the C.Fn settings included in the flash unit. The EL-100 has only two Custom Functions, while the more top-of-the-line model EX600 II-RT, has 23 Custom Functions (see Figure 9.11). To set flash Custom Functions, rotate the QCD to choose the C.Fn number to be adjusted, then press SET. Rotate the Quick Control Dial again to choose from that function's options, then press SET again to confirm.

Clear Settings

Select this menu entry, located at the bottom of the screen, and you'll be asked if you want to change all the flash settings to their factory default values. You have two choices: Clear Flash Settings (the settings internal to the EOS RP) and Clear All Speedlite C.Fn's, which returns all the *attached* Speedlite's Custom Function settings to their factory defaults. The only exception is C.Fn-0: Distance Indicator Display, which will remain at its set value.

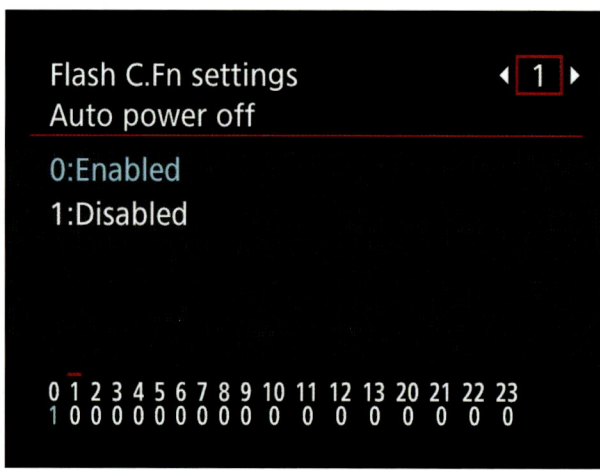

Figure 9.11
Custom Functions for your Speedlite can be set from the camera's Flash C.Fn menu.

Using Flash Settings

This section includes some tips for using the available Flash settings.

When to Disable Flash Firing

There are a few applications where I always disable my flash and AF-assist beam, even though my EOS RP won't fire an attached flash without my intervention anyway. Some situations are too important to take chances.

- **Venues where flash is forbidden.** I've discovered that many No Photography signs actually mean "No Flash Photography," either because those who make the decisions feel that flash is distracting or they fear it may potentially damage works of art. Tourists may not understand the difference between flash and available-light photography, or may be unable to set their camera to turn off the flash. One of the first phrases I learn in any foreign language is "Is it permitted to take photos if I do not use flash?" Fortunately, the word "flash" has come to mean camera electronic flash in many languages, and quite a few tongues have adopted the English expression "OK," too. So "OK (sin, sans, senza, sem) flash?" usually works in Spanish, French, Italian, and Portuguese, respectively with no problem. A polite request, while brandishing an advanced camera like the EOS RP (which may indicate you know what you are doing), can often result in permission to shoot away.

- **Venues where flash is ineffective anyway.** We've all seen the concert goers who stand up in the last row to shoot flash pictures from 100 yards away. I tend to not tell friends that their pictures are not going to come out, because they usually come back to me with a dismal, grainy shot (actually exposed by the dim available light) that they find satisfactory, just to prove I was wrong.

- **Venues where flash is annoying.** If I'm taking pictures in a situation where flash is permitted, but mostly supplies little more than visual pollution, I'll disable or avoid using it. Concerts or religious ceremonies may *allow* flash photography, but who needs to add to the blinding bursts when you have a camera that will take perfectly good pictures at ISO 3200? Of course, I invariably see one or two people flashing away at events where flash is not allowed, but that doesn't mean I am eager to join in the festivities.

More on Flash Modes

In choosing Flash mode, you have up to four main choices. The available modes are E-TTL II, the standard mode for EX-series Speedlites; Manual flash, which you can use to set a fixed flash output, from full power (1/1) to 1/128th power; MULTI flash, used to produce stroboscopic effects; and CSP, to preserve your battery power and allow grabbing more shots continuously.

E-TTL II

You'll leave Flash mode at this setting most of the time. In this mode, the camera fires a pre-flash prior to the exposure, and measures the amount of light reflected to calculate the proper settings. As noted earlier, when you've selected the E-TTL II flash mode, you can also choose either Evaluative or Average metering methods. If you select Manual flash or MULTI flash, that option is removed from the menu.

Manual Flash

Use this setting when you want to specify exactly how much light is emitted by the flash, and don't want the EOS RP's E-TTL II exposure system to calculate the f/stop for you. When you activate this option, a new entry appears in the Flash Func. Setting menu, with a sliding scale from 1/1 (full power) to 1/128th power. Highlight the scale and press the SET button. You can then rotate the Quick Control Dial and choose any of the settings. (Only 1/4, 1/2, 1/1, and the intermediate settings between them appear when 1/1 is chosen; view the other power settings by rotating the QCD counterclockwise.) A blue dot appears under the 1/1 setting, and a white dot appears under your new setting, a reminder that you've chosen something other than full power.

Here are some situations where you might want to use manual flash settings:

- **Close-ups.** You're shooting macro photos and the E-TTL II exposure is not precisely what you'd like. You can dial in exposure compensation, or set the output manually. Close-up photos are problematic, because the power of the flash may be too much (choose 1/128 power to minimize the output), or the reflected light may not be interpreted accurately by the through-the-lens metering system. Manual flash gives you greater control.

- **Fill flash.** Although E-TTL II can be used in full daylight to provide fill flash to brighten shadows or add a catchlight to a human subject's eyes, using manual flash allows you to tweak the amount of light being emitted in precise steps. Perhaps you want just a little more illumination in the shadows to retain a dramatic lighting effect without the dark portions losing all detail. Again, you can try using exposure compensation to make this adjustment, but I prefer to use manual flash settings. (See Figure 9.12.)

- **Action stopping.** The lower the power of the flash, the shorter the effective exposure. Use 1/128th power in a darkened room (so that there is no ambient light to contribute to the exposure and cause a "ghost" image) and you can end up with a "shutter speed" that's the equivalent of 1/50,000th second!

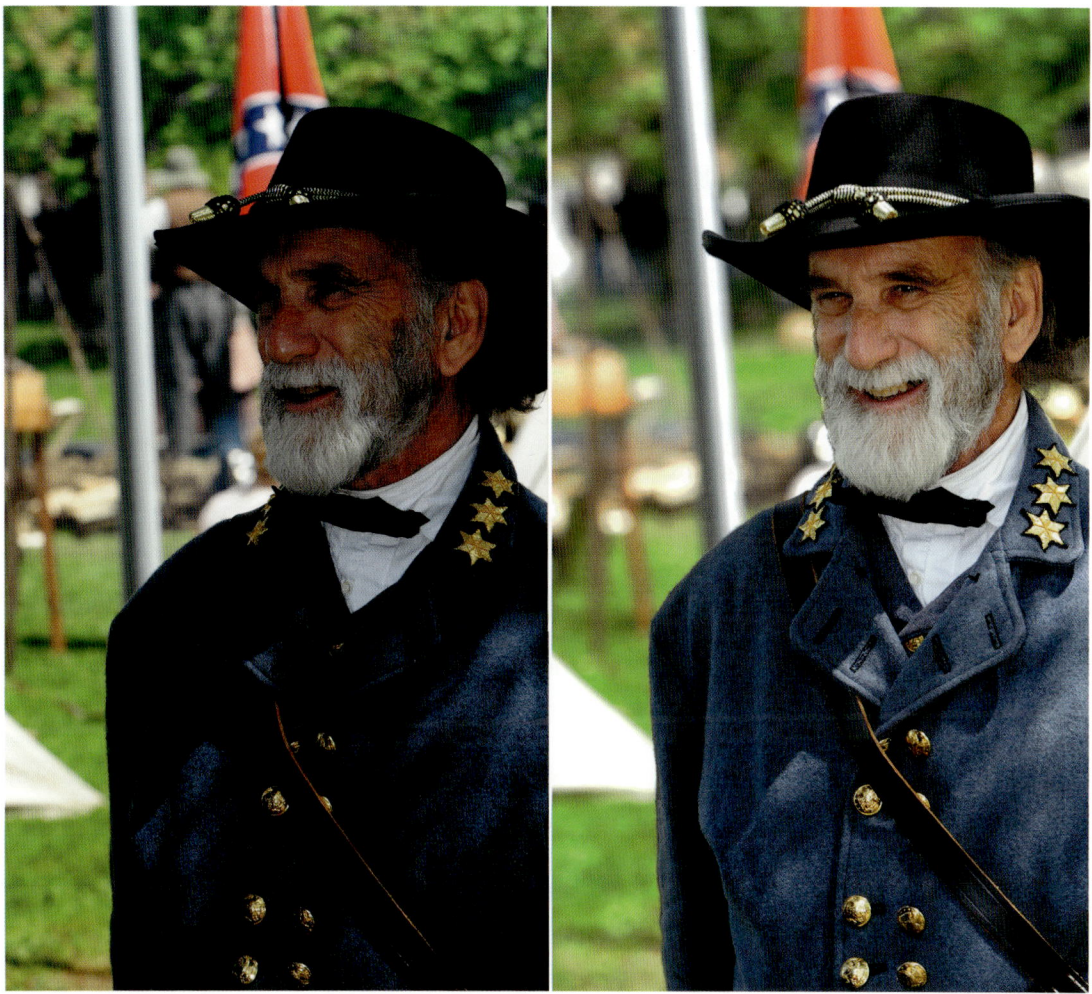

Figure 9.12 You can fine-tune fill illumination by adjusting the output of your camera's flash manually.

MULTI Flash

The MULTI flash setting makes it possible to shoot cool stroboscopic effects, with the flash firing several times in quick succession. You can use the capability to produce multiple images of moving objects, to trace movement (say, your golf swing). When you've activated MULTI flash, three parameters appear on the Flash Function Setting menu, as shown in Figure 9.13.

These factors work together to determine the maximum number of flashes you can string together in a single shot. The exact number will vary, depending on your settings and your Speedlite model.

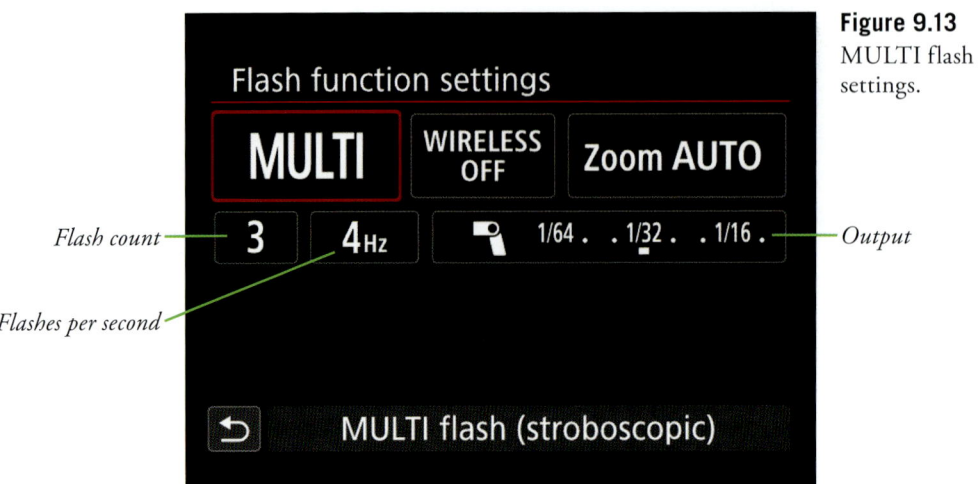

Figure 9.13
MULTI flash settings.

Flash count — 3

Flashes per second — 4 Hz

Output — 1/64 . . 1/32 . . 1/16 .

Flash function settings

MULTI   WIRELESS OFF   Zoom AUTO

MULTI flash (stroboscopic)

Here are some guidelines you can use:

- **Output.** As you cut the power from 1/4 to 1/128th, the output of the flash drops dramatically, and so does the maximum distance you can shoot at any particular f/stop. The 1/4 power setting, the most powerful setting available with MULTI flash, will give you the greatest flash range in this mode. With your EOS RP's sensitivity set to ISO 1600, your flash will allow you to photograph a subject at 10 feet using f/8 and one-quarter power. (If you remember the discussion of guide numbers from earlier in this chapter, the flash would have an effective GN of 80 at ISO 1600.)

  If you wanted to use the 1/16th power setting instead, you'd need to use f/4 to account for the reduced output of the flash. By the time you dial down to 1/128th power, your flash has a feeble guide number of about 14 (at ISO 1600!), so to shoot at f/4 you'd be able to locate your subject *no farther* than 3.5 feet from the camera.

  The output level also determines the maximum number of flashes that are possible before the charge stored in your flash's capacitor is depleted. The capacitor partially recharges itself as you shoot, so the number of flashes also varies by the flashes-per-second rate. At the 1Hz (one flash per second) rate and 1/4 power, you can expect about 6 to 7 flashes before the Speedlite's power poops out. By the time you reach 10Hz (10 flashes per second) and higher, the unit can crank out no more than two flashes per second at 1/4 power.

  Logically, as output levels decrease, more flashes can be pumped out in a given time period. At 1/128th power, you can expect as many as 100 flashes at the 1Hz rate, and up to 40 consecutive flashes at the 20Hz to 199Hz frequency.

- **Flashes per second.** Cycles per second are, by convention, measured using an increment called *Hertz*. The more flashes you want during the time the shutter is open, the higher the rate you must select. You can select rates of 1Hz to 199Hz, or 1 to 199 flashes per second, plus "- -" (more on that later). To maximize the number of flashes in a second, you'll also need to choose the lowest power output level that you find acceptable. The flash unit can emit a lot more fractional 1/128th power bursts in a given period of time than it can more robust (relatively) 1/4 power bursts.

When you choose "- -" for your frequency, the flash will continue firing until the shutter closes, or its internal storage is depleted. (In any case, you should not use the MULTI flash feature for more than 10 consecutive pictures. At that point, you should allow the flash to "rest" for at least 15 minutes. But don't worry, the unit will shut down automatically to avoid overheating.)

I like to shoot "strobing" flash pictures in dark rooms against a dark backdrop, and use a long exposure to capture multiple images in a single frame, like the (yet another) plummeting fruit example seen in Figure 9.14.

■ **Flash count.** Chose the number of flashes, from 1 to 30, that you want in your multiple exposure, given the output and flash frequency constraints described above.

Figure 9.14
Four bursts during
the exposure yielded
this exciting photo
of a drowning lime.

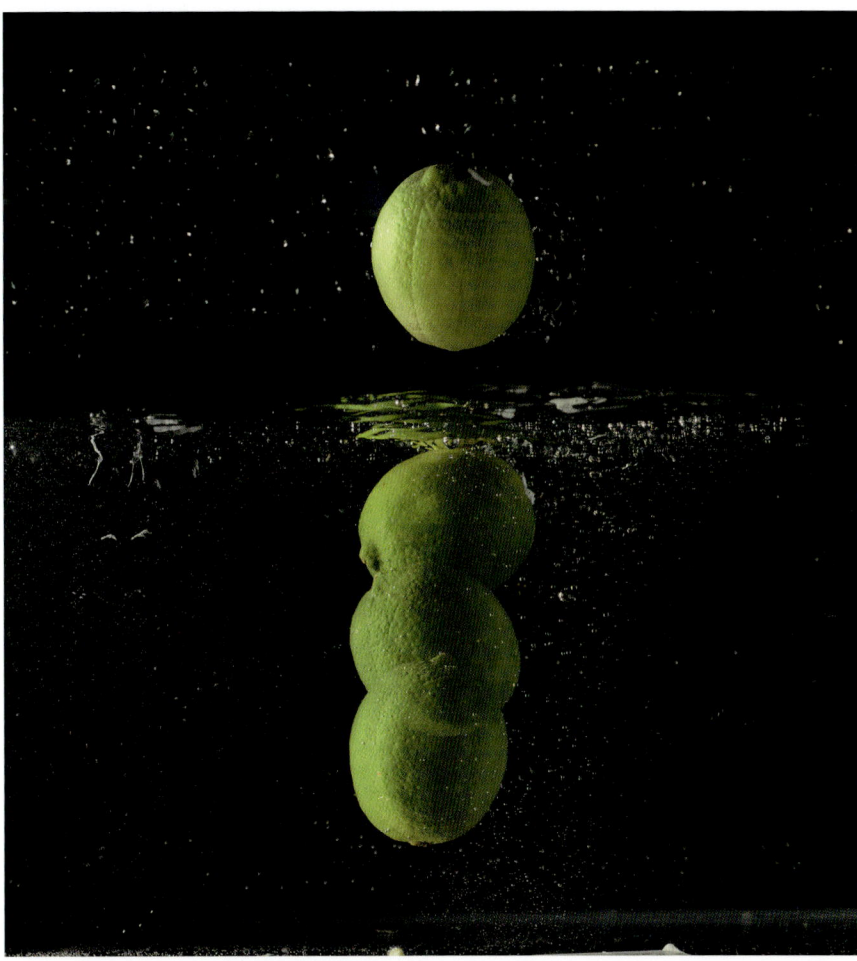

High-Speed Sync

High-speed sync is a special mode that allows you to synchronize a compatible external flash at all shutter speeds, rather than just 1/180th second and slower. The entire frame is illuminated by a series of continuous bursts as the shutter opening moves across the sensor plane, so you do *not* end up with a horizontal black band, as shown earlier in Figure 9.6.

HSS is especially useful in three situations, all related to problems associated with high ambient light levels:

- **Eliminate "ghosts" with moving images.** When shooting with flash, the primary source of illumination may be the flash itself. However, if there is enough available light, a secondary image may be recorded by that light (as described under "Ghost Images" earlier in this chapter). If your main subject is not moving, the secondary image may be acceptable or even desirable. But if your subject is moving, the secondary image creates a ghost image.

    High-speed sync gives you the ability to use a higher shutter speed. If ambient light produces a ghost image at 1/180th second, upping the shutter speed to 1/500th or 1/1000th second may eliminate it.

    Of course, HSS *reduces* the amount of light the flash produces. If your subject is not close to the camera, the waning illumination of the flash may force you to use a larger f/stop to capture the flash exposure. So, while shifting from 1/180th second at f/8 to 1/500th second at f/8 *will* reduce ghost images, if you switch to 1/500th second at f/5.6 (because the flash is effectively less intense), you'll end up with the same ambient light exposure. Still, it's worth a try.

- **Improved fill flash in daylight.** The EOS RP can use an attached flash unit to fill in inky shadows—both automatically and using manually specified power ratios, as described earlier in this chapter. However, both methods force you to use a 1/180th second (or slower) shutter speed. That limitation can cause three complications.

    First, in very bright surroundings, such as beach or snow scenes, it may be difficult to get the correct exposure at 1/180th second. You might have to use f/16 or a smaller f/stop to expose a given image, even at ISO 100. If you want to use a larger f/stop for selective focus, then you encounter the second problem—1/180th second won't allow apertures wider than f/8 or f/5.6 under many daylight conditions at ISO 100. (See the discussion of fill flash with Aperture-priority in the next bullet.)

    Finally, if you're shooting action, you'll probably want a shutter speed faster than 1/180th second, if at all possible, under the current lighting. That's because, in fill flash situations, the ambient light (often daylight) provides the primary source of illumination. For many sports and fast-moving subjects, 1/500th second, or faster, is desirable. HSS allows you to increase your shutter speed and still avail yourself of fill flash. This assumes that your subject is close enough to your camera that the fill flash has some effect; forget about using fill and HSS with subjects a dozen feet away or farther. The flash won't be powerful enough to have much effect on the shadows.

■ **When using fill flash with Aperture-priority.** The difficulties of using selective focus with fill flash, mentioned earlier, become particularly acute when you switch to Av exposure mode. Selecting f/5.6, f/4, or a wider aperture when using flash is guaranteed to create problems when photographing close-in subjects, particularly at ISO settings higher than ISO 100. If you own a compatible external flash unit, HSS may be the solution you are looking for.

To use High-speed sync, just follow these steps:

1. **Attach the flash.** Mount/connect the external flash on the EOS RP, using the hot shoe or a dedicated flash cable. (HSS cannot be used in wireless radio mode with the 600EX II-RT, nor with a flash linked through the PC terminal.)

2. **Power up.** Turn the flash and camera on.

3. **Select HSS in the camera.** Set the External Flash Function setting *in the camera* to HSS as the EOS RP's sync mode.

4. **Choose HSS on the flash.** Activate HSS (FP flash) on your attached external flash. With the older (but still common) Speedlite 580EX II, press the High-speed sync/Sync button on the back of the flash unit (it's the second from the right under the LCD). If you're using the 600EX II-RT, press the #4 function button (of the array under the LCD) until the HSS icon appears on the LCD.

5. **Confirm HSS is active**. The HSS icon will be displayed on the flash unit's LCD (at the upper-left side with the 580EX II and 600EX II-RT), and at bottom left in the EOS RP's viewfinder. If you choose a shutter speed of 1/180th second or slower, the indicator will not appear in the viewfinder, as HSS will not be used at slower speeds.

6. **View minimum/maximum shooting distance.** Choose a distance based on the maximum shown in the line at the bottom of the flash's LCD display (from 0.5 to 18 meters).

7. **Shoot.** Take the picture. To turn off HSS, press the button on the flash again. Remember that you can't use MULTI flash or Wireless flash when working with high-speed sync.

Using External Electronic Flash

Once the capacitor is charged, the burst of light that produces the main exposure can be initiated by a signal from the EOS RP that commands the internal or connected flash units to fire. External strobes can be linked to the camera in several different ways:

■ **Camera-mounted/hardwired external dedicated flash.** Units offered by Canon or other vendors that are compatible with Canon's lighting system can be clipped onto the accessory "hot" shoe on top of the camera or linked through a wired system such as the Canon Off Shoe Camera Cord OC-E3.

- **Wireless dedicated flash.** A compatible unit can be triggered by signals produced by a pre-flash (before the main flash burst begins), which offers two-way communication between the camera and flash unit. The triggering flash can be an external flash unit in Master mode, or a wireless non-flashing accessory, such as the Canon Speedlite Transmitter ST-E2 and radio-controlled wireless trigger, the Speedlite Transmitter ST-E3-RT, which each do nothing but "talk" to the external flashes. You'll find more on this mode in Chapter 10.

- **Wired, non-intelligent mode.** If you connect a flash to a PC/X adapter attached to the hot shoe, you can use non-dedicated flash units, including studio strobes, through a non-intelligent camera/flash link that sends just one piece of information, one way: it tells a connected flash to fire. There is no other exchange of information between the camera and flash. The PC/X adapter can be used to link the EOS RP to studio flash units, manual flash, flash units from other vendors that can use a PC cable, or even Canon-brand Speedlites that you elect to connect to the EOS RP in "unintelligent" mode.

- **Infrared/radio transmitter/receivers.** Another way to link flash units to the EOS RP is through third-party wireless infrared or radio *transmitters*, like a Godox, PocketWizard, Radio Popper, or the Paul C. Buff CyberSync trigger. These are generally mounted on the accessory shoe of the camera, and emit a signal when the EOS RP sends a command to fire through the hot shoe. The simplest of these function as a wireless dumb (PC/X-type) connector, with no other communication between the camera and flash (other than the instruction to fire). However, sophisticated units have their own built-in controls and can send additional commands to the receivers when connected to compatible flash units. I use one to adjust the power output of my Alien Bees studio flash from the camera, without the need to walk over to the flash itself.

- **Simple slave connection.** In the days before intelligent wireless communication, the most common way to trigger off-camera, non-wired flash units was through a *slave* unit. These can be small external triggers connected to the remote flash (or built into the flash itself), and set off when the slave's optical sensor detects a burst initiated by the camera itself. When it "sees" the main flash (from the EOS RP's attached external flash, or another flash), the slave flash units are triggered quickly enough to contribute to the same exposure. The main problem with this type of connection—other than the lack of any intelligent communication between the camera and flash—is that the slave may be fooled by any pre-flashes that are emitted by the other strobes, and fire too soon. Modern slave triggers have a special "digital" mode that ignores the pre-flash and fires only from the main flash burst.

Canon offers a broad range of accessory electronic flash units for the EOS RP. They can be mounted to the flash accessory shoe, or used off-camera with a dedicated cord that plugs into the flash shoe to maintain full communications with the camera for all special features. (Non-dedicated flash units, such as studio flash, can be connected using a PC/X adapter.) They range from the Speedlite

600EX II-RT and Speedlite 580EX II, which can correctly expose subjects up to 24 feet away at f/11 and ISO 200, to the 270EX II, which is good out to 9 feet at f/11 and ISO 200. (You'll get greater ranges at even higher ISO settings, of course.) There are also two electronic flash units specifically for specialized close-up flash photography.

I power my Speedlites with Panasonic Eneloop AA nickel metal hydride batteries, seen in Figure 9.15. These are a special type of rechargeable battery with a feature that's ideal for electronic flash use. The Eneloop cells, unlike conventional batteries, don't self-discharge over relative short periods of time. Once charged, they can hold onto most of their juice for a year or more. That means you can stuff some of these into your Speedlite, along with a few spares in your camera bag, and not worry about whether the batteries have retained their power between uses. There's nothing worse than firing up your strobe after not using it for a month, and discovering that the batteries are dead.

Figure 9.15
Panasonic's Eneloop AA batteries are a perfect power source for Canon Speedlites.

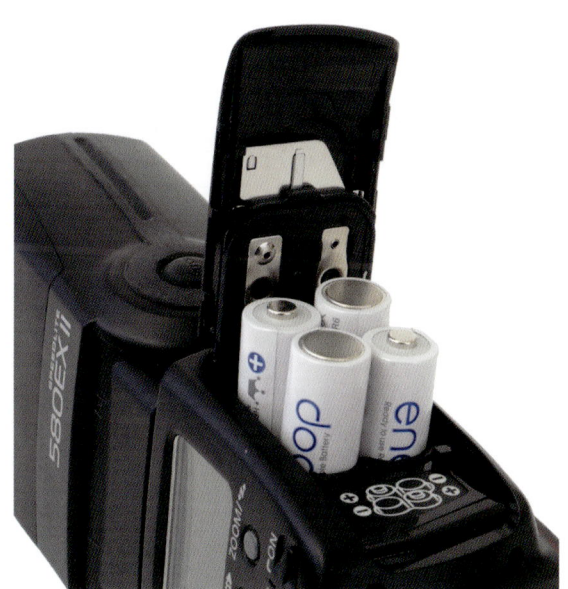

Speedlite 600EX-RT/600EX II-RT

This flagship of the Canon accessory flash line (and most expensive at about $550) is the most powerful unit the company offers, with a GN of 197 and a manual/automatic zoom flash head that covers the full frame of lenses from 24mm wide angle to 200mm telephoto. (There's a flip-down, wide-angle diffuser that spreads the flash to cover a 14mm lens's field of view, too.) All angle specifications given by Canon refer to full-frame sensors, but this flash unit automatically converts its field of view coverage to accommodate the crop factor of the EOS RP and the other 1.6X crop Canon dSLRs. The latest 600EX II-RT version was not available while this book was being written, but Canon states it will have improved continuous flash firing rates (up to 2X faster with an optional CP-E4N battery pack).

The 600EX-RT shares its basic features with the discontinued (but still widely used) 580EX II, described next, so I won't repeat them here, because the typical veteran Canon owner is more likely to own multiple Speedlites.

The killer feature of this unit is the new wireless two-way radio communication between the camera and this flash (or ST-E3-RT wireless controller and the flash) at distances of up to 98 feet. You can link up to 15 different flash units with radio control, using *five* groups (A, B, C, D, and E), and no line-of-sight connection is needed. (You can hide the flash under a desk or in a potted plant.) With the latest Canon cameras having a revised "intelligent" hot shoe (which includes the EOS RP), a second 600EX-RT/600EX II-RT can be used to trigger a *camera* that also has a 600EX-RT/600EX II-RT mounted, from a remote location. That means you can set up multiple cameras equipped with multiple flash units to all fire simultaneously! For example, if you were shooting a wedding, you could photograph the bridal couple from two different angles, with the second camera set up on a tripod, say, behind the altar.

600EX (NON-RADIO)

If you see references to a 600EX model (non-RT), you'll find that a version with the radio control crippled is sold only outside the USA in countries where obtaining permission to use the relevant radio spectrum is problematic.

The 600EX II-RT maintains backward compatibility with optical transmission used by earlier cameras. However, it's a bit pricey for the average EOS RP owner, who is unlikely to be able to take advantage of all its features. If you're looking for a high-end flash unit and don't need radio control, I still recommend the Speedlite 580EX II (described next), which is still widely available and is the most-used high-end flash Canon has ever offered.

Remember that with the 600EX II-RT, you can't use radio control and some other features unless you own at least *two* radio-controlled Speedlites, such as a 600EX II-RT or 430EX III-RT (described later) or one 600EX II-RT plus the ST-E3-RT, which costs about $300. Radio control is possible only between a camera that has a radio-capable flash or ST-E3-RT in the hot shoe, and an additional radio-capable flash or ST-E3-RT.

Some 18 Custom Functions of the 600EX II-RT can be set using the EOS RP's External Flash C.Fn Setting menu. Additional Personal Functions can be specified on the flash itself.

The EOS RP–friendly functions include:

C.Fn-00 Distance indicator display (Meters/Feet)

C.Fn-01 Auto power off (Enabled/Disabled)

C.Fn-02 Modeling flash (Enabled-DOF preview button/Enabled-test firing button/ Enabled-both buttons/Disabled)

C.Fn-03 FEB Flash exposure bracketing auto cancel (Enabled/Disabled)

C.Fn-04 FEB Flash exposure bracketing sequence (Metered > Decreased > Increased Exposure/Decreased > Metered > Increased Exposure)

C.Fn-05 Flash metering mode (E-TTL II/E-TTL/TTL/External metering: Auto/External metering: Manual)

C.Fn-06 Quickflash with continuous shot (Disabled/Enabled)

C.Fn-07 Test firing with autoflash (1/32/Full power)

C.Fn-08 AF-assist beam firing (Enabled/Disabled)

C.Fn-09 Auto zoom adjusted for image/sensor size (Enabled/Disabled)

C.Fn-10 Slave auto-power-off timer (60 minutes/10 minutes)

C.Fn-11 Cancellation of slave unit auto power off by master unit (within 8 hours/within 1 hour)

C.Fn-12 Flash recycling on external power (Use internal and external power/Use only external power)

C.Fn-13 Flash exposure metering setting button (Speedlite button and dial/Speedlite dial only)

C.Fn-20 Beep (Enable/Disable)

C.Fn-21 Light distribution (Standard, Guide number priority, Even coverage)

C.Fn-22 LCD panel illumination (On for 12 seconds, Disable, Always on)

C.Fn-23 Slave flash battery check (AF-assist beam/Flash lamp, Flash lamp only)

The Personal Functions available include the following. Note that you can set the LCD panel color to differentiate at a glance whether a given flash is functioning in Master or Slave mode.

P.Fn-01 LCD panel display contrast (Five levels of contrast)

P.Fn-02 LCD panel illumination color: Normal (Green, Orange)

P.Fn-03 LCD panel illumination color: Master (Green, Orange)

P.Fn-04 LCD panel illumination color: Slave (Green, Orange)

P.Fn-05 Color filter auto detection (Auto, Disable)

P.Fn-06 Wireless button toggle sequence (Normal > Radio > Optical, Normal < > Radio, Normal < > Optical)

P.Fn-07 Flash firing during linked shooting (Disabled, Enabled)

Speedlite 580EX II

If you were using Canon cameras prior to purchasing your EOS RP, you might already own this deposed flagship of the Canon accessory flash line. Despite the introduction of the 600EX-RT/ 600EX II-RT, this unit is still the most widely used Canon Speedlite, popular because of its relatively lower price and wide availability new (from some retailers) or used. The 580EX II is the second-most powerful unit the company offers, with a GN of 190, and a manual/automatic zoom flash head that covers the full frame of lenses from 24mm wide angle to 105mm telephoto, as well as 14mm optics with a flip-down diffuser.

Like the 600EX II-RT, this unit offers full swivel, 180 degrees in either direction, and has its own built-in AF-assist beam and an exposure system that's compatible with the nine focus points of the EOS RP. Powered by economical AA-size batteries, the unit recycles in 0.1 to 6 seconds, and can squeeze 100 to 700 flashes from a set of alkaline batteries.

The 580EX II automatically communicates white balance information to your camera, allowing it to adjust WB to match the flash output. You can even simulate a modeling light effect: When you press the depth-of-field preview button on the EOS RP, the 580EX II emits a one-second burst of light that allows you to judge the flash effect. If you're using multiple flash units with Canon's wireless E-TTL system, this model can serve as a master flash that controls the slave units you've set up (more about this later) or function as a slave itself.

It's easy to access all the features of this unit, because it has a large backlit LCD panel on the back that provides information about all flash settings. There are 14 Custom Functions that can be controlled from the flash, numbered from 00 to 13. These functions are (the first setting is the default value):

C.Fn-00   Distance indicator display (Meters/Feet)

C.Fn-01   Auto power off (Enabled/Disabled)

C.Fn-02   Modeling flash (Enabled-DOF preview button/Enabled-test firing button/ Enabled-both buttons/Disabled)

C.Fn-03   FEB Flash exposure bracketing auto cancel (Enabled/Disabled)

C.Fn-04   FEB Flash exposure bracketing sequence (Metered > Decreased > Increased Exposure/Decreased > Metered > Increased Exposure)

C.Fn-05   Flash metering mode (E-TTL II-E-TTL/TTL/External metering: Auto/External metering: Manual)

C.Fn-06   Quickflash with continuous shot (Disabled/Enabled)

C.Fn-07   Test firing with autoflash (1/32/Full power)

C.Fn-08   AF-assist beam firing (Enabled/Disabled)

C.Fn-09   Auto zoom adjusted for image/sensor size (Enabled/Disabled)

C.Fn-10   Slave auto power off timer (60 minutes/10 minutes)

C.Fn-11   Cancellation of slave unit auto power off by master unit (within 8 hours/within 1 hour)

C.Fn-12   Flash recycling on external power (Use internal and external power/Use only external power)

C.Fn-13   Flash exposure metering setting button (Speedlite button and dial/Speedlite dial only)

Speedlite 430EX III-RT

This less pricey electronic flash (available for less than $300) is an affordable replacement for the 580EX II for those who don't need the beefy power of the older Speedlite. It also makes radio control wireless triggering available to those who can't afford the 600EX-RT's price tag. The 430EX III-RT has automatic and manual zoom coverage from 24mm to 105mm, and the same wide-angle pullout panel found on the 600EX-RT/600EX II-RT that covers the area of a 14mm lens on a full-frame camera, and automatic conversion to the cropped frame area of the EOS RP and other 1.6X crop Canon dSLRs. The 430EX III-RT also communicates white balance information with the camera, and has its own AF-assist beam. Compatible with Canon's wireless E-TTL system, it makes a good slave unit, but cannot serve as a master flash. It, too, uses AA batteries, and offers recycle times of 0.1 to 3.7 seconds for 200 to 1,400 flashes, depending on subject distance.

This long-overdue replacement for the 430EX II has as its biggest selling point the ability to communicate either optically (as a slave) with any compatible master flash, or by radio transmission (as either master or slave) with other RT flashes, including the 600EX RT. Previously, you needed either two of the expensive 600EX RT/600EX II-RT units or one 600EX RT/600EX II-RT and an ST-E3-RT trigger to use radio communications.

The Canon Speedlite 430EX III-RT offers a sophisticated set of features, including an LCD panel that allows you to navigate the unit's menu and view its status. These features, along with powerful output and automatic zoom means this unit has more in common with Canon's high-end Speedlites than it does with the 320EX or the 270EX II. The Speedlite 430EX III-RT is compatible with E-TTL II and earlier flash technologies. It can serve as a slave unit in an optical wireless configuration. The Speedlite 430EX III-RT has a Guide Number of 43/141 (meters/feet) at ISO 100, at 105mm focal length.

Speedlite 320EX

This $249 flash has a GN of 105. Lightweight and more pocket-sized than the 430EX III-RT and 600EX-RT, this bounceable (both horizontally and vertically) flash has some interesting features, including a built-in LED video light that can be used for shooting movies with the EOS RP, or as a modeling light or even AF-assist beam when shooting with live view. Canon says that this efficient LED light can provide up to four hours of illumination with a set of AA batteries. (See Figure 9.16.) It can be used as a wireless slave unit, and has a new flash release function that allows the shutter to be triggered remotely with a two-second delay.

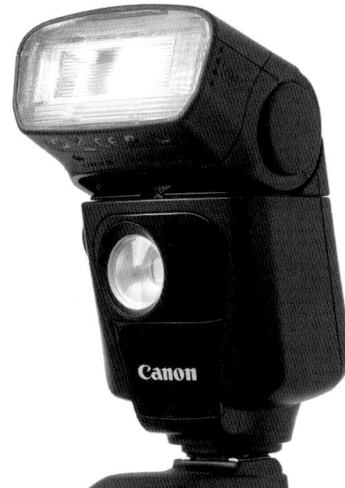

Figure 9.16
The Speedlite 320EX has a built-in video lamp.

Speedlite EL-100

I got this compact little flash when it was first introduced and have grown especially fond of it since the introduction of the EOS RP and EOS R. At $199, it's clearly the high-value bargain flash among Canon Speedlites, because it does so many things you don't expect from such an inexpensive unit. If you want to keep your EOS RP kit's weight reasonable, the EL-100 has most of what you really need, with the only cost being total light output.

It's pleasantly small at about 2.5 × 3.6 × 2.8 inches and weighs less than eight ounces with two AA batteries. (See Figure 9.17, left.) The flash head rotates 180 degrees and pivots up and down from zero to 90 degrees, so you can easily bounce light off a nearby wall or ceiling. (Keep in mind that bounce flash really soaks up a strobe's illumination, and the EL-100 has a guide number of only 85 at ISO 100 when using the 50mm flash coverage setting to begin with.) It recycles in less than six seconds, and signals that it's ready to go with a flash-ready indicator.

Figure 9.17
The EL-100 is
Canon's most versa-
tile low-cost
Speedlite.

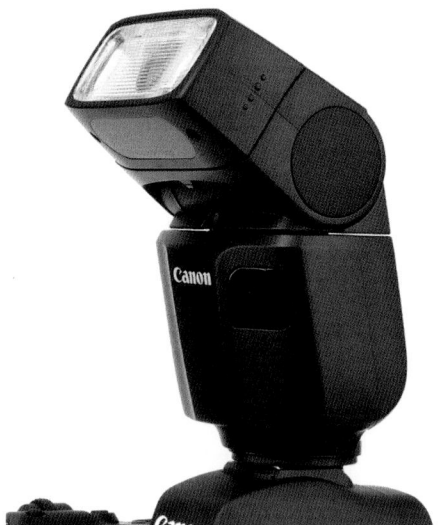
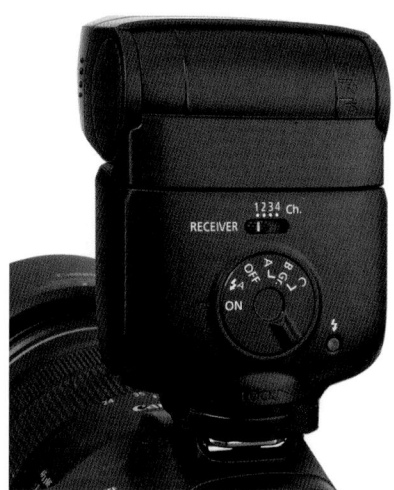

The EL-100's controls are simplicity itself; there is no LCD and a plethora of buttons or dials. One switch labeled Receiver allows you to choose Channels 1–4, a rotating dial chooses Off, On, Auto Flash (which allows the EOS RP to decide whether to use flash or not), and assigns the flash to Groups A, B, or C for wireless applications. There's also a flash Test button. That's it. (See Figure 9.17, right.)

The number of flash modes available make this unit quite versatile. You can use E-TTL, Manual, MULTI, or CSP modes using External Flash Functions settings described earlier. In wireless mode, it can serve as an optical master or slave, and access the ratio and exposure compensation options described earlier, including light ratio controls and separate Group C exposure compensation. Its burst will normally fill the frame captured by a 24mm lens or zoom setting, but you can adjust it for a 50mm focal length, which gives the unit a bit more range.

The EL-100 can clearly be a strong choice for someone who's already working with a variety of Canon equipment. But any creative photographer can enjoy the Speedlite EL-100 as the highly competent tool it is. In the right hands, it can brighten shots with precision, help you evade over-exposure, and enable you to be ready to take on challenging lighting circumstances.

I like this unit as an on-camera flash for fill light outdoors, and to trigger wireless Speedlights opti-cally (in such cases, you may not want an extra-powerful flash mounted on the camera anyway). The EL-100 is an economical choice for both functions.

Speedlite 270EX II

The Canon Speedlite 270EX II is designed to work with compatible EOS cameras utilizing E-TTL II and E-TTL automatic flash technologies. This flash unit is entirely controlled from the camera, making it as simple to use as a built-in flash. Its options can be selected and set via the camera's menu system. The 270EX II can also be used as an off-camera slave unit when controlled by a master Speedlite, transmitter unit, or a camera with an integrated Speedlite transmitter. One interesting feature of this unit is that it is also a remote control transmitter, allowing you to wirelessly release the shutter on cameras compatible with certain remote controller units. The Speedlite 270EX II has a Guide Number of 27/89 (meters/feet) at ISO 100, with the flash head pulled forward.

This $170 ultra-compact unit is Canon's entry-level Speedlite, and suitable for EOS RP owners who want a simple strobe for occasional use, without sacrificing the ability to operate it as a wireless slave unit. With its modest guide number, it provides a little extra pop for fill-flash applications. It has vertical bounce capabilities of up to 90 degrees, and can be switched between Tele modes to Normal (28mm full-frame coverage) at a reduced guide number of 72.

The 270EX II functions as a wireless slave unit triggered by any Canon EOS unit or flash (such as the 430EX III-RT) with a Master function. It also has the new flash release function with a two-second delay that lets you reposition the flash. There's a built-in AF-assist beam, and this 5.5-ounce, 2.6 × 2.6 × 3–inch unit is powered by just two AA-size batteries.

Close-Up Lites

Canon has offered three *lites*, especially suitable for close-up photography: the Macro Ring Lite MR-14EX and EX II and Macro Twin Lite flash MD-24EX-RT. As you might guess from their names, these lites are especially suitable for close-up, or macro photography, because they provide a relatively shadowless illumination. It's always tricky photographing small subjects up close, because there often isn't room enough between the camera lens and the subject to position lights effectively. Ring lites, in particular, especially those with their own modeling lamps to help you visualize the illumination you're going to get, mount around the lens at the camera position, and help solve many close-up lighting problems.

But, in recent years, the ring lite has gone far beyond the macro realm and is now probably even more popular as a light source for fashion and glamour photography. The right ring lite, properly used, can provide killer illumination for glamour shots, while eliminating the need to move and reset lights for those shots that lend themselves to ring lite illumination. As you, the photographer, move around your subject, the ring lite moves with you.

One of the key drawbacks to ring lites (whether used for macro or glamour photography) is that they are somewhat bulky and clumsy to use (they must be fastened around the camera lens itself, or the photographer must position the ring lite, and then shoot "through" the opening or ring). That means that you might not be moving around your subject as much as you thought and will, instead, mount the ring lite and camera on a tripod, studio stand, or other support.

Another drawback is the cost. The MR-14EX/MR-14EX II and MR-24EX-RT close-up lites are priced in the $550 and $989 range, respectively. You have to be planning a *lot* of macro or fashion work to pay for one of those. Specialists take note. I tend to favor a third-party substitute for close-up photography, the Alien Bees ABR800 Ringflash. It's priced at about $400, and, besides, it integrates very well with my other Alien Bees studio flash units.

10

Working with Wireless Flash

As I mentioned in the last chapter, one of the chief objections to the use of electronic flash is the stark, flat look of direct/on-camera flash. But as flash wizard Joe McNally, author of *The Hotshoe Diaries*, has proven, small flash units can produce amazingly creative images when used properly.

The key to effective flash photography is to get the flash off the camera, so its illumination can be used to paint your subject in interesting and subtle ways from a variety of angles. But, sometimes, using a cable to liberate your flash from the accessory shoe isn't enough. Nor is the use of just a single electronic flash always the best solution. What we really have needed is a way to trigger one—or more—flash units wirelessly, giving us the freedom to place the electronic flash anywhere in the scene and, if our budgets and time allow, to work in this mode with multiple flashes.

Wireless Evolution

Most Canon interchangeable-lens cameras with a built-in flash introduced since 2009 include internal wireless triggering capabilities using the on-camera flash. Because the EOS RP doesn't have a flash to serve as a wireless master, we must rely on using other flash units or add-ons to trigger our wireless Speedlites. Fortunately, most users of this camera are advanced photographers and can generally abide the equipment requirements that accompany useful wireless capabilities.

It's not possible to cover every aspect of wireless flash in one chapter. There are too many permutations involved. For example, you can use the EOS RP's external flash, or the ST-E2 optical transmitter (or ST-E3-RT radio transmitter) as the master. You may have one external "slave" flash, or use several. It's possible to control all your wireless flash units as if they were one multi-headed flash, or you can allocate them into "groups" that can be managed individually. You may select one of several "channels" to communicate with your strobes (or any of multiple wireless IDs when using radio-controlled units like the 600EX II-RT). These are all aspects that you'll want to explore as you become used to working with the EOS RP's amazing wireless capabilities.

What I hope to do in this chapter is provide the introduction to the basics that you won't find in other guidebooks, so you can learn how to operate the EOS RP's wireless capabilities quickly, and then embark on your own exploration of the possibilities.

YOUR STEPS MAY VARY

This chapter is intended to teach you the basics of wireless flash: why to use it, how a dedicated flash or add-on controller can be used to trigger and manipulate additional units, and what lighting ratios, channels, and groups are. I'm going to provide instructions on getting set up with wireless flash, but, depending on what flash unit you're working with (and how many you have), your specific steps may vary. The final authority on working with wireless flash has to be the manual furnished with your flash unit.

Elements of Wireless Flash

Here are some of the key concepts to electronic flash and wireless flash that I'll be describing in this chapter. Learn what these are, and you'll have gone a long way toward understanding how to use wireless flash. You need to understand the various combinations of flashes that can be used, how they can be controlled individually and together, and why you might want to use multiple and off-camera flash units. I'm going to address all these points in this section.

Flash Combinations

Your EOS RP's attached on-camera external flash can be used alone, or, if it has the capability to serve as a *master or controller flash* (not all Canon Speedlites do), in combination with other, external *remote* or *slave* flash units. (While Canon sometimes uses the terms *sender* and *receiver* to refer to master/controller and remote/slave, respectively, I'll use the industry standard terminology.) Here's a quick summary of the permutations available to you.

■ **On-camera flash used alone.** Your on-camera flash can function as the only flash illumination used to take a picture. In that mode, the flash can provide the primary illumination source (the traditional "flash photo") with the ambient light in the scene contributing little to the overall exposure. (See Figure 10.1, left.) Or, the on-camera flash can be used in conjunction with the scene's natural illumination to provide a balanced lighting effect. (See Figure 10.1, center.) In this mode, the flash doesn't overpower the ambient light, but, instead, serves to supplement it. Finally, the on-camera flash can be used as a "fill" light in scenes that are illuminated predominantly by a natural main light source, such as daylight. In this mode, the flash serves to brighten dark shadows created by the primary illumination, such as the glaring daylight in Figure 10.1, right.

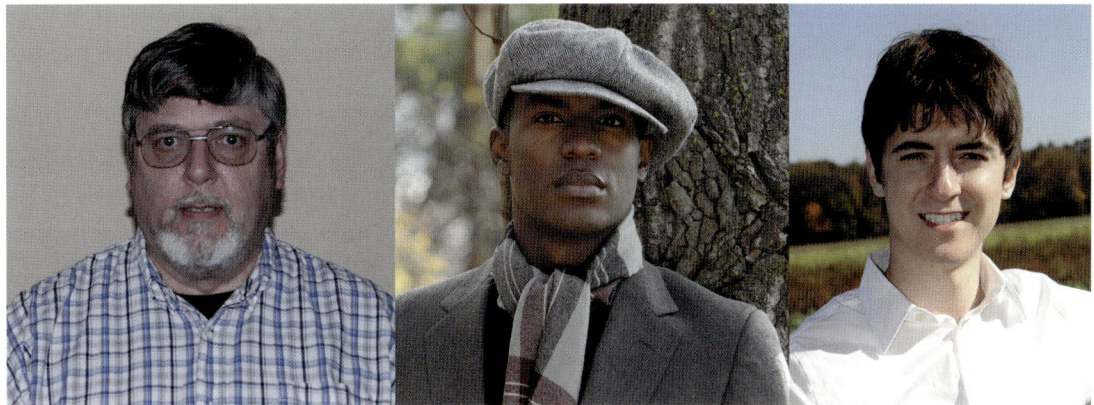

Figure 10.1 On-camera flash alone (left), as a supplement (center), and for fill flash (right).

- **On-camera flash used simultaneously with off-camera flash.** You can use the off-camera flash as a *main light* and supply *fill light* from the on-camera flash to produce interesting effects and pleasing portraits.

- **On-camera flash used as a trigger only for off-camera flash.** Use the EOS RP's on-camera wireless flash controller to command single or multiple Speedlites for studio-like lighting effects, without having the flash contribute to the exposure itself.

Controlling Flash Units

There are multiple ways of controlling flash units, both through direct or wired connections and wirelessly. Here are the primary methods used:

- **Direct connection.** The on-camera flash, of course, is directly connected to the EOS RP, and triggered electronically when a picture is taken. External flash units can also be controlled directly by linking them to a camera with a dedicated flash cord that in turn attaches to the accessory hot shoe, such as the Canon OC-E3 EOS Dedicated TTL off-camera shoe cord.

  When used in these modes, the camera has full communication with the flash, which can receive information about zoom lens position, correct exposure required, and the signals required to fire the flash. You can also plug a non-dedicated strobe, such as studio flash units, into the PC/X adapter plugged into the hot shoe. The adapter's PC/X connection is "dumb" and conveys no information other than the signal to fire.

- **Dedicated wireless optical signals.** In this mode, external flash units communicate with the camera through a pre-flash, which is used to measure exposure prior to the "real" flash burst an instant later. The pre-flashes can also wirelessly send information from the camera to the flash unit, to determine the duration of the burst to achieve the desired exposure. The pulses also can be used to adjust zoom head position (if the flash has that feature). In the case of Canon flash units, the pre-flash information is sent and received as visible light, sent so quickly just before the main burst that you may not be able to distinguish them from the "real" flash.

- **Dedicated wireless infrared signals.** Some devices, such as the Canon ST-E2 Speedlite Transmitter, can communicate with dedicated flash units through infrared signals—much like the remote control of your television. (And, also like your TV remote, the IR signal can bounce around the room somewhat, but you more or less need a line-of-sight connection for the communication to work properly.) (See Figure 10.2, left, for front and back views.) The transmitter attaches to the accessory shoe or is connected to the accessory shoe through a dedicated cable. It was an option for wireless flash for Canon cameras prior to the EOS 7D (and later models with an in-camera wireless controller), as well as for Canon cameras that have no flash unit at all (such as the EOS R and RP). Although the ST-E2 costs about $220, it's still less expensive than using a unit like the 600EX II as a master controller, particularly when on-camera flash is not desired. However, the EL-100 flash, priced at about $200, may be an even better choice as a controller, because it gives you the option to use it as a conventional on-camera or off-camera flash.

- **Canon and third-party IR and radio transmitters.** The 600EX-RT/600EX II-RT, 430EX III-RT, and ST-E3-RT from Canon can communicate as master flash units using radio signals. The 600EX-RT/600EX II-RT can also serve as a master optical flash, and as a radio or optical slave, while the 430 EX III-RT functions as a slave only in optical mode. The ST-E3-RT, shown at right in Figure 10.2, functions *only* as a radio trigger and cannot communicate with flashes that recognize only optical signals. It's priced at about $285.

In addition, some excellent wireless flash controllers that use IR or radio signals to operate external flash units are available from sources like Godox, PocketWizard, and RadioPopper. One advantage some of these third-party units has is the ability to dial in exposure/output adjustments from the transmitter mounted on the accessory shoe of the camera.

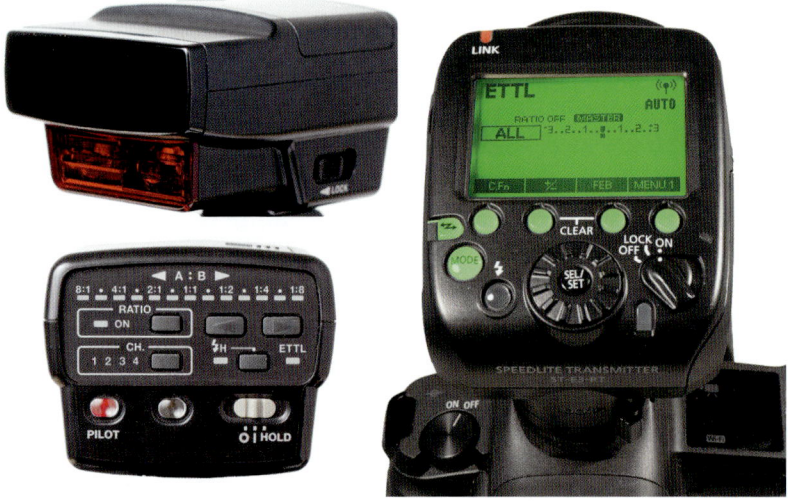

Figure 10.2
The ST-E2 infrared transmitter (left) and ST-E3-RT radio transmitter (right).

■ **Optical slave units.** A relatively low-tech/low-versatility option is to use optical slave units that trigger the off-camera flash units when they detect the firing of the main flash. Slave triggers are inexpensive, but dumb: they don't allow making any adjustments to the external flash units, and are not compatible with the EOS RP's E-TTL II exposure system. Moreover, you should make sure that the slave trigger responds to the *main* flash burst only, rather than a pre-flash, using a so-called *digital* mode. Otherwise, your slave units will fire before the main flash, and not contribute to the exposure.

Why Use Wireless Flash?

Canon's wireless flash system gives you a number of advantages that include the ability to use directional lighting, which can help bring out detail or emphasize certain aspects of the picture area. It also lets you operate multiple strobes; with models like the old favorite 580EX II that's as many as four flash units in each of three groups, or twelve in all (although most of us won't own 12 Canon Speedlites). With the 600EX-RT/600EX II-RT and 430EX III-RT, which also have radio control in addition to optical transmission, you can control many more flash units optically, but only 15 radio-controlled Speedlites, in five different groups.

You can set up complicated portrait or location lighting configurations. Since the two top Canon Speedlites pump out a lot of light for a shoe-mount flash, a set of these units can give you near studio-quality lighting. Of course, the cost of these high-end Speedlites approaches or exceeds that of some studio monolights—but the Canon battery-powered units are more portable and don't require an external AC or DC power source.

Key Wireless Concepts

There are three key concepts you must understand before jumping into wireless flash photography: channels, groups, and flash ratios. Here is an explanation of each:

■ **Channel controls.** Canon's wireless flash system offers users the ability to determine on which of four possible channels the flash units can communicate. (The pilots, ham radio operators, or scanner listeners among you can think of the channels as individual communications frequencies.) When using optical transmission, the channels are numbered 1, 2, 3, and 4, and each flash must be assigned to one of them. Moreover, in general, each of the flash units you are working with should be assigned to the *same* channel, because the slave Speedlites will respond *only* to a master flash that is on the same channel.

When using the 600EX-RT or 430EX III-RT in radio control mode, there are 15 different channels, plus an Auto setting that allows the flash to select a channel. In addition, you can assign a four-digit Wireless Radio ID that further differentiates the communications channel your flashes use.

The channel ability is important when you're working around other photographers who are also using the same system. Photojournalists, including sports photographers, encounter this situation frequently. At any event populated by a sea of "white" lenses, you'll often find photographers who are using Canon flash units triggered by Canon's own optical or (now) radio control. Third-party triggers from PocketWizard or RadioPopper are also popular, but Canon's technology remains a mainstay for many shooters.

Each photographer sets flash units to a different channel so as to not accidentally trigger other users' strobes. (At big events with more than four photographers using Canon flash and optical transmission, you may need to negotiate.) I use this capability at workshops I conduct where we have two different setups. Photographers working with one setup use a different channel than those using the other setup, and can work independently even though we're at opposite ends of the same large room.

There is less chance of a channel conflict when working with radio control and all radio-compatible Canon flash units. With 15 channels to select from, and almost 10,000 wireless radio IDs to choose from, any overlap is unlikely. (It's smart not to use a radio ID like 0000, 1111, 2222, etc., to avoid increasing the chances of conflicts. I use the last four digits of my mother-in-law's Social Security Number.) Remember that you must use either all optical or all radio transmission for all your flash units; you can't mix and match.

- **Groups.** Canon's wireless flash system lets you designate multiple flash units in separate groups. There can be as many as three groups with earlier Speedlites like the 580EX II, and newer models like the EL-100, labeled A, B, and C.

With the 600EX-RT, 430EX III-RT, and ST-E3-RT, up to five groups (A, B, C, D, and E) can be used with as many as 15 different flash units. All the flashes in all the groups use the exact same *channel* and all respond to the same master controller, but you can set the output levels of each group separately. So, Speedlites in Group A might serve as the main light, while Speedlites in Group B might be adjusted to produce less illumination and serve as a fill light. It's convenient to be able to adjust the output of all the units within a given group simultaneously. This lets you create different styles of lighting for portraits and other shots.

TIP

It's often smart to assign flash units that will reside to the left of the camera to the A group, and flashes that will be placed to the right of the camera to the B group. It's easier to adjust the comparative power ratios because you won't have to stop and think where your groups are located. That's because the adjustment controls in the *menus* are always arranged in the same A-B-C left-to-right alignment.

For example, if your A group is used as a main light on the left, and the B group as fill on the right, you intuitively know to specify more power to the A group, and less output to the B group. Reserve the C group (if used) to some other purpose, such as background or hair lights.

■ **Flash ratios.** This ability to control the output of one flash (or set of flashes) compared to another flash or set allows you to produce lighting *ratios*. You can control the power of multiple off-camera Speedlites to adjust each unit's relative contribution to the image, for more dramatic portraits and other effects.

Which Flashes Can Be Operated Wirelessly?

A particular Speedlite can have one of two functions. It can serve as a *master* flash that's capable of triggering other compatible Canon units that are on the same channel. Or, a Speedlite can be triggered wirelessly as a *slave unit* that's activated by a *master*, with full control over exposure through the camera's eTTL flash system. The second function is easy: all current and many recent Canon shoe-mount flash, including the 600EX-RT, 580EX II, 430EX II, 430EX III, 430EX III-RT, EL-100, 320EX, and 270EX II can be triggered wirelessly. In addition, some Speedlites have the ability to serve as a master flash.

I'm not going to discuss older flash units in this chapter; if you own one, particularly a non-Canon unit, it may or may not function as a slave. For example, the early Speedlite 380EX lacked the wireless capabilities added with later models, such as the 420EX, 430EX, 430EX II, 430EX III, and 430EX III-RT.

Here's a quick rundown of current flash capabilities:

■ **Canon Speedlite 600EX-RT/600EX II-RT.** These top-of-the-line flashes can function as a master flash when physically attached to any Canon EOS model, using either optical or radio transmission, and can be triggered wirelessly by another master flash, such as a compatible EOS model, another 600EX-RT/600EX II-RT or 580EX II, or the ST-E2/ST-E3-RT transmitters.

■ **Canon Speedlite 580EX II.** This discontinued flash can function as a master flash when physically attached to any Canon EOS model, and can be triggered wirelessly by an optical (not radio) transmission from another master flash from a compatible EOS camera, another 580EX II, a 600EX-RT, 600EX II-RT, 430EX III-RT, or the ST-E2 transmitter. (The ST-E3-RT transmitter operates in radio mode only.)

■ **Canon Speedlite 430EX III.** This sibling of the radio-compatible version described next cannot function as a master, but can be used as a slave when working with optical triggering technology.

■ **Canon Speedlite 430EX III-RT.** This newer flash can function as a master (in radio mode only) and as a slave when using both optical and radio technology.

■ **Canon Speedlite 430EX II.** This discontinued flash cannot function as a master, but can be triggered wirelessly by a master flash, including a compatible EOS camera, a Speedlite 600EX-RT/580EX II, or the ST-E-2 transmitters.

■ **Canon Speedlite 320EX.** This flash can be triggered wirelessly by a master flash, including a compatible EOS camera, a 600EX-RT/600EX II-RT, 580EX II, or the ST-E-2 transmitter.

- **Canon Speedlite 270EX II.** This flash can be triggered wirelessly by a compatible camera's master flash, a 600EX-RT/600EX II-RT, 580EX II, or the ST-E-2 transmitter in optical mode.
- **Canon Speedlite EL-100.** This flash can be triggered wirelessly by a compatible camera's master flash, a 600EX-RT/600EX II-RT, 580EX II, or the ST-E-2 transmitter in optical mode.

You can use any combination of compatible flash units in your wireless setup. You can use an attached 600EX-RT/600EX II-RT, 580EX II, 430EX III-RT, EL-100, or ST-E2/ST-E3-RT as a master, with any number of 600EX-RT, 580EX II, 430EX III, 430EX III-RT, EL-100, 430EX II, 320EX, or 270EX II units (or older compatible Speedlites not discussed in this chapter) as wireless slaves. I'll get you started assigning these flash to groups and channels later on.

Setting Up a Master Flash or Controller

The first step in working with wireless flash is to set up one unit (either a flash or controller) as the *master*. You can mount a Speedlite EL-100, 580EX, 580EX II, or 600EX-RT/600EX II-RT to your camera, which can serve as the master unit, transmitting E-TTL II optical signals to one or more off-camera Speedlite *slave* units. The master unit can have its flash output set to "off" so that it controls the remote units with the pre-flash, but omitting the main flash so the master unit does not contribute any illumination of its own to the exposure. This is useful for images where you don't want noticeable flash illumination coming in from the camera position. The next sections explain your options for setting up a master unit for fully automatic, E-TTL II exposure. You can also use manual exposure instead of E-TTL II automatic exposure in wireless mode. Setting up your master flash for manual operation is beyond the scope of this introductory wireless chapter.

Using a Speedlite as an Optical Master

Here are the steps to follow with the on-flash controls to set up and use compatible Speedlites as a camera-mounted master unit for automatic exposure. (The EL-100 is set up as a master using the Flash Function settings rather than controls on the flash; when you activate Wireless functions, Channel, Group, and Flash Ratio adjustments become available.) For each individual flash unit described below, check your flash's manual if you have any questions about particular button location.

600EX-RT/600EX II-RT

1. Press the Wireless button repeatedly until the NO LCD PANEL indicates you are in optical wireless master mode.
2. Press MODE to cycle through the ETTL, M, and Multi modes.
3. Use the menu system to control and make changes to RATIO, output, and other options on the master and slave units.

580EX II

1. Press and hold the ZOOM button to bring up the wireless options. Use the Select dial to cycle through the OFF, MASTER on, and SLAVE on options. Select and confirm MASTER on.

2. Press MODE to cycle through the ETTL, M, and Multi modes.

3. Press the ZOOM button repeatedly to cycle through the following options: Flash zoom, RATIO, CH., and flash emitter ON/OFF. Use the Select dial and Select/SET button to make any changes to these options.

4. Use the Select/SET button to select and confirm the output power settings when using Manual and Multi modes, or to use FEC or FEB when in ETTL mode.

580EX

1. Slide the OFF/MASTER/SLAVE wireless switch near the base of the unit to MASTER.

2. Press MODE to cycle through the ETTL, M, and Multi modes.

3. Press the ZOOM button repeatedly to cycle through the following options: Flash zoom, RATIO, CH., and flash emitter ON/OFF. Use the Select dial and Select/SET button to make any changes to these options.

4. Use the Select/SET button to select and confirm the output power settings when using Manual and Multi modes, or to use FEC or FEB when in ETTL mode.

Using the ST-E2 Transmitter as Master

Canon's Speedlite Transmitter (ST-E2) is mounted on the camera's hot shoe and provides a way to control one or more Speedlites and/or units assigned to Groups A and B. The ST-E2 does not provide any flash output of its own and will not trigger units assigned to Group C. It has the following features and controls:

■ **Transmitter.** Located on the top front of the unit, the transmitter emits E-TTL II pulses through an infrared filter.

■ **AF-assist beam emitter.** Just below the transmitter, the AF-assist beam emitter works similarly to the Speedlite 430EX II and higher models.

■ **Battery compartment.** The ST-E2 uses a 6.0V 2CR5 lithium battery. The battery compartment is accessed from the top of the unit.

■ **Lock slider and mounting foot.** The lock slider is located on the right side of the unit when facing the front. Sliding it to the left lowers the lock pin in the mounting foot (located on the bottom of the unit) to secure it to the camera's hot shoe.

■ **Back panel.** The rear of the unit features several indicators and controls:

- **Ratio indicator.** A series of red LED lights indicating the current A:B ratio setting.

- **Flash ratio control lamp.** A red LED that lights up when flash ratio is in use.

- **Flash ratio setting button.** Next to the flash ratio control lamp. Press this button to activate flash ratio control.

- **Flash ratio adjustment buttons.** Two buttons with raised arrows (same color as buttons) pointing left and right. Use these to change the A:B ratio setting.

- **Channel indicator.** The channel number in use (1–4) glows red.

- **Channel selector button.** Next to the channel indicator. Press this button to select the communication channel.

- **High-speed sync (FP flash) indicator.** A red LED that glows when high-speed sync is in use.

- **High-speed sync button.** Press this button to activate/deactivate high-speed sync.

- **ETTL indicator.** A red LED that glows when E-TTL II is in use.

- **Off/On/HOLD switch.** Slide this switch to turn the unit off, on, or on with adjustments disabled (HOLD). The ST-E2 will power off after approximately 90 seconds of idle time. It will turn back on when the shutter button or test transmission button is pressed.

- **Pilot lamp/Test transmission button.** This lamp works similarly to the Speedlite pilot lamp/test buttons. The lamp glows red when ready to transmit. Press the lamp button to send a test transmission to the slave units.

- **Flash confirmation lamp.** This lamp glows green for about three seconds when the ST-E2 detects a good flash exposure.

Here are the steps to follow to set up and use the ST-E2 transmitter (shown previously at left in Figure 10.2) as a camera-mounted master unit:

1. Mount the ST-E2 unit on your EOS RP.

2. Make sure both the ST-E2 unit and your camera are powered on.

3. Make sure the slave units are set to E-TTL II, assigned to the appropriate group(s), and that all units are operating on the same channel.

4. If you'd like to set a flash ratio between Groups A and B, press the flash ratio setting button and flash ratio adjustment buttons to select the desired ratio. Press the high-speed sync button to use high-speed sync (often helpful with outdoor shooting).

Using the Speedlite 600EX-RT/600EX II-RT as Radio Master

The Speedlite 600EX-RT/600EX II-RT can serve as the master unit when mounted to your camera, transmitting radio signals to one or more off-camera Speedlite 600EX-RT/600EX II-RT slave units. The master unit can have its flash output set to "off" so that it controls the remote units without contributing any flash output of its own to the exposure. This is useful for images where you don't want noticeable flash illumination coming in from the camera position.

Here are the steps to follow to set up and use a Speedlite 600EX-RT/600EX II-RT as a camera-mounted master unit for radio wireless E-TTL II operation.

1. Mount the Speedlite 600EX-RT/600EX II-RT to your EOS RP.
2. Make sure the 600EX-RT master units, slave units, and the camera are powered on.
3. Set the camera-mounted unit to radio wireless MASTER mode. Press the Wireless button until the NO LCD PANEL indicates you are on radio wireless master mode.
4. Set the slave 600EX-RT/600EX II-RT or 430EX III-RT units to radio wireless SLAVE mode. For each 600EX-RT unit, press the Wireless button until the NO LCD PANEL indicates you are on radio wireless slave mode. For each 430EX III-RT slave, press the left directional key and rotate the Select dial until Slave appears on the LCD. Then press the Select button to confirm.
5. Confirm that all units are set to E-TTL II, assigned to the appropriate group(s), and that all units are operating on the same channel and ID number. The LINK lamps on all units should glow green.

Using the Speedlite 430EX III-RT as Radio Master

The Speedlite 430EX III-RT can serve as a radio master unit to trigger another 430EX III-RT or a 600EX-RT flash. Just follow these steps:

1. Press the left directional key on the Select dial. It's marked with a lightning bolt symbol.
2. Rotate the Select dial until MASTER appears on the LCD.
3. Press the Select button in the center of the Select dial.
4. Set any 600EX-RT or 430EX III-RT units that you will be using as slaves to the Slave mode.
   - For the 600EX-RT, press the Wireless button until the NO LCD PANEL indicates you are in radio wireless slave mode.
   - For any 430EX III-RT slaves, press the left directional key and rotate the Select dial until Slave appears on the LCD. Then press the Select button to confirm.
5. Repeat Step 4 for any additional Slave units.
6. When master and slaves are communicating, the LINK lamps on all units will glow green.

Using the ST-E3-RT as Radio Master

The ST-E3-RT transmitter can be mounted to the camera's hot shoe and used as a master controller to one or more slave Speedlite 600EX-RT units. The ST-E3-RT and the 600EX-RT share essentially the same radio control capabilities except that the ST-E3-RT does not produce flash, provide AF-assist, or otherwise emit light and is therefore incapable of optical wireless transmission.

The layout of the ST-E3-RT's control panel is virtually identical to the 600EX-RT. So is the menu system and operation, except that, as stated earlier, it will only operate as a radio wireless transmitter. Here are the steps to follow to set up and use the ST-E3-RT transmitter as a camera-mounted master unit for radio wireless E-TTL II operation:

1. Mount the ST-E3-RT unit on your EOS RP.
2. Make sure both the ST-E3-RT unit and your camera are powered on.
3. Set the slave 600EX-RT or 430EX III-RT units to radio wireless SLAVE mode. For each 600EX-RT unit, press the Wireless button until the NO LCD PANEL indicates you are on radio wireless slave mode. For each 430EX III-RT slave, press the left directional key and rotate the Select dial until Slave appears on the LCD. Then press the Select button to confirm.
4. Confirm that all units are set to E-TTL II, assigned to the appropriate group(s), and that all units are operating on the same channel and ID number. The LINK lamps on all units should glow green.

The ST-E3-RT controls slave units as described earlier in the section, "Using the Speedlite 600EX-RT/600EX II-RT as Radio Master."

Setting Up a Slave Flash

The whole point of working wirelessly is to have a master flash/controller trigger and adjust one or more slave flash units. So, once you've defined your master flash, the next step is to switch your remaining Speedlites into slave mode. That's done differently with each particular Canon Speedlite.

- **Speedlite 600EX-RT/600EX II-RT.** Press the Wireless button repeatedly until the NO LCD PANEL indicates that the unit is in optical wireless slave mode or radio wireless slave mode. In this mode, the 600EX-RT is assigned a flash mode by the master transmitter, either a flash or ST-E2 or ST-E3-RT.

- **Speedlite 580EX II.** Press and hold the ZOOM button until the wireless setting options appear. Use the Select dial and Select/SET button to select and confirm that wireless is on and in slave mode.

- **Speedlite 430EX III/430EX III-RT.** For each 430EX III-RT slave, press the left directional key and rotate the Select dial until Slave appears on the LCD. Then press the Select button to confirm.

■ **Speedlite 430EX II.** Press and hold the ZOOM button for two seconds or more until the wireless setting options appear. Use the Select dial and Select/SET button to select and confirm that wireless is on and in slave mode.

■ **Speedlite 320EX.** This flash has an On/Off/Slave switch at the lower left of the back panel. In Slave mode, you can use the flash's C.Fn-10 setting to tell the unit to power down after either 10 or 60 minutes of idle time. That can help preserve the 320EX's batteries. The unit's C.Fn-11 setting can be set to allow the master transmitter to "wake" a sleeping 320EX after your choice of within 1 hour or within 8 hours. Note that the C.Fn settings of the 320EX and 270EX II (described next) can be set only while the Speedlites are connected to the camera with the hot shoe.

■ **Speedlite 270EX II.** This flash has an Off/Slave/On switch. If left on and idle, the 270EX II will power itself off after approximately 90 seconds. C.Fn-1 can be used to disable auto power off. As with the 320EX, in Slave mode, you can use the flash's C.Fn-10 setting to tell the unit to power down after either 10 or 60 minutes of idle time. The unit's C.Fn-11 setting can be set to allow the master transmitter to "wake" a sleeping unit after your choice of within 1 hour or within 8 hours.

■ **Speedlite EL-100.** Using this flash as a remote is ridiculously easy. Set the Receiver switch on the back of the unit to the same channel used by the master, and rotate the mode dial to the appropriate Group (usually A).

Choosing a Channel

In optical mode, Canon's wireless flash system can work on any of four channels, so if more than one photographer is using the Canon system, each can set his gear to a different channel so they don't accidentally trigger each other's strobes. You need to be sure all of your gear is set to the same channel. Selecting a channel is done differently with each particular flash model. The EL-100 is the easiest in this regard: just slide the Receiver switch to the Channel you want to use.

The ability to operate flash units on a particular channel isn't really important unless you're shooting in an environment where other photographers are also using the Canon wireless flash system. If the system only offered one channel, then each photographer's wireless flash controller would be firing every Canon flash set for wireless operation. By having four channels available, the photographers can coordinate their use to avoid that problem. Such situations are common at sporting events and other activities that draw a lot of shooters.

It's always a good idea to double-check your flash units before you set them up to make sure they're all set to the same channel, and this should also be one of your first troubleshooting questions if a flash doesn't fire the first time you try to use it wirelessly.

You do this as follows:

1. **Set flash units to the channel you want to use for all your groups.** Before you use the EOS RP's controls to configure your flash exposures, you must first make adjustments on the external Speedlite. Each flash unit may use its own procedure for setting that strobe's channel. Consult your Speedlite's manual for instructions. With the 580EX II, press the Zoom button repeatedly until the CH. Indicator blinks, then rotate the control dial to select Channel 1, 2, 3, or 4. Press the control dial center button to confirm. With the 600EX-RT/600EX II-RT, press Fn Button 4 until Menu 2 appears, then press Fn Button 1 to select a channel.

2. **Activate wireless operation.** From the External Speedlite Control entry in the Shooting 2 menu, navigate to the Flash Function Settings choice, Flash Functions. Highlight the second icon from the left in the top row (as seen in Figure 10.3, left) and press SET. Then choose Wireless: Optical Transmission from the screen that appears (Figure 10.3, right). Press SET to confirm and exit.

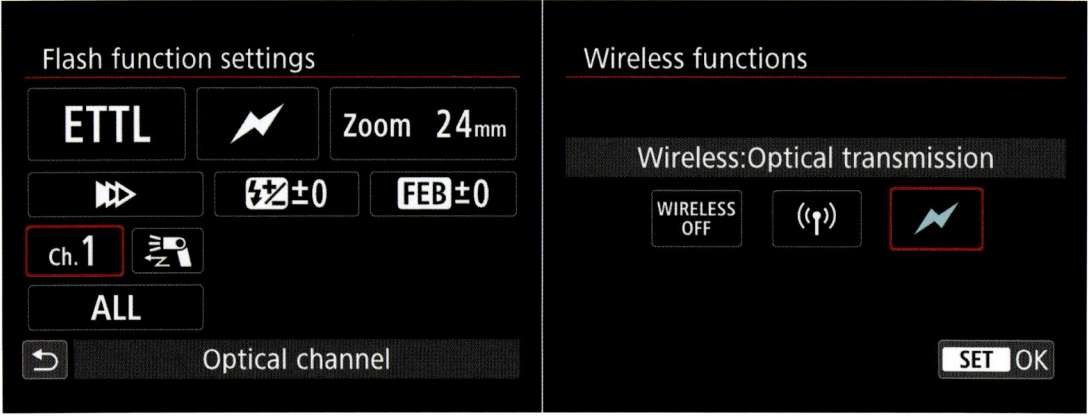

Figure 10.3 You can choose the Channel, Groups, and other parameters from the Flash Function settings screen (left); activate wireless functions (right).

3. **Navigate to the EOS RP's channel selection option.** Navigate to the Channel Setting (highlighted in red at left in Figure 10.3) and push the SET button.

4. **Select the channel your flashes are set to.** You can then use the QCD to cycle the channel number from 1 to 4.

5. **Enable/disable master flash firing.** The icon to the immediate right of the Channel Setting icon allows you to enable or disable firing of the master flash. When disabled, the master flash will still control external flashes wirelessly with a pre-flash burst, but won't contribute to the exposure. This is useful if you want all the illumination to come from your slave flash units, such as when shooting close-up or macro images, or when you're simulating a studio flash setup with Speedlites.

6. **Double-check to make sure your off-camera flash units are set to the appropriate channel.** Your wireless flash units must be set to the same channel as the EOS RP's wireless flash controller; otherwise, the Speedlites won't fire.

Working with Groups

With what you've already learned, you can shoot wirelessly using your camera's on-camera flash and one or more external flash units. All these strobes will work together with the EOS RP for automatic exposure using E-TTL II exposure mode. You can vary the power ratio between your on-camera flash and the external units. As you become more comfortable with wireless flash photography, you can even switch the individual external flash units into manual mode, and adjust their lighting ratios manually.

But there's a lot more you can do if you've splurged and own two or more compatible external flash units (some photographers I know own five or six Speedlite 580EX II or 600EX II-RT units). Canon wireless photography lets you collect individual strobes into *groups*, and control all the Speedlites within a given group together. You can operate as few as two strobes in two groups or three strobes in three groups, while controlling more units if desired. You can also have them fire at equal output settings (A+B+C mode) versus using them at different power ratios (A:B or A:B C modes). Setting each group's strobes to different power ratios gives you more control over lighting for portraiture and other uses.

This is one of the more powerful options of the EOS wireless flash system. I prefer to keep my Speedlites set to different groups normally. I can always set the power ratio to 1:1 if I want to operate the flash units all at the same power. If I change my mind and need to make adjustments, I can just change the wireless flash controller and then manipulate the different groups' output as desired.

Canon's wireless flash system works with a number of Canon flashes and even some third-party units. I routinely mix a 600EX-RT, 600EX II-RT, 580EX II, 550EX, and 420EX. I control these flash units either with the EOS RP's on-camera external flash or using a Canon ST-E2 Speedlite Transmitter.

The ST-E2 is a hot-shoe mount device that offers wireless flash control for a wide variety of Canon wireless-flash-capable strobes and can even control flash units wirelessly for high-speed sync (HSS) photography. (HSS is described in Chapter 9.) The ST-E2 can only control two flash groups though.

Here's how you set up groups (for flashes other than the EL-100, which has Group positions on its mode dial):

1. **Set flash units to the group you want to assign them to.** Each flash unit may use its own procedure for setting that strobe's group. Consult your Speedlite's manual for instructions.

2. **Navigate to the EOS RP's group selection option.** From the External Speedlite Control entry in the Shooting 1 menu, navigate to the Flash Function Settings choice, Flash Functions. Navigate to the Group setting (located just below the Channel and Master Flash Firing options) and push the SET button.

3. **Select the group configuration you want.** You can then use the QCD to cycle to select ALL, A:B, or A:B C. If you're using the 600EX-RT/600EX II-RT in radio control mode, you can also activate Groups D and E.

4. **Double-check to make sure your flash units are set to the appropriate channel.** Your wireless flash units must be set to the same channel as the EOS RP's wireless flash controller; otherwise, the Speedlites won't fire.

Ratio Control

By default, all the flashes in each group will fire at full power. However, for more advanced lighting setups, you can select lighting ratios.

Your on-camera master flash and your wireless slave flash units have their own individual *oomph*—how much illumination they put out. This option lets you choose the relationship between these units, a *power ratio* between your on-camera flash and your wireless flash units—the relative strength of each. That ability can be especially useful if you want to use the on-camera flash for just a little fill light, while letting your off-camera units do the heavy work.

Having the ability to vary the power of each flash unit or group of flash units wirelessly gives you greater flexibility and control. Varying the light output of each flash unit makes it possible to create specific types of lighting (such as traditional portrait lighting, which frequently calls for a 3:1 lighting ratio between main light and fill light) or to use illumination to highlight one part of the photo while reducing contrast in another.

Lighting ratios determine the contrast between the main light (sometimes called a "key" light) and fill light. For portraiture, usually the main light is placed at a 45-degree angle to the subject (although there are some variations), with the fill-in light on the opposite side or closer to the camera position. Choosing the right lighting ratio can do a lot to create a particular look or mood. For instance, a 1:1 ratio produces what's known as "flat" lighting. While this is good for copying or documentation, it's not usually as interesting for portraiture. Instead, making the main light more powerful than the fill light creates interesting shadows for more dramatic images. (See Figure 10.4.)

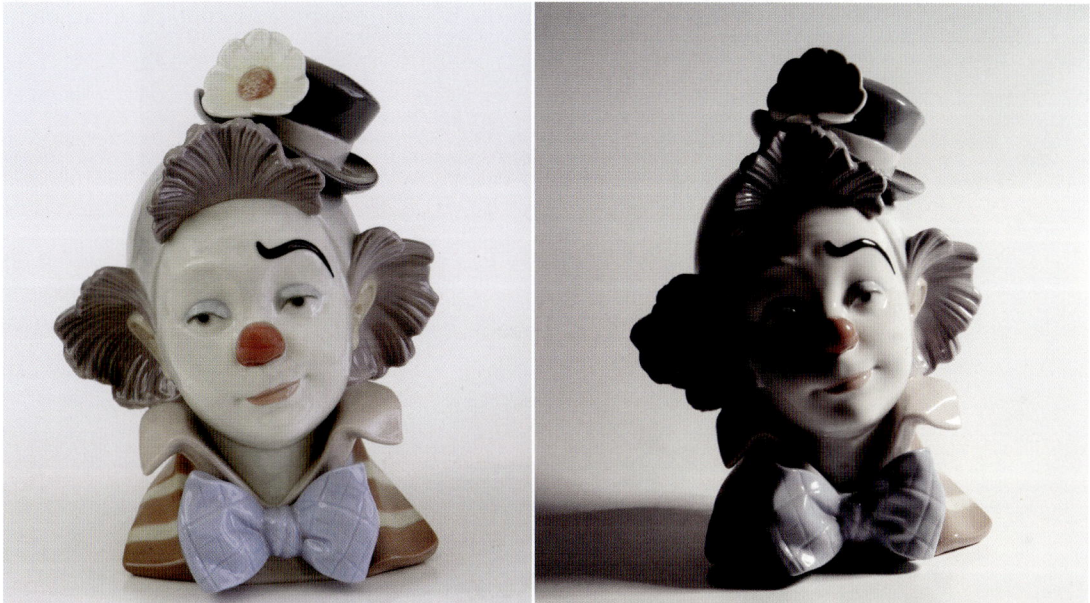

Figure 10.4 More dramatic lighting ratios produce more dramatic-looking illumination.

By selecting the power ratio between the flash units, you can change the relative illumination between them. Figure 10.5 shows a series of four images with a single main flash located at a 45-degree angle off to the right and slightly behind the model. The on-camera flash at the camera provided illumination to fill in the shadows on the side of the face closest to the camera. The ratio between the two Speedlites flash was varied using 2:1 (upper left), 3:1 (upper right), 4:1 (lower left), and 5:1 (lower right) ratios.

Here's how to set the lighting ratio between the master flash and one additional external wireless flash unit:

1. **Navigate to the EOS RP's Flash Group selection option.** With wireless flash already activated, visit the External Speedlite Control entry in the Shooting 2 menu, navigate to the Flash Function Settings choice, Flash Functions. Navigate to the Flash Group choice at the lower left of the screen, and push the SET button.

2. **Choose Group Configuration.** You can select ALL, A:B, or A:B C. If you're using the 600EX-RT/600EX II-RT in radio transmission mode, you can also select Groups D and E. Press SET to confirm.

3. **Select Ratio.** If you've chosen A:B C, use the QCD to navigate to the A:B Ratio Control option, highlighted in red at left in Figure 10.6, press SET and select a ratio from 8:1 to 1:8 (see Figure 10.6, right). Group A at 1:8 supplies 1/8th the output of Group B. At 8:1, the ratio is reversed.

4. **Confirm.** Press SET to confirm your ratio.

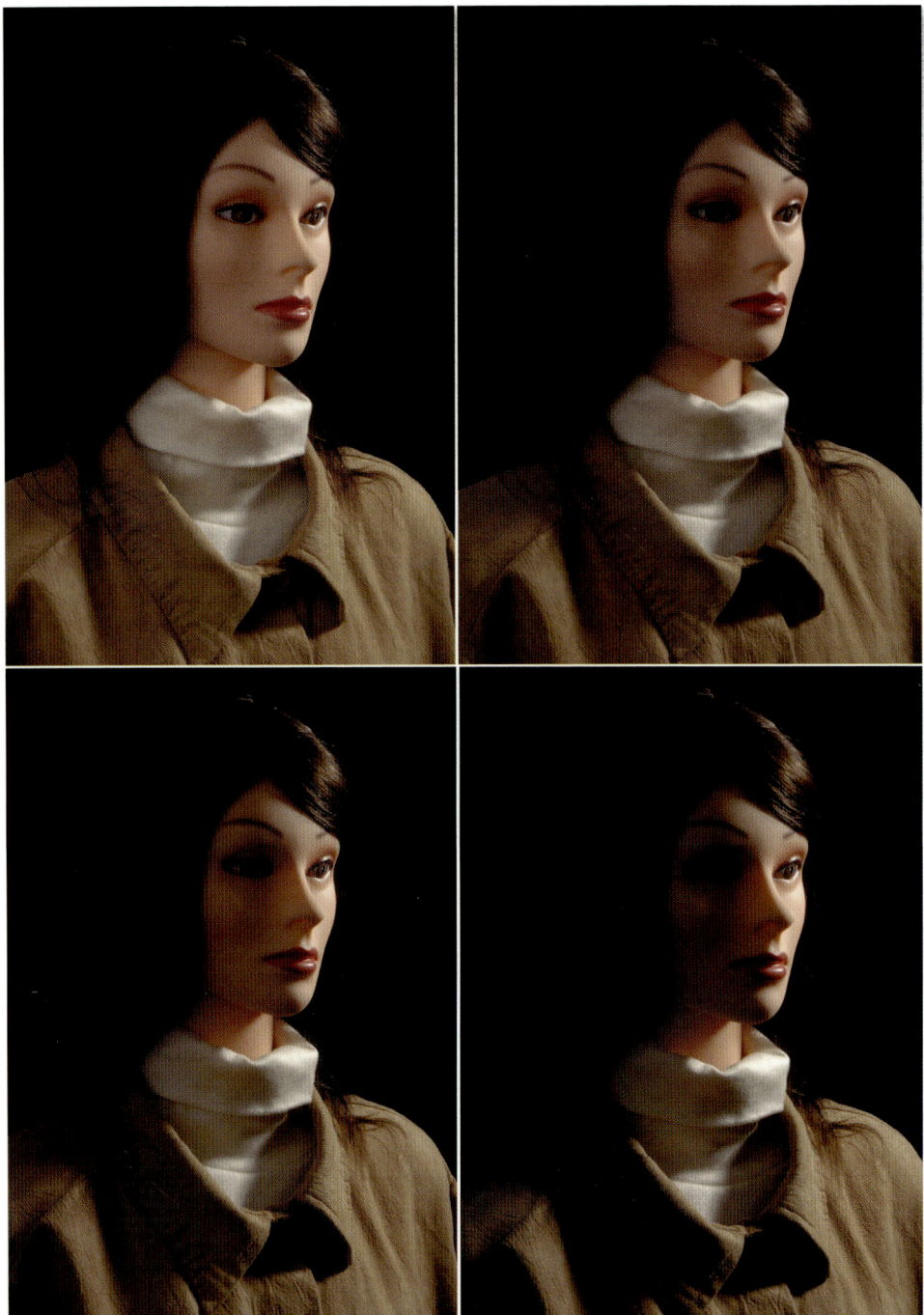

Figure 10.5 The main light (to the right and behind the model) and fill light (at the camera position) were varied using 2:1 and 3:1 (top row, left to right) as well as 4:1 and 5:1 (bottom row, left to right) ratios.

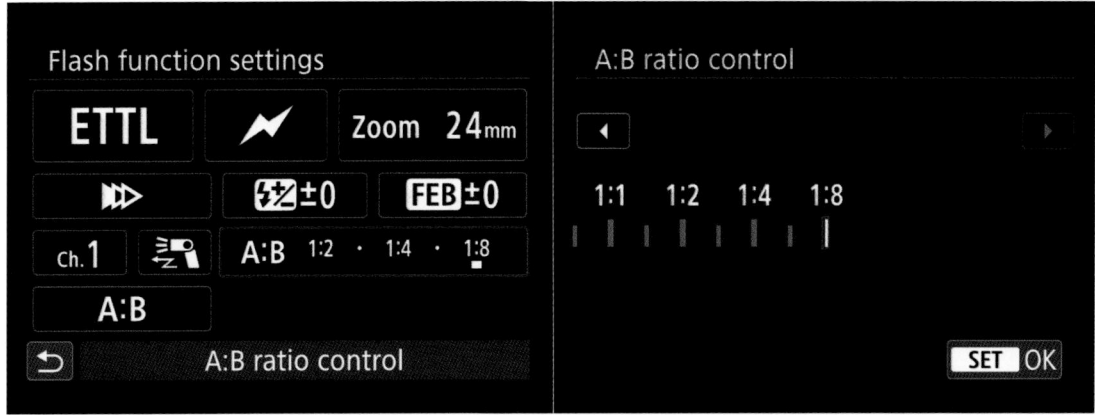

Figure 10.6 Select your Group Configuration.

Here's how the various basic Group Configurations work:

- **ALL.** All groups will fire at the power level set at the flash unit itself. That may be full power, or you may have set individual flashes to fire at some other power level. It's usually simpler to set your flashes at full power and allow the master to control their output.

- **A:B.** In this configuration, you can specify the ratio of the power levels of Groups A and B, as described in Step 3 above.

- **A:B C.** In this Group configuration, you can specify the power ratio between Groups A and B, but *not* the output of Group C flashes. Those can be controlled only using Flash Exposure Compensation, the option labeled FEB immediately above the A:B Power Ratio setting in Figure 10.6 (left).

Remote Release Function/Linked Shooting

Unfortunately, the EOS RP is not compatible with the optical mode of the Remote Release function found on certain Canon Speedlites, as the feature requires an infrared sensor remote control, which the mirrorless camera lacks. I'm mentioning this for owners of previous Canon models who have used this feature in the past with their Canon Speedlite 600EX-RT, 600EX II-RT, 430EX III, 320EX, 270EX II, or ST-E3-RT transmitter.

However, the 600EX-RT/600EX II-RT and ST-E3-RT transmitter *do* have their own remote release function, which allows you to use a slave unit to trigger your camera by remote control when using *radio transmission* mode. EOS cameras released since 2012, including the EOS RP, can be triggered in this way through the intelligent hot shoe, using a 600EX-series flash or ST-E3-RT transmitter mounted on the camera as a receiver, and the slave 600EX-RT/600EX II-RT off camera as the remote trigger. Older cameras can still be used in this mode, but you'll need to connect the on-camera "receiver" to the camera's N3 three-pin remote control terminal using an optional Release Cable SR-N3. The remote release/linked shooting features operate within a perimeter of about 33 feet.

Check your transmitter/flash menu for a more complete explanation, but setup is relatively simple. On the 600EX-series, press the Menu 2 button on the unit which will be used as a remote/slave flash and choose REL (release). Thereafter, a release signal is sent from the slave to the master/controller flash on the camera, and the EOS RP will be triggered to take a picture and fire all the remote units. Remote release can be triggered only when autofocus can be achieved and is performed only using Single Shooting, regardless of the camera's drive mode.

Linked shooting is also possible, and allows triggering the shutter of a slave unit *camera* by linking it to a master unit camera. You can then trigger all the camera and flash units simultaneously. Each camera must have a flash that supports radio transmission wireless shooting, or you can use the ST-E3-RT transmitter on one or more of the slave cameras. You're better off using manual focus when triggering multiple cameras, because if even one camera is unable to achieve autofocus, linked shooting with that camera is disabled.

You'll need to set the flash/transmitter on the master camera as the master of the multi-camera array, and the slave flash/transmitters to linked slave mode. On each slave ST-E3-RT, you'll need to press the Wireless/Linked Shooting button until Linked Shot appears. (The button is located on the left edge of the back panel, labeled with a double-headed lightning bolt icon, as shown earlier in Figure 10.2.) On the master transmitter, press the button again to make it the master. Note that each time you switch a unit from slave to master modes, any other units that had been set as "master" will automatically switch to slave mode. The Link light (at the top left of the back panel) of the slave and master units should be lit green.

Setting up the master/slave Speedlites is similar. The 600EX-series flash have their own Wireless/Linked Shooting button in roughly the same location on their back panels. Press that button and rotate the large select dial until Linked Shot appears, then press the Select/SET button. Use the control wheel to set each flash as Master or Slave, then press the Select/SET button.

Then press the button again to set the "master" unit of the linked shooting configuration. When the Channel and ID are specified and ready, the Link lamp on the slave unit(s) will illuminate in green. Then, point the remote/slave flash used as a trigger at the front of the camera/master flash within 16 feet of the camera, and press the remote control button on the side of the flash. During the two-second delay, you can then point the flash in a different direction (as is likely, because you're probably using this feature to illuminate the scene, not the camera). That's the real reason for the two-second delay, by the way: giving you the ability to reposition the "remote" release flash.

11

Customizing with the Shooting Menu

This chapter and the next three will help you sort out the settings you can make to customize how your Canon EOS RP uses its features, shoots photos, displays images, and processes the pictures after they've been taken. I'm not going to waste a lot of space on some of the more obvious menu choices. For example, you can probably figure out that the Touch Shutter option in Shooting 5 deals with whether or not the Touch Shutter option is enabled or disabled. In this chapter, I'll devote no more than a sentence or two to the blatantly obvious settings and concentrate on the more confusing aspects of EOS RP setup, such as Automatic Exposure Bracketing.

The nine Shooting menu tabs discussed in this chapter are those available in still shooting mode. If you switch to a Movie mode, only the first four Shooting menus are available. I'll explain the Movie Shooting menus in Chapter 16, where I've collected all the basic video capture information for the EOS RP. For now, let's start off with an overview of the EOS RP's menus themselves.

Anatomy of the EOS RP's Menus

The EOS RP divides the entries into five major sections—Shooting, Playback, Set-up, Custom Functions, and My Menu—each of which (except for the last) is further subdivided into separate pages. Each page's listings are shown as a separate screen with no scrolling.

The menus are easy to use, too. Just press the MENU button, spin the Main Dial to highlight the menu tab and page you want to access, and then scroll up and down within a menu with the Quick Control Dial. What could be easier?

Tapping the MENU button brings up a typical menu like the one shown in Figure 11.1. (If the camera goes to "sleep" while you're reviewing a menu, you may need to wake it up again by tapping the shutter release button.) Different menu tabs are provided, depending on the shooting mode, shown in Table 11.1.

The EOS RP's tabs are color-coded: red for Shooting, blue for Playback, amber yellow for Set-up, brown for Custom Functions, and Green for My Menu. The currently selected menu tab's icon is white within a background corresponding to its color code. A lineup immediately underneath shows the page numbers available, and, at far right, the name of the page (for example, SHOOT1). The current screen's number is highlighted. All the inactive menus are gray and dimmed.

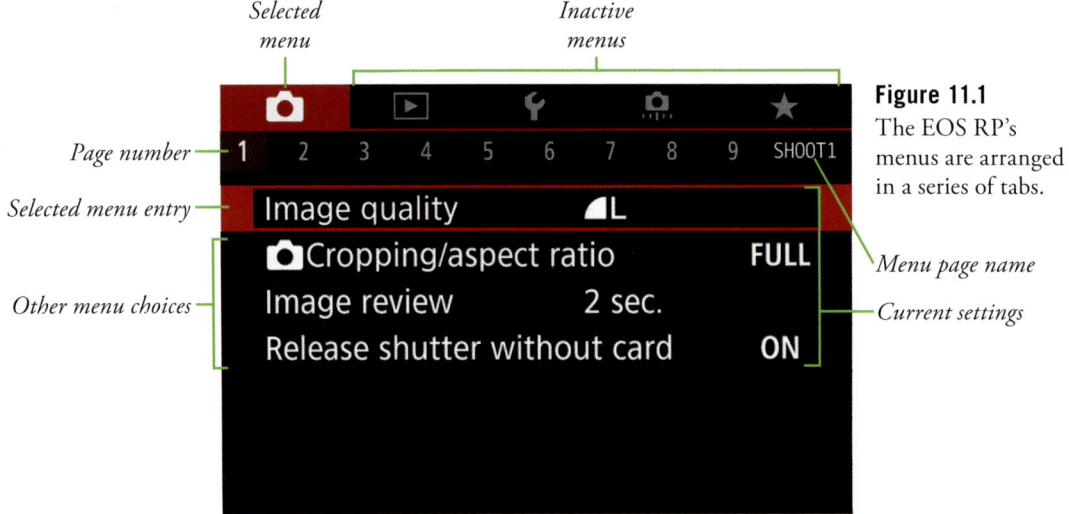

Figure 11.1
The EOS RP's menus are arranged in a series of tabs.

Table 11.1 Available Menus

Modes	Available Menu Tabs
Bulb, M, Tv, Av, Fv, P modes	Shooting 1–9, Playback 1–4, Set-up 1–6, Custom Functions 1, My Menu
Scene Intelligent Auto, Scene	Shooting 1–5, Playback 1–4, Set-up 1–6
Movie mode	Shooting 1–6, Playback 1–4, Set-up 1–6, Custom Functions 1, My Menu

HYPER MENU NAVIGATION

As I mentioned, you can use the Main Dial to move from menu to menu, and the Quick Control Dial to highlight a menu entry. Press the SET button to select a menu item. That procedure is probably the best way to start out, because those controls are used to make so many settings with the EOS RP that they quickly become almost intuitive. But, you can use the touch screen to tap on a specific menu tab, page number, and individual entry, if you like.

It gets even better. You can jump from tab to tab even if you've highlighted a menu setting on another tab—and the EOS RP will remember which menu entry you've highlighted when you return to that menu. The memorization works even if you leave the menu system or turn off your camera. The EOS RP always remembers the last menu entry you used with a tab. So, if you generally use the Format command each time you access the Set-up 1 menu, that's the entry that will be highlighted when you choose that tab. The camera remembers which tab was last used, too, so, potentially, formatting your memory card might take just a couple presses (the MENU button, the SET button to select the highlighted Format command, then a click of the Quick Control Dial to choose OK, and another press of SET to start the format process).

Here are the things to watch for as you navigate the menus:

■ **Menu tabs.** In the top row of the menu screen, the menu that is currently active will be highlighted as described earlier. The numbers within the tab let you know if you are in, say, Set-up 1, Set-up 2, Set-up 3, or another tab. Just remember that the red camera icons stand for still and movie shooting options; the blue right-pointing triangles represent playback options; the yellow wrench icons stand for set-up options; the brown camera icons represent Custom Functions; and the green star stands for personalized menus defined for the star of the show—you.

■ **Selected menu.** The currently selected menu entry within a given tab will have a black background and will be surrounded by a box the same hue as its color code.

■ **Other menu choices.** The other menu items visible on the screen will have a dark gray background.

■ **Current setting.** The current settings for visible menu items are shown in the right-hand column, until one menu entry is selected (by pressing the SET key). Current settings aren't appropriate for some menu entries (for example, the Protect Images or Resize options in the Playback 1 and 2 screens), so the right column is left blank.

When you've moved the menu highlighting to the menu item you want to work with, press the SET button to select it. The current settings for the other menu items in the list will be hidden, and a list of options for the selected menu item (or a submenu screen) will appear. Or, you may be shown a separate settings screen for that entry. Within the menu choices, you can scroll up or down with the Quick Control Dial; press SET to select the choice you've made; and press the MENU button again to exit.

Shooting Menu Options

You'll find that the Shooting menu options are those that you access second most frequently when you're using your EOS RP. You might make such adjustments as you begin a shooting session, or when you move from one type of subject to another. Canon makes accessing these changes very easy.

This section explains the options of the first eight Shooting menu tabs and how to use them. There are additional movie-oriented entries on in the Shooting 9 menu (not discussed in this chapter), and in the differently organized Shooting menus that appear when the Mode Dial is rotated to the Movie position. The options you'll find in these first eight red-coded menus include:

- Image Quality
- Cropping/Aspect Ratio
- Image Review
- Release Shutter without Card
- Lens Aberration Correction
- External Speedlite Control
- Exposure Compensation/AEB (Automatic Exposure Bracketing)
- ISO Speed Settings
- Movie ISO Speed Settings
- Auto Lighting Optimizer
- Highlight Tone Priority
- Metering Timer
- Exposure Simulation
- White Balance
- Custom White Balance
- WB Shift/Bkt
- Color Space
- Picture Style

- Long Exposure Noise Reduction
- High ISO Speed Noise Reduction
- Dust Delete Data
- Touch Shutter
- Multiple Exposure
- HDR Mode
- Focus Bracketing
- Interval Timer
- Bulb Timer
- Anti-flicker Shooting
- High Speed Display
- AF Operation
- AF Method
- Eye Detection AF
- Continuous AF
- Touch & Drag AF Settings
- Lens Electronic MF
- AF-Assist Beam Firing
- MF Peaking Settings

Image Quality

Options: Resolution: Large (default), Medium, Small 1, Small 2; JPEG Compression: Fine (default), Normal; JPEG (default), RAW, or RAW+JPEG

My preference: Resolution: Large; JPEG Compression: Fine; RAW+JPEG

You can choose the image quality settings used by the EOS RP to store its files. You have choices to make when selecting a quality setting:

- **Resolution.** The number of pixels captured determines the absolute resolution of the photos you shoot with your EOS RP. Your choices range from 26 megapixels (Large or L), measuring 6240 × 4160; 12 megapixels (Medium or M), measuring 4160 × 2768; 6.5 megapixels (Small 1 or S1), measuring 3120 × 2080; and 3.8 megapixels (Small 2 or S2), measuring 2400 × 1600. You can also choose RAW-only sizes of RAW and C RAW (6240 × 4160; 26MP). Both RAW formats have the same resolution, but C RAW (Compact RAW) produces a smaller file size: 17.1MB compared to 29.1MB for standard RAW.

- **JPEG compression.** To reduce the size of your image files and allow more photos to be stored on a given memory card, the EOS RP uses JPEG compression to squeeze the images down to a smaller size. This compacting reduces the image quality a little, so you're offered your choice of Fine compression and Normal compression. The symbols help you remember that Fine compression (represented by a quarter-circle) provides the smoothest results, while Normal compression (signified by a stair-step icon) provides "jaggier" images. The Small 2 (S2) file option has no quality option icon, but it is Fine quality.

- **JPEG, RAW, or both.** You can elect to store only JPEG versions of the images you shoot or you can save your photos as uncompressed, loss-free RAW files, which consume about four times as much space on your memory card. Or, you can store both at once as you shoot. Many photographers elect to save *both* a JPEG and a RAW file, so they'll have a JPEG version that might be usable as-is, as well as the original "digital negative" RAW file in case they want to do some processing of the image later. You'll end up with two different versions of the same file: one with a JPG extension, and one with the CR3 extension that signifies a Canon RAW file.

To choose the combination you want, access the menus, scroll to Image Quality, and press the SET button. A screen similar to the one shown in Figure 11.2 will appear with two rows of choices. Spin the Main Dial to choose from:—(no RAW), RAW, or C RAW. Rotate the QCD to select one of the JPEG choices:—(no JPEG), Large, Medium, or Small in Fine or Normal compression (represented by smooth and stepped icons, respectively), plus Small 2 (with Fine compression), at the resolutions listed above. A red box appears around the currently selected choice. If you choose "--" for both RAW and JPEG, then JPEG Fine will be used. As always, when you've highlighted your selection, press SET to confirm.

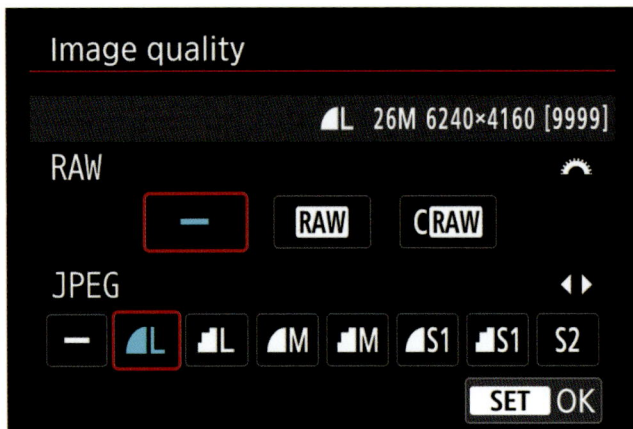

Figure 11.2
Choose your resolution, JPEG compression, and file format from this screen.

Why so many choices? There are some limited advantages to using the Medium and Small resolution settings, Normal JPEG compression setting, and the two lower resolution RAW formats. They all allow stretching the capacity of your memory card so you can shoehorn quite a few more pictures onto a single memory card. That can come in useful when on vacation and you're running out of storage, or when you're shooting non-critical work that doesn't require full resolution. The Small 2 setting can be useful for photos taken for real estate listings, web page display, photo ID cards, or similar non-critical applications.

For most work, using lower resolution and extra compression is often false economy. You never know when you might need that extra bit of picture detail. Your best bet is to have enough memory cards to handle all the shooting you want to do until you have the chance to transfer your photos to your computer or a personal storage device.

However, reduced image quality can sometimes be beneficial if you're shooting sequences of photos rapidly, as the EOS RP is able to hold more of them in its internal memory buffer before transferring to the memory card. Still, for most sports and other applications, you'd probably rather have better, sharper pictures than longer periods of continuous shooting.

JPEG vs. RAW

You'll sometimes be told that RAW files are the "unprocessed" image information your camera produces, before it's been modified. That's nonsense. RAW files are no more unprocessed than camera film is after it's been through the chemicals to produce a negative or transparency. A lot can happen in the developer that can affect the quality of a film image—positively and negatively—and, similarly, your digital image undergoes a significant amount of processing before it is saved as a RAW file. Canon even applies a name (DIGIC 8) to the digital image processing (DIP) chip used to perform this magic.

A RAW file is more like a film camera's processed negative. It contains all the information, captured in 14-bit channels per color (and stored in a 16-bit space), with no compression, no sharpening, and no application of any special filters or other settings you might have specified when you took the picture. Those settings are *stored* with the RAW file so they can be applied when the image is converted to a form compatible with your favorite image editor. However, using RAW conversion software such as Adobe Camera Raw or Canon's Digital Photo Professional, you can override those settings and apply settings of your own. You can select essentially the same changes there that you might have specified in your camera's picture-taking options.

RAW exists because sometimes we want to have access to all the information captured by the camera, before the camera's internal logic has processed it and converted the image to a standard file format. RAW doesn't save as much space as JPEG. What it does do is preserve all the information captured by your camera after it's been converted from analog to digital form. Of course, the EOS RP's RAW format preserves the *settings* information.

So, why don't we always use RAW? Although some photographers do save only in RAW format, it's more common to use either RAW plus one of the JPEG options or just shoot JPEG and avoid RAW altogether. That's because having only RAW files to work with can significantly slow down your workflow. While RAW is overwhelmingly helpful when an image needs to be fine-tuned, in other situations working with a RAW file, when all you really need is a good-quality, un-tweaked JPEG image, consumes time that you may not want to waste. For example, RAW images take longer to store on the memory card, and require more post-processing effort, whether you elect to go with the default settings in force when the picture was taken, or just make minor adjustments.

Thus, those who depend on speedy access to images or who shoot large numbers of photos at once may prefer JPEG over RAW. Wedding photographers, for example, might expose several thousand photos during a bridal affair and offer hundreds to clients as electronic proofs for possible inclusion in an album or transfer to a CD or DVD. These wedding shooters, who want JPEG images as their final product, take the time to make sure that their in-camera settings are correct, minimizing the need to post-process photos after the event. Given that their JPEGs are so good (in most cases thanks, in large part, to the pro photographer's extensive experience), there is little need to get bogged down shooting RAW.

JPEG was invented as a more compact file format that can store most of the information in a digital image, but in a much smaller size. JPEG predates most digital SLRs, and was initially used to squeeze down files for transmission over slow dial-up connections. Even if you were using an early dSLR with 1.3 megapixel files for news photography, you didn't want to send them back to the office over a modem (Google it) at 1,200 bps.

But, as I noted, JPEG provides smaller files by compressing the information in a way that loses some image data. JPEG remains a viable alternative because it offers several different quality levels. At the highest-quality Fine level, you might not be able to tell the difference between the original RAW file and the JPEG version. You've squeezed the image significantly without losing much visual information at all. (See Figure 11.3.)

In my case, I shoot virtually everything at RAW+JPEG Fine. Most of the time, I'm not concerned about filling up my memory cards, as I usually have a minimum of five fast 64GB memory cards with me. If I think I may fill up all those cards on a trip, I usually have a laptop with me and can transfer photos to that device. As I mentioned earlier, when shooting sports, I'll shift to JPEG Fine (with no RAW file) to squeeze a little extra speed out of my EOS RP's continuous shooting mode, and to reduce the need to wade through eight-photo bursts taken in RAW format. On the other hand, on my last trip to Europe, I took only RAW (instead of my customary RAW+JPEG) photos to fit more images onto my laptop, as I planned on doing at least some post-processing on many of the images for a travel book I was working on.

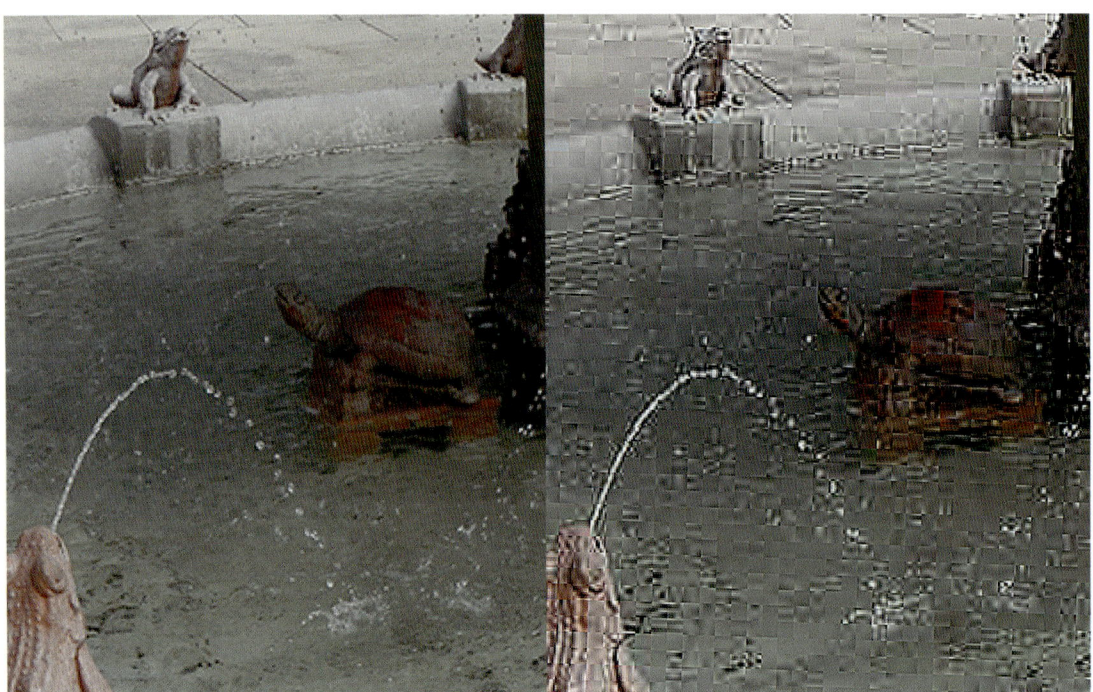

Figure 11.3 Low compression yields the best image (left); at high compression, pixelation and artifacts rear their ugly heads.

Cropping/Aspect Ratio

Options: FULL (default), 1.6X, 1:1, 4:3, 16:9; Shooting area display: Masked, Outlined

My preference: FULL

Your EOS RP allows you to crop images in the camera. Instead of the full sensor frame of 36mm × 24mm, you can select a 1.6X APS-C crop (with a 3:2 crop ratio that's the same as the FULL setting), or aspect ratios of 1:1 (square), 4:3, or 16:9 (which corresponds to high-definition/ ultra-high-definition movie frames). You can also choose whether the shooting area is displayed within the frame—either outlined with blue lines or masked so that only the current crop or aspect ratio is displayed.

The 1.6X crop is significant, because it means that the EOS RP, unlike other Canon full-frame cameras, can, when equipped with an EF/EF-S mount adapter, use APS-C format EF-S lenses. You can use the 1.6X crop to increase the telephoto "reach" of RF and EF lenses (with adapter), giving you a 3888 × 2592–pixel, 10.1MP image. If you are using an EF-S lens, then the 1.6X crop is chosen automatically and the other aspect ratios are not available.

If you've selected the 1.6X crop or have mounted an EF-S lens, the EOS RP magnifies the image so the cropped portion fills the display, as the APS-C aspect ratio of 3:2 is identical to that of the full-frame image. If shooting RAW (or when using an EF-S lens), the area outside the 1.6X crop will not be captured. For other aspect ratios, only the captured image area will be shown on the display. The crop/aspect ratio options are shown in Figure 11.4, and the relative resolutions are shown in Table 11.2.

Figure 11.4
Crop/Aspect Ratio options.

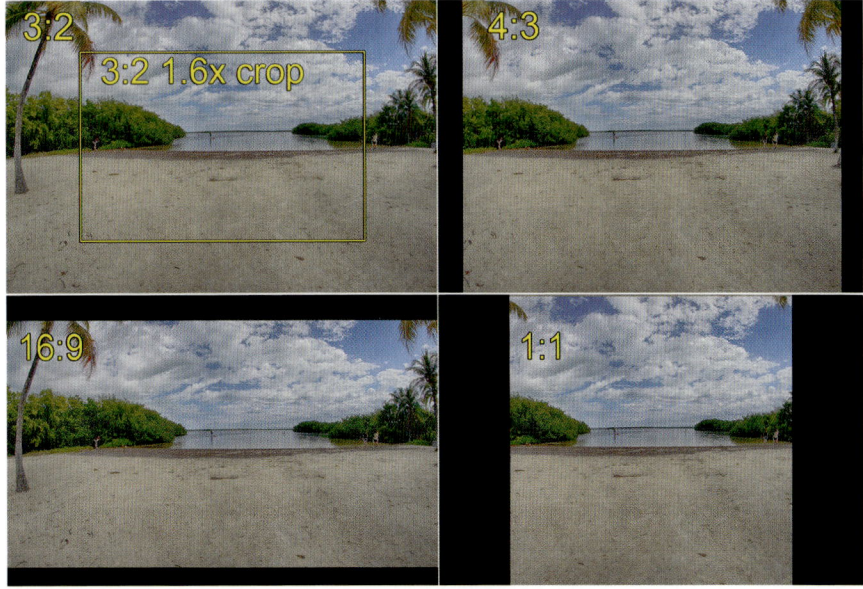

Table 11.2 Crop/Aspect Ratio Image Sizes

Size Ratio	JPEG Large RAW/C RAW	JPEG Medium	JPEG Small 1	JPEG Small 2
Full Frame (3:2)	6240 × 4160 (26MP)	4160 × 2768 (11.5MP)	3120 × 2080 (6.5MP)	2400 × 1600 (3.8MP)
1.6X Crop (3:2)	3888 × 2592 (10.1MP)	N/A	N/A	2400 × 1600 (3.8MP)
1:1	4160 × 4160 (17.3MP)	2768 × 2768 (7.7MP)	2080 × 2080 (4.3MP)	1600 × 1600 (2.6MP)
4:3	5536 × 4160 (23MP)	3680 × 2768 (10.2MP)	2768 × 2080 (5.8MP)	2112 × 1600 (3.4MP)
16:9	6240 × 3504 (21.9MP)	4160 × 2336 (9.7MP)	3120 × 1752 (5.5MP)	2400 × 1344 (3.2MP)

Image Review

Options: 2 sec. (default), Off, 4 sec., 8 sec., Hold

My preference: 2 sec.

You can adjust the amount of time an image is displayed for review on the LCD after each shot is taken. You can elect to disable this review entirely (Off), or choose display times of 2, 4, or 8 seconds. You can also select Hold, an indefinite display, which will keep your image on the screen until you use one of the other controls, such as the shutter button, Main Dial, or Quick Control Dial. Turning the review display off or choosing a brief duration can help preserve battery power. However, the EOS RP will always override the review display when the shutter button is partially or fully depressed, so you'll never miss a shot because a previous image was on the screen. Choose Image Review from the Shooting 1 menu, and select Off, 2 sec., 4 sec., 8 sec., or Hold. If you want to retain an image on the screen for a longer period, but don't want to use Hold as your default, press the Erase button under the LCD monitor. The image will display until you choose Cancel or Erase from the menu that pops up at the bottom of the screen. A longer review time gives you an opportunity to delete a non-keeper quickly without a visit to the menu system.

Release Shutter without Card

Options: Enable (default), Disable

My preference: Disable

This entry in the Shooting menu gives you the ability to snap off "pictures" without a memory card installed—or to lock the camera shutter release if that is the case. It is sometimes called Play mode, because you can experiment with your camera's features or even hand your EOS RP to a friend to let him/her fool around, without any danger of pictures being taken. Back in our film days, we'd sometimes finish a roll, rewind the film back into its cassette surreptitiously, and then hand the camera to a child to take a few pictures—without wasting any film. It's hard to waste digital film, but Release Shutter without Card mode is still appreciated by some, especially camera vendors who want to be able to demo a camera at a store or trade show, but don't want to have to equip every demonstrator model with a memory card. Choose this menu item, press SET, select Enable or Disable, and press SET again to turn this capability on or off.

Lens Aberration Correction

Options: Peripheral illumination correction: Enable (default)/Disable; Distortion correction: Enable/Disable (default); Digital Lens Optimizer (Chromatic Aberration): Enable (default)/Disable; Diffraction Correction: Enable/Disable (default)

My preference: Use the default values. However, if working with small apertures frequently, say for macro photography, disable Digital Lens Optimizer and enable Diffraction Correction. (They are mutually exclusive.)

This is the first entry on the Shooting 2 menu (see Figure 11.5). The EOS RP can automatically partially correct for lens aberrations in several different ways using three different settings, if you

Figure 11.5
The Shooting 2 menu.

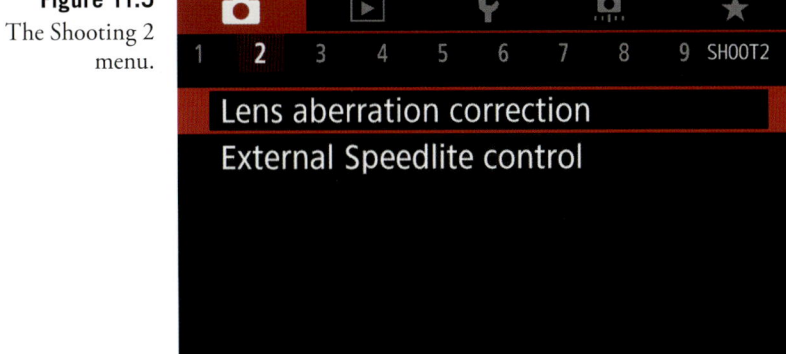

are using a lens for which correction data is available. Previously, several of these corrections were available only when post-processing the image in Digital Photo Professional or another utility. The three choices (see Figure 11.6), all described in detail in the next section, are as follows:

- **Peripheral illumination correction.** Fixes light fall-off at the edges of an image.
- **Distortion correction.** Adjusts for barrel and pincushion distortion.
- **Digital lens optimizer.** Corrects for a variety of characteristics, taking into account the lens, subject distance, focal length, aperture, and low-pass (anti-aliasing) filter over the sensor. It corrects for both chromatic aberration (color fringes around the edges of subjects) and diffraction for moiré effects produced when shooting at a very small aperture.
- **Diffraction correction.** This choice appears only when Digital Lens Optimizer is disabled. It corrects a loss of sharpness due to scattering of light as photons strike the edges of the lens diaphragm; it is generally most pronounced at small f/stops.

I'll explain what each of these components do one at a time, and include some examples of those aspects that can be easily illustrated.

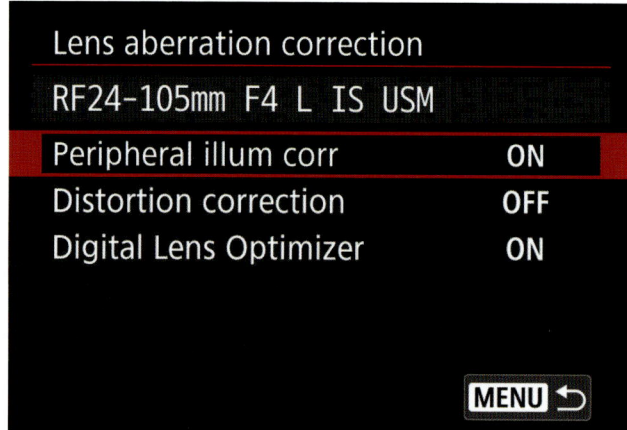

Figure 11.6
The Lens Aberration Correction screen.

Peripheral Illumination Correction

One defect is caused by a phenomenon called *vignetting*, which is a darkening of the four corners of the frame because of a slight amount of fall-off in illumination at those nether regions. This menu option allows you to activate Peripheral Illumination Correction, a clever feature built into the EOS RP that partially (or fully) compensates for this effect for any lens included in the camera's internal, updateable (through firmware upgrades) database. Depending on the f/stop you use, the lens mounted on the camera, and the focal length setting, vignetting can be non-existent, slight, or may be so strong that it appears you've used a too-small hood on your camera. (Indeed, the wrong lens hood can produce a vignette effect of its own.) Vignetting can be affected by the use of a telephoto converter (more on those in Chapter 7, too).

Peripheral illumination drop-off, even if pronounced, may not be much of a problem. I actually *add* vignetting, sometimes, when shooting portraits and some other subjects. Slightly dark corners tend to focus attention on a subject in the middle of the frame. On the other hand, vignetting with subjects that are supposed to be evenly illuminated, such as landscapes, is seldom a benefit.

To minimize the effects of corner light fall-off, you can process RAW files using Digital Photo Professional or, if you want your JPEG files fixed as you shoot them, by using this menu option. Figure 11.7 shows an image at top left without peripheral illumination correction, and a corrected image at bottom left. I've exaggerated the vignetting a little to make it more evident on the printed page. Keep in mind that the amount of correction available with Digital Photo Pro can be a little more intense than that applied in the camera. In addition, the higher the ISO speed, the less correction is applied. If you see severe vignetting with a particular lens, focal length, or ISO setting, you might want to turn off this feature, shoot RAW, and apply correction using DPP instead.

When you select this menu option from the Shooting 2 menu, a screen appears with the name of the lens currently attached to the camera, along with a notation whether correction data needed to brighten the corners is already registered in the camera. (Information about the most popular lenses is included in the EOS RP's firmware.) If so, you can use the Quick Control Dial to choose Enable

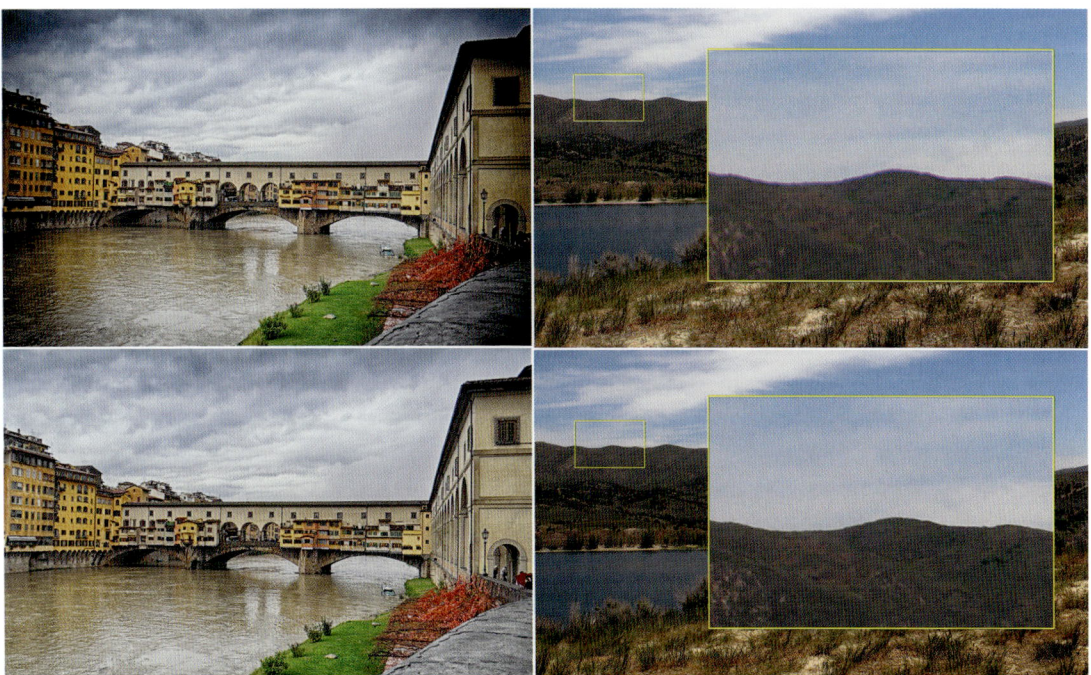

Figure 11.7 Left: Vignetting (top) is undesirable. You can correct this defect in the camera (bottom). Right: Color fringes can be corrected using the lens aberration correction feature (right top and bottom).

to activate the feature, or Disable to turn it off. Press the SET button to confirm your choice. Note that in-camera correction must be specified *before* you take the photo, so that the DIGIC 8 processing engine can lighten the corners of your photo before it is saved to the memory card.

Distortion Correction

This option adjusts to correct barrel and pincushion distortion, based on information in the camera's database.

Barrel distortion is found in some wide-angle lenses, and causes straight lines to bow outward, with the strongest effect at the edges. In fisheye (or *curvilinear*) lenses, this defect is a feature. When distortion is not desired, you'll need to use a lens that has corrected barrel distortion. Manufacturers like Canon do their best to minimize or eliminate it (producing a *rectilinear* lens), often using *aspherical* lens elements (which are not cross-sections of a sphere). You can also minimize less severe barrel distortion simply by framing your photo with some extra space all around, so the edges where the defect is most obvious can be cropped out of the picture. If none of the above work, you can apply this feature, which is disabled by default, to "undistort" your image with some bending of its own.

Pincushion distortion is a trait of many telephoto lenses, producing lines that curve inward toward the center of the frame. You might find after a bit of testing that it is worse at certain focal lengths with your particular zoom lens. Like chromatic aberration, it can be partially corrected using tools like Photoshop's Lens Correction filter and Photoshop Elements' Correct Camera Distortion filter, Digital Photo Professional, or this in-camera feature.

Digital Lens Optimizer

This option is a general-purpose fixer-upper based on the EOS RP's database understanding of its list of lenses and characteristics of the camera and sensor. It applies a whole range of corrections and can apply them separately to the center or edges of the frame, fixing spherical aberration, axial chromatic aberration, curvature of field, astigmatism, chromatic aberration, sagittal halo, and chromatic magnification. Many of these are technical aspects that are beyond the scope of this book.

Another defect fixed by the Digital Lens Optimizer involves fringes of color around backlit objects, produced by *chromatic aberration*, which comes in two forms: *longitudinal/axial*, in which all the colors of light don't focus in the same plane; and *lateral/transverse*, in which the colors are shifted in one direction. (See Figure 11.7, top right.) When this feature is enabled, the camera will automatically correct images taken with one of the supported lenses to reduce or eliminate the amount of color fringing seen in the final photograph. (See 11.7, bottom right.)

Diffraction Correction

The final defect that can be corrected is *diffraction*, a phenomenon that can cause a reduction in the apparent sharpness of your image due to scattering and interference of photons as they pass through smaller lens openings. In effect, the edges of your lens aperture affect proportionately more photons as the f/stop grows smaller. The relative amount of space available to pass freely decreases, and the amount of edge surface that can collide with incoming light increases.

The best analogy I can think of is a pond with two floating docks sticking out into the water, as shown in Figure 11.8, left. Throw a big rock in the pond, and the ripples pass between the docks relatively smoothly if the structures are relatively far apart (top). Move them closer together (bottom), and some ripples rebound off each dock to interfere with the incoming wavelets. In a lens, smaller apertures produce the same effect.

Reminder: Diffraction Correction appears on the screen *only* when Digital Lens Optimizer is disabled. In addition, Multiple Exposures cannot be captured when Digital Lens Optimizer is Enabled.

The EOS RP's sensor also includes a so-called "anti-aliasing" filter (technically known as an *optical low-pass filter,* or OLPF), designed to eliminate moiré. You might see it on your television when a guest wears a checked shirt with a pattern that's very close to the interval, or frequency, of the lines that produce the video image. Or, it might show up when photographing a window screen (see Figure 11.8, right). The optical low-pass filter blocks most of that moiré by blurring the image slightly.

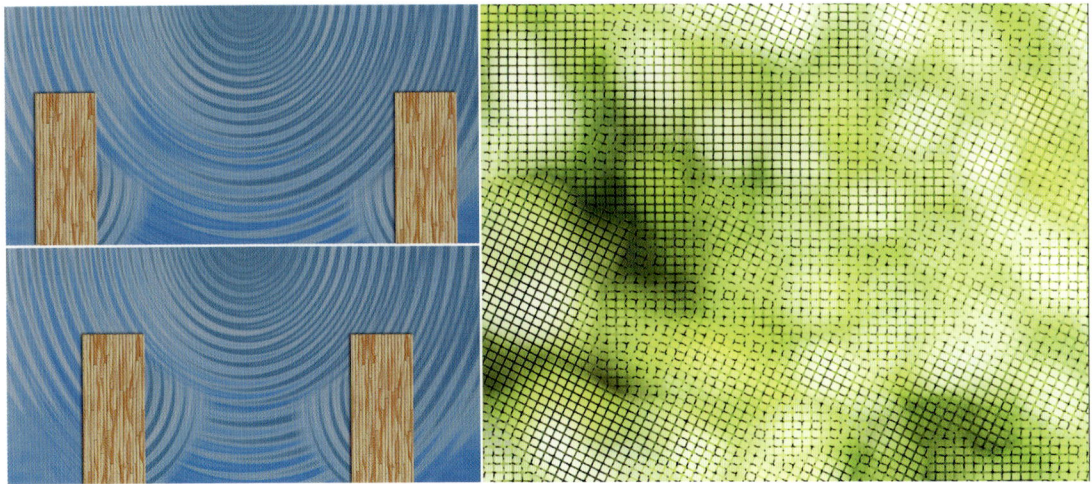

Figure 11.8 Diffraction interference can be visualized as ripples on a lake (left). Patterns, such as window screens, can create moiré effects (right).

With the EOS RP, Canon has greatly expanded the list of lens data included within the camera itself. However, if lens aberration correction information for your lens is not registered in the camera, you can often remedy that deficit using the most recent version of the EOS Utility. Just follow these steps:

1. **Link up your camera.** Mount the lens you want to register, then connect your EOS RP to your computer using the USB cable supplied with the camera.

2. **Launch the EOS utility.** Load the utility on your computer and click on Camera Settings from the splash screen that appears. (See Figure 11.9, upper left.)

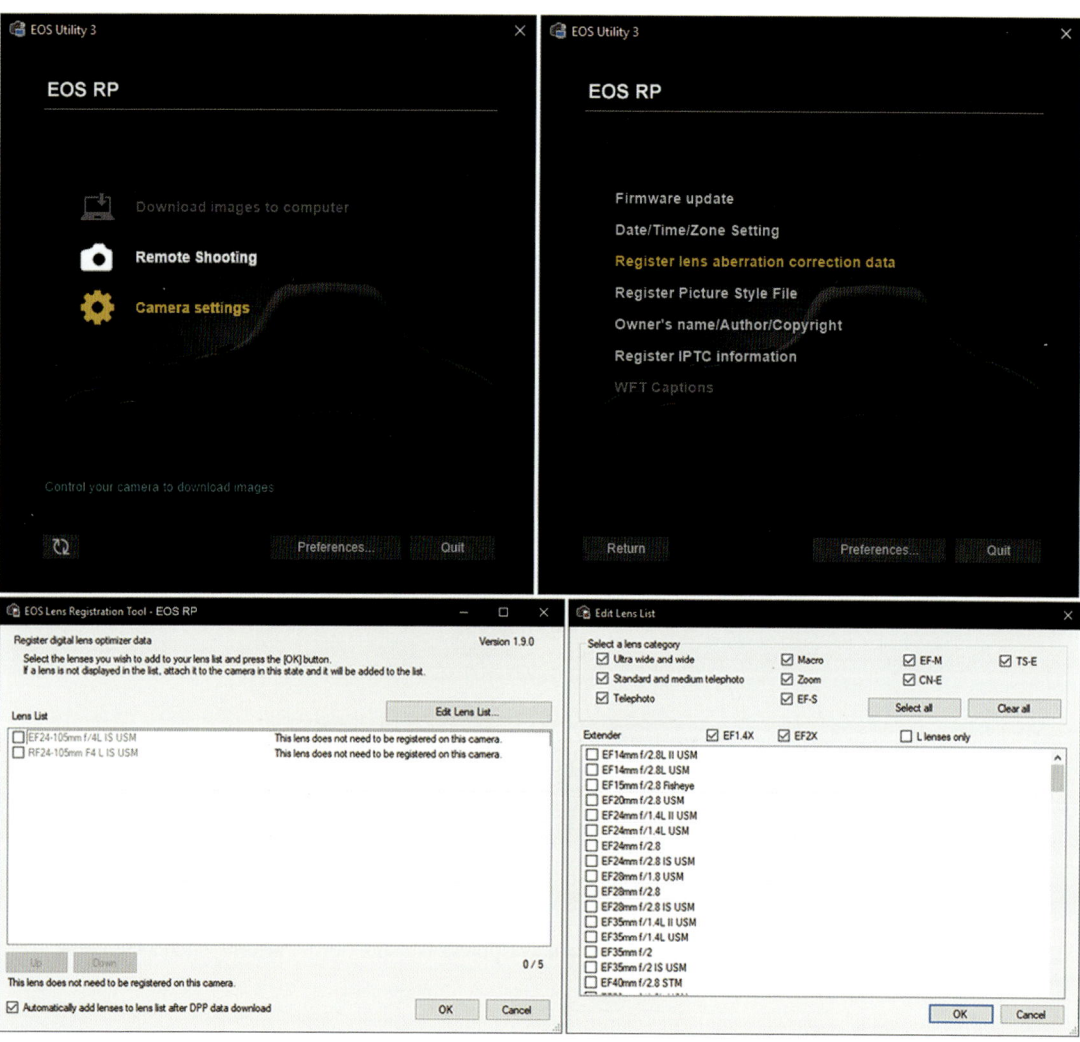

Figure 11.9 Add lens correction data using the EOS Utility.

3. **Click on the Register Lens Aberration Correction Data choice.** The Camera Settings options screen is shown in Figure 11.9, upper right.

4. **Choose your lens.** The current lenses you own that have been mounted on your camera will appear in the EOS RP Lens Registration Tool, shown at lower left in Figure 11.9. You can place a check next to a lens you want to add, then click OK to confirm. If the message "This lens does not need to be registered on this camera" appears next to a lens, the EOS RP already has correction data for it, and you do not need to add it.

5. **Add another lens.** You can add one or more lenses without mounting them on the camera by clicking on the Edit Lens List option, seen at upper right of the Lens Registration Tool. The Edit Lens List screen is shown in Figure 11.9, lower right.

6. **View and select lenses.** Select the category containing the lens you want to register from the panels at the top of the new screen; then place a check mark next to all the lenses you'd like to register in the camera.

7. **Confirm your choice.** Click OK to send the data from your computer to the EOS RP and register your lenses.

8. **Activate correction.** When a newly registered lens is mounted on the camera, you will be able to activate the Peripheral Illumination Correction (anti-vignetting) feature for that lens from the Shooting 2 menu.

External Speedlite Control

This multi-level menu entry includes settings for controlling the Canon EOS RP's accessory flash units attached to the camera (see Figure 11.10). I'll provide in-depth coverage of how you can use these options in Chapters 9 and 10, but will list the main options here for reference.

Figure 11.10
The External Speedlite Control menu entry has six options, plus Clear Settings.

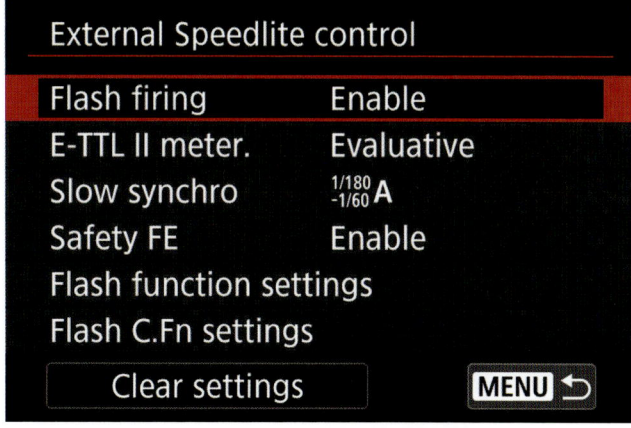

Flash Firing

Use this option to enable or disable the attached electronic flash. Choose Enable, and the flash fires normally when it's attached to the camera and powered up. Select Disable, and the flash itself will not fire, but the AF-assist beam emitted by the unit will function normally. You might want to use the latter option when you prefer to shoot under low levels of existing light, but still need the auto-focusing boost the flash's AF beam provides.

E-TTL II Metering

You can choose Evaluative (Matrix) or Average metering modes for the electronic flash exposure meter. Evaluative looks at selected areas in the scene to calculate exposure, and is the best choice for most images because it attempts to interpret the type of scene being shot; Average calculates flash exposure by reading the entire scene, and it is possibly a good option if you want exposure to be calculated for the overall scene.

Slow Synchro

You can select the flash synchronization speed that will be used when working in Av (Aperture-priority) or P (Program) exposure modes; choose from 1/180th–30 sec Auto (the EOS RP selects the shutter speed from 30 seconds to 1/180th second), to a range embracing only the speeds from 1/180th–60 sec Auto, or fixed at 1/180th second.

Normally, in Aperture-priority mode when using flash, you specify the f/stop to be locked in. The camera then adjusts exposure by varying the output of the electronic flash. In Program mode, the camera chooses the f/stop. Because the primary exposure comes from the flash, the main effect of the shutter speed selected is on the secondary exposure from the ambient light remaining on the scene.

Auto is your best choice under most conditions. The EOS RP will choose a shutter speed that balances the flash exposure and available, ambient light. The 1/180th–1/60th second setting locks out slower shutter speeds, preventing blur from camera/subject movement in the secondary ("ghost") exposure. However, the background may be rendered dark if the flash is not strong enough to illuminate it. The 1/180th second (fixed) setting further reduces the chance of getting those blurry ghosts, but there is more of a chance the background will be dark. You'll find a more detailed explanation of these options in Chapter 9.

Safety FE

Enabling this setting helps avoid overexposure from an attached and powered-up external flash when used during bright daylight or close to your subject. The EOS RP will automatically lower the ISO speed when sensitivity is set to ISO Auto.

Flash Function Settings

There is a total of six possible choices for this menu screen, plus Clear Settings. These additional options are grayed out unless you're working in wireless flash mode. All these are explained in Chapters 9 and 10.

- **ETTL Flash mode.** This entry allows you to choose from automatic exposure calculation (E-TTL II), manual flash exposure, multi (repeating) flash, or Continuous Shooting Priority (CSP). The latter setting, which increases flash output and ISO speed each by one stop, uses less battery power and enables the EOS RP to use flash when shooting continuously.

- **Wireless functions.** These choices include Mode, Channel, Firing Group, and other options used only when you're working in wireless mode to control a wireless-capable external flash. If you've disabled wireless functions, the other options don't appear on the menu. I'm going to leave the explanation of these options for Chapter 10, which is an entire chapter dedicated to using the EOS RP's wireless shooting capabilities.

- **Zoom.** Use this to select a flash zoom head setting to adjust coverage area of compatible Speedlites.

- **Shutter sync.** You can choose first-curtain sync, which fires the pre-flash used to calculate the exposure before the shutter opens, followed by the main flash as soon as the shutter is completely open. This is the default mode, and you'll generally perceive the pre-flash and main flash as a single burst. Alternatively, you can select second-curtain sync, which fires the pre-flash as soon as the shutter opens, and then triggers the main flash in a second burst at the end of the exposure, just before the shutter starts to close. (If the shutter speed is slow enough, you may clearly see both the pre-flash and main flash as separate bursts of light.) This action allows photographing a blurred trail of light of moving objects with sharp flash exposures at the beginning and the end of the exposure. This type of flash exposure is slightly different from what some other cameras produce using second-curtain sync. I explained how it works in Chapter 9.

  If you have an external compatible Speedlite attached, you can also choose high-speed sync, which allows you to use shutter speeds faster than 1/180th second, using the External Flash Function Setting menu.

- **Flash exposure compensation.** If you'd rather adjust flash exposure using a menu than with the ISO/Flash exposure compensation button, you can do that here. (If you happen to specify a value with both, this menu entry overrides the button-selected value.) Select this option with the SET button, then dial in the amount of flash EV compensation you want using the Quick Control Dial. The EV that was in place before you started to make your adjustment is shown as a blue indicator, so you can return to that value quickly. Press SET again to confirm your change, then press the MENU button twice to exit.

- **Flash exposure bracketing.** Use these settings to specify options for adjusting the output of your unit when using bracketing with your compatible electronic flash.

Flash Custom Function Settings

Many external Speedlites from Canon include their own list of Custom Functions, which can be used to specify things like flash metering mode and flash bracketing sequences, as well as more sophisticated features, such as modeling light/flash (if available), use of external power sources (if attached), and functions of any slave unit attached to the external flash. This menu entry allows you to set an external flash unit's Custom Functions from your EOS RP's menu. The exact functions available will vary by flash unit. For example, with the Speedlite 320EX, only Custom Functions 1 (Auto Power Off), 6 (Quick Flash with Continuous Shot), 10 (Slave Auto Power Off Timer), and 11 (Slave Auto Power Off Cancel) are available. With high-end units, like the Speedlite 600EX-RT, a broader range of choices (described in Chapter 9) are at your disposal.

Clear Settings

This entry allows you to zero-out any changes you've made to your external flash's settings and Custom Functions settings, and return them to their factory default settings. The exception is C.Fn-00 Distance Indicator Display (if available for your flash). That setting remains as adjusted until you change it yourself. Note that a flash's Personal Functions (P.Fn) cannot be set or reset from the camera; you must use the Speedlite's controls instead.

Exposure Compensation/Automatic Exposure Bracketing

Options: Exposure comp/Auto exposure bracketing

My preference: N/A

The first entry on the Shooting 3 menu is Expo. Comp./AEB, or exposure compensation and automatic exposure bracketing. (See Figure 11.11.) As you learned in Chapter 4, exposure compensation increases or decreases exposure from the metered value. You can set it from this screen, or, in Fv, P, Tv, or Av modes by simply pressing the shutter release halfway and then rotating the Quick Control Dial to add or subtract exposure. A plus/minus exposure compensation indicator is displayed while compensation is in effect.

Exposure bracketing using the EOS RP's AEB feature is a way to shoot several consecutive exposures using different settings, to improve the odds that one will be exactly right. Automatic exposure bracketing is also an excellent way of creating the base exposures you'll need when you want to combine several shots to create a high dynamic range (HDR) image. (You'll find a discussion of HDR photography in Chapter 4, too.)

Figure 11.11
Exposure compensation/AEB is the first entry in the Shooting 3 menu.

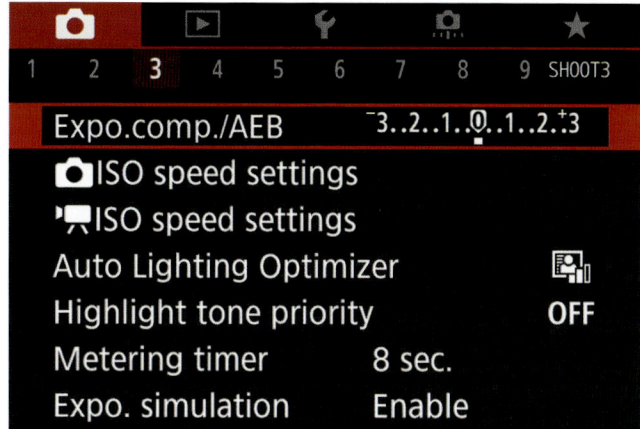

To activate automatic exposure bracketing, select this menu choice, then rotate the Main Dial to spread or contract the three lines beneath the scale until you've defined the range you want the bracket to cover, which can be up to plus/minus three stops from the base exposure, as shown in Figure 11.12. Then, use the Quick Control Dial (or left/right buttons) to move the bracket set right or left, moving the base exposure point from the metered (0) value and biasing the bracketing toward underexposure (rotate left) or overexposure (rotate right).

When AEB is activated, the bracketed shots will be exposed in this sequence: metered exposure, decreased exposure, increased exposure. You'll find more information about exposure bracketing in Chapter 4.

Figure 11.12
Set the range of the bracketed exposures.

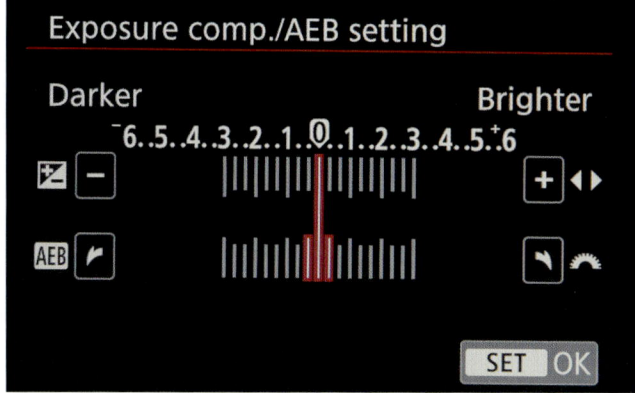

ISO Speed Settings

Options: ISO Speed, ISO Speed Range, Auto Range, Minimum Shutter Speed

My preference: N/A

Use this entry to select a specific ISO speed using a menu instead of the Quick Control menu, or to limit the range of ISO settings and shutter speeds that the camera selects automatically.

The four subentries include:

- **ISO Speed.** This scale allows you to choose from the enabled ISO speeds, plus Auto, using a sliding scale that can be adjusted using the QCD or the touch screen. Press INFO when the scale is visible to activate Auto.

- **ISO Speed Range.** You can specify the minimum and maximum ISO sensitivity available, including "expanded" settings you may have enabled such as Low (ISO 50 equivalent) and H1 or H2 (ISO 51200 and 102400 equivalent, respectively). I find myself using this feature frequently to keep me from accidentally switching to a setting I'd rather (or need to) avoid. For example, at concerts I may switch from ISO 1600 to 6400 as the lighting changes, and I set those two values as my minimum or maximum. Outdoors in daylight, I might prefer to lock out ISO values lower than ISO 100 or higher than ISO 800.

- **Auto Range.** This is the equivalent "safety net" for Auto ISO operation. You can set the minimum no lower than ISO 100 and the maximum to ISO 40000, and no further. Use this to apply your own "smarts" to auto ISO setting.

- **Minimum Shutter Speed.** You can choose whether to allow the EOS RP to select the slowest shutter speed used before Auto ISO kicks in. The idea here is that you'll probably want to boost ISO sooner if you're using a long lens with P and Av modes (in which the camera selects the shutter speed). If you specify, for example, a minimum shutter speed of 1/250th second, if P or Av mode needs a slower shutter speed for the proper exposure, it will boost ISO instead, within the range you've specified with Auto Range.

  This setting has two modes. In Auto mode, the camera decides when the shutter speed is too low. You can fine-tune this by choosing Slower or Faster on the scale (–3 to +3) that appears. Or, you can manually select the "trigger" shutter speed, from 1 second to 1/8000th second.

  However, if you've handicapped the EOS RP by selecting an Auto ISO range that doesn't include a sensitivity high enough, the camera will *override this setting* and use a shutter speed lower than the minimum you specify anyway. The camera assumes (rightly or wrongly) that your upper ISO boundary is more important than your lower shutter speed limit. The lesson here is that if you really, really want to enforce a minimum shutter speed when using Auto ISO, make sure your upper limit is high enough. Note that the Minimum Shutter Speed setting is ignored when using flash.

Movie ISO Speed Settings

Options: Maximum for Auto: 6400, 12800, 25600 (default), H1 (51200), H2 (102400)

My preference: 6400

Although its name is similar to the entry that precedes it, this setting only allows specifying the maximum ISO sensitivity that can be selected when an automatic exposure setting (rather than Manual exposure) is specified while shooting movies. Ordinarily, in autoexposure modes, the EOS RP will choose an ISO setting in the range 100–25600 automatically for Full HD and Standard HD video. For 4K Ultra High Definition video, the maximum is one stop less: 12800. If you feel the top speeds will not be satisfactory, you can limit ISO Auto to a lower figure (down to ISO 6400), or even a higher number (up to H2/ISO 202400 equivalent). Note that when Highlight Tone Priority (located two slots down from this one in the Shooting 3 menu) is enabled, the automatic speed range *minimum* is ISO 200.

Auto Lighting Optimizer

Options: Disable, Low, Standard (default), High, Disabled in Manual or Bulb modes

My preference: Disable

The Auto Lighting Optimizer provides a partial fix for images that are too dark or flat. Such photos typically have low contrast, and the Auto Lighting Optimizer improves them—as you shoot—by increasing both the brightness and contrast as required. The feature can be activated in Program, Aperture-priority, and Shutter-priority modes. You can select from four settings: Standard (the default value, which is always selected when using Scene Intelligent Auto mode, and used for Figure 11.13), plus Low, High, and Disable. Press the INFO button to add/remove a check mark icon that indicates the Auto Lighting Optimizer is disabled during manual exposure and bulb modes. Since you're likely to be specifying an exposure in those modes, you probably don't want the optimizer to interfere with your settings, so disabling the feature is the default.

Highlight Tone Priority

Options: Disable (default), Enable D+, Enhanced D+2

My preference: Disable

This setting concentrates the available tones in an image from the middle grays up to the brightest highlights, in effect expanding the dynamic range of the image at the expense of shadow detail. You'd want to activate this option when shooting subjects in which there is lots of important detail in the highlights, and less detail in shadow areas. Highlight tones will be preserved, while shadows will be allowed to go dark more readily (and may exhibit an increase in noise levels). Bright beach or snow scenes, especially those with few shadows (think high noon, when the shadows are smaller) can benefit from using Highlight Tone Priority.

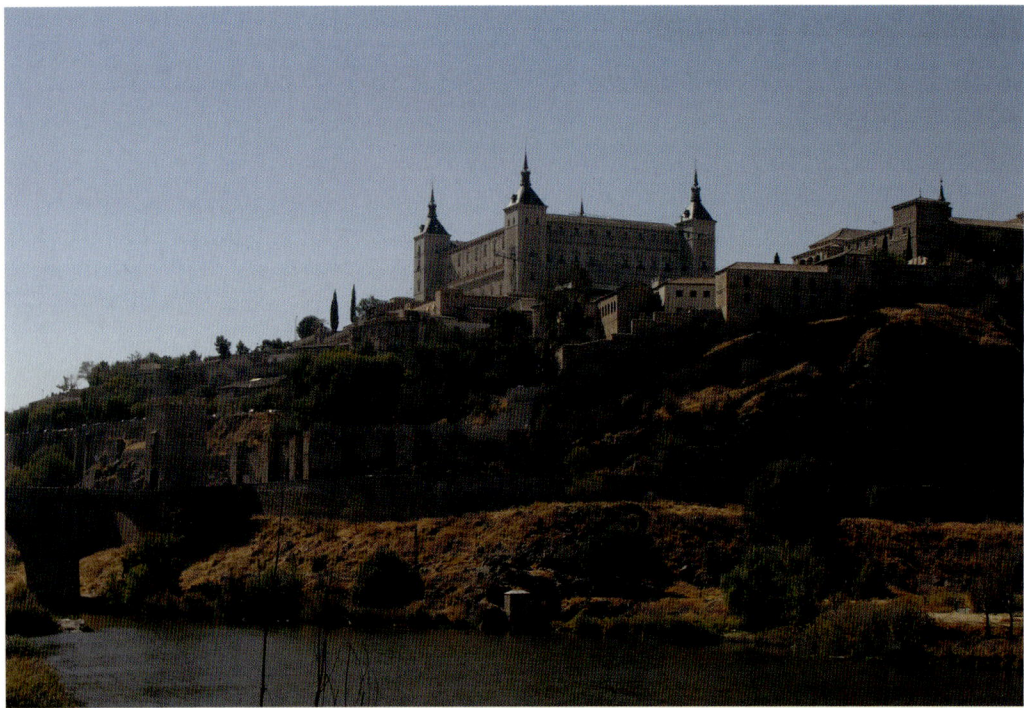

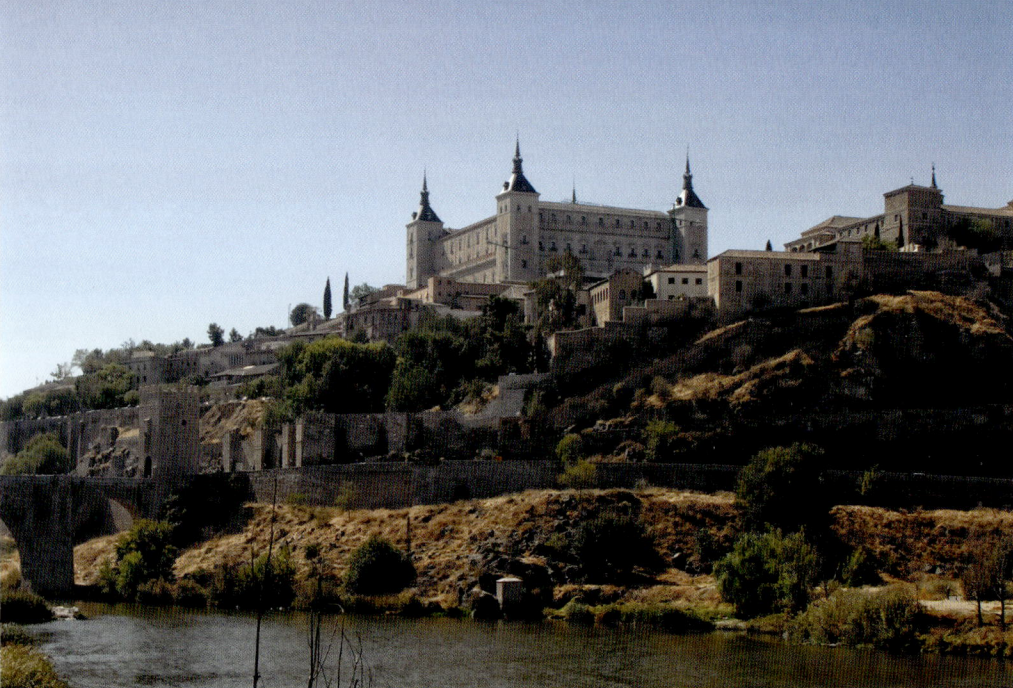

Figure 11.13 Auto Lighting Optimizer can brighten dark, low-contrast images (top), giving them a little extra snap and brightness (bottom).

Your choices:

- **Disable/OFF.** The EOS RP's normal dynamic range is applied. Note that when Highlight Tone Priority is switched off, the related Auto Lighting Optimizer setting (discussed earlier in this chapter) functions normally.

- **Enable D+.** Highlight areas are given expanded tonal values, while the tones available for shadow areas are reduced. The ISO 100 sensitivity setting is disabled and only ISO 200 to ISO 40000 (or ISO 200–12800 for movies) are available. You can tell that this restriction is in effect by viewing the D+ icon shown in the viewfinder, on the ISO Selection screen, and in the shooting information display for a particular image. Image noise may slightly increase as the camera manipulates the image. Note that this setting disables the Auto Lighting Optimizer.

- **Enhanced D+2.** More aggressive preservation of overexposed highlights. Use this with caution, as your images can be changed rather drastically. This setting is not available when shooting movies.

Metering Timer

Options: 4 sec., 8 sec. (default), 16 sec., 30 sec., 1 min., 10 min., 30 min.

My preference: 8 sec. most of the time; I switch to 10 min. when shooting sports.

This option allows you to specify how long the EOS RP's metering system will remain active before switching off. Tap the shutter release to start the timer again after it switches off.

Exposure Simulation

Options: Enable (default), During DOF Preview, Disable

My preference: During DOF Preview

This option allows you to choose whether the live view image mimics the exposure level of the final image, or whether the screen displays a bright image (dependent on the Display Brightness settings you've specified in the Set-up 2 menu for the electronic viewfinder and LCD screen) that may be easier to view under high-ambient-lighting conditions. Your choices are as follows:

- **Enable.** The image on the display corresponds to the brightness level of the actual image based on the current exposure settings, including any exposure compensation you've specified. Use this option when you want to be able to roughly (but not precisely) monitor the effects of your exposure settings in live view.

- **During DOF Preview.** The viewed image is displayed at standard brightness, but will be adjusted to simulate your exposure settings when you press any button you may have defined as a depth-of-field preview button. This is your best option when you might want to check exposure from time to time during a shooting session. It's the setting I use most often, because I can compose with a big, bright screen, but still stop down to the aperture that will be used and view the effects.

■ **Disable.** The EOS RP ignores any exposure settings and compensation, and shows the image at standard brightness. This setting is useful outdoors in full sunlight when using the LCD screen, instead of the electronic viewfinder, because any exposure simulation causing a dimmed LCD will be difficult to interpret under high ambient lighting anyway.

White Balance

Options: Auto (default), Daylight, Shade, Cloudy, Tungsten, White Fluorescent, Flash, Custom, Color Temperature
My preference: N/A

This is the first entry in the Shooting 4 menu. (See Figure 11.14.) If automatic white balance or one of the preset settings available (Auto, Daylight, Shade, Cloudy, Tungsten, White Fluorescent, or Flash) aren't suitable, you can set a custom white balance using the Custom menu option or a specific color temperature value. The screen shown in Figure 11.15 is identical to the one that pops up

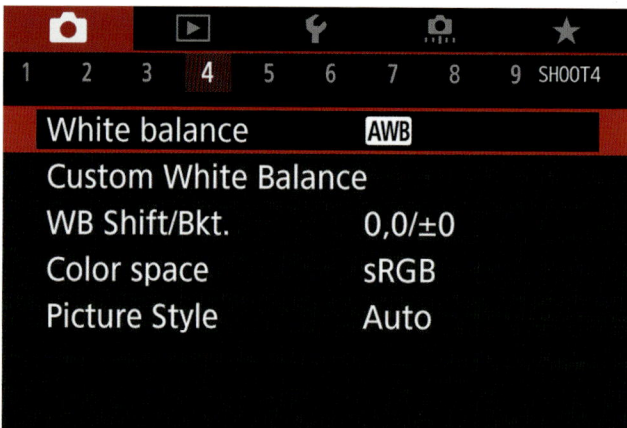

Figure 11.14
The Shooting 4 menu.

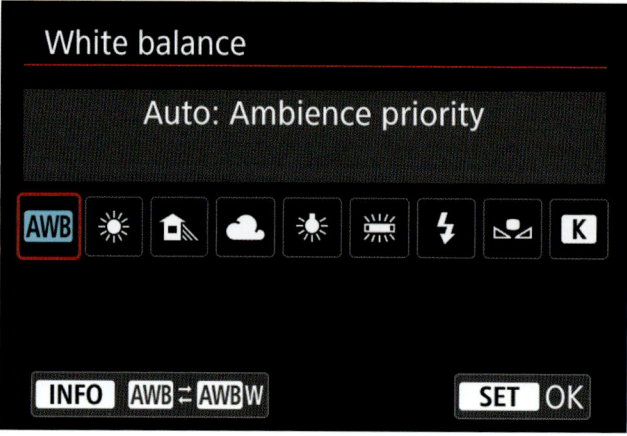

Figure 11.15
White balance presets can be chosen here.

when you select White Balance from the Quick Control screen. If you choose the "K" entry, you can select an exact color temperature from 2,500K to 10,000K using the Main Dial.

Of course, unless you own a specialized tool called a color temperature meter, you probably won't know the exact color temperature of your scene. However, knowing the color temperatures of the preset options can help you if you decide to tweak them by choosing a different color temperature setting. The values used by the EOS RP are as follows, with two options available for Auto:

- **Auto (AWB).** 3,000K–7,000K. Press the INFO button when this is selected to toggle between Ambience-priority (to keep warm color under tungsten light) or White-priority (to produce neutral whites even under tungsten illumination).
- **Daylight.** 5,200K
- **Shade.** 7,000K

- **Cloudy.** 6,000K
- **Tungsten.** 3,200K
- **White Fluorescent.** 4,000K
- **Flash.** 6,000K
- **Custom.** 2,000K–10,000K
- **Color temperature.** 2,500K–10,000K (Settable in 100K increments)

Choosing the right white balance can have a dramatic effect on the colors of your image, as you can see in Figure 11.16.

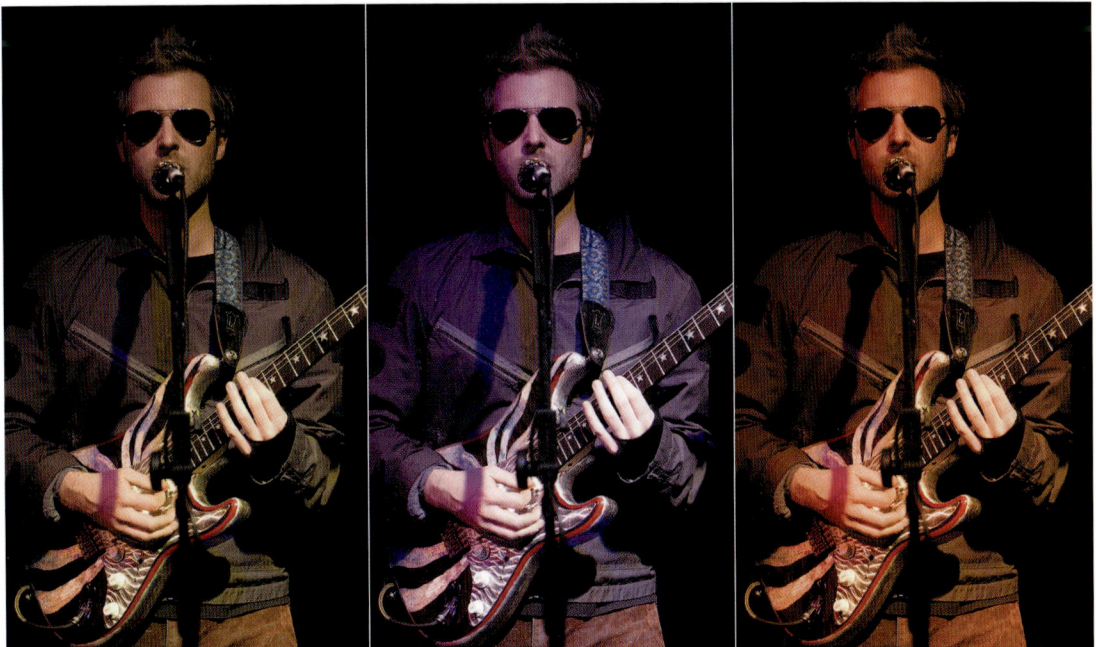

Figure 11.16
Adjusting color temperature can provide different results of the same subject at 3,400K (left), 5,000K (center), and 2,800K (right).

The problem with the available presets (Daylight, Shade, etc.) is that you have only seven of them, and in any given situation, all of them are likely to be wrong—strictly speaking. The good news is that they are likely to be only a *little bit* wrong. The human eye is very adaptable, so in most cases you'll be perfectly happy with the results you get if you use Auto, or choose a preset that's in the white balance ballpark.

But if you absolutely must have the correct color balance, or are frequently dissatisfied with the color balance the EOS RP produces when using Auto or one of the presets, you can always shoot RAW, and adjust the final color balance in your image editor when converting the .cr2 file. Or, you can use a custom white balance procedure, described next.

If automatic white balance or one of the preset settings aren't suitable, you can set a custom white balance using this menu option. The custom setting you establish will then be applied whenever you select Custom using the White Balance menu entry described earlier.

To set the white balance to an appropriate color temperature under the current ambient lighting conditions, focus manually (with the lens set on MF) on a plain white or gray object, such as a card or wall, making sure the object fills the spot metering circle in the center of the viewfinder. Then, take a photo. Next, press the MENU button and select Custom WB from the Shooting 4 menu. Use the Quick Control Dial until the reference image you just took appears and press the SET button to store the white balance of the image as your Custom setting.

Using an ExpoDisc

As I mentioned in Chapter 8, many photographers prefer to use a gadget called an ExpoDisc, from ExpoImaging, Inc. (www.expoimaging.com), which fits over (or attaches to) the front of your lens and provides a diffuse neutral (or semi-neutral) subject to measure with your camera's custom white balance feature. ExpoDiscs cost $75 to $100 or so, depending on the filter size of your lens, but many just buy the 77mm version and hold it in front of their lens. (There's a strap attached, so you won't lose it.) Others have had mixed success using less-expensive alternatives (such as the lid of a Pringles can). ExpoImaging also makes ExpoCap lens caps with similar diffusing features, and you can leave one of them on your lens at all times (at least, when you're not shooting).

There are two models, the standard ExpoDisc Neutral, and a Portrait model that produces a slightly warmer color balance suitable for portraits. The product produces the best results when you use it to measure the *incident light*; that is, the light falling onto your subject. In other words, instead of aiming your camera at your subject from the shooting position, take the time (if it's possible) to position yourself at the subject position and point your ExpoDisc-equipped lens toward the light source that will illuminate the scene. (However, don't point your camera directly at the Sun! Aim at the sky instead.)

I like to use the ExpoDisc in two situations:

- **Outdoors under mixed lighting.** When you're shooting outdoors, you'll often find that your scene is illuminated by direct sunlight as well as by open shade, full shade, or a mixture of these. A custom white balance reading can help you zero in on the correct color balance in a situation that's hard to judge visually.

- **When using studio flash.** It's a nasty secret that many studio flash units change color temperature when you adjust the power slider to scale down the output. Perhaps your 1600ws (watt second) flash puts out too much light to allow you to use a larger f/stop for selective focus. So, you dial it down to 1/4 power. That will likely change the color temperature of the unit slightly, particularly when compared to your 800ws fill light, which you've reduced to *half* power. You can use the ExpoDisc to measure the color temperature of your main light at its new setting, or aim it between two lights to obtain an average reading. The result will probably be close enough to the correct color temperature to satisfy most studio shooters.

Custom White Balance

Options: White balance setting

My preference: N/A

If automatic white balance (Auto) or one of the preset settings (Daylight, Shade, Cloudy, Tungsten, White Fluorescent, or Flash) aren't suitable, you can set a custom white balance using this menu option. The custom setting you establish will then be applied whenever you select Custom using the White Balance menu.

To set the white balance to an appropriate color temperature under the current ambient lighting conditions, focus manually (with the lens set on MF) on a plain white or gray object, such as a card or wall, making sure the object fills the spot metering circle in the center of the viewfinder. Then, take a photo. Next, press the MENU button and select Custom WB from the Shooting 4 menu. Rotate the Quick Control Dial until the reference image you just took appears and choose SET to store the white balance of the image as your Custom setting. Only compatible images that can be used to specify a custom white balance will be shown on the screen. Custom white balance images are marked with a custom icon, and cannot be removed (although they can be replaced with a new custom white balance image).

A WHITE BALANCE LIBRARY

Shoot a selection of blank-card images under a variety of lighting conditions on a spare memory card. If you want to "recycle" one of the color temperatures you've stored, insert the card and set the Custom white balance to that of one of the images in your white balance library, as described above.

White Balance Shift/Bracketing

Options: WB bias and WB bracketing

My preference: N/A

White balance shift allows you to dial in a white balance color bias along the blue/amber dimensions, and/or magenta/green scale. In other words, you can set your color balance so that it is a little bluer or yellower (only), a little more magenta or green (only), or a combination of the two bias dimensions. You can also bracket exposures, taking several consecutive pictures each with a slightly different color balance biased in the directions you specify.

The process is a little easier to visualize if you look at Figure 11.17. The center intersection of lines BA and MG (remember high school geometry!) is the point of zero bias. Move the point at that intersection using the directional buttons to locate it at any point on the graph using the blue/amber and magenta/green coordinates. The amount of shift will be displayed in the SHIFT box to the right of the graph.

White balance bracketing is like white balance shifting, only the bracketed changes occur along the bias axis you specify. This form of bracketing is like exposure bracketing, but with the added dimension of hue. Bias bracketing can be performed in any JPEG-only mode. You can't use any RAW format or RAW+JPEG format because the RAW files already contain the information needed to fine-tune the white balance and white balance bias.

When you select WB SHIFT/BKT, the adjustment screen appears. First, you rotate the Quick Control Dial to set the range of the shift in either the magenta/green dimension (rotate to the left to change the vertical separation of the three dots representing the separate exposures) or in the blue/amber dimension by rotating to the right. Use the up/down/left/right buttons to move the bracket set around within the color space, and outside the MG or BA axes.

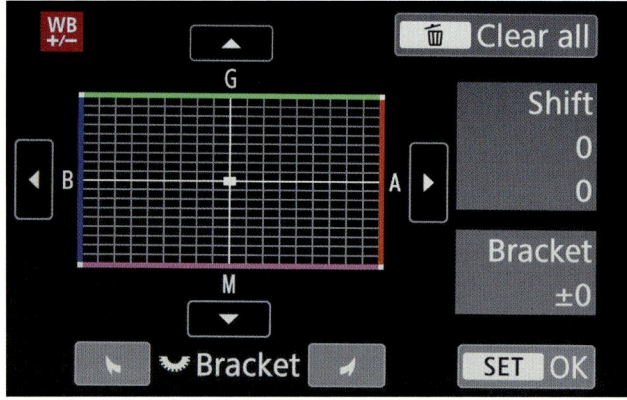

Figure 11.17
Use the Quick Control Dial to specify color balance bracketing using magenta/green bias or to specify blue/amber bias.

In most cases, it's easy to determine if you want your image to be more green, more magenta, more blue, or more amber, although judging your current shots on the LCD screen can be tricky unless you view the screen in a darkened location so it will be bright and easy to see. Bracketing is covered in Chapter 4.

Color Space

Options: sRGB (default), Adobe RGB

My preference: I use the expanded Adobe RGB color space.

When you are using one of the Creative Zone modes, you can select one of two different color spaces (also called *color gamuts*) using this menu entry. One color space is named *Adobe RGB* (because it was developed by Adobe Systems in 1998), while the other is called *sRGB* (supposedly because it is the *standard* RGB color space). These two color gamuts define a specific set of colors that can be applied to the images your EOS RP captures.

The Color Space menu choice applies directly to JPEG images shot using P, Tv, Av, and M exposure modes. When you're using Scene Intelligent Auto mode, the EOS RP uses the sRGB color space for all the JPEG images you take. RAW images are a special case. They have the information for *both* sRGB and Adobe RGB, but when you load such photos into your image editor, it will default to sRGB (with Scene Intelligent Auto or Creative Auto shots) or the color space specified here, unless you change that setting while importing the photos. (See the "Best of Both Worlds" sidebar that follows for more information.)

You may be surprised to learn that the EOS RP doesn't automatically capture *all* the colors we see. Unfortunately, that's impossible because of the limitations of the sensor and the filters used to capture the fundamental red, green, and blue colors, as well as that of the elements used to display those colors on your camera and computer monitors. Nor is it possible to *print* every color our eyes detect, because the inks or pigments used don't absorb and reflect colors perfectly. In short, your sensor doesn't capture all the colors that we can see, your monitor can't display all the colors that the sensor captures, and your printer outputs yet another version.

On the other hand, the EOS RP does capture quite a few more colors than we need. A 14-bit RAW image contains a possible 281 *trillion* different hues (16,384 colors per red, green, or blue channel), which are condensed down to a mere 16.8 million possible colors when converted to a 24-bit (eight bits per channel) image.

The set of colors, or gamut, that can be reproduced or captured by a given device (scanner, digital camera, monitor, printer, or some other piece of equipment) is represented as a color space that exists within the larger full range of colors. That full range is represented by the odd-shaped splotch of color shown in Figure 11.18, as defined by scientists at an international organization back in 1931. The colors possible with Adobe RGB are represented by the black triangle in the figure, while the sRGB gamut is represented by the smaller white triangle. The location of the corners of each triangle represent the position of the primary red, green, and blue colors in the gamut.

A third color space, ProPhoto RGB, represented by the yellow triangle in the figure, has become more popular among professional photographers as more and more color printing labs support it. While you cannot *save* images using the ProPhoto gamut with your EOS RP, you can convert your photos to 16-bit ProPhoto format using Adobe Camera RAW when you import RAW photos into an image editor. ProPhoto encompasses virtually all the colors we can see (and some we can't), giving advanced photographers better tools to work with in processing their photos. It has richer reds, greens, and blues, although, as you can see from the figure, its green and blue primaries are imaginary (they extend outside the visible color gamut). Those with exacting standards need not use a commercial printing service if they want to explore ProPhoto RGB: many inkjet printers can handle cyans, magentas, and yellows that extend outside the Adobe RGB gamut.

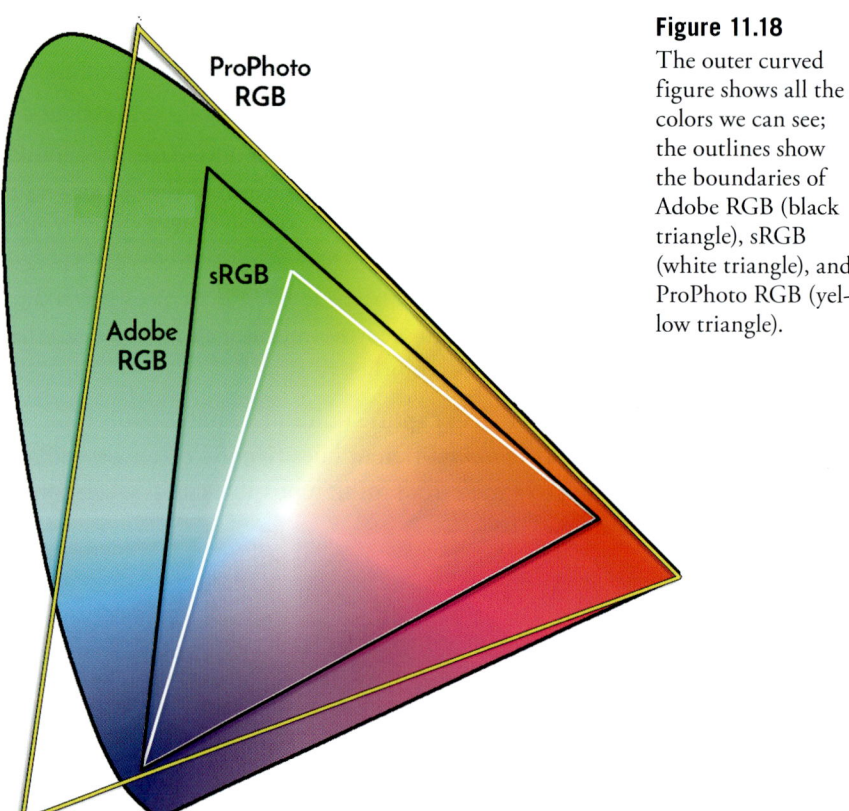

Figure 11.18
The outer curved figure shows all the colors we can see; the outlines show the boundaries of Adobe RGB (black triangle), sRGB (white triangle), and ProPhoto RGB (yellow triangle).

Regardless of which triangle—or color space—is used by the EOS RP, you end up with some combination of 16.8 million different colors that can be used in your photograph. (No one image will contain all 16.8 million! Think about it: the only way a 24-megapixel image could include that many colors would be if two-thirds of the pixels were each a unique hue!) But, as you can see from the figure, the colors available will be *different*.

Adobe RGB, like ProPhoto RGB, is an expanded color space useful for commercial and professional printing, and it can reproduce a wider range of colors. It can also come in useful if an image is going to be extensively retouched, especially within an advanced image editor, like Adobe Photoshop, which has sophisticated color management capabilities that can be tailored to specific color spaces. As an advanced user, you don't need to automatically "upgrade" your EOS RP to Adobe RGB, because images tend to look less saturated on your monitor and, it is likely, significantly different from what you will get if you output the photo to your personal inkjet. (You can *profile* your monitor for the Adobe RGB color space to improve your on-screen rendition using widely available color calibrating hardware and software.)

While both Adobe RGB and sRGB can reproduce the exact same 16.8 million absolute colors, Adobe RGB spreads those colors over a larger portion of the visible spectrum, as you can see in the figure. Think of a box of crayons (the jumbo 16.8 million crayon variety). Some of the basic crayons from the original sRGB set have been removed and replaced with new hues not contained in the original box. Your "new" box contains colors that can't be reproduced by your computer monitor, but which work just fine with a commercial printing press. For example, Adobe RGB has more "crayons" available in the cyan-green portion of the box, compared to sRGB, which is unlikely to be an advantage unless your image's final destination is the cyan, magenta, yellow, and black inks of a printing press.

The other color space, sRGB, is recommended for images that will be output locally on the user's own printer, as this color space matches that of the typical inkjet printer fairly closely. You might prefer sRGB, which is the default for the Canon EOS RP and most other cameras, as it is well suited for the range of colors that can be displayed on a computer screen and viewed over the Internet. If you plan to take your image file to a retailer's kiosk for printing, sRGB is your best choice, because those automated output devices are calibrated for the sRGB color space that consumers use.

BEST OF BOTH WORLDS

If you plan to use RAW+JPEG for most of your photos, go ahead and set sRGB as your color space. You'll end up with JPEGs suitable for output on your own printer, but you can still extract an Adobe RGB version from the RAW file at any time. It's like shooting two different color spaces at once—sRGB and Adobe RGB—and getting the best of both worlds.

Of course, choosing the right color space doesn't solve the problems that result from having each device in the image chain manipulating or producing a slightly different set of colors. To that end, you'll need to investigate the wonderful world of *color management*, which uses hardware and software tools to match or *calibrate* all your devices, as closely as possible, so that what you see more closely resembles what you capture, what you see on your computer display, and what ends up on a printed hardcopy. Entire books have been devoted to color management, and most of what you need to know doesn't directly involve your Canon EOS RP, so I won't detail the nuts and bolts here.

To manage your color, you'll need, at the bare minimum, some sort of calibration system for your computer display, so that your monitor can be adjusted to show a standardized set of colors that is repeatable over time. (What you see on the screen can vary as the monitor ages, or even when the room light changes.) I use the Spyder5 Pro monitor color correction system from Datacolor (www.datacolor.com) for my computer's three 26-inch widescreen LCD displays. The unit checks room light levels every five minutes and reminds me to recalibrate every week or two using a small sensor device, which attaches temporarily to the front of the screen and interprets test patches that the software displays during calibration. The rest of the time, the sensor sits in its stand, measuring the room illumination, and adjusting my monitors for higher or lower ambient light levels. Datacolor has recently introduced SpyderX available in Pro ($170) and Elite ($270) versions with faster, more accurate color correction.

If you're willing to make a serious investment in equipment to help you produce the most accurate color and make prints, you'll want a more advanced system (up to $500) like the various Spyder products from Datacolor or Colormunki from X-Rite (www.colormunki.com).

Picture Style

Options: Auto (default), Standard, Portrait, Landscape, Fine Detail, Neutral, Faithful, Monochrome, three User Styles

My preference: Auto

This feature is one of the most important tools for customizing the way your Canon EOS RP renders its photos. Picture Styles are a type of fine-tuning you can apply to your photos to change certain characteristics of each image taken using a particular Picture Style setting. The parameters you can specify for full-color images include the amount of sharpness, degree of contrast, the richness of the color, and the hue of skin tones. For black-and-white images, you can tweak the sharpness and contrast, but the two color adjustments (meaningless in a monochrome image) are replaced by controls for filter effects (which I'll explain shortly), and sepia, blue, purple, or green tone overlays.

The Canon EOS RP has preset Picture Styles for Standard, Portrait, Landscape, Fine Detail, Neutral, and Faithful pictures, plus Auto, and three user-definable settings called User Def. 1, User Def. 2, and User Def. 3, which you can define to apply to any sort of shooting situation you want, such as sports, architecture, or baby pictures. There is also a seventh, Monochrome, Picture Style that allows you to adjust filter effects or add color toning to your black-and-white images. See Figure 11.19 for the main Picture Style menu.

Figure 11.19
Picture Styles are available from this scrolling menu; these six, plus Faithful, Monochrome, and three User Def. styles that become visible when you scroll down the list.

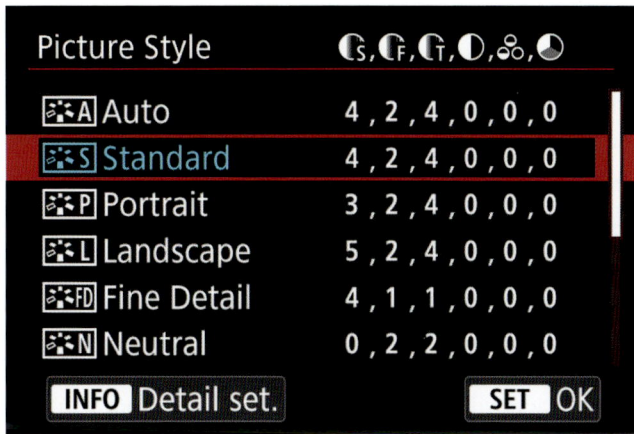

Picture Styles are extremely flexible. Canon has set the parameters for Auto and the predefined color Picture Styles and the single monochrome Picture Style to suit the needs of most photographers. But you can adjust any of those "canned" Picture Styles to settings you prefer. Better yet, you can use those three User Definition files to create brand-new styles that are all your own. If you want rich, bright colors to emulate Velvia film or the work of legendary photographer Pete Turner, you can build your own color-soaked style. If you want soft, muted colors and less sharpness to create a romantic look, you can do that, too. Perhaps you'd like a setting with extra contrast for shooting outdoors on hazy or cloudy days.

The current settings for each are arrayed along the top in Figure 11.19 as icons, left to right: S (sharpness strength), F (sharpness fineness), T (sharpness threshold), Contrast (a half white/half black circle), Saturation (a triangle composed of three circles), and Color Tone (a circle divided into thirds). When you scroll down within the Monochrome Picture Style, Filter Effect (overlapping circles) and Toning Effect (paintbrush tip) appear. These parameters applied when using Picture Styles are described next.

Here are the parameters:

- **Sharpness.** This parameter determines the apparent contrast between the outlines or edges in an image, which we perceive as image sharpness. When adjusting sharpness, remember that more is not always a good thing. A little softness is necessary (and is introduced by a blurring "anti-alias" filter in front of the sensor) to reduce or eliminate the moiré effects that can result when details in your image form a pattern that is too close to the pattern, or frequency, of the sensor itself. The default levels of sharpening were chosen by Canon to allow most moiré interference to be safely blurred to invisibility, at the cost of a little sharpness. As you boost sharpness (either using a Picture Style or in your image editor), moiré can become a problem, plus, you may end up with those noxious "halos" that appear around the edges of images that have been oversharpened. Use this adjustment with care. You have three individual parameters within this setting that you can adjust individually:

  - **Strength.** Set the intensity of the sharpening on an eight-step scale from 0 (weak outline emphasis) to 7 (strong outline emphasis). Adding too much strength can result in a halo and excess detail around the edges within your image.

  - **Fineness.** This determines which edges will be emphasized, on a scale of 1 (sharpens the finest lines in your image) to 5 (sharpens only larger, coarser lines). Use a lower number if you anticipate your image will have a wealth of fine detail that you want to emphasize, such as a heavily textured subject. A larger number might be better for portraits, so that eyes and hair might be sharpened, but not skin defects. Changes in Fineness and Threshold (which follows) do not apply when shooting movies.

  - **Threshold.** This setting uses contrast between the edges being sharpened and the surrounding areas, to determine the degree of sharpening applied to the outlines. It uses a scale from 1 to 5, with lower numbers allowing sharpening when there is less contrast between the edge and surroundings. There is an increase in noise when a low threshold is set. Higher numbers produce sharpening only when the contrast between edge and adjacent pixels is already high. The highest numbers can produce excessive contrast and a posterlike effect.

- **Contrast.** Use this control, with values from −4 (low contrast) to +4 (higher contrast), to change the number of middle tones between the deepest blacks and brightest whites. Low-contrast settings produce a flatter-looking photo, while high-contrast adjustments may improve the tonal rendition while possibly losing detail in the shadows or highlights.

- **Saturation.** This parameter, adjustable from −4 (low saturation) to +4 (high saturation) controls the richness of the color, making, say, a red tone appear to be deeper and fuller when you increase saturation, and tend more toward lighter, pinkish hues when you decrease saturation of the reds. Boosting the saturation too much can mean that detail may be lost in one or more of the color channels, producing what is called "clipping." You can detect this phenomenon when using the RGB histograms, as described in Chapter 4.

- **Color tone.** This adjustment has the most effect on skin tones, making them either redder (0 to −4) or yellower (0 to +4).

- **Filter effect (Monochrome only).** Filter effects do not add any color to a black-and-white image. Instead, they change the rendition of gray tones as if the picture were taken through a color filter. I'll explain this distinction more completely in the sidebar "Filters vs. Toning" later in this section.

- **Toning effect (Monochrome only).** Using toning effects preserves the monochrome tonal values in your image, but adds a color overlay that gives the photo a sepia, blue, purple, or green cast.

The predefined Picture Styles are as follows:

- **Auto.** Adjusts the color to make outdoor scenes look more vivid, with richer colors.

- **Standard.** This Picture Style applies a set of parameters, including boosted sharpness, that are useful for most picture taking, and which are applied automatically when using Basic Zone modes other than Portrait or Landscape.

- **Portrait.** This style boosts saturation for richer colors when shooting portraits, which is particularly beneficial for women and children, while reducing sharpness slightly to provide more flattering skin texture. The Basic Mode Portrait setting uses this Picture Style. You might prefer the Faithful style for portraits of men when you want a more rugged or masculine look, or when you want to emphasize character lines in the faces of older subjects of either gender.

- **Landscape.** This style increases the saturation of blues and greens, and increases both color saturation and sharpness for more vivid landscape images. The Basic Zone Landscape mode uses this setting.

- **Fine detail.** As you might expect, this setting uses sharpening and contrast to produce an image with optimum detail, at the expense of possibly adding some visual noise.

- **Neutral.** This Picture Style is a less-saturated and lower-contrast version of the Standard style. Use it when you want a more muted look to your images, or when the photos you are taking seem too bright and contrasty (say, at the beach on a sunny day).

- **Faithful.** The goal of this style is to render the colors of your image as accurately as possible, roughly in the same relationships as seen by the eye.

- **Monochrome.** Use this Picture Style to create black-and-white photos in the camera. If you're shooting JPEG only, the colors are gone forever. But if you're shooting JPEG+RAW you can convert the RAW files to color as you import them into your image editor, even if you've shot using the Monochrome Picture Style. Your EOS RP displays the images in black-and-white on the screen during playback, but the colors are there in the RAW file for later retrieval.

Tip

You can use the Monochrome Picture Style even if you are using one of the RAW formats alone, without a JPEG version. The EOS RP displays your images on the screen in black-and-white, and marks the RAW image as monochrome so it will *default* to that style when you import it into your image editor. However, the color information is still present in the RAW file and can be retrieved, at your option, when importing the image.

Selecting Picture Styles

Canon makes selecting a Picture Style for use very easy, and, to prevent you from accidentally changing an existing style when you don't mean to, divides *selection* and *modification* functions into two separate tasks. There are different ways to choose from among your existing Picture Styles:

- **Picture Styles menu.** Use this menu entry and scroll down the list shown earlier in Figure 11.19 with the Quick Control Dial until the style you want to use is highlighted. Then press SET.

- **Quick Control screen.** Press the Q button and navigate to the Picture Styles icon in the right column. With the icon highlighted, you can rotate either dial or use the left/right directional buttons to choose the Style you want to use and press SET to confirm.

Defining Picture Styles

Canon makes interpreting current Picture Style settings and applying changes very easy. As you saw in Figure 11.19, the current settings of the visible Picture Style options are shown as numeric values on the menu screen. Some camera vendors use word descriptions, like Sharp, Extra Sharp, or Vivid, More Vivid that are difficult to relate to. You can change one of the existing Picture Styles or define your own whenever the Picture Styles menu is visible. Just follow these steps:

1. **Choose a style to modify.** Highlight the style you'd like to adjust.

2. **Activate adjustment mode.** Press the INFO button to choose Detail Set. The screen that appears next will be like the one shown in Figure 11.20 for the six color styles or three User Def. styles. In addition to the Sharpness and Contrast adjustments shown in the figure, you can scroll down to two more: Saturation and Color Tone. The Monochrome screen looks similar, but substitutes Filter Effect and Toning Effect (discussed later) for Saturation and Color Tone.

Figure 11.20
Each parameter can be changed separately for color Picture Styles, such as the Standard style pictured.

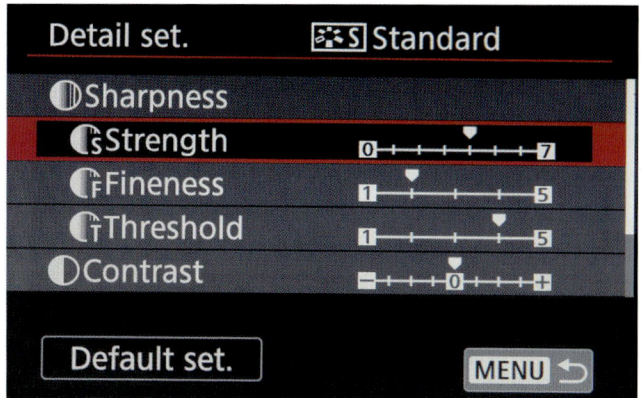

3. **Choose a parameter to change.** Use the Quick Control Dial to scroll among the parameters, plus Default Set. at the bottom of the screen, which restores the values to the preset numbers.

4. **Activate changes.** Press SET to change the values of a highlighted parameter.

5. **Adjust values.** Use the Quick Control Dial to move the triangle to the value you want to use. Note that the previous value remains on the scale, represented by a gray triangle. This makes it easy to return to the original setting if you want.

6. **Confirm changes.** Press the SET button to lock in that value, then press the MENU button three times to back out of the menu system.

Any Picture Style that has been changed from its defaults will be shown in the Picture Style menu with blue highlighting the altered parameter. You don't have to worry about changing a Picture Style and then forgetting that you've modified it. A quick glance at the Picture Style menu will show you which styles and parameters have been changed.

Making changes in the Monochrome Picture Style is slightly different. As I mentioned, the Saturation and Color Tone parameters are replaced with Filter Effect and Toning Effect options. (Keep in mind that once you've taken a JPEG photo using a Monochrome Picture Style, you can't convert the image back to full color.) You can choose from Yellow, Orange, Red, or Green filters, or None, and specify Sepia, Blue, Purple, or Green toning, or None. You can still set the Sharpness and Contrast parameters that are available with the other Picture Styles.

FILTERS VS. TONING

Although some of the color choices overlap, you'll get very different looks when choosing between Filter Effects and Toning Effects. Filter Effects add no color to the monochrome image. Instead, they reproduce the look of black-and-white film that has been shot through a color filter. That is, Yellow will make the sky darker and the clouds will stand out more, whereas Orange makes the sky even darker and sunsets more full of detail. The Red filter produces the darkest sky of all and darkens green objects, such as leaves. Human skin may appear lighter than normal. The Green filter has the opposite effect on leaves, making them appear lighter in tone. Figure 11.21, left, shows the same scene shot with no filter, then Yellow, Green, and Red filters.

The Sepia, Blue, Purple, and Green Toning Effects, on the other hand, all add a color cast to your monochrome image. Use these when you want an old-time look or a special effect, without bothering to recolor your shots in an image editor. Figure 11.21, right, shows the various Toning Effects available.

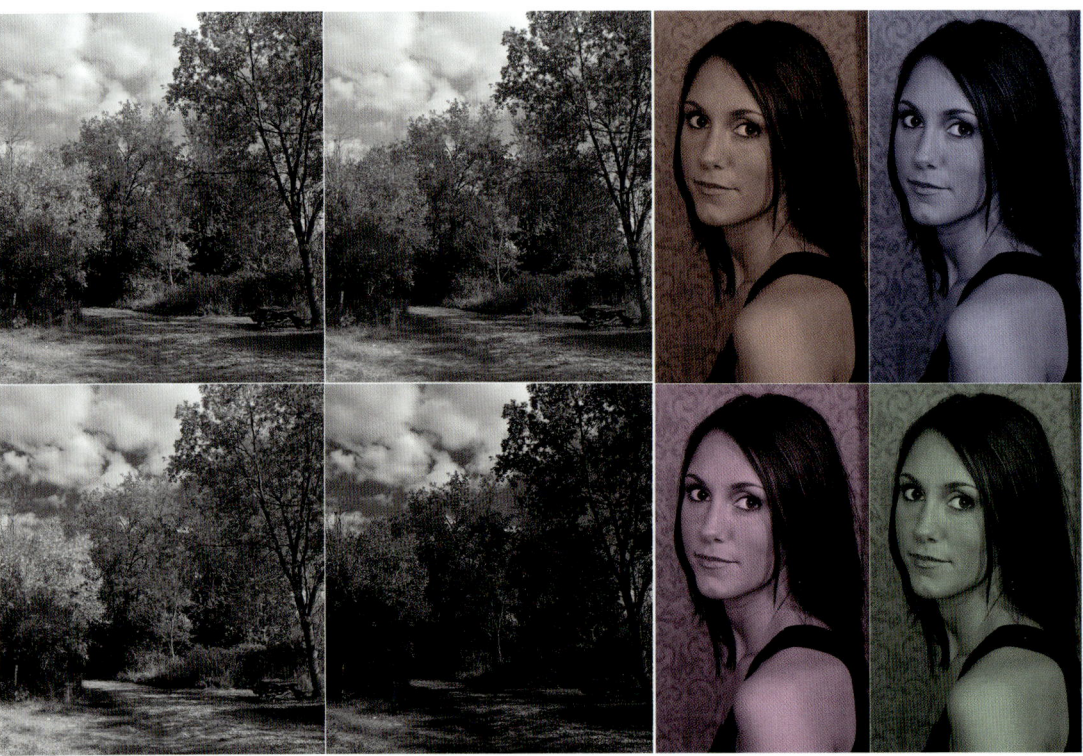

Figure 11.21 Left: Applying color filters: No filter (upper left); Yellow filter (upper right); Green filter (lower left); and Red filter (lower right). Right: Toning: Sepia (top left); Blue (top right); Purple (lower left); and Green (lower right).

Adjusting Styles with the Picture Style Editor

If you'd rather edit Picture Styles in your computer, the Picture Style Editor supplied for your camera in versions for both Windows and Macs allows you to create your own custom Picture Styles, or edit existing styles, including the Standard, Landscape, Faithful, and other predefined settings already present in your EOS RP. You can change sharpness, contrast, color saturation, and color tone—and a lot more—and then save the modifications as a PF2 file that can be uploaded to the camera, or used by Digital Photo Professional to modify a RAW image as it is imported.

To create and load your own Picture Style, just follow these steps:

1. **Load the editor.** Launch the Picture Style Editor (PSE, not to be confused with the *other* PSE, Photoshop Elements).

2. **Access a RAW file.** Load a RAW CR3 image you'd like to use as a reference into PSE. You can drag a file from a folder into the editor's main window, or use the Open command in the File menu.

3. **Choose an existing style to base your new style on.** Select any of the base styles except for Standard. Your new style will begin with all the attributes of the base style you choose, so start with one that already is close to the look you want to achieve ("tweaking" is easier than building a style from the ground up).

4. **Split the screen.** You can compare the appearance of your new style with the base style you are working from. Near the lower-left edge of the display pane are three buttons you can click to split the old/new styles vertically, horizontally, or return to a single image.

5. **Dial in basic changes.** Click the Advanced button in the Tool palette to pop up the Advanced Picture Style Settings dialog box that appears at left in the figure. These are the same parameters you can change in the camera. Click OK when you're finished.

6. **Make advanced changes.** The Tool palette has additional functions for adjusting hue, tonal range, and curves. Use of these tools is beyond the scope of a single chapter, let alone a notation in a list, but if you're familiar with the advanced tools in Photoshop, Photoshop Elements, Digital Photo Pro, or another image editor, you can experiment to your heart's content. Note that these modifications go way beyond what you can do with Picture Styles in the camera itself, so learning how to work with them is worth the effort.

7. **Save your Picture Style.** When you're finished, choose Save Picture Style File from the File menu to store your new style as a PF2 file on your hard disk. Add a caption and copyright information to your style in the boxes provided. If you click Disable Subsequent Editing, your style will be "locked" and protected from further changes, and the modifications you did make will be hidden from view (just in case you dream up your own personal, "secret" style). But you'll be unable to edit that style later. If you think you might want to change your custom Picture Style, save a second copy without marking the Disable Subsequent Editing box.

Uploading a Picture Style to the Camera

Now it's time to upload your new style to your Canon EOS RP into one of your three User Def. slots in the Picture Style array. Just follow these steps:

1. **Link your camera for upload.** Connect your camera to your computer using the USB cable, turn the EOS RP on, launch the EOS Utility, and click the Camera Settings/Remote Shooting choice in the splash screen.

2. **Choose the Shooting menu.** It's marked with an icon of a white camera on a red background, from the menu bar located about midway in the control panel that appears on your computer display.

3. **Select Register User Defined Style.** Click on the box, outlined in red in the figure, to produce the Register Picture Style dialog box.

4. **Choose a User Def. tab.** Click on one of the three tabs, labeled User Def. 1, User Def. 2, or User Def. 3. Each tab will include the name of the current Picture Style active in that tab.

5. **Click the Open File button and choose the Picture Style file to load.** The Picture Styles you've saved (or downloaded from another source) will appear with a PF2 extension. Click on the one you want to use, and then click the Open button in the Open dialog box.

6. **Upload Picture Style to the camera.** The Register Picture Style File dialog box will return. Click OK and the Picture Style will be uploaded to the camera in the User Def. "slot" represented by the tab you've chosen. The name of the Picture Style will appear in the EOS RP's menu in place of User Def. 1 (or User Def. 2/User Def. 3).

Changing a Picture Style's Settings from the EOS Utility

You can modify the settings of a Picture Style that's already loaded into your camera from the EOS Utility when your camera is linked to your computer. Just follow these steps:

1. **Link your camera to the computer.** Connect your camera to your computer using the USB cable, turn the EOS RP on, launch the EOS Utility, and click the Camera Settings/Remote Shooting choice in the splash screen.

2. **Choose the Shooting menu.** It's marked with an icon of a white camera on a red background, from the menu bar located about midway in the control panel that appears on your computer display.

3. **Access the Picture Style.** Click on the Picture Style choice. The currently active Picture Style in the camera will be shown, along with its detail settings.

4. **Choose a Picture Style to modify.** Click the Picture Style box to produce a listing of all the available Picture Styles.

5. **Click Detail Set**. At lower left, Landscape is now highlighted. When you click on Detail Set., a dialog box appears. You can move the sliders to change the settings, as described earlier. You can also click the Default Set. button to return the settings to their original values.

6. **Confirm choice.** Click Return when you've finished making changes, and the Picture Style you've modified will be changed in the camera.

7. **Exit EOS Utility.** Disconnect your camera from your computer, and your modified style is ready to use.

Getting More Picture Styles

I've found that careful Googling can unearth other Picture Styles that helpful fellow EOS owners have made available, and even a few from the helpful Canon company itself. My own search turned up this link: https://global.canon/en/imaging/picturestyle/index.html, where Canon offers a half dozen or more useful PF2 files you can download and install on your own using the EOS Utility. Select Register Picture Style File from the EOS RP Utility screen shown earlier in Figure 11.9, upper right.

Remember that Picture Style files are compatible between various Canon EOS camera models (that is, you can use a style created for the Canon 40D with your EOS RP), but you should be working with the latest software versions to work with the latest cameras and Picture Styles. If you owned an earlier Canon EOS camera and haven't re-installed the EOS Utility software since your camera upgrade, you might need to re-install the software. It's available for download from the Canon website.

Try the additional styles Canon offers. They include:

■ **Studio Portrait.** Compared to the Portrait style built into the camera, this one, Canon says, expresses translucent skin in smooth tones, but with less contrast. (Like films in the pre-digital age that were intended for studio portraiture.)

■ **Snapshot Portrait.** This is another "translucent skin" style, but with increased contrast with enhanced contrast indoors or out.

■ **Nostalgia.** This style adds an amber tone to your images, while reducing the saturation of blue and green tones.

■ **Clear.** This style adds contrast for what Canon says is additional "depth and clarity."

■ **Twilight.** Adds a purple tone to the sky just before and after sunset or sunrise.

■ **Emerald.** Emphasizes blues and greens.

■ **Autumn Hues.** Increases the richness of browns and red tones seen in Fall colors.

■ **Video Camera X Series Look.** Provides image characteristics similar to images shot with Canon's professional digital video camera (X series) and contrast is softer than Standard in Picture style.

Long Exposure Noise Reduction

Options: Off/Disable (default), Auto, On/Enable

My preference: Auto

This entry is the first in the Shooting 5 menu. (See Figure 11.22.) It allows you to enable or disable long exposure noise reduction, or allow the EOS RP to evaluate your scene and decide whether to use this noise-canceling adjustment. Visual noise is that graininess that shows up as multicolored specks in images, and this setting helps you manage it. In some ways, noise is like the excessive grain found in some high-speed photographic films. However, while photographic grain is sometimes used as a special effect, it's rarely desirable in a digital photograph.

The visual noise-producing process is something like listening to a CD in your car, and then rolling down all the windows. You're adding sonic noise to the audio signal, and while increasing the CD player's volume may help a bit, you're still contending with an unfavorable signal-to-noise ratio that probably mutes tones (especially higher treble notes) that you really want to hear.

The same thing happens when the analog signal is amplified: You're increasing the image informa-tion in the signal, but boosting the background fuzziness at the same time. Tune in a very faint or distant AM radio station on your car stereo. Then turn up the volume. After a certain point, turn-ing up the volume further no longer helps you hear better. There's a similar point of diminishing returns for digital sensor ISO increases and signal amplification as well.

These processes create several different kinds of noise. Noise can be produced from high ISO set-tings. As the captured information is amplified to produce higher ISO sensitivities, some random noise in the signal is amplified along with the photon information. Increasing the ISO setting of your camera raises the threshold of sensitivity so that fewer and fewer photons are needed to register as an exposed pixel. Yet, that also increases the chances of one of those phantom photons being counted among the real-life light particles, too.

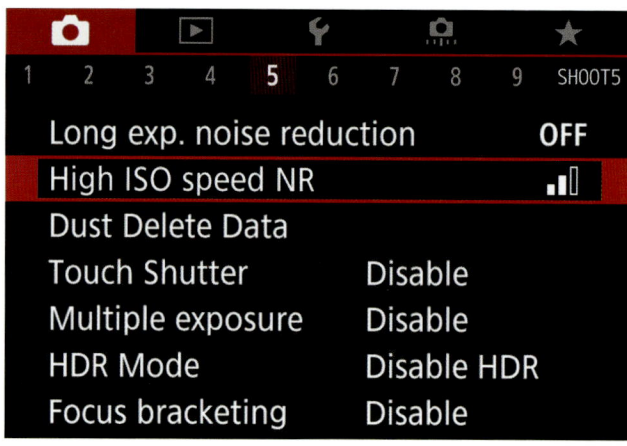

Figure 11.22
The Shooting 5 menu.

Fortunately, the EOS RP's sensor and its digital processing chip are optimized to produce the low noise levels, so ratings as high as ISO 800 or ISO 1600 can be used routinely (although there will be some noise, of course), and even ISO 3200 can generate good results.

A second way noise is created is through longer exposures. Extended exposure times allow more photons to reach the sensor, but increase the likelihood that some photosites will react randomly even though not struck by a particle of light. Moreover, as the sensor remains switched on for the longer exposure, it heats, and this heat can be mistakenly recorded as if it were a barrage of photons. This entry can be used to tailor the amount of noise-canceling performed by the digital signal processor.

■ **Off/Disable.** Disables long exposure noise reduction. Use this setting when you want the maximum amount of detail present in your photograph, even though higher noise levels will result. This setting also eliminates the extra time needed to take a picture caused by the noise reduction process. If you plan to use only lower ISO settings (thereby reducing the noise caused by ISO amplification), the noise levels produced by longer exposures may be acceptable. For example, you might be shooting a river spilling over rocks at ISO 100 with the camera mounted on a tripod, using a neutral-density filter and long exposure to cause the pounding water to blur slightly. To maximize detail in the non-moving portions of your photos, you can switch off long exposure noise reduction. Because the noise-reduction process used with Auto and On can effectively double the time required to take a picture, Off is a good setting to use when you want to avoid this delay when possible.

■ **Auto.** The EOS RP examines your photo taken with an exposure of one second or longer, and if long exposure noise is detected, a second, blank exposure is made and compared to the first image. Noise found in the "dark frame" image is subtracted from your original picture, and only the noise-corrected image is saved to your memory card.

■ **On/Enable.** When this setting is activated, the EOS RP applies dark frame subtraction to all exposures longer than one second. You might want to use this option when you're working with high ISO settings (which will already have noise boosted a bit) and want to make sure that any additional noise from long exposures is eliminated, too. Noise reduction will be applied to some exposures that would not have caused it to kick in using the Auto setting.

Tip

While the "dark frame" is being exposed, the LCD screen will be blank during Live View mode, and the number of shots you can take in continuous shooting mode will be reduced. White balance bracketing is disabled during this process.

High ISO Speed Noise Reduction

Options: Disable, Low, Standard (default), High, Multi Shot Noise Reduction

My preference: Low, with further noise reduction as required in an image editor

The other type of noise results from using higher ISO settings. This entry allows you to specify just how much or how little of this noise reduction to apply, which can be a valuable option because noise reduction does eliminate detail while blurring the amount of noise. The default is Standard noise reduction, but you can specify Low or High noise reduction, or disable noise reduction entirely. At lower ISO values, noise reduction improves the appearance of shadow areas without affecting highlights; at higher ISO settings, noise reduction is applied to the entire photo. Note that when the High option is selected, the maximum number of continuous shots that can be taken will decrease significantly, because of the additional processing time for the images.

- **Disable.** No additional noise reduction will be applied.
- **Low.** A smaller amount of noise reduction is used. This will increase the grainy appearance, but preserve more fine image detail.
- **Standard.** At lower ISO values, noise reduction is applied primarily to shadow areas; at higher ISO settings, noise reduction affects the entire image.
- **High.** More aggressive noise reduction is used, at the cost of some image detail, adding a "mushy" appearance that may be noticeable and objectionable. Because of the image processing applied by this setting, your continuous shooting maximum burst will decrease significantly.
- **Multi Shot Noise Reduction.** When this option is active, the EOS RP takes four separate shots continuously. It then aligns them (in case there was movement between images) and then merges them, using the dark frame subtraction technique to ignore random pixels caused by noise. The result is a JPEG image that is of better quality than the High setting.

  Multi Shot NR works best if the camera is mounted on a tripod and your subject is not moving. It is not available when Image Quality is set to RAW or RAW+JPEG or Dual Pixel RAW, nor when using flash, live view, shooting multiple or Bulb exposures, or performing autoexposure/white balance bracketing.

Dust Delete Data

Options: Store Delete Data

My preference: N/A

This menu choice lets you "take a picture" of any dust or other particles that may be adhering to your sensor. The EOS RP will then append information about the location of this dust to your photos, so that the Digital Photo Professional software can use this reference information to identify dust in your images and remove it automatically. You should capture a Dust Delete Data photo from time to time as your final line of defense against sensor dust.

To use this feature, select Dust Delete Data, select OK, and press the SET button. The camera will first perform a self-cleaning operation by applying ultrasonic vibration to the low-pass filter that resides on top of the sensor. Then, a screen will appear asking you to press the shutter button. Point the EOS RP at a solid-white card with the lens set on manual focus and rotate the focus ring to infinity. When you press the shutter release, the camera takes a photo of the card using Aperture-priority and f/22 (which provides enough depth-of-field [in this case, *depth-of-focus*] to image the dust sharply). The "picture" is not saved to your memory card but, rather, is stored in a special memory area in the camera. Finally, a "Data obtained" screen appears.

The Dust Delete Data information is retained in the camera until you update it by taking a new "picture." The EOS RP adds the information to each image file automatically.

Touch Shutter

Options: Enable (default), Disable

My preference: Disable

The Touch Shutter feature allows you to tap the LCD screen to focus and snap a picture with one gesture. It's easy to accidentally trigger the Touch Shutter, so I generally leave it off. However, it's quite useful when your camera is on a tripod and you want to be able to snap a picture of some portion of your scene quickly and with minimal vibration.

Multiple Exposure

Options: Multiple exposure: Disable (Default), Enable; Multiple exposure control: Additive (default), Average; Number of exposures: 2–9 (default 2), Continue multiple exposure: 1 Shot Only (default), Continuously; Select image for multi-exposure

My preference: N/A

This option lets you combine two to nine separate images into one photo without the need for an image editor like Photoshop. It can be an entertaining way to return to those thrilling days of yes-teryear, when complex photos were created in the camera itself. In truth, prior to the digital age, multiple exposures were a cool, groovy, far-out, hep/hip, phat, sick, fabulous way of producing composite images. Today, it's more common to take the lazy way out, snap two or more pictures, and then assemble them in an image editor like Photoshop.

However, if you're willing to spend the time planning a multiple exposure (or are open to some happy accidents), there is a lot to recommend the multiple exposure capability that Canon has bestowed on the EOS RP. For one thing, the camera can combine two or more images using the RAW data from the sensor, producing photos that are blended together more smoothly than is likely for anyone who's not a Photoshop guru. In addition, Canon has eliminated one annoying aspect of the feature found in some cameras: it's not necessary to return to the menu to activate multiple exposure for every set. If you want to take a series of pictures, you can set it once, and forget it. (But don't forget to turn it off when you're done!)

Multiple exposures cannot be captured if white balance bracketing, HDR shooting, or movie-making modes are in use. Before you begin snapping your own multi-exposures, you'll need to set your parameters using the options discussed below. (See Figure 11.23.)

■ **Multiple Exposure.** The Disable option deactivates the multi-exposure feature; Enable turns it on. This is the "master control" that allows you to turn multiple exposure on and off (leaving the other parameters you've set unchanged).

■ **Multi-Expos Ctrl.** This essential parameter can determine how successful your multiple exposure is, by controlling how each individual exposure is merged with the overlapping portions of the other images in the series. Picture an image like the one shown at top in Figure 11.24. The performer, Todd Cooper of the Alan Parsons Live Project, was photographed against a plain, dark background. He happened to be moving, so neither of the two images overlapped with each other, or with any details of the featureless background. But in Figure 11.24, bottom, the dancer remained in place, so that each subsequent image overlapped the others slightly. The Multi-Exposure Control feature allows you to specify how the images are combined with these choices:

• **Additive.** Each individual shot in the series is, by default, given the full exposure, which is what I used for Figure 11.24, top. Because the background was totally black and the subject was moving and did not overlap, the cumulative exposure effect was to combine two separate images into one image.

However, you can manually adjust the amount of exposure each shot is given by dialing in exposure compensation, making this mode useful for overlapping images as well. The customary procedure is to specify –1-stop exposure compensation for two shots, –1.5 EV for three-shot multiple exposures, and –2 EV for four-shot multis. Manually calculating the amount of negative exposure compensation allows you to fine-tune the look of overlapping images.

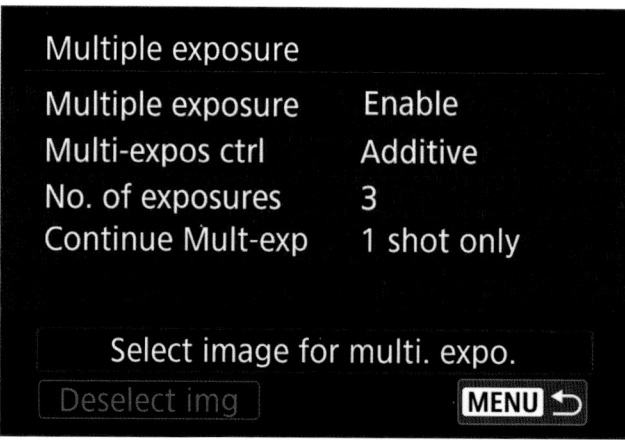

Figure 11.23

Set these parameters to configure your multiple exposures.

Figure 11.24
Top: Multiple
exposure using
Additive exposure,
and no exposure
compensation.
Bottom: Multiple
exposure using
Average exposure.

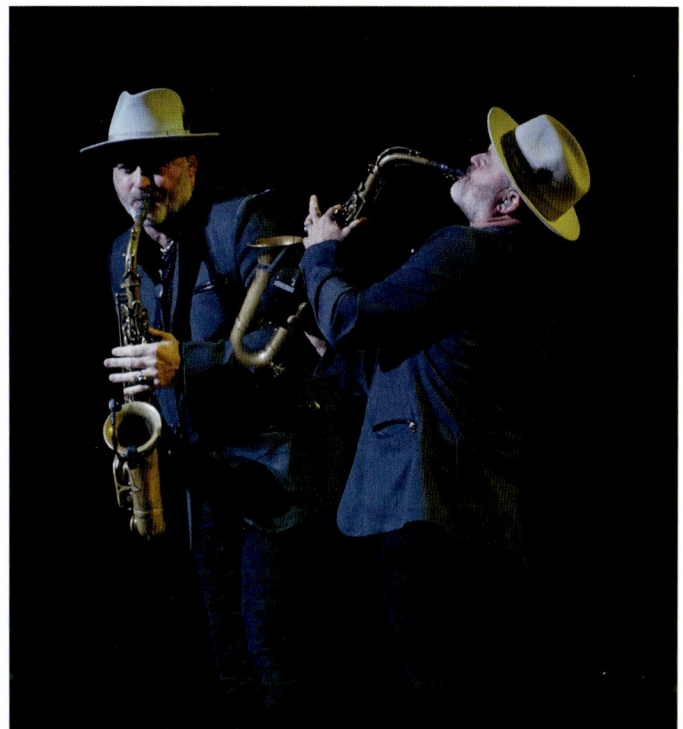

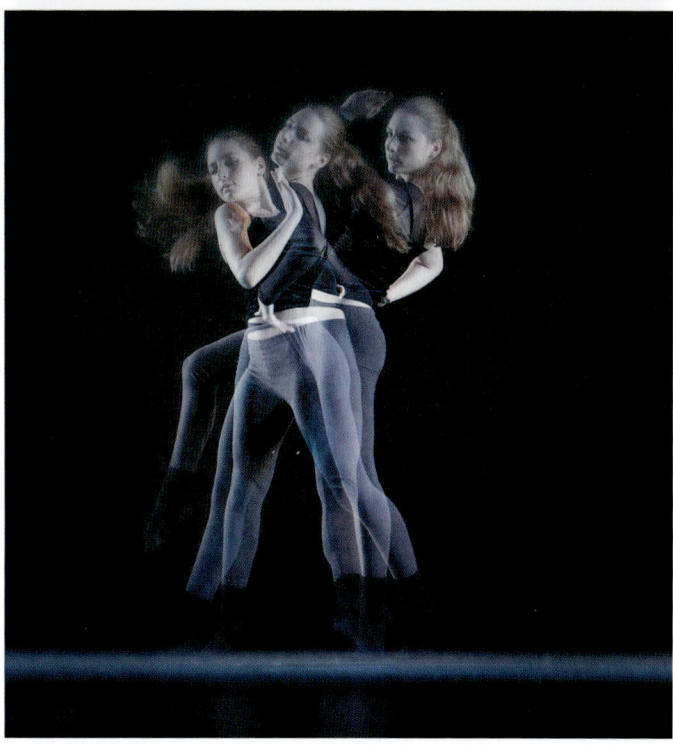

- **Average.** Choose this option and the EOS RP will apply appropriate negative exposure compensation for you, based on the number of exposures you're combining into a single image. If your multiple exposures happen to be of the same scene (rather than separate subjects), the camera will attempt to ensure that the background receives the equivalent of a full exposure. I used this option for Figure 11.24, bottom.

- **No. of Exposures.** You can choose from 2 to 9 exposures in each multiple exposure set. Highlight the option, press SET, and spin the QCD to choose the number of exposures. I recommend starting out with three multiple exposures when you begin exploring this tool; you'll quickly discover picture opportunities that call for more or fewer combined shots in a single image.

- **Continue Mult-exp.** Choose 1 Shot Only or Continuously. Choose the former if you want to take a single multiple exposure series and then return to normal shooting with Multiple Exposure then disabled. Select Continuously if you plan to shoot a batch of different multiple exposures and don't want to return to the menu system to reactivate the feature after each shot.

- **Select Image for Multi-Exposure.** If you like, you can use an image you already took as the base image for a subsequent multi-exposure. The base image can only be a RAW image (not M RAW or S RAW). When RAW images *taken with your camera* (other RAW images on the card cannot be used) are available, this option will be selectable. However, a RAW image that is already a multiple exposure *can* be used as your base image (the mind boggles at the possibilities).

  With the option highlighted, press SET and choose the image you want to use. Rotate the QCD to view compatible RAW images and press SET to choose one. Press OK. You can then take the *remaining* exposures in your set. That is, if you've chosen to combine three shots in a multiple exposure, the base image counts as one, so you'll be able to add two more by pressing and holding the shutter release.

  Note that images using Highlight Tone Priority or an Aspect Ratio other than 3:2 cannot be used as your base image, and Lens Aberration Correction and Auto Lighting Optimizer will not be applied to your set. If the RAW image specifies the Auto Picture Style, the camera will revert to Standard for the rest of the images.

MULTI NOTES

Some special conditions are required for your EOS RP to shoot multiple exposures. Some features are disabled, and others are locked in at particular values.

■ Auto Lighting Optimizer, Highlight Tone Priority, and Lens Aberration Correction are disabled, and the Standard Picture Style will be used if you've chosen the Auto Picture Style setting. Multiple exposures are disabled if your camera is connected to a computer or printer via the USB cable.

■ Most settings used for the first shot in a series are locked in for all subsequent images in that series, including image recording quality, ISO sensitivity, Picture Style, high ISO noise reduction, and color space.

■ Other functions that cannot be changed while shooting multiple exposures will be dimmed in the camera menu.

HDR Mode

Options: Adjust Dynamic Range, Effect, Continuous HDR, Auto Image Align

My preference: N/A

I described using the EOS RP's HDR Mode in detail in Chapter 4. To recap, this menu entry has four subentries you can adjust:

■ **Adjust Dynamic Range.** Select Disable HDR, allow the camera to select a dynamic range automatically, or select the range yourself to achieve a particular look. You can choose plus/minus 1, 2, or 3 EV.

■ **Effect.** You can add special effects on top of any Picture Style you are using to produce an even more dramatic HDR image. Your choices are as follows:

• **Natural.** Provides the most useful range of highlight and shadow details.

• **Art Standard.** Offers a great deal of highlight and shadow detail, but with lower overall contrast and outlines accentuated, making the image look more like a painting. Saturation, bold outline, and brightness are adjusted to the default levels, and tonal range is lower in contrast.

• **Art Vivid.** Like Art Standard, but saturation is boosted to produce richer colors, and the bold outlines not as strong, producing a poster-like effect.

• **Art Bold.** Even higher saturation than Art Vivid, with emphasized edge transitions, producing what Canon calls an "oil painting" effect.

• **Art Embossed.** Reduced saturation, darker tones, and lower contrast give the image a faded, aged look. The edge transitions are brighter or darker to emphasize them.

- **Continuous HDR.** Choose 1 Shot Only if you plan to take just a single HDR exposure and want the feature disabled automatically thereafter, or Every Shot to continue using HDR mode for all subsequent exposures until you turn it off. This is like the multiple exposure option described earlier.
- **Auto Image Align.** You can choose Enable to have the camera attempt to align all three HDR exposures when shooting hand-held, or select Disable when using a tripod. The success of the automatic alignment will vary, depending on the shutter speed used (higher is better), and the amount of camera movement (less is better!).

Focus Bracketing

Options: Focus bracketing: Enable, Disable; Number of shots: 2 to 999; Focus increment: 1 (narrow) to 10 (wide); Exposure smoothing: Enable, Disable

My preference: N/A

If you are doing macro (close-up) photography of flowers, or other small objects at short distances, the depth-of-field often will be extremely narrow. In some cases, it will be so narrow that it will be impossible to keep the entire subject in focus in one photograph. Although having part of the image out of focus can be a pleasing effect for a portrait of a person, it is likely to be a hindrance when you are trying to make an accurate photographic record of a flower, or small piece of precision equipment. One solution to this problem is focus stacking (which Canon calls "Focus Bracketing"), a procedure that can be considered like HDR translated for the world of focus—taking multiple shots with different settings, and, using software as explained below, combining the best parts from each image in order to make a whole that is better than the sum of the parts. Focus bracketing requires a non-moving object, so some subjects, such as flowers, are best photographed in a breezeless environment, such as indoors.

With the EOS RP's Focus Bracketing feature, the camera takes a series of pictures, adjusting the focus slightly between each image, refocusing from closest to your subject to the farthest point that needs to appear sharp. You end up with a series of up to 999 different images that can be combined using two simple Photoshop commands, which I will describe shortly.

You can visualize how focus stacking works if you examine Figure 11.25, which is cropped versions of three actual frames from one of my own Focus Bracketing series. All three used an exposure of 1/30th second at f/5.6. At left is the original exposure, with the lens focused on the third row of crayons. The center image shows the 35th exposure in the series, in which the Focus Bracketing feature had adjusted focus on the last row. In between were 33 intermediate-focus shots that I merged in Photoshop to produce the finished image at right.

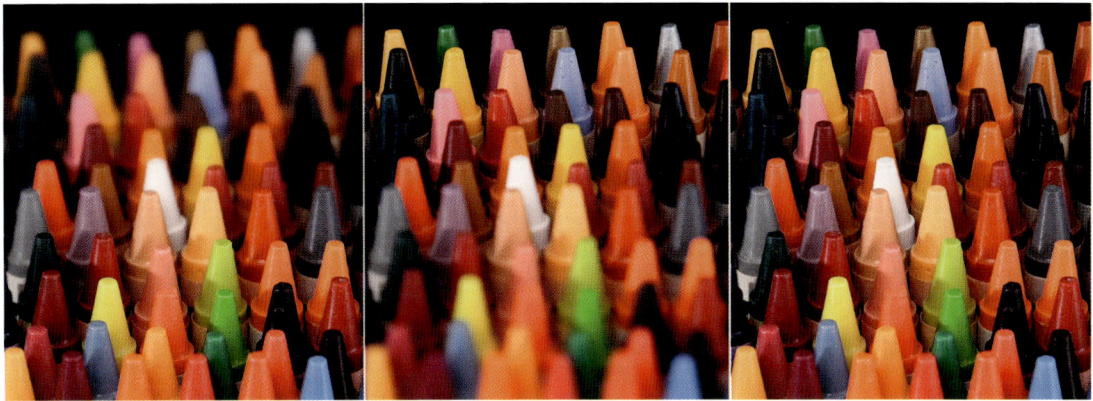

Figure 11.25 Closest focus (left), farthest focus (center), merged image (right).

Here are the detailed steps you can take to use Focus Bracketing for your own deep-focus images:

1. **Set the camera firmly on a solid tripod.** A tripod or other equally firm support is absolutely essential for this procedure. You don't want the camera (or the subject) to move at all during the exposures.

2. **Attach a remote release.** You want to be able to trigger the camera without moving it. However, the procedure does pause for a short period of time once you activate it, perhaps giving your tripod/camera time to settle down even if you begin by poking the OK button with your finger.

3. **Attach an autofocus lens with an appropriate close-focus range.** Focus Bracketing uses the lens's built-in autofocus motor and will not work with manual focus lenses or with an AF lens set to manual focus. You can use any of the RF-mount lenses offered to date, plus (with a mount adapter) the EF 16-35mm f/4L IS USM, EF 24-70mm f/4L IS USM, EF 100mm f/2.8L Macro IS USM, EF 180mm f/3.5L Macro USM, EF-S 60mm f/2.8 Macro USM, and EF-S 35mm f/2.8 Macro IS USM optics.

4. **Set the focus modes.** Choose One-Shot (single focus) and the 1-point or Spot AF.

5. **Set the quality of the images to JPEG FINE.** You'll want the highest image quality possible.

6. **Set the exposure, ISO, and white balance manually.** Use test shots if necessary to determine the best values. This step will help prevent visible variations from arising among the multiple shots that you'll be taking. You don't want the camera to change the ISO setting or white balance between shots.

   Note: Even though you'll be effectively increasing depth-of-field through focus stacking, you should still avoid the widest apertures of your lens, as they are rarely the sharpest f/stops.

I always stop down at least 1.5 f/stops—using f/5.6 in the example. Shutter speed is not as important, because the camera is on a tripod, but I tend to avoid very slow speeds anyway. You can manually set a slightly higher ISO sensitivity, if needed, to obtain the shutter speed/aperture combination you want to use.

7. **Turn off image stabilization.** If your lens has IS, slide the IS switch to Off.

8. **Access the Focus Bracketing menu.** Select an appropriate setting for each of the following parameters (shown in Figure 11.26), using my guidelines:

   - **Focus bracketing.** Select Enable to activate the feature.

   - **Number of Shots.** You can choose from 1 to 999 individually refocused shots. The number of images captured will depend on how finely you want to have the EOS RP change focus between shots (and you'll combine this with the step width option described next). I rarely need more than 50 shots, and used only 35 for the example shown earlier in Figure 11.25.

   - **Focus Increment.** You can specify values from 1 (a narrow slice per adjustment) and 10 (a much wider focus change). Canon does not specify how much each increment changes the focus, for a very good reason: it *can't*. Depending on the focal length of your lens and your f/stop, the effective plane of apparent focus may vary from narrow, to very narrow, to super-narrow in macro shooting environments. (If you're confused, see "Circles of Confusion" in Chapter 5.)

   You may need some trial-and-error to choose the correct number of shots and focus step width. For example, with 50 shots and a wide focus step, the first 10 may encompass your entire subject and the last 40 may be wasted on completely out-of-focus images. It's often worthwhile to take a test shot, view a slide show of all your images, and decide whether to increase/decrease the number of shots and/or focus step width.

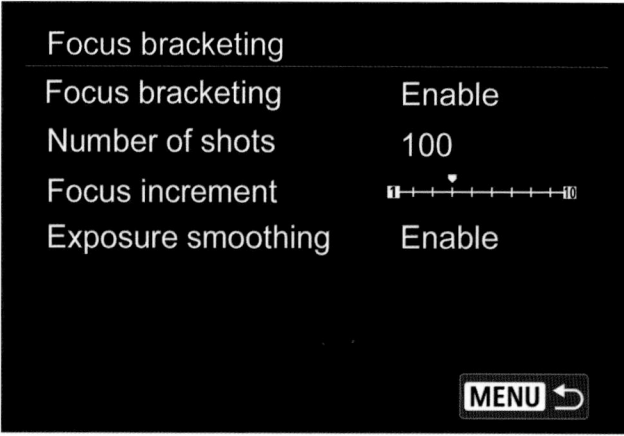

Figure 11.26
Focus Bracketing Shooting options.

- **Exposure Smoothing.** I recommend shooting under a steady, constant source of illumination and using Manual exposure. However, if you're working outdoors that may not be possible. In that case, in semi-automatic modes turn Exposure Smoothing On and allow the EOS RP to match exposure between frames. Exposure Smooth works in Manual exposure mode, too, if you enable Auto ISO Sensitivity so the camera can change ISO sensitivity during your sequence if required. Don't use smoothing with the following Canon lenses: EF 100mm f/2.8L Macro IS USM, EF 180mm f/3.5L Macro USM, and EF-S 60mm f/2.8 Macro USM.

9. **Prepare to shoot.** When all the parameters are locked in, press MENU to return to the shooting screen. A "folder" icon will appear (just above the magnifying glass icon.) I recommend tapping it to create a new folder for your images, in order to keep them separate from the other shots you've captured.

10. **Set focus point to nearest object.** Press the AF Point button and use the directional buttons to position the red focus box on the subject nearest the camera lens.

11. **Capture images.** Press the shutter button to begin shooting.

12. **Combine your images.** I'll describe the steps for that next.

The next step is to process the images you've taken in Digital Photo Pro or Photoshop. For maximum flexibility, I recommend using Photoshop. Transfer the images to your computer, and then follow these steps:

1. In Photoshop, select File > Scripts > Load Files into Stack. In the dialog box that then appears, navigate on your computer to find the files for the photographs you have taken, and highlight them all.

2. At the bottom of the next dialog box that appears, check the box that says, "Attempt to Automatically Align Source Images," then click OK. The images will load; it may take several minutes for the program to load the images and attempt to arrange them into layers that are aligned based on their content.

3. Once the program has finished processing the images, go to the Layers panel and select all of the layers. You can do this by clicking on the top layer and then Shift-clicking on the bottom one.

4. While the layers are all selected, in Photoshop go to Edit > Auto-Blend Layers. In the dialog box that appears, select the two options, Stack Images and Seamless Tones and Colors, then click OK. The program will process the images, possibly for a considerable length of time.

5. If the procedure worked well, the result will be a single image made up of numerous layers that have been processed to produce a sharply focused rendering of your subject. If it did not work well, you may have to take additional images the next time, specifying smaller slices of the subject as you move progressively farther away from the lens.

6. You'll want to flatten the final image before saving it. Given the 26MP resolution of the EOS RP, the stack of individual shots will sometimes be more than 2GB, which exceeds the maximum file size of some storage media and/or OS file systems.

Although this procedure can work very well in Photoshop, you also may want to try it with programs that were developed more specifically for focus stacking and related procedures, such as Helicon Focus (www.heliconsoft.com), PhotoAcute (www.photoacute.com), or CombineZM (www.hadleyweb.pwp.blueyonder.co.uk).

Interval Timer

Options: Interval: 1 second to 99 hours, 59 minutes, 59 seconds; Number of shots: 1 to 99
My preference: N/A

This feature, the first in the Shooting 6 menu, was covered in depth in Chapter 6 and I will not repeat that information here. The feature is easy to use: just choose how long you want the EOS RP to pause between shots, and specify the number of exposures you want to capture. (See Figure 11.27.)

Bulb Timer

Options: Disable (default), Enable, Exposure time
My preference: N/A

This feature is available only when the Mode Dial is set to the B (Bulb) position. It allows you to specify exposure times up to 99 hours, 59 minutes, and 59 seconds. I described use of this feature, too, in Chapter 6.

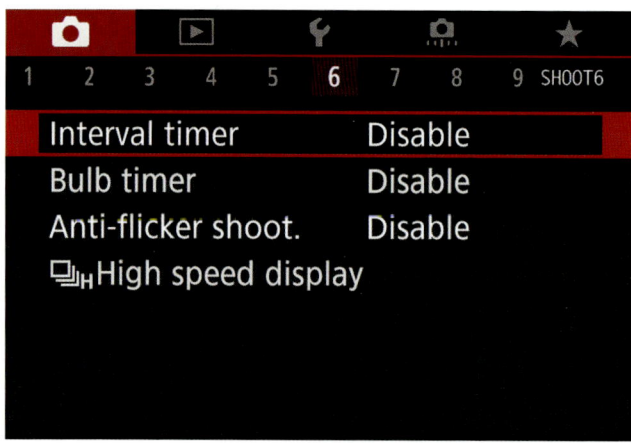

Figure 11.27
The Shooting 6 menu.

Anti-Flicker Shooting

Options: Enable, Disable (default)

My preference: Disable, unless shooting under flickering light source

Novice sports photographers often ask me why shots they take in certain gymnasiums or arenas have inconsistent exposure, wildly varying color, or banding. The answer is that certain types of artificial lighting have a blinking cycle that is imperceptible to the eye, but which the camera can capture. This setting, when enabled, detects the frequency (it's optimized for 100 to 120 Hz illumination and may not detect other frequencies) of the light source that is blinking, and takes the picture at the moment when the flicker has the least effect on the final image.

You may experience a slight shutter release time lag as the camera "waits" for the proper instant, and your continuous shooting speed may be reduced, which makes this setting a necessary evil for sports and other activities involving action. Your results may vary when using P or Av modes, because the shutter speed can change between shots as proper exposure requires. You're better off using Tv or M mode, so the shutter speed remains constant.

If you want to detect flicker manually, once this feature is enabled, you can press the Q button, choose Anti-Flicker Shooting from the Quick Control menu, and press the INFO button. The camera will tell you whether or not flicker has been detected.

Anti-Flicker is disabled when using Basic Zone modes, and may not work as well with dark backgrounds, a bright light within the image area, when using wireless flash, and under other shooting conditions. Canon recommends taking test shots to see how effective the feature is under the light source you are working with.

High-Speed Display

Options: Enable, Disable (Default)

My preference: Enable

This function activates a high-speed display that is more responsive, switching between the shot you've taken and the live image. Sports shooters will find it particularly useful when they're trying to follow action, as the default display is limited to about 5 frames per second. To use high-speed display, these conditions must be met:

■ **Using RF lens.** High-speed display does not work when an adapted EF/EF-S lens is mounted on the EOS RP.

■ **Servo AF.** You must set AF Operation to Servo AF to allow continuous focusing of your moving subject.

■ **High-Speed Continuous.** Drive mode must be set to High-Speed Continuous. You don't need this feature at slower shooting speeds, anyway.

■ **No Anti-Flicker Shooting.** Set Anti-Flicker to Disable.

■ **Exposure Simulation.** You must enable Exposure Simulation.

AF Operation

Options: One-Shot AF, Servo AF

My preference: N/A

This menu entry, the first in the Shooting 7 menu (see Figure 11.28), is an alternative to using the Quick Control or M-Fn button options to set autofocus operation. If the AF/MF switch on the lens is set to MF, then only MF appears in this entry and the other two are not available. **Reminder:** when focus is achieved, the focus point turns green or blue (in Servo mode); if focus cannot be achieved the point turns orange.

To recap:

- **One-Shot AF.** Single autofocus locks in a focus point when the shutter button is pressed down halfway. Green boxes will appear when the image is in focus at the active focus points, or orange if the EOS RP is unable to achieve sharp focus. The focus will remain locked until you release the button or take the picture.

- **Servo AF.** This continuous autofocus mode sets focus when you partially depress the shutter button, but continues to monitor the frame and refocuses if the camera or subject is moved. The focus area turns blue when focus is achieved, or orange if the EOS RP is unable to focus.

AF Method

Options: Face+Tracking, Spot AF, 1-point AF, Expand AF area, Expand AF area: Around, Zone AF

My preference: N/A

You can use this menu entry instead of the Quick Control screen or M-Fn button options. You can check focus with 5X and 10X magnified views by pressing the Magnify/Reduce button in all modes except Face+Tracking.

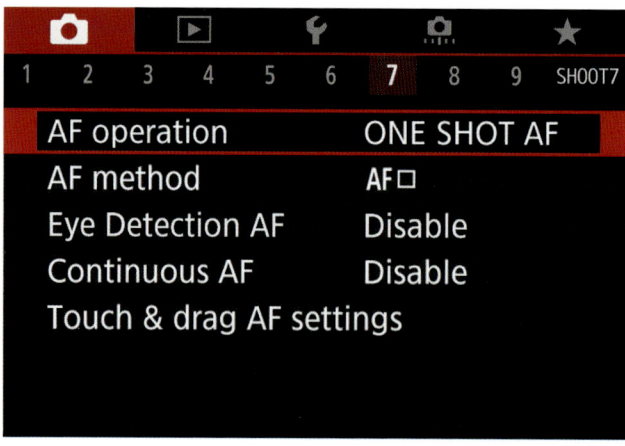

Figure 11.28
The Shooting 7 menu.

Your choices, as explained in more detail in Chapter 5 are as follows:

- **Face+Tracking.** The EOS RP uses intelligent algorithms to locate and focus on human faces, and track them and refocus if your subject moves. If no face is found, it will use all the focus points within the frame. You can select the initial position for autofocus when using Servo AF.
- **Spot AF.** Uses a single, small, reduced-size manually selected AF point.
- **1-point AF.** Allows you to manually select a larger AF point.
- **Expand AF area.** You can manually select a single AF point, as well as the four points located above, below, and to the left/right of it.
- **Expand AF area: Around.** You can manually select a single AF point, as well as *up to* eight points surrounding it (above, below, left, right, and diagonally from the selected point).
- **Zone AF.** AF points are segregated into square-shaped zones that cover about one-sixth of the frame, and you can select which zone to use. In this Zone mode the EOS RP will seek out faces and attempt to focus on them.

Eye Detection AF

Options: Enable, Disable (default)

My preference: N/A

Turns Eye Detection AF on or off, as described in Chapter 5. In use, an AF point is displayed around a detected eye. Eye Detection is available only with One-Shot AF and the Face+Tracking AF method. Temporarily disable Eye Detection AF by pressing the AF Point Selection button, followed by the M-Fn and the INFO button. Press INFO a second time to reactivate Eye Detection.

Continuous AF

Options: Enable, Disable (default)

My preference: N/A

When Continuous AF is enabled, the EOS RP refocuses all the time (even in One-Shot mode) until you press the shutter release halfway. Then it refocuses (and locks, in One-Shot mode) and resumes refocusing (in Servo mode) until you press the shutter release all the way. The net effect is that when you're ready to take a picture, the camera has focused and refocused continually and therefore should be ready for the final focusing when you take the photo. Canon warns that if you want to switch to manual focus when Continuous AF is active, you should turn the camera off first, slide the lens switch to MF, and then turn the camera back on.

Touch & Drag AF Settings

Options: Touch & Drag AF: Enable, Disable (default); Positioning method: Absolute, Relative (default); Active Touch Area: Whole Panel, Right (default), Left, Top, Bottom, Top Right, Bottom Right, Top Left, Bottom Left

My preference: When enabled, I prefer Relative Positioning and Whole Panel Active Touch Area.

As I've mentioned before, your touch screen can be useful even when you're working exclusively with the electronic viewfinder. When you access this entry you are given three options:

- **Touch & Drag AF.** Choose Enable to activate, or Disable to turn the feature off. When enabled, you can touch and drag according to the parameters that follow. In Face+Tracking mode, a round orange frame appears in the viewfinder while you are dragging. As soon as you are satisfied with that position, lift your finger and the frame changes to a square frame and tracking of the subject begins. Press the Trash button to cancel selection of that subject.

- **Positioning method.** You have two options for this setting:

  - **Absolute.** While looking through the viewfinder, touch the LCD screen with a finger on the active area and drag to any position on the screen. The AF point will move to that location. This option may be more precise, but it requires you to be aware of approximately where you are touching the screen. When the active touch area (as described next) is the whole panel, that's not difficult, but the behavior is more touch and go (so to speak) with smaller screen active areas.

  - **Relative.** You can touch and drag *anywhere* within the active area and move the AF point in that direction by an amount corresponding to the size of the motion.

- **Active Touch Area.** It's simplest if you select Whole Panel, so the entire LCD screen is active for the Touch & Drag feature. However, you can choose to make only the left, right, top, or bottom halves active, or the top and bottom left and right corners. A smaller area requires less dragging to move the focus point to a particular location, but is also less precise. The Whole Panel choice is generally more accurate, even if a bit slower than the alternatives.

Lens Electronic MF

Options: Enable after One-Shot AF (default), Disable after One-Shot AF, Disable in AF
My preference: Enable after One-Shot AF

This is the first entry in the Shooting 8 menu. (See Figure 11.29.) You may need this entry's capabilities if you frequently use EF/EF-S-mount lenses with an adapter. A limited number of extra-fast Canon prime lenses and one zoom—all of them L lenses with USM or STM motors—feature super-sensitive electronic manual focusing rings you can use to fine-tune focus after focus has been locked in using One-Shot AF. You might want to disable the use of this ring when using one of the compatible lenses, because even a casual bump against the ring can change focus significantly.

Figure 11.29
The Shooting 8 menu.

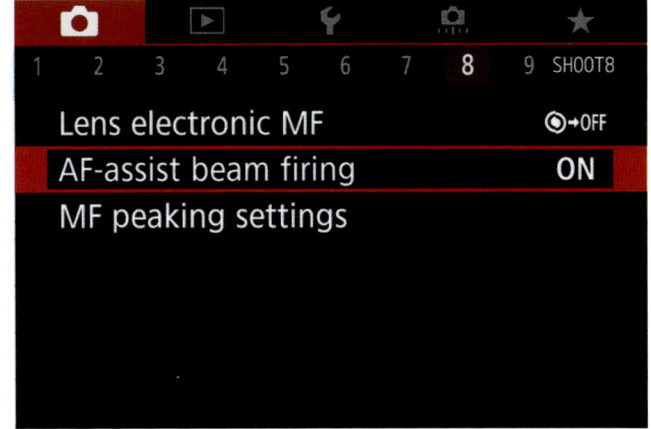

Note: Even if you've enabled One-Shot: Enabled (Magnify), the LCD screen or viewfinder display may not be magnified when you turn the focus ring while pressing the shutter button halfway following a shot. If that happens, release the shutter button, wait for the magnified display, and then press the shutter release halfway again while turning the focus ring. (This is a rather esoteric capability; I don't expect many readers of this book to need it.) The lenses in question are as follows as of this writing:

EF50mm f/1.0L USM	EF300mm f/2.8L USM	EF600mm f/4L USM
EF85mm f/1.2L USM	EF400 f/2.8L USM	EF1200 f/5.6L USM
EF85mm f/1.2L II USM	EF400mm f/2.8L II USM	EF200mm f/1.8L USM
EF500mm f/4.5L USM	EF28-80mm f/2.8-4L USM	EF40mm f/2.8 STM
EF50mm f/1.8 STM	EF24-105mm f/3.5-5.6 STM	

You have three choices:

- **Enable after One-Shot AF.** When active, you can continue to hold the shutter release halfway, while adjusting focus manually. I use this when shooting portraits with my 85mm f/1.2 lens at a large aperture, allowing me to zero focus in on the near eye of a subject seated on a diagonal angle.

- **Disable after One-Shot AF.** Manual focus is disabled. Use this when you are satisfied with the focus set by the camera's autofocus system and don't want to manually tweak it. Remember that if you truly want to use manual focus and bypass the AF system entirely, just slide the AF/MF switch on the lens to the MF position.

- **Disable in AF.** Turns off the feature entirely.

AF-Assist Beam Firing

Options: Enable (default), Disable, LED AF-assist beam only

My preference: LED AF-assist beam only

This setting determines when bursts from a compatible external electronic flash or the camera's built-in LED are used to emit a pulse of light that helps provide enough contrast for the EOS RP to focus on a subject. You can select Enable to use the camera's LED or an attached Canon Speedlite to produce a focus assist beam. Use Disable to turn this feature off if you find it distracting. Keep in mind that if you select Enable and the Speedlite's own AF-Assist Beam Firing is set to Disable, the AF-assist beam will not be emitted (the flash's setting takes precedence).

- **Enable.** The AF-assist light is emitted by the camera's LED or an attached, powered-up external flash whenever light levels are too low for accurate focusing using the ambient light.
- **Disable.** The AF-assist illumination is disabled. You might want to use this setting when shooting at concerts, weddings, or darkened locations where the light might prove distracting or discourteous.
- **LED AF-Assist Beam Only.** Some Canon flash units have an LED AF-assist lamp. Select this option to activate only the Speedlite's beam. If your flash does not have an LED, the EOS RP's LED will be used instead. Again, if you've turned off the external flash's AF-assist beam using its own controls, this function is disabled.

MF Peaking Settings

Options: Peaking: On, Off; Level: High, Low; Color: Red, Yellow, White

My preference: On, High, Red

MF Peaking Settings deals only with manual focus and therefore available only when focusing in Manual modes. *Focus peaking* is a technique that outlines the area in sharpest focus with a color that can be red, white, or yellow. The colored area shows you at a glance what will be very sharp if you take the photo at that moment. If you're not satisfied, simply change the focused distance (with manual focus). As the focus gets closer to ideal for a specific part of the image, the color outline develops around hard edges that are in focus. You can choose how much peaking is applied (High, Medium, and Low), select a specific accent color (Red, Yellow, or White), or turn the feature off.

Peaking Color allows you to specify which color is used to indicate peaking when you use manual focus. White is the default value, but if that color doesn't provide enough contrast with a similarly hued subject, you can switch to a more contrasting color, such as red or yellow.

12

Customizing with the Playback Menu

In the last chapter, I introduced you to the layout and general functions of the Canon EOS RP's menu system, with specifics on how to customize your camera with the Shooting menu. In this chapter, you'll learn how to work with the Playback menu. If you're jumping directly to this chapter and need some guidance in how to navigate the EOS RP's menu system, review the first few pages of Chapter 11. Otherwise, you're welcome to dive right in.

Playback Menu Options

The four blue-coded Playback menus are where you select options related to the display, review, transfer, and printing of the photos you've taken. Most of these entries are functions rather than settings, and thus only a few have actual default values, such as Image Jump with Main Dial (10 images), Magnification (2X), and Control over HDMI (Disable). So, in most cases I won't be providing recommendations.

The choices you'll find include:

- Protect Images
- Rotate Image
- Erase Images
- Print Order
- Photobook Set-up
- RAW Image Processing
- Creative Assist
- Quick Control RAW Processing
- Create Album
- Cropping
- Resize

- Rating
- Slide Show
- Set Image Search Conditions
- Image Jump with Main Dial
- Playback Information Display
- Highlight Alert
- AF Point Disp.
- Playback Grid
- View From Last Seen
- Magnification (apx)

Protect Images

Options: Select Images, Select Range, All Images in Folder, Unprotect All Images in Folder, All Images on Card, Unprotect All Images on Card

My preference: N/A

This is the first of five entries in the Playback 1 menu (see Figure 12.1). If you want to keep an image from being accidentally erased (either with the Erase button or by using the Erase Images entry in the Playback menu), you can mark that image for protection. Use the Protect entry in the Playback version of the Quick Control menu (described next), or use this menu item. To protect one or more images, press the MENU button while viewing an image and choose Protect from the Playback 1 menu. Then, select from the following options:

- Select Images
- Select Range
- All Images in Folder

- Unprotect All Images in Folder
- All Images on Card
- Unprotect All Images on Card

If you choose the first option, you can view and select individual images with the left/right directional controls, Main Dial, or touch screen, followed by pressing the SET button when the image you want to protect is displayed on the screen. A key icon will appear at the upper edge of the information display while still in the protection screen, and when reviewing that image later. Choose Select Range and you can mark the first of a string of images by highlighting it and pressing SET. Then navigate to the last image to be protected and press SET again.

Figure 12.1
The Playback 1
menu.

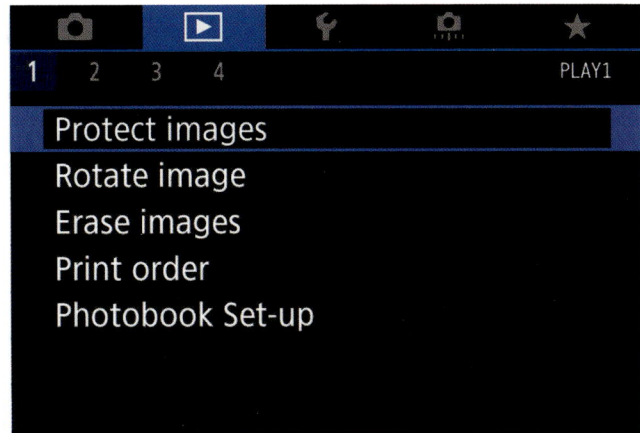

To remove protection, repeat the process. You can scroll among the other images on your memory card and protect/unprotect them in the same way. Image protection will not save your images from removal when the card is reformatted.

A fast way to protect images is to press the Q button when an image is displayed, then navigate to the Protect "key" icon that appears at top in the left-hand column. (See Figure 12.2.) When Enable is highlighted, press SET to protect the current image, or press INFO to select multiple images using the Select Range, All Images on Card, or Unprotect All Images on Card options that appear.

Figure 12.2
Protected images
can be locked
against accidental
erasure (but not
preserved from
formatting).

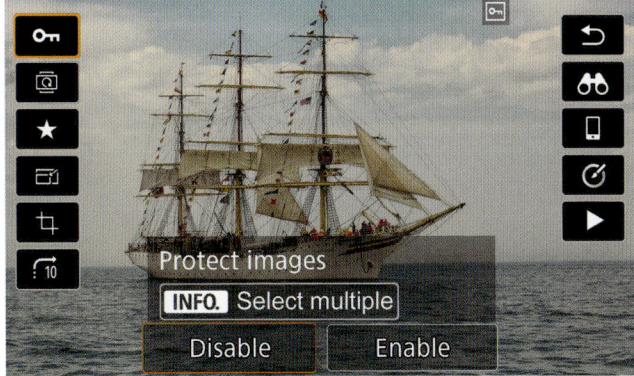

Rotate Image

Options: Rotate image

My preference: N/A

While you can set the EOS RP to automatically rotate images taken in a vertical orientation using the Auto Rotate option in the Set-up 1 menu (as described in Chapter 13), you can manually rotate an image during playback using this menu selection. Select Rotate Image from the Playback 1 menu, use the Quick Control Dial to page through the available images on your memory card until the one you want to rotate appears, then press SET. The image will appear on the screen rotated 90 degrees. Press SET again, and the image will be rotated 270 degrees. (See Figure 12.3.) Note that you can also rotate images from the Quick Control menu that appears when you press the Q button during Playback. It's the second icon from the top in the left column, as shown earlier in Figure 12.2.

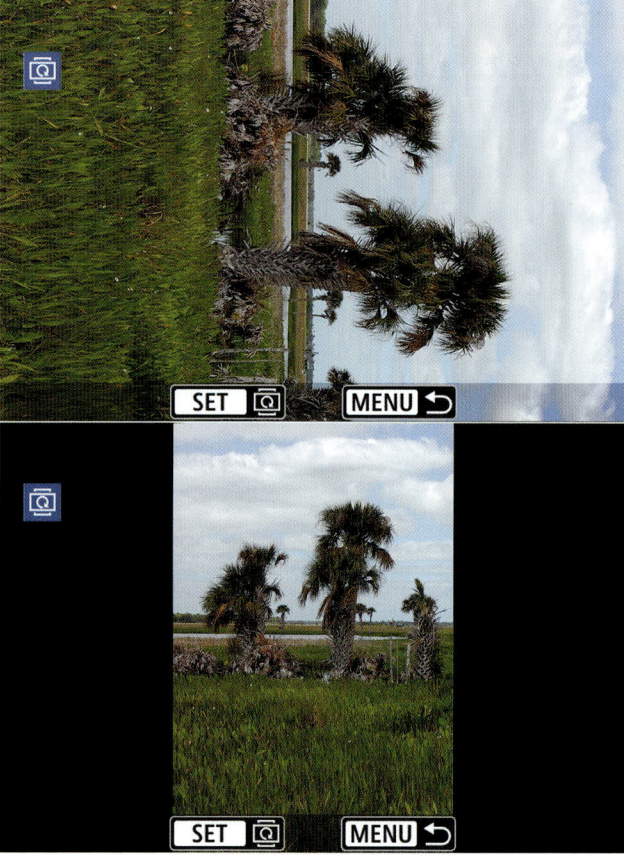

Figure 12.3
A vertically oriented image that isn't rotated appears larger on the LCD (top), but rotation allows viewing the photo without turning the camera (bottom).

Erase Images

Options: Select and Erase Images, Select Range, All Images in Folder, All Images on Card
My preference: N/A

Choose this menu entry and you'll be given four choices: Select and Erase Images, Select Range, All Images in Folder, and All Images on Card. You can use the first three to selectively remove images, while the fourth option deletes all the pictures on a card. But, using the Format command is usually faster and more thorough.

- **Select and Erase Images.** View the images on your card by pressing the left/right directional buttons to scroll through them. To mark an image for deletion or to remove a check mark, press the SET button. When you're finished selecting, press the Trash button (to the lower right of the LCD) and you'll be asked to confirm. Choose Cancel or OK and SET to finish.

- **Select Range.** Operates similarly to the range protect option listed earlier. Choose Select Range and you can mark the first of a string of images by highlighting it and pressing SET. Then navigate to the last image to be erased and press SET again.

- **All Images in Folder.** You'll be shown a list of the available folders on your memory card. Select SET, and a prompt will appear asking you to confirm, and reminding you that Protected images will not be removed.

- **All Images on Card.** A prompt will ask you to confirm this step. The All Images on Card choice removes all the pictures on the card, except for those you've marked with the Protect command, and does not reformat the memory card.

Print Order

Options: Select Image, Multiple: Select Range, Mark/Clear All in Folder, Mark All/Clear All on Card; Set Up: Print type (Standard, Index, Both); Date (On/Off); File Number (On/Off)
My preference: N/A

The EOS RP supports the DPOF (Digital Print Order Format) that is now almost universally used by digital cameras to specify which images on your memory card should be printed, and the number of prints desired of each image. This information is recorded on the memory card, and can be interpreted by a compatible printer. Photo labs are also equipped to read this data and make prints when you supply your memory card to them.

Once marked for DPOF printing, you can print the selected images, or take your memory card to a digital lab or kiosk, which is equipped to read the print order and make the copies you've specified. (You can't "order" prints of RAW images or movies.)

To create a DPOF print order, just follow these steps:

1. **Access Print Order screen.** In the Playback 1 menu, navigate to Print Order. Press SET.

2. **Access Set-up.** The Print Order screen will appear. (See Figure 12.4.) Use the directional buttons to highlight Set Up. Press SET.

3. **Select Print type.** Choose Print Type (Standard, Index/Thumbnails print, or Both), and specify whether Date or File Number imprinting should be turned on or off. (You can turn one or the other on, but not both Date and File Number imprinting.) You cannot set print type individually; all images in the print order will use the same print type. Press MENU to return to the Print Order screen.

4. **Choose selection method.** Highlight Sel. Image (choose individual images) or Multiple.

   - **Select individual images.** With Sel. Image, use the directional buttons to view the images, and press SET to mark or unmark an image for printing. If you'd rather view thumbnails of images, press the Thumbnail/Zoom In button. Press the Magnify/Zoom Out button to return to single-image view.

   - **Multiple.** Allows you to select a Range, Mark All in Folder, Clear All in Folder, Mark All on Card, Clear All on Card. Press SET to choose a range or folder, and MENU to return to the print order screen.

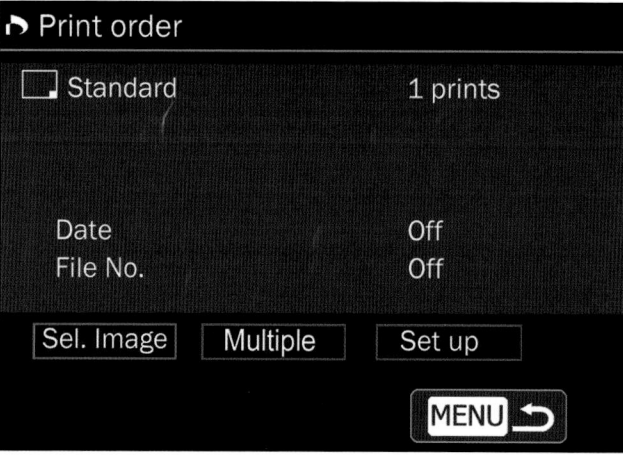

Figure 12.4
Select the images to be printed individually, by folder, or all the images on your memory card.

5. **Choose number of prints.** If you've selected individual images (rather than a range, folder, or card) as an image is selected, you can press the up/down directional buttons to specify 1 to 99 prints for that image. (For Index prints, you can only specify whether the selected image is included in the index print, not the number of copies.) Press SET to confirm. You can then use the up/down buttons to select additional images. Press MENU when finished selecting to return to the Print Order screen.

6. **Output your hardcopies.** If the camera is linked to a PictBridge-compatible printer, an additional option appears on the Print Order screen—Print. You can select that; optionally, adjust Paper Settings as described in the previous section, and start the printing process. Alternately, you can exit the Print Order screen by tapping the shutter release button. Then turn off the camera and printer, remove the memory card, and insert it in the memory card slot of a compatible printer, retailer kiosk, or digital minilab.

Photobook Set-up

Options: Select Images, Multiple

My preference: N/A

You can select up to 998 images on your memory card, and then use the EOS Utility to copy them all to a specific folder on your computer. This is a handy way to transfer only specific images to a particular folder, and is especially useful when you're collecting photos to assemble in a photobook. Your choices include:

- ■ **Select images.** You can mark individual images from any folder on your memory card.
- ■ **Multiple.** You can choose Select Range, All Images in Folder, Clear All in Folder, All Images on Card, Clear All on Card.

Once you marked the images you want to transfer to the specified folder, use the EOS Utility to copy them.

RAW Image Processing

Options: Select Images, Select Range; Use Shot Settings; Customize RAW Processing: Brightness, White balance, Picture Style, Auto Lighting Optimizer, High ISO Noise Reduction, Image Quality, Color Space, Lens Aberration Correction

My preference: N/A

This is the first entry on the Playback 2 menu. (See Figure 12.5.) You can produce JPEG versions of your full-size RAW and C RAW images. The original RAW shot is not modified. When you select this menu entry, only compatible RAW images are offered for your selection.

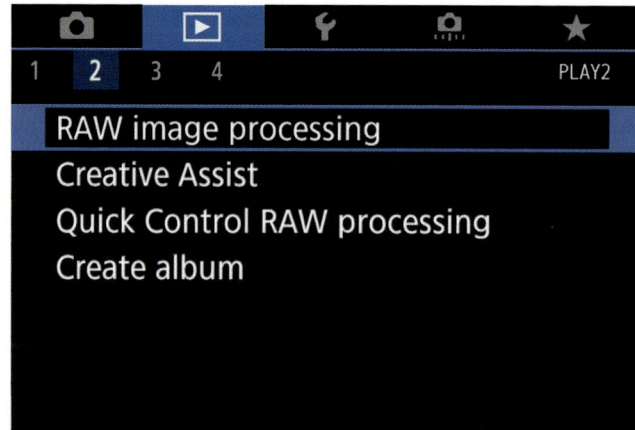

Figure 12.5
The Playback 2 menu.

Just follow these steps:

1. **View RAW images.** From the first screen that appears, select either Select Images (to choose individual RAW images) or Select Range (to choose a continuous series of images). Rotate the QCD to scroll through compatible images. Press the Magnify button and rotate the Main Dial counterclockwise to view a selection of index images instead.

2. **Select image to process.** Press SET to select an image for processing. A check mark will appear next to it. When you are done choosing, press MENU to move on to the next step.

3. **Use Shot Settings or Customize RAW Processing.** If you select Use Shot Settings in the next screen, the EOS RP will immediately create JPEG copies of the RAW image(s) you specified. If you want to customize settings, proceed to Step 4.

4. **Specify parameters.** A screen appears with a selection of parameters you can adjust. (See Figure 12.6.) Navigate to the parameter you want to manipulate using the directional buttons. Your choices include:

   - Brightness
   - White Balance
   - Picture Style
   - Auto Lighting Optimizer
   - High ISO Noise Reduction
   - Image Quality
   - Color Space
   - Lens Aberration Correction

5. **Make adjustments.** All parameters will already be set to those specified when you exposed the RAW file. When a parameter you want to change is highlighted, press SET, then rotate either dial to select an option. Some changes are difficult to see; press the Magnify button to enlarge a portion of the image for review. Press SET to confirm your option, and return to the main screen.

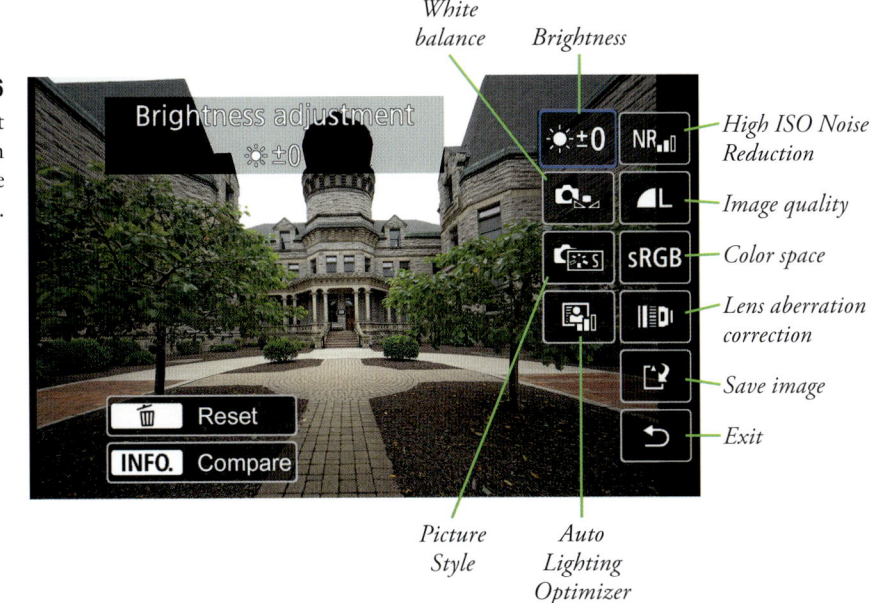

Figure 12.6
Select from eight types of correction using RAW Image Processing.

White balance

Brightness

High ISO Noise Reduction

Image quality

Color space

Lens aberration correction

Save image

Exit

Picture Style

Auto Lighting Optimizer

6. **Repeat Step 5 (optional).** You can continue making adjustments to any or all of the other parameters. At any time you can press the Trash/Erase button to cancel all the changes you've made so far.

7. **Compare before/after.** Here's the cool part. After you've made adjustments, you can press the INFO button to compare your before and after images. The image will be shown in the After Change version (and labeled as such) with the parameters you've modified highlighted in orange in the upper-right corner of the screen. Rotate the QCD to toggle between the After Change image and the Shot Settings (original) version. Press MENU to exit Compare mode.

8. **Save JPEG.** When you're satisfied with your changes, navigate to the Save icon at the bottom right of the screen (just above the Return arrow) and press SET. Choose OK to save as a new file, or Cancel to abort the process. If the original was shot using an aspect ratio other than 3:2, the image will be displayed in those proportions, and the JPEG will be saved in that aspect ratio.

QUICK CONTROL PROCESSING

RAW Image Processing can be performed from the Playback version of Quick Control menu. You can also summon an alternate type of RAW adjustment—Creative Assist special effects (described next). Only one of the two types of processing can appear in the Quick Control menu, and will be located in the fourth position from the top of the right-hand column, as seen earlier in Figure 12.2. Enable either of the two using the Quick Control RAW Processing setting, described shortly.

Creative Assist

Options: Preset, Brightness, Contrast, Saturation, Color Tone 1, Color Tone 2, Monochrome

My preference: N/A

This entry lets you take a RAW image and create a new JPEG after applying your choice of an array of Picture Styles–like special effects to the image. It's particularly useful when you'd like to make adjustments to an image you've already captured, but don't want to (or can't) use an image editor. Just follow these steps:

1. Access the Creative Assist entry and press SET.

2. Navigate among available RAW images using the left/right directional buttons. Press SET to select an image to process.

3. A screen similar to the one shown in Figure 12.7 appears, with an array of effects displayed along the bottom.

4a. To work with a Preset adjustment, highlight the Preset icon and press SET. Auto1, Auto2, and Auto3 presets can be selected from the array that appears, along with others, including Vivid, Soft, Cool, Green, Shine, Lime, Peach, B&W, Blue, Purple, and Normal. As each effect is highlighted, a preview of its effect is shown on the display. Press SET to select.

4b. To make your own adjustments, instead, highlight the Brightness, Contrast, Saturation, Color Tone 1, Color Tone 2, or Monochrome adjustments. Press SET to modify the highlighted setting with the left/right directional buttons. Reset a particular effect by pressing the Trash button, or the AF Point button to confirm.

5. When finished, highlight OK and press SET to save a new JPEG version of the image.

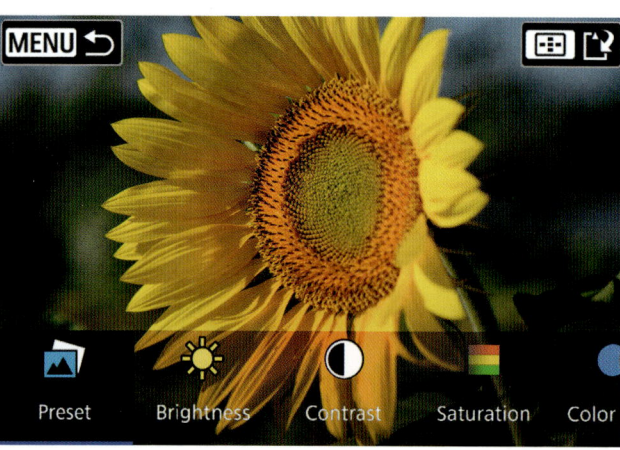

Figure 12.7
Creative Assist adjustments.

Quick Control RAW Processing

Options: Creative Assist, RAW Image Processing

My preference: N/A

This setting determines which of the two RAW adjustment options appears in the Quick Control menu. Your choice should be based on whether you want to be able to apply special effects quickly (Creative Assist) or perform more traditional RAW settings while creating a new JPEG file with those adjustments.

Create Album

Options: Select Movies, Rearrange, Save

My preference: N/A

Your EOS RP allows you to create video snapshots in Movie mode, each clip 4, 6, or 8 seconds long (your choice). You can save any snapshot as a separate album, or keep adding snapshots to a single video album to create a longer clip. This entry adds the ability to *combine* individual albums into one longer sequence, and to rearrange them in any order you like. I'll provide complete instructions for shooting, saving, and editing albums in Chapter 15.

Cropping

Options: Crop, Aspect Ratio

My preference: N/A

This entry is the first on the Playback 3 menu. (See Figure 12.8.) If you need to crop an image, you can do it here. You don't have as much control as you would have in an image editor, but if you, say, need to crop an image for emailing or uploading to a social media site, this may do the job. You can crop *only* JPEG images. This function does not work on RAW images, or frames grabbed from 4K movies.

Figure 12.8
The Playback 3 menu.

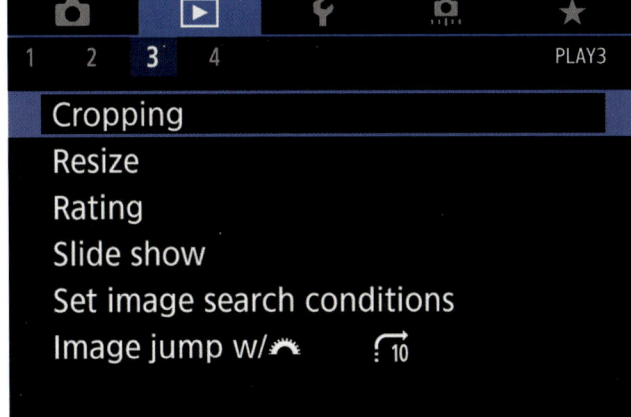

Simply select this menu entry and press SET. A compatible JPEG image appears. Use the QCD to select an image for cropping. Press the Magnify/Reduce button and rotate the Main Dial counterclockwise to view and select a thumbnail image in index view. Press SET when you've chosen your image and MENU to go to the screen shown in Figure 12.9. (Note that you can also crop images from the Quick Control menu that appears when you press the Q button during Playback. See note in Resize option—shown next.

In the cropping screen you can apply one of these tools:

- **Select adjustment.** Arrayed along the top row of the screen are function icons. Rotate the QCD to highlight any of these (from left to right):

  - **Enlarge/reduce crop.** Rotate the Main Dial to enlarge and reduce the green cropping frame, seen in Figure 12.9. Use the directional buttons to relocate the position of the cropping frame within the image.

  - **Correct for tilt.** Up to plus/minus 10 degrees of tilt can be corrected. Rotating the QCD will adjust orientation in 0.1-degree increments. Rotational arrows appear in the top row that you can tap on the touch screen to adjust in 0.5-degree increments. A grid appears to help you straighten your image. Press SET to finish this correction and confirm.

  - **Change aspect ratio.** Rotate the QCD to cycle the cropping frame's proportions among 3:2, 16:9, 4:3, 1:1, 2:3, 9:16, or 3:4 aspect ratios.

- **Save cropped image.** Press SET and select OK to save your cropped image as a new file with a new file number. Your original image is retained unharmed.

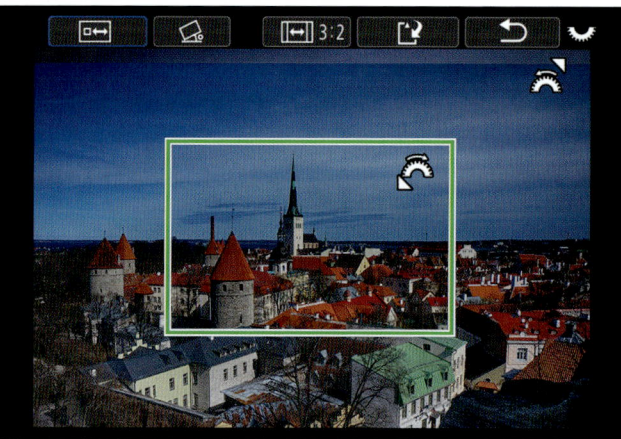

Figure 12.9
The green frame represents the cropped area.

Resize

Options: Medium, Small 1, Small 2 image sizes

My preference: N/A

If you've already taken an image and would like to create a smaller version (say, to send by e-mail), you can create one from this menu entry. Just follow these steps:

1. **Choose Resize.** Select this menu entry from the Playback 3 menu.

2. **View images to resize.** You can scroll through the available images with the touch screen or directional buttons, or press the Thumbnail/Reduce Image button to view thumbnails and select from those. Only images that can be resized are shown. They include JPEG Large, Medium, Small 1, and Small 2 images. Small 3 and RAW images of any type cannot be resized.

3. **Select an image.** Choose SET to select an image to resize. A pop-up menu will appear on the screen offering the choice of reduced-size images. These include M (Medium: 11.5 MP, 4160 × 2768 pixels); S1 (Small 1: 6.5 MP, 3120 × 2080 pixels); or S2 (Small 2: 3.8 MP, 2400 × 1600 pixels). You cannot resize an image to a size that is larger than its current size; that is, you cannot save a JPEG Medium image as JPEG Large.

4. **Resize and save.** Choose SET to save as a new file, and confirm your choice by selecting OK from the screen that pops up, or cancel to exit without saving a new version. The old version of the image is untouched.

As with some other entries in the Playback menu, you can also apply resize images from the Quick Control menu that appears when you press the Q button during Playback.

Rating

Options: Select Images (Range, All Images in Folder, All Images on Card); One to five stars

My preference: N/A

If you want to apply a quality rating to images or movies you've shot (or use the rating system to represent some other criteria), you can simply press the Rating button during playback multiple times to apply a rating. Or, alternatively, use this entry to give images one, two, three, four, or five stars, or turn the rating system off. The Image Jump function can display only images with a given rating. Suppose you were photographing a track meet with multiple events. You could apply a one-star rating to jumping events, two stars to relays, three stars to throwing events, four stars to hurdles, and five stars to dashes. Then, using the Image Jump feature, you could review only images of one type.

With a little imagination, you can apply the rating system to all sorts of categories. At a wedding, you could classify pictures of the bride, the groom, guests, attendants, and parents of the couple. If you were shooting school portraits, one rating could apply to first grade, another to second grade, and so on. Given a little thought, this feature has many more applications than you might think. Ratings can be used to specify images for a slide show, too, or to select images in Digital Photo Professional. Note that you can also apply ratings from the Quick Control menu that appears when you press the Q button during Playback. It's the third icon from the top in the left column, as shown earlier in Figure 12.2.

To use the Ratings menu entry, just follow these steps:

1. Choose the Rating menu item.

2. Choose Select Images, Select Range, All Images in Folder, or All Images on Card to specify images to be rated.

3. When an image or movie you want to rate is visible, press SET.

4. Now rotate the QCD or press the up/down buttons to apply a one- to five-star rating, or turn a rating off. You can rate up to 999 images.

5. When finished rating, choose MENU to exit.

Slide Show

Options: Image Selection, Display Time, Repeat, Transition Effect

My preference: N/A

Slide Show is a convenient way to review images one after another, without the need to manually switch between them. To activate, just choose Slide Show from the Playback 3 menu. During playback, you can press the SET button to pause the "slide show" (in case you want to examine an image more closely), or the INFO button to change the amount of information displayed on the screen with each image. For example, you might want to review a set of images and their histograms to judge the exposure of the group of pictures. To set up your slide show, follow these steps:

1. **Choose images.** By default, the Slide Show feature chooses all images on the card, and Start is highlighted by default. If you want to begin a slide show using all the available still and video images, jump to Step 8. If you want to choose specific types of images to display, continue to Step 2.

2. **Specify certain image types.** You can "filter" which kinds of images will be displayed in your slide show. The parameters can include Rating, Date, Folder, Protected, File Type (RAW, RAW+JPEG, JPEG, or Movie). You'll find instructions for filtering images in the entry described after Slide Show: Set Image Search Conditions.

3. **Choose Set Up.** Highlight the Set Up option and press SET to begin choosing display parameters.

4. **Choose Display time.** Highlight Display Time and press SET to produce a screen with a choice of playing times (1, 2, 3, 5, 10, or 20 seconds per image). Press SET to confirm.

5. **Repeat.** If you want the show to keep playing, highlight Repeat, press SET, and Enable.

6. **Transition Effect.** This sub-entry has five possible effects (slide in from left, right, and three fade-in transitions), plus Off.

7. **Exit Set Up.** Press MENU to exit Set Up.

8. **Start the show.** Highlight Start and press SET to begin your show. (If you'd rather cancel the show you've just set up, press MENU instead.) **Note:** the display time of each slide will vary, depending on the file size of the image.

9. **Use show options during display.** Press SET to pause/restart; INFO to cycle among the four information displays; and MENU to stop the show. The EOS RP auto-power-off feature will not turn the camera off during playback. Sound volume can be adjusted by rotating the Main Dial, and during playback or pause, you can press the left/right buttons to view a different slide.

Adding Music

Use the EOS Utility to add music files to your memory card, so you can play them back during your slide shows. Just follow these steps:

1. **Connect.** Link your EOS RP to your computer and then launch the EOS Utility application.

2. **Choose Register Background Music.** When the Camera Settings screen appears, select Register Background Music to view the Background Music window.

3. **Add tunes (optional).** The EOS Utility includes several background music files with themes like sports, memories, and travel. You can also add your own music files in .WAV format to the catalog, using the Add button or by dragging and dropping the files. Up to a total of 20 different background tracks can be stored, each up to 29 minutes, 59 seconds long.

4. **Register to card.** Select the music files you want to include and click Register. They will be copied to your memory card, overwriting any music files already stored there.

Set Image Search Conditions

Options: Filter by: Rating, Date, Folder, Protection, or File Type
My preference: N/A

You don't need to see every image on your memory card as you play them back. This entry allows you to specify which images are shown during image review, available in a slide show, or subject to the Protect and Erase features.

Just follow these steps:

1. **Choose Set Image Search Conditions.** Highlight the entry and press SET.

2. **Select condition.** A vertical column at left appears with the conditions available, listed, from top to bottom: Rating, Date, Folder, Protection, or File Type. Use the up/down buttons to highlight a condition.

3. **Enter parameter.** Use the left/right buttons to set the parameter for a particular condition:

   - **Rating.** You can choose one to five stars.

   - **Date.** Select a specific date *that includes photos taken.* (That is, you cannot select a date on which no images where taken with this card.)

   - **Folder.** Select from among the various folders on your card. If only one folder is available, that is chosen by default.

   - **Protected.** Choose Protected or Unprotected images.

   - **Type of File.** Choose to show only stills, various combinations of RAW, RAW+JPEG, and JPEG, plus movie files.

4. **Set condition.** When parameters are set for a condition, press INFO to add it to your conditions. You can press INFO again to unselect it. Mix and match conditions, choosing any one, or any combination of the five parameters. Press Trash to remove all conditions.

5. **Confirm.** Press SET to exit. An informational screen will appear. Press OK to confirm.

Image Jump with Main Dial

Options: 1 Image, 10 Images (default), Specified number (1–100), Date, Folder, Movies, Stills, Protected, Rating

My preference: 10 Images

As first described in Chapter 2, you can leap ahead or back during picture review by swiping across the touch screen with two fingers, or by rotating the Main Dial. You can select from a variety of increments that will be used with this menu entry. The Jump method is shown briefly on the screen as you leap ahead to the next image displayed, as shown in Figure 12.10. Your options are as follows:

- **1 image.** Rotating the Main Dial one click or swiping jumps forward or back 1 image.

- **10 images.** Rotating the Main Dial one click or swiping jumps forward or back 10 images.

- **Specified number.** When this option is highlighted, rotate the Main Dial to choose the increment between jumps, from one image to 100.

- **Date.** Rotating the Main Dial one click or swiping jumps forward or back to the first image taken on the next or previous calendar date.

Figure 12.10
The Jump method is shown on the LCD briefly when you leap forward or back using the Main Dial or a two-fingered touch screen swipe.

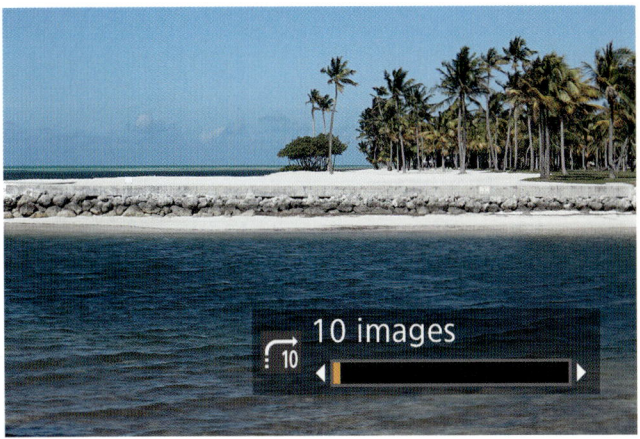

- **Folder.** Rotating the Main Dial one click or swiping jumps forward or back to the first image in the next folder available on your memory card (if one exists).

- **Movies.** Rotating the Main Dial one click or swiping jumps forward or back, displaying movies you captured only.

- **Stills.** Rotating the Main Dial one click or swiping jumps forward or back, displaying still images only.

- **Protected.** Rotating the Main Dial jumps between Protected images only. This is a good way to review images you deemed worthy of protection, or which you have marked with the protected attribute for some other reason (say, you wanted to group some favorite shots for review, but not apply a specific star rating).

- **Rating.** Rotating the Main Dial one click or swiping jumps forward or back, displaying images by the ratings you've applied (as described earlier). Tap the touch screen or rotate the Main Dial to choose the rating parameter.

Playback Information Display

Options: Enable or Disable 9 different informational screens

My preference: N/A

This is the first entry on the Playback 4 menu. (See Figure 12.11.) When you press the INFO button during Playback, the EOS RP cycles among three different screens, shown in Figure 12.12. They include an uncluttered screen with no overlaid information, a basic information screen, and a shooting information screen that provides more complete information, and can include several additional optional panels of data. Use this entry to specify which of the optional screens you want to display.

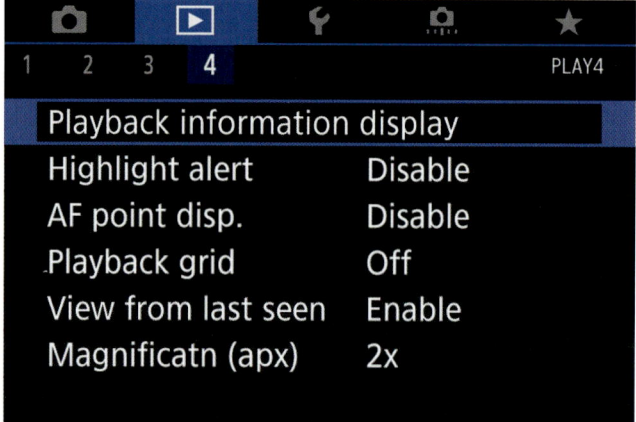

Figure 12.11
The Playback 4 menu

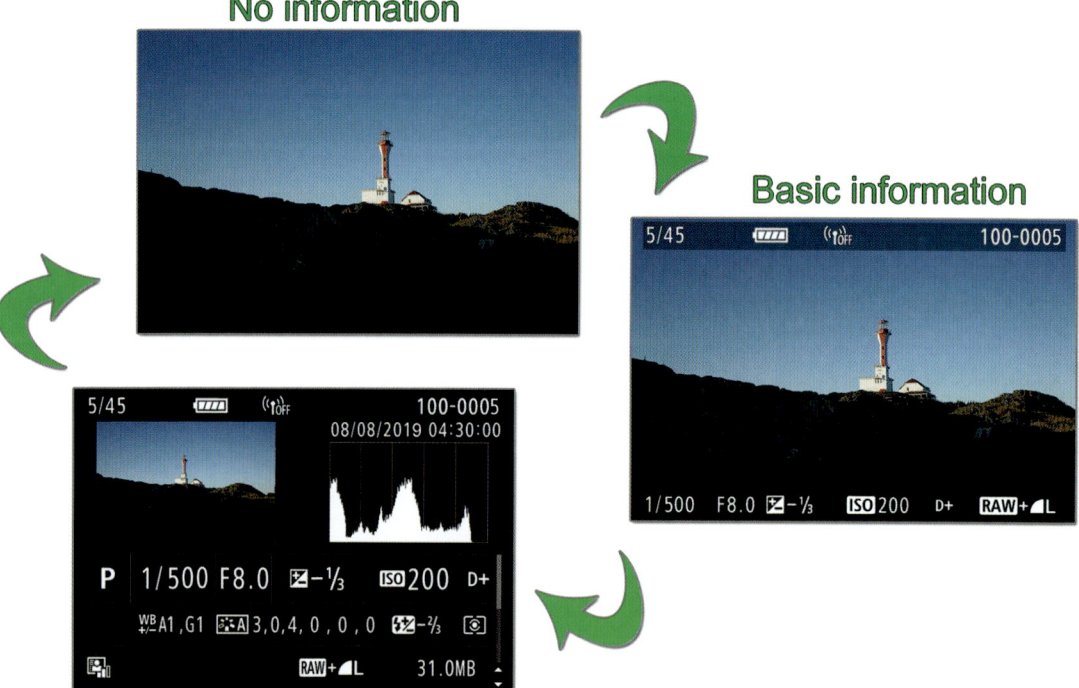

Figure 12.12 Press INFO to cycle among these three screens: No information (upper left); Basic information (center right); Shooting information (lower left). You can enable or disable all but the No Information version.

Just follow these steps to include/exclude the available displays.

1. Access with menu entry. A screen similar to the one shown in Figure 12.13 appears. Check marks appear next to any of the available screen options.

2. Highlight the screens that you want to see, and press SET to add a check mark. To hide a display, highlight a check marked option and press SET to unmark it.

3. You can mark or unmark any or all. If none are selected, only the No Information screen will be displayed during Playback. (See Figure 12.12, upper left.)

4. The available screens are as follows:

   • **The Basic Information screen.** (See Figure 12.12, center, right.) This shows a limited amount of information, such as battery status, picture number, shutter speed, aperture, exposure compensation, ISO setting, highlight priority, and image quality.

   • **The Shooting Information screen,** which provides more detailed information like that shown in Figure 12.12, lower left. Note the scroll bar at lower right. Options 2–9 in the Playback Information Display represent additional panels that can be appended to the scroll, and described next. By default, a brightness/luminance histogram is displayed at upper right in the Shooting Information Screen. You can press INFO while activating this entry to substitute an RGB histogram instead. I showed you how to work with histograms in Chapter 4.

   • **Lens information/alternate histogram.** Activate this option and scrolling down from the main Shooting Information screen displays information about the lens used to take the current photo, as well as the *other* histogram display. (If the main screen shows the Brightness histogram, the RGB histogram appears here, and vice versa.) You can press INFO and exchange the order of the two histograms if you wish.

Figure 12.13
Mark any, all, or none of the Playback display options using this screen.

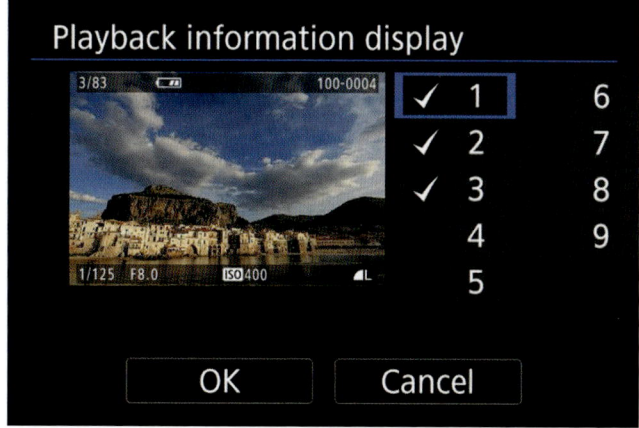

- **White balance.** Adds WB information to the scrolling screen, including a color bias display.

- **Picture Control.** Displays current Picture Control settings.

- **Color Space/Noise Reduction.** Appends these details to the display.

- **Peripheral Illumination/Distortion Correction.** Shows whether correction features are enabled or disabled.

- **Image Sent To.** Lets you know that the image has been transferred to your smart device.

- **GPS Information.** Appears if the image was taken using a GPS device.

5. When finished adding screen options, highlight OK at the bottom left of the Playback Information Display screen and press SET.

6. During Playback, when the Shooting Information screen is displayed (press INFO to make it appear, if necessary), you can scroll among the activated options using the up/down directional buttons.

Highlight Alert

Options: Enable, Disable (default)

My preference: N/A

Choose Enable, and overexposed highlight areas will blink on the LCD screen during picture review (these are commonly known as "blinkies"). Set to Disable if you find this alert distracting. Many EOS RP users use the histogram displays during playback as a more precise indicator of over- and underexposure.

AF Point Disp.

Options: Enable, Disable (default)

My preference: N/A

Select Enable, and the exact AF point(s) used to determine focus will be highlighted in red. If automatic AF point selection was used, you may find multiple points highlighted.

Playback Grid

Options: 3 × 3, 6 × 4, 3 × 3+ diagonal lines, Off (default)

My preference: N/A

You can superimpose a 3 × 3, 6 × 4, or 3 × 3 plus diagonal lines grid over your image during playback, or disable the grid display entirely. (See Figure 12.14.) The same selection of grids can be displayed as you shoot, using the Set-up 4 menu entry Shooting Information Display, which I'll explain in Chapter 13.

Figure 12.14
Playback grid
options.

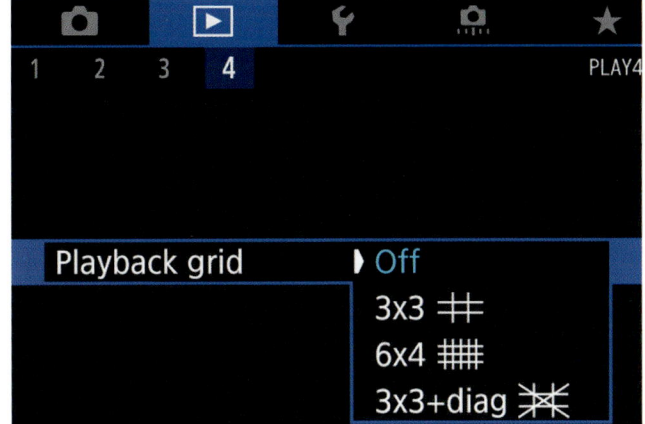

View from Last Seen

Options: Enable (default), Disable

My preference: N/A

This option allows you to specify which image is shown first when you press the Playback button.

■ **Enable.** The EOS RP will show you the last image you were viewing during picture review. This is useful when you check your shots, exit Playback, and then want to pick up where you left off. However, if you take a photo in the meantime, the camera will start from the image you just captured instead.

■ **Disable.** Playback always begins from your most recent shot. This may be your best option when shooting events or sports and you always want quick access to the last photo you captured.

Magnification (apx)

Options: 1X, 2X (default), 4X, 8X, 10X, Actual size, Same as last magnification

My preference: Same as last magnification

This setting allows you to specify the initial magnification for magnified view during playback, as well as the starting position on the screen. Choose your starter magnification based on how often you tend to take a close-up look at your images during review. If you're a pixel-peeper, you might want an in-depth 10X view each time you magnify your image. If you're more sedate in your zooming habits, the 1X magnification will start you off with a full-screen view you can zoom in on. I like to use the same magnification I most recently used, because I am likely to examine a series of similar images at the same zoom level during a shooting or review session.

Your options are as follows:

- **1X (no magnification).** When you press the Magnify button, the initial view will be the single image display with no magnification. Continue pressing Magnify to zoom in.
- **2X, 4X, 8X, 10X (from the center of the frame).** The initial magnified view will be 2X, 4X, 8X, or 10X (your choice), centered around the middle of the frame.
- **Actual size (from selected point).** Magnified view starts at 100 percent, centered around the autofocus point used to achieve focus; if manual focus was used, the image will be centered around the middle of the frame.
- **Same as last magnification (from the center point).** The EOS RP uses the same magnification value you last used, centered around the middle of the frame.

13

Customizing with the Set-up Menu

There are six amber-coded Set-up menu screens where you adjust how your camera *behaves* during your shooting session, as differentiated from the Shooting menu, which adjusts how the pictures are taken. Your choices include:

- Select Folder
- File Numbering
- Auto Rotate
- Format Card
- Mode Guide
- Feature Guide
- Eco Mode
- Power Saving
- Display Brightness
- Date/Time/Zone
- Language
- Video System
- Touch Control
- Beep
- Battery Information
- Sensor Cleaning

- HDMI Resolution
- HDMI HDR Output
- Shooting Information Display
- Viewfinder Performance
- Display Settings
- Shutter Button Function for Movies
- Help Text Size
- Wireless Communication Settings
- GPS Device Settings
- Multi-Function Lock
- Custom Shooting Mode (C1–C3)
- Clear All Camera Settings
- Copyright Information
- Manual/Software URL
- Certification Logo Display
- Firmware

Select Folder

Options: Select Folder, Create Folder

My preference: N/A

Choose this menu option, the first in the Set-up 1 menu (see Figure 13.1) to create a folder where the images you capture will be stored on your memory card, or to switch between existing folders. Just follow these steps:

1. **Choose Select Folder.** Access the option from the Set-up 1 menu.
2. **View list of available folders.** The Select Folder screen pops up with a list of the available folders on your memory card, with names like 100CANON, 101CANON, etc. (See Figure 13.2.)

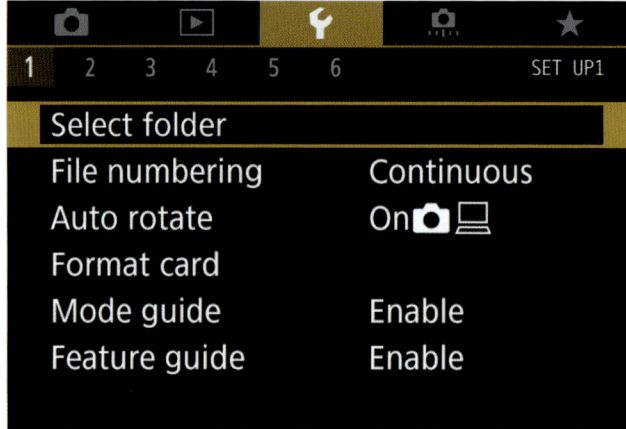

Figure 13.1
The Set-up 1 menu.

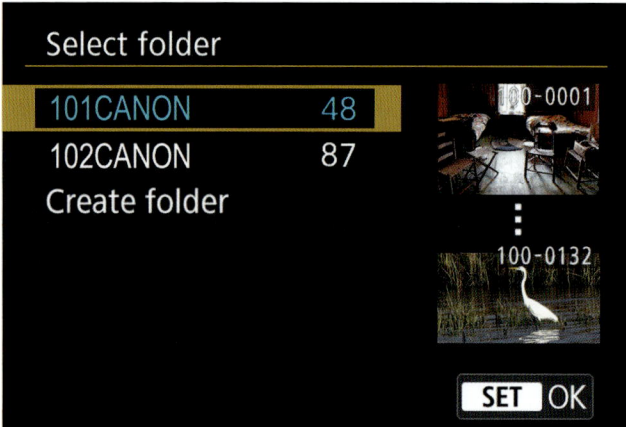

Figure 13.2
Choose a folder or create a new one.

3. **Choose a different folder.** To store subsequent images in a different existing folder, use the touch screen or directional buttons to highlight the label for the folder you want to use. When a folder that already has photos is selected, two thumbnails representing images in that folder are displayed at the right side of the screen.

4. **Confirm the folder.** Choose SET to confirm your choice of an existing folder.

5. **Create new folder.** If you'd rather create a new folder, highlight Create Folder in the Select Folder screen and choose SET. The name of the folder that will be created is displayed, along with a choice to Cancel or OK creating the folder. Choose SET to confirm your choice.

6. **Exit.** Press MENU to return to the Set-up 1 menu.

The folders your EOS RP creates *always* follow the *nnn*CANON convention. You can also use your computer to create folders with names that depart from this arrangement, as long as you adhere to the camera's general rules for memory card folder names. Here's how to create folders with personalized names:

1. **Access the memory card from your computer.** There are two ways to do this.

   a. **USB link.** Plug the USB cable into the port on the left side of the EOS RP and connect to a USB connector on your computer. In Windows, the EOS RP will appear as a generic digital camera icon. A similar icon will appear on the Mac OS X desktop.

   b. **Use a card reader.** Remove the card from the EOS RP and insert it in a card reader attached to your computer.

2. **Open the camera/memory card in your computer.** A folder called DCIM will appear at the top level. All the folders your EOS RP can access must be located inside the DCIM folder.

3. **Create a new folder within the DCIM folder.** Although you're not limited to the *nnn*CANON arrangement, you must adhere to the rules in the steps that follow.

4. **Type in a three-digit folder number.** You can use any three numbers from 100 to 999, as long as those numbers are not already in use on that memory card. In other words, you can't have folders named 101CANON and 101SPAIN.

5. **Add a five-character description of your choice.** I use "EOSRP." However, you can use any uppercase or lowercase letters from A to z, plus the underscore character (to represent a space). You cannot use an actual space, nor any other characters, even if your computer allows them in a file name. An invalid folder name will end up being "invisible" to the EOS RP, even if it actually exists on your memory card.

With a little imagination (and caution, to avoid creating "bad" folder names), you can develop some useful folder names, and switch among them at will. I find this capability especially useful when working with very large cards, because I can do a great deal of organizing right on the card itself. Perhaps I have some images in a particular folder that I use as a "slide show" for display on my EOS RP's LCD screen. Or, I might want to sort images by location or date. For example, I could use 104_USA_, 105SPAIN, 106FRANC, or 107GBRIT to indicate the location where the images were shot.

File Numbering

Options: Continuous (default), Automatic Reset, Manual Reset

My preference: Continuous

The EOS RP will automatically apply a file number to each picture you take, using consecutive numbering for all your photos over a long period, spanning many different memory cards, starting over from scratch when you insert a new card, or when you manually reset the numbers. Numbers are applied from 0001 to 9999, at which time the camera creates a new folder on the card (100, 101, 102, and so forth), so you can have 0001 to 9999 in folder 100, then numbering will start over in folder 101.

The camera keeps track of the last number used in its internal memory. That can lead to a few quirks you should be aware of. For example, if you insert a memory card that had been used with a different camera, the EOS RP may start numbering with the next number after the highest number used by the previous camera. (I once had a brand-new Canon camera start numbering files in the 8,000 range.) I'll explain how this can happen next.

On the surface, the numbering system seems simple enough: In the menu, you can choose Continuous, Automatic Reset, or Manual Reset. Here is how each works:

- **Continuous.** If you're using a blank/reformatted memory card, the EOS RP will apply a number that is one greater than the number stored in the camera's internal memory. If the card is not blank and contains images, then the next number will be one greater than the highest number on the card *or* in internal memory. (In other words, if you want to use continuous file numbering consistently, you must always use a card that is blank or freshly formatted.) Here are some examples.

  - You've taken 4,235 shots with the camera, and you insert a blank/reformatted memory card. The next number assigned will be 4,236, based on the value stored in internal memory.

  - You've taken 4,235 shots with the camera, and you insert a memory card with a picture numbered 2,728. The next picture will be numbered 4,236.

  - You've taken 4,235 shots with the camera, and you insert a memory card with a picture numbered 8,281. The next picture will be numbered 8,282, and that value will be stored in the camera's menu as the "high" shot number (and will be applied when you next insert a blank card).

- **Automatic Reset.** If you're using a blank/reformatted memory card, the next photo taken will be numbered 0001. If you use a card that is not blank, the next number will be one greater than the highest number found on the memory card. Each time you insert a memory card, the next number will either be 0001 or one higher than the highest already on the card. Note that when your Folder number reaches 999 (that's potentially a lot of folders on one card!) and that folder has 9999 images, you will not be able to continue shooting until you replace the card with a different one.

■ **Manual Reset.** The EOS RP creates a new folder numbered one higher than the last folder created, and restarts the file numbers at 0001. Then, the camera uses the numbering scheme that was previously set, either Continuous or Automatic reset, each time you subsequently insert a blank or non-blank memory card.

Auto Rotate

Options: On: Camera, Computer (default); On: Computer Only; Off

My preference: Camera+Computer

You can turn this feature On or Off. When activated, the EOS RP rotates pictures taken in vertical orientation on the display screen so you don't have to turn the camera to view them comfortably. However, this orientation also means that the longest dimension of the image is shown using the shortest dimension of the display, so the picture is reduced in size. You have three options. The image can be autorotated when viewing in the camera *and* on your computer screen using your image-editing/viewing software (this choice is represented by a pair of camera/computer screen icons). The image can be marked to autorotate *only* when reviewing your image in your image editor or viewing software (just a computer screen icon is used). This option allows you to have rotation applied when using your computer, while retaining the ability to maximize the image on your display in the camera. The third choice is Off. The image will not be rotated when displayed in the camera or with your computer. Note that if you switch Auto Rotate off, any pictures shot while the feature is disabled will not be automatically rotated when you turn Auto Rotate back on; information embedded in the image file when the photo *is taken* is used to determine whether autorotation is applied.

Format Card

Options: Format Card, Low Level Format

My preference: N/A

Use this item to erase everything on your memory card and set up a fresh file system ready for use. When you select Format Card, a display appears showing the capacity of the card, how much of that space is currently in use, and two choices at the bottom of the screen to Cancel or OK (proceed with the format). Press the Trash button if you'd like to do a low-level format. That's a more basic format that removes all sectors from the card and creates new ones, which can help speed up a card that seems to be slow (because the camera must skip over "bad" sectors left behind from previous uses). An orange bar appears on the screen to show the progress of the formatting step.

Mode Guide

Options: Enable (default), Disable

My preference: Disable

When the Mode Guide is enabled, when you rotate the Mode Dial to a new shooting mode, a screen appears describing that mode (see Figure 13.3, left). Press the down directional button to see additional information (Figure 13.3, right). The descriptions are minimal, at best, and not really useful once you've been using the EOS RP for, say, 30 minutes or more. I recommend shutting the Mode Guide off once you've gained some familiarity with your camera.

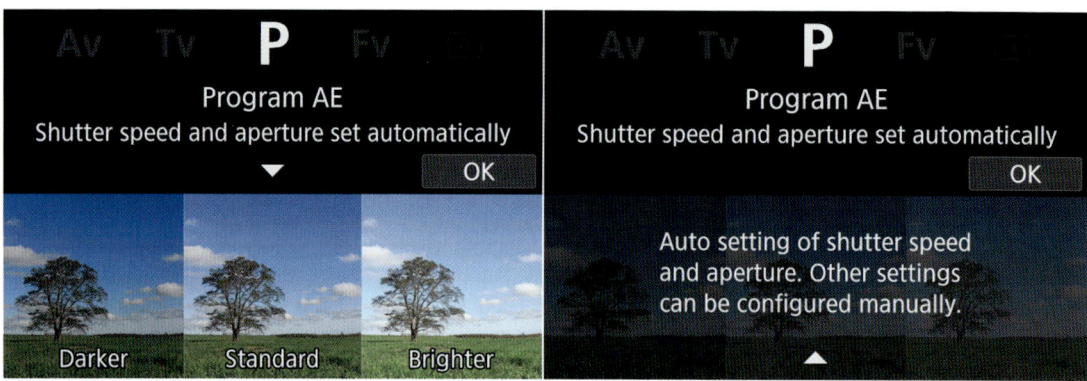

Figure 13.3 Mode Guide screens.

Feature Guide

Options: Enable (default), Disable

My preference: Disable

Like the Mode Guide, the tip message, which appears when you highlight an option on the Quick Control screen, is not especially helpful. For example, when you highlight the AF Method icon, a message is displayed "Choose the Autofocus Method." Thanks a bunch, Canon. I recommend turning this feature off.

Eco Mode

Options: On, Off (default)

My preference: Off. Carry multiple batteries so you don't have to worry about this.

This setting is the first in the Set-up 2 menu (see Figure 13.4). Even though your EOS RP uses the same LP-E17 battery pack supplied with some of Canon's digital SLRs, it is inherently more power hungry than traditional dSLRs you may have used. The sensor is energized any time you are using the viewfinder or LCD screen (rather than only when capturing a photo), and the EVF and LCD themselves suck up juice. Based on Canon's own specifications, you may expect to shoot only a few hundred exposures or capture just 2 hours, 20 minutes of movies with a single fully charged battery.

When Eco Mode is enabled, the LCD screen (but not the viewfinder) darkens drastically if the camera is not used for approximately two seconds, and turns off completely after 10 seconds. To reactivate, tap the shutter release to gain yourself another 2 to10 seconds of LCD viewing. While Eco Mode is a thoughtful feature on Canon's part, in practice it can be a major inconvenience, especially if you are using the LCD to compose your image (say, the camera is mounted on a tripod). In such cases, you'd definitely want to make sure Eco Mode is turned off. Even better, you can turn Eco Mode off and leave it off for the rest of your life though the simple expedient of buying a reasonable number of batteries. Swapping power cells every few hours is preferable to losing your LCD image at a critical moment. I use this feature only when I am down to my last battery (due to unforeseen circumstances, or, stupidity) and want to squeeze every bit of juice I can out of my remaining LP-E17.

Figure 13.4
The Set-up 2 menu.

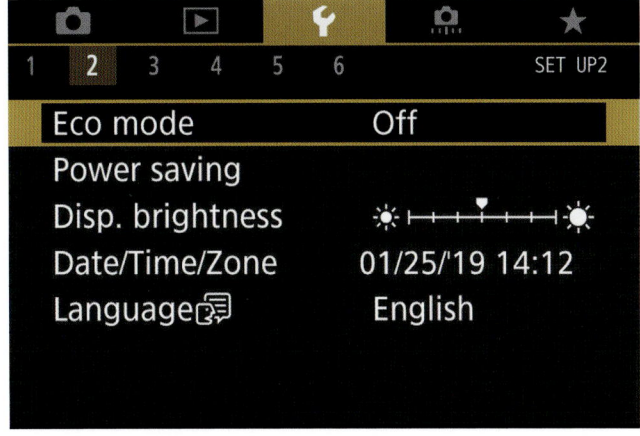

Power Saving

Options: Display Off: Default, 1 min.; Auto Power Off: Default, 1 min.; Viewfinder Off: Default, 3 min.

My preference: Display Off: 3 min.; Auto Power Off: 5 min.; Viewfinder Off: 3 min.

This setting allows you to adjust how long the EOS RP remains active before features are turned off to save power. As I noted with the Eco Mode explanation, intelligent power saving can be crucial with mirrorless cameras. This option is more useful and flexible than Eco Mode; you have three choices:

- **Display Off.** In this case, by "display," Canon is referring to the LCD screen. You can specify a delay of 15 seconds to 30 minutes. While the default value is 1 minute, as long as I have a spare battery or two with me, I'm more comfortable with a longer delay of 3 minutes. That gives me time to stop and think about what I am doing if I am working with menus or reviewing an image on the LCD. In special cases, longer delays are appropriate, say, if you have the camera on a tripod and are monitoring a live scene while waiting for wildlife or another subject to appear before taking a picture. If Eco Mode is active, this setting and Auto Power Off are disabled.

- **Auto Power Off.** This setting controls the amount of time the camera can remain idle before powering down. You can bring the EOS RP back to live by tapping the shutter button. I usually set this option for five minutes, but set a longer delay when shooting sports or taking street photos and I want the camera to be ready for a quick shot.

- **Viewfinder Off.** Power savings from switching off the electronic viewfinder are relatively minimal, which is why your only options are 1 minute, 3 minutes, and Disable. Regardless of the setting, the viewfinder reactivates when you bring the camera up to your eye, so a three-minute delay is reasonable. If you're in sports or photojournalism mode, you might want to disable automatic power down. Eco Mode doesn't turn off the viewfinder, so if Eco Mode is active, you can still use this setting to specify a delay of your choice.

Display Brightness

Options: Adjust brightness of viewfinder and/or LCD screen

My preference: N/A

I hope the Canon engineer who designed this feature got a bonus for cleverness. Like every other mirrorless camera I've used, the EOS RP allows you to adjust the brightness of the electronic viewfinder and LCD screen separately. But, unlike the others, when you access this particular entry, the camera automatically defaults to whichever display you happen to be using. Bring the camera up to your eye and press the left/right directional buttons to brighten or darken the electronic viewfinder display. Fix your attention on the LCD instead, and the adjustment screen switches to the back-panel display. You can then use the directional buttons or touch screen to make your adjustment.

Use the example image and the gray patches shown (see Figure 13.5) to decide whether the brightness is satisfactory. The thumbnail shows the last image viewed during Playback, so you can actually "calibrate" your display for your current shooting environment. You want to be able to see both the lightest and darkest steps at top and bottom of the gray scale, and not lose any of the steps in the middle. Brighter settings use more battery power, but can allow you to view an image on the LCD outdoors in bright sunlight. When you have the brightness you want, press the SET button to lock it in and return to the menu. At concerts, I tend to review my images using the electronic viewfinder; if I want to share images with a companion, I often dial down the brightness of the LCD screen to the minimum to avoid disturbing the other paying customers who might not be as interested in my results.

Figure 13.5
Adjust electronic viewfinder and LCD screen brightness for easier viewing under varying ambient lighting conditions.

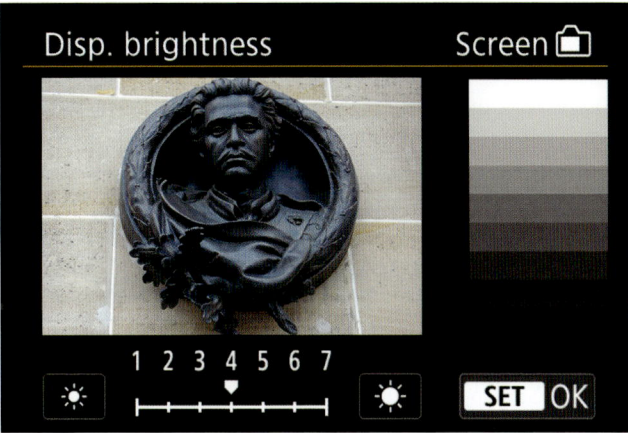

Date/Time/Zone

Options: Date, Time, Zone, Daylight Savings
My preference: N/A

Use this option to set the date and time, which will be embedded in the image file along with exposure information and other data. As first outlined in Chapter 1, you can set the date and time by following these steps:

1. Access this menu entry from the Set-up 2 menu.
2. Rotate the QCD to move the highlighting down to the Date/Time entry.
3. Press the SET button in the center of the QCD to access the Date/Time setting screen.
4. Rotate the QCD to select the value you want to change. When the gold box highlights the month, day, year, hour, minute, or second format you want to adjust, press the SET button to activate that value. A pair of up-/down-pointing triangles appears above the value.
5. Rotate the QCD to adjust the value up or down. Press the SET button to confirm the value you've entered.

6. Repeat steps 4 and 5 for each of the other values you want to change. The date format can be switched from the default mm/dd/yy to yy/mm/dd or dd/mm/yy; you can turn Daylight Savings time on or off, and choose an appropriate time zone.

7. When finished, rotate the QCD to select either OK (if you're satisfied with your changes) or Cancel (if you'd like to return to the Set-up 2 menu without making any changes). Press SET to confirm your choice.

8. When finished setting the date and time, press the MENU button to exit, or just tap the shutter release.

Language

Options: 29 languages

My preference: N/A

Choose from 29 languages for menu display, rotating the Quick Control Dial or using the directional buttons until the language you want to select is highlighted. Press the SET button to activate.

Video System

Options: For NTSC, For PAL

My preference: N/A

This setting, the first on the Set-up 3 screen (see Figure 13.6), controls the output of the EOS RP through the HDMI cable when you're displaying images on an external monitor. You can select either NTSC, used in the United States, Canada, Mexico, many Central, and South American, and Caribbean countries, much of Asia, and other countries; or PAL, which is used in the UK, much of Europe, Africa, India, China, and parts of the Middle East.

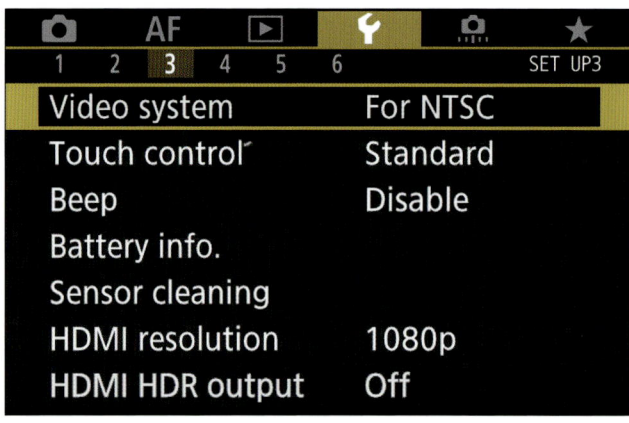

Figure 13.6
The Set-up 3 menu.

VIEWING ON A TELEVISION

Canon makes it quite easy to view your images on a high-definition television (HDTV). Purchase the optional HDMI Cable HTC-100 (or equivalent HDMI Micro C cable) and connect it to the HDMI OUT terminal just below the USB Type-C port on the left side of the camera.

Connect the other end to an HDMI input port on your television or monitor (my 42-inch HDTV has three of them; my 26-inch monitor has just two). Then turn on the camera and press the Playback button. The image will appear on the external TV/HDTV/monitor and will not be displayed on the camera's LCD. Most HDTV systems automatically show your images at the appropriate resolution if you set HDMI Resolution to Auto using the Set-up 3 entry described later in this chapter.

Touch Control

Options: Standard (default), Sensitive, Disable

My preference: Standard

Here you can specify how sensitive the touch screen is to your taps and strokes. Note that the screen responds to changes in capacitance (changes in an electrical charge), rather than pressure, so using a stylus or other object instead of a finger isn't advised. Moisture or protective covers for the LCD screen may also interfere with touch operation, although I've had no problems with GGS screens available from Amazon and elsewhere. If you find that your everyday handling of the EOS RP frequently triggers unwanted actions, you can disable touch control entirely if you never want to use it. Otherwise, set the amount of sensitivity that works best for digital control, so to speak. While Standard works best for most, those who use touch control frequently may want to try the Sensitive setting. However, at that setting, very rapid, light movements may not register.

Beep

Options: Enable (default), Touch Screen, Disable

My preference: Disable

The EOS RP's internal beeper provides a helpful chirp to signify various functions, such as the countdown of your camera's self-timer, when an image is in focus, and during touch operations. You can switch it off entirely if you want to avoid the beep because it's annoying, impolite, or distracting (at a concert or museum), or undesired for any other reason. In the Beep screen, choose Enable to activate, Disable to silence all beeps, or Touch Screen (which silences the beep only during touch screen operations), as you prefer. Press SET to activate your choice and exit.

Battery Information

Options: Register, Delete Info.

My preference: N/A

This entry is an exceptionally useful feature that allows you to view battery condition information and performance. I also own other Canon cameras which use the same battery, so I'm able to justify four batteries to shuttle between my multiple cameras. This feature makes it possible to see exactly how each battery you own is performing. When you select this menu choice, a Battery info screen like the one shown in Figure 13.7 appears:

- **Battery position.** The second line of the screen includes an icon that shows where the battery currently being evaluated is installed (usually the hand grip).

- **Power type.** Next to the position icon is an indicator that shows the model number of the battery installed, or shows that the DC power adapter is being used instead.

- **Remaining capacity.** The Battery check icon appears showing the remaining capacity visually, along with a percentage number that reads out in 1% increments. You can use this as a rough gauge of how much power you have remaining. If you're in the middle of an important shooting session, you might want to switch to a fully charged battery at the 25%–33% level to avoid interruptions at the worst probable time. (If you're using six AA batteries in the BG-E6 grip instead of LP-E6 packs, only this battery capacity notice will appear; the other indicators are not shown.)

- **Recharge performance.** This indicator shows how well your battery pack is accepting and holding a charge. Three green bars mean that the pack's performance is fine; two bars show that recharge performance is degraded a little. A red bar indicates that your pack is on its last legs and should be replaced soon. To lengthen the service time of your batteries, you might want to rotate usage among several different packs, so they all "age" at roughly the same rate.

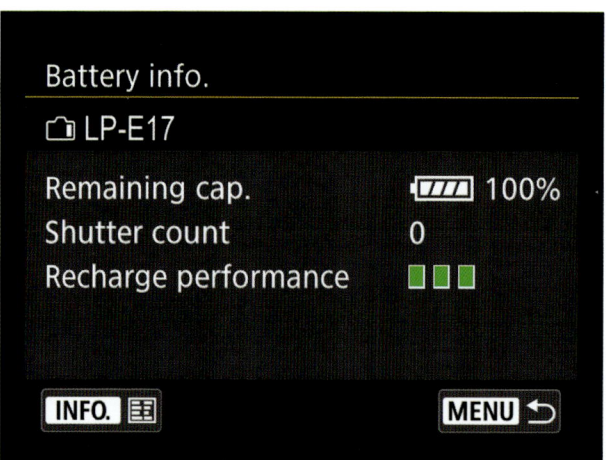

Figure 13.7
View the battery type and position, remaining capacity, and the performance of your pack.

Sensor Cleaning

Options: Auto Cleaning, Clean Now (default), Clean Manually

My preference: N/A

One of the Canon EOS RP's most useful features is the automatic sensor cleaning system that reduces or eliminates the need to clean your camera's sensor manually using brushes, swabs, or bulb blowers. Canon has applied anti-static coatings to the sensor and other portions of the camera body interior to counter charge build-ups that attract dust. A separate filter over the sensor vibrates ultrasonically each time the EOS RP is powered on or off, shaking loose any dust.

Use this menu entry to enable or disable automatic sensor cleaning on power up (select Auto Cleaning to choose) or to activate automatic cleaning during a shooting session (select Clean Now). You can also choose the Clean Manually option to open the EOS RP's shutter and clean the sensor yourself with a blower, brush, or swab. If the battery level is too low to safely carry out the cleaning operation, the EOS RP will let you know and refuse to proceed, unless you use the optional AC Adapter Kit ACK-E6N with the DC Coupler DR-E6.

HDMI Resolution

Options: Auto (default), 1080p

My preference: 1080p if your device accepts it

As I mentioned earlier, your EOS RP can output to an external monitor or video recorder, using a cable that has an HDMI Mini-C connector to fit the camera and a standard HDMI connector on the other end to link to your device. You can set this option to Auto, in which case the camera will attempt to ascertain the correct resolution for the connected device, and then direct its output in that format. There may be some delay while the appropriate resolution is achieved, but if you know your device can accept 1080p video, you can go ahead and select that setting to avoid the time lag.

The only problem with this procedure is that the EOS RP has a nasty habit of *not* adjusting to the correct resolution for some devices, complicated by the fact that you cannot then select the right setting yourself. I've encountered several devices, including my BlackMagic Intensity Shuttle capture device, that the EOS RP is unable to recognize automatically, and which require a setting that Canon does not allow you to make manually. I checked with Canon and they offer no solution; there is no way to manually specify a resolution other than 1080p.

HDMI HDR Output

Options: Off/On

My preference: N/A

Television innovations come and go, but some are more likely than others to catch on, and Canon is keeping abreast of the curve. Unlike, say, 3D TV (which suffered from a lack of content and consumer desire and had mercifully died by 2018), High Dynamic Range (HDR) TV is here to stay. If your current television doesn't have HDR, it's likely your next one will (along with 4K display). In that case, you'll be able to output your EOS RP's RAW images for display on your nifty new set. They'll look marvelous (at least, that's what I'm told).

In addition to an HDR-compatible TV, you'll need to remember to set up your television's input to accept HDR images. While viewing HDR output from your camera, some features, such as RAW processing, are not available. The camera will also send JPEG images instead of RAW to your HDR TV when displaying multiple-exposure RAW images and photos shot with the L (ISO 50 equivalent) sensitivity setting.

Shooting Information Display

Options: Screen Information Settings, Viewfinder Info/Toggle Settings, Viewfinder Vertical Display, Grid Display, Histogram Display, Focus Distance Display, Reset

My preference: N/A

This is the first entry in the Set-up 4 menu (see Figure 13.8). One of the advantages of cameras that have electronic displays for both viewfinder and LCD screen is that a wealth of relevant information can remain in constant view as you shoot. You're not forced to remove your eye from the viewfinder to check shooting information, to review images in Playback, or to make changes using the Quick Control and conventional menu systems. Everything you need to know can be shown on both displays.

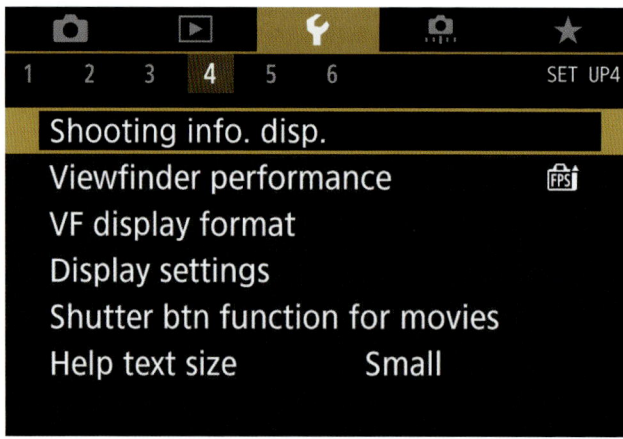

Figure 13.8
The Set-up 4 menu.

One of the *disadvantages* of cameras that have electronic displays for both viewfinder and LCD screen is that all that data must be overlaid on the image frame, which can be quite cluttered—sometimes with information that you really don't care about at the moment. Fortunately, you can customize what information appears on the shooting information displays, segregating some data onto alternate screens, and cycle among the screens you *do* want to see at the press of the INFO button.

You can define up to five different LCD screen layouts, and three different viewfinder configurations using this menu entry. When you choose it in the Set-up 4 menu, a sub-menu like the one shown in Figure 13.9 appears, with six options, plus Reset. I'm going to explain each of them in turn.

Figure 13.9
Shooting Information Display Options.

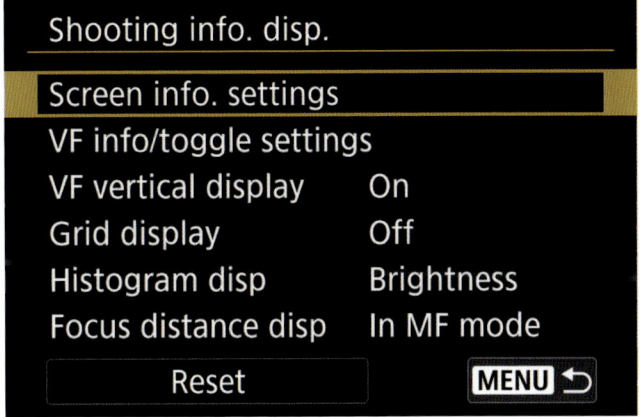

Screen Info Settings

This is where you activate/deactivate and edit up to five LCD screen displays. Figure 13.10 (left) shows the enable/disable options, shown numbered from 1 to 5 in the right column. To enable one of the five screens, highlight it using the up/down buttons and press SET to activate (marking with a check) or deactivate (removing a check that is already there). At least one screen must be active; you can't hide them all.

To edit the type of information that appears on a given screen, highlight it and press INFO. An Edit Screen like the one shown at right in Figure 13.10 appears. Five information types appear in the right column, representing (top to bottom) Basic Shooting Information, Detailed Shooting Information, On-Screen Buttons (display of icons, such as Focus Method, you can tap to make adjustments), Histogram Display, and Electronic Level. As with the numbered screens, you can activate any combination of information types for a given screen.

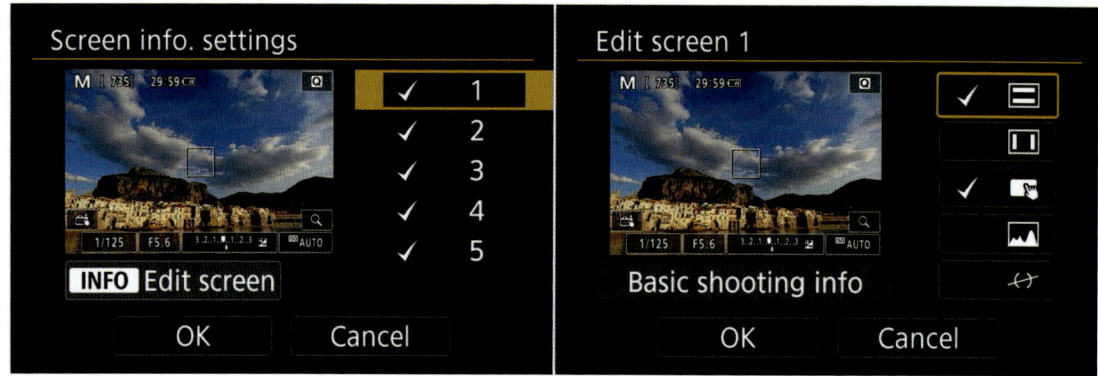

Figure 13.10 Enable/disable specific screens (left); edit each screen's contents (right).

You obviously won't want all information to appear on all screens; it makes sense to reserve one screen for Basic Shooting Information, another for Detailed Shooting Information, and using the others either to provide one specific type of data, or a combination you find useful. When you're finished, highlight OK to confirm or Cancel to eliminate your changes, then SET to exit.

When you're using the LCD screen, cycle among the displays you've set up by pressing the INFO button.

Viewfinder Info/Toggle Settings

This option operates very much like the LCD screen setup, except (on the theory that the viewfinder should be kept free of clutter as much as possible) only three screens can be enabled/disabled, and the choices for each of the three are limited to a single trio of settings: Detailed Shooting Information, Histogram, and Electronic viewfinder. Set up any or all three of the available screens with appropriate options, as described above. (See Figure 13.11.)

When you're using the electronic viewfinder, cycle among the displays you've set up by pressing the INFO button.

Vertical Viewfinder Display

Even though your electronic viewfinder may bristle with overlaid information, you can still read it when shooting vertically oriented pictures. This one's a no brainer: set to On, and when you rotate the camera, the information display rotates with it, so you can still read it.

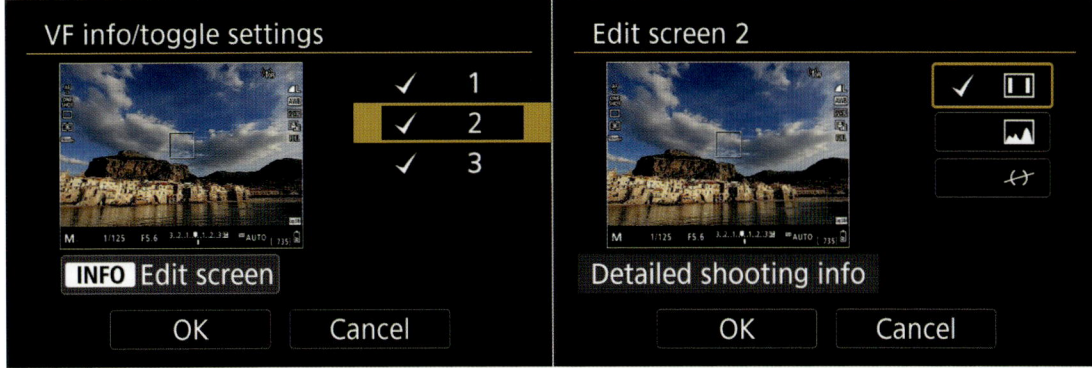

Figure 13.11 Enable/disable specific viewfinder screens (left); edit each screen's information (right).

Grid Display

Those helpful grids discussed earlier in this chapter in the Playback section are also available for use while shooting. You can superimpose a 3 × 3, 6 × 4, or 3 × 3 plus diagonal lines grid over your image during shooting, or disable the grid display entirely.

Histogram Display

There's only room for one histogram on the screen when shooting, but you can choose whether the histogram displayed by your selected LCD screens is a brightness or RGB histogram, and whether it is displayed in large or small size. Choose the configuration you prefer, but for most the brightness histogram provides sufficient information while shooting. The RGB histogram may be one to study during playback to see exactly what went right (or wrong) with the tonal rendition of your image.

Focus Distance Display

Canon RF-mount lenses communicate a remarkable amount of information to the camera, so you have the option of showing the actual focus distance on the display. It's arrayed as a scale on the bottom of the display. Best of all, you can choose *when* this information is supplied: in Manual Focus mode, any time you are actually focusing (either with autofocus or manual focus), always, or never (Disable). Close-up and macro photographers will particularly find this feature useful.

Reset

Highlight Reset and press SET to return all the shooting information displays to their default values. The Screen Info/VF Info screens are all enabled with preset values; viewfinder vertical rotation and grid display are on, histograms are set to Brightness, and focus distance display is returned to In MF Mode only.

Viewfinder Performance

Options: Power Saving, Smooth (default)

My preference: Smooth

One objection that mirrorless cameras like the EOS RP have handily overcome is the quality of the electronic viewfinder display. Early EVFs were low resolution, slow in refresh rate, and often looked jerky when compared to the smooth display of the optical viewfinders found in dSLRs. With 2.63 million dots, your camera's viewfinder has very high resolution and boasts a 0.70X magnification factor that make it almost indistinguishable from an optical display. All that visual horsepower comes with a power penalty. If juice is at a premium, you can use this setting to switch to a slightly slower refresh rate with a display that's still good. However, most of the time—and especially when shooting sports or other action—you can safely leave this setting on Smooth and enjoy one of the best viewfinder displays available in a mirrorless camera.

Viewfinder Display Format

Options: Display 1 (default), Display 2

My preference: N/A

Your EOS RP offers two slightly different viewfinder display formats. Your choice is just a matter of preference. With Display 1, the image fills the viewfinder, with information along the bottom displayed in a black bar, and any information shown at left and right sides overlaid over the image area. Display 2 shrinks the image display slightly to provide room for black bars at right and left sides, so information icons can be displayed in those bars rather than overlaid on the image. If you prefer to declutter your image area as much as possible, choose Display 2. I'm accustomed to shooting mirrorless cameras and don't mind the overlaid data when it appears.

Display Settings

Options: Auto (default), Manual: Viewfinder, Screen

My preference: Auto

This option controls how the EOS RP switches between the LCD screen and electronic viewfinder:

- **Auto.** The LCD screen is used for display by default, but the camera switches to the viewfinder when you bring the camera up to your eye, or anything else approaches the eye sensor next to the viewfinder.

- **Manual.** Specify either viewfinder or LCD screen, and the EOS RP will use only that display. I use this frequently at concerts and stage performances when I don't want the LCD screen illuminating and bothering the other paying customers. I set the display to Manual: Viewfinder, and I can then do all my composing, picture review, and menu navigation using only the electronic viewfinder.

Shutter Button Function For Movies

Options: Half press: Metering and Movie Servo AF, Metering and One-Shot AF, Metering Only; Full press: Disable during movie shooting, Shoots Movies

My preference: Half press: Metering and One-Shot AF; Full press: Disable during movie shooting

This setting specifies what a half-press and a full press of the shutter release will do during movie shooting. **Note:** The Full press option is available *only* when the camera's Mode Dial is set to Movie mode.

- **Half press.** Partially depressing the shutter release during movie shooting always starts exposure metering. You can choose whether *only* metering occurs as well, or whether Movie Servo AF *or* One-Shot AF are initiated when you half-press the shutter release.
- **Full press.** I prefer to use the Movie button to start video capture, so I set this to No Function. If you prefer, you can choose Start/Stop Movie Recording and use the shutter release as an alternate Movie button.

Help Text Size

Options: Small (default), Large

My preference: Large

When you first begin using your EOS RP, you may find yourself pressing the INFO button when the INFO Help message is displayed below a menu. Pressing it will pop up a screen with information on how to choose options for that menu item. You won't need this help after you've had your camera for a while, but as long as you avail yourself of this aid, you might as well have it displayed in large, clear text. You can press the up/down directional buttons to scroll within the help text display.

Wireless Communications Settings

Options: Wi-Fi Settings, Wi-Fi Function, Bluetooth Function, Send Images to Smartphone, Nickname, Clear Settings

My preference: See Chapter 6

This entry, one of only two in the Set-up 5 menu (not shown), allows you to specify wireless communication settings. I explained these functions in detail in Chapter 6, and won't repeat those instructions here.

GPS Device Settings

Options: Disable GPS, Select GPS Receiver, Smartphone

My preference: See Chapter 6

This is the other entry in the Set-up 5 menu. Your options for using the Canon GP-E2 were explained in more detail in Chapter 6, and won't be repeated here.

Multi-Function Lock

Options: Main Dial, Quick Control Dial, Touch Control, Control Ring

My preference: N/A

This is the first entry on the Set-up 6 menu (see Figure 13.12). Your EOS RP includes a sliding lock switch concentric with the Quick Control Dial. Slide it to forward when you want to prevent the use of the Main Dial, Quick Control Dial, Touch Controls, or Control Ring from accidentally changing a setting. You can select any or all four of the controls to lock, while freeing the others (or none) to act normally. I use this sometimes when I am using manual exposure, especially when I'm fumbling around in a darkened environment, and don't want to unintentionally manipulate my settings. The Multi-Function Lock screen has one option for each control; highlight the control and press SET to lock or unlock it. A check mark appears next to the control's name when it's locked, and an L/Lock indicator appears in the viewfinder, top-panel LCD, and LCD screen (see Figure 13.13). In Scene Intelligent Auto mode, only touch control can be locked.

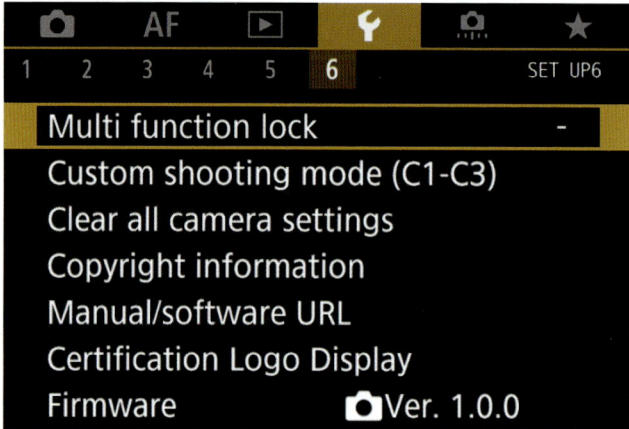

Figure 13.12
Set-up 6 menu.

Figure 13.13
Lock any or all of these four: Main Dial, Quick Control Dial, Touch Control, and Control Ring.

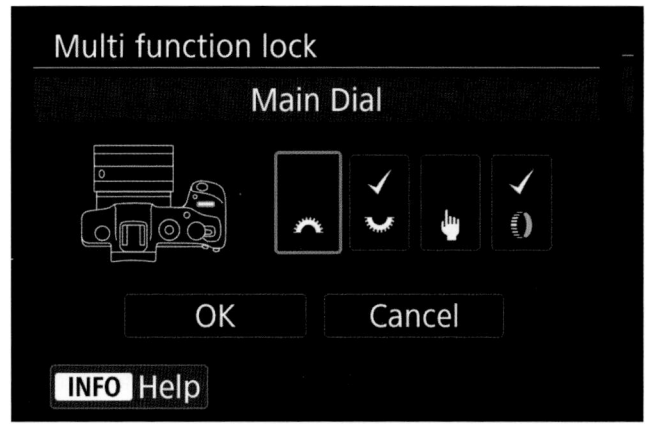

Custom Shooting Mode (C1–C3)

Options: Register Settings; Clear Settings; Auto Update Settings, Enable/Disable

My preference: N/A

This entry allows you to register your EOS RP's current camera shooting settings and file them away in the C1, C2, or C3 positions and access them when pressing the MODE button. Doing this overwrites any settings previously stored at that position. You can also clear the settings for any of the three MODE positions individually, returning them to their factory default values.

Register your favorite settings for use in particular situations. I have stored settings for sports, portraits, and landscapes. If you switch to C1, C2, or C3 and forget what settings you've made for that slot, just press the INFO button to view the current settings. Keep in mind that My Menu settings are not stored individually. You can have only one roster of My Menu entries available for all the Mode Dial's positions.

This menu choice has only three options: Register Settings (which stores your current settings in your choice of C1, C2, or C3), Clear Settings (which erases the settings in C1, C2, or C3), and Auto Update Settings. When the latter is set to Enable, any changes you make to your settings in C1, C2, or C3 modes will be stored in that memory slot; use Disable to preserve your registered setting as-is, ignoring any changes you made while using that Custom Shooting mode. Note that you must use this menu entry to clear your settings; when using C1, C2, or C3, the Clear Settings option in the Set-up 3 menu is disabled. The Clear all Custom Func. (C.Fn) option in the Custom Functions menu is disabled as well.

To perform these tasks, just follow these steps:

1. **Make your settings.** Set the EOS RP to an exposure mode other than Scene Intelligent Auto.

2. **Access Camera user settings.** Navigate to the Custom shooting mode option in the Set-up 6 menu, and press SET.

3. **Choose function.** Choose Register Settings if you want to store your EOS RP's current settings in C1, C2, or C3; or select Clear Settings if you want to erase the settings stored in either location. Press SET to access the settings screen for your choice.

4. **Store/Clear settings.** The individual screens for storing/clearing are virtually identical. Use the QCD to highlight Mode Dial: C1, Mode Dial: C2, or Mode Dial: C3, and press SET to store or clear the settings for that position. (You'll be given a choice to proceed or cancel first.)

5. **Auto update.** Keep in mind that if you change a setting while using one of the custom shooting modes and want to retain the new settings, your stored settings can be automatically updated to reflect the modifications. Select Auto Update Set. and choose Enable to activate this option. If you'd rather retain your custom settings until you manually decide to update, select Disable instead.

6. **Exit.** When you confirm, you'll be returned to the Set-up 6 menu. Press the MENU button or tap the shutter release button to exit the menu system entirely.

Clear All Camera Settings

Options: Clear settings

My preference: N/A

This menu choice resets all the settings to their default values. Regardless of how you've set up your EOS RP, it will be adjusted to One-Shot AF mode, Automatic AF-point selection, Evaluative metering, JPEG Fine Large image quality, Automatic ISO, sRGB color mode, Automatic White Balance, and Standard Picture Style. Any changes you've made to exposure compensation, flash exposure compensation, and white balance will be canceled, and any bracketing for exposure or white balance nullified. Custom white balances and Dust Delete Data will be erased. Tables showing the factory default settings and my recommendations were provided in Chapter 3.

Remember, Custom Functions and Camera User Settings will *not* be cleared. If you want to cancel those as well, you'll need to use the Custom shooting mode option (described previously) and the Custom Functions clearing option.

Copyright Information

Options: Display Copyright Information, Enter Author's Name, Enter Copyright Details, Delete Copyright Information

My preference: N/A

Here's where you can give yourself credit for the great photos you're shooting with your EOS RP:

- **Display Copyright Info.** Enable or disable embedding copyright information in your image files. If you're a double-naught secret agent who wants to submit spy photos anonymously, you'll definitely want to disable copyright information.

- **Enter Author's Name.** You can add your own name (up to 63 characters) to each image file.

- **Enter Copyright Details.** You can add more information using the expanded character set. Up to 63 characters can be entered. Note that no copyright symbol is available. While some use a lowercase *c* within parentheses, technically the correct notification would be (Copyright) or (Copr.).

- **Delete Copyright Information.** This removes all the data you've entered and gives you a clean slate, so to speak.

Manual/Software URL

Options: None

My preference: N/A

This entry displays a URL you can type in to access manuals and software for your EOS RP, as well as a QR code you can scan with your smart device to whisk you off to the same web page.

Certification Logo Display

Options: None

My preference: N/A

This is an informational screen, which allows Canon to add certification data (similar to what is printed on the bottom panel of the camera) via a firmware upgrade, and without the need to manufacture new stickers for the camera bottom.

Firmware

Options: Update firmware

My preference: N/A

You can see the current firmware release in use in the menu listing. If you want to update to a new firmware version, insert a memory card containing the binary file, and press the SET button to begin the process.

14

The Custom Functions and My Menus

Custom Functions let you tailor the behavior of your camera in a variety of different ways, such as the function carried out when the SET button is pressed. If you don't like the default way the camera carries out a particular task, you may be able to do something about it. You can find the Custom Functions in their own one-page menu, color-coded orange-brown, and visible whenever you are using P, Fv, Tv, Av, M, and B exposure modes. The menu has three groups of commands (Custom Functions I, II, and III), and two entries that return your Custom Functions and customized settings to their factory defaults. (See Figure 14.1.)

Figure 14.1
The Custom
Settings menu.

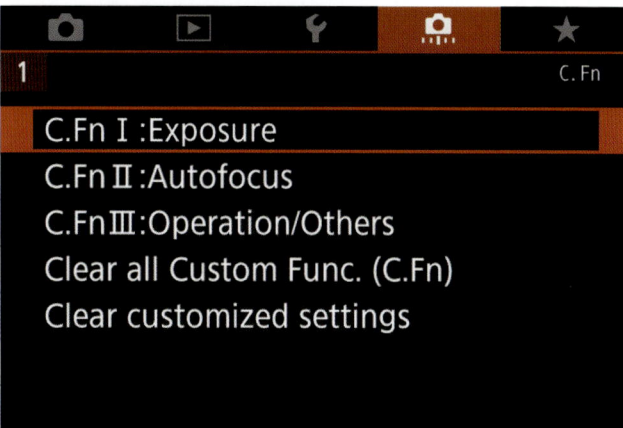

The Custom Functions menu contains these entries:

- **C.Fn I: Exposure**
  - Exposure Level Increments
  - ISO Speed Setting Increments
  - Bracketing Auto Cancel
  - Bracketing Sequence
  - Number of Bracketed Shots
  - Safety Shift
  - AE Lock Metering Mode After Focus

- **C.Fn II: Autofocus**
  - Tracking Sensitivity
  - Acceleration/Deceleration Tracking
  - AF Point Auto Switching
  - Lens Drive when AF Impossible
  - Limit AF Methods
  - Orientation Linked AF Point
  - Initial Servo AF Point for Face Tracking

- **C.Fn III: Operation/Others**
  - Dial Direction During Tv/Av
  - Control Ring Rotation
  - Focus Ring Rotation
  - RF Lens MF Focus Ring Sensitivity
  - Customize Buttons
  - Customize Dials
  - Release Shutter Without Lens
  - Retract Lens on Power Off
  - Audio Compression

- **Clear commands:**
  - Clear Customized Settings
  - Clear All Custom Functions

Of the 23 Custom Functions, 16 consist of Custom Functions that have from two to four numbered options, as you can see in Figure 14.2. I'll explain what each of those choices do, but not bog you down with a bunch of illustrations showing how to make this setting or that. The remaining seven use graphical screens to make adjustments and may merit an illustration or two.

Navigating Custom Functions

This quick overview is all you need to know to be able to adjust the Custom Functions that have numbered options. These non-graphical entries all work in the same way. (I'll explain the graphical entries later in this chapter.)

■ **Custom Functions category.** Choose the settings screen for each of the main Custom Function categories and press SET to produce a screen like the one shown in Figure 14.2. At the top of the settings screen is a label that tells you which category that screen represents, either C.Fn I (Exposure), C.Fn II (Autofocus), or C.Fn III (Operation/Others).

■ **Name of currently selected Current Function.** Use the touch screen arrows at the left and right of the screen or the left/right directional buttons to select the function you want to adjust. The name of the function currently selected appears at the top of the screen, and its number is marked with an overscore in the row of numbers at the bottom of the screen. You don't need to memorize the function numbers.

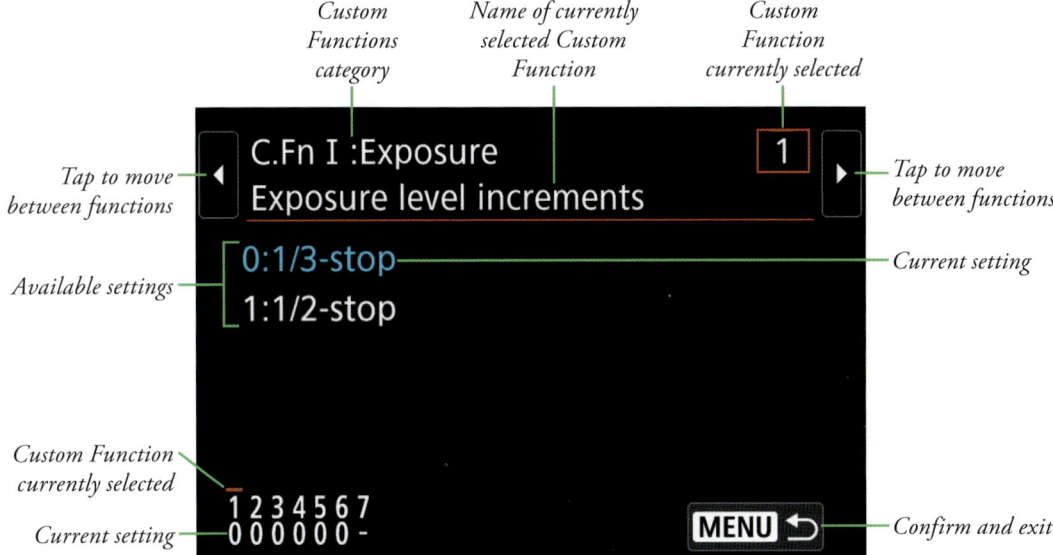

Figure 14.2 Each C.Fn screen with numbered settings has two to four options numbered 0 to 3, represented by the numbers at the bottom of the screen. The currently selected function has a gold line above it.

- **Function currently selected.** The function number appears in two places. In the upper-right corner you'll find a box with the current function clearly designated. In the lower half of the screen are two lines of numbers. The upper row has numbers from 1 to 7 (for C.Fn I and C.Fn II) or 1 to 9 (for C.Fn III), representing the individual Custom Function. The second row shows the number of the current setting. If the setting is other than the default value (a zero), it will be colored blue, so you can quickly see which Custom Functions have been modified. The currently selected function will have a gold line above it.

- **Available settings.** The setting options are numbered. Many have only two choices, several have a total of three or four. The current setting is highlighted in blue. You can use the up/down directional buttons to scroll to the option you want and then choose SET to select it; then press MENU to confirm and back out of the Custom Functions menus.

- **Current setting.** Underneath each Custom Function in the row at the bottom left is a number from 0 to 4 that represents the current setting for that function.

- **Custom function currently selected.** When a function is selected, the currently selected option appears in a highlighted box at upper right. As you scroll up and down the option list, the setting in the box changes to indicate an alternate value. Press SET to activate that setting's option selection.

Custom Function I (C.Fn I): Exposure

This is the Custom Function category you can use to set the increments for exposure and ISO, define bracketing parameters, and change a few other settings.

C.Fn I-1: Exposure Level Increments

Options: 1/3 stop (default), 1/2 stop

My preference: 0: 1/3 stop

This setting tells the EOS RP the size of the "jumps" it should use when making exposure adjustments—either one-third or one-half stop. The increment you specify here applies to f/stops, shutter speeds, EV changes, and autoexposure bracketing.

- **0: 1/3 stop.** Choose this setting when you want the finest increments between shutter speeds and/or f/stops. For example, the EOS RP will use shutter speeds such as 1/60th, 1/80th, 1/100th, and 1/125th second, and f/stops such as f/5.6, f/6.3, f/7.1, and f/8, giving you (and the autoexposure system) maximum control.

- **1: 1/2 stop.** Use this setting when you want larger and more noticeable changes between increments. The EOS RP will apply shutter speeds such as 1/60th, 1/125th, 1/250th, and 1/500th second, and f/stops including f/5.6, f/6.7, f/8, f/9.5, and f/11. These coarser adjustments are useful when you want more dramatic changes between different exposures.

C.Fn I-2: ISO Speed Setting Increments

Options: 1/3 stop (default), 1 stop

My preference: 1/3 stop

This setting determines the size of the "jumps" made when adjusting ISO—either one-third or one full stop. At the one-third stop setting, typical ISO values would be 100, 125, 160, 200, and so forth. Switch to the one-stop setting, and ISO values would be 100, 200, 400, 800, and so forth. The larger increment can help you leap from an ISO setting to one that's twice (or half) as sensitive with one click.

- **0: 1/3 stop.** Choose this setting when you want the finest increments between ISO settings.

- **1: 1 stop.** Use this setting when you want larger increments between ISO settings. Because one-third stop adjustments may not make much of a difference, those who want to be able to make ISO changes more quickly may value the coarser increments. I'm usually not rushed, so I do tend to keep the default 1/3 stop setting. Note that even though ISO 40000 is not a full-stop change (from ISO 32000) it is available even when this 1 stop increment is in effect.

C.Fn I-3: Bracketing Auto Cancel

Options: Enable (default), Disable

My preference: 0: Enable

When this Auto Cancel feature is activated (the default), AEB (Auto Exposure Bracketing) and WB-BKT (White Balance Bracketing) are cancelled when you turn the EOS RP off, change lenses, use the flash, or change memory cards; when Auto Cancel is deactivated, bracketing remains in effect until you manually turn it off or use the flash. When Auto Cancel is switched off, the AEB and WB-BKT settings will be kept even when the power switch is turned to the OFF position. The flash still cancels autoexposure bracketing, but your settings are retained.

I prefer the Enable setting, because I generally shoot a series of bracketed exposures and then turn off the camera when I am finished.

C.Fn I-4: Bracketing Sequence

Options: 0−+ (default), −0+, +0−

My preference: −0+

You can define the sequence in which AEB and WB-BKT series are exposed. For exposure bracketing, you can determine whether the order is metered exposure, decreased exposure, increased exposure or decreased exposure, metered exposure, increased exposure. Or with white balance bracketing, if your bias preference is set to blue/amber in the WB SHIFT/BKT adjustments in the Shooting 4 menu, the white balance sequence when option 0 is selected will be current WB, more blue, more amber. If your bias preference is set to magenta/green, then the sequence for option 0 will be current WB, more magenta, more green. Because I shoot so many HDR images to merge in Photoshop, I prefer the −0+ sequence, which starts with less exposure, metered exposure, and plus exposure, as that is the way I bracketed back in the film days.

■ **0: 0−+.** Exposure sequence is metered exposure, decreased exposure, increased exposure (0,−,+). White balance sequence is current WB, more blue/more magenta (depending on how your bias is set), more amber/more green (ditto).

■ **1: −0+.** The sequence is decreased exposure, metered exposure, increased exposure (−, 0, +). White balance sequence is more blue/more magenta, current WB, more amber/more green.

■ **2: +0−.** The sequence is increased exposure, metered exposure, decreased exposure. White balance sequence is more amber/more green, current WB, more blue/more magenta.

C.Fn I-5: Number of Bracketed Shots

Options: 2, 3 (default), 5, or 7 shots

My preference: 3

Your choices are 2, 3, 5, or 7 shots in a bracket sequence. I find that with an increment of 2/3 or one full stop, three bracketed exposures are enough that one of them will be close to optimum.

C.Fn I-6: Safety Shift

Options: Disable (default), Shutter Speed/Aperture, ISO Speed

My preference: Disable

Ordinarily, both Aperture-priority and Shutter-priority modes work fine, because you'll select an f/stop or shutter speed that allows the EOS RP to produce a correct exposure using the other type of setting (shutter speed for Av; aperture for Tv). However, when lighting conditions change, it may not be possible to select an appropriate setting with the available exposure options, and the camera will be unable to take a picture at all. (**Note:** for this and other similar discussions, Fv mode is considered the same as Av or Tv mode when you select either aperture or shutter speed manually.)

For example, you might be at a concert shooting the performers and, to increase your chances of getting a sharp image, you've selected Tv or Fv mode and a shutter speed of 1/250th second. Under bright lights and with an appropriate ISO setting, the EOS RP might select f/5.6, f/4, or even f/2.8. Then, in a dramatic moment, the stage lights are dimmed significantly. An exposure of 1/250th second at f/2 is called for, but your lens has an f/2.8 maximum aperture. If you've used this Custom Function to allow the EOS RP to override your selection, the camera will automatically switch to 1/125th second to allow the picture to be taken at f/2.8.

Safety Shift will make similar adjustments if your scene suddenly becomes too bright; although, in practice, you'll find that the override will be needed most often when using Tv mode. It's easier to "run out of" f/stops, which generally range no smaller than f/22 or f/32, than to deplete the available supply of shutter speeds, which can be as brief as 1/8000th second. For example, if you're shooting at ISO 400 in Tv mode at 1/1000th second, an extra-bright beach scene could easily call for an f/stop smaller than f/22, causing overexposure. However, Safety Shift would bump your shutter speed up to 1/2000th second with no problem.

On the other hand, if you were shooting under the same illumination in Av mode with the preferred aperture set to f/16, the EOS RP could use 1/1000th, 1/2000th, 1/4000th, or 1/8000th second shutter speeds to retain that f/16 aperture under conditions that are 2X, 4X, 8X, or 16X as bright as normal daylight. No Safety Shift would be needed, even if the ISO were (for some unknown reason) set much higher than the ISO 400 used in this example. These are your options:

- **0: Disable.** Turn off Safety Shift. Your specified shutter speed or f/stop remains locked in, even if conditions are too bright or too dim for an appropriate exposure. Use this option if you'd prefer to have the shot taken at the shutter speed, aperture, or ISO you've selected under all circumstances, even if it means an improperly exposed photo. You might be able to salvage the photo in your image editor.

- **1: Shutter Speed/Aperture.** Safety Shift is activated for Tv and Av modes. The EOS RP will adjust the preferred shutter speed or f/stop to allow a correct exposure. If you don't mind having your camera countermand your orders, this option can save images that otherwise might be incorrectly exposed. Use when working with a shutter speed or aperture that is *preferable,* but not critical.

- **2: ISO Speed.** This option operates in Program AE (P) mode as well as Tv and Av modes. Think of it as an "emergency" Auto ISO option. You can manually select your preferred ISO setting, and the EOS RP will generally stick with that, but you can adjust the ISO setting if required to produce an acceptable exposure. If you've selected a minimum and maximum allowable ISO range in the ISO Speed Settings entry of the Shooting 2 menu (as explained in Chapter 11), this setting will honor those limits *unless* your current manually selected ISO is outside those boundaries.

For example, if you've chosen a minimum and maximum Auto ISO range of ISO 200–800, this setting will stay within that range when adjusting ISO (even though you have Auto ISO off), but if your camera is currently manually set to ISO 100 or a value higher than ISO 800, it will go ahead and use the extra values, too.

C.Fn I-7: AE Lock Metering Mode After Focus

Options: Lock: Evaluative (default), Partial, Spot, Center-weighted Average metering (Any or all)

My preference: N/A

If you find yourself frequently using the * button to lock exposure, you may find this entry handy. You can order the EOS RP to automatically lock the exposure as soon as autofocus is achieved in One-Shot AF mode by pressing the shutter release halfway. There is no need to press the * button; simply keep the shutter release depressed halfway until you press it all the way down to take a picture, or release it. Highlight any of the four metering mode options (Evaluative, Partial, Spot, or Center-weighted Averaging) and press SET to enable exposure lock for that mode. A check mark appears above the metering mode, and you can enable or disable the feature for any, all, or none. (See Figure 14.3.) The exposure lock does not apply to Servo mode.

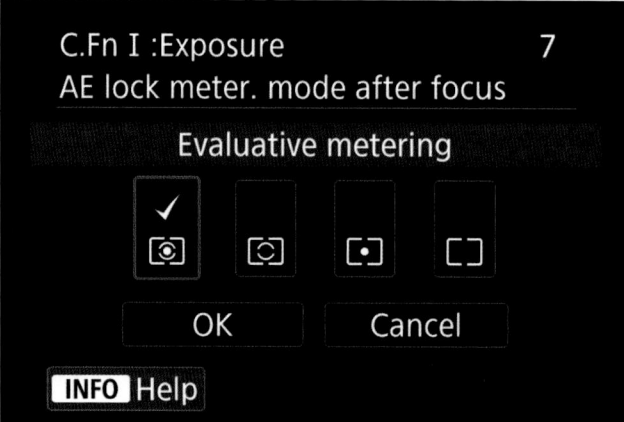

Figure 14.3

Lock exposure after autofocusing for any of the four metering modes.

Custom Function II (C.Fn II): Autofocus

This menu tab offers several options for autofocus, including important tracking functions. The first three entries are graphical, but their adjustments consist only of a slider you can adjust with the left/right directional buttons or the touch screen.

C.Fn II-1: Tracking Sensitivity

Options: Locked On (−2) to Responsive (+2); Default: Standard (0)

My preference: N/A

This feature determines how quickly the camera unlocks focus from the subject it is currently tracking in Servo AF mode, and focuses instead on another subject that intervenes. For example, if you're shooting a football game as a running back is breaking through the line and a referee bolts along the sideline in front of you. With this feature set to Responsive, the camera will very quickly switch to the ref, and then should return its attention to the running back—but often, not quickly enough. A better choice would be to use Locked On, so that the camera briefly ignores the referee, who is likely to have moved on in a second or two. Focus tracking will remain on your running back. Your options include:

- **0: Standard.** At the 0 setting, response to movement is a bit slower, so that the camera doesn't constantly refocus as subjects move about the frame. This is the default and should be used when there is only moderate movement, and especially if the movement is across the width or height of the frame (rather than coming toward you or away from you), and when you're using a small f/stop, because the increased depth-of-field will eliminate the need for most re-focusing.

- **1: Locked On (–1 or –2).** At the –1 and –2 settings, the EOS RP will lock onto the initial subject and follow it until it leaves the frame. Use this setting when you know you'll have intervening subjects often and are certain that you want to ignore them. Many sports events fall into this category.

- **2: Responsive (+1 or +2).** At the +1 or +2 settings, the camera quickly responds to new subjects that cross the frame. This is the best setting to use for fast-moving subjects, such as sports or frenetic children, *as long as you don't expect intervening subjects*. The camera will smoothly follow your subjects. It works well when subjects within the frame are at significantly different distances.

C.Fn II-2: Acceleration/Deceleration Tracking

Options: –2 to +2; Default: 0

My preference: N/A

In Servo AF mode, this setting specifies how sensitive the EOS RP is to sudden changes in speed when a subject starts moving or stops unexpectedly. It helps the camera respond to movement in sports, including basketball, soccer, and hockey, that involve some unpredictable action. You might also find it useful for young children or pets! Your options are as follows:

- **0: 0.** Use this for subjects that are moving at a steady pace, such as people walking, vehicles in motor sports, and similar events.

- **1: –2 or –1.** If your subject may change speed slightly, or other objects may intervene between the camera and the subject (say, a referee crossing in front of a speeding wide receiver), one of these settings may work better than the default 0 value.

- **2: +1 or +2.** These settings make the AF system very sensitive to dramatic changes in movement, such as sudden acceleration or, even more likely, an unexpected stop. The EOS RP will be able to continue refocusing as the subject moves, and won't be fooled if a subject abruptly heads in your direction. While the camera will more reliably track the subject, the quick response may overcompensate so that focus briefly becomes unstable. Use with caution!

C.Fn II-3: AF Point Auto Switching

Options: 0 (default), +2/+1

My preference: +1 for most action

Your EOS RP has a full toolbox when it comes to adjusting how its autofocus system responds. Tracking sensitivity (how quickly the camera locks and unlocks focusing on the current focus) and Acceleration/Deceleration (how it responds to changes in speed) are only part of the equation. The camera is also able to adjust *which* focus points it uses to track a subject. AF Point Auto Switching is strictly two-dimensional: it accounts for how the EOS RP selects which focus points to use as it tracks objects that move dramatically up, down, left, or right within the frame.

This adjustment is active when using Face+Tracking, Expand AF area, Expand AF area: Around, and Zone AF. With the default 0 setting, as your subject moves in the x or y directions, the camera will gradually switch to adjacent focus points to follow it.

At the +1 or +2 settings, dramatic moves in the up/down/left/right directions will impel the camera to switch more quickly to neighboring focus points. The EOS RP's smarts use the subject's past movements and contrast with its surroundings to predict which focus points to use next; however, the feature can become confused if the subject is too small within the frame (making predictions of movement more difficult), or when a wide-angle lens with lots of depth-of-field is in use. Extra responsiveness in focus point selection can come in handy at air shows or track events, such as pole-vaulting or high-jumping, that involve lots of movement in the x/y directions.

C.Fn II-4: Lens Drive When AF Impossible

Options: Continue focus search, Stop focus search

My preference: Stop focus search

Although the EOS RP's autofocus is largely fast and accurate, it can have difficulty when confronted with low-contrast scenes and dim light levels. This is often the case with long telephotos or lenses with a relatively small maximum aperture. Tele lenses that don't have a constant maximum aperture are the worst offenders. They may have a maximum aperture of f/3.5 at their widest zoom setting, but no better than, say, f/6.3 at maximum zoom. When you're shooting wildlife or sports you may not have the time (or patience) to allow the camera to keep hunting for focus over a "deep" area. In that case, switching from the default 0: Continue Focus Search to 1: Stop Focus Search may be your best bet.

C.Fn II-5: Limit AF Methods

Options: Face+Tracking, Spot AF, 1-point AF, Expand AF area, Expand AF area: Around, Zone AF

My preference: All options checked

Here you can choose which of the six AF area selection modes are available. In effect, you can enable the modes you use most often, and disable those that you rarely or never work with. The 1-point AF mode cannot be disabled, however.

When you access this entry, a screen with all six modes is displayed (see Figure 14.4). Use the Quick Control Dial or directional buttons to highlight a mode you want to activate/deactivate and press SET. A check mark above the icon indicates that the mode will be available. Select OK to confirm your choices. To cycle among the modes you've checked, press the AF Point Selection button on the upper-right corner of the back of the camera and press the M-Fn button until the mode you want to use is selected.

Figure 14.4
Enable or disable any of the six AF Area Selection modes.

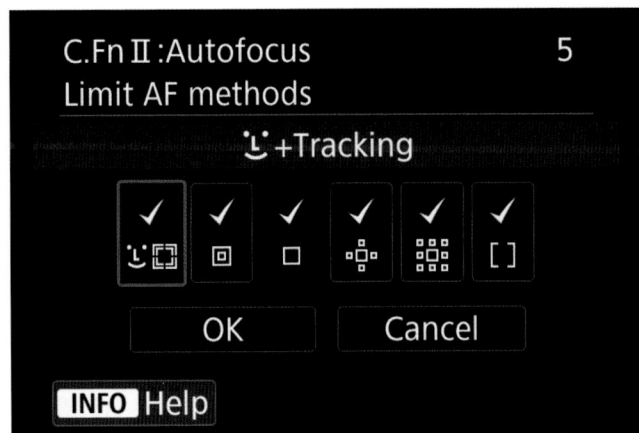

C.Fn II-6: Orientation Linked AF Point

Options: Same for both vertical and horizontal (default), Separate AF points: Point Only

My preference: Separate AF Points: Point Only

If you have a preference for a particular manually selected AF point or Zone AF frame when composing vertical or horizontal pictures, you can specify that preference using this menu entry, by choosing select Separate AF Points. Or, you can indicate that you want to use the same mode/point in all orientations (Same for Both Vert/Horiz).

If you'd like to differentiate, there are different orientations to account for:

- **0: Same for both vertical and horizontal.** The AF area selection mode *and* the AF point or zone that you select manually are used for both vertical and horizontal images.

- **1: Separate AF points: Point Only.** The AF area mode remains the same regardless of camera orientation, but you can specify a different AF point in manual point selection modes for each of three orientations. The specified point will remain in force even if you switch from one manual selection mode to another. The orientations are as follows:

  - **Camera held horizontally.** This orientation assumes that the camera is positioned so the viewfinder/shutter release are on top.

  - **Camera held vertically** with the grip/shutter release above the Mode Dial.

  - **Camera held vertically** with the Mode Dial above the grip/shutter release.

I provided instructions for setting your focus points and illustrations in Chapter 5 and won't repeat that information here.

C.Fn II-7: Initial Servo AF Point for Face+Tracking

Options: Auto (default); Initial AF Point Set for Face+Tracking; AF Point Set for Spot, 1-point AF, Expand AF, Expand AF: Around

My preference: Auto

Do you feel that your EOS RP's AF-point selection is *too* automated for you? If you'd like to regain a little control, because you feel you know exactly where your subject is most likely to reside in the frame, this is the override for you. You can manually specify the starting point that will be used in AI Servo (continuous autofocus) mode when the AF Method is set to Face+Tracking. If you're confused, this description of your options should clear things up:

- **0: Auto.** The initial AF point for Servo AF when using Face+Tracking is determined by the camera. I find this option to be the simplest and least prone to unintended errors.

- **1: Initial AF Point Set for Face+Tracking.** When Servo AF starts to focus in Face+Tracking mode, it will first use the AF point you specify here before seeking other points as the EOS RP evaluates your scene. You could use this option when you know that your main subject will *probably* be located in a particular area of the frame (say, a distance runner approaching from the left), but still want the camera to refocus as the subject moves. This helps reduce AF confusion from movement elsewhere in the frame that is not your main subject.

- **2: AF Point Set for Spot, 1-point AF, Expand AF Area, Expand AF Area: Around.** If you are using one of these four AF methods, and *then* switch to Face+Tracking, Servo AF initially uses the AF point you specified after you've activated Face+Tracking. This can be a convenient mode to use, because you can define a button to switch from another mode to Face+Tracking, using a defined Custom Control. I'll explain the use of Custom Controls later in this chapter.

Custom Function III (C.Fn III): Operation/Others

This menu category offers several options for display and controls, including the important Customize Buttons feature.

C.Fn III-1: Dial Direction During Tv/Av

Options: Normal (–+) (default), Reverse direction(+–)

My preference: Normal

This setting reverses the result when rotating the Quick Control Dial and Main Dial when using Shutter-priority or Aperture-priority (Tv and Av). That is, rotating the Main Dial to the right will decrease the shutter speed rather than increase it; f/stops will become larger rather than smaller. Use this if you find the default rotation scheme in Tv and Av modes are not to your liking. Activating this option also reverses the dial direction in Manual exposure mode. In other shooting modes, only the Main Dial's direction will be reversed.

- **0: Normal.** The Main Dial and Quick Control Dial change shutter speed and aperture normally.
- **1: Reverse direction.** The dials adjust shutter speed and aperture in the reverse direction when rotated.

C.Fn III-2: Control Ring Rotation

Options: Normal (–+) (default), Reverse direction (+–)

My preference: Normal

This setting reverses the rotational direction of the control ring on RF-mount lenses and the control ring mount adapter, as well. This is strictly a preference setting; I prefer the normal rotational direction, which coincides with the direction used for the focusing ring.

C.Fn III-3: Focus Ring Rotation

Options: Normal (–+) (default), Reverse direction (+–)

My preference: Normal

If you're converting to the Canon world from another camera platform (Nikon), you may prefer to stick with the focus ring direction you are accustomed to rather than train your fingers to adjust. Because RF lenses focus by wire (rather than using a mechanical linkage), it was easy for Canon to provide this feature. The Focus Ring Rotation setting reverses the rotational direction of the control ring on RF-mount lenses and the control ring mount adapter, as well. I use both camera systems daily and have never had a problem when swapping cameras, but that's not the case for everyone. If you do reverse the direction of the focus ring, you'll probably want to do the same for the control ring, for consistency.

C.Fn III-4: RF Lens MF Focus Ring Sensitivity

Options: Varies with rotation speed (default), Linked to rotation degree

My preference: Varies with rotation speed for stills; Linked to rotation degree for video

You probably haven't given much thought to how sensitive your focus ring is when you rotate it to fine-tune focus or when focusing manually. But focus ring response *can* be a big deal. For still photography, particularly when you're shooting sports, you want the ring to be more responsive when you're focusing rapidly. You want the focus to change as quickly as possible in those cases.

But if you're shooting video, having manual focusing respond to the *amount* of rotation can be crucial. Remember that during video capture, when the EOS RP is refocusing, the focus change is visible in the real-time image when it's played back. While you may not be changing focus while shooting video often, doing so has some special applications, particularly in *pull focus* shots, which are used to change the emphasis from one subject to another. An example is when a desk phone in the foreground is out of focus while people in the background are in sharp focus; the phone rings, and focus changes to the phone to draw our attention hence. (This example is a bit retro now that most homes don't have landlines.) Hollywood productions have full-time *focus pullers* (or first assistant camera operator) to perform this task using *follow focus* devices.

If you're serious about video, you'll find there are knobbed devices that attach to the focus ring to make pull focus easier. In such cases, you'd want focus to be more precise and not vary with focusing speed. That's where the Linked to Rotation Degree setting comes in handy. You can actually mark focus points for the beginning and end manual focus positions, and repeat precise focus planes reliably.

C.Fn III-5:Customize Buttons

Options: Redefine 15 buttons

My preference: N/A

If you're eager to totally confuse any poor soul who is not equipped to deal with a custom-configured EOS RP (or, perhaps, even yourself), Canon allows you to redefine the behavior of no less than 15 different buttons in interesting, and potentially hilarious ways. Just highlight any of the options (some are shown in Figure 14.5), press SET to view the functions you can assign, and make your choice. If you see the INFO icon at bottom left, there are even more decisions to make. You can truly manipulate your camera to work in a way that's fastest and most efficient for you. There are dozens of combinations of control possibilities, spelled out in a huge matrix+legend description starting on Page 538 of your factory manual. Those huge tables and explanations would take up half this chapter, so I won't duplicate that information here. The default values are shown in Table 14.1.

Figure 14.5
Some of the assign-
able buttons.

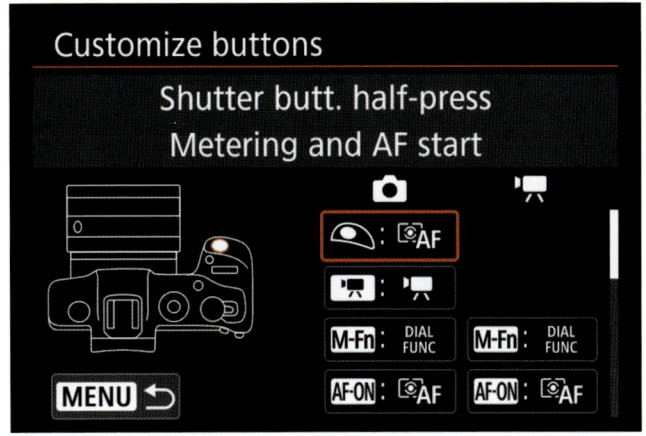

Table 14.1 Default Button Assignments

Control	Default Function: Stills	Default Function: Movies
Shutter button half-press	Metering and AF Start	None
Movie button	Shoot Movies	None
M-Fn button	Dial Function Settings	Dial Function Settings
AF-ON button	Metering and AF Start	Metering and AF Start
AE lock/FE lock button	AE Lock/FE Lock	AE Lock
AF point/Index/Magnify/ Reduce button	Shooting: AF Point Selection Playback: Index/Magnify Reduce	Shooting: AF Point Selection Playback: Index/Magnify/ Reduce
Lens AF stop button	Stop AF	Stop AF
Up button	Directional FV mode: Reset selected item	Directional
Left button	Directional FV mode: Reset selected item	Directional
Right button	Directional FV mode: Reset Tv/Av/ Exposure Comp./ISO	Directional
Down button	Directional FV mode: Reset Tv/Av/ Exposure Comp./ISO	Directional
SET button	Quick Control screen	Quick Control screen

When the button set-up screen reads "Dial Functions" it means that button summons a list of functions that can be accessed separately. For example, when you press the M-Fn button (without first pressing the AF Point button), a scrollable list of functions like the one shown in Figure 14.6 appears. Rotating the QCD dial moves the highlighting in the bottom row from ISO to Drive Mode to Focus Mode to White Balance to Flash Exposure Compensation. Once a function is highlighted, you can rotate the Main Dial to adjust the settings for the highlighted function.

If you customize the M-Fn button, you can keep its default Dial Functions behavior or choose from alternate individual functions, including Metering and AF Start, AF Stop, AE Lock, AF Stop, AF Point Selection, plus 34 *additional* behaviors and Off. The initial screen showing the first ten options appears in Figure 14.7. Other buttons are customizable with their own behaviors, and not all are assignable to every control. For example, Shutter button half-press can invoke Metering and AF Start, Metering Start (only), or AE Lock (while button is pressed), and no other functions. The best way to learn what each button can do is to work your way through the Customize Buttons screen.

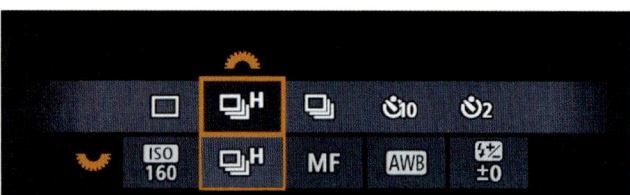

Figure 14.6
Default dial functions for the M-Fn button.

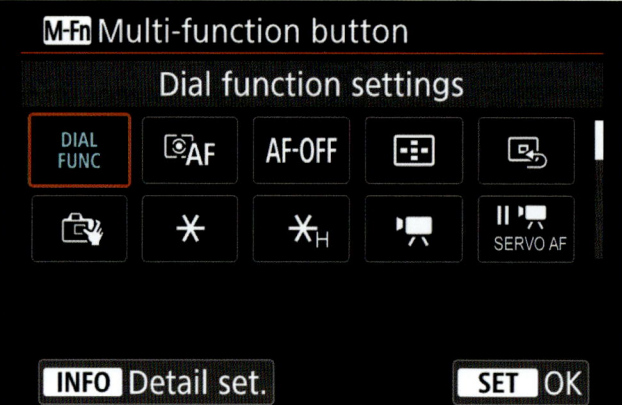

Figure 14.7
Some of the behaviors available for the M-Fn button.

C.Fn III-6: Customize Dials

Options: Redefine Main Dial, Quick Control Dial, and Control Ring

My preference: N/A

Each of these three dials can also be redefined with a customized behavior, but, fortunately, the possibilities are more limited. (See Figure 14.8.) All these are a matter of personal taste, and don't need to be changed to "improve" anything.

Figure 14.8
Customize dials.

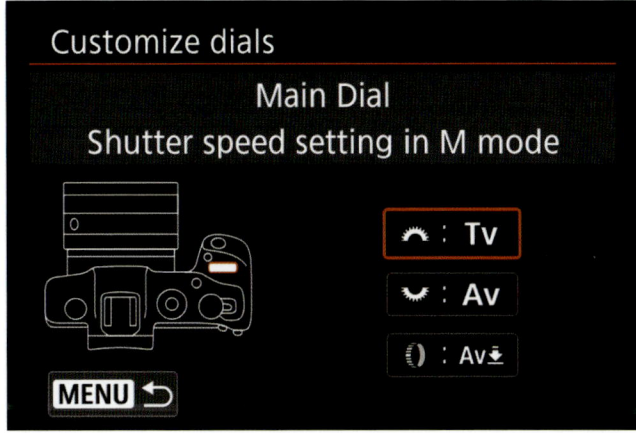

Your choices are as follows:

- **Redefine Main Dial.** By default, the Main Dial adjusts the shutter speed in Tv and Manual exposure modes, and in Fv mode if you haven't set the EOS RP to adjust shutter speed automatically. The dial's behavior can be changed *only* for Manual exposure mode. You can set it to adjust shutter speed (the default), aperture, or disable it so that the dial does nothing in Manual exposure mode.

- **Quick Control Dial.** By default, the Quick Control Dial adjusts the aperture in Av and Manual exposure modes, and in Fv mode if you haven't set the EOS RP to adjust aperture automatically. The dial's behavior can be changed *only* for Manual exposure mode. You can set it to adjust aperture (the default), switch it to change the shutter speed, or disable it so that the dial does nothing in Manual exposure mode.

■ **Control Ring.** The Control Ring on the lens or mount adapter has a little more flexibility. By default, you can use it to change the aperture of the lens by rotating it as you hold the shutter release (or other Metering Start button you may have defined). In effect, this gives you an old-school lens aperture adjustment ring, and is very convenient if you want to adjust the f/stop while cradling the lens in your left hand. (That may be more comfortable than using a thumb on the QCD for some users.)

If you prefer, the Control Ring can be defined to set aperture, shutter speed, ISO, or exposure compensation when rotated, and you can choose to require holding down the shutter release, or skip so that any of these adjustments can be performed just by spinning the dial, with no need to hold a button down. The no-hold options are faster, but make it easier for you to accidentally adjust a setting when you grip the Control Ring instead of the Focus Ring by mistake. Like the other two, the Control Ring can also be set to Off to disable it.

C.Fn III-7: Release Shutter without Lens

Options: 0: Disable (default), 1: Enable, Disable (default)

My preference: 1: Enable

Ordinarily, you don't want the camera to be capable of actuating the shutter to take stills, or to capture movies when no lens is attached. However, if you are using optics that the EOS RP does not recognize as a lens—such as a microscope, telescope, or a lens mounted on a bellows, you do want to take a photo or shoot movies using your manual exposure controls (ISO, shutter speed, and whatever aperture your device offers).

C.Fn III-8: Retract Lens on Power Off

Options: 0: Enable (default), 1: Disable

My preference: 0: Enable

Some lenses that focus using a gear mechanism (such as the EF40mm f/2.8 STM) can retract when the camera is turned off, regardless of whether the lens's focus mode switch is set to AF or MF. The retracted lens is smaller and its reduced surface area is better protected against bumps, so I usually leave this setting enabled. Make sure the lens is retracted before detaching it.

C.Fn III-9: Audio Compression

Options: 0: Enable (default), 1: Disable

My preference: 0: Enable

The default value tells the EOS RP to use compression for audio when recording movies. If you need higher audio quality and are willing to accept larger movie file sizes, choose Disable. But wait, there's more: if you *edit* movie files that have uncompressed audio and then save your edited video using compression, the audio will be compressed as well. The Disable setting is ignored if your Movie Recording Size is FHD IPB (Light) at 29.97P (NTSC) or 25.00P (PAL), and audio will be compressed. Finally, audio for video snapshots is always compressed, regardless of how this Custom Function is set.

Clear Customized Settings

Options: Clear customized buttons and dials

My preference: N/A

This entry can be used to erase all your customization of controls (only), should you need to do that. Note that the Clear All Custom Functions entry does *not* reset the controls settings (fortunately); you have to do it here.

Clear All Custom Func. (C.Fn)

Options: Clear

My preference: N/A

Select this entry and choose Cancel (if you chicken out) or OK to return all your Custom Functions to their default values. But don't panic—your matrix of customized buttons, dials, and M-Fn bar adjustments is retained.

My Menu

Options: Add My Menu tab, Delete all My Menu tabs, Delete all items, Menu display

My preference: N/A

The Canon EOS RP has a great feature that allows you to define your own menu with multiple tabs, each with just the items listed that you want. Remember that the EOS RP always returns to the last menu and menu entry accessed when you press the MENU button. So, you can setup My Menu to include just the items you want, and jump to those items instantly by pressing the MENU button. Or, you can set your camera so that My Menu appears when the MENU button has been pressed, regardless of what other menu entry you accessed last.

To create your own My Menu, you have to *register* the menu items you want to include. When no items have been registered, the initial My Menu tab looks like the one at left in Figure 14.9. Just follow these steps:

1. Press the MENU button and use the Main Dial or directional buttons to select the My Menu tab. When you first begin, the personalized menu will be empty except for the My Menu settings shown at left in the figure.

2. Rotate the Quick Control Dial to select Add My Menu Tab, then press the SET button. Highlight OK in the screen that appears, and press SET once again.

3. The Configure choice will appear. Press SET to view a list of options. Choose Select Items to Register, located at the top of the options screen. (See Figure 14.9, right.)

4. Use the Quick Control Dial to scroll down through the continuous list of menu entries to find one you would like to add. Press SET.

5. Confirm your choice by selecting OK in the next screen and pressing SET again.

6. Continue to select more entries for your My Menu tab. You can add up to six for each tab. If you try to add a seventh, you'll be told that you cannot register more items for the current tab.

7. When you're finished, press the MENU button twice to return to the My Menu screen to see your customized menu, which might look like my example in Figure 14.10.

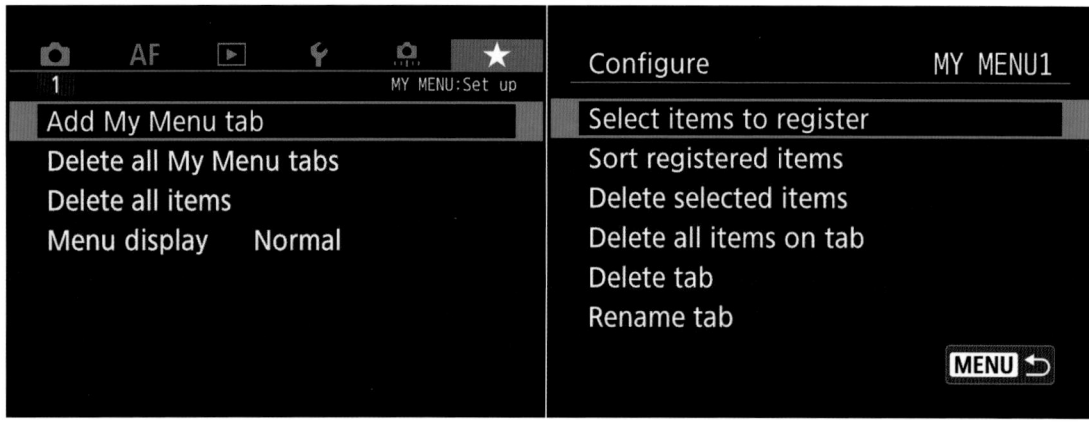

Figure 14.9 Initial My Menu screen (left); Configure tab screen (right).

Figure 14.10
Typical user-created
My Menu tab.

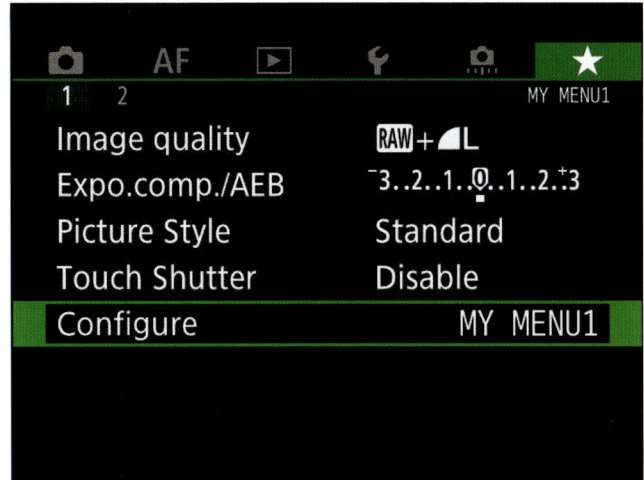

The Configure choice now appears at the bottom of the My Menu tab you have just created (and will be repeated at the bottom of any additional My Menu tabs you add). If you want to modify this tab (or any tabs created later, just select Configure and use the options that appear in the screen shown in Figure 14.9, right, shown earlier. Those items include:

■ **Select items to register.** Use this entry to add additional items to My Menu. As a tab fills up, a new tab will be created, and will be assigned names, like MY MENU1, MY MENU2, etc. The original MY MENU: Set-up tab will move to the farthest position in the tab lineup. You can have a maximum of five new tabs, plus the sixth Set-up tab.

■ **Sort registered items.** Choose this entry to reorder the items in each My Menu tab. Select the menu item and press the SET button. Rotate the Quick Control Dial to move the item up and down within the menu list. When you've placed it where you'd like it, press the MENU button to lock in your selection and return to the previous screen. When finished, press MENU again to exit.

■ **Delete selected items, Delete all items on tab, Delete tab.** Use these to remove an individual menu item or all menu items on a tab, or to delete the entire tab itself.

■ **Rename tab.** You're not stuck with the MY MENU1, MY MENU2 monikers. This entry allows you to apply a new name for a tab with up to 16 characters. For example, if you created customized Shooting or Autofocus settings, you could name them My Shooting and My Autofocus, respectively. As with any of the EOS RP's text-entry screens, this is one example of when the touch screen is highly preferable.

The Configure entry operates only on the currently selected tab. However, once you've created your first tab, a new Set-up tab appears automatically. It looks like Figure 14.11, left, and contains the following options:

- **Add My Menu Tab.** Use this to create a new, blank tab, which will be assigned the next available number.

- **Delete All My Menu Tabs.** Removes your existing tabs and all the items in them so you can start fresh.

- **Delete All Items.** This deletes all the registered items on all the tabs you have added. The options in the MY MENU: Set-up tab remain. When you delete all items, each will still contain a Configure choice, which allows you to register more entries. The tabs themselves are not removed.

- **Menu Display.** This determines which menu screen appears first when the MENU button is pressed. You can choose:

  - **Normal display (default).** Shows the *most recently displayed* menu tab from the Shooting, AF, Playback, Set-up, Custom Settings, and My Menu choices. You'd want this if you prefer to jump back to whichever menu you were working with recently.

  - **Display from My Menu tab.** Shows the My Menu tab only. Use this if you want to bypass the conventional menus and make your menu choices only from your custom My Menu tabs. The other menu tabs are still shown and can be selected.

  - **Display only My Menu tab.** Only the My Menu tabs are available. The others are hidden. Use this only if you do not need to use the conventional menus as you work. You can return to this entry and restore Normal display at any time.

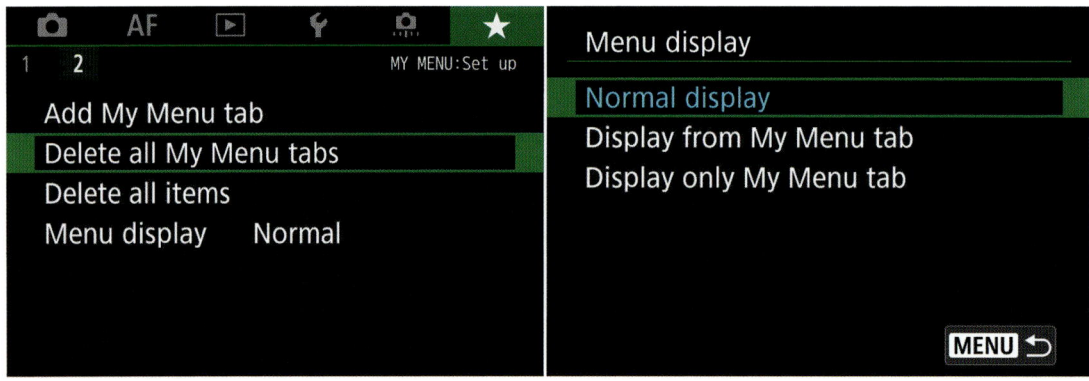

Figure 14.11 Add or delete tabs (left) and customize My Menu display (right).

15

Capturing Video

The Canon EOS RP can shoot full HDTV movies with stereo sound at 3840 × 2160 (4K) resolution, 1920 × 1080 (Full HD) resolution, or video at 1280 × 720 (Standard HD) resolution.

Shooting movies on the spur of the moment is easy, even if you are currently in any still shooting mode. Just press the Movie button (located on top of the camera to the southwest of the shutter release and marked with a red dot). To stop shooting, press the button again. That's all there is to it. Unless you've changed the default settings, Movie Autoexposure and Movie Servo AF will be enabled and you won't need to concern yourself with exposure or focus. ISO sensitivity is set automatically. If you like, you can lock exposure at any point (press the * button) or change exposure using exposure compensation of +/–3 stops, just as you can in still photo mode.

However, if you need the most flexibility and full control over your settings, you'll want to switch to one of the "official" movie modes. Just rotate the Mode Dial to the Movie position and proceed. Note that while you can shoot movies in still photography mode, you can't take still photos once you've changed the Mode Dial to movie mode. You can, however, select a frame from a 4K movie and save an 8.3-megapixel 3840 × 2160–pixel JPEG image to your memory card, as described later. Most of this chapter will deal with the options available using the Movie Shooting menus.

Movie Shooting Menus

The Movie Shooting menus contain many of the same options, such as Lens Aberration Correction (on the Movie Shoot 2 menu), Exposure Compensation, Auto Lighting Optimizer, Highlight Tone Priority, Metering Timer, White Balance, and Picture Styles (found in the Movie Shooting 3 and 4 menus). I explained how to use the common settings in Chapter 11 and won't repeat that information here. This chapter will deal with the adjustments unique to Movie Shooting. I'll explain them in more detail later in this chapter.

Movie Shooting 1 Menu

In this menu, shown in Figure 15.1, you'll make most of the basic movie shooting settings; the other Movie menus contain a mixture of movie-oriented entries and options that are virtually identical to their still photo counterparts.

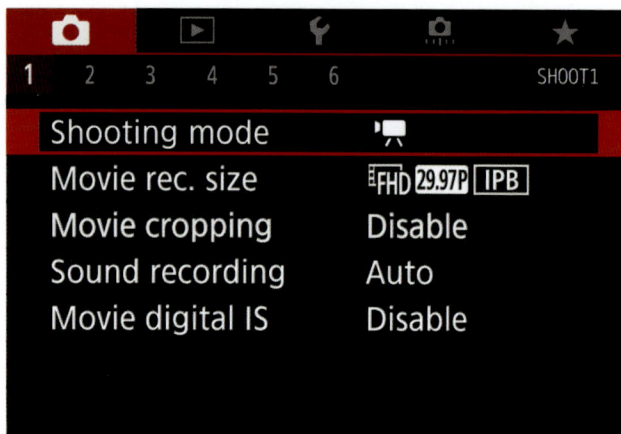

Figure 15.1
The Movie Shooting 1 menu.

Shooting Mode

Much of the time, you'll want to let the camera make your exposure decisions, so the default Movie Auto Exposure mode is usually the best choice. However, once you've rotated the Mode Dial to the Movie position you can use this menu entry (or just press SET to jump directly to the Shooting Mode adjustment) and press the up/down directional buttons to select from Movie Autoexposure, Movie Manual Exposure, or HDR Movies.

Movie Recording Size

The Canon EOS RP has a large number of video recording quality settings, including ultra-high-resolution 4K video. (See Figure 15.2.) I'll explain the use of these settings in more detail later in this chapter, but, in brief, your choices include the following:

- **Image size.** This is the resolution of the movie, either 4K (3840 × 2160), Full HD (1920 × 1080), or Standard HD (1280 × 720).

- **Frame Rate.** The number of individual frames or fields captured per second. These are commonly expressed as 60 fps, 30 fps, and 24 fps (in NTSC mode, used in North American, Japan, and other countries; frame rates are different in Europe and other areas using the PAL specification). Note that the actual frames-per-second is a fraction less than the nominal value, as I'll explain below. Frame rates of 24p are available for 4K video, and 60p and 30p for Full HD and Standard HD video.

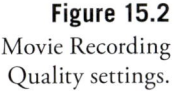

Figure 15.2
Movie Recording
Quality settings.

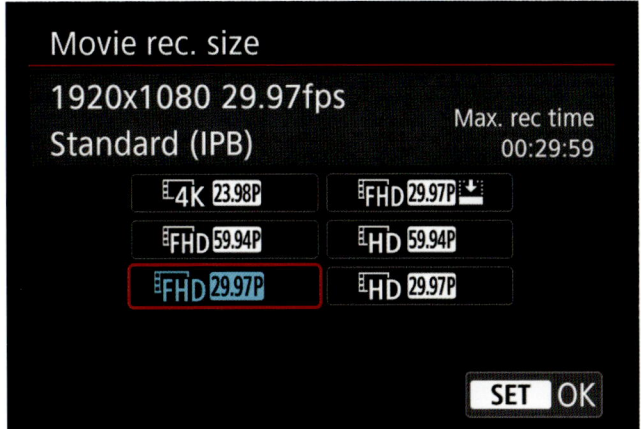

- **Compression method.** To save space and reduce demands on the transmission rates of the captured frames to your storage device, each frame is compressed, using either IPB Standard or IPB Light formats. There is no direct setting for compression: if you choose FHD 29.97P (shown at the bottom of the left column in Figure 15.2), then IPB Standard is used; select the alternate FHD 29.97P (at the top of the right column), then IPB Light compression is applied instead. I'll explain these in more detail later.

All movies are stored using the MP4 format as the "container" for your video files, with the MPEG4 AVC/H.264 codec (coder/decoder). MP4 is an international standard and widely supported/used and recorded using progressive scan, described shortly.

Movie Cropping

The actual area of the EOS RP's full image size that is captured is always cropped to a certain extent. Because the High Definition and Ultra High Definition aspect ratios are 16:9 rather than the 3:2 ratio used for still photography, a certain amount is cropped off the top and bottom of your frame. The remaining area may be further cropped depending on your movie mode and the lenses you are using. This setting gives you some control over the image crop used.

- **Movie Cropping: Disable.** This mode is suitable for use with RF-mount and EF-mount lenses attached using an adapter (typical full-frame lenses). As shown in Figure 15.3, top, the full width of the sensor is used for Full HD and Standard HD video, as well as 4K Time-lapse and Full HD Time-lapse movies, as these are assembled in the camera using still frames captured using the full width of the frame.

However, the EOS RP records 4K Ultra HD movies using a cropped portion of the sensor, outlined in green in Figure 15.3, top, producing a 1.6X crop effect (explained in more detail in Chapter 7). This crop ratio means that the EOS RP is functioning more or less as a Super 35/ ASP-C video camera. It also means that while you'll gain extra "telephoto reach," you'll need lenses with shorter focal lengths if you need a wider perspective; your 24mm zoom setting offers the same field of view as a 38mm optic.

■ **Movie Cropping: Enable.** With this setting, your video is *always* cropped, and the resulting image area corresponds to that of Canon APS-C lenses with the EF-S designation. You can also use RF- and EF-mount lenses, which will have their field of view cropped similarly. 4K UHD will be cropped using the area within the red frame in Figure 15.3, bottom. 4K Time-lapse and Standard HD Time-lapse movies are cropped to the slightly larger green frame. **Note:** Full HD recording is *not* available when Movie Cropping is set to enable. You can record *only* using the two time-lapse modes (4K and Full HD time-lapse), 4K video, and Standard HD (1280 × 720) video.

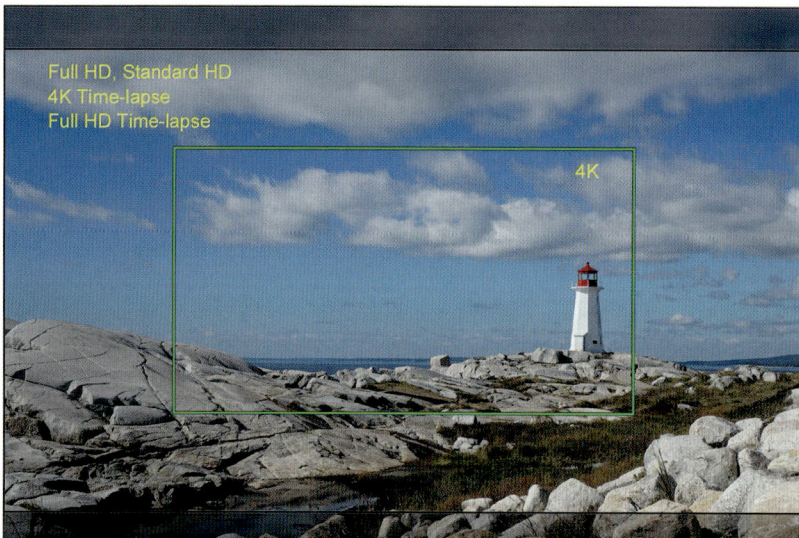

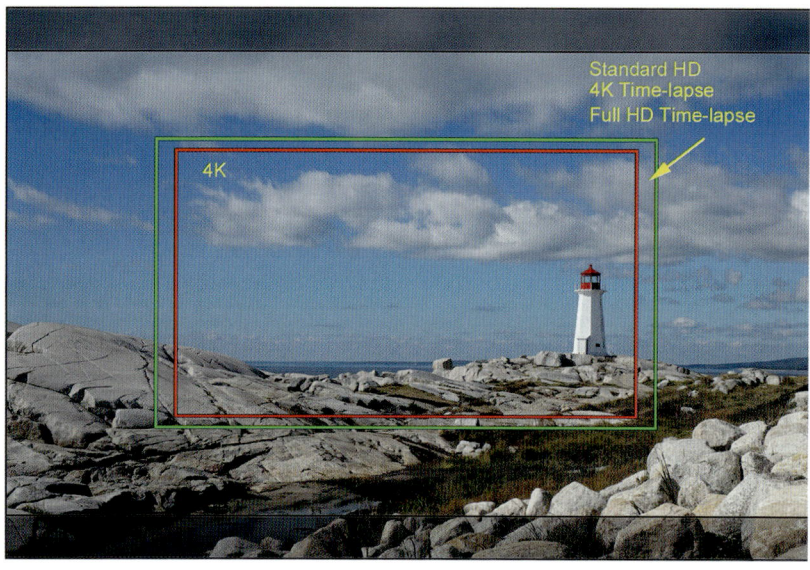

Figure 15.3
Movie cropping.

Note that when using Movie Digital Image Stabilization (described later) a slight additional crop is applied to allow adjusting the frame to compensate for camera motion.

Sound Recording

This setting lets you choose Auto, Manual, or Disable; plus, Enable or Disable the wind filter. (See Figure 15.4.)

■ **Auto.** The EOS RP sets the audio level for you.

■ **Manual.** Choose from 64 different sound levels. Select Rec Level and rotate the QCD while viewing the decibel meter at the bottom of the screen to choose a level that averages –12 dB for the loudest sounds. (See Figure 15.4.)

■ **Disable.** Shoot silently, and add voice over, narration, music, or other sound later in your movie-editing software. Note that if you are connected to an external device, including recorders using HDMI, sound is not output when sound recording is disabled in the camera.

■ **Wind filter/Attenuator.** Enable to reduce the effects of wind noise on the built-in microphone. This also reduces low tones in the sound recording. If wind is not a problem, you'll get better quality audio with this option disabled. Even better is to use an external microphone with a wind shield. The Attenuator suppresses distortion caused by loud noises, which can affect audio even when Auto sound level is in use.

You can use your EOS RP's built-in stereo microphone or plug in a stereo microphone into the 3.5mm jack on the left side of the camera. An external microphone is a good idea because the built-in microphone can easily pick up camera operation, such as the autofocus motor in a lens. Headphones are useful for monitoring sound. Press the Q button, select Headphone, and rotate the Main Dial to adjust headphone volume.

Figure 15.4
Sound recording options.

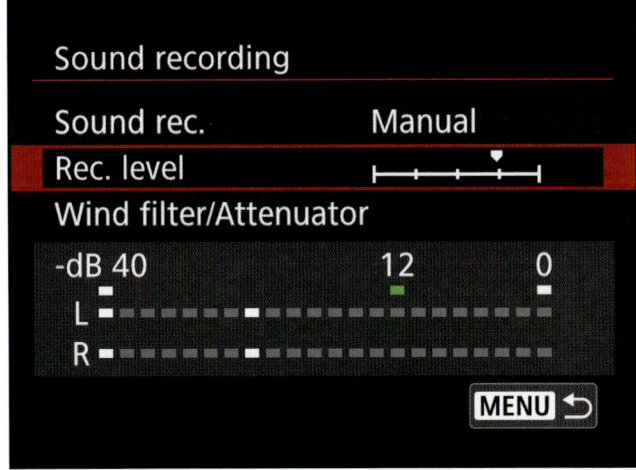

Movie Digital Image Stabilization

Although the EOS RP relies on the image stabilization built into some RF- and EF/EF-S-mount lenses, it can supplement this optical image stabilization (OIS) with an electronic version that can be activated when shooting movies. Note that this additional IS can be applied even with lenses that lack stabilization entirely (including EF/EF-S lenses).

Digital image stabilization takes advantage of the fact that cropped video frames contain some image information outside the boundaries of the actual frame displayed. The camera is able to monitor movement and compensate for it by shifting the pixels of the entire frame slightly so that subject matter that is not moving remains in the same relative position in the frame. That is, if the camera image shakes a few pixels to the left, the frame area is moved an equivalent amount the same number of pixels to the right. Because some pixels at the edges of the frame must be trimmed to compensate for this adjustment, the resulting movie is slightly cropped, adding a small amount of magnification. If you're using EF-S lenses, or have selected the Movie Cropping feature, additional cropping/magnification is applied.

You must use this feature in conjunction with the built-in optical image stabilization of your lenses that have stabilization (it won't work if your lens has IS and it is turned off). Canon provides a list of lenses that are compatible with what it terms "combination IS" (when both digital and optical image stabilization are combined). Movie IS does not work with lenses with a focal length greater than 800mm and is not recommended with tilt/shift (TS-E), fisheye, or third-party lenses. Your options are as follows:

- **Disable.** No digital IS is applied. Use this setting when the camera is mounted on a tripod.
- **Enable.** A great deal of camera shake will be corrected; the image will be slightly cropped, producing a slight magnification effect. This setting works best with wide-angle lenses.
- **Enhanced.** Even more pronounced camera shake is compensated for, and the image will be magnified a bit more. Use this as a last result, as there may be a noticeable blurring of the image *while viewing* and an increase in visual noise.

Movie Shooting 2 Menu

The Movie Shooting 2 menu, shown in Figure 15.5, has four entries. The Lens Aberration Correction entry at the top of the menu has the same functions as its Shooting 2 menu counterpart, described in Chapter 11, and I described techniques for shooting time-lapse movies in Chapter 6. I won't repeat any of that information here. The third entry, Remote Control, is a specialized feature for those who own the Canon BR-E1 wireless remote control. The BR-E1 wireless remote is a Bluetooth device that can be used to start and stop movies, including time-lapse recordings. You must first pair the remote with your EOS RP using the instructions supplied with the remote. Then, set the Remote Control entry to Enable. The final entry, Video Snapshot, is a useful way of creating short movie clips compiled from four- to eight-second sequences. I'll explain that capability here.

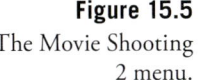

Figure 15.5
The Movie Shooting
2 menu.

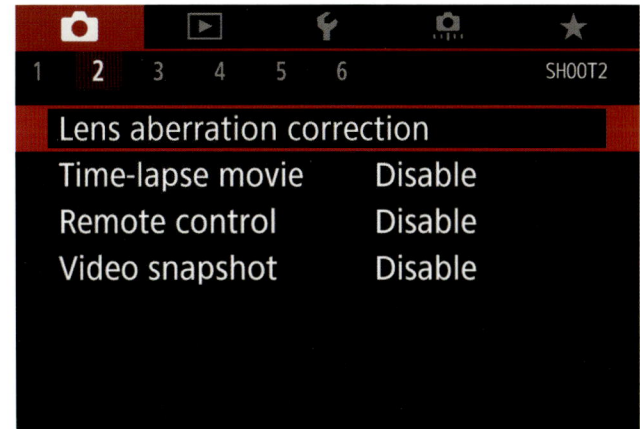

Video Snapshot

Video snapshots are movie clips, all the same length, assembled into video albums as a single movie. You can choose a fixed length of 2, 4, or 8 seconds for all clips in an album. I use the 2-second length to compile mini-movies of fast-moving events, such as parades, giving me a lively album of clips that show all the things going on without lingering too long on a single scene. The 8-second length is ideal for landscapes and many travel clips, because the longer scenes give you time to absorb all the interesting things to see in such environments. The 4-second clips are an excellent way to show details of a single subject, such as a cathedral or monument when traveling, or an overview of the action at a sports event. The Playback 2 menu's Create Album entry, discussed in Chapter 12, allows you to assemble individual albums into a longer snapshot movie.

First, activate the video snapshot feature in the Movie Shooting 2 menu:

1. **Activate.** Select Video Snapshot from the Movie Shooting 2 menu.

2. **Enable Snapshots.** Highlight the Video Snapshot entry, press SET, select Enable, then press SET again to confirm. The screen shown in Figure 15.6 will appear.

3. **Select Album.** Next, highlight Album Settings and choose either Create a New Album or Add to Existing Album.

4. **Specify Snapshot Length.** If you choose to Create a New Album, you can choose Snapshot Length. Select 2 Sec., 4 Sec., or 8 Sec. Press SET to confirm your choice.

5. **Choose Playback Effect.** You can have your video snapshots play back in slow motion (1/2X speed), normal speed (1X speed), or double-time (2X speed). Highlight your choice and press SET to confirm.

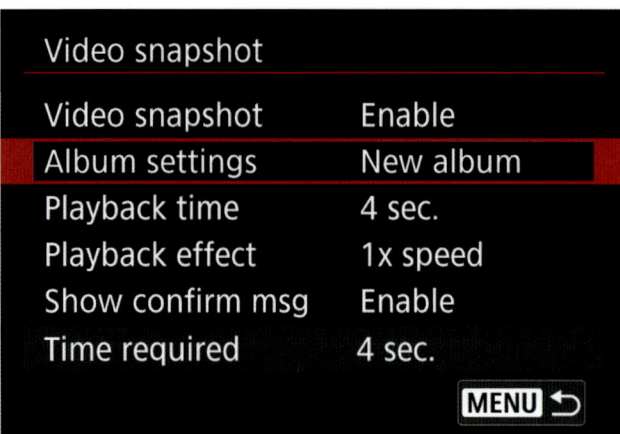

Figure 15.6
Select Video
Snapshot options.

6. **Enable/Disable Confirm Msg.** When enabled, a message will appear on the screen inviting you to Add to Album, Save As a New Album, Playback Video Snapshot, or Delete Without Saving to Album. If you select Disable, the camera *skips* this step, automatically saves your video snapshot, and is then ready to capture another. You'd want to disable the confirmation message if you planned to shoot several video snapshots one after the other and not have to respond to the confirmation message each time.

7. **Exit.** Press/Tap MENU to exit Video Snapshot setup. The next section will show you how to use the feature in a little more detail.

When Video Snapshot is enabled, conventional movie shooting is disabled. Instead, every time you press the Movie button, the EOS RP captures a clip of the length you've specified. The procedure goes something like this:

1. **Capture Video Snapshot.** In Movie mode, press the Live View/Movie button. The EOS RP will begin shooting a clip, and a blue bar appears showing you how much time remains before shooting stops automatically. (See Figure 15.7.)

2. **Save your clip as a video snapshot album.** If you've disabled the confirmation message, the clip will be saved to the current album, and be ready to capture another snapshot. Note that the confirmation message is overlaid on whichever Playback screen you've specified using the INFO button. The figure illustrates the display when No Information is shown on playback.

3. **Choose confirmation option.** The screen shown in Figure 15.8 appears. You can use the left/right directional buttons or touch screen to select Save As Album/Add To Album (depending on whether this is the first clip for an album, or an additional clip), Save to New Album, Playback Video Snapshot (that you just took), or Do Not Save to Album/Delete Without Saving to Album (exit without adding to an album).

4. **Press SET.** Your first clip will be saved as the start of a new album.

Figure 15.7
Recording a video snapshot.

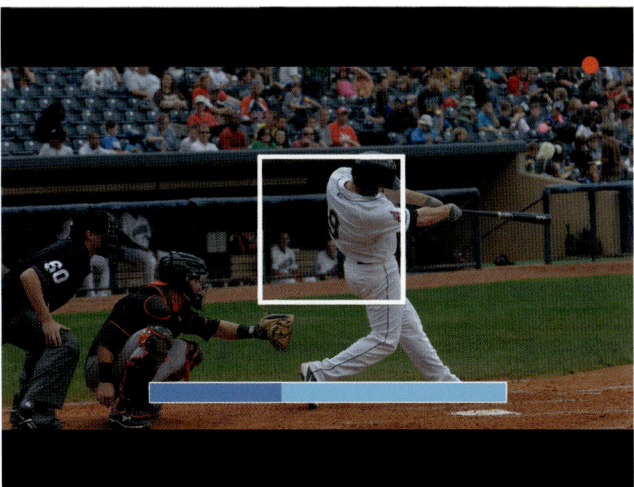

Figure 15.8
The video snapshot confirmation screen includes options (bottom, left to right) to Save as Album/Add to Album, Save to New Album, Playback Video Snapshot, and Do Not Save to Album/Delete Without Saving to Album.

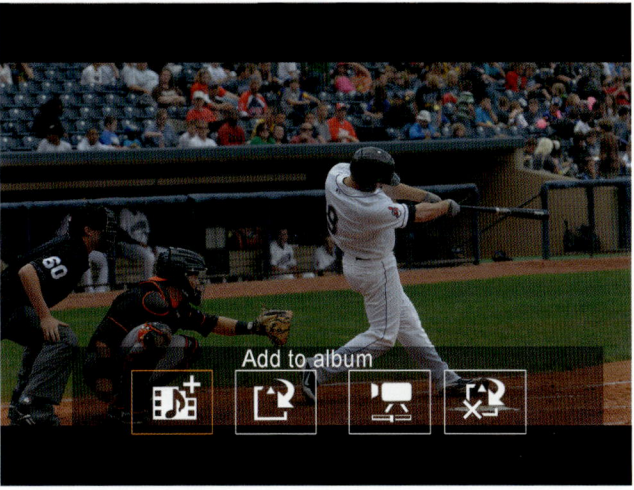

5. **Shoot additional clips.** Press the Movie button to shoot more clips of the length you have chosen, and indicated by the blue bars at the bottom of the frame. At the end of the specified time, the confirmation screen will appear again.

6. **Add to album or create new album.** Select the left-most icon again if you want to add the most recent clip to the album you just started. Alternatively, you can press the left/right directional buttons to choose the second icon from the left, Save as a New Album. That will complete your previous album, and start a new one with the most recent clip.

   Or, if you'd like to review the most recent clip first to make sure it's worth adding to an album, select the Playback Video Snapshot icon (second from the right) and review the clip you just shot. You can then Add to Album, Create New Album, or Delete the Clip.

7. **Delete most recent clip.** If you decide the most recent clip is not one you'd like to add to your current album, you can select Do Not Save to Album/Delete without Saving to Album (the right-most icon).

8. **Switch from Video Snapshots to conventional movie clips.** If you want to stop shooting video snapshots and resume shooting regular movie clips (of a variable length), navigate to the Movie 5 menu again, and disable Video Snapshot.

Note: Once you've set up the Video Snapshot feature, you can quickly enable or disable it using the Quick Control menu, which is illustrated later in this chapter. The Video Snapshot icon is the bottom icon in the left row of the Quick Control menu.

Movie Shooting 3 Menu

The Movie Shooting 3 menu, shown in Figure 15.9, has seven entries. Four of them are similar to their Shooting menu counterparts: Exposure Compensation, Auto Lighting Optimizer, Highlight Tone Priority, and Metering Timer. (The Exposure Compensation entry has no Bracketing feature, however.) I won't repeat those descriptions here. The more specialized entries are Movie ISO Speed Settings, Movie Auto Slow Shutter, and Movie Av 1/8th Stop Increments, explained next.

Movie ISO Speed Settings

You can separately specify ISO parameters for movie shooting using this entry. Select a specific ISO speed or specify limits on the range of ISO settings and shutter speeds that the camera selects automatically.

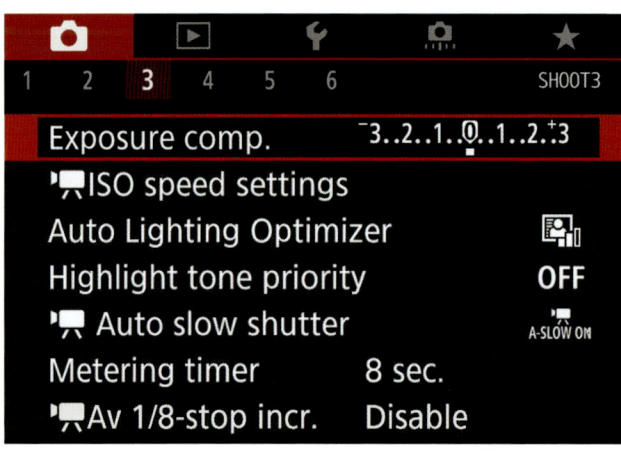

Figure 15.9
The Movie Shooting 3 menu.

The subentries include:

■ **ISO speed.** In Movie M (Manual exposure) mode, you can select a specific ISO speed from ISO 100 to 25600, or choose Auto to allow the EOS RP to select an appropriate sensitivity. The latter effectively gives you an autoexposure mode when using manual exposure: you select the shutter speed and aperture manually, and the camera adjusts the ISO to produce the right exposure.

■ **ISO Speed Range.** Available when recording Standard HD and Full HD movies, or Full HD time-lapse movies, you can specify an ISO range from a *minimum* of ISO 100 to H1 (ISO 51200 equivalent) and a maximum of ISO 200 to H2 (ISO 102400 equivalent). The default range is ISO 100 to ISO 25600. I find myself using this feature frequently to keep me from accidentally switching to a setting I'd rather (or need to) avoid. For example, at concerts I may switch from ISO 1600 to 6400 as the lighting changes, and I set those two values as my minimum or maximum. Outdoors in daylight, I might prefer to lock out ISO values lower than ISO 100 or higher than ISO 800.

■ **Range for 4K.** This is the equivalent to the ISO Speed Range setting, but for 4K UHD video or 4K time-lapse movies. Its defaults are a range of ISO 100 to ISO12800, but you can set the same minimums and maximums as for Standard HD/Full HD movies, listed above.

■ **Max for Auto.** This is the equivalent "safety net" for Auto ISO operation for a maximum setting. The default maximum is ISO 25600, but you can specify another value between ISO 6400 and H2.

■ **4K Max for Auto.** Set the maximum ISO for 4K movie shooting in Program, Tv, Av, or Manual exposure mode and ISO Auto. The default maximum is 12800, but you can specify another value between ISO 6400 and H2.

■ **Time-lapse Max for Auto.** Set the maximum for ISO Auto for 4K/Full HD time-lapse movie shooting in Movie Auto Exposure or Movie Manual Exposure modes. The default maximum is 12800, but you can specify another value between ISO 400 and 25600.

Movie Auto Slow Shutter

Use this setting to allow the EOS RP to select a slower shutter speed no faster than 1/30th second when shooting with Program or Av (Aperture-priority) at a frame rate of 60p. (I'll provide more detail on how choice of frame rates affects your movies later in this chapter.) You can select Enable or Disable. Here's the difference:

■ **Disable.** Frame rates of 1/60th second or faster will be chosen. The video will be smoother and more natural looking, and individual frames will be sharper because of this "higher" shutter speed. However, under low light, your video may appear to be underexposed.

■ **Enable.** Shutter speeds of 1/30th second or slower are enabled, producing better-exposed movies that may have less noise (because a lower ISO setting may be used). However, moving subjects may be blurry or leave a visible "trail" caused by the longer exposure.

Movie Av 1/8th Stop Increment

The EOS RP's RF-mount lenses have apertures that can be controlled much more precisely than those found in EF/EF-S lenses, and Canon takes advantage of that by offering the ability to adjust f/stops in increments of 1/8th stop. While such fine increments are not essential for still photography, when movie shooting it's important to have consistent exposure, especially with sequences of shots. This feature is available only in the sole movie exposure mode in which you have full control over the aperture—M mode. Choose Enable to allow selection in 1/8th stop increments rather than the 1/2 or 1/3 stop jumps you may have set in the Shooting 1 menu's Exposure Level Increments entry. This feature does not work with EF or EF-S lenses.

Movie Shooting 4 Menu

The Movie Shooting 4 menu, shown in Figure 15.10, has six entries. Only one of them, HDMI Information Display, is especially for movie shooting. I won't repeat the descriptions of the others—the three White Balance entries, plus Picture Styles and High ISO Speed Noise Reduction—that appeared in Chapter 11.

HDMI Information Display

This entry controls how image information is displayed when the EOS RP's output is directed to an external monitor or recorder using an HDMI cable. There are three choices:

- **With Info.** In this case, shooting information, including AF points and other data, are overlaid on the image sent to the monitor or recorder over the HDMI cable. The EOS RP's own LCD screen is blank, *and the video is recorded only on the camera's memory card.* You might want to use this entry if you wanted to monitor your video as it was shot on a larger display screen, accompanied by the overlaid shooting information, while recording the video on the camera's memory card.

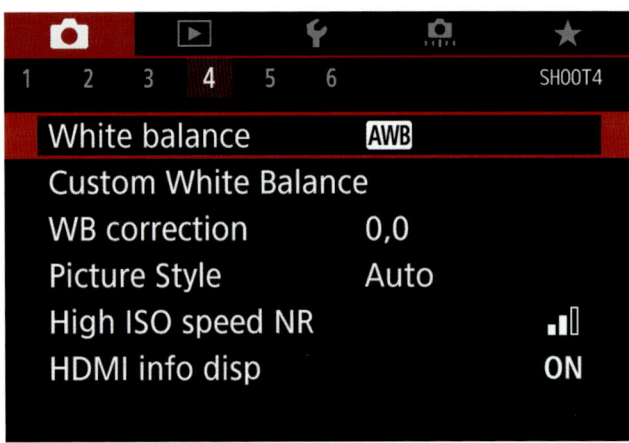

Figure 15.10
The Movie Shooting 4 menu.

- **Clean/4K Output.** The clean video information is output to your external device in 4K format, and is not saved to the memory card. However the EOS RP's LCD screen is live and shows shooting information and AF points. Wi-Fi communication is disabled. With this mode, you can store the video on the external recorder while still being able to view our output on the camera's screen.

- **Clean/FHD Output.** Functions exactly the same as the previous option, but HDMI output is Full HD.

Movie Shooting 5 Menu

In Movie mode, the Movie Shooting 5 menu has four entries, as seen in Figure 15.11. Three of them—AF Method, Eye Detection AF, and Touch & Drag AF Settings function exactly the same as their Shooting menu counterparts described in Chapter 11, and their options won't be repeated here. The additional entry, Movie Servo AF, is discussed next.

Movie Servo AF

If you enable this menu item, the EOS RP will focus continually during movie shooting, even if you are not pressing the shutter release halfway. To stop focusing or to pause, tap the Servo AF icon at the lower-left corner of the LCD screen. Movie Servo AF will reactivate automatically if you resume shooting after performing tasks such as using menus, using Playback, or adjusting the AF method. Choose Disable, and AF will take place only when you press the AF-ON button or press the shutter release halfway.

Figure 15.11
The Movie Shooting 5 menu.

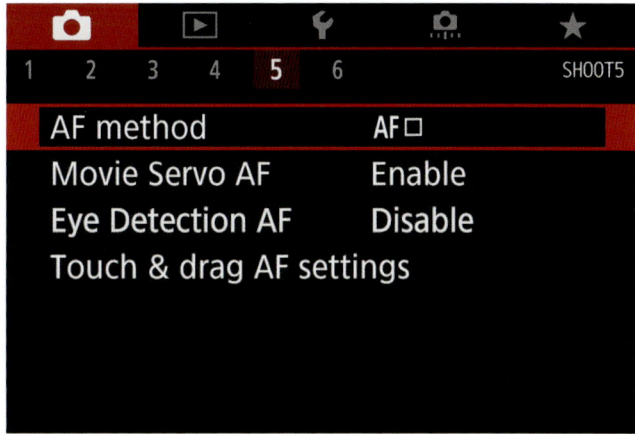

Movie Shooting 6 Menu

The Movie Shooting 6 menu has four entries, as seen in Figure 15.12. Lens Electronic Manual Focus and Manual Focus Peaking Settings operate the same as their still photography counterparts, as described in Chapter 11. Movie Servo AF Track Sensitivity and Movie AF Speed are explained in the next two sections.

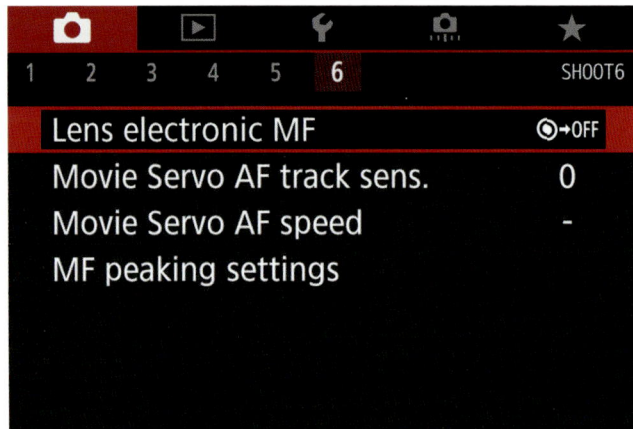

Figure 15.12
The Movie Shooting 6 menu.

Movie Servo AF Tracking Sensitivity

Here you can specify how quickly the Movie Servo AF tracking locks onto a moving subject. It's similar to the Tracking Sensitivity option described in Chapter 11. As with its still photo counterpart, changing the tracking sensitivity can come in useful when an intervening subject passes through the frame in front of the subject you were capturing. It's also helpful when panning. A sliding scale (shown in Figure 15.13) can be adjusted from Locked On (–3 to –1) to Responsive (+1 to +3) or standard at the 0 position. Locked On tells the camera to stick with the subject currently in focus—like that referee at a football game, or a passerby in an urban scene. Responsive settings tell the camera to switch to track a subject located at the current focus point, even if it's the same subject now moving toward you at a rapid rate, or a different subject that comes into view.

This setting requires Movie Servo AF to be enabled, and the AF method to be set to 1-point AF. If you choose another AF method, the EOS RP defaults to the standard (0) setting and does not vary. It is disabled when recording 4K video.

Figure 15.13
Movie AF Tracking
Sensitivity.

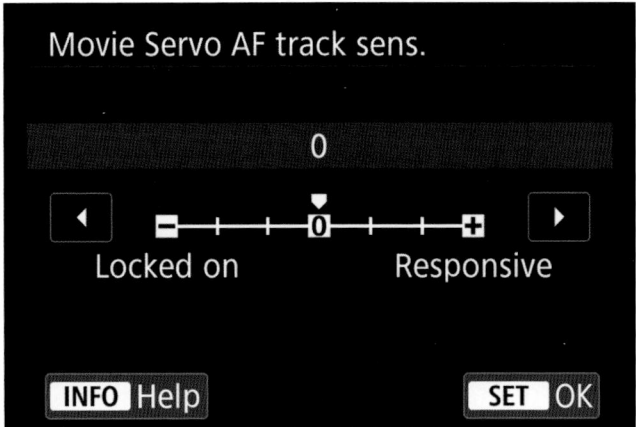

Movie Servo AF Speed

This choice is available when Movie Servo AF is set to Enable, and AF Method is set to 1-point AF. The function can be used when working with lenses released after 2009 that have USM or STM motors and support slow focus transition during movie shooting. (Check the Canon website in your country for the most recent updated listing of compatible lenses.) It's disabled when capturing 4K video. Your choices, shown in Figure 15.14, are as follows:

■ **When Active.** Always On activates the AF adjustment speed setting automatically before and during movie shooting. If you select During Shooting AF, then the speed adjustment is active *only* when you are actually capturing video.

■ **AF Speed.** Highlight this option and press SET. You can then adjust the AF speed using the touch screen, QCD, or directional buttons along a sliding scale from Slow (–7 to 0) to Standard (0) to Fast (+1 to +2).

FOCUS ON 4K VIDEO

In addition to the forced cropping of your image, shooting 4K video has one other disadvantage. Dual Pixel AF (using the sensor's phase detect pixels) is disabled, and the EOS RP uses slower contrast detection to focus. That's not ideal and is another factor that makes this camera less than perfect for 4K video shooting.

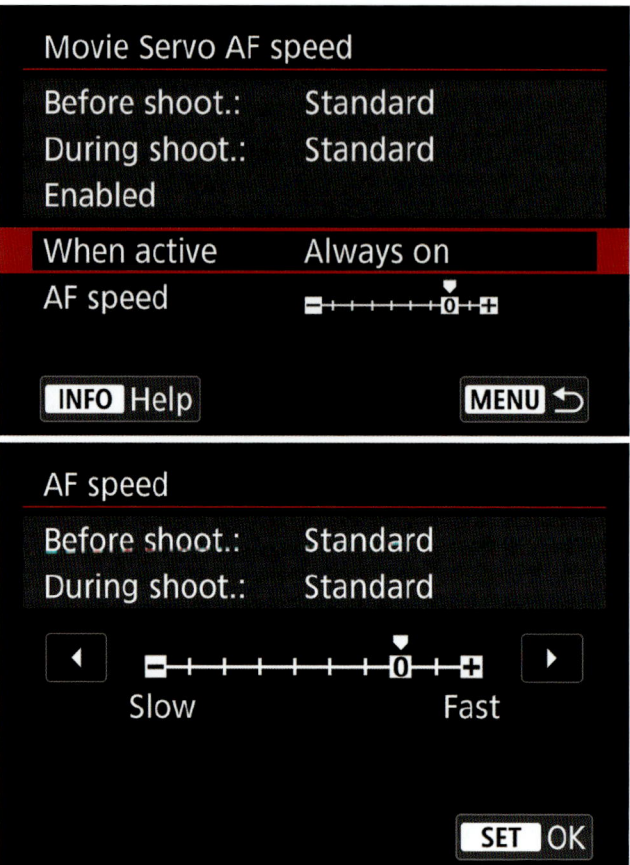

Figure 15.14
Movie Servo AF speed.

Compression, Resolution, and Frame Rates

I've explained how to make and use settings first, and saved explanations of some of the technical terms for now. The information in this section will help you make your choices. Even intermediate movie shooters can be confused by the number of different options for compression, resolution, and frame rates. This section will help clarify things for you.

Compression

Compression is easiest to understand, so I'll get it out of the way first. As I mentioned earlier, the EOS RP stores files using the standard H.264/MPEG-4 codec ("coder-decoder"). Compression is either IPB (Standard) or the less demanding IPB (Light) version.

■ **IPB (Standard).** This is a newer compression method that is considered Standard by Canon. It uses *interframe* compression; that is, only certain "key" frames are saved, with other frames "simulated" or interpolated from information contained in the frames that precede and succeed them. I-frames are the complete or *intraframes*; P-frames are "predicted picture" frames, which record *only the pixel changes* from the previous frame (say, a runner traveling across a fixed background); B-frames are "bi-predictive picture" frames, created by using the differences from the preceding *and* following frames. This interpolation produces image quality that is a bit lower and which requires more of your camera's DIGIC 8 processing power, but file sizes are smaller.

Video encoded using IPB must be converted, or transcoded to a format compatible with your video-editing software. The compression scheme can produce more artifacts, particularly in frames with lots of motion throughout the frame. I use this method only when the ability to shoot longer is very important.

■ **IPB (Light).** It is recorded at a bit rate that is lower than IPB (Standard), producing files that are smaller, transfer more quickly, have higher playback compatibility, and provide longer maximum shooting times. If you don't need the maximum resolution possible, this choice can be very useful.

"CLEAN" HDMI OUTPUT

The video is directed through the HDMI port with embedded time code to an external monitor or recorder. As mentioned earlier, you can simultaneously display the video on the color LCD as it is recorded to your memory card. You can choose whether to display the captured image and scene and camera shooting information on the LCD as you shoot. This capability allows professional videographers (or other advanced shooters) more latitude in color correction through the enhanced color space, improved monitoring during the shoot, and more versatile post-production workflow. You can, for example, synchronize the EOS RP's video capture with the start/stop of the external video recorder.

Movie files are limited to 4GB in size if you are using an SDHC card (those with a capacity of 32GB or less). The EOS RP formats such cards using the FAT32 file system, which cannot store files larger than 4GB. If a clip stored on such a card reaches that size, the EOS RP will create a new file and continue shooting. The separate files must be viewed separately and/or combined in a movie editor.

On the other hand, SDXC (with capacities of 64GB or more) are formatted in the camera using the exFAT file system and files can exceed 4GB. However, your *computer's operating system* may have some restrictions on file size.

In any case, the maximum recording time for a movie clip is 29 minutes, 59 seconds, regardless of file size. Movie shooting will stop automatically, but you can begin shooting a new movie immediately by pressing the Movie button again. The EOS Movie Utility can merge multiple MP4 files into one longer file. You can also use third-party movie-editing software to edit and combine your clips.

The 4GB limitation is not as noxious as you might think, and you can continue capture without, in practice, a significant interruption. Roughly 30 seconds before the 4GB file size is reached, the elapsed shooting time displayed on the LCD will begin blinking. The maximum shooting time of 29 minutes, 59 seconds was established because some jurisdictions classify equipment that can capture more than 30 minutes as "camcorders" at higher tax rates.

Resolution

Resolution choices are a little less techie:

- **3840 × 2160 (4K).** This ultra-high-definition format is the wave of the future, even if content and display choices are limited at present. As you advance in the video world, you'll probably find yourself shooting 4K a lot, even if you intend to distribute Full HD video. Many editors swear that 4K video converted to Full HD is better than Full HD video captured natively. The EOS RP's inability to use Dual Pixel AF in 4K mode is the only thing that keeps UHD mode from being the standard format for avid video shooters.

- **1920 × 1080 (1080p).** This resolution is so-called "full HD" and is the maximum resolution displayed when using the HDTV format. Many monitors and most HD televisions can display this resolution, and you'll have the best image quality when you use it. Use this resolution for your "professional" productions, especially those you'll be editing and converting to nifty-looking DVDs. However, the top-of-the-line resolution requires the most storage space, as mentioned earlier. This means you can fit a collection of individual clips amounting to no more than about or 1 hour 4 minutes (using IPB) on a single 16GB memory card.

- ■ **1280 × 720.** "Standard HD" provides less resolution, and can be displayed on any monitor or television that claims HDTV compatibility. If your production will appear only on computer monitors with 1280 × 720 resolution, or on HDTVs that max out at 720p, this resolution will be fine. Don't choose this resolution to stretch your memory cards; it uses a 60/30 fps capture rate that streams an amount of data similar to that of 1080p shooting, so the elapsed time of your clips on a single card will be roughly the same.

Frame Rate

In the EOS RP world, in which all video is shot using *progressive scan* with no *interlaced scan* option, frame rates are easy to choose. (Interlacing is a capture method in which even/odd numbered lines of each frame are captured alternately; with progressive scan, all the lines in a frame are captured consecutively.) Fortunately, one seemingly confusing set of alternatives can be dispensed with quickly: The 50/25 fps and 60/30 fps options can be considered as pairs of *video*-oriented frame rates. The 60/30 fps rates are used only where the NTSC television standard is in place, such as North America, Japan, Korea, and a few other places. The 50/25 frame rates are used where the PAL standard reigns, such as Europe, Russia, China, Africa, Australia, and other places. For simplicity, I'll refer just to the 60/30 frame rates in this section; if you're reading this in India, just convert to 50/25.

The third possibility is 24 fps, available with 4K shooting, which is a standard frame rate used for motion pictures. Keep in mind that the rates are *nominal*. A 24 fps setting yields 23.976 frames per second; 30 fps gives you 29.97 actual "frames" per second.

The difference lies in the two "worlds" of motion images—film and video. The standard frame rate for motion picture film is 24 fps, while the video rate, at least in the United States, Japan, and those other places using the NTSC standard, is 30 fps. Computer-editing software can handle either type, and convert between them. The choice between 24 fps and 30 fps is determined by what you plan to do with your video.

The short explanation is that shooting at 24 fps gives your movie a "film" look, excellent for showing fine detail. However, if your clip has moving subjects, or you pan the camera, 24 fps can produce a jerky effect called "judder." A 30 or 60 fps rate produces a home-video look that some feel is less desirable, but which is smoother and less jittery when displayed on an electronic monitor. I suggest you try both and use the frame rate that best suits your tastes and video-editing software.

Another consideration that we can't do much about is the difference between a *rolling shutter* and *global shutter*. In progressive scan mode, each line is captured one after another, so that a moving subject may have perceptibly relocated (part of it anyway) during the capture of a frame. The EOS RP's rolling shutter may produce Jell-O-like effects with such motion. A global shutter, like those used in professional video cameras, captures the entire frame at once, eliminating that problem. Without benefit of a global shutter in our EOS RP, we at least need to be aware of the possible result when shooting action.

HDR Movies

You can extend the dynamic range of your movies in high-contrast situations by shooting HDR movies. Effectively, this mode is a type of in-camera bracketing to provide an expanded dynamic range and improved highlight rendition. The Movie Recording Size setting under Movie Recording Quality must be set to Full HD 29.9P IPB or Full HD 25.00P IPB. Highlight Tone Priority and Time Lapse Movies must be disabled.

With the Mode Dial set to the Movie position, press SET and use the up/down directional buttons to choose HDR Movie. Then shoot a movie conventionally. Multiple frames are merged to create an HDR movie. You may see excessive noise or some distortion, so you'll want to experiment with this feature to see how useful it is to you.

You should be using an RF- or EF-mount lens to shoot HDR movies in Full HD. If you're using EF-S lenses with an adapter or when you use the Movie Cropping entry, movies are recorded in Standard HD. HDR movies are not available when using Highlight Tone Priority, Canon Log, or when shooting time-lapse movies.

Exposure Options

You can select fully automatic exposure, or elect to specify exposure manually for creative reasons. The EOS RP will select an ISO speed for you automatically in all cases, generally sticking to the range ISO 100 to ISO 12800. (Some oddball exceptions are applied for various combinations of exposure mode and ISO speed settings made in the Shooting 2 menu.) Exposure can be locked with the * button, and cancelled with the AF point selection button located to the right of the * button. Here are your options:

- **Fully automatic exposure.** The EOS RP will automatically select an appropriate exposure for you if the Mode Dial is set to Scene Intelligent Auto, P (program auto exposure), or B (bulb exposure). Note that B will not produce a bulb or time exposure; the camera defaults to P when you use the B position. The idea is to prevent you from losing video capture capabilities if you accidentally select B by mistake. In Scene Intelligent Auto, the EOS RP will analyze your subject and select a Scene type and display it on the upper-left corner of the LCD monitor.

- **Manual exposure.** Choose Movie Manual and you can specify ISO speed, shutter speed, and aperture.
  - **ISO.** Press the ISO/Flash Exposure Compensation button on top of the camera to view the ISO speed setting screen. Adjust with the Main Dial. Choose Auto and the camera will select an appropriate ISO based on the shutter speed and aperture you have selected. During Manual exposure, the * button locks ISO at its current setting if you have selected Auto.
  - **Shutter speed.** Use the Main Dial to select a shutter speed.
  - **Aperture.** Use the Quick Control Dial to adjust aperture.

Tip

When choosing shutter speed or aperture, you can monitor exposure using the exposure level scale at the bottom of the LCD screen. For an additional check, you can press the INFO button to view a live histogram.

More on Shutter Speeds

You might think that setting your camera to a faster shutter speed will help give you sharper video frames. But the choice of a shutter speed for movie making is a bit more complicated than that. As you might guess, it's almost always best to leave the shutter speed at 1/30th or 1/60th second, and allow the overall exposure to be adjusted by varying the aperture and/or ISO sensitivity. We don't normally stare at a video frame for longer than 1/30th or 1/24th second, so while the shakiness of the *camera* can be disruptive (and often corrected by your camera's in-lens and in-body image stabilization), if there is a bit of blur in our *subjects* from movement, we tend not to notice. Each frame flashes by in the blink of an eye, so to speak, so a shutter speed of 1/30th or 1/60th second works a lot better in video than it does when shooting stills. Even shots with lots of movement are often sufficiently sharp at 1/60th second.

Higher shutter speeds introduce problems of their own. If you shoot a video frame using a shutter speed of 1/250th second, the actual moment in time that's captured represents only about 12 percent of the 1/30th second of elapsed time in that frame. Yet, when played back, that frame occupies the full 1/30th of a second, with 88 percent of that time filled by stretching the original image to fill it. The result is often a choppy/jumpy image, and one that may appear to be *too* sharp.

The reason for that is more social imprinting than scientific: we've all grown up accustomed to seeing the look of Hollywood productions that, by convention, were shot using a shutter speed that's half the reciprocal of the frame rate (that is, 1/48th second for a 24 fps movie). Professional movie cameras use a rotary shutter (achieving that 1/48th-second exposure by using a 180-degree shutter "angle"), but the effect on our visual expectations is the same. For the most "film-like" appearance, use 24 fps and 1/60th second shutter speed.

Faster shutter speeds do have some specialized uses for motion analysis, especially where individual frames are studied. The rest of the time, 1/30th or 1/60th of a second will suffice. If the reason you needed a higher shutter speed was to obtain the correct exposure, use a slower ISO setting, or a neutral-density filter to cut down on the amount of light passing through the lens. A good rule of thumb is to use 1/60th second or slower when shooting at 24 fps; 1/60th second or slower at 30 fps; and 1/125th second or slower at 60 fps.

Playback and Editing

Select a movie during playback and press SET to commence viewing. As a movie is being played back, press the SET button again to pause and produce a set of options at the bottom of the screen. When the icons are shown, use the QCD, touch screen, or directional buttons to highlight one, and then press the SET button to activate a function. Left to right at the bottom of the figure in the upper-left corner of Figure 15.15, the functions are as follows:

- **Playback.** Begins playback of the movie or album. To pause playback, press the SET button again. That restores the row of icons so you can choose a function.

- **Slow motion.** Displays the video in slow motion.

- **First frame.** Jumps to the first frame of the video, or the first scene of an album's first video snapshot.

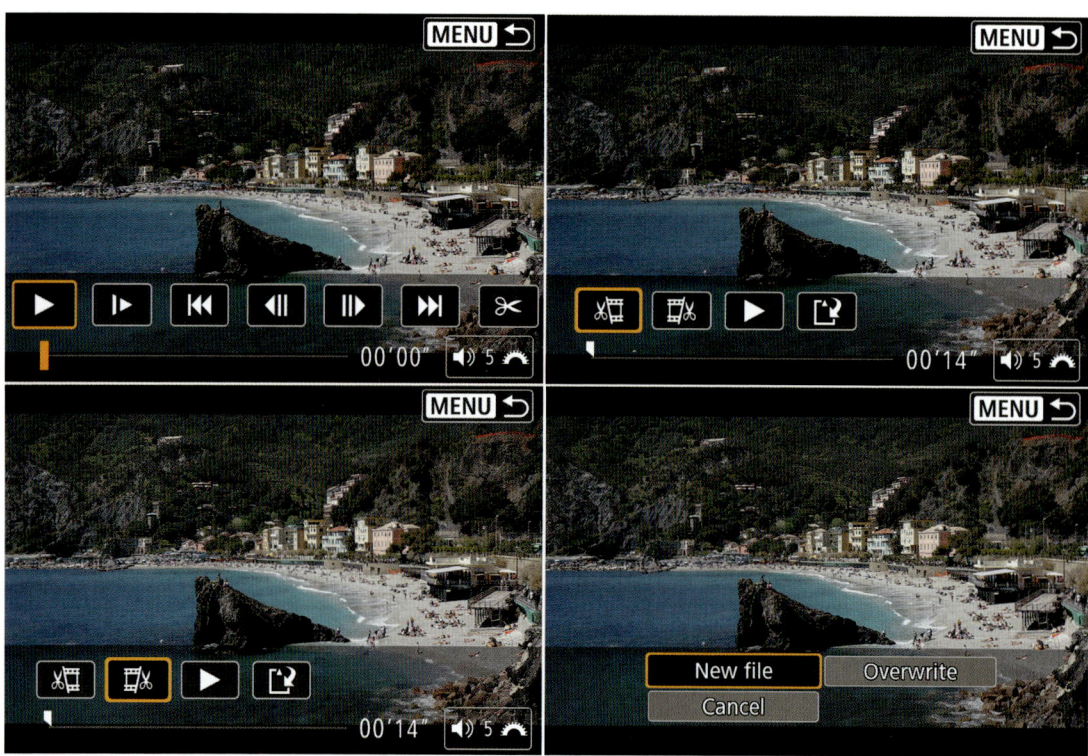

Figure 15.15 Playback and editing options.

- **Previous frame.** Press SET to view previous frame; hold down SET to rewind movie.

- **Next frame.** Press SET to view next frame; hold down SET to fast forward movie.

- **Last frame.** Jumps to last frame of the video, or the last scene of the album's last video snapshot.

- **Edit.** Summons an editing screen.

- **Frame grab (not shown).** This icon is located to the right of the Edit scissor icon, and available only when a 4K movie is being viewed. You can grab the displayed frame and save it as a JPEG image. I'll explain Frame Grab at the end of Chapter 16.

- **Playback position.** A bar at the bottom of the screen shows the amount of the clip that has been played so far.

- **Playback time.** In minutes and seconds with Movie Play Count: Rec Time enabled.

- **Volume.** Rotate the Main Dial to adjust the volume of the audio.

- **Menu.** Return to single-image display of the movie.

When you select Edit, the screen shown at upper right in Figure 15.15 appears. While reviewing your video, you can trim from the beginning or end of your video clip. Press SET to pause the video at the edit position, and select the scissors symbol. The icons that appear have the following functions:

- **Cut beginning.** Trims off all video prior to the current point. (Figure 15.15, upper right.)

- **Cut end.** Removes video after the current point. (Figure 15.15, lower left.)

- **Play video.** Play back your video to reach the point where you want to trim the beginning or end.

- **Save.** Saves your video to the memory card. A screen appears offering to save the clip as a New File, or to Overwrite the existing movie with your edited clip. (Figure 15.15, lower right.)

- **Menu.** Exits editing mode.

- **Adjust volume.** Modifies the volume of the sound.

16

Tips for Shooting Better Video

Once upon a time, the ability to shoot video with a digital still camera was one of those "gee whiz" gimmicks camera makers seemed to include just to have a reason to get you to buy a new camera. That hasn't been true for many years now, as the video quality of many digital still cameras has gotten quite good. Indeed, feature films have been shot entirely or in part using Canon dSLRs. The EOS RP really ups the ante by incorporating video capabilities that have been enhanced or were simply not available with previous Canon still cameras.

The Canon EOS RP provides advanced color- and tonal-correcting capabilities to a lightweight but powerful camera that can capture Ultra HD (4K) and HD-quality video while outperforming typical modestly priced digital video camcorders—especially when you consider the range of lenses and other helpful accessories available for it that are not possible with more limited video-only devices.

Using an External Recorder/Monitor

If you're truly becoming an advanced videographer, you'll probably be working with the EOS RP's ability to output "clean" non-compressed HDMI video to an external monitor or video recorder, including the Atomos Shogun lineup, which includes versions that are quite affordable, at least in terms of professional video gear. You can choose models both with and without an external LCD monitor, and capture to solid-state drives (SSD), a laptop's internal or connected hard drive, or to CFast memory cards (the latter chiefly as a nod to those still using the "fast" version of Compact Flash cards). Such equipment allows very high transfer rates and is certainly your best choice if you're shooting 4K video.

Probably the best of the lot for Canon EOS RP owners is the Atomos Ninja V, an extremely portable unit with a 5.2-inch screen and a $695 price tag that's currently the lowest for this type of device. (The only comparable monitor/recorder, the Video Devices PX-E5, costs $995.) Its size is a definite plus—if you're shooting video with a smaller, lightweight camera, you're going to need an equally compact recorder/monitor, such as the roughly 13-ounce Ninja V. Add a battery, HDMI cable, and a 2.5-inch solid-state drive, and you're ready to go.

The Ninja V has HDMI input and output jacks on its left edge, which you can see in Figure 16.1. The latter allows you to daisy-chain an even larger monitor or other device. A power button, headphone jack, microphone/audio input, and remote jack reside on the other edge. The touch screen enables you to view your video and access the monitor/recorder's menus and controls, which is convenient (except outdoors in cold weather when you're wearing gloves and might wish you had a few buttons to press instead). The only other "defect" of the unit is the noise produced by its fan; even when you're using an external microphone with your EOS RP, the fan noise may be picked up in a quiet room.

If you simply want a monitor and don't want to record your camera's output, the $400 Atomos Shinobi is a lightweight 1920 × 1080 HDMI monitor introduced in February 2019 that has the same display as the Ninja V, but lacks recording capabilities. It does have a headphone jack so you can output to an external recorder if you want. Like the screen on the Ninja V, the Shinobi can display full HD or 4K video (despite its native 1920 × 1080 resolution) with 10 stops worth of dynamic range, and includes presets to adjust the display for Canon Log output.

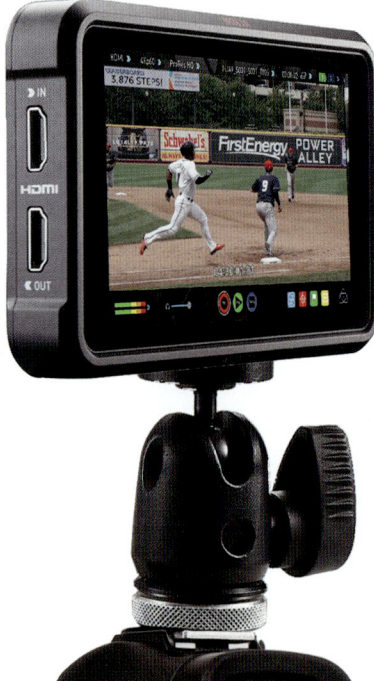

Figure 16.1
The Atomos Ninja V monitor/recorder.

Why use an external monitor or a monitor/recorder like the Ninja V, when your EOS RP has its own nifty monitor and can store quite a lot of video on its memory card? From a monitor standpoint, an external unit's screen is larger, easier to see, and offers more flexibility in positioning. The Ninja V's screen tilts up or down; mounted on a ballhead like the one in the figure, you can adjust an external screen to any angle, including reversing it to point in the same direction as the lens, so vloggers can monitor themselves as they record or stream their video blog.

But the best value may come from the recording capabilities of such a device. Internal video is saved to your memory card in the standard H.264/MPEG-4 as an MP4 file, which compresses that stream of images as much as 50X. Fortunately, the EOS RP can also direct its video output through the HDMI port in "clean" uncompressed 4:2:2 8-bit at up to UHD (ultra-high-definition) resolution.

TECH ALERT

Unless you're venturing into professional videography, you probably aren't obsessed with all those numbers in the previous paragraph. However, if you're terminally curious, the important things to keep in mind are:

■ **Transfer bit rate.** This is the speed the EOS RP outputs its video to your memory card or external recorder. High transfer rates (such as the 120 megabits per second required for 4K IPB, as mentioned in Chapter 15) require fast memory cards; an external recorder should be able to suck up video as quickly as your camera can deliver it.

■ **Encoding.** Although the "clean" video output to the HDMI port is not compressed, it is *encoded* using a procedure called *chroma subsampling,* which does reduce the amount of information that needs to be transferred. Chroma subsampling takes advantage of the fact that human beings don't detect changes in color (chroma) as easily as they do for brightness (luma). The designation 4:2:2 simply indicates that the full amount of brightness information is passed along ("4") while the two chroma values are sampled at half that rate ("2:2"). Subsampling in this way reduces the bandwidth of the otherwise uncompressed video signal by as much as one-third with no visual difference.

The HDMI port on the EOS RP accepts an HDMI mini-C cable. Canon offers the HTC-100, but I prefer to purchase less-pricey third-party cables, which I buy in convenient lengths of 3 feet, 6 feet, 10 feet, or longer. The cable can be connected to the monitor, recorder, or other device of your choice. (Some of the video screen shots in this book were output to a Blackmagic Intensity shuttle that allowed capturing stills of the EOS RP's menus, and video.)

But producing good-quality video is more complicated than just buying good equipment. There are techniques that make for gripping storytelling and a visual language the average person is very accustomed to seeing, but also unaware of. After all, by comparison we're used to watching the best productions that television, video, and motion pictures can offer. While this book can't make you a professional videographer, there is some advice I can give you that will help you improve your results with the camera.

There are many different things to consider when planning a video shoot, and when possible, a shooting script and storyboard can help you produce a higher-quality video.

Lens Craft

I covered the use of lenses with the EOS RP in more detail in Chapter 7, but a discussion of lens selection when shooting movies may be useful at this point. In the video world, not all lenses are created equal. The two most important considerations are depth-of-field, or the beneficial lack thereof, and zooming. I'll address each of these separately.

Depth-of-Field and Video

One thing that makes digital still cameras so attractive for professional video shooters—especially now that cameras like the EOS RP support 4K video—is that they have relatively large sensors, which provides improved low-light performance and results in the oddly attractive reduced depth-of-field, compared with many professional video cameras.

But wait! you say. No matter what size sensor is used to capture, say, a full HD video frame, isn't the number of pixels in that video frame exactly the same—1920 × 1080 pixels? That's true—the final resolution of the video image is precisely 1920 × 1080 pixels, whether you're capturing that frame with a point-and-shoot camera, a professional video camera, or a full-frame digital SLR like the Canon EOS RP. But that's only the *final* resolution. The number of pixels used to capture each video frame varies by sensor size.

For example, your EOS RP does *not* use only its central 1920 × 1080 pixels to capture a full HD video frame. If it did that, you'd have to contend with a significant "crop" factor, and the field of view of a wide-angle lens would be sharply curtailed. Instead, the EOS RP captures a full HD video frame using the full width of its 6240 × 4160 full-frame sensor, trimmed to the proportions of a 16:9 area, producing a negligible crop factor. Your wide-angle and telephoto lenses retain roughly their same fields of view, and you can frame and compose your video through the viewfinder normally, with only the top and bottom of the frame and a little off each side cropped off to account for the wider video aspect ratio. That's why the EOS RP gives you such great video quality, and why your video images retain roughly the same field of view and exact same depth-of-field you get with full-frame still images in Full HD mode.

It's a different story when capturing 4K video, however. The EOS RP uses a smaller area of the sensor, providing a crop that's similar to the area used for APS-C format stills and Super 35 video. Indeed, the EOS RP in 4K mode is very close to Super 35 format. Canon says this cropping is necessary to reduce heat buildup when shooting 4K with a small camera that limits head dissipation options.

Figure 16.2 shows at upper left the approximate capture areas for still photos, Full HD, and 4K video. You can also see that a 4K video frame *isn't* captured from the entire 36 × 24mm still frame. A smaller area measuring 3840 × 2160 in a 16:9 aspect ratio is captured instead. That means that any 4K video you shoot will be cropped from the full image, and result in a "magnification" or crop factor of about 1.8X compared to the 3:2 aspect ratio full frame for stills. You'll need to take that into consideration, especially when using wide-angle lenses.

Also shown in lower left and lower center of the figure are the video capture areas for some professional video sensors, the sensor in many snapshot cameras, and (at lower right) the APS-C sensor found in non-full-frame Canon EOS RP models.

As I noted in Chapter 7, a larger sensor calls for the use of longer focal lengths to produce the same field of view, so, in effect, a larger sensor has reduced depth-of-field. And *that's* what makes cameras like the EOS RP attractive from a creative standpoint. Less depth-of-field means greater control over the range of what's in focus. Your EOS RP, with its larger sensor, has a distinct advantage over consumer camcorders in this regard, and even does a better job than many professional video cameras. With a really fast lens, such as the Canon 85mm f/1.2 or 50mm f/1.2, some sensational selective focus effects can be achieved.

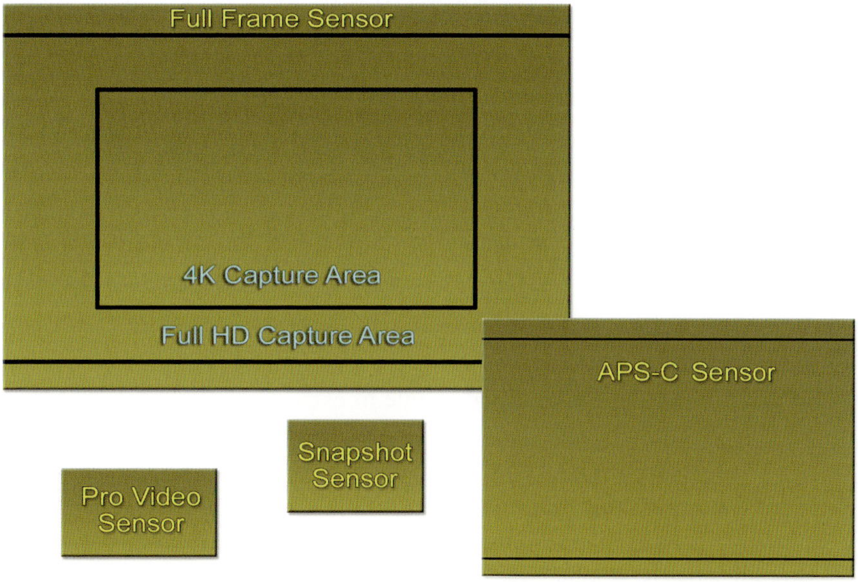

Figure 16.2
Video capture areas.

Zooming and Video

When shooting still photos, a zoom is a zoom is a zoom. The key considerations for a zoom lens used only for still photography are the maximum aperture available at each focal length ("How *fast* is this lens?), the zoom range ("How far can I zoom in or out?"), and its sharpness at any given f/stop ("Do I lose sharpness when I shoot wide open?").

When shooting video, the priorities may change, and there are two additional parameters to consider. The first two I listed, lens speed and zoom range, have roughly the same importance in both still and video photography. Zoom range gains a bit of importance in videography, because you can always/usually move closer to shoot a still photograph, but when you're zooming during a shot most of us don't have that option (or the funds to buy/rent a dolly to smoothly move the camera during capture). But, oddly enough, overall sharpness may have slightly less importance under certain conditions when shooting video. That's because the image changes in some way many times per second (24/30/60 times per second with the EOS RP in NTSC mode), so any given frame doesn't hang around long enough for our eyes to pick out every single detail. You want a sharp image, of course, but your standards don't need to be quite as high when shooting video.

Here are the remaining considerations:

- **Zoom lens maximum aperture.** The speed of the lens matters in several ways. A zoom with a relatively large maximum aperture lets you shoot in lower light levels, and a big f/stop allows you to minimize depth-of-field for selective focus. Keep in mind that the maximum aperture may change during zooming. A lens that offers an f/3.5 maximum aperture at its widest focal length may provide only f/5.6 worth of light at the telephoto position. If shooting wide open you may want to retain the same maximum aperture regardless of focal length, so depth-of-field (and, along with it, focus) will increase or decrease more predictably from shot to shot, because the *focal length* has changed (that is, going from wide-angle to tele, or the reverse), and not because the *effective aperture* has changed, too.

  In that case, you'll want to use a *constant aperture* lens (sometimes called a *fixed aperture* lens, which can be interpreted two ways). Often, such lenses are Canon L lenses; with less expensive optics with a similar focal length range having a variable maximum aperture. A typical example is the RF 24-105mm f/4L. The L lens's maximum aperture is f/4 from 24mm right up to 105mm.

- **Zoom range.** Use of zoom during actual capture should not be an everyday thing, unless you're shooting a kung-fu movie. However, there are effective uses for a zoom shot, particularly if it's a "long" one from extreme wide angle to extreme close-up (or vice versa). Most of the time, you'll use the zoom range to adjust the perspective of the camera *between* shots, and a longer zoom range can mean less trotting back and forth to adjust the field of view. Zoom range also comes into play when you're working with selective focus (longer focal lengths have less depth-of-field), or want to expand or compress the apparent distance between foreground and background subjects. A longer range gives you more flexibility.

■ **Linearity.** Interchangeable lenses may have some drawbacks, as many photographers who have been using the video features of their digital SLRs have discovered. That's because, unless a lens is optimized for video shooting, zooming with a particular lens may not necessarily be linear. Rotating the zoom collar manually at a constant speed doesn't always produce a smooth zoom. There may be "jumps" as the elements of the lens shift around during the zoom. Keep that in mind if you plan to zoom during a shot, and are using a lens that has proved, from experience, to provide a non-linear zoom. (Unfortunately, there's no easy way to tell ahead of time whether you own a lens that is well-suited for zooming during a shot.)

Keep Things Stable and on the Level

Camera shake's enough of a problem with still photography, but it becomes even more of a nuisance when you're shooting video. The image-stabilization feature found in many Canon lenses (and some third-party optics) can help minimize this. Any of them make an excellent choice for video shooting if you're planning on going for the hand-held cinema verité look.

Just realize that while hand-held camera shots—even image stabilized—may be perfect if you're shooting a documentary or video that intentionally mimics traditional home movie making, in other contexts it can be disconcerting or annoying. And even IS can't work miracles. As I'll point out in the next section, it's the camera movement itself that is distracting—not necessarily any blur in your subject matter.

If you want your video to look professional, putting the EOS RP on a tripod will give you smoother, steadier video clips to work with. It will be easier to intercut shots taken from different angles (or even at different times) if everything was shot on a tripod. Cutting from a tripod shot to a hand-held shot, or even from one hand-held shot to another one that has noticeably more (or less) camera movement can call attention to what otherwise might have been a smooth cut or transition.

Remember that telephoto lenses and telephoto zoom focal lengths magnify any camera shake, even with IS, so when you're using a longer focal length, that tripod becomes an even better idea. Tripods are essential if you want to pan from side to side during a shot, dolly in and out, or track from side to side (say, you want to shoot with the camera in your kid's coaster wagon). A tripod and (for panning) a fluid head built especially for smooth video movements can add a lot of production value to your movies.

Shooting Script

A shooting script is nothing more than a coordinated plan that covers both audio and video and provides order and structure for your video when you're in planned, storytelling mode. A detailed script will cover what types of shots you're going after, what dialogue you're going to use, audio effects, transitions, and graphics. A good script needn't constrain you: as the director, you are free to make changes on the spot during actual capture. But, before you change the route to your final destination, it's good to know where you were headed, and how you originally planned to get there.

When putting together your shooting script, plan for lots and lots of different shots, even if you don't think you'll need them. Only amateurish videos consist of a bunch of long, tedious shots. You'll want to vary the pace of your production by cutting among lots of different views, angles, and perspectives, so jot down your ideas for these variations when you put together your script.

If you're shooting a documentary rather than telling a story that's already been completely mapped out, the idea of using a shooting script needs to be applied more flexibly. Documentary filmmakers often have no shooting script at all. They go out, do their interviews, capture video of people, places, and events as they find them, and allow the structure of the story to take shape as they learn more about the subject of their documentary. In such cases, the movie is typically "created" during editing, as bits and pieces are assembled into the finished piece.

Storyboards

A storyboard makes a great adjunct to a detailed shooting script. It is a series of panels providing visuals of what each scene should look like. While the storyboards produced by Hollywood are generally of very high quality, there's nothing that says drawing skills are important for this step. Stick figures work just fine if that's the best you can do. The storyboard helps you visualize locations, placement of actors/actresses, props and furniture, and also helps everyone involved get an idea of what you're trying to show. It also helps show how you want to frame or compose a shot. You can even shoot a series of still photos and transform them into a "storyboard" if you want, such as in Figure 16.3.

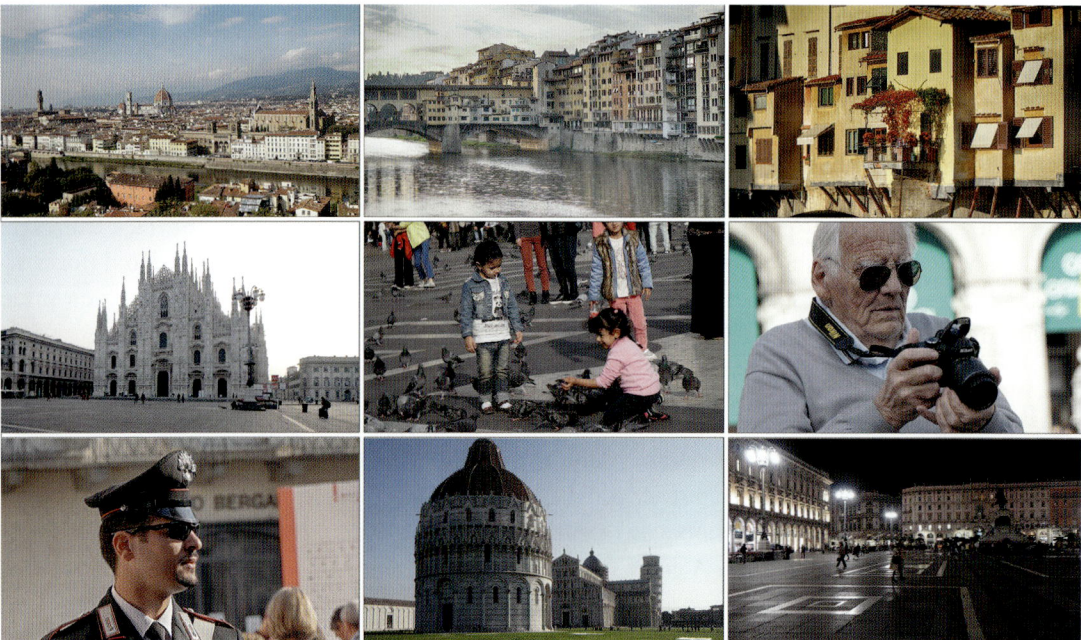

Figure 16.3 A storyboard is a series of simple sketches or photos to help visualize a segment of video.

Storytelling in Video

Today's audience is used to fast-paced, short-scene storytelling. To produce interesting video for such viewers, it's important to view video storytelling as a kind of shorthand code for the more leisurely efforts print media offers. Audio and video should always be advancing the story. While it's okay to let the camera linger from time to time, it should only be for a compelling reason and only briefly.

Above all, look for movement in your scene as you shoot. You're not taking still photographs! Perhaps your ideal still picture of an old castle in Segovia, Spain might be to show the edifice in its modern-day surroundings, but a movie needs to show something *moving,* like the hang glider that soared overhead when I captured the image shown in Figure 16.4. The juxtaposition of old and new added an interesting contrast to the video image (and later narration). If you've seen too many travel videos that looked like they could have been assembled from a series of still photos (a "slide show" so to speak), you'll know that motion is what brings many otherwise static scenes to life.

It only takes a second or two for an establishing shot to impart the necessary information. For example, many of the scenes for a video documenting a model being photographed in a Rock 'n' Roll music setting might be close-ups and talking heads, but an establishing shot showing the studio where the video was captured helps set the scene.

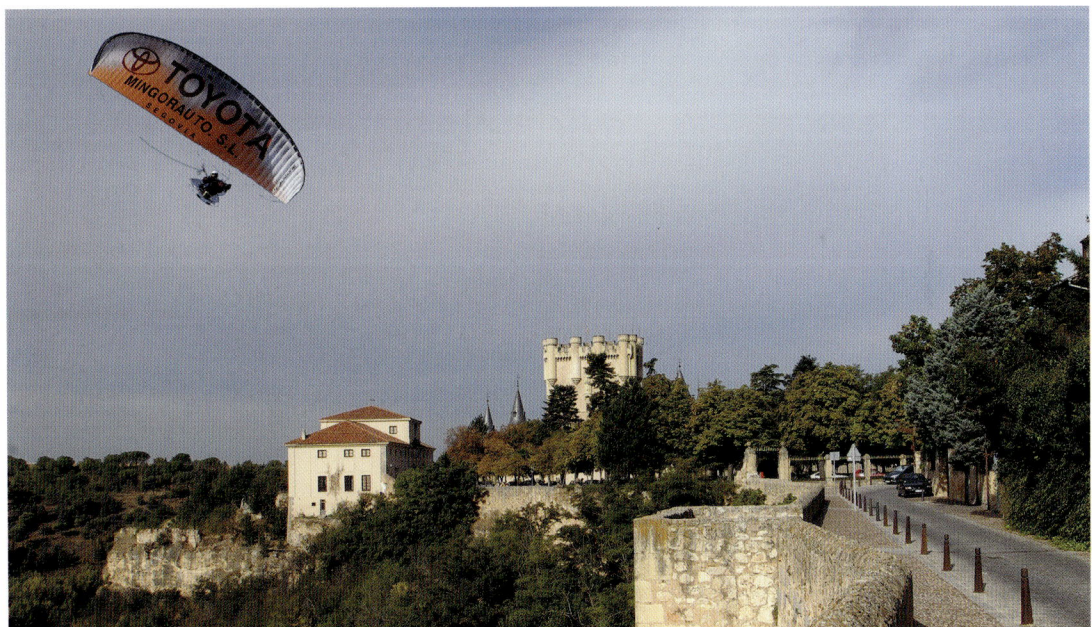

Figure 16.4 Movies need motion to come alive.

Provide variety too. If you put your shooting script together correctly, you'll be changing camera angles and perspectives often and never leave a static scene on the screen for a long period. (You can record a static scene for a reasonably long period and then edit in other shots that cut away and back to the longer scene with close-ups that show each person talking.)

When editing, keep transitions basic. I can't stress this enough. Watch a television program or movie. The action "jumps" from one scene or person to the next. Fancy transitions that involve exotic "wipes," dissolves, or cross fades take too long for the average viewer and make your video ponderous.

Composition

In movie shooting, several factors restrict your composition, and impose requirements you just don't always have in still photography (although other rules of good composition do apply). Here are some of the key differences to keep in mind when composing movie frames:

- **Horizontal compositions only.** Some subjects, such as basketball players and tall buildings, just lend themselves to vertical compositions. But movies are shown in horizontal-format only. So, if you're interviewing a local basketball star, you can end up with a worst-case situation like the one shown in Figure 16.5. If you want to show how tall your subject is, it's often impractical to move back far enough to show him full-length. You really can't capture a vertical composition. Tricks like getting down on the floor and shooting up at your subject can exaggerate the perspective, but aren't a perfect solution.

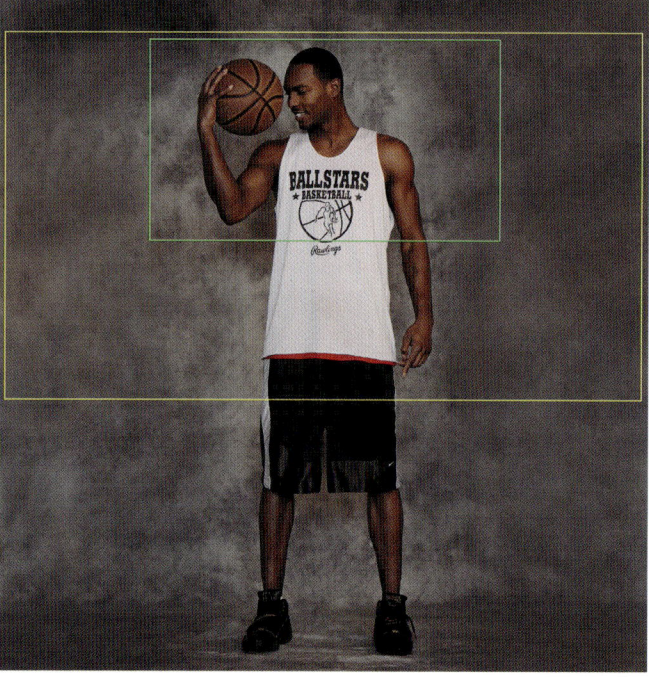

Figure 16.5
Movie shooting requires you to fit all your subjects into a horizontally oriented frame.

■ **Wasted space at the sides.** Moving in to frame the basketball player as outlined by the yellow box in Figure 16.5 means that you're still forced to leave a lot of empty space on either side. (Of course, you can fill that space with other people and/or interesting stuff, but that defeats your intent of concentrating on your main subject.) So, when faced with some types of subjects in a horizontal frame, you can be creative, or move in *really* tight. For example, if I was willing to give up the "height" aspect of my composition, I could have framed the shot as shown by the green box in the figure, and wasted less of the image area at either side.

■ **Seamless (or seamed) transitions.** Unless you're telling a story with a photo essay, still pictures often stand alone. But with movies, each of your compositions must relate to the shot that preceded it, and the one that follows. It can be jarring to jump from a long shot to a tight close-up unless the director—you—is very creative. Another common error is the "jump cut" in which successive shots vary only slightly in camera angle, making it appear that the main subject has "jumped" from one place to another. (Although everyone from French New Wave director Jean-Luc Goddard to Guy Ritchie—Madonna's ex—have used jump cuts effectively in their films.) The rule of thumb is to vary the camera angle by at least 30 degrees between shots to make it appear to be seamless. Unless you prefer that your images flaunt convention and appear to be "seamy."

■ **The time dimension.** Unlike still photography, with motion pictures there's a lot more emphasis on using a series of images to build on each other to tell a story. Static shots where the camera is mounted on a tripod and everything is shot from the same distance are a recipe for dull videos. Watch a television program sometime and notice how often camera shots change distances and directions. Viewers are used to this variety and have come to expect it. Professional video productions are often done with multiple cameras shooting from different angles and positions. But many professional productions are shot with just one camera and careful planning, and you can do just fine with your EOS RP.

Here's a look at the different types of commonly used compositional tools:

■ **Establishing shot.** Much like it sounds, this type of composition, as shown in Figure 16.6, upper left, establishes the scene and tells the viewer where the action is taking place. Let's say you're shooting a video of your offspring's move to college; the establishing shot could be a wide shot of the campus with a sign welcoming you to the school in the foreground. Another example would be for a child's birthday party; the establishing shot could be the front of the house decorated with birthday signs and streamers or a shot of the dining room table decked out with party favors and a candle-covered birthday cake. I wanted to show the studio where the video was shot.

■ **Medium shot.** This shot is composed from about waist to head room (some space above the subject's head). It's useful for providing variety from a series of close-ups and makes for a useful first look at a speaker. (See Figure 16.6, upper right.)

■ **Close-up.** The close-up, usually described as "from shirt pocket to head room," provides a good composition for someone talking directly to the camera. Although it's common to have your talking head centered in the shot, that's not a requirement. In Figure 16.6, center left, the subject was offset to the right. This would allow other images, especially graphics or titles, to be superimposed in the frame in a "real" (professional) production. But the compositional technique can be used with EOS RP videos, too, even if special effects are not going to be added.

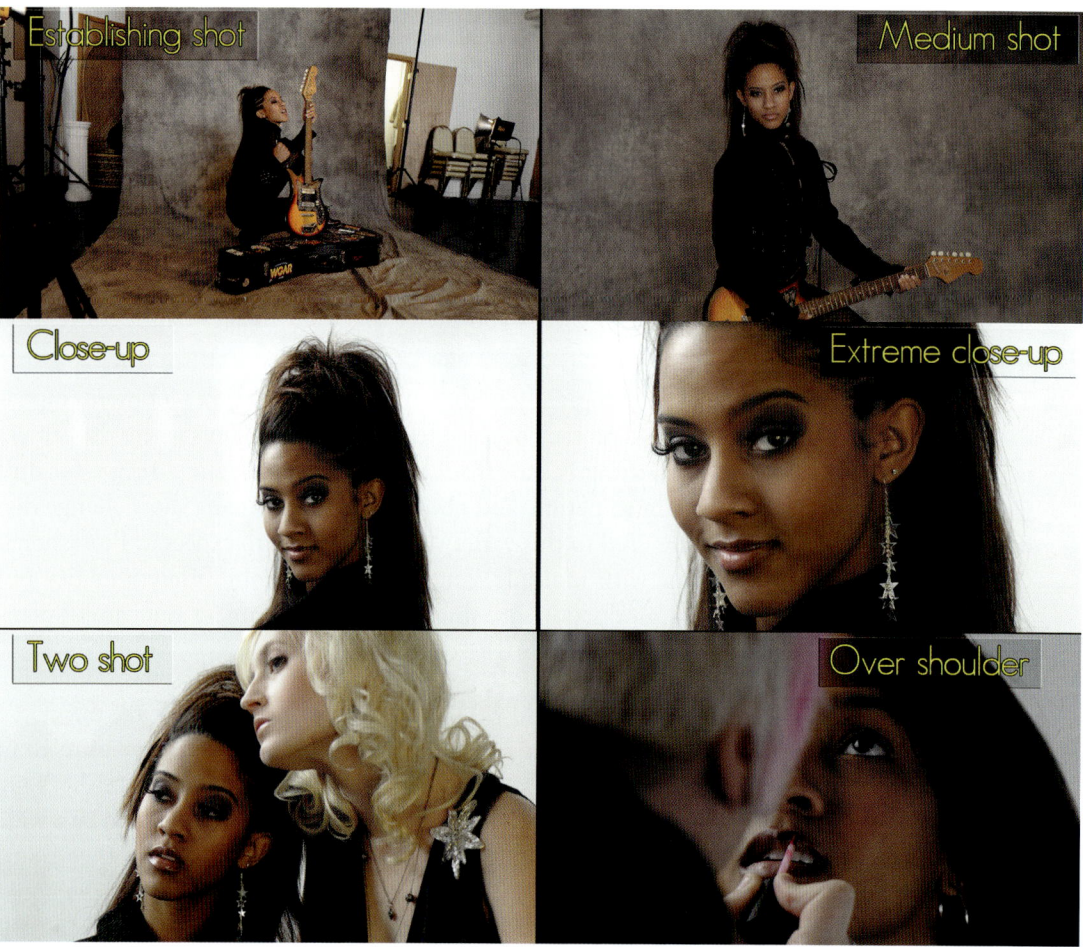

Figure 16.6 Shot choice provides different perspectives on a scene.

- **Extreme close-up.** When I went through broadcast training back in the '70s, this shot was described as the "big talking face" shot and we were actively discouraged from employing it. Styles and tastes change over the years and now the big talking face is much more commonly used (maybe people are better looking these days?) and so this view may be appropriate. Just remember, the EOS RP is capable of shooting in high-definition video and you may be playing the video on a high-def TV; be careful that you use this composition on a face that can stand up to high definition or 4K resolution. (See Figure 16.6, center right.)

- **"Two shot".** A two shot shows a pair of subjects in one frame. They can be side by side or one in the foreground and one in the background. (See Figure 16.6, lower left.) This does not have to be a head-to-ground composition. Subjects can be standing or seated. A "three shot" is the same principle except that three people are in the frame.

- **Over-the-shoulder shot.** Long a composition of interview programs, the "over-the-shoulder shot" uses the rear of one person's head and shoulder to serve as a frame for the other person. This puts the viewer's perspective as that of the person facing away from the camera. (See Figure 16.6, lower right.)

Lighting for Video

Much like in still photography, how you handle light pretty much can make or break your videography. Lighting for video can be more complicated than lighting for still photography, since both subject and camera movement are often part of the process.

Lighting for video presents several concerns. First off, you want enough illumination to create a useable video. Beyond that, you want to use light to help tell your story or increase drama. Let's take a better look at both.

Illumination

You can significantly improve the quality of your video by increasing the light falling in the scene. This is true indoors or out, by the way. While it may seem like sunlight is more than enough, it depends on how much contrast you're dealing with. If your subject is in shadow (which can help them from squinting) or wearing a ball cap, a video light can help make them look a lot better.

Lighting choices for amateur videographers are a lot better these days than they were a decade or two ago. An inexpensive incandescent video light, which will easily fit in a camera bag, can be found for $15 or $20. You can even get a good-quality LED video light for less than $100. Work lights sold at many home improvement stores can also serve as video lights since you can set the camera's white balance to correct for any color casts. You'll need to mount these lights on a tripod or other support, or, perhaps, to a bracket that fastens to the tripod socket on the bottom of the camera.

Much of the challenge depends upon whether you're just trying to add some fill-light on your subject versus trying to boost the light on an entire scene. A small video light will do just fine for the former. It won't handle the latter. Fortunately, the versatility of the EOS RP comes in quite handy here. Since the camera shoots video in Auto ISO mode, it can compensate for lower lighting levels and still produce a decent image. For best results, though, better lighting is necessary.

Creative Lighting

While ramping up the light intensity will produce better technical quality in your video, it won't necessarily improve the artistic quality of it. Whether we're outdoors or indoors, we're used to seeing light come from above. Videographers need to consider how they position their lights to provide even illumination while up high enough to angle shadows down low and out of sight of the camera.

When considering lighting for video, there are several factors. One is the quality of the light. It can either be hard (direct) light or soft (diffused) light. Hard light is good for showing detail, but can also be very harsh and unforgiving. "Softening" the light, but diffusing it somehow, can reduce the intensity of the light but make for a kinder, gentler light as well.

While mixing light sources isn't always a good idea, one approach is to combine window light with supplemental lighting. Position your subject with the window to one side and bring in either a supplemental light or a reflector to the other side for reasonably even lighting.

Lighting Styles

Some lighting styles are more heavily used than others. Some forms are used for special effects, while others are designed to be invisible. At its most basic, lighting just illuminates the scene, but when used properly it can also create drama. Let's look at some types of lighting styles:

- **Three-point lighting.** This is a basic lighting setup for one person. A main light illuminates the strong side of a person's face, while a fill light lights up the other side. A third light is then positioned above and behind the subject to light the back of the head and shoulders. (See Figure 16.7, top.)

- **Flat lighting.** Use this type of lighting to provide illumination and nothing more. It calls for a variety of lights and diffusers set to raise the light level in a space enough for good video reproduction, but not to create a mood or emphasize a scene or individual. With flat lighting, you're trying to create even lighting levels throughout the video space and minimize any shadows. Generally, the lights are placed up high and angled downward (or possibly pointed straight up to bounce off a white ceiling). (See Figure 16.7, bottom.)

- **"Ghoul lighting."** This is the style of lighting used for old horror movies. The idea is to position the light down low, pointed upward. It's such an unnatural style of lighting that it makes its targets seem weird and "ghoulish."

- **Outdoor lighting.** While shooting outdoors may seem easier because the sun provides more light, it also presents its own problems. As a general rule of thumb, keep the sun behind you when you're shooting video outdoors, except when shooting faces (anything from a medium shot and closer) since the viewer won't want to see a squinting subject. When shooting another human this way, put the sun behind her and use a video light to balance light levels between the foreground and background. If the sun is simply too bright, position the subject in the shade and use the video light for your main illumination. Using reflectors (white board panels or aluminum foil–covered cardboard panels are cheap options) can also help balance light effectively.

Figure 16.7
With three-point lighting (top) and flat lighting (bottom).

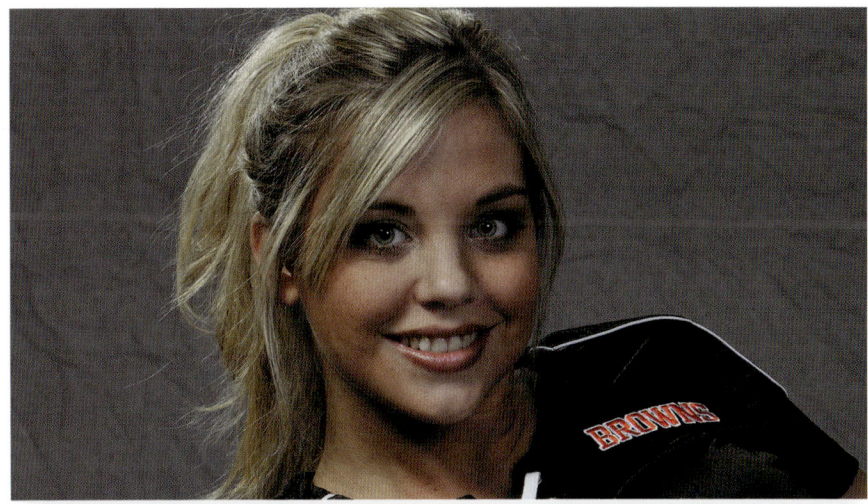

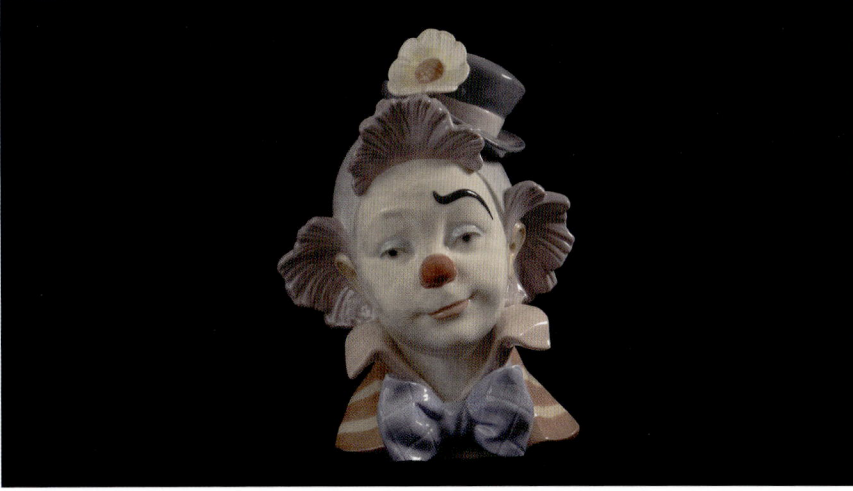

Audio

When it comes to making a successful video, audio quality is one of those things that separates the professionals from the amateurs. We're used to watching top-quality productions on television and in the movies, yet the average person has no idea how much effort goes in to producing what seems to be "natural" sound. Much of the sound you hear in such productions is recorded on carefully controlled sound stages and "sweetened" with a variety of sound effects and other recordings of "natural" sound.

Tips for Better Audio

Since recording high-quality audio is such a challenge, it's a good idea to do everything possible to maximize recording quality. Here are some ideas for improving the quality of the audio your camera records:

- **Get the camera and its microphone close to the speaker.** The farther the microphone is from the audio source, the less effective it will be in picking up that sound. While having to position the camera and its built-in microphone closer to the subject affects your lens choices and lens perspective options, it will make the most of your audio source. Of course, if you're using a very wide-angle lens, getting too close to your subject can have unflattering results, so don't take this advice too far. It's important to think carefully about what sounds you want to capture. If you're shooting video of an acoustic combo that's not using a PA system, you'll want the microphone close to them, but not so close that, say, only the lead singer or instrumentalist is picked up, while the players at either side fade off into the background.

- **Use an external microphone.** You'll recall the description of the camera's external microphone port in Chapter 2. As noted, this port accepts a stereo mini-plug from a standard external microphone, allowing you to achieve considerably higher audio quality for your movies than is possible with the camera's built-in microphones (which are disabled when an external mic is plugged in). An external microphone reduces the amount of camera-induced noise that is picked up and recorded on your audio track. (The action of the lens as it focuses can be audible when the built-in microphones are active.)

The external microphone port can provide plug-in power for microphones that can take their power from this sort of outlet rather than from a battery in the microphone. Canon provides optional compatible microphones such as the Canon Directional Microphone DM-E1 (around $240, see Figure 16.8); you also may find suitable microphones from companies such as Shure and Audio-Technica. If you are on a quest for superior audio quality, you can even obtain a portable mixer that can plug into this jack. Or, you might be using an Atomos recorder with professional microphone jacks. One good thing about the EOS RP is that so many pro videographers are using it that a wealth of add-on video gear, from monitors to cages and stabilizers are available for it.

Figure 16.8
External micro-
phones can improve
the sound quality of
your video.

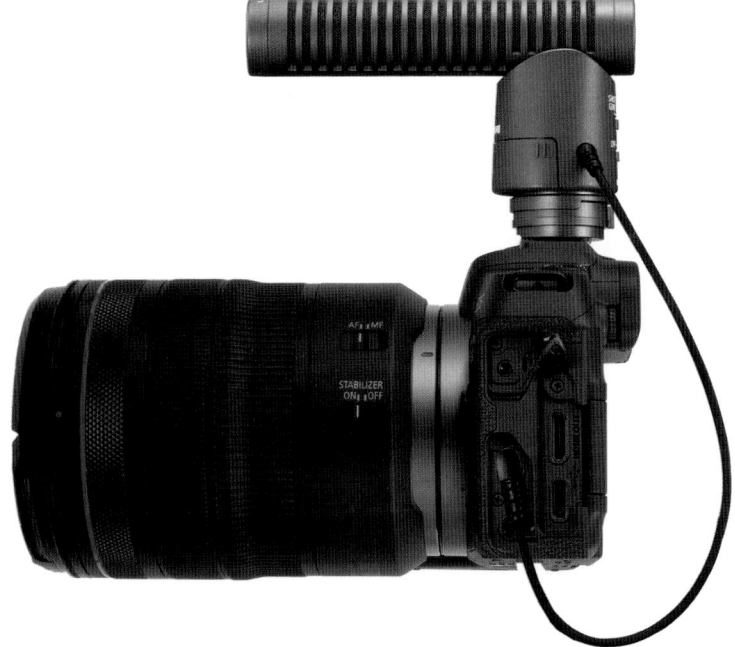

- **Hide the microphone.** Combine the first few tips by using an external mic, and getting it as close to your subject as possible. If you're capturing a single person, you can always use a lapel microphone (described in the next section). But if you want a single mic to capture sound from multiple sources, your best bet may be to hide it somewhere in the shot. Put it behind a vase, using duct tape to fasten the microphone, and fix the mic cable out of sight (if you're not using a wireless microphone).

- **Turn off any sound makers you can.** Little things like fans and air handling units aren't obvious to the human ear, but will be picked up by the microphone. Turn off any machinery or devices that you can plus make sure cell phones are set to silent mode. Also, do what you can to minimize sounds such as wind, radio, television, or people talking in the background.

- **Make sure to record some "natural" sound.** If you're shooting video at an event of some kind, make sure you get some background sound that you can add to your audio as desired in post-production.

- **Consider recording audio separately.** Lip-syncing is probably beyond most of the people you're going to be shooting, but there's nothing that says you can't record narration separately and add it later. It's relatively easy if you learn how to use simple software video-editing programs like iMovie (for the Macintosh) or Windows Movie Maker (for Windows PCs). Any time the speaker is off-camera, you can work with separately recorded narration rather than recording the speaker on-camera. This can produce much cleaner sound.

External Microphones

The single most important thing you can do to improve your audio quality is to use an external microphone. The EOS RP's internal stereo microphones mounted on the front of the camera will do a decent job, but they have some significant drawbacks, partially spelled out in the previous section:

■ **Camera noise.** There are plenty of noise sources emanating from the camera, including your own breathing and rustling around as the camera shifts in your hand. Manual zooming is bound to affect your sound, and your fingers will fall directly in front of the built-in mics as you change focal lengths. An external microphone isolates the sound recording from camera noise.

■ **Distance.** Anytime your EOS RP is located more than 6 to 8 feet from your subjects or sound source, the audio will suffer. An external unit allows you to place the mic right next to your subject.

■ **Improved quality.** Obviously, Canon wasn't able to install a super-expensive, super-high-quality microphone, even on an advanced camera. Not all owners of the EOS RP would be willing to pay the premium, especially if they didn't plan to shoot much video themselves. An external microphone will almost always be of better quality.

■ **Directionality.** The EOS RP's internal microphone generally records only sounds directly in front of it. An external microphone can be either of the directional type or omnidirectional, depending on whether you want to "shotgun" your sound or record more ambient sound.

You can choose from several different types of microphones, each of which has its own advantages and disadvantages. If you're serious about movie making with your EOS RP, you might want to own more than one. Common configurations include:

■ **Shotgun microphones.** These can be mounted directly on your EOS RP, although, if the mic uses an accessory shoe mount, you'll need the optional adapter to convert the camera's shoe to a standard hot shoe. I prefer to use a bracket, which further isolates the microphone from any camera noise. One thing to keep in mind is that while the shotgun mic will generally ignore any sound coming from *behind* it, it will pick up any sound it is pointed at, even *behind* your subject. You may be capturing video and audio of someone you're interviewing in a restaurant, and not realize you're picking up the lunchtime conversation of the diners seated in the table behind your subject. Outdoors, you may record your speaker, as well as the traffic on a busy street or freeway in the background.

■ **Lapel microphones.** Also called *lavalieres*, these microphones attach to the subject's clothing and pick up their voice with the best quality. You'll need a long enough cord or a wireless mic (described later). These are especially good for video interviews, so whether you're producing a documentary or grilling relatives for a family history, you'll want one of these.

■ **Hand-held microphones.** If you're capturing a singer crooning a tune, or want your subject to mimic famed faux newscaster Wally Ballou, a hand-held mic may be your best choice. They serve much the same purpose as a lapel microphone, and they're more intrusive—but that may be the point. A hand-held microphone can make a great prop for your fake newscast! The speaker can talk right into the microphone, point it at another person, or use it to record ambient sound. If your narrator is not going to appear on-camera, one of these can be an inexpensive way to improve sound.

■ **Wired and wireless external microphones.** This option is the most expensive, but you get a receiver and a transmitter (both battery-powered, so you'll need to make sure you have enough batteries). The transmitter is connected to the microphone, and the receiver is connected to your EOS RP. In addition to being less klutzy and enabling you to avoid having wires on view in your scene, wireless mics let you record sounds that are physically located some distance from your camera. Of course, you need to keep in mind the range of your device, and be aware of possible signal interference from other electronic components in the vicinity.

WIND NOISE REDUCTION

Always use the wind screen provided with an external microphone to reduce the effect of noise produced by even light breezes blowing over the microphone. Many mics include a low-cut filter to further reduce wind noise. However, these can also affect other sounds. You can disable the low-cut filters for some units by changing a switch on the back from L-cut (low cutoff) to Flat.

Stills from Movies

You cannot capture stills while shooting movies. You must stop video capture first, take your stills, and then resume movie shooting. However, you *can* grab an 8.3-megapixel 3840 × 2160 JPEG still image from any 4K video or 4K time-lapse movie during playback, using the EOS RP's Frame Grab feature. Just follow these steps:

1. Press the Playback button and select a 4K movie/time-lapse video. They are designated with a 4K icon on the shooting information screen. Press SET to begin playing the video.

2. As the movie plays, the movie playback panel appears. Press Pause to stop the movie on the frame you want to grab.

3. Use the directional buttons to select the Frame Grab icon (see Figure 16.9). It's located at lower far right, next to the Scissors icon.

4. A message "Save as a New Still Image" appears. Highlight OK to save that frame as a still JPEG.

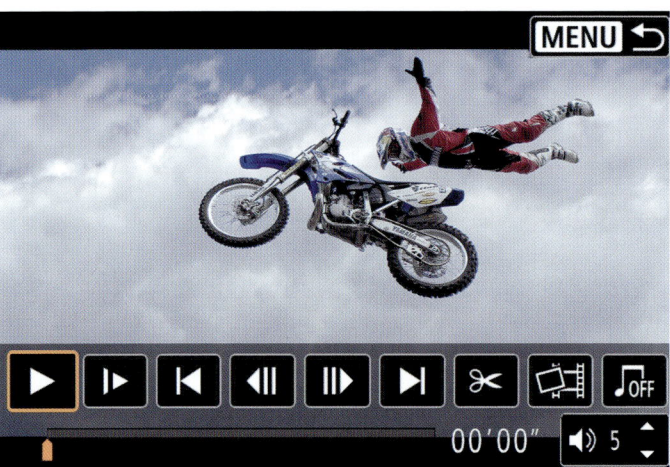

Figure 16.9
Grab a still frame from a 4K video.

17

Troubleshooting and Prevention

One of the nice things about modern electronic cameras like the Canon EOS RP is that they have fewer mechanical moving parts to fail, so they are less likely to "wear out." No film transport mechanism, no wind lever or motor drive, and no complicated mechanical linkages from camera to lens to physically stop down the lens aperture. Instead, tiny, reliable motors are built into each lens (and you lose the use of only that lens should something fail), and the EOS RP dispenses with one of the few major moving parts that digital SLRs have—the mirror that flips up and down with each shot not taken using live view.

Of course, the camera also has a moving shutter that can fail, but the shutter is built rugged enough that you can expect it to last 100,000 shutter cycles or more. Unless you're shooting sports in continuous mode day in and day out, the shutter on your EOS RP is likely to last as long as you expect to use the camera.

The only other things on the camera that move are switches, dials, buttons, the LCD screen, and the door that slides open to allow you to remove and insert the memory card. Unless you're extraordinarily clumsy or unlucky, there's not a lot that can go wrong mechanically with your EOS RP.

There are numerous other electrical and electronic connections in the camera (many connected to those mechanical switches and dials), and components like the color LCD screen that can potentially fail or suffer damage. The camera also relies on its "operating system," or *firmware*, which can be plagued by bugs that cause unexpected behavior. Luckily, electronic components are generally more reliable and trouble-free, especially when compared to their mechanical counterparts from the pre-electronic film camera days. Digital cameras have problems unique to their breed, too; the most troublesome being the need to clean the sensor of dust and grime periodically. This chapter will show you how to diagnose problems, fix many common ills, and, importantly, learn how to avoid them, when possible, in the future.

Updating Your Firmware

As I said, the firmware in your EOS RP is the camera's operating system, which handles everything from menu display (including fonts, colors, and the actual entries themselves), what languages are available, and even support for specific devices and features. Upgrading the firmware to a new version makes it possible to add new features while fixing some of the bugs that sneak in. As I write this, Canon has released only one firmware revision for the EOS RP—Version 1.1.0, which added a new silent shooting mode and fixed a few bugs. In addition, Canon has released updated firmware for the RF 24-105mm (an enhancement to ensure compatibility in the new silent shooting mode) and RF 35mm f/1.8 (which adds support for a "panning" scene mode that is available for the EOS RP's stablemate, the EOS R).

Most of the updates are minor. You can now use continuous shooting mode when the electronic shutter's silent shooting is enabled. Other changes corrected rare phenomena that could occur when large numbers of files in a specific format were saved to the memory card, and linear noise ("banding") appeared when specific lenses and image quality settings were combined. A rare abnormal viewfinder display error was corrected, too.

Official Firmware

Official firmware for your EOS RP is given a version number that you can view by turning the power on, pressing the MENU button, and scrolling to Firmware Ver. x.x.x in the Set-up 6 menu. The first number in the version string represents the major release number, while the second and third represent less significant upgrades and minor tweaks, respectively. Theoretically, a camera should have a firmware version number of 1.0.0 when it is introduced, but vendors have been known to do some minor fixes during testing and unveil a camera with a 1.0.1 firmware designation. It's likely, however, that any camera you buy new will have the latest firmware, or lag only one release behind. Most updating is done for currently owned cameras that need to keep pace with progress. Firmware upgrades are used most frequently to fix bugs in the software, and much less frequently to add or enhance features. Some of the bug fixes can affect only a tiny number of users or applications.

The exact changes made to the firmware are generally spelled out in the firmware release announcement. My recommendation is always to examine the remedies provided and decide if a given firmware patch is important to you. If not, you can usually safely wait a while before going through the bother of upgrading your firmware—at least long enough for the early adopters to report whether the bug fixes have introduced new bugs of their own. Check with the camera forums to see if the firmware caused more problems than it fixed before proceeding. Each new firmware release incorporates the changes from previous releases, so if you skip a minor upgrade you should have no problems.

Upgrading Your Firmware

If you're computer savvy, you might wonder how your EOS RP can overwrite its own operating system—that is, how can the existing firmware be used to load the new version on top of itself? It's a little like lifting yourself by reaching down and pulling up on your bootstraps. Not ironically, that's almost exactly what happens: At your command (when you start the upgrade process), the EOS RP shifts into a special mode in which it is no longer operating from its firmware but, rather, from a small piece of software called a *bootstrap loader*, a separate, protected software program that functions only at startup or when upgrading firmware. The loader's function is to look for firmware to launch or, when directed, to copy new firmware from a memory card or your computer to the internal memory space where the old firmware is located. Once the new firmware has replaced the old, you can turn your camera off and then on again, and the updated operating system will be loaded.

Because the loader software is small in size and limited in function, there are some restrictions on what it can do. For example, the loader software isn't set up to go hunting through your memory card for the firmware file. It looks only in the top or root directory of your card, so that's where you must copy the firmware you download. Once you've determined that a new firmware update is available for your camera and that you want to install it, just follow these steps. (If you chicken out, any Canon service center can install the firmware upgrade for you.)

Using a Card Reader

Note that, from time to time, Canon changes the firmware updating procedure. The Canon website will always provide directions for the latest method. Follow those directions if the steps below are slightly different.

WARNING

Use a fully charged battery or Canon's optional ACK-E6N AC adapter kit to ensure that you'll have enough power to operate the camera for the entire upgrade. Moreover, you should not turn off the camera while your old firmware is being overwritten. Don't open the memory card door or do anything else that might disrupt operation of the EOS RP while the firmware is being installed.

AC Adapter Kit ACK-E6N. This device is used with a *DC coupler*, the DR-E18, that replaces the LP-E17 battery and powers the Canon EOS RP from AC current. Note that the ACK-E6N adapter can be used with other Canon EOS models with an appropriate coupler; the EOS R, for example, requires the DR-E6 unit.

1. Download the firmware from Canon (you'll find it in the Downloads section of the Support portion of Canon's website) and place it on your computer's hard drive. The firmware is contained in a self-extracting file for either Windows or Mac OS. It will have a name such as EOSR0110.fir.

2. In your camera, format a memory card. Choose Format from the Set-up menu, and initialize the card (make sure you don't have images you want to keep before you do this!).

3. You can copy the upgrade software to the card using a card reader.

4. Insert the card in the camera. With the EOS RP set to P, turn the camera on, press MENU and scroll to Firmware Ver. x.x.x at the bottom of the Set-up 6 menu and press the SET button. The camera displays a message listing the current firmware version, and offering to update. Select OK, and it will check to see if there is a firmware file on the card.

5. If a firmware file is found, you'll see the current firmware version, and an option to update. Choose OK and press the SET button to begin loading the update program.

6. A confirmation screen will appear. Select OK and press SET to continue. As the Firmware Update Program loads, you'll see a progress screen.

7. Next, you'll get the opportunity to confirm that the version you're upgrading to is the one you want. You can press the MENU button to cancel. (Yes, I know there are a lot of confirmation screens; Canon wants to make sure you don't upgrade your firmware by accident, or, possibly, intentionally.)

8. Finally, the very last confirmation screen. Select OK, and press SET, and, I promise, the actual firmware update will really begin.

9. While the firmware updates, you'll be warned not to turn off the power switch or touch any of the EOS RP's buttons.

10. When the update complete screen appears, you can turn off the EOS RP, remove the AC adapter, if used, and reinsert the battery. Then turn the camera on to boot up your camera with the new firmware update.

11. Be sure to reformat the card before returning it to regular use to remove the firmware software.

Using Direct Camera USB Link to Copy the Software

The procedure is slightly different (and a little more automated) if you choose to transfer the firmware software to the camera through a USB linkup. Follow these instructions to get started:

1. Connect the camera (with a freshly charged battery or attached to an AC Adapter) to the computer using the USB cable and turn it on.

2. Set the mode dial to P mode.

3. Insert an SD card that has been formatted in the camera.

4. Load the EOS Utility.

5. Click the Camera/Settings/Remote Shooting button.

6. Select the firmware update option. When the Update Firmware window appears at the bottom of the EOS Utility, choose OK.

7. Click Yes in the confirmation screen.

8. Follow the instructions in the dialog boxes that pop up next by pressing the SET button on the camera.

Protecting Your LCD

The 3-inch color LCD screen on the back of your EOS RP almost seems like a target for banging, scratching, and other abuse. Fortunately, it's quite rugged, and a few errant knocks are unlikely to shatter the protective cover over the LCD, and scratches won't easily mar its surface. However, if you want to be on the safe side, there are several protective products you can purchase to keep your LCD safe—and, in some cases, make it a little easier to view.

As I've noted before, placing a protector on your screen can reduce the sensitivity of the touch screen. However, I have not had any problems with the plastic overlays and GGS glass shields I've used. Keep in mind that the screen detects capacitance changes, so pressing the touch screen with a stylus or other tool instead of your finger is not going to work very well. Here's a quick overview of your options.

■ **Plastic overlays.** The simplest solution (although not always the cheapest) is to apply a plastic overlay sheet or "skin" cut to fit your LCD. These adhere either by static electricity or through a light adhesive coating that's even less clingy than stick-it notes. You can cut down overlays made for PDAs (although these can be pricey at up to $19.95 for a set of several sheets), or purchase overlays sold specifically for digital cameras. These products will do a good job of shielding your EOS RP's LCD screen from scratches and minor impacts, but will not offer much protection from a good whack.

■ **Acrylic/glass shields.** These scratch-resistant panels, laser cut to fit your camera perfectly, are my choice as the best protection solution, and what I use on my own EOS RP. A company called GGS/Larmour makes some nice glass protectors (see Figure 17.1); they're available for about $12–$20 from eBay, Amazon.com, and other online vendors. The ones I've tested do not interfere with the EOS RP's capacitive touch screen.

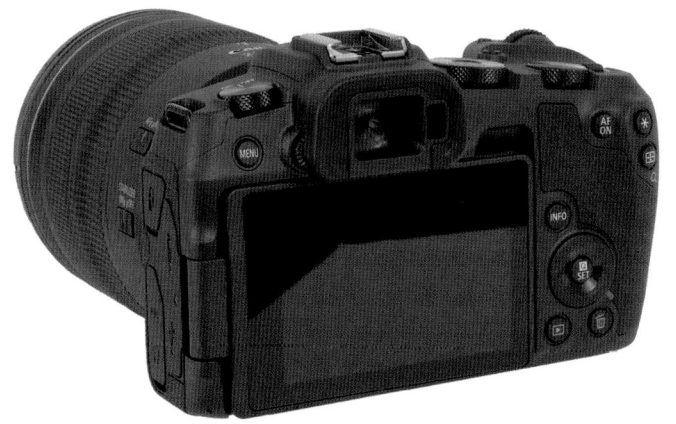

Figure 17.1
A tough glass shield can protect your LCD from scratches.

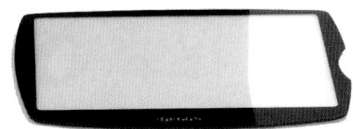

Troubleshooting Memory Cards

Sometimes good memory cards go bad. Sometimes good photographers can treat their memory cards badly. It's possible that a memory card that works fine in one camera won't be recognized when inserted into another. In the worst case, you can have a card full of important photos and find that the card seems to be corrupted and you can't access any of them. Don't panic! If these scenarios sound horrific to you, there are lots of things you can do to prevent them from happening, and a variety of remedies available if they do occur. You'll want to take some time—before disaster strikes—to consider your options.

All Your Eggs in One Basket?

The debate about whether it's better to use one large memory card or several smaller ones has been going on since even before there were memory cards. I can remember when computer users wondered whether it was smarter to install a pair of 200MB (not *gigabyte*) hard drives in their computer, or if they should go for one of those new-fangled 500MB models. By the same token, a few years ago, the user groups were full of proponents who insisted that you ought to use 128MB memory cards rather than the huge 512MB versions. Today, most of the arguments involve 32GB cards versus 64GB or 128GB cards, and I expect that as prices for 256GB and the still-scarce 512GB memory cards continue to drop, they'll eventually find their way into the debate as well. Size is especially important when you're using a camera like the EOS RP that captures 30-megapixel images.

Why all the fuss? Are 64GB memory cards more likely to fail than 32GB cards? Are you risking all your photos if you trust your images to a larger card? Isn't it better to use several smaller cards, so that if one fails you lose only half as many photos? Or, isn't it wiser to put all your photos onto one larger card, because the more cards you use, the better your odds of misplacing or damaging one and losing at least some pictures?

In the end, the "eggs in one basket" argument boils down to statistics, and how you happen to use your EOS RP. The rationales can go both ways. If you have multiple smaller cards, you do increase your chances of something happening to one of them, so, arguably, you might be boosting the odds of losing some pictures. If all your images are important, the fact that you've lost 100 rather than 200 pictures isn't very comforting.

Also, consider that the eggs/basket scenario assumes that the cards that are lost or damaged are always full. It's actually likely that a 32GB card might suffer a mishap when it's less than half-full (indeed, it's more likely that a large card won't be filled before it's offloaded to a computer), so you really might not lose any more shots with a single 64GB card than with multiple 32GB cards.

If you shoot photojournalist-type pictures, you probably change memory cards when they're less than completely full in order to avoid the need to do so at a crucial moment. (When I shoot sports, my cards rarely reach 80 to 90 percent of capacity before I change them.) Using multiple smaller cards means you must change them that more often, which can be a real pain when you're taking a lot of photos.

There are only two good reasons to justify limiting yourself to smaller memory cards when larger ones can be purchased at the same cost per-gigabyte. One of them is when every single picture is precious to you and the loss of any of them would be a disaster. If you're a wedding photographer, for example, and unlikely to be able to restage the nuptials if a memory card goes bad, you might even have an assistant ready to copy each card removed from the camera onto a backup hard drive.

To be even safer, you'd want to alternate cameras or have a second photographer at least partially duplicating your coverage so your shots are distributed over several memory cards simultaneously. (Strictly speaking, the safest route of all is to backup as you shoot to an on-site external drive through Wi-Fi in tethered shooting mode.)

If you deem none of these options sufficient, consider *interleaving* your shots. Say you don't shoot weddings, but you do go on vacation from time to time. Take 250 or so pictures on one card, or whatever number of images might fill about 25 percent of its capacity. Then, replace it with a different card and shoot about 25 percent of that card's available space. Repeat these steps with diligence (you'd have to be determined to go through this inconvenience), and, if you use four or more memory cards, you'll find your pictures from each location scattered among the different memory cards. If you lose or damage one, you'll still have *some* pictures from all the various stops on your trip on the other cards. That's more work than I like to do (I usually tote around a portable hard disk and copy the files to the drive as I go), but it's an option.

What Can Go Wrong?

There are lots of things that can go wrong with your memory card, but the ones that aren't caused by human stupidity are statistically very rare. Yes, a memory card's internal bit bin or controller can suddenly fail due to a manufacturing error or some inexplicable event caused by old age. However, if your card works for the first week or two that you own it, it should work forever. There's not a lot that can wear out.

The typical memory card is rated for a Mean Time Between Failures of 1,000,000 hours of use. That's constant use 24/7 for more than 100 years! Per the manufacturers, they are good for 10,000 insertions in your camera, and should be able to retain their data (and that's without an external power source) for something on the order of 11 years. Of course, with the millions of memory cards in use, there are bound to be a few lemons here or there.

Given the reliability of solid-state memory, compared to magnetic memory, though, it's more likely that your memory problems will stem from something that you do. Memory cards, particularly the SD variety, are small and easy to misplace if you're not careful. For that reason, it's a good idea to keep them in their original cases or a "card safe" offered by Gepe, Pelican, and others. Always placing your memory card in a case can provide protection from the second-most common mishap that befalls memory cards: the common household laundry. If you slip a memory card in a pocket, rather than a case or your camera bag, often enough, sooner or later it's going to end up in the washing machine and probably the clothes dryer, too. There are plenty of reports of relieved digital camera owners who've laundered their memory cards and found they still worked fine, but it's not uncommon for such mistreatment to do some damage.

Memory cards can also be stomped on, accidentally bent, dropped into the ocean, chewed by pets, and otherwise rendered unusable in myriad ways. It's also possible to force a card into your EOS RP's memory card slot incorrectly if you're diligent enough. Or, if the card is formatted in your computer with a memory card reader, your EOS RP may fail to recognize it. Occasionally, I've found that a memory card used in one camera would fail if used in a different camera (until I reformatted it in Windows, and then again in the camera). Every once in a while, a card goes completely bad and—seemingly—can't be salvaged.

Another way to lose images is to do commonplace things with your memory card at an inopportune time. If you remove the card from the EOS RP while the camera is writing images to the card, you'll lose any photos in the buffer and may damage the file structure of the card, making it difficult or impossible to retrieve the other pictures you've taken. The same thing can happen if you remove the memory card from your computer's card reader while the computer is writing to the card (say, to erase files you've already moved to your computer). You can avoid this by *not* using your computer to erase files on a memory card but, instead, always reformatting the card in your EOS RP before you use it again.

What Can You Do?

Pay attention: If you're having problems, the *first* thing you should do is *stop* using that memory card. Don't take any more pictures. Don't do anything with the card until you've figured out what's wrong. Your second line of defense (your first line is to be sufficiently careful with your cards that you avoid problems in the first place) is to *do no harm* that hasn't already been done. Read the rest of this section and then, if necessary, decide on a course of action (such as using a data recovery service or software described later) before you risk damaging the data on your card further.

Now that you've calmed down, the first thing to check is whether you've actually inserted a card in the camera. If you've set the camera in the Shooting menu so that Shoot w/o Card has been turned on, it's entirely possible (although not particularly plausible) that you've been snapping away with no memory card to store the pictures to, which can lead to massive disappointment later. Of course, the No Card Message appears on the LCD when the camera is powered up, and it is superimposed on the review image after every shot, but maybe you're inattentive, or aren't using picture review.

Things get more exciting when the card itself is put in jeopardy. If you lose a card, there's not a lot you can do other than take a picture of a similar card and print up some Have You Seen This Lost Flash Memory? flyers to post on utility poles all around town.

If all you care about is reusing the card, and have resigned yourself to losing the pictures, try reformatting the card in your camera. You may find that reformatting removes the corrupted data and restores your card to health. Sometimes I've had success reformatting a card in my computer using a memory card reader (this is normally a no-no because your operating system doesn't understand the needs of your EOS RP), and *then* reformatting again in the camera.

If your memory card is not behaving properly, and you *do* want to recover your images, things get a little more complicated. If your pictures are very valuable, either to you or to others, you can always turn to professional data recovery firms. Be prepared to pay hundreds of dollars to get your pictures back, but these pros often do an amazing job. You wouldn't want them working on your memory card on behalf of the police if you'd tried to erase some incriminating pictures. There are many firms of this type, and I've never used them myself, so I can't offer a recommendation. Use a

Google search to turn up a ton of them. A more reasonable approach is to try special data recovery software you can install on your computer and use to attempt to resurrect your "lost" images yourself. They may not actually be gone completely. Perhaps your card's "table of contents" is jumbled, or only a few pictures are damaged in such a way that your camera and computer can't read some or any of the pictures on the card. Some of the available software was written specifically to reconstruct lost pictures, while other utilities are more general-purpose applications that can be used with any media, including floppy disks and hard disk drives. They have names like OnTrack, Photo Rescue 2, Digital Image Recovery, MediaRecover, Image Recall, and the aptly named Recover My Photos. I use a software program called RescuePro, which came free with one of my SanDisk memory cards.

DIMINISHING RETURNS

Usually, once you've recovered any images on a memory card, reformatted it, and returned it to service, it will function reliably for the rest of its useful life. However, if you find a card going bad more than once, you'll almost certainly want to stop using it forever. See if you can get it replaced by the manufacturer, if you can, but, in the case of card failures, the third time is never the charm.

Cleaning Your Sensor

There's no avoiding dust. No matter how careful you are, some of it is going to settle on your camera and on the mounts of your lenses, eventually making its way inside your camera. As you take photos, the shutter opening and closing causes the dust to become airborne and eventually come to rest on the anti-aliasing filter atop your sensor. There, dust and particles can show up in every single picture you take at a small enough aperture to bring the foreign matter into sharp focus. No matter how careful you are and how cleanly you work, eventually you will get some of this dust on your camera's sensor. But even the cleanest-working photographers using Canon cameras are far from immune.

Fortunately, one of the EOS RP's most useful features is the automatic sensor cleaning system that reduces or eliminates the need to clean your camera's sensor manually. Canon has applied anti-static coatings to the sensor and other portions of the camera body interior to counter charge build-ups that attract dust. A separate filter over the sensor vibrates ultrasonically each time the EOS RP is powered on or off, shaking loose any dust.

Although the automatic sensor cleaning feature operates when you power the camera up or turn it off, you can activate it at any time. Choose Sensor Cleaning from the Set-up 3 menu, and select Clean Now. If you'd rather turn the feature on or off, choose Auto Cleaning instead, and then choose either Enable or Disable with the Quick Control Dial. Press SET, then press the MENU button to return to the Set-up 3 menu.

If some dust does collect on your sensor, you can often map it out of your images (making it invisible) using software techniques with the Dust Delete Data feature in the Shooting 5 menu. Operation of this feature is described in Chapter 11. Of course, even with the EOS RP's automatic sensor cleaning/dust-resistance features, you may still be required to manually clean your sensor from time to time. This section explains the phenomenon and provides some tips on minimizing dust and eliminating it when it begins to affect your shots.

Dust the FAQs, Ma'am

Here are some of the most frequently asked questions about sensor dust issues.

Q. I see tiny specks in my viewfinder. Do I have dust on my sensor?

A. If you see sharp, well-defined specks, they are clinging to the underside of your focus screen and not on your sensor. They have absolutely no effect on your photographs, and are merely annoying or distracting.

Q. I see a bright spot in the same place in all of my photos. Is that sensor dust?

A. You've probably got either a "hot" pixel or one that is permanently "stuck" due to a defect in the sensor. A hot pixel is one that shows up as a bright spot only during long exposures as the sensor warms. A pixel stuck in the "on" position always appears in the image. Both show up as bright red, green, or blue pixels, usually surrounded by a small cluster of other improperly illuminated pixels, caused by the camera's interpolating the hot or stuck pixel into its surroundings, as shown in Figure 17.2. A stuck pixel can also be permanently dark. Either kind is likely to show up when they contrast with plain, evenly colored areas of your image.

Finding one or two hot or stuck pixels in your sensor is unfortunately fairly common. They can be "removed" by telling the EOS RP to ignore them through a simple process called *pixel mapping*. If the bad pixels become bothersome, Canon can remap your sensor's pixels with a quick trip to a service center.

Bad pixels can also show up on your camera's color LCD panel, but, unless they are abundant, the wisest course is to just ignore them.

Figure 17.2
A stuck pixel is surrounded by improperly interpolated pixels created by the EOS RP's demosaicing algorithm.

Q. I see an irregular out-of-focus blob in the same place in my photos. Is that sensor dust?

A. Yes. Sensor contaminants can take the form of tiny spots, larger blobs, or even curvy lines if they are caused by minuscule fibers that have settled on the sensor. They'll appear out of focus because they aren't on the sensor surface but, rather, a fraction of a millimeter above it on the filter that covers the sensor. The smaller the f/stop used, the more in-focus the dust becomes. At large apertures, it may not be visible at all.

Q. I never see any dust on my sensor. What's all the fuss about?

A. Those who never have dust problems with their EOS RP fall into one of four categories: those for whom the camera's automatic dust removal features are working well; those who seldom change their lenses and have clean working habits that minimize the amount of dust that invades their cameras in the first place; those who simply don't notice the dust (often because they don't shoot many macro photos or other pictures using the small f/stops that makes dust evident in their images); and those who are very, very lucky.

Identifying and Dealing with Dust

Sensor dust is less of a problem than it might be because it shows up only under certain circumstances. Indeed, you might have dust on your sensor right now and not be aware of it. The dust doesn't settle on the sensor itself, but, rather, on a protective filter a very tiny distance above the sensor, subjecting it to the phenomenon of *depth-of-focus.* Depth-of-focus is the distance the focal plane can be moved and still render an object in sharp focus. At f/2.8 to f/5.6 or even smaller, sensor dust, particularly if small, is likely to be outside the range of depth-of-focus and blur into an unnoticeable dot.

However, if you're shooting at f/16 to f/22 or smaller, those dust motes suddenly pop into focus. Forget about trying to spot them by peering directly at your sensor with the shutter open and the lens removed. The period at the end of this sentence, about .33mm in diameter, could block a group of pixels measuring 40 × 40 pixels (160 pixels in all!). Dust spots that are even smaller than that can easily show up in your images if you're shooting large, empty areas that are light colored. Dust motes are most likely to show up in the sky, as in Figure 17.3, or in white backgrounds of your seamless product shots and are less likely to be a problem in images that contain lots of dark areas and detail.

To see if you have dust on your sensor, take a few test shots of a plain, blank surface (such as a piece of paper or a cloudless sky) at small f/stops, such as f/22, and a few wide open. Open Photoshop, copy several shots into a single document in separate layers, then flip back and forth between layers to see if any spots you see are present in all layers. You may have to boost contrast and sharpness to make the dust easier to spot.

Figure 17.3
Only the dust spots
in the sky are appar-
ent in this shot.

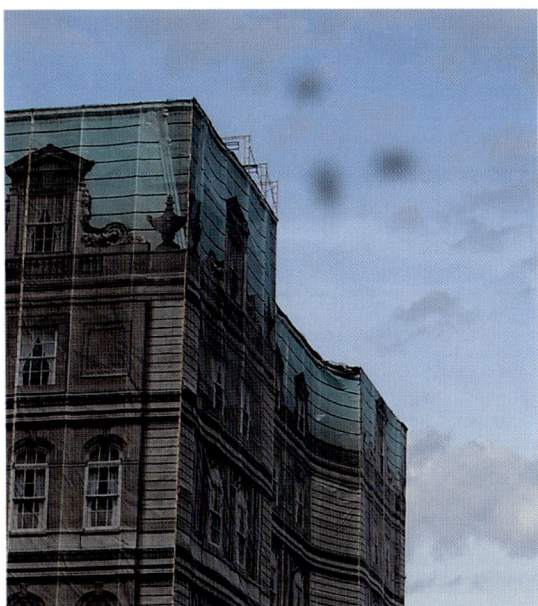

Avoiding Dust

Of course, the easiest way to protect your sensor from dust is to prevent it from settling on the sensor in the first place. Some Canon lenses come with rubberized seals around the lens mounts that help keep dust from infiltrating, but you'll find that dust will still find a way to get inside. Here are my tips for eliminating the problem before it begins.

■ **Clean environment.** Avoid working in dusty areas if you can do so. Hah! Serious photographers will take this suggestion with a grain of salt, because it usually makes sense to go where the pictures are. Only a few of us are so paranoid about sensor dust (considering that it is so easily removed) that we'll avoid moderately grimy locations just to protect something that is, when you get down to it, just a tool. If you find a great picture opportunity at a raging fire, during a sandstorm, or while surrounded by dust clouds, you might hesitate to take the picture, but, with a little caution (don't remove your lens in these situations, and clean the camera afterward!) you can still shoot. However, it still makes sense to store your camera in a clean environment. One place cameras and lenses pick up a lot of dust is inside a camera bag. Clean your bag from time to time, and you can avoid problems.

■ **Clean lenses.** There are a few paranoid types that avoid swapping lenses to minimize the chance of dust getting inside their cameras. It makes more sense just to use a blower or brush to dust off the rear lens mount of the replacement lens first, so you won't be introducing dust into your camera simply by attaching a new, dusty lens. Do this before you remove the lens from your camera, and then avoid stirring up dust before making the exchange.

■ **Work fast.** Minimize the time your camera is lensless and exposed to dust. That means having your replacement lens ready and dusted off, and a place to set down the old lens as soon as it is removed, so you can quickly attach the new lens.

■ **Let gravity help you.** Face the camera downward when the lens is detached so any dust in the camera will tend to fall away from the sensor. Turn your back to any breezes, indoor forced air vents, fans, or other sources of dust to minimize infiltration.

■ **Protect the lens you just removed.** Once you've attached the new lens, quickly put the end cap on the one you just removed to reduce the dust that might fall on it.

■ **Clean out the vestibule.** From time to time, remove the lens while in a relatively dust-free environment and use a blower bulb like the one shown in Figure 17.4 (*not* compressed air or a vacuum hose) to clean out the area behind the lens mount. A blower bulb is generally safer than a can of compressed air, or a strong positive/negative airflow, which can tend to drive dust further into nooks and crannies.

■ **Be prepared.** If you're embarking on an important shooting session, it's a good idea to clean your sensor *now*, rather than come home with hundreds or thousands of images with dust spots caused by flecks that were sitting on your sensor before you even started. Before I left on my recent trip to Spain, I put both cameras I was taking through a rigid cleaning regimen, figuring they could remain dust-free for a measly 10 days. I even left my bulky blower bulb at home. It was a big mistake, but my intentions were good.

■ **Clone out existing spots in your image editor.** Photoshop and other editors have a clone tool or healing brush you can use to copy pixels from surrounding areas over the dust spot or dead pixel. This process can be tedious, especially if you have lots of dust spots and/or lots of images to be corrected. The advantage is that this sort of manual fix-it probably will do the least damage to the rest of your photo. Only the cloned pixels will be affected.

■ **Use filtration in your image editor.** A semi-smart filter like Photoshop's Dust & Scratches filter can remove dust and other artifacts by selectively blurring areas that the plug-in decides represent dust spots. This method can work well if you have many dust spots, because you won't need to patch them manually. However, any automated method like this has the possibility of blurring areas of your image that you didn't intend to soften.

Figure 17.4
Use a robust air bulb for cleaning your sensor.

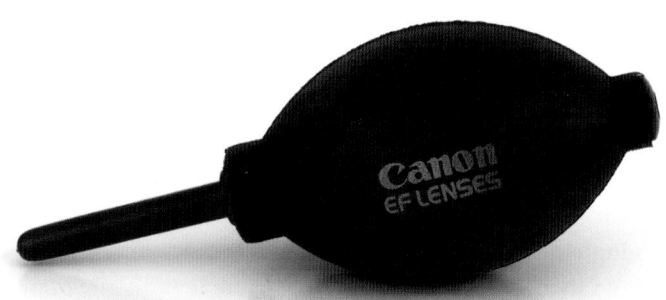

Sensor Cleaning

Those new to the concept of sensor dust actually hesitate before deciding to clean their camera themselves. Isn't it a better idea to pack up your EOS RP and send it to a Canon service center so their crack technical staff can do the job for you? Or, at the very least, shouldn't you let the friendly folks at your local camera store do it?

Of course, if you choose to let someone else clean your sensor, they will be using methods that are more or less identical to the techniques you would use yourself. None of these techniques are difficult, and the only difference between their cleaning and your cleaning is that they might have done it dozens or hundreds of times. If you're careful, you can do just as good a job.

Of course, vendors like Canon won't tell you this, but it's not because they don't trust you. It's not that difficult for a real goofball to mess up his camera by hurrying or taking a shortcut. Perhaps the person uses the "Bulb" method of holding the shutter open and a finger slips, allowing the shutter curtain to close on top of a sensor cleaning brush. Or, someone tries to clean the sensor using masking tape, and ends up with goo all over its surface. If Canon recommended *any* method that's mildly risky, someone would do it wrong, and then the company would face lawsuits from those who'd contend they did it exactly in the way the vendor suggested, so the ruined camera is not their fault. If you visit Canon's website, you'll find this recommendation: "If the image sensor needs cleaning, we recommend having it cleaned at a Canon service center, as it is a very delicate component."

You can see that vendors like Canon tend to be conservative in their recommendations, and, in doing so, make it seem as if sensor cleaning is more daunting and dangerous than it really is. Some vendors recommend only dust-off cleaning, using reasonably gentle blasts of air, while condemning more serious scrubbing with swabs and cleaning fluids. However, these cleaning kits for the exact types of cleaning they recommended against are for sale in Japan only, where, apparently, your average photographer is more dexterous than those of us in the rest of the world. These kits are like those used by official repair staff to clean your sensor if you decide to send your camera in for a dust-up.

As I noted, sensors can be affected by dust particles that are much smaller than you might be able to spot visually on the surface of your lens. The filters that cover sensors tend to be hard compared to optical glass. Cleaning the 24mm × 36mm sensor in your Canon EOS RP within the tight confines of the body call for a steady hand and careful touch. If your sensor's filter becomes scratched through inept cleaning, you can't simply remove it yourself and replace it with a new one.

There are three basic kinds of cleaning processes that can be used to remove dusty and sticky stuff that settles on your camera's sensor.

- **Air cleaning.** This process involves squirting blasts of air inside your camera with the shutter locked open. This works well for dust that's not clinging stubbornly to your sensor.

- **Brushing.** A soft, very fine brush is passed across the surface of the sensor's filter, dislodging mildly persistent dust particles and sweeping them off the imager.

- **Liquid cleaning.** A soft swab dipped in a cleaning solution such as ethanol is used to wipe the sensor filter, removing more obstinate particles.

Air Cleaning

Your first attempts at cleaning your sensor should always involve gentle blasts of air. Many times, you'll be able to dislodge dust spots, which will fall off the sensor and, with luck, out of the vestibule. Attempt one of the other methods only when you've already tried air cleaning and it didn't remove all the dust. First, remove the lens to give you access to the exposed sensor. (See Figure 17.5.)

Here are some tips for air cleaning:

- **Use a clean, powerful air bulb.** Your best bet is bulb cleaners designed for the job, like the Giottos Rocket. Smaller bulbs, like those air bulbs with a brush attached sometimes sold for lens cleaning or weak nasal aspirators, may not provide sufficient air or a strong enough blast to do much good.

- **Hold the EOS RP upside down.** Then look up into the body cavity as you squirt your air blasts, increasing the odds that gravity will help pull the expelled dust downward, away from the sensor. You may have to use some imagination in positioning yourself. (See Figure 17.6.)

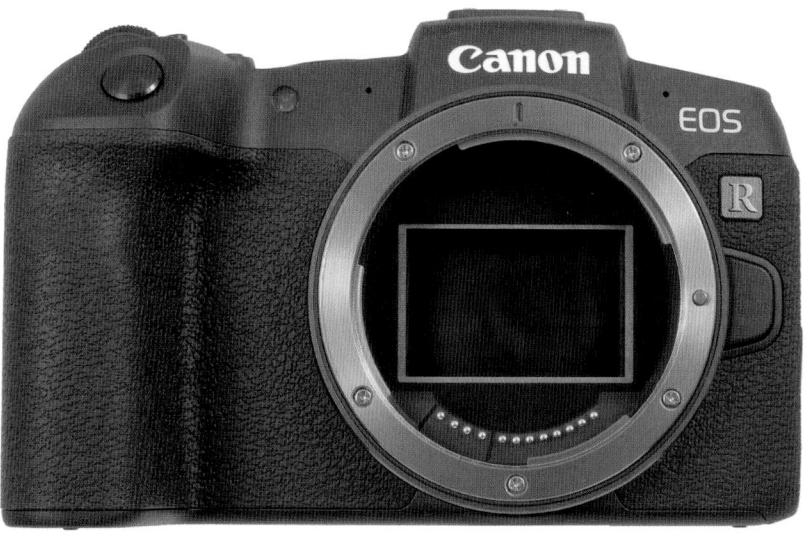

Figure 17.5
With the lens removed, you can commence cleaning the exposed sensor.

Figure 17.6
Hold the camera upside down when cleaning to allow dust to fall out.

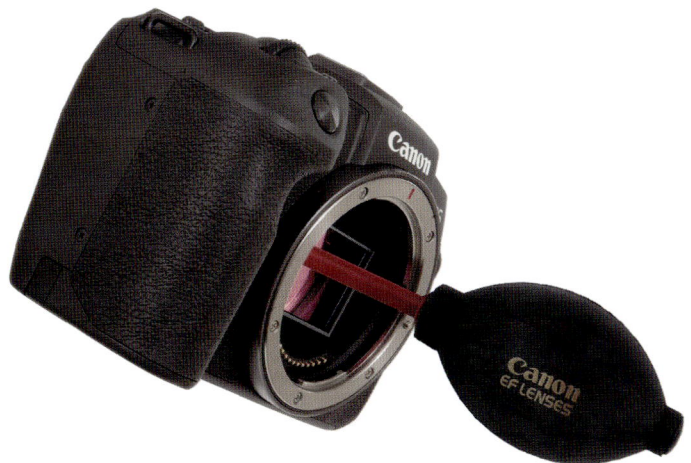

- **Never use air canisters.** The propellant inside these cans can permanently coat your sensor if you tilt the can while spraying. It's not worth taking a chance.
- **Avoid air compressors.** Super-strong blasts of air are likely to force dust under the sensor filter.

Brush Cleaning

If your dust is a little more stubborn and can't be dislodged by air alone, you may want to try a brush, charged with static electricity that can pick off dust spots by electrical attraction. One good, but expensive, option is the Sensor Brush sold at www.visibledust.com. You need one like the Artic Butterfly shown in Figure 17.7, that can be stroked across the short dimension of your EOS RP's sensor.

Figure 17.7
The motor in the Arctic Butterfly flutters the brush tips for a few minutes to charge them for picking up dust (left). Then, turn off the power and flick the tip above the surface of the sensor (right).

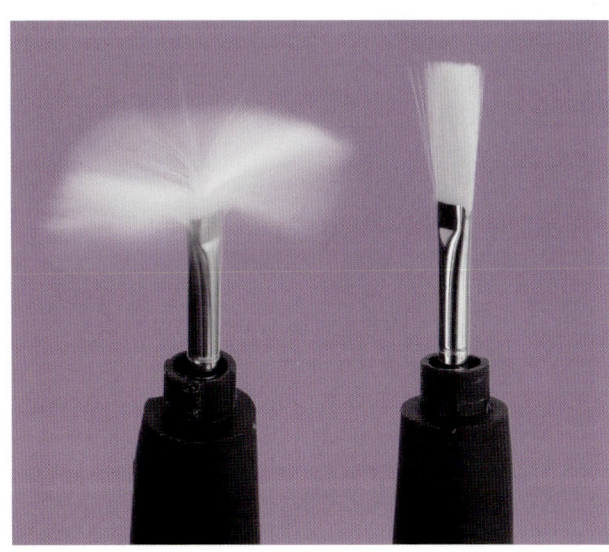

Ordinary artist's brushes are much too coarse and stiff and have fibers that are tangled or can come loose and settle on your sensor. A good sensor brush's fibers are resilient and described as "thinner than a human hair." Moreover, the brush has a non-conducting handle that reduces the risk of static sparks.

Brush cleaning is done with a dry brush by gently swiping the surface of the sensor filter with the tip. The dust particles are attracted to the brush particles and cling to them. You should clean the brush with compressed air before and after each use, and store it in an appropriate air-tight container between applications to keep it clean and dust-free. Although these special brushes are expensive, one should last you a long time.

Liquid Cleaning

Unfortunately, you'll often encounter stubborn dust spots that can't be removed with a blast of air or flick of a brush. These spots may be combined with some grease or a liquid that causes them to stick to the sensor filter's surface. In such cases, liquid cleaning with a swab may be necessary. During my first clumsy attempts to clean my own sensor, I accidentally got my blower bulb tip too close to the sensor, and some sort of deposit from the tip of the bulb ended up on the sensor. I panicked until I discovered that liquid cleaning did a good job of removing whatever it was that took up residence on my sensor.

You can make your own swabs out of pieces of plastic (some use fast-food restaurant knives, with the tip cut at an angle to the proper size) covered with a soft cloth or Pec-Pad, as shown in Figure 17.8. However, if you've got the bucks to spend, you can't go wrong with good-quality commercial sensor cleaning swabs, such as those sold by Photographic Solutions, Inc. (www.photosol.com).

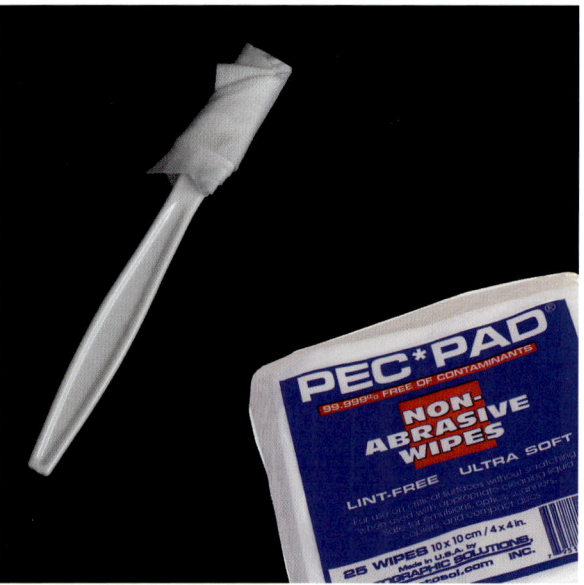

Figure 17.8
You can make your own sensor swab from a plastic knife that's been truncated.

You want a sturdy swab that won't bend or break so you can apply gentle pressure to the swab as you wipe the sensor surface. Use the swab with methanol (as pure as you can get it, particularly medical grade; other ingredients can leave a residue), or the Eclipse solution also sold by Photographic Solutions. Eclipse is quite a bit purer than even medical-grade methanol. A couple drops of solution should be enough, unless you have a spot that's extremely difficult to remove. In that case, you may need to use extra solution on the swab to help "soak" the dirt off.

Once you overcome your nervousness at touching your EOS RP's sensor, the process is easy. You'll wipe continuously with the swab in one direction, then flip it over and wipe in the other direction. You need to completely wipe the entire surface; otherwise, you may end up depositing the dust you collect at the far end of your stroke. Wipe; don't rub.

If you want a close-up look at your sensor to make sure the dust has been removed, you can pay $50–$100 for a special sensor "microscope" with an illuminator. Or, you can do like I do and work with a plain old Carson MiniBrite PO-55 illuminated 5X magnifier, as seen in Figure 17.9. It has a built-in LED and, held a few inches from the lens mount with the lens removed from your EOS RP, provides a sharp, close-up view of the sensor, with enough contrast to reveal any dust that remains. If you'd like to buy one for less than $10, I provide a link at my website, www.dslrguides.com/carson.

Figure 17.9
An illuminated magnifier like this Carson MiniBrite PO-55 can be used as a 'scope to view your sensor.

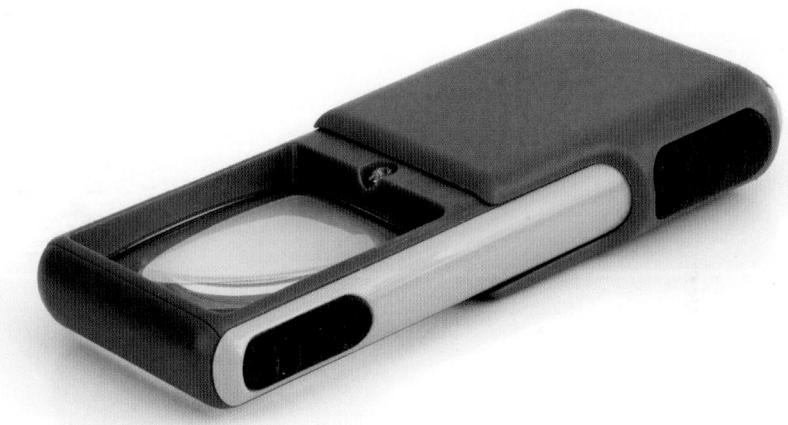

Index

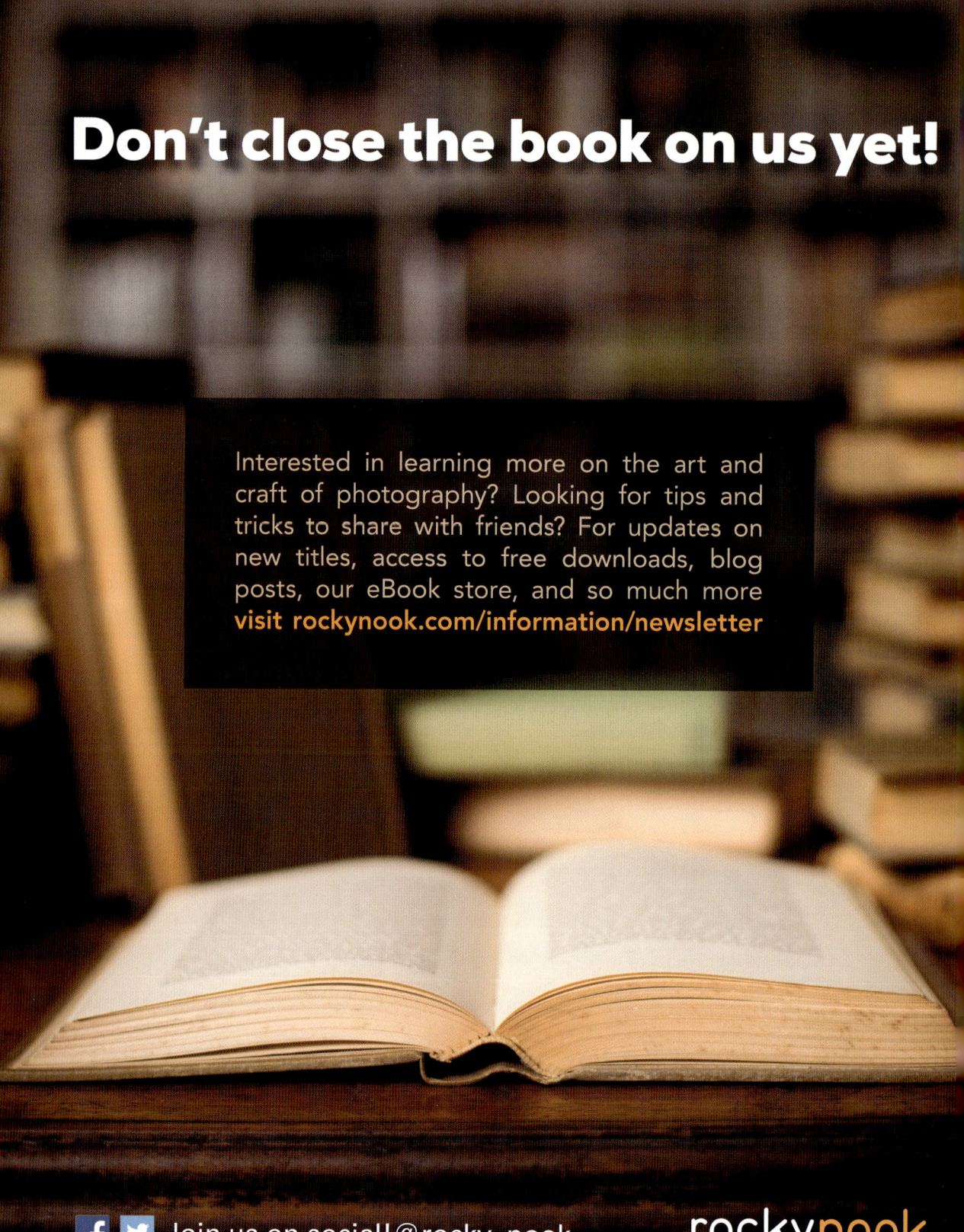